WORLD ECONOMIC DEVELOPMENT

D. W. FRYER

Department of Geography
University of Hawaii

McGraw-Hill Book Company

New York St. Louis San Francisco Toronto London Sydney

World Economic Development

Library of Congress Catalog Card Number 64-21629

22584

3456789HD72106987

Photographic editing by SAM HOLMES

PREFACE

In the present work the author has endeavored to provide a more analytical treatment of the vast, complex, and constantly changing world economy than is currently available in other introductory texts in economic geography, and if this has led him more deeply into the marginal territory between economics and geography than is customary, it is because he feels that such an excursion is long overdue. Short of descending to platitude there is no way of reducing the study of the world economy to a matter of simplicity, and students usually perceive that facile explanations of the distribution of certain economic activities do not stand critical analysis. The author feels strongly that it is not enough merely to learn the facts concerning the distribution of various types of economic activities or even to appreciate the basic causation of such patterns; it is the consequences of such distributions that the student should reflect on to comprehend many of the pressing economic problems facing the world. There is no suggestion in the present text that "that that is, is best." For the geography student who knows little of economics, simple explanations of unfamiliar terms and concepts have been provided, but the author hopes that the text will also prove a valuable window on the world for those students of economics required to undertake some empirical study of the world economy.

As a result of the emphasis placed on a world view the allocation of space is rather different from other introductory texts. The United States has been accorded a treatment commensurate with its status in the world economy; but this has not been exceeded, and the author hopes that his American readers particularly will appreciate the wider prospect of the world that this has made possible.

Any writer of a world economic geography must accept that his work will be out of date by the time it appears in print. From his vantage point in time, therefore, he should not only survey what is going on around him but also peer ahead and try to ascertain the probable direction of march. The author suggests that there are four powerful influences that are shaping the world economy and that appear likely to operate strongly for some time to come.

The first is this: despite minor oscillations, the world economy has resumed the course of expansion which was checked by World War I; with the advantage of hindsight, it appears that the general depression of the interwar period was a temporary phenomenon. Although opinion is divided on the possibility of another slump of the magnitude of the Great Depression, it is clear that in any country of the Western world, no government prepared to accept a level of unemployment even remotely approaching that of the early Thirties could possibly survive. Moreover, governments have not only come to accept responsibility for the maintenance of full employment and the general health of the economy; they have also been compelled to redress or to counteract any gross imbalance in employment opportunities between regions within the national territory.

The second factor of major importance is the wave of nationalism that has swept over Asia and Africa, producing since World War II a crop of often raw and brash new nations determined to create the industrial underpinnings of a modern society as rapidly as possible. These new nations are slowly coming to face the unpalatable fact that the gap between rich and poor countries is steadily enlarging. Though independent for nearly a century and a half, the countries of Latin America have been scarcely less affected by the upsurge of nationalism than those parts of the underdeveloped world that experienced the greatest impact of World War II, it should be added.

The third great force has been the creation of the Sino-Soviet bloc and the growing economic strength of the U.S.S.R. The rapidity of Russian economic growth has greatly influenced the present economically backward countries, and some of the techniques of Russian economic development have become widely copied. The concept of the Sino-Soviet bloc itself, however, appears ready for some revaluation; China is determined to challenge the U.S.S.R., not only for leadership of the communist world, but also for the allegiance of the present uncommitted nations.

Finally, the rate of growth of world population is a fundamental fact of the world economy that the economic geographer cannot possibly ignore. A rapidly growing population may be either a stimulus or an impediment to economic growth; much depends on the preexisting level of economic activity. In some parts of the world an expanding population offers the possibility of substantial economic growth and enhanced incomes; in others it is difficult to view the present rate of increase with anything but deep concern.

In this work the author has tried to come to terms with these realities of the post-World War II world. Western Europe, Japan, and Australia, with their booming economies, are given an analysis which reflects their enhanced stature in the world economy; due account is taken of the fact that Western Europe, moreover, has indeed embarked on a program of economic unification which in the near future could produce a state with a population and productive capacity greater than those of either the United States or the U.S.S.R. Because of their repercussions on the world economy, particular attention has been paid to the so called "growth" industries—petroleum, motor vehicles, aluminum and chemicals—and an attempt has been made to assess the problems and the probable course of industrialization in economically backward nations. The growing importance of industrial activity including its supreme political importance in the underdeveloped world, has necessitated that less relative space is given to agriculture than in most other introductory texts, but here also attention has been focused on developmental problems.

A large scale survey can become extremely tedious. The author has tried to avoid encyclopedism, and a vigorous comparative approach has been adopted to make the facts more palatable; particular attention has been paid throughout to those factors making for change. The author has not hesitated to draw his own conclusions from the evidence before him, and appreciates that some of his views will appear controversial. This is as it should be; all economic activity serves ends which are decided in the political arena, and in a free society every citizen has the right to say what those ends should be.

Statistical tables have been provided wherever appropriate, for although a considerable range of statistical material is now widely available, the author has found that students are often reluctant to seek it out, and where it is not provided in a text, the instructor often finds himself distributing statistical information. United Nations sources have been used wherever possible, and the metric units of the United Nations Statistical Office have been retained in tables, which generally relate either to 1962 or 1963. For some tables 1961 has had to be used, but in this year business activity generally was at a lower level than in preceding years.

Any broad review must rely heavily on secondary sources. The author is indebted to all those regional and topical specialists whose material he has used, and trusts that he has made adequate acknowledgment. Many people have assisted the preparation of this work either with information or advice, but the author is especially appreciative of the contribution of his former colleagues of the Department of Commerce of the University of Melbourne—Miss Mollie Bayne, Mr. C. S. Woods and in particular, Dr. R. Kent Wilson, whose expert knowledge of land use, especially of Australia and New Zealand, was freely placed at the author's disposal. Dr. Wilson played a major part in helping the author to arrive at most of his conclusions, and whatever merit the work has is in large part the result of his influence. Others who have given valuable advice on the manuscript are Professors Norton Ginsburg, James Parsons, and John Weaver. The author is also anxious to record his gratitude to Professor Karl Pelzer for clarifying the author's ideas on land use in the humid tropics, and to Professor Charles Fisher for suggesting the initial conceptions that constitute the theme of this work. The author alone, however, must accept responsibility for any errors, for which the opportunities in a work such as this are considerable. He has done his best to keep them to a minimum, but he will be grateful to his readers for bringing to his notice any that have escaped him. Miss Ivy Ang was of great assistance in revising the manuscript, which was typed by Miss Elizabeth Amaloo and Miss Yeoh Soh See; to all of these and to Mr. V. Palani who prepared the diagrams, the author is greatly indebted.

D. W. FRYER

CONTENTS

Preface *v*

I. THE PATTERN OF WORLD ECONOMIC DEVELOPMENT

1. Types of Economies 3

Criteria of Development The Four Basic National Patterns Occupations and Their Productivity over the World

2. World Populations and Urbanism 28

Geographic Distribution of Population Urbanization and Industrialization Population Growth and Structure

II. AGRICULTURE, FORESTRY, AND FISHING

3. Agriculture in the World Economy 47

The Economic Status of the Farmer Scarcity and Abundance Agricultural Structure

4. Types of Agriculture and Their Distribution 67

Primitive Subsistence Agriculture Sawah Agriculture Intensive Dry-field Agriculture Plantation-crop Agriculture Pastoral Nomadism Commercial Grazing Commercial Grain Farming Crop Farming and Horticulture, with Subsidiary Livestock Commercial Crop and Livestock Farming (Mixed Farming) Dairy Farming Specialized Horticulture The Agricultural Types and Economic Development

5. Food Crops 119

Cereals Vegetable Oils Sugar Beverages

6. Industrial Crops 165

Cotton Other Vegetable Fibers Natural Rubber Tobacco The Prospects for Industrial Crops

7. Livestock and Livestock Products 192

Man's Choice and Development of Livestock Cattle Sheep Hogs and Poultry

8. **Forestry and Forest Industries** 217

Forest Utilization Forest Industries of the United States and Other Lands

9. **Fishing and Fisheries** 236

Distribution of Fish and Fisheries Whaling The Outlook for the World's Fisheries

III. MINING AND MANUFACTURING INDUSTRIES

10. **Industry and Power in the World Economy** 257

Industry and Level of Development The Location of Modern Industry Industrialization and Power

11. **The Petroleum Industry** 276

The Growth of Production Structure and Major Locations of the Industry Refining, Consumption, and Trade Natural Gas Social and Political Problems

12. **The Coal Industry** 308

Nature and Occurrence of Coal Coal-mining Technology World Coal Production and Coal Reserves

13. **Electric Energy** 335

The Place of Electricity in the World Economy Power-supply Systems and Their Operation Methods of Generating Electricity Atomic Energy

14. **The Iron and Steel Industry** 359

The Changing Technology of Iron and Steel The Iron and Steel Industry of the United States The British Industry Iron and Steel in Western Europe The Russian Industry Other Producing Countries

15. **Nonferrous-metal Industries** 398

General Characteristics of the Industries Copper and Aluminum Lead and Zinc Tin and Nickel The Precious Metals

16. **Engineering Industries** 430

Agricultural Machinery Machine Tools Textile and Mining Machinery Locomotives Shipbuilding The Electrical Industries

17. Motor-vehicle and Aircraft Industries 452

The Motor-vehicle Industry of the United States The Motor-vehicle Industry in Western Europe The Aircraft Industry Yesterday and Today

18. Textile Industries 473

Cotton Wool Man-made Fibers

19. Chemical Industries 500

Historical Development and World Organization Heavy Chemicals Fine Chemicals and Pharmaceuticals Plastics Petrochemicals The United States and Other Major Chemical Producers

IV. SERVICE INDUSTRIES

20. Building, Commercial Services, and Government 525

Building and Construction Large-scale Commerce and Finance Distribution: The Marketing Revolution Government Services

21. Transportation Industries 542

Transport in the World Economy Railways Roads Inland Waterways Ocean Transport Air Transport

22. International Trade 572

The Bases and Traditions of World Trade The Composition of World Trade The Network of International Tradc Tradc Blocs and Trade Agreements

V. CONCLUSION

23. Towards Five Billion People 597

Problems of the Resource Basis International Aid for Economic Development

Photograph Credits 612

Index 613

…vehicle and Aircraft Industries 153

…Commercial Services and Government

…Industry

PART I

The pattern of world economic development

PART I

Chapter 1

TYPES OF ECONOMIES

In one of the classics of the literature of economics, Alfred Marshall began to define his subject by calling it "a study of mankind in the ordinary business of life . . . the attainment and use of the material requisites of well-being."[1]

It is obvious that this ordinary business of life means one thing in the Red Basin of Szechwan in western China, another in the mining valleys of south Wales, and another still on the farms of Iowa. To some extent, differences in the natural environment help to explain such contrasts, but of much greater significance are the dissimilarities in the social and cultural superstructures erected on the framework provided by nature. Essentially similar environments can be used in very varying ways, and the same environment has different significance for human activity at various points of time. Only the most primitive people, moreover, are unable to effect some change in their environment. It may indeed be doubted if there is any sizable portion of the globe, apart from the polar regions and the great seas and oceans, that remains in a state of nature, and the changes wrought by highly organized and technologically advanced peoples are immense.

The level of material welfare, of "the material requisites of well-being" attained and used, is very closely dependent on the general way of life. There is overwhelming evidence that the traditional way of life of the great majority of the world's population involves a low and static or even declining productivity per worker, and this leads to low income and deplorable standards of living. Grinding poverty is the inevitable lot of most of the world's people, and it is only very recently that even the citizens of the world's most opulent countries have escaped from penury. In 1850 the structure of the American economy was not greatly different from that of Brazil or Turkey at the present, and in most aspects of material welfare—employment opportunities, working hours, expectations of life, and education—the average

[1] **Alfred Marshall,** *Principles of Economics,* **8th ed., Macmillan & Co., Ltd., London, 1959, p. 1.**

Fig. 1-1 Major world regions.
After N. Ginsburg, *Atlas of Economic Development.*

American citizen was little better off than his present Turkish or Brazilian counterpart. Writing at the end of the nineteenth century, Marshall still considered poverty the foremost problem of Western society. Poverty in the Western world today is largely a consequence of unemployment; no family whose breadwinner is in regular work need suffer serious diet deficiencies or even semistarvation. Yet even Western poverty must be judged modest opulence by the standards of much of Asia and of Africa; here the battle against want has scarcely been joined.

Since the end of World War II there has been a remarkable awakening of the peoples of the world to their economic backwardness, very largely in consequence of the wave of nationalism that has swept across Asia, Africa, and Latin America (Fig. 1-1). The study of economic development has become perhaps the most fashionable and certainly one of the most productive branches of economics. The wealthy nations of the West have recognized considerable responsibility for improving the living standards of others, and annually expend vast sums in foreign aid. This interest has sometimes had political overtones which have rendered aid much less effective than it might have been. Nevertheless, there is every indication that foreign aid has come to stay, and it represents a momentous step forward in improving human relations.

CRITERIA OF DEVELOPMENT

A considerable number of tests have been used to throw light on the level of economic development attained by the various countries

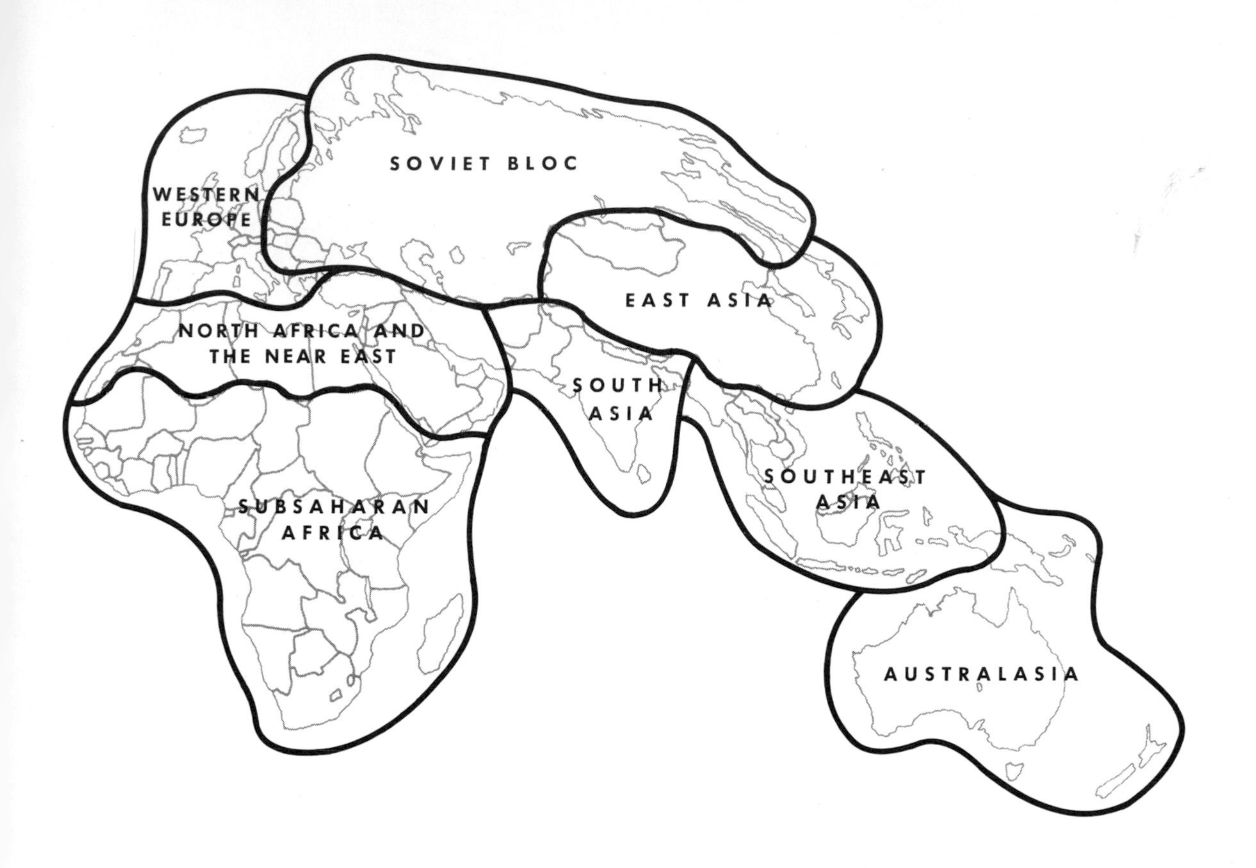

of the world. These tests may relate to either the technological or the demographic situation of a nation, but by and large, they all tell the same story.[2] The criteria used here to determine the main patterns of development in the world are (*a*) per capita national product, (*b*) the occupational distribution of the population, (*c*) the urban-rural population ratio, (*d*) the age structure of the population, and (*e*) the rate of economic growth. The world situation in relation to the first four can be presented in cartographic form (Figs. 1-2 through 1-5); unfortunately the statistical information available at present is inadequate for the construction of a world map of the last, but can support some statements of broad validity.

[2] B. J. L. Berry, "A Statistical Analysis," in Norton Ginsburg, *Atlas of Economic Development,* The University of Chicago Press, Chicago, 1961, part 8.

Per Capita National Product

National product may be defined as the value in monetary terms of all goods and services produced in one year by the total population of a given country, and for some countries it is possible to make a refinement by allowing for capital consumption and depreciation (net national product). *Per capita national product* represents the arithmetical result of dividing national product by total population. The use of per capita product in place of per capita income avoids any implication of a direct measurement of welfare and has the practical advantage that production statistics are more plentiful than those of consumption.[3]

A number of changes have occurred since

[3] Ginsburg, *ibid.*, p. 1. The two concepts merely represent different ways of looking at the same flow of goods and services, and in most instances are monetarily identical.

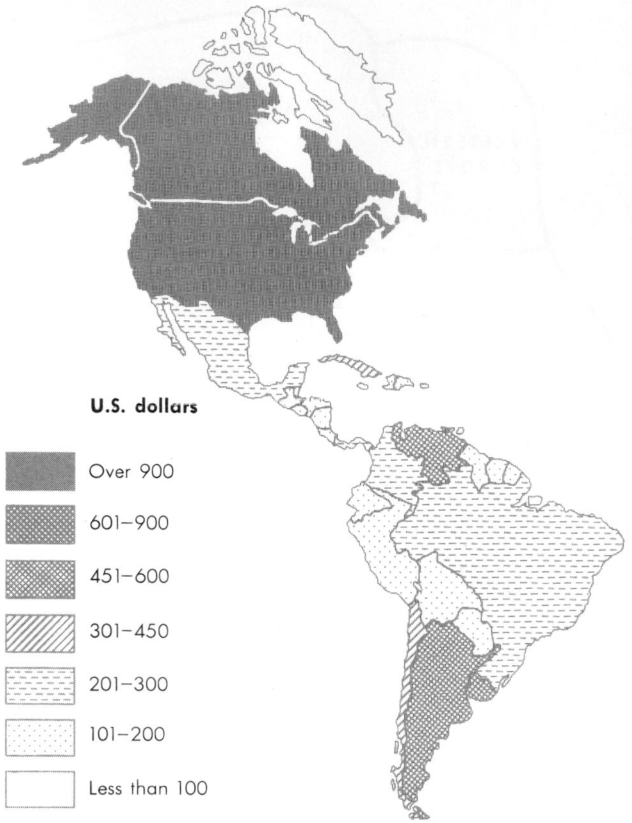

Fig. 1-2 Per capita national product. Based mainly on United Nations, *Statistical Papers,* series E, no. 4, 1957, with certain later estimates.

the estimates that form the basis of Fig. 1-2 were prepared in the middle Fifties; Japan, Italy, the U.S.S.R., and West Germany would rank considerably higher at present, and Cuba and some other Latin American countries would need to be downgraded. Nevertheless, the general picture would not be substantially different. Considerable caution is necessary, however, in interpreting the low rank of much of Africa, Asia, and Latin America. Countries which have overwhelmingly subsistence economies are inevitably undervalued, because it is impossible to make an accurate assessment of the money value of all the goods and services that subsistence farmers and their families provide for themselves or for their neighbors. Moreover, figures of per capita national product suggest a degree of precision which is quite unmerited, as the difficulties of estimating all its various components and translating them into common monetary terms (United States dollars) are very considerable and often have to be settled by approximations based on the limited evidence available.

The differences are nevertheless remarkable. In the premier position is the United States, the only nation to record a figure exceeding $2,000. (Throughout the present work, dollars are United States dollars unless otherwise specified.) This arises from the fact that the United States, with but 6 per cent of world population, produces about 40 per cent of gross world product (the sum of the gross national products). On the other hand, large areas of Africa and Asia record figures of less than $100; with about 30 per cent of world population,

South and Southeast Asia generate a mere 4 per cent of world product. Latin America in general ranks higher than does either Africa or Asia; the effect of huge oil and iron-ore royalties is clearly visible in the case of Venezuela, although the political and social turmoil in that country suggests that this relative opulence affects few of its people. Countries of Eastern and southeast Europe stand at about the same rank as those of Latin America; Spain and Portugal, historically an integral part of Western Europe, appear to have economies that are considerably less productive than those of their Western European neighbors. A high per capita product is apparently not a prerogative of large countries; Switzerland, Belgium, and Denmark outrank many European countries with far larger populations and with greater physical resources. The dominance of Anglo-Saxon countries in the highest rank is very striking.

National averages, however, conceal wide regional variations. In the southern United States per capita product still stands well below that of the country as a whole, while that of the entire Pacific Coast is well above it. Other disparities suggest themselves—Quebec and British Columbia, Calabria and Lombardy, Castile and Catalonia, Connacht and Ulster, Moravia and Bohemia, and many more.

Occupational Distribution

A high per capita national product is invariably associated with a wide range of employment opportunities and with a low

Fig. 1-3 **Percentage of work force engaged in agriculture.**
FAO, Yearbook, 1960.

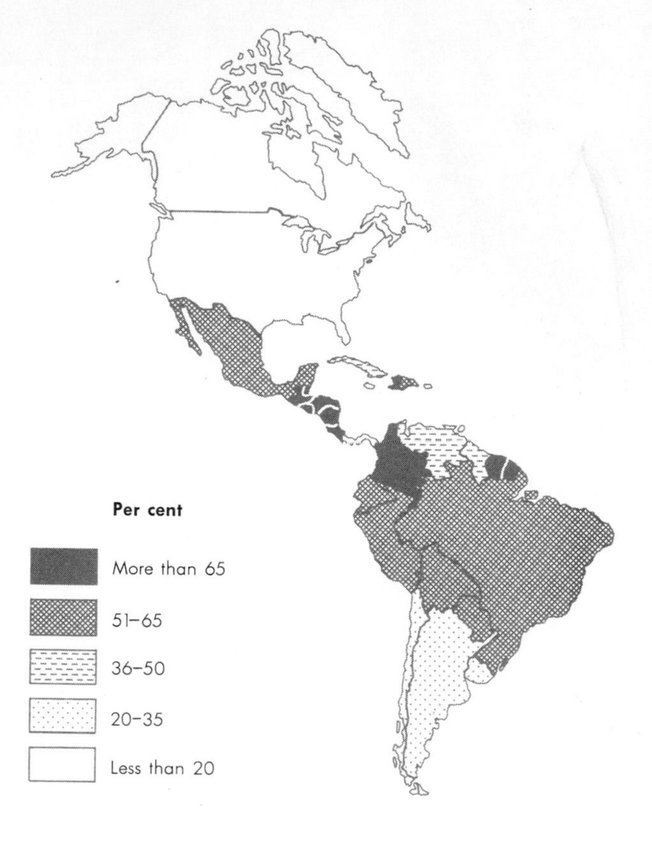

Fig. 1-4 **Percentage of population classified as urban according to local definitions.**
United Nations, Demographic Yearbook, 1955.

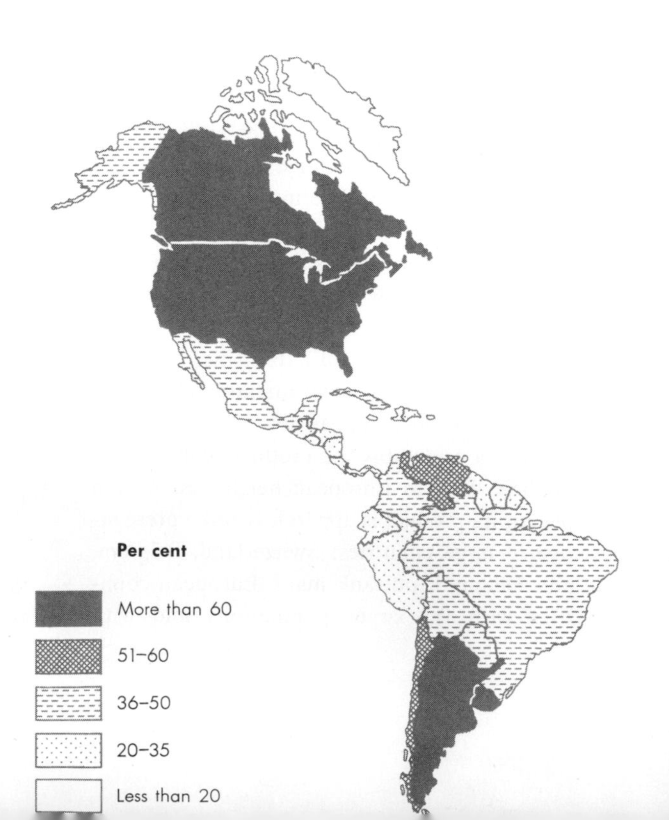

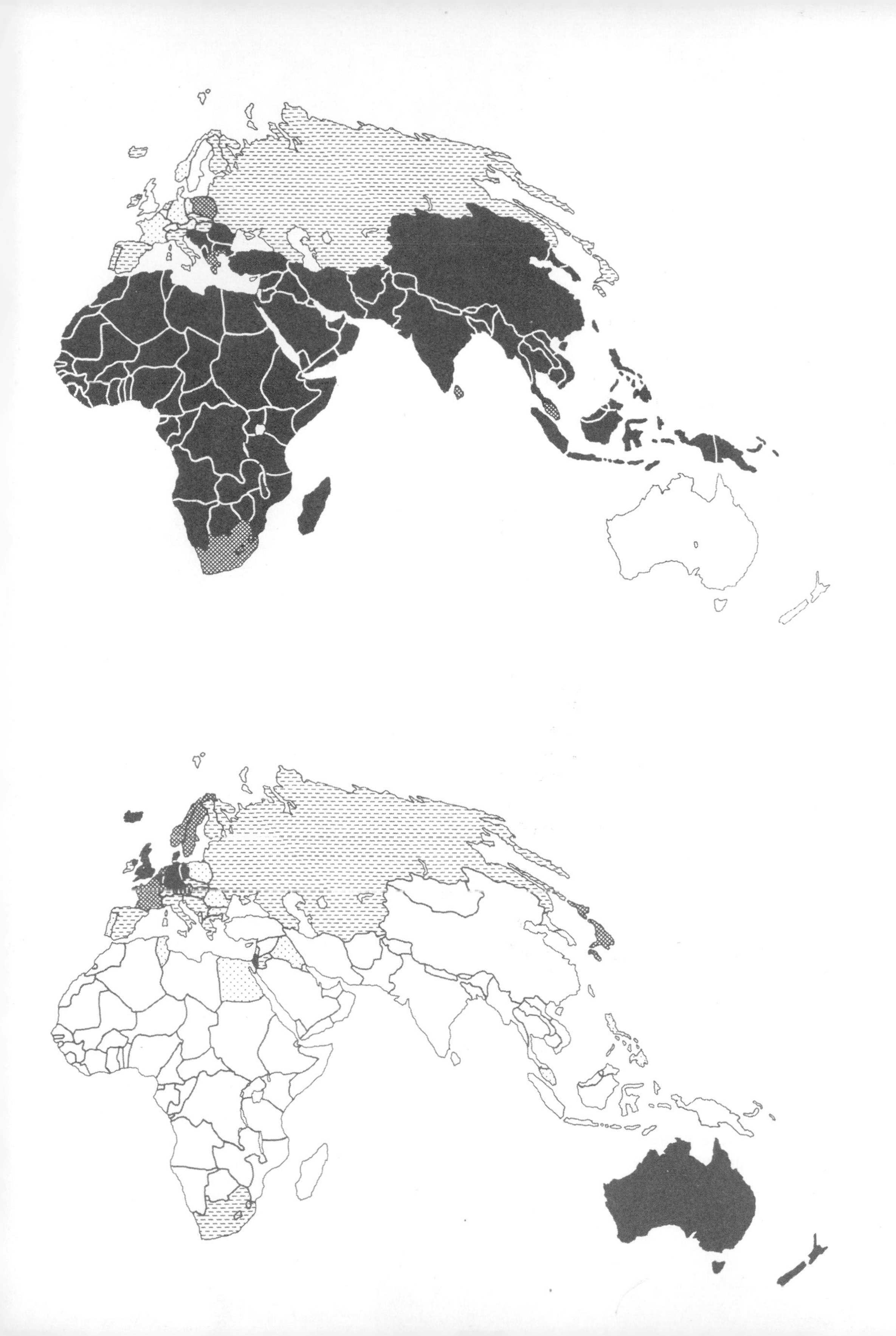

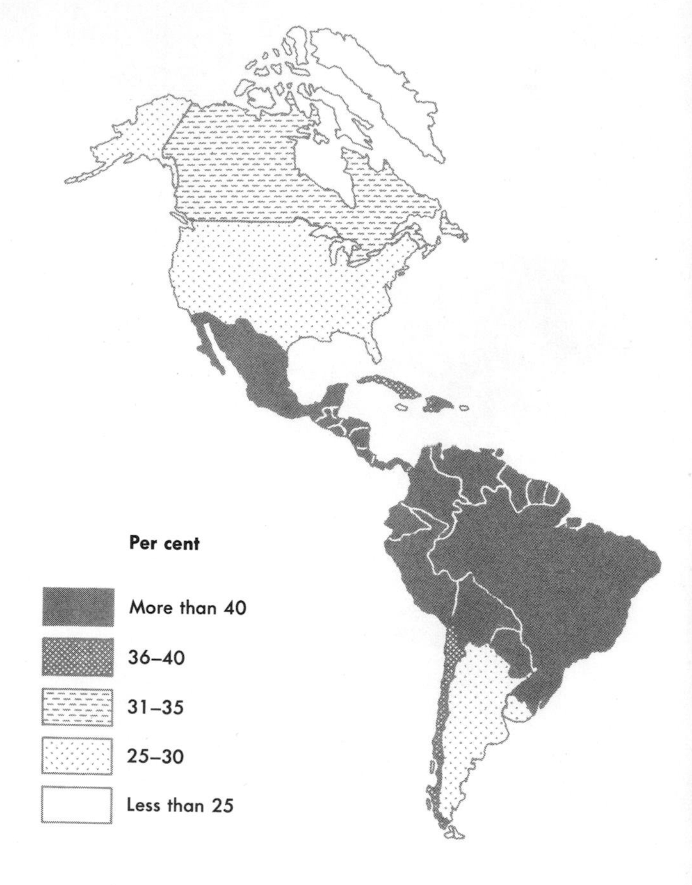

Fig. 1-5 Percentage of population below fifteen years of age.
United Nations, Demographic Yearbook, 1960.

proportion of the working population in agriculture. As economic development proceeds, improved technology raises the productivity of the agricultural worker and makes possible an increasing agricultural production from a diminishing labor force. The redundant labor is thus available for deployment in other activities, such as manufacturing and commerce, and as the economy grows, these activities come to employ more of the total work force. Manufacturing does not continually absorb a progressively larger proportion of the work force, at least in the noncommunist world; even in the most highly industrialized nations its share does not rise much above 30 per cent and is more commonly around 25 per cent. The collective share of nonmanufacturing and service industries such as transport, commerce, and administration does continue to grow, however, and in all countries with a high per capita national product these activities absorb a very large proportion of the labor force.

These observations apply to all countries with a high per capita national product, even to Denmark, Australia, and New Zealand, which are often termed agricultural countries.[4] Conversely, a high proportion of the national labor force engaged in agriculture is a clear sign of a backward and impoverished economy; it cannot be anything else, for the working

[4] These countries are agricultural only in the sense that a large share of their *export* earnings is produced by agriculture. In fact, they are among the most highly urbanized countries on earth. In all of them, agriculture generates about one-sixth of national product and employs less than one-fifth of the work force; its share of both is rapidly falling. Moreover, Denmark's industrial exports now equal in value its exports of dairy products, and Australian industrial exports are growing rapidly.

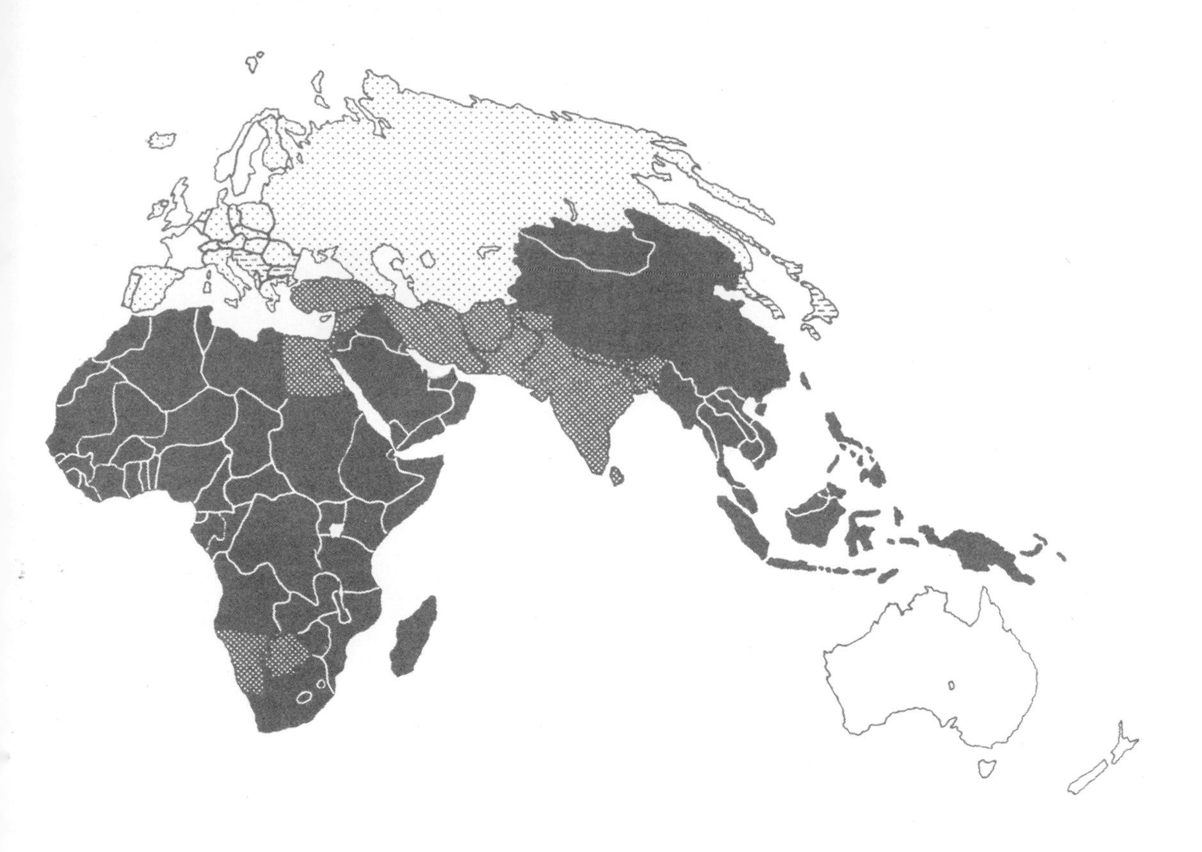

population is mainly occupied with the basic problem of providing enough to eat. It follows that low-income countries desirous of raising their level of development must endeavor first to enlarge productivity in the agricultural sector of the economy and then to transfer workers to nonagricultural activities.

The Urban-Rural Ratio

As economic development proceeds and workers leave agricultural employment, a greater proportion of the population comes to live in cities and more particularly in large cities. Population distribution thus becomes more discontinuous. There is a close correlation between per capita national product and the proportion of the total population living in urban conditions (Figs. 1-2 and 1-4). Anomalies arise for the most part from varying national definitions of the urban population; Switzerland, for example, is considerably more urbanized than Fig. 1-4 indicates. However, Britain, the most highly urbanized of all nations, does not have the highest per capita national product.

The Age Structure of the Population

Economic development produces considerable changes in the size and age structure of the population. Total population increases very substantially. Under the influence of urban conditions, through some still imperfectly understood mechanism, powerful new social forces are generated which gradually depresses birth rates. Increased living standards, the fruits of a higher level of economic develop-

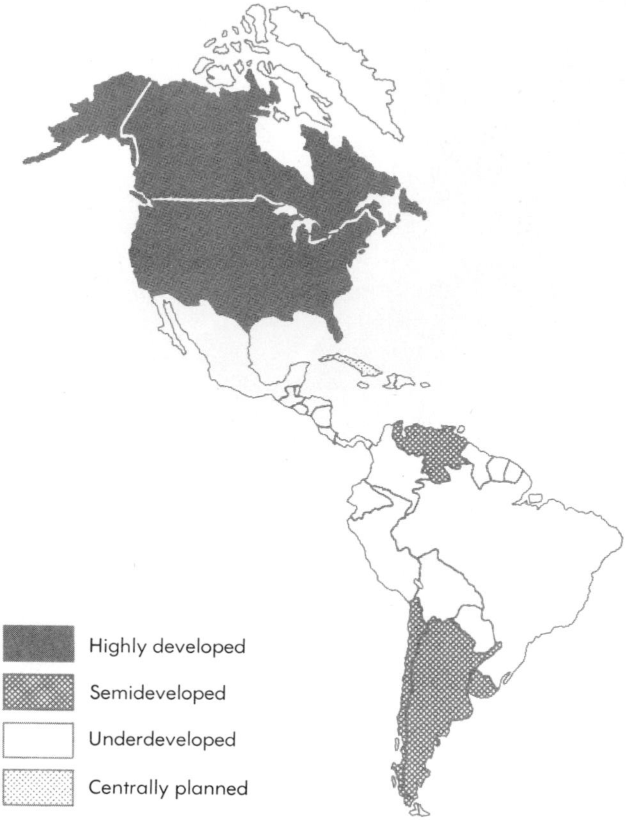

Highly developed
Semideveloped
Underdeveloped
Centrally planned

Fig. 1-6 Types of economies.

ment, prolong the expectation of life, and slowly but inevitably the proportion of children and young persons in the total population declines. There is a clear correlation between the juvenile population and the level of per capita income (Fig. 1-5). Countries with very low incomes all have a large proportion of population below the age of fifteen, although, as Fig. 1-5 indicates, the two countries with the highest per capita incomes are not those with the lowest proportion of children and young people.

The Rate of Economic Growth

Information concerning rates of economic growth is available only for countries that are quite clearly at a high level of economic development. Thus for countries that lack detailed statistical services it is impossible to do more than hazard a guess of the general rate of growth, but in most cases it is certain that it is very small. Every country with a high per capita national product saves a considerable proportion of its gross national product; the higher the proportion saved, the faster is the rate of economic growth. Countries with low per capita national products can save little; thus investment in productive enterprises is low, and the cycle of poverty is perpetuated. Some countries with modest levels of per capita national product, such as Italy, Japan, and the U.S.S.R., have quite obviously experienced very high rates of economic growth over the past decade. For the world as a whole, however, the gap between the rich and the poor is widening.

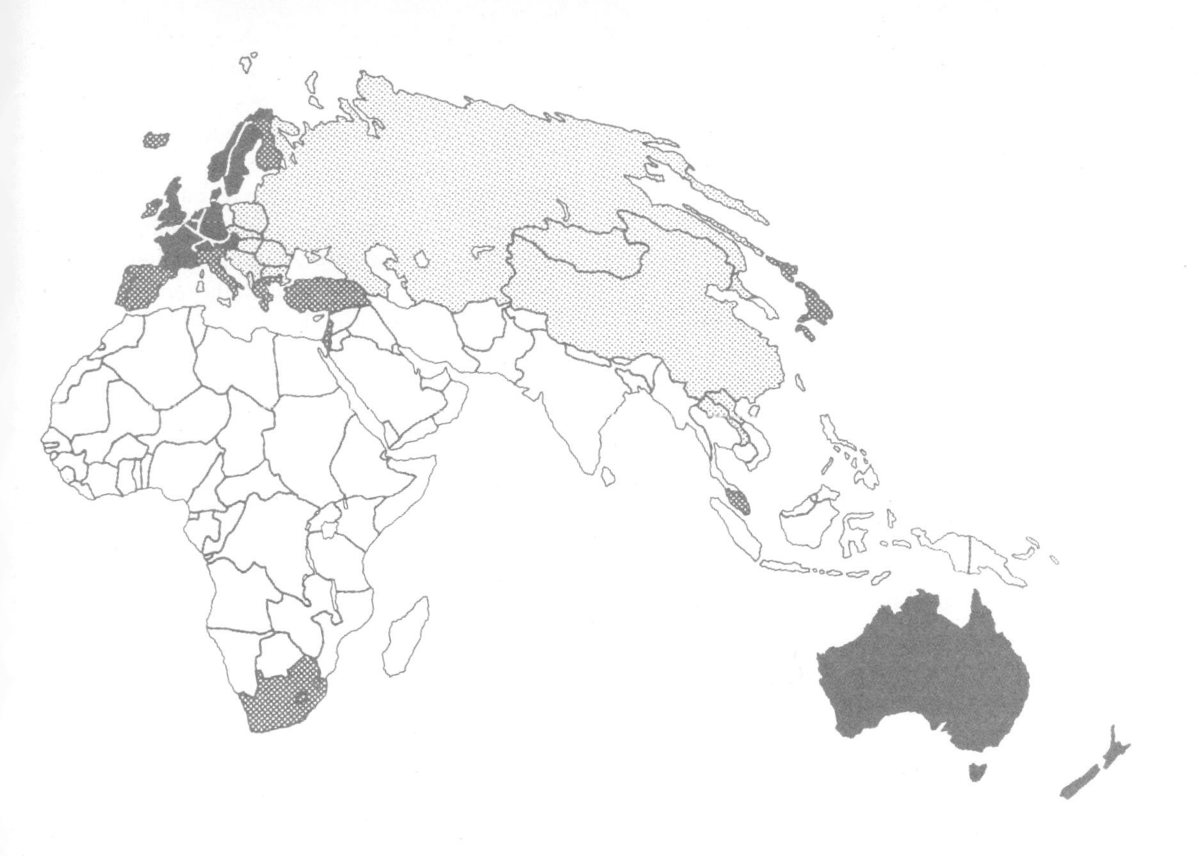

THE FOUR BASIC NATIONAL PATTERNS

Analysis of the above criteria suggests that it is possible to classify national economies in four basic categories. The world has:

1. Highly developed, or industrial-commercial, economies. Economies of this type support only about 8 per cent of world population.
2. Semideveloped, or mixed industrial-agricultural, economies, supporting about 12 per cent of world population.
3. Underdeveloped, or predominantly agricultural, economies. These very widespread economies support almost 50 per cent of world population.
4. Centrally planned economies, which are essentially either type 2 or type 3, but which have some of the characteristics of type 1 and so many other special characteristics that they are best considered as a separate category. The centrally planned economies at present include about 30 per cent of world population.

The distribution of these four basic economies is shown in Fig. 1-6.

The Highly Developed Economies

The highly developed countries include Anglo-American and most countries of Western Europe. Outside these areas only Australia and New Zealand can be numbered among the wealthy nations of the world.

These countries are the economic aristocrats of the world. Not only are they the wealthiest in any sense; they also have high rates of economic growth and are therefore leaving poorer countries further and further behind. Of course, this wealth is not spread evenly throughout the community, and even the richest nation in the world, the United States, can show plenty of poverty. Twenty-seven per cent of American families received total incomes of less than $2,000 and had a standard of living which was well below socially acceptable standards in 1948. Ten years later the average cash income of all farm workers was still less than $1,500.[5] But inequality of wealth is certainly no worse than in other types of economies, and there has been a marked improvement in the fortunes of the lowest-paid workers in Western industrialized countries since World War II.

The economies with the highest levels of per capita national product all have less than 20 per cent of their labor force employed in agriculture. Moreover, in all of them the size of the agriculture labor force continues to decline, both absolutely and relatively to total employment. Between 1940 and 1950 agricultural employment in the United States fell from 19 per cent to 12 per cent of total employment and by 1960 was below 8 per cent. Nevertheless, food output expanded by considerably more than half during this time.

Manufacturing accounts for about 25 to 30 per cent of total employment in highly developed economies, but the figure for Britain is somewhat higher, reflecting a dependence on manufactured exports in order to make good the large deficit in domestic agricultural production.[6]

In all highly developed economies employment in nonmanufacturing and service industries—transport, commerce, administration, etc.—(sometimes collectively called the tertiary industries) exceeds that in manufacturing by a substantial margin. The share of total employment in commerce has been claimed to be of particular significance as an index of the level of economic development, and it is for this reason that these economies have been termed industrial-commercial.[7]

There are wide disparities among the highly developed countries, for the highly developed countries of Europe have a considerable way to go to reach American or Canadian levels of per capita national product. With the exception of Britain, however, their rate of economic growth since 1950 has been considerably greater than that of the United States, and the same is also true of Australia and New Zealand. In addition, disparities among countries at the upper end of the scale of wealth are of little significance in terms of health, nutrition, expectation of life, and education.

It is sometimes argued that because the highly developed economies have already used up a substantial proportion of their natural resources, their economic prospects must become progressively gloomier. This view largely arises from a misunderstanding of the nature of resources; resources represent the application of technological, managerial, and financial skills

[5] In 1964 President Johnson sent Congress a $220 million assistance plan to rehabilitate "Appalachia," the poorest part of the country, and to provide direct relief to families whose total income amounted to less than $3,000 per year.

[6] The distribution of employment between types of manufacturing differs greatly from one level of economic development to another; highly developed economies all show a concentration in metal making and the metalworking industries. See also pp. 260–261.

[7] Colin Clark, *The Conditions of Economic Progress,* 3d ed., Macmillan & Co., Ltd., London, 1957, pp. 490–520. See also pp. 530–531 of the present work. Clark's thesis has been strongly criticized. Some economists have asserted that there is no correlation between the level of economic development and the share of the work force in commerce.

In the highly developed economies, a relatively small number of large-scale, highly mechanized producers accounts for a very large share of total farm output. The balance is derived from a multiplicity of small, undercapitalized farmers, whose continued existence is largely the result of state assistance of various kinds.

to the handiwork of nature, and while some resources are being used up or destroyed, many new ones are continually being created. Culture, operating on the background of nature, produces resources; hence an expanding cultural equipment broadens the resource base of the economy and makes possible increasing productivity and income.

In a sense, even the richest nations can be regarded as underdeveloped, as the scope for economic development is infinite. Many people clearly recognize the great potentialities of such countries as Australia and Canada; great potentialities exist equally in the United States and Western Europe. Economic development will cease only when cultural change itself comes to a halt and the social framework congeals.

A hallmark of highly developed economies is a high level of urbanization, including the existence of very large cities. In several countries originally separate towns have grown explosively and coalesced into sprawling conurbations covering more than 100 square miles and sometimes very much more. This stage of city evolution has been described as *megalopolis.*[8]

The citizens of highly developed countries enjoy the highest expectation of life in the world, and the proportion of the population which is of working age is exceedingly high.

The Semideveloped Economies

The semideveloped countries are very widely distributed, with representatives in every continent. They form a very diverse assemblage, including countries as varied as Japan, Italy, Argentina, South Africa, and Finland. The range of per capita national product between members of this group is considerable, but in all except Argentina and Uruguay the proportion of the working population in agriculture is much higher than in the highly developed countries, ranging from 35 per cent to as much as 55 per cent; the urban-rural population ratio is thus much lower. Argentina and Uruguay, which are in many ways pale replicas of Australia and New Zealand, are anomalies. In both, the proportion of the labor force in agriculture is almost commensurate with that of highly developed economies, a consequence of the relatively great importance of livestock farming in the agricultural sector. In the semideveloped economies there are relatively few of the machines that give a high productivity to the agricultural worker.

The semideveloped economies, with their lower per capita national products, save proportionately less than the highly developed ones, though for short periods some have been able to achieve comparable rates of saving. In the decade following 1950 Japan and Italy maintained very high rates of economic growth, that of the former being the highest so far recorded by any country at any period of time. Both now stand on the threshold of passing into the highly developed category.

Social obstacles to economic growth are much more powerful in semideveloped countries than in highly developed ones. The racial policies of South Africa and the social structure of Argentina (a country which might have developed in the manner of Australia had the British military invasion of the early nineteenth century been successful) have prevented these countries from realizing a higher rate of economic growth. A reappraisal of the position and function of the landlord could produce very beneficial effects in many semideveloped countries, even in Europe; in Italy and Spain the political and social strength of the large landowners and the wide extent of *mezzadria*

[8] **Lewis Mumford,** *The Culture of Cities,* **Harcourt, Brace and Company, Inc., 1938, p. 289.**

Tokyo's Ginza epitomizes Japan's economic maturity, but the country's agricultural labor force is still relatively much larger than that of the highly developed economies.

(sharecropping) and rural indebtedness duplicate some of the worst features of Asian agrarian organization. In Japan, the traditional obligation of the employer to maintain all his workers even when he can no longer find a profitable use of their labor tends to keep costs high and hampers economic mobility.

Nevertheless, the semideveloped countries have already taken the most difficult steps along the road to a high level of economic development.

Most of the semideveloped countries have been able to accomplish this largely with their own resources, although Argentina, Uruguay, and South Africa owe much to the investment of foreign capital. However, *none ever possessed such an unfavorable ratio of population to resources as occurs at present in the underdeveloped economies*. The experience of Japan provides little comfort for other countries anxious to industrialize; its high degree of literacy and a tradition of large-scale economic activity dating back to the sixteenth century for some of the country's great clans, find no parallel elsewhere in Asia.

South Africa and Southern Rhodesia are somewhat anomalous. In both there is a relatively small white community with an economy in the highly developed stage, linked in the political framework with a large African population whose economy is in the underdeveloped stage. Both countries provide examples of an economic dualism which has racial rather than regional divisions. As there is no prospect of an early integration, it appears best to allocate these countries to the semideveloped category.

The Underdeveloped Economies

Underdeveloped economies are the most extensive on earth. They include the whole of Africa with the exception of South Africa, the greater portion of South and Central America, and virtually the whole of Asia outside Soviet Asia, Japan, and Malaysia. As stated before, these economies support nearly 50 per cent of world population (a figure that becomes 70 per cent when the underdeveloped countries of the Eastern bloc are included).

Per capita national products in the underdeveloped countries are very low. At the very lowest level are those of the African continent. Over wide areas deforestation and overgrazing have resulted in extensive soil erosion and laterization, and living conditions are such that infection by such diseases as malaria and yaws and infestation by helminthic parasites are virtually inevitable. Poor health is a powerful factor in the low productivity of the African farmer, and resistance to infection is lowered by poor diet, which may be little above starvation level before harvests. Certain of the Pacific islands and much of New Guinea are little different from Africa in these respects.

Asia presents many variations on the same basic theme of poverty; a solution for the economic problems of one country may by no means be applicable to those of a near neighbor. The enormous rural slums of East and South Asia present the most massive and intractable problems of economic development anywhere in the world. While there are exceptions such as Thailand or Sumatra, both of which could accommodate many more people than they do at present without reducing living standards, there is considerable evidence that over considerable parts of East, Southeast, and South Asia population pressure is extremely severe.

In Latin America problems of population pressure are much less acute than in Asia and are confined to certain intermontane basins in the cordilleran systems of Central and South America and some Caribbean islands. It is even possible to maintain that by and large, Latin America is underpopulated even in relation to existing resources and techniques, though this view implies the acceptance of a higher degree of economic liberalism than most Latin American republics are probably prepared to countenance.[9]

Underdeveloped economies are essentially agricultural economies. Everywhere the proportion of the working population in agricultural pursuits is very high, reaching about 60 per cent in many of the cordilleran states of Latin America, 70 per cent in much of East, Southeast, and South Asia, and a still higher per cent in Africa. Techniques are primitive and frequently even inferior to those of classical times. Many cultivators, it is true, demonstrate considerable ability in appraising environmental potentialities and in adapting techniques accordingly. Examples of this capacity are rice cultivation with two or three stages of transplanting as in the Mekong plain of Cambodia and Vietnam, the elaborate terraces and irrigation systems of Bali and south China, and even some of the practices of shifting cultivators in many parts of the intertropical world. But all such adaptations involve the acceptance of a low productivity per worker; almost everywhere there are too many farmers in relation to the land and capital at their disposal.

Underdeveloped countries are thus overwhelmingly rural. Generally, the proportion of the total population living in cities or towns is less than one-quarter; often it is very much less. Large cities are few in number. In 1960 India had a total population more than four times as great as that of Japan; yet India had only 7 cities with a population exceeding 1 million, compared with 6 such cities in Japan (and 20 in the United States). Collectively the 107 Indian cities with a population exceeding 100,000 accounted for less than 9 per cent of India's population.[10]

Several underdeveloped countries in Central America and Southeast Asia have high rates of population growth—as much as 3 per cent per annum. A population increasing at such a rate doubles itself in twenty-three years. This high rate of population increase has come about largely through a reduction in death rates; birth rates, determined by social custom and tradition, have changed little. Even where the present rate of increase is not particularly high, as in India, the absolute increase is formidable. The expectation of life at birth is only half that in a highly developed country. The result is a population structure with a high proportion of children and young persons, who constitute a great burden on the economy.

In underdeveloped countries the proportion of the gross national product that is saved seldom reaches 5 per cent, and relatively little of this saving is invested in productive enterprises that enlarge gross national product. It is generally assumed by economists that in underdeveloped countries an increase in population of 1 per cent per annum requires the investment of about 4 per cent of gross national product in order to maintain living standards. While this figure may be questioned, it is clear that with a high rate of population increase the rate of saving in underdeveloped economies offers no possibility of a higher level of economic development in the near future. Thus incomes remain low, savings are scanty, and the economy stagnates.

It is not surprising, therefore, that many governments of underdeveloped countries have attempted to use some of the techniques of the centrally planned economies to produce a high rate of economic growth and that almost every Asian and African nation has a national development plan.

The Centrally Planned Economies

The centrally planned economies are essentially either mixed industrial-agricultural

[9] It is just possible that the Latin American Free Trade Area (LAFTA) may help to bring such acceptance about.

[10] United Nations, *Demographic Yearbook, 1960*, New York, 1961, table 7.

Agricultural techniques in the underdeveloped economies are extremely primitive, and over much of Africa, the plow is replaced by the hoe or digging stick. The large proportion of children in the total population (right) imposes a heavy economic burden.

(semideveloped) or predominantly agricultural (underdeveloped). Even the most economically advanced country with a centrally planned economy, the U.S.S.R., has not yet reached the industrial-commercial stage of the highly developed economies. However, the U.S.S.R. is already second only to the United States in total industrial production, and its output of coal, steel, and electric power exceeds the combined outputs of Britain and West Germany, the most highly industrialized nations of Western Europe. In the development of thermonuclear energy, rocket propulsion, and other extremely complex and capital-intensive technologies, the U.S.S.R. appears to be little, if at all, behind the United States. The economy of the U.S.S.R. is thus very different from that of the semideveloped economies and is clearly observable as such.

A striking characteristic of the centrally planned economies is that over certain periods they have shown a very high rate of economic growth. It has taken a long time for this fact to become widely accepted, and there are still economists who deny that the long-term rate of economic growth in the U.S.S.R. is anything but extremely modest. Other writers claim that while the Russian economy is expanding rapidly, it would have done better still with a free-enterprise system—an observation which,

The greatest investment in centrally planned economies, such as Communist China, is made in heavy industry; agriculture and consumer-goods industries receive low priority. The few manifestations of commercial advertising, so obtrusive in highly developed economies, appear crude to Westerners.

even if correct, does not offer much comfort.[11] Still other economists are entirely convinced of the considerably superior economic growth of the U.S.S.R. and even of the Soviet satellites, in comparison with that of the West. In the decade following the death of Stalin, Russian industrial output increased by at least 100 per cent;[12] certainly the rate of growth of the Soviet economy is far too high for complacency on their part.

Marxists attribute the high growth rate of communist countries to the adoption of the principle of central planning, under which the allocation of factors of production is determined, not by the market as in free-enterprise economies, but by an elaborate state plan. There is abundant evidence that the adoption of this principle, which is of course fundamental in Marxist-Leninist philosophy, has retarded rather than promoted economic growth; the innumerable bottlenecks of the Russian type of economy are an inevitable consequence of a stifling, overcentralized bureaucracy. It is the high rate of saving and capital formation that is the key to the rapid economic advance of the Eastern bloc, for given the political and economic framework, the rate of saving can be virtually what government cares to make it.

In addition, the U.S.S.R. puts a larger proportion of total investment than highly developed countries into activities that increase the capacity of the system for further growth and increase real economic strength—fuel and power, iron and steel, chemicals, cement, communications, etc. Since 1953, however, Russia has pursued a fitful policy of giving the consumer rather more than he enjoyed in the past, and it is common knowledge that the government is under considerable pressure to increase investment in housing and consumer-goods industries. This would tend to slow down the rate of economic advance, and it is probable that such investment will be kept at a minimum consistent with political expediency.

The spectacular performances of the Eastern bloc countries[13] in mining and manufacturing have not been matched in agriculture. All these countries are faced with agricultural problems of varying degrees of severity, and at a time when agricultural productivity in the highly developed economies and in many of the semideveloped economies is increasing by leaps and bounds. The depressed condition of agriculture is a direct result of developmental policy, for agriculture has not been provided with sufficient investment to offset the drain on its labor force and output arising from rapid industrialization and urbanization. Thus the U.S.S.R. is obliged to maintain almost 40 per cent of its labor force in agriculture, but shortages of foodstuffs repeatedly occur.

Even more remarkable than the recent economic growth of the U.S.S.R. was the attempted transformation of China in the "great leap forward" of 1958; laboring unceasingly, summer and winter, the 700 million Chinese endeavored to "do in a day what took other countries years." As a result, China's steel production expanded from 3 million to 11 million tons between 1955 and 1959, and fantastic increases in agricultural production were claimed. It is now clear that virtually all the stupendous advances actually achieved were at the expense

[11] See, for example, Demitri Skimkin, "Economic Regionalization in the Soviet Union," *Geographical Review*, vol. 42, pp. 591–614, 1952, and Harry Schwartz, *Russia's Soviet Economy*, 2d ed., Prentice-Hall, Inc., Englewood Cliffs, N.J., 1954.

[12] *The Economist*, vol. 206, p. 784, 1963. The Russian official index claimed 170 per cent. The large Russian grain purchases from the West in 1964 revealed, however, that the agriculture sector was badly lagging, and between 1962 and 1964 the rate of economic growth was probably very low.

[13] The conception of a monolithic Eastern bloc requires some modification in the light of the acrimonious Sino-Soviet dispute over leadership of world communism. But there is nothing to suggest that this dispute is likely to result in basic changes in the economic organization of either Russia or China.

of consolidated long-term gains; China has found to its cost that it will have to be content with a considerably more modest rate of growth. China still has probably more than 60 per cent of its labor force engaged in agriculture, and there is little reason for thinking that it will be any more successful than the U.S.S.R. in solving its agricultural problems; they are, in any case, much more severe.

There are few studies of economic growth in the satellite countries. But there is no reason for believing that their rates of growth have been significantly lower than those of Western European countries. As in the U.S.S.R., a greater share of investment in consumer industries is now being made than in the Stalinist era. By 1964, however, both Poland and Czechoslovakia had found that overinvestment in basic industries had resulted in a neglect of higher manufactures, and their respective industrial products were becoming increasingly unacceptable on world markets.

A high rate of economic development is not a prerogative of any particular type of political organization. It is highly likely, moreover, that continuing competition between the U.S.S.R. and the West for world leadership will cause both parties to adopt many features of each other's economies that make for a high rate of growth and these can be employed without substantially modifying political institutions. Thus there is growing Western recognition of the advantage given the U.S.S.R. by its rigorous educational system with a strong emphasis on the sciences—the U.S.S.R. graduates three times as many engineers per year as the United States and as many geologists as the rest of the world.[14] Similarly, the excessive bureaucratic centralization which has stifled local economic development in the U.S.S.R. could ultimately be swept away. Any nation can have a high rate of economic growth if it really desires it.

[14] **Although this may not be such an advantage as it seems. Automation may economize in scientific personnel just as the use of machinery has economized in manual workers.**

OCCUPATIONS AND THEIR PRODUCTIVITY OVER THE WORLD

The world labor force is distributed in three principal categories of occupation:

1. Agriculture in the broadest sense, hunting, forestry, and fishing (sometimes called primary industry).
2. Manufacturing, mining, and building and construction (or secondary industry).
3. Nonmanufacturing and service industry, including transportation, communications, commerce, distribution, administration, and professional services (or tertiary industry).

Rudimentary service industries must of course exist for the appearance of any civilized society, and their development is ultimately bound up with the foundation and expansion of cities. Initially, however, these only employ a small proportion of a labor force which is almost entirely deployed in agricultural pursuits. An economy moves to the semideveloped stage by improving the productivity of agriculture and transferring workers into mining and manufacturing. In the final transition to the highly developed stage more workers leave agriculture for employment in manufacturing and service industries, and with increasing productivity in manufacturing and mining, workers in these industries may also transfer to service industries.

Variations in Economic Evolution The course of economic evolution just described was followed by most of the highly developed

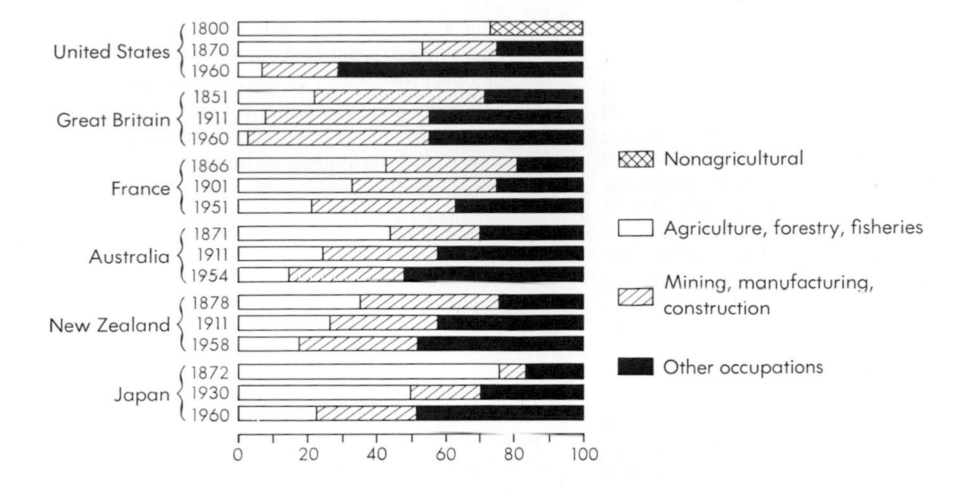

Fig. 1-7 Percentage distribution of labor force over time in selected countries.
Economic development greatly reduces the proportion of the work force engaged in agriculture. Note the rapid approach of Japan to the highly developed pattern.

countries; at certain points of time their economies were not so very different from those of countries at present lower on the scale of economic development (Fig. 1-7). The exceptions, and they are striking, are Australia and New Zealand, although both countries have shown a steady decline in the proportion of the total labor force engaged in agriculture. These Dominions never had, as did Western Europe and Anglo-America, a majority of workers engaged in agriculture, for the physical environment and the "squattocracy" (the large graziers who settled on land to which they had no legal title) combined to prevent the successive waves of pioneering settlement which were so prominent a feature in American economic history. From their earliest years these remote southern lands had a population concentrated in a few port settlements, and the growth of a large export trade in animal products which needed little farm labor merely confirmed the growth of the port cities. The Australian economy, in particular, has always possessed a large proportion of workers in service industries, and the establishment of manufacturing industries followed rather than preceded the expansion of the tertiary sector.

There is another important particular in which Australia and New Zealand are anomalous. They are the only countries in the world in which productivity (and therefore income) per agricultural worker is equivalent to that in nonagricultural pursuits; indeed, there are some who claim that it is superior.[15]

The lower the level of economic develop-

[15] **This is a contention long maintained by Colin Clark, but the author cannot accept it. Estimates of productivity per agricultural worker in Australia and New Zealand are artificially inflated because they fail to take into account the substantial unrecorded labor of the farmer's wife and family, particularly in dairying, which is a very important branch of farming in both countries.**

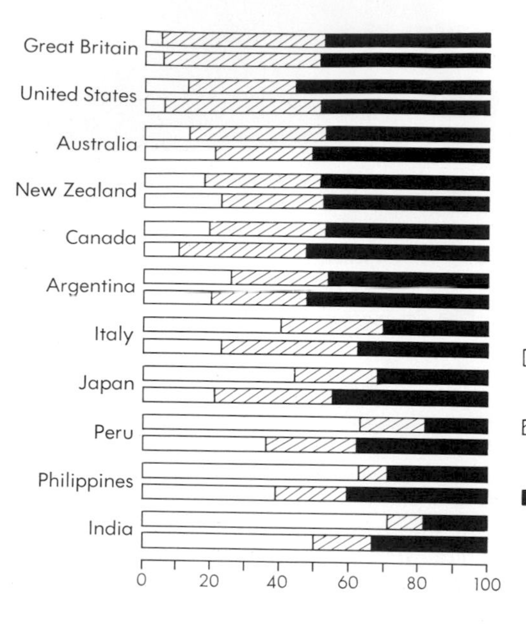

Fig. 1-8 Percentage distribution of labor force (upper bar) and national product (lower bar) by sectors of economy. Note the great disparities between the two distributions in economies at low levels of development, and the apparently anomalous positions of Australia and New Zealand.

ment, the greater the disparity between agricultural and nonagricultural incomes per capita, but in every type of economy agriculture's share of national product is lower than its share of employment (Fig. 1-8). This strongly suggests that agriculture everywhere is overpopulated, even in highly developed economies, and the continuous decline in farm population lends support to this view.

The main reason for such inequality lies in the much lower capitalization of agriculture; investment per worker in farming is usually lower, often very much lower, than that in either mining or manufacturing. Another important reason is that agriculture does not discharge its surplus labor fast enough, for the obstacles to the mobility of farm labor are much greater than those facing the worker in manufacturing or in a service industry.

In the comparatively recently settled and still thinly populated temperate lands of the Southern Hemisphere, however, physical and economic conditions alike encouraged an early specialization in capital-intensive livestock farming, and this has become steadily more pronounced. The productivity of the agricultural worker is thus extremely high. New Zealand and Australia lead the world in value of output per farm worker, and before World War II both Argentina and Uruguay also ranked very high. In Anglo-American and Western Europe, where agricultural productivity is extremely high by world standards, the output of the farm worker is still considerably below that of his nonagricultural counterpart. In centrally planned economies the niggardliness of agricultural investment has produced a disparity between the output of the agricultural and the industrial worker which is known to be very large; in underdeveloped economies the primitive techniques of agriculture are responsible for agricultural incomes per head that are frequently less than a quarter of those in other economic activities.

Occupations under the Four National Patterns In the highly developed countries the whole economy is integrated in the world market. Agriculture operates at a high level of efficiency with a relatively small labor force but still has lower per capita income than other activities. In manufacturing, the processing and working of minerals and metals are extremely well developed. The highly organized market is made possible by, and equally has made necessary, an elaborate system of distributive trades, transport, communications, and financial institutions.

In semideveloped countries some features of the highly developed economies are found, but they exist alongside an agricultural organization which still retains many of its traditional characteristics.

In underdeveloped countries only a very small portion of the economy has experienced the impact of the world market, and this portion is embedded in a rural and traditional economy largely aimed at local self-sufficiency. This "capitalist" sector is largely devoted to the production of commodities required by more highly developed countries, and serves needs which are international rather than national in origin. Manufacturing activities are largely concerned with processing the products of the "capitalist" sector for export. Large-scale capital-intensive industries scarcely exist, although they figure prominently in national development plans.

In the centrally planned economies, agriculture is backward, but manufacturing industry is even more specialized in mineral and metal processing and fabrication than in the highly developed economies. Consumer-goods industries receive the barest minimum of investment. Within the limitations of a central planning authority, the organization of the whole economy is directed at ensuring the maximum rate of economic growth with minor consideration for social cost.

SELECTED REFERENCES

Bauer, Peter T., and B. S. Yamey: "Economic Progress and Occupational Distribution," *Economic Journal,* vol. 61, pp. 741–755, 1951.

——— and ———: *Economics of Underdeveloped Countries,* Nisbet, London, 1957.

Clark, Colin: *The Conditions of Economic Progress,* 3d ed., Macmillan & Co., Ltd., London, 1957, pp. 490–520.

Dewhurst, J. Frederic, et al.: *Europe's Needs and Resources,* The Twentieth Century Fund, New York, 1961, pp. 61–106.

Ginsburg, Norton: *Atlas of Economic Development,* The University of Chicago Press, Chicago, 1961.

Johnston, B. F.: "Agricultural Productivity and Economic Development in Japan," *Journal of Political Economy,* vol. 59, pp. 498–513, 1951.

Kuznets, Simon: "Quantitative Aspects of the Economic Growth of Nations: II. Industrial Distribution of National Product and Labor Force," *Economic Development and Cultural Change,* vol. 5, supplement, 1957.

Lewis, W. A.: *The Theory of Economic Growth,* George Allen & Unwin, Ltd., London, 1960.

Rostow, W. W.: *Stages of Economic Growth,* Cambridge University Press, Cambridge, England, 1960.

Schwartz, Harry: *Russia's Soviet Economy,* 2d ed., Prentice-Hall, Inc., Englewood Cliffs, N.J., 1954.

Shimkin, Demitri: "Economic Regionalization in the Soviet Union," *Geographical Review,* vol. 42, pp. 591–614, 1952.

Wiles, P. J. D.: "Soviet Economy Outpaces the West," *Foreign Affairs,* vol. 31, pp. 566–580, 1953.

Woytinsky, W. S., and E. S. Woytinsky: *World Population and Production,* The Twentieth Century Fund, New York, 1953, pp. 413–450.

Chapter 2

WORLD POPULATION AND URBANISM

Many aspects of population exert a powerful effect on economic activity—total size, geographic distribution, the age and sex structure, health and the expectation of life, and whether population is increasing, stationary, or declining. The fact that world population now exceeds 3 billion is not *in itself* of much importance, for it is only in national and regional contexts that the relationship of population to resources becomes of practical significance.

GEOGRAPHIC DISTRIBUTION OF POPULATION

The great disparities in population distribution are among the most significant elements of human and economic geography, on both macrogeographic and microgeographic levels. It is far from easy to provide an explanation of this inequality, for the factors which influence population distribution are numerous and exceedingly complex. They are, moreover, continuously changing, though in the short period there is an appearance of stability.

The pattern of population distribution reflects the opportunities of gaining a livelihood. For the highly developed economies it could be claimed that this statement is absolutely true, but some qualifications need to be made concerning those at a lower level of development. The greatest concentrations in such economies are likely to be found in areas which have the highest capacity for supporting population with existing and traditional agricultural techniques; to support such concentrations usually entails the acceptance of a large volume of unemployed and/or underemployed, whose "marginal product," to use the term of the economist, is zero.

The negative areas are easiest disposed of, for though these areas are very extensive, the reasons for their emptiness are clear. Some 60 per cent of the land surface of the earth contains less than 5 per cent of the world population; in this portion of the world physical controls operate strongly. Rugged topography, climates that are very cold or dry or are hot and humid, and a thin, infertile soil all severely limit the capacity of peoples using traditional techniques to augment their numbers.

In numerous areas these factors are reinforced by spatial factors which result in isolation and limited possibilities of commercial contact. Such areas include the great mountain and plateau systems of the earth, the great deserts, whose wide extent is one of the most striking and significant features of the earth's physical geography, and the permanent ice caps. Almost in the same category are the vast and very scantily populated expanses of intertropical Africa, South America, and Southeast Asia, where high temperatures and heavy precipitation produce environments offering few opportunities for gaining a living except in a few restricted areas which have been modified by the importation of nonindigenous techniques. In more densely settled agricultural regions lacunae in the pattern of population distribution arise very largely from less favorable considerations of topography and soil.

The areas of greatest population concentration are more easily described than accounted for. The eastern and southern margins of Asia can be said to contain the greatest agglomeration of humanity, though this major concentration can be divided into two portions, the Far East and the Indian subcontinent. These are separated by the less densely populated Southeast Asia. Southeast Asia, however, has a few areas, such as the north Java plain and the Tonkin delta, where population densities approach or even exceed those of the most overcrowded parts of the Far East or of India. Another concentration appears in Europe; it is a matter of opinion whether the thickly populated east central portion of North America should be included to make one major concentration bordering the North Atlantic.

A number of secondary areas of concentration can also be distinguished. These include the Nile valley and the Guinea coastlands of Africa, the southeastern margin of South America and the intermontane basins of both South and Central America, certain of the Caribbean islands, the Pacific Coast of the United States, and southeast Australia.

It is striking fact that the overwhelming majority of the world's population lives at low elevations; 90 per cent of the world's people live in areas with an elevation of less than 1,200 feet.[1] Under certain conditions, mountains can support quite dense populations, as in the *tierra templada* of the highlands of Central and South America. But the limited area of cultivable land, the difficulty of working poor and stony soils, and the high cost of transport are great handicaps to most mountain dwellers, who almost everywhere in the world have a distinctive culture of their own. Mountain people are traditionally self-sufficient, highly independent, and, from the point of view of plains dwellers, lawless and troublesome people; the hill folk of the Appalachians and Ozarks, the Highlanders of Scotland, and the Montenegrins are examples that readily suggest themselves.

Plains offer enormous advantages for sedentary agriculturists. The growing season is longer than in upland areas, soils are deeper, and the level terrain permits the use of more productive equipment than the hoe or foot plough used by many mountain people. Main-

[1] Pierre George, *Introduction à l'étude géographique de la population du monde,* Presses Universitaires de France, Paris, 1951, p. 29.

tenance costs are markedly lower, and the relative ease of transport makes possible extensive commercial contact and offers the possibility of higher productivity (and hence higher living standards) through increased specialization.

Hardly less remarkable than the concentration of world population on plains is the enormous attraction of coastal and peripheral areas, particularly in temperate latitudes. Physical and climatic conditions are generally more favorable than those of the continental interiors, but these marginal agglomerations owe more, perhaps, to the greatly enhanced opportunities for cultural and commercial contacts that arise from greater mobility. As commercial contacts grow, the advantages of established route centers are confirmed and augmented, and those with maritime locations enjoy new opportunities denied to rivals inland. Concentrations, once initiated, tend to expand as the opportunities for specialization are increased. A small and scattered population has little chance of achieving a higher level of productivity because such a population by its very nature must be largely self-sufficient. One very important consequence of specialization is the growth of cities.

It appears certain that in all types of economies population distribution will continue to become more uneven; the great concentrations of population in the world will become more marked, and the present comparatively empty areas will continue to support only a minute fraction of the world's inhabitants, even though in absolute numbers their populations may increase. Evidence for this view is provided by the course of industrialization and city development, by the fact that the greatly needed increases in world food production appear more likely to eventuate through raising yields on the existing cultivated area rather than large additions to it, and by world demographic trends.

URBANIZATION AND INDUSTRIALIZATION

Economic development inevitably entails an increase in urbanization; in fact, the two are almost synonymous. In the modern world the impetus for economic growth originates in the cities, and is directed towards activities that must result in a further increase in the number and size of citics. *Urban populations are capital-accumulating; rural populations are generally capital-consuming.* In highly developed economies and in some semideveloped economies, it is the cities that support the rural areas; agricultural incomes are always higher than they would be in a completely free economy. The cities produce equipment and fertilizers which enable agriculture to replace the natural capital removed from the soil in cultivation.

Cities are as old as civilization itself, but they could not have developed without the production of a local agricultural surplus by sedentary agriculturists. The first cities were thus supported by the countryside, and this is still the situation in underdeveloped economies, where, through cheap-food policies and disproportionate taxation and in many other ways, the peasant is made to pay for industrialization programs.

It seems probable that the transition from the underdeveloped to the semideveloped stage takes place when capital accumulation in the cities exceeds that in the countryside. Even in classical times the profits of trade were frequently applied to country estates, and this tendency has been recurrent in European economic history since the Middle Ages. One reason for the low rate of capital accumulation in underdeveloped economies is that their urban populations are so small; the cities, moreover, make little investment in increasing agricultural productivity.

Cities have been founded for a number of reasons—as strategic centers or strongpoints, at places of religious significance, or as trade centers. In some parts of the world, such as Southeast Asia, city development only occurred with a favorable concurrence of princely, religious, and commercial interests; elsewhere in Asia the establishment of large political units or empires generally confirmed the royal seat as an urban center of some magnitude. But cities grow on what they feed, and the main sustenance of cities has always been commerce; trade of some kind probably predates civilization itself. Simple manufacturing may well have developed from trading interests; conversely, trading interests may have appeared in response to some handicraft based on local skill or raw materials. Skilled handicrafts serving the needs of princely courts or religious temples or shrines have been a feature of every indigenous Asian city and of every past civilization. Manufacturing and service industries have almost certainly been associated with cities from their first beginnings.

But the cities' almost complete monopoly of manufacturing, at least outside underdeveloped economies, is of comparatively recent origin. The concentration of manufacturing in towns is largely a consequence of the application of power, particularly steam power based on coal. Technological change has produced alternative sources of power which might, indeed, make possible a continuation of some industrial production outside the towns at competitive cost levels. Japan is outstanding in the way in which small-scale industries[2] have been able to maintain a place in a rapidly industrializing economy, but these are mainly located in towns rather than in the countryside. Electric power or small internal-combustion engines can effect great increases in the productivity of village industries, but it appears out of the question for an economy to industrialize without greatly expanding its urban population both absolutely and relatively.

[2] See p. 259.

A very powerful stimulus to city growth over the last 150 years has been the growth of manufacturing, which has been greatly influenced by the occurrence of suitable raw materials and above all by the existence of deposits of metalliferous minerals and sources of fuel and power. Outstanding, of course, is the great attraction of coalfields, for coal is both a major source of power and an indispensable raw material in the iron and steel and chemical industries; it is also essential for the reduction of many other metalliferous ores. At a stage of technological development which necessitated the consumption of 8 tons of coal for the production of 1 ton of pig iron, the attraction of coalfields for the production of iron and steel and for related heavy industries was irresistible. On this coal-iron combination grew up a great series of population concentrations, which have continued to constitute the primary markets for all other power and mineral industries. For this reason, alternative sources of fuel such as petroleum and natural gas have not exercised anything like as great an attraction for industrial development as coal, although the greater ease of transporting these products and their frequent occurrence in extremely unattractive environments have also been important contributory factors.

The Large City

As economic development proceeds, a greater proportion of the population lives in large cities (Table 2-1). This happens because manufacturing grows through increasing specialization and a considerable number of "external economies" appear as a result of a concentration of producers in a particular area. Knowledge of processes and markets are more easily shared, and opportunities for the profitable use of by-products arise more easily, as do those for further specialization. The end products of one industry become the raw

Table 2-1

Percentage of Population Living in Urban Areas of 100,000 or More, in Selected Countries

COUNTRY	YEAR	TOTAL POPULATION (MILLIONS)	PERCENTAGE IN URBAN AREAS OF 100,000 OR MORE
United States	1960	179.3	61.7
Australia	1960	10.3	56.3
Britain	1959	50.7	51.0
West Germany	1959	53.0	35.1
Canada	1960	17.8	34.8
New Zealand	1960	2.4	33.3
Japan	1959	93.0	41.2
Argentina	1958	20.2	39.6
Italy	1959	49.1	23.8
Portugal	1959	9.1	13.2
Brazil	1960	65.7	18.3
India	1960	408.1	9.8
Philippines	1960	27.5	9.8
Indonesia	1959	90.3	9.4

SOURCE: United Nations, Demographic Yearbook, 1960.

materials of another, or the particular requirements of one industry make necessary the establishment of others to supply them. Moreover, *manufacturing creates not only its markets but also its labor supply;* under the impact of industrialization population grows rapidly, and the greater part of this increase occurs in the cities, partly through natural increase and partly through immigration from the rural areas. Once established, manufacturing develops considerable momentum, and population tends to grow fastest where industrial growth is proceeding most rapidly. The advantages of the large cities are thus steadily augmented—they constitute the industrial complexes from which new industries are most likely to rise and the largest markets and reservoirs of labor. Success breeds success.

Industrialization has produced conurbation extending over hundreds of square miles in advanced economies, but the very large city is now of worldwide distribution. Many underdeveloped economies support one city with a population of 1 million, and some have more. The growth of the large city proceeds apace in underdeveloped economies even though relatively little expansion in industrial capacity may be involved. Despite the lack of jobs for newcomers, the very large cities of underdeveloped countries continue to attract large numbers of in-migrants from the rural areas.

The great majority of city in-migrants in countries that are not highly developed are little better off than they were before, but they find city life immensely more satisfying than life in the villages. In mainland China the perpetual influx into the great cities has provoked the government to conduct periodic roundups of in-migrants and to return them to the country. The U.S.S.R. has long operated a passport system to control internal movement and to check the drift of farm workers to the cities. Precisely similar measures are taken to deal with in-migrants into the cities of southern Africa. The appeal of the city is universal.

It is tempting, therefore, to distinguish between a "true" urbanization which reflects an expansion of nonagricultural activities and constitutes a step forward in economic development, and a "false" or "spurious" urbanization which is the result of the social and political attraction of city life. Of course, many in-migrants to the cities of highly developed economies, particularly the largest cities, are thus attracted, but this scarcely matters, for the new population is soon absorbed in the expanding manufacturing and service industries. In the underdeveloped economies, however, the growing number of city dwellers, for whom there is little hope of permanent employment, is producing a highly explosive political situation—the result of desire to enjoy the fruits of a higher level of economic development before they have been realized.

Even the largest urban agglomerations of the world are not exclusively located in the highly developed economies. As the centers of industrial and commercial empires with world-wide ramifications, London and New York are in a class by themselves; London is the major administrative center of the British Commonwealth, and New York stands in the center of world politics as the home of the United Nations. Both of these supergiant cities have a population exceeding 10 million.[3] Yet of the same order of magnitude, and rapidly acquiring a similar world-embracing network of economic and financial relationships, is Tokyo, sometimes claimed to be the world's largest city.

The giant cities of the second order, those with a population exceeding 4 million, are 9 in number. The highly developed economies possess 4—Chicago, Los Angeles, Philadelphia, and Paris; but for partition and the flight of a substantial population to West Germany, Berlin might have been added to this number. West Germany does in fact have a conurbation with a population exceeding 4 million in the North Rhine–Westphalia conurbation, but each of its many centers is enumerated separately in German censuses. The semi-developed economies possess only 1 city of this order of magnitude, Buenos Aires. The centrally planned economies have 3 such cities—Moscow, Shanghai, and Peking. Calcutta is the only city of this size category in an underdeveloped economy.

In 1935 there were 56 cities with a population of over 1 million;[4] by 1960 the number had risen to 100.[5] Of these 100 "million cities," 41 are situated in the highly developed economies; several additional cities in these economies have substantially more than a million inhabitants within their effective metropolitan areas. The semideveloped economies possess 20 "million cities"; centrally planned economies contain 21; while the underdeveloped economies, with not far short of half the world's population, have only 18. Thus the urban revolution that such cities symbolize has so far affected only a small fraction of the world's population; but the number of "million cities" seems certain to go on expanding—in part, of course, reflecting the rapid increase in world population.

[3] The population of the Greater London Region of the Ministry of Planning and Local Government exceeds 10 million. Though the region includes considerable rural areas, it by no means embraces all the smaller urban centers which are entirely tributary to London.

[4] Audrey M. Lambert, "Millionaire Cities," *Economic Geography,* **vol. 32, p. 285, 1956.**

[5] United Nations, Demographic Yearbook, 1960, New York, 1961, table 7.

Inchoate urban sprawl produces formidable problems, of which traffic congestion and atmospheric pollution are merely among the more obvious. Even the underdeveloped economies may possess great cities, whose downtown districts differ little from those of Western cities. The city margins, however, as visible in Hong Kong (right), are invariably the sites of continually poliferating slums created by in-migrants from rural areas.

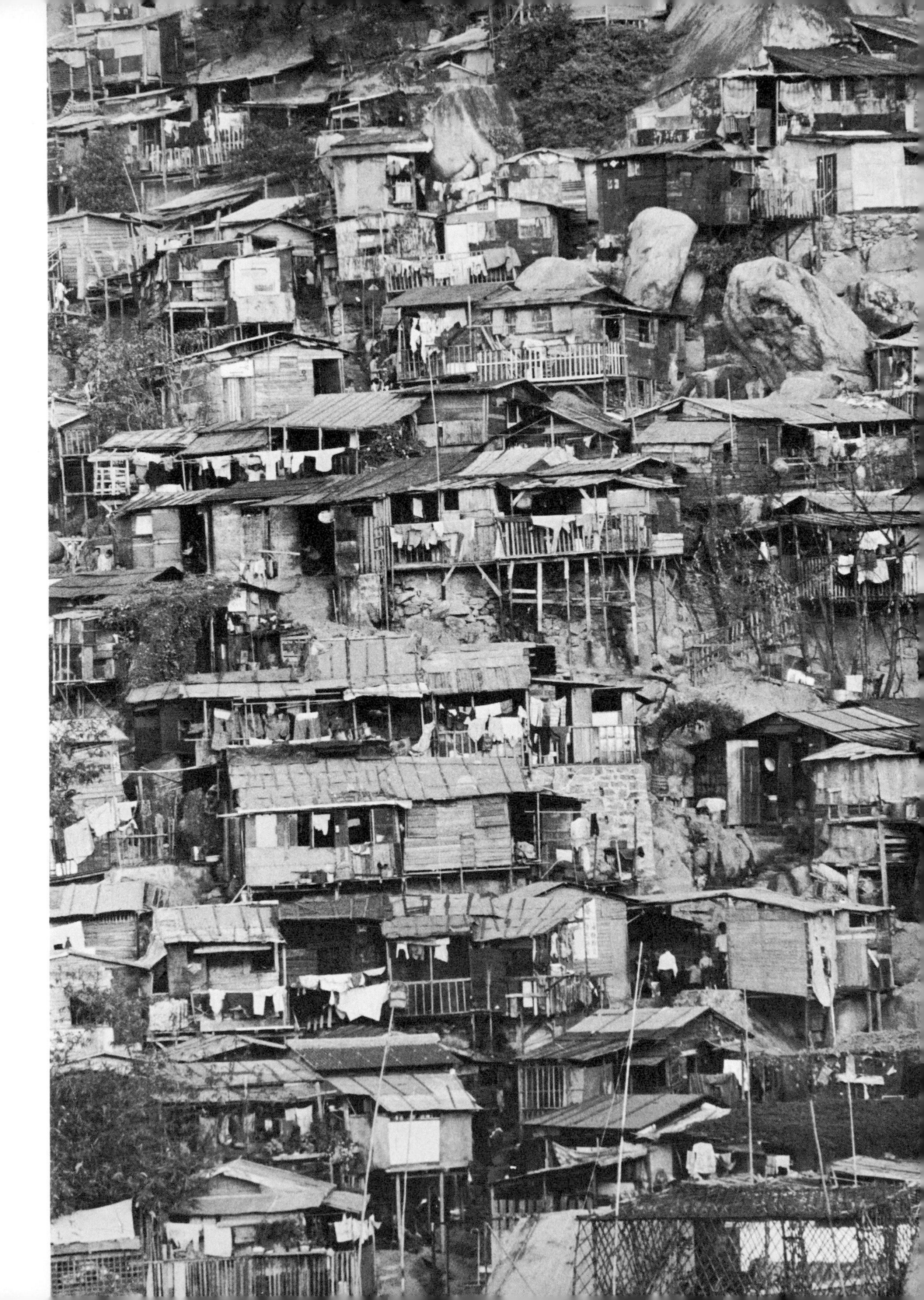

Table 2-2

Estimates of World Population by Continents, 1650–2000 (Millions)

	1650	1750	1850	1950	2000
Africa	100	95	95	198	520
North America	1	1	26	166	310
Central America	6	5	13	51	200
South America	6	6	20	111	400
Asia	330	479	749	1,302	3,870*
Europe	100	140	266	559	570*
Oceania	2	2	2	13	30
WORLD TOTAL	545	728	1,179	2,400	6,280†

* Excluding U.S.S.R., estimated at 380 million in 2000.
† Figures have been rounded off. Total includes U.S.S.R., 380.
SOURCE: W. S. Woytinsky and E. S. Woytinsky, *World Population and Industries, 1953,* United Nations Population Studies, no. 28, 1958.

POPULATION GROWTH AND STRUCTURE

Whether an expanding population constitutes an impediment or a stimulus to economic growth is still debated by economists and sociologists. Considerable evidence can be produced to support either view, and the question is heavily charged with political and religious overtones; Marxists and Catholics, for example, both regard an expanding population as advantageous and denounce, for different reasons, any attempt at limiting the rate of growth. But population and economic growth are not independent: they profoundly influence each other. A rapid rate of population growth at an advanced level of economic development can have consequences vastly different from those of a similar rate of population growth in a backward economy.

There is no doubt, however, that world population is expanding very rapidly. Only a world catastrophe of an unprecedented scale, such as a thermonuclear war and the complete breakdown of social order, can prevent world population from reaching a level of between 6 and 7 billion by the end of the century. The virtual certainty that by about 1980 world population will be double what it was in 1950 transcends all economic considerations; in the words of a United Nations report, "We should do well to ponder the significance of this development in terms of the destiny of our species."[6]

World population in 1960 totaled some 3 billion. It is clear that for very long periods of time population can only have grown slowly, and must have suffered many setbacks from natural and man-made disasters. It is probably only within the last 150 years that population growth in Europe has exceeded an annual rate of 0.1 per cent, and it appears likely that in no half-century prior to 1650 did total world population increase by more than about 10 per cent. Since 1650, however, the world proportionate increase has grown half-century by half-century, and it probably amounted to over 50 per cent between 1901 and 1950 (Table 2-2).

It is not necessary to postulate any increase

[6] United Nations, Department of Social and Economic Affairs, *The Future Growth of World Population,* Population Studies, no. 28, New York, 1958, p. 20.

in the capacity of the human species to reproduce itself to account for this remarkable growth over the past three centuries, or even any desire on the part of humanity to do so. It may have been that the addition to the family income that could be made by putting children to work at an early age occasionally tended to encourage larger families; Defoe comments on the employment of very young children in the Yorkshire woolen industry in the early eighteenth century.[7] It has sometimes been suggested that a major reason for the rapid growth of population in Java in the nineteenth century was the encouragement given to the production of large families by the "culture system," a system of forced deliveries of exportable crops. But it is equally probable that children have always constituted an economic liability of greater or lesser extent. There is nothing in the demographic history of Java to suggest that it has differed materially from that of any other underdeveloped economy. The birth rate in England in the early eighteenth century and that in Java in the nineteenth century were probably not far short of the theoretical maximum, but early, universal marriage and large families have always been the fundamental pattern of human society, and are still so today over large parts of the world. Only by such social organization have populations been able to maintain themselves against periodic ravages of famine, pestilence, war, and an extremely high infant mortality.

The explanation of the quickening rate of population growth in the last three centuries almost certainly resides in the great reduction in mortality achieved through the growth of scientific knowledge and its widening application throughout the world. The reduction has been achieved above all through control of infectious diseases such as bubonic plague (the Black Death of the Middle Ages), typhoid, and cholera, which have been prevented from reaching epidemic proportions. The establishment of strong governments, the elimination of internecine warfare, and improved transport have converted famine from a major local or regional disaster into an essentially administrative problem.

The reduction in mortality appeared first in Europe, where from the mid-seventeenth century there was a remarkable quickening in the pace of scientific discovery. With the passing of enormous areas of the world under the political control of Europeans, the decline in mortality became firmly established. The discovery of the causes of malaria, yellow fever, sleeping sickness, and other diseases finally gave promise of a tremendous reduction in mortality in the intertropical world; this was not fully realized, however, until after World War II, when extremely effective and relatively cheap insecticides at last became available. Between 1945 and 1950 Ceylon achieved a reduction in mortality commensurate with that achieved by Britain in about six decades of the nineteenth century.

Contemporary accounts leave little doubt of the highly insalubrious conditions that existed in the new and rapidly industrializing cities of Britain during the Industrial Revolution. But real incomes and standards of living slowly mounted during the Victorian "age of improvement"; better diet assisted in reducing mortality, and the expectation of life grew. With a birth rate that remained at a high level, the population of Britain began to expand rapidly (Fig. 2-1). Towards the end of the nineteenth century, however, a decline in fertility was established, which has persisted. Higher living standards, the city way of life, the realization that children in large families cannot receive such a favorable preparation for

[7] **Daniel Defoe,** *A Tour through England and Wales,* **Everyman ed., J. M. Dent & Sons, Ltd., Publishers, London, 1928, vol. 2, p. 195.**

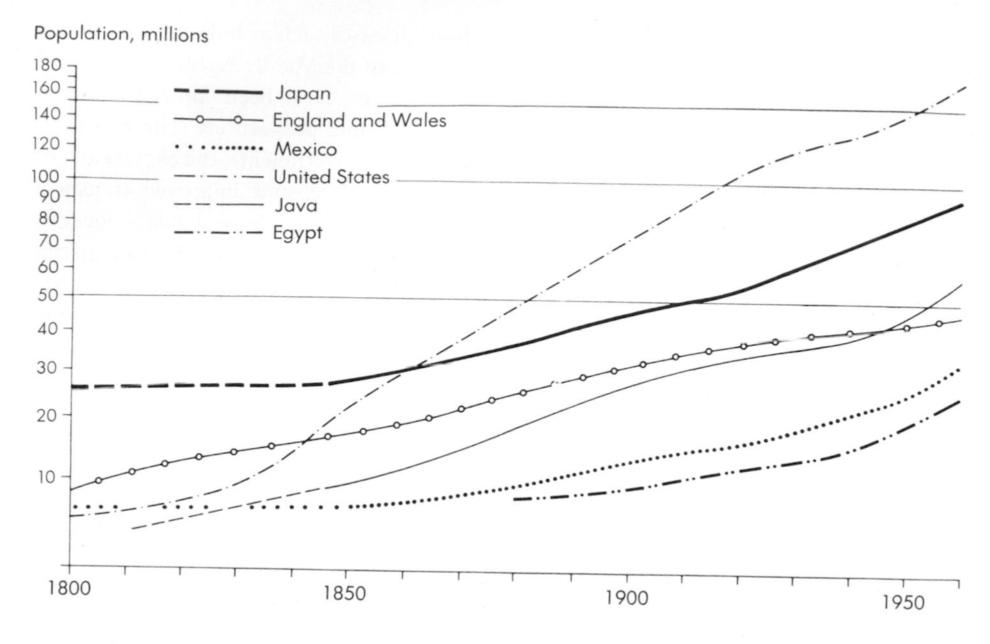

Fig. 2-1 Population growth in selected countries, 1800–1955. Rapid population growth has been experienced in countries at all levels of economic development over the past century.

life as is possible in small families, and, perhaps most importantly, the spread of techniques of family limitation all help to account for the reduction in fertility. It is significant that in rural areas where these influences have been less felt, fertility has remained substantially higher than in the cities.

Every country passing through a process of rapid industrialization has experienced an essentially similar demographic evolution, and there is strong evidence that the countries that have recently commenced their industrial development will also do so. The effect of urbanization and industrialization appears essentially the same throughout the world.

The application of Western medical knowledge in dependent territories, however, resulted in a population growth *unaccompanied by any proportional increase in urbanization and industrialization.* Java experienced a pattern of population growth similar to that of Great Britain, but in Java the far-reaching changes in population structure which took place in Britain with the final balance of a low death rate against a low birth rate have not so far occurred. It has been a comparatively easy matter to effect marked reductions in death rates through the use of only limited capital investment. It is very much more difficult to bring pressure to bear on the complex of social forces which results in a high rate of population replacement no longer biologically necessary. Moreover, there is still scope for further substantial declines in death rates in many parts of the world, particularly through the reduction of infant mortality. Thus it is clear that the capacity of world population for growth will augment as more infants and children survive. The total increase from 1950 to 1975 is expected to be about 54 per cent; from 1975 to 2000 a further increase of 64 to 79 per cent is expected.[8]

In underdeveloped economies birth rates are very high. Crude birth rates of more than 40 per thousand of population are found in many countries of Latin America, in much of Southeast and East Asia, in many of the island groups of the Pacific, and, though there are only very incomplete and imperfect statistics, over the greater part of Africa. Most highly developed economies, on the other hand, have crude birth rates of around 20 per thousand, and in several countries of Western Europe the rates are well below this. But there has been a marked increase in birth rate in such economies since the end of World War II, and it now seems clear that the very low rates recorded during the Thirties, which greatly colored demographic writing at the time,[9] were the result of acute economic depression. Semideveloped economies generally have moderately high birth rates, although several are now approaching the low rates characteristic of the highly developed economies.

Death rates show much less variation, and the trend is markedly downward throughout the world. There are, however, very great differences in infant mortality rates between the various types of economies, and there is an enormous field for their reduction over much of the world (Fig. 2-2). The high infant mortality in underdeveloped economies arises from lack of medical care and attention, from inadequate housing and sanitation, and, above all, from an inadequate diet both for mother and infant. In highly developed economies, reductions in infant mortality now mirror the success achieved in saving premature babies. The lower mortality of the highly developed economies gives to their citizens an expectation of life at birth which is twice as high as that of the underdeveloped economies (Fig. 2-3).

With high infant and child mortality and low expectation of life, the working life of the average individual in an underdeveloped country is very short—often too short to repay even the limited amount of capital invested in him. A high birth rate and a high mortality rate produce a population structure in which there are too few adults and too many children for economic efficiency. In most underdeveloped economies the proportion of the total population that is below fifteen years of age is around 40 per cent. Thus a large proportion of the population contributes little to production, despite the fact that children are frequently used for certain agricultural tasks. The child workers drag down the average productivity per head, and it is commonly found that there is a marked shortage of skilled and semiskilled labor.

In contrast, the population structure of the highly developed economies shows a comparatively small proportion of children and young dependents and a large proportion of population of working age (fifteen to sixty-five years). Only about 25 per cent of the population consists of children and young people; 60 per cent or more of the population is of working age, compared with 55 per cent or less in the underdeveloped economies. The greater expectation of life also results in a proportion of population over the age of sixty-five about twice as great as that of the underdeveloped economies. These varying structures are clearly visible in Fig. 2-4.

The Population Cycle

Reviewing these changes in birth and death rates and the changes in population structure that result from them, it is possible to distin-

[8] United Nations, *op. cit.*, p. 21.

[9] An estimate of 160 million for the population of the United States in the year 1960, made in 1937 on the basis of the balance of births and deaths in the Depression years, had already been greatly exceeded by 1953.

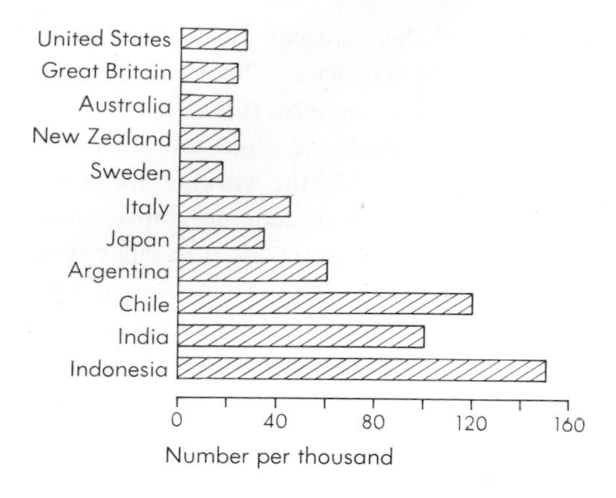

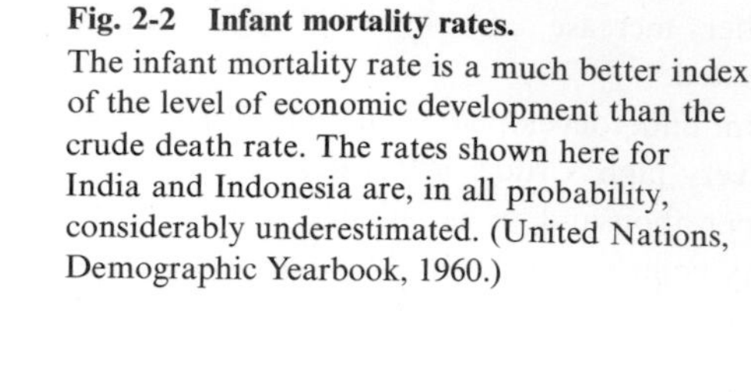

Fig. 2-2 Infant mortality rates.
The infant mortality rate is a much better index of the level of economic development than the crude death rate. The rates shown here for India and Indonesia are, in all probability, considerably underestimated. (United Nations, Demographic Yearbook, 1960.)

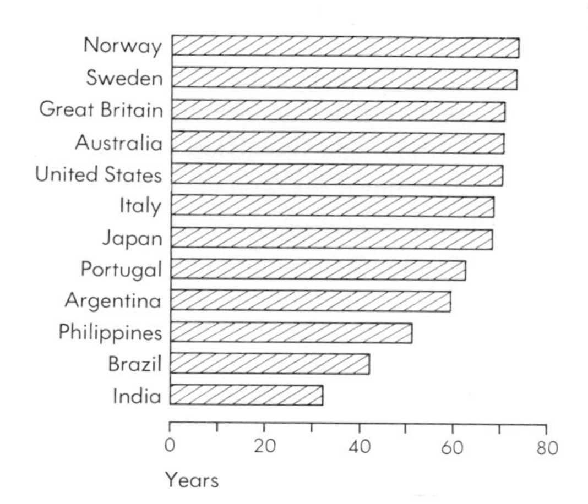

Fig. 2-3 Expectation of life at birth.
The expectation of life at birth in an underdeveloped economy is only about half that of an economy at a high level of development.

guish four main stages of demographic evolution which together comprise the *cycle of population*, or *demographic transition.*

The first stage is that which has existed through the greater part of historical time, terminating in Europe about the middle of the seventeenth century. This stage is characterized by high birth and death rates; population growth proceeds only very slowly, and is punctuated by periods of decline.

The next stage is marked by declining mortality, though fertility remains at a high level. This is the stage of Western Europe before the Industrial Revolution and of the

Fig. 2-4 (opposite) Population structure.
The typically pyramidal pattern of population structure in underdeveloped economies contrasts markedly with the bell-shaped pattern of the highly developed economies; in the recent past, however, the latter possessed population structures not so very different from those of the present underdeveloped economies. Japan's approaching economic maturity is reflected in rapid demographic change.

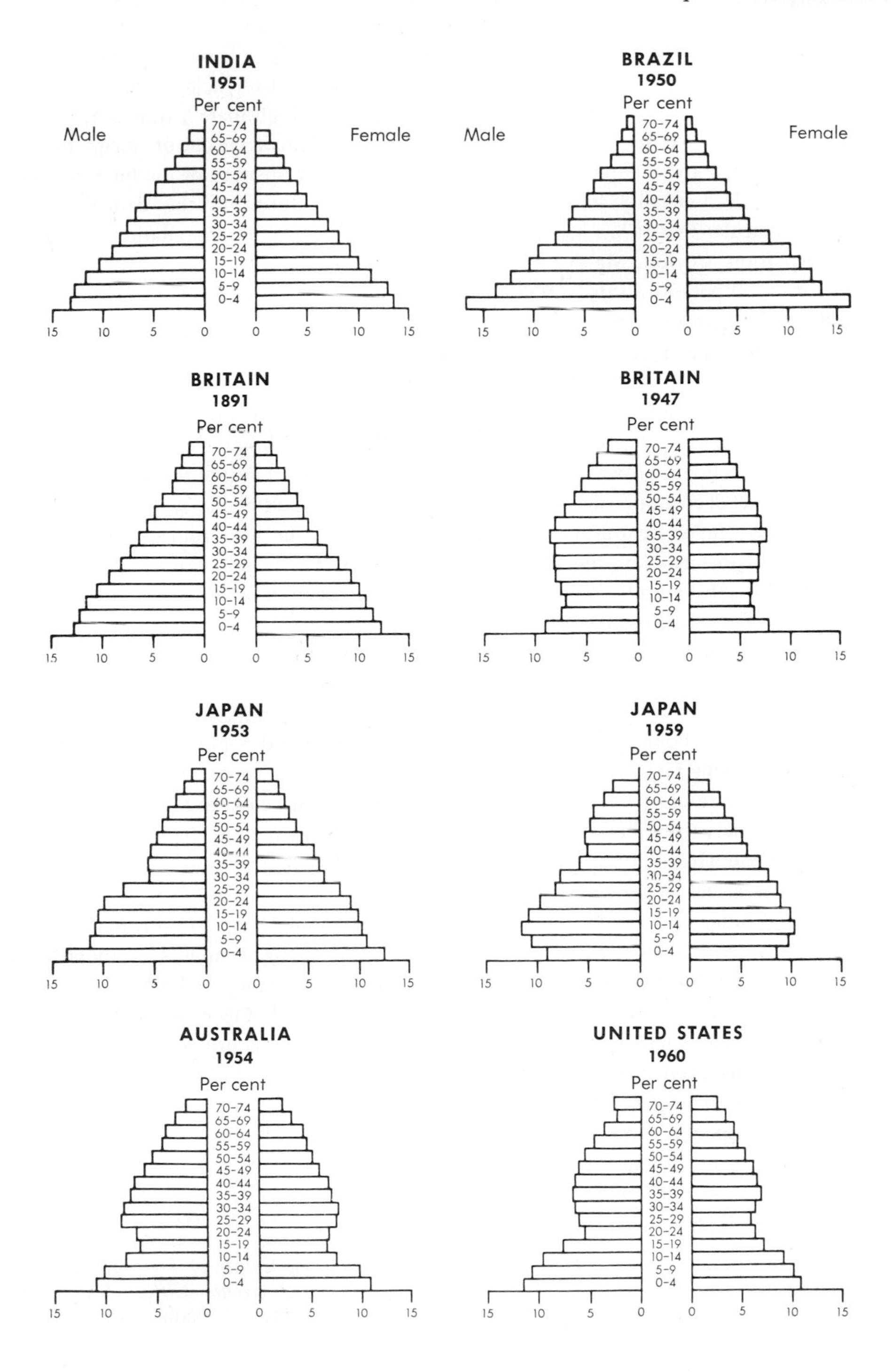
INDIA
1951
Per cent
Male
Female
BRAZIL
1950
Per cent
Male
Female
BRITAIN
1891
Per cent
BRITAIN
1947
Per cent
JAPAN
1953
Per cent
JAPAN
1959
Per cent
AUSTRALIA
1954
Per cent
UNITED STATES
1960
Per cent
70-74
65-69
60-64
55-59
50-54
45-49
40-44
35-39
30-34
25-29
20-24
15-19
10-14
5-9
0-4
15 10 5 0
0 5 10 15

greater part of Asia, Africa, and Latin America at the present day. Notestein calls this stage of development one of "high growth potential," for with the changing balance of birth and death rates, population grows rapidly. In some countries the fall in mortality has been so sudden and spectacular that it has produced a population explosion; Ceylon, Malaya, Singapore, and Taiwan all possess a rate of population growth of 3.5 per cent per annum. A population growing at this rate would increase itself tenfold in sixty-seven years, but it is inconceivable, of course, that such a rate of growth could endure for so long.

The stage of transitional growth is attained when the higher level of economic development has begun to exert influence on the factors responsible for a high birth rate. Fertility declines but is still substantially higher than mortality, which falls more rapidly than before. This is the demographic stage of Western Europe in the full flush of industrialization and that of the semideveloped economies and the U.S.S.R. at the present. Population continues to grow but at a declining rate.

The final stage is reached with the transformation of the society from a predominantly rural to an urban one. Higher living standards, a greatly changed social outlook, and widespread use of techniques of family limitation produce a marked decline in the birth rate. With a low birth rate and death rate the population is once more in balance, though at a much higher numerical level than initially. The excess of births over deaths produces only a slow growth of population. This is the situation of all the highly developed economies and one which will probably be attained by several semideveloped economies and the U.S.S.R. before the end of the century.

The very low birth rates in the highly developed economies during the years of the Great Depression gave rise to a number of gloomy statements that the white populations of the world were not replacing themselves and were in danger of ultimate extinction; thus Notestein called this stage one of "incipient decline." The postwar upswing of the birth rate in these economies illustrates the dangers of basing estimates of future population on current or past trends.

Only a very small portion of the world's population has achieved this final demographic balance; what are the prospects of a more widespread demographic transition in the future? To this complex problem there is no clear answer. It is quite clear, however, that the proportionate distribution of the world's population by continents will undergo marked changes in the near future. The effect of the rapid growth of population in Europe and in other continents in which Europeans settled in large numbers was to reduce the share of world population of Africa and Asia. Now it is certain that Asia, which has always been the most populous continent, will contain a larger proportion of world population than it ever has in the past; from some 54 per cent in 1950 its share will rise to about 62 per cent by the year 2000, by which time it will probably possess almost 4 billion people, virtually three times the 1950 figure (Table 2-2, p. 36).

This would seem to indicate that the task of raising living standards in underdeveloped economies is going to be far harder than is often supposed; the prospect that greatly inflated populations are going to be attained so quickly makes the task of matching population growth with an enhanced resource basis considerably more difficult.

SELECTED REFERENCES

Alexanderson, Gunnar: *The Industrial Structure of American Cities,* University of Nebraska Press, Lincoln, Nebr., 1956.

Bennett, M. K.: *The World's Food,* Harper & Row, Publishers, Incorporated, 1954, New York, pp. 3–57.

Broek, Jan O. M.: "Climate and Future Settlement," *Climate and Man,* Yearbook of Agriculture, 1941, U.S. Department of Agriculture, 1941, pp. 227–236.

Conference on the Role of Cities in Economic Development and Cultural Change: *Economic Development and Cultural Change,* vol. 3, nos. 1 and 2, 1955.

Gottman, Jean: "Megalopolis, or the Urbanization of the Northeastern Seaboard," *Economic Geography,* vol. 33, pp. 189–200, July, 1957.

Hoselitz, B. F.: "The City, the Factory and Economic Growth," *American Economic Review,* vol. 45, pp. 166–184, May, 1955.

Huntington, Ellsworth: *Civilization and Climate,* Yale University Press, New Haven, Conn., 1939, chap. 18.

Lee, Douglas H. K.: *Climate and Economic Development in the Tropics,* Harper & Row, Publishers, Incorporated, New York, 1957.

Markham, S. F.: *Climate and the Energy of Nations,* Oxford University Press, London, 1944.

Mumford, Lewis: *The Culture of Cities,* Harcourt, Brace and Company, Inc., New York, 1938.

Notestein, F. W., et al.: *The Future Population of Europe and the U.S.S.R.,* League of Nations, Geneva, 1944.

United Nations: *Determinants and Consequences of Population Trends,* New York, 1953.

———: *The Future Growth of World Population,* Population Studies, no. 28, New York, 1958.

PART II

Agriculture, forestry, and fishing

Chapter 3

AGRICULTURE IN THE WORLD ECONOMY

It has often been observed that agriculture is, and always has been, the leading occupation of mankind. It is less often remarked that this fact is indicative of the generally low level of economic development of the world as a whole and of the enormous scope that exists for economic progress. Perhaps at some future date the statement may no longer be true; when agriculture employs only about one-quarter of the world's working population instead of almost two-thirds as at present, the world will be a pleasanter place for the great majority of its inhabitants. They may or may not be happier, but their working lives will certainly be more rewarding in terms of real income.

THE ECONOMIC STATUS OF THE FARMER

World agriculture comprises two great divisions—*subsistence* and *commercial.* The great majority of the world's farmers are subsistence farmers; that is, their production is primarily intended for the needs of the cultivator himself and his family. Only when these needs have been met and an allowance has been made for seed is any surplus offered for sale. There are very few farmers who are not obliged to earn some cash income for the purchase of certain essentials and for the payment of taxes, but there are many farmers who are not even able to produce enough for their own sustenance. These farmers survive through becoming continually more indebted to moneylenders or through taking jobs with other employers wherever they can. In advanced economies agriculture is commercialized and forms an integral part of a monetary economy; output is for sale, and final consumption may take place many thousands of miles from the farm on which the crop was grown. The requirements of the commercial farmer's household are purchased from the proceeds of the sale of farm products, but in addition the commercial farmer expects to receive a reasonable return on the capital invested in the farm and a profit to encourage him to remain in business. At times, however, these expectations may not be realized.

But whether agriculture is of the subsistence or the commercial kind, it is a form of economic activity that on the whole offers only meager returns to those engaged in it. It is true that at times great fortunes may be made in certain lines of agricultural production. But the wheel of fortune spins rapidly, and a graph of the movement of world prices for many farm products during the present century resembles a series of alpine peaks and precipitous drops.

In subsistence agriculture what the farmer receives in return for his labor depends primarily on the bounty or otherwise of nature and on his social obligations; he may be compelled to turn over half or more of his crop to the landlord or to dispose of it to moneylenders or middlemen at a substantial discount. The commercial farmer is scarcely less dependent on nature, but his real income depends upon the *relationship of the prices of the farm products that he sells to the prices of the things he needs to purchase.* The commercial farmer usually has no more control over these two sets of prices than he has over the forces of nature, though he will certainly bring pressure to bear upon his government to compensate him for any marked disparity.

It has already been remarked that in all economies incomes per head in agriculture are lower than in nonagricultural pursuits. One major reason is that the capital investment per agricultural worker is generally much lower than for his nonagricultural counterpart. The size of the productive unit is smaller; even in many advanced countries the family farm is still regarded as socially and economically desirable, although the small family unit has long ceased to be of importance in manufacturing. Another major disability of agriculture is its dependence on soil and water supply, weather, and the biological processes of plant and animal life. In manufacturing, every stage of production is under complete control, and output can easily be varied to meet changes in demand.

Under certain conditions some control can be exercised over the natural influences on agriculture; the magnitude of a crop, however, is never really certain until it is harvested, and an increase in the demand for agricultural products can seldom be satisfied as quickly as in the case of industrial products. Tree crops require several years to come into bearing; if the increased demand is not sustained, the additional output is likely to produce a considerable price drop. Even with annual crops it is not easy to effect a sudden increase in output; unless the land is prepared at the right time and weather conditions are favorable, a whole season can be lost. Downward adjustments of output are even more difficult. Unlike manufacturers, farmers can seldom reduce output when prices fall, because to do so makes little difference to their costs. In agriculture fixed costs are generally a large proportion of total costs, and are incurred whatever the level of farm production; only in types of farming where fixed costs are relatively low, as in smallholder rubber production, does output show rapid response to price stimuli.[1]

Moreover, demand for most agricultural products is inelastic; a fall in price does not stimulate demand to any great extent, as is usually the case with manufactured products. Agriculture is mainly concerned with food production, but people's capacity to consume food is limited; their capacity for consuming manufactured products, on the other hand, is virtually unlimited. Once people have attained

[1] **See p. 87–88.**

an adequate diet, they do not react to a fall in the price of foodstuffs by consuming very much more. Moreover, as economic development proceeds and people become richer, they will, in accordance with Engel's law, spend proportionately less of their income on food and more on other things; most of the extra income of the community thus flows to the producers of manufactured goods and services.

To some extent, however, the diminishing share of agriculture in total expenditure may be offset by the substitution of more expensive foodstuffs for cheaper ones. With increasing wealth the proportion of the diet that is composed of starchy staples (that is, cereals, potatoes, and other tubers, which have a high calorie content) declines, but the consumption of milk and dairy products, eggs, meat, and fresh fruit tends to increase. The latter foods possess relatively few calories, but they are essential for the preservation of bodily health and efficiency. A diet that contains a high proportion of starchy foods is an unbalanced one, for though providing bodily energy, it is inadequate to provide resistence against infection and may give rise to deficiency diseases, such as beriberi, pellagra, and kwashiorkor, a protein deficiency common among children in the tropics.

A country with high living standards gets a substantial portion of its foodstuffs from animal products, which alone contain first-class protein.[2] Animal products are expensive because their production takes more time than is required for that of starchy foods, and in the process there is a considerable calorie loss; only a small portion of the vegetable calories consumed by the animal appear as usable animal calories. Animal farming thus yields a high return wherever it can be carried on, but it generally requires a favorable ratio of land to farmers. In countries where the land at the disposal of the farmer is very limited, the animal can occupy only a minor place in the farm economy; it must be restricted to land that cannot be used for growing food for direct human consumption, or it must earn its keep as a work animal. In south China the land required to support one water buffalo would feed many men if planted to rice. The land area needed to support a family, if reliance is placed upon vegetable crops alone, is incredibly small. It was the potato, the crop with the highest calorie yield of all, that permitted mid-nineteenth-century Ireland to support a population of 8 million people; under the "conacre" system a family of six with a daily potato consumption of 14 pounds was adequately nourished on a quarter of an acre.[3]

There appears to be a fairly close correlation between the level of economic development and the per capita consumption of proteins, particularly animal protein (Table 3-1). Countries with a high per capita income invariably have a high per capita consumption of animal protein in the form of meat, but in underdeveloped economies any considerable meat consumption is generally reserved for special occasions such as weddings and feasts. Religious and social taboos reinforce the economic necessity for a diet low in animal protein: Chinese reject milk and dairy products, Muslims do not consume pork, and Hindus will not eat beef. It is not suggested that there is any economic motivation behind these

[2] **First-class protein contains all essential amino acids; vegetable proteins are of lower biological value. A *varied* vegetable diet, however, will compensate for any individual deficiency if the total protein intake is sufficient; it is the overall shortage of protein that is the trouble with most vegetable diets. The soybean is unique in containing amino acids that do not normally occur in plant proteins and is a very valuable constituent of many Asian diets.**

[3] **Redcliffe N. Salaman,** *The History and Social Influence of the Potato,* **Cambridge University Press, Cambridge, England, 1949, p. 278. After surveying the effects of the potato on Irish life from the sixteenth to the nineteenth century, Salaman concludes: "It is not too much to say that for close on three hundred years the potato both stabilized and perpetuated the misery of the Irish masses."**

Table 3-1

Calorie and Protein Content of Estimated Daily per Capita Food Consumption in Selected Countries, 1960–1961

COUNTRY	NUMBER OF CALORIES	PROTEIN (g)	PERCENTAGE OF PROTEIN FROM ANIMAL PRODUCTS
United States	3120	92	65
United Kingdom	3270	87	52
Canada	3100	94	62
Australia (1959–1960)	3260	93	61
New Zealand	3490	110	75
West Germany	2950	80	48
Argentina (1959)	2950	91	48
Japan	2240	68	18
Italy	2740	80	28
India	1990	53	6
Philippines	1950	49	15
Peru (1959)	2060	52	13

SOURCE: FAO, *State of Food and Agriculture,* 1962.

customs, but is is noteworthy that increasing wealth often tends to diminish their force.

SCARCITY AND ABUNDANCE

In the underdeveloped economies, where subsistence farming is widespread, it is often quite difficult to maintain per capita food consumption; production trends slowly upwards but is matched by population growth. Food requirements vary greatly according to climatic conditions, the age and weight of the individual, and his energy output. The Food and Agriculture Organization (FAO) has estimated that in many countries the daily per capita calorie intake is often reduced below the level of subsistence, and that the population, though not actually starving, must frequently experience considerable hunger; some writers, however, have denied that there is any such widespread malnutrition.[4] There is some truth on both sides, perhaps, but it can scarcely be doubted that a substantial increase in domestic food production is urgently required in the underdeveloped economies. Its realization is obstructed partly by great difficulties in augmenting the capital and land at the disposal of the farmer and partly by the fact that many governments discourage peasant initiative by paying low prices for farm products which they then dispose of at a considerably higher price; the latter situation exists in several countries of Latin America, West Africa, and Southeast Asia.

The centrally planned economies also suffer from a shortfall of agricultural output in relation to demand, which can occasionally be extreme, as in China in 1961 and 1962, when semistarvation was experienced in most parts

[4] **M. K. Bennett,** *The World's Food,* **Harper & Row, Publishers, Incorporated, New York, 1954, pp. 189–212.**

of the country. China's problems arose mainly from a precipitate reorganization of the whole agrarian structure which coincided with a series of the natural misfortunes to which China is particularly prone. But it is clear that agricultural production in the U.S.S.R. and in Eastern Europe is basically inadequate; Russia's enormous wheat purchases in 1963 and 1964 strongly suggest a degree of inadequacy far larger than previously supposed. Unwillingness to make large investments in agriculture and the payment of prices which are too low to provide incentives to farm workers are the principal reasons for the shortcomings of agriculture in the centrally planned economies. The exploitation of rural workers is considerably more severe than in underdeveloped economies; on produce obtained from collective farms the state may make a markup of several thousand per cent.[5]

In the highly developed economies and in many semideveloped economies, agriculture is heavily pampered; in *none* of the former are governments prepared to allow agriculture to stand on the basis of its own efficiency in a free market, a fact which should be borne in mind when the more obvious shortcomings of Soviet agriculture are discussed. Even so, agriculture incomes per capita are still lower than those in nonagricultural activities, largely because agriculture does not or cannot discharge its surplus labor fast enough with increases in technical efficiency. The result is the familiar and depressing one of recurring surpluses—products that cannot be sold at prices sufficient to cover their costs of production. These costs are maintained at levels which are far too high for consumers to be able to absorb the whole output through government price-support policies.

State assistance to agriculture can take many forms—guaranteed prices, "deficiency payments," direct subsidies or bounties, protective duties or embargoes on the import of designated agricultural produce—and all these forms of assistance result in the transference of income from the nonfarming to the farming community. All countries use many methods of transferring and redistributing income among citizens, and these have to be judged in the light of social ends they are designed to serve; in European countries, defense requirements have often been advanced as justification for policies of heavy assistance to agriculture. But it is not difficult to show that these policies work to the long-term economic disadvantage of the country concerned and even of its agriculture. A case can be made out for helping the less efficient and small farmers to improve their competitive position and for helping farmers who wish to withdraw from production to do so. In practice, however, it is always the large farmers who benefit most from such schemes, and these efficient producers do not require assistance. Small farmers tend to receive too little to enable them to raise their productivity to more competitive levels and become entirely dependent upon the preservation of subsidies; moreover, there are far too many of them to make success possible for all. A very large proportion of the astronomical sums paid out by the United States government under its price-support programs has gone to the owners of large holdings. Thus in practice the American price-support policy has merely conferred another advantage on large farms, which already produce so much of the country's output that the removal of all small farmers from production would make little difference to total output. European countries that pay high subsidies on cereal production hinder transfer of interest towards greater livestock production and, by delaying the removal of workers to nonagricultural activities, slow down the rate of economic advance.

That agricultural support policies of one

[5] **John Gunther,** *Inside Russia Today,* **Harper & Row, Publishers, Incorporated, New York, 1962, p. 392.**

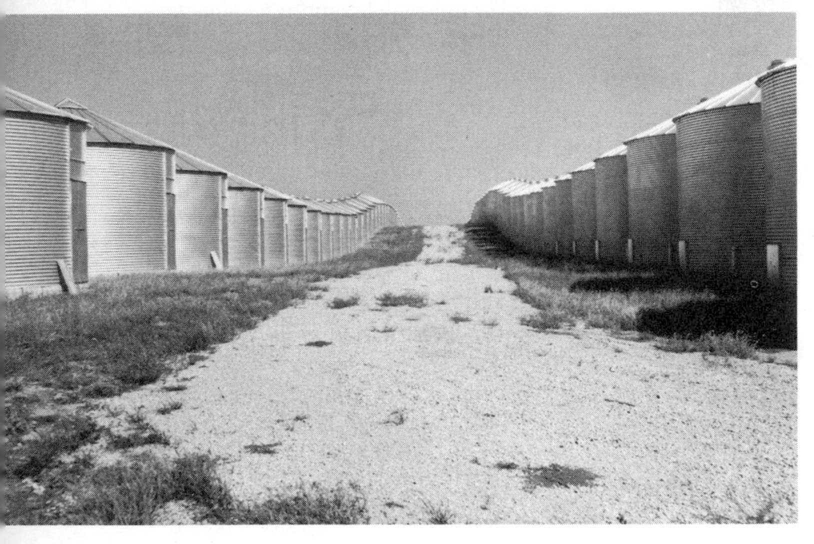

Corn and cotton have been the American crops most prone to oversupply, but huge surpluses of wheat and small grains have also been created. At times, storage facilities of all kinds have been overwhelmed by the productivity of the American farmer, and grain has been dumped in city streets.

Surplus food has been given away to those who are unemployed or to others in need; it has been used, too, for financing economic development or for the relief of distress in various parts of the world.

kind or another are found in all highly developed economies is entirely the result of the political strength of agriculture, which is grossly disproportionate to its contribution to national product. This arises from the fact that in democratic countries the system of electoral representation invariably makes one rural vote worth many urban votes. Cities are always the foremost centers of social change; those wishing to arrest the social and economic changes which take their origin in cities tend to ally themselves with agricultural interests in order to preserve the *status quo.* Large cities are thus prevented from achieving an electoral representation proportionate to their populations.[6] Since 1789 no French government has been able to defy the peasants; even in highly urbanized Australia and New Zealand, one rural vote may be worth from two to ten urban votes.

So long as governments continue to provide heavy direct and indirect subsidies to agriculture, the problem of agricultural surpluses will be insoluble. It can only be overcome by ensuring a high rate of economic growth in the economy as a whole and by the prompt removal to other occupations of agricultural workers made redundant through technological progress. Every diminution in the numbers employed in agriculture is a step forward in economic development and reduces the disparity in incomes between those who remain in farming and those engaged in other occupations.

AGRICULTURAL STRUCTURE

Agricultural structure is the whole complex of social and economic relations existing between the producers of agricultural products and consumers, though the term is often used in a more restricted sense. It includes farm size and layout, tenure (that is, the economic, legal, and political relations between owners of the land and cultivators), and the marketing arrangements for the products. Often all are an integral part of a rigid social and institutional framework, and without changes in social attitudes it is often impossible to introduce technical improvements which would result in a higher productivity both of the land and of the worker. Examples of defective agricultural structure can be gathered from all types of economies; the great majority of small owner-occupier farmers in England are worse off than agricultural laborers.

Farm Size

It is difficult to make statements of broad general validity about the size of the world's farms; terrain, climate, soil, the type of farming itself, and general social organization combine to produce an enormous diversity of farm sizes. At the upper extremity, the world's largest holding is the famous Alexandria "station," sprawling over 7¼ million acres of the Barkly Tableland of the Northern Territory of Australia (Fig. 3-1); but it is a euphemism to call Alexandria a farm, for its 70,000 shorthorns range over land virtually in a state of nature. The famous King ranch of coastal southwest Texas extends over 920,000 acres, and several *sovkhozy* (state farms) in the U.S.S.R. exceed 100,000 acres. Before World War II the HAPM estate of the U.S. Rubber Co. extended over 76,000 acres of east Sumatra. At the other end of the scale, the average farm size in the less congested parts of India is about 4 acres, in areas of dense rural settlement less than 2 acres; in Java it falls to about 1.5 acres. There appears to be a relationship between the

[6] In three decisions since 1962, the United States Supreme Court has ruled unconstitutional electoral systems that produce a heavy preponderance of rural interests in state legislatures; but opposition is still strong.

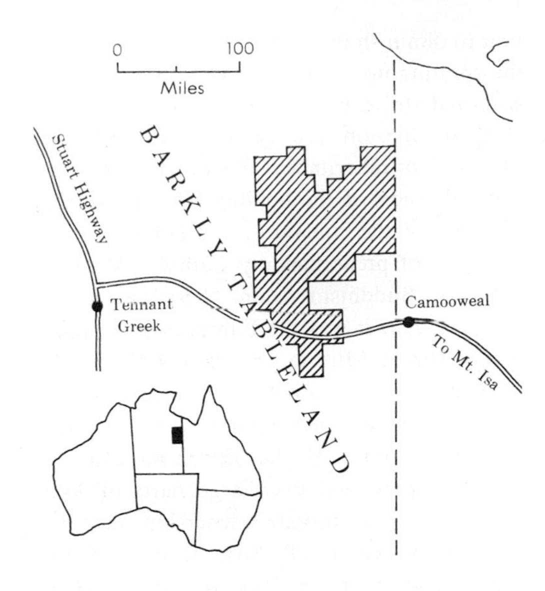

Fig. 3-1 Alexandria Station. Alexandria Station, the world's largest cattle ranch, leases over 7 million acres of Crown land in the Northern Territory. Prior to its subdivision before World War II, the Victoria Station was even larger.

level of economic development and farm size; the average size for the United States is about 160 acres, for England and Wales about 75 acres, for most countries of Eastern Europe about 10 to 15 acres, and over much of Asia less than 5 acres. Yet there are very substantial regional variations.

It is clear, however, that in many parts of the world the average farm size is uneconomic. "Uneconomic," of course, is a word which permits of several interpretations. It may mean, as is usually the case in highly developed economies, that the farm is too small to provide the occupier with the minimum level of income that is socially acceptable; many small farmers in the United States and Britain would earn a higher income as wage earners. In countries at a lower level of economic development, "uneconomic" signifies that the land at the disposal of the cultivator is too small to provide continuous employment for the farmer's equipment and labor; in Malaya, rice farmers, even with their present equipment, could cultivate three times the present rice area, so that for much of the year they are underemployed. On the other hand, there is evidence that in some parts of the world farm size may be too large. This is particularly true of countries with a Latin cultural background, in which large estates, or *latifundia,* are dominant, although, of course, these large properties may occur side by side with very small ones. Under these conditions redistribution through land reform can be very beneficial to economic growth.

The type of farming practiced is closely related to farm size. In those parts of the world with an average farm size of below 5 acres, animals, apart from pigs and poultry, can have little place in the farm economy. In highly developed economies, a farm of less than 100 acres must specialize either in dairying or in horticulture, but such farms provide only a small margin of economic security. Belgium possesses an average farm size of about 4 acres, which is minute for a country at a high level of economic development. This is largely accounted for by the existence of a large number of horticultural small holdings, for many Belgians combine part-time farming with employment in coal mining or in manufacturing.

Two widely distributed phenomena of world farming are the tendency for the farm unit to diminish in size through *subdivision* and the splitting up of the holding between several scattered strips, which is known as *fragmentation.* Subdivision usually arises through the operation of inheritance laws which require an equal division of the holding between all the offspring of the cultivator, and is common in countries of predominantly Catholic, Muslim, Hindu, or Buddhist religion. There is evidence, however, that it was the European interpretation of Hindu, Muslim, or local law that made excessive subdivision possible; indigenous conceptions of land ownership were very much less rigid than those of the European colonial administrators, and over large parts of Asia the concept of private ownership of land scarcely existed at all. Strip farms are still common in parts of Western Europe (Fig. 3-2), though in Britain they were swept away by the waves of enclosure and consolidation that took place between the sixteenth and the nineteenth centuries (Fig. 3-3), and areas settled by British colonists never experienced the fragmented preenclosure pattern. Fragmentation of farms is a great obstacle to increasing productivity, and though consolidation is expensive to undertake, the enhanced production that it makes possible amply repays the costs involved, at least under European conditions. But in Asia, fragmentation has proceeded to an excessive degree; a 5- to 7-acre holding may be composed of as many as twenty strips, some lying perhaps a mile or more from the cultivator's dwelling. Under such a system of agrarian organization, the obstacles to improved efficiency are enormous; a third or more of the farmer's working day may be spent in traveling.

The fragmentation of the farm into a number of widely scattered strips is of considerable antiquity, and may have arisen in order to ensure an equitable distribution of good and poor soil among cultivators; this has also been encouraged by the practice of period redistribution in some instances.

Subdivision and fragmentation are still proceeding (Fig. 3-4); in Malaya and in India holdings on new irrigation schemes originally large enough to yield an adequate income to the cultivator are being steadily reduced in size through the operation of inheritance laws. In Anglo-Saxon countries the operation of the law of primogeniture effectively prevents such division, and the desirability of preserving the farm intact in the absence of such a law has been frequently advanced as a reason for the long period of low birth rates in France.

Land Tenure

There is probably no more powerful cause of unrest in the world than a system of land tenure that no longer meets social needs. An inadequate tenure system was an important factor in the Chinese revolution, and over large parts of Asia and Latin America the present system of land tenure is overripe for reform; in many parts of the Middle East, farmers are at the mercy of owners of water rights. Security of tenure is perhaps the greatest desire of cultivators in most underdeveloped countries.

Though there are great regional variations in the laws governing the ownership of land and the right to its use, there are four major systems of widespread occurrence: (*a*) communal tenure, (*b*) large estates, (*c*) free-holds, or owner-occupied farms, and (*d*) tenancy.

Communal Tenure Communal tenure is a very ancient and widespread form of agrarian structure found in many parts of South and Southeast Asia, in much of intertropical Africa, and in some parts of Latin America. Though usually considered a primitive type of organization, it has been revived in the present century in the Israeli *kibbutz,* or communal settlement; in the Mexican *ejido;* in the *kolkhoz,* or collec-

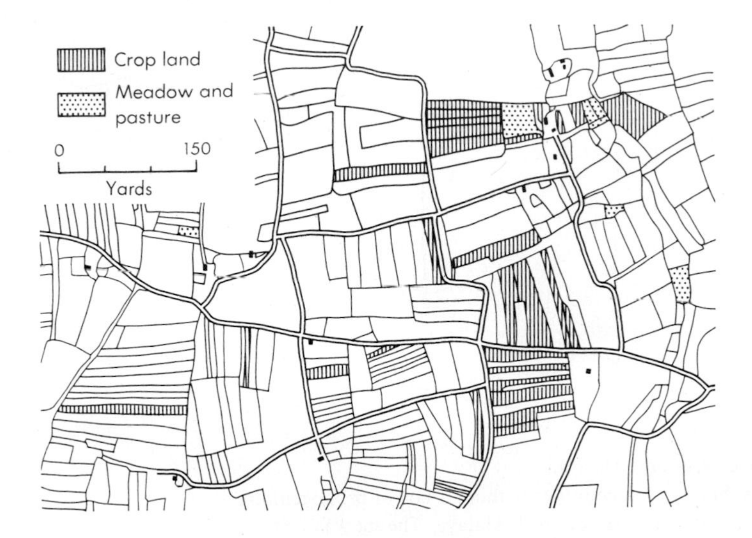

Fig. 3-2 Fragmentation of crop land and meadow and pasture in Brittany, France.
Fragmentation of the farm is common in much of Western Europe; this farm in a district of Brittany is by no means an extreme example. (After Uhlig.)

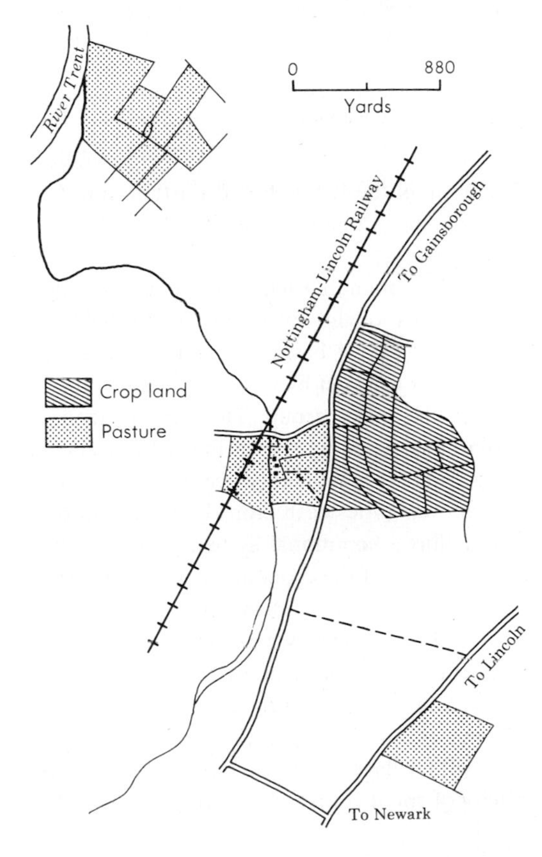

Fig. 3-3 A fragmented British farm.
Although widely separated, the units of this mixed farm in Nottinghamshire, England, consist of compact blocks. (After Edwards.)

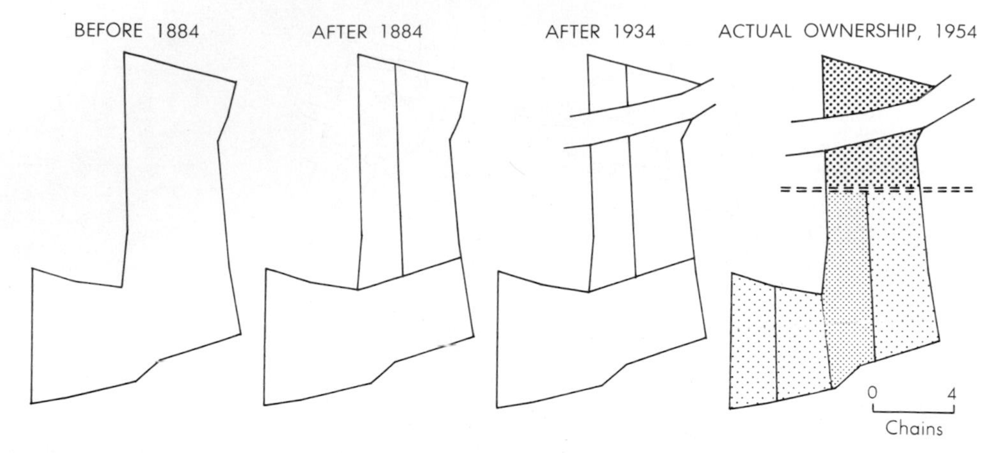

Fig. 3-4 History of a lot in Province Wellesley, Malaya.
The process of fragmentation and subdivision in countries without a law of primogeniture is well exemplified by this lot in a rice growing area of north Malaya. The lot was first registered about 1870 and consisted of about 11 acres of forest; it was finally cleared about 1884 and was then subdivided into three lots shared between two owners. With the construction of an irrigation canal in 1934, the original 10-acre lot was split between 5 holdings in which 11 owners had shares, making 55 claims in all. In practice, however, the ownership pattern was less complicated; in 1954 there were 9 coowners in three closely related family groups, but with the exception of one part time cultivator, none of the owners themselves engaged in cultivation. (T. B. Wilson, *The Economics of Padi Production in North Malaya.*)

tive farm, of the U.S.S.R. and Eastern Europe; and in the Chinese agricultural producers' cooperative.

Under communal tenure there are no individual rights to land ownership; land is held on a tribal or village basis, and individuals have the right of usufruct by virtue of their membership in the social group. This type of tenure system has generally shown limited powers of adaptation to a monetary economy. In some African territories cash crops have been introduced into a communal system, but with the monetization of the economy there is a general tendency for the custodians of the communal land to become the owners. Thus in Java the renting of village rice land by farmers for sugar cultivation helped to preserve the communal system, as sugar companies found it easier to deal with village headmen than with a multiplicity of small cultivators. Throughout Southeast Asia, North Africa, and the Middle East, tribal chieftains and petty rulers have become large landowners and their subjects have been reduced to tenant status.

That communal tenure is not, however, inherently incompatible with a monetary economy is shown by some modern variations. Perhaps the most remarkable of all is the *kibbutz,* whose members lead a completely communal life. These flourishing settlements carved out of land of low productivity or desert represent one of the greatest achievements of Zionism (Fig. 3-5).[7] The *ejido,* a purely Mexican institution first established in the Thirties, is a form of land redistribution aimed at removing the shortcomings of the large estates, which, as elsewhere in Latin America, have dominated the agrarian scene.

[7] **Their political and economic importance in the Israeli nation, however, tends progressively to decline.**

In the *ejido* (literally, outlet), land acquired by the state from the large *haciendas* is returned to the village; each villager receives a plot which he retains so long as he continues to cultivate it, but the land cannot be sold or mortgaged, and remains the property of the village. *Ejidos* were originally created in irrigated oases in Northern Mexico and were mainly engaged in cotton cultivation. Since 1960, however, a run of dry years has brought several such settlements to the verge of disaster.

The *kolkhoz,* the collective farm of the U.S.S.R. and satellite countries, in some ways resembles a state plantation. The member of the collective possesses no rights of usufruct and is essentially a worker whose labor is ruthlessly exploited. Averaging about 1,000 acres after their creation in the Thirties, Russian collectives have been progressively merged until the average size now stands at about 15,000 acres. Peasants have, however, been permitted to retain small plots of about 1 to 2½ acres for their own use, and these private plots account for about half the total animal population. The *kolkhoznik* is paid according to the number of work day units he has acquired during the year, but in practice he prefers to put in as much time on his private plot as he can.[8] Since 1957 some of the grosser forms of exploitation of the collectives have been abolished, such as the motor-tractor stations, which made exorbitant charges for the use of machinery and equipment; higher prices have also been paid to the peasants for the produce of their private plots, but these are still below those obtainable on the small free market. Nevertheless, the collective does possess some slight control over its own destinies and is infinitely preferable from the peasants' point of view to the *sovkhoz,* or state-owned farm. It is significant that Poland, which has rejected collectivization, has had considerably better success in its agricultural program than other Soviet satellites.

In China private ownership of land is of considerable antiquity, and there is no his-

[8] The yield per acre of potatoes on private plots is about twice that on collectives' land.

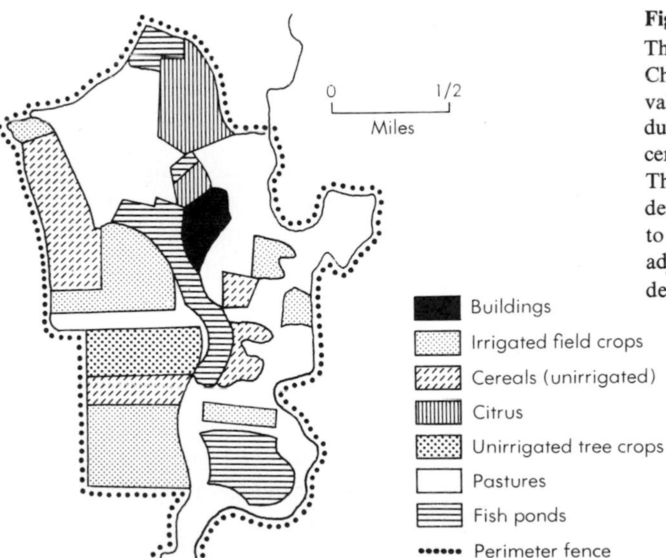

Fig. 3-5 An Israeli *kibbutz.*
This large Israeli *kibbutz* in the Beth Chean (Beisan) district of the Jordan valley has a considerable area under industrial crops (cotton, sugar beets) while cereals are grown on unirrigated land. The irrigated orchard land is mainly devoted to citrus; carob, a tree crop fed to cattle, is unirrigated. As the *kibbutz* adjoins the Jordan frontier, it is heavily defended. (After *Dov Nir.*)

torical tradition of communal tenure as in Russia. Agrarian reorganization began in 1950, when the new government instituted a land-reform program which was claimed to have involved the confiscation from landlords and rich peasants of almost a third of the cultivated land of the country. The redistribution of this land to the poorer peasants appeared to confirm the prevailing system of private ownership. Experiments were then made with forms of cooperative labor called mutual aid teams, which worked in groups on a few farms; by 1954 they covered about half the farm households of the country, and in 1955 were succeeded by a more advanced form of agricultural cooperatives. Members contributed land, implements, livestock, and their own labor to cooperative farming, and were paid rent in proportion to their contribution and a dividend commensurate with their labor input. Rent payments were later dropped, and small cooperatives were merged in larger units which by 1957 covered almost all farms.

In the new organizations tiny fields were eliminated, and new techniques and seeds could be more easily introduced. The new organizations could also more easily construct dams and irrigation channels, which formerly would have involved the resettlement of displaced individuals. Methods of farming remained essentially unchanged, however, and widespread mechanization lies well into the future.

In 1958 appeared the *commune,* a further aggregation of large cooperatives, but its main significance lay in the assumption of local government powers, in the promotion of village manufacture, and in an aspiration for a more thoroughly communal life for its members. The Chinese agricultural revolution was carried out with remarkable speed and apparently without the catastrophic fall in production that accompanied Russian collectivization. This, however, was to prove illusory; the Chinese planners had moved too far and too fast, and with the disasters of 1959 to 1961 the *communes* were quietly dropped.

Large Estates Large estates, or *latifundia,* were well established in classical times and are still widespread in Portugal, Spain, southern Italy, large parts of Latin America, and in the Philippines. They also occur in many parts of Asia, such as the Middle East, Pakistan, and in many areas of India. In Asia, however, the indigenous estate is essentially an assemblage of tenancies, and the landowner is primarily dependent upon rents; in Latin America the estate is usually a unit of production whose output is intended for sale.

The estate has successively made use of slave, serf, and wage labor; the first has virtually disappeared save for a few small pockets in North Africa and the Middle East, but serfdom, or peonage, though legally abolished in all Latin American countries, is still not uncommon in several cordilleran republics. In the *inquilino* system of Chile the peasant is allowed to cultivate a plot in return for a certain number of days of work per week on the estate, and a somewhat similar system of relations between landlord and tenant existed in both Argentina and Brazil before World War II. The *colono,* usually an Italian immigrant, prepared the land and planted the main crop: alfalfa on the *estancias* of Argentina, coffee on the *fazendas* of São Paulo. In Argentina land remains under alfalfa for several years, and once it had become established, the *colono* was obliged to move on. In Brazil the *colono* was allowed to intercrop between the young coffee trees until they were old enough to begin bearing. *Patron*-tenant relations of this kind clearly do not encourage a high level of productive efficiency.

The great estates of the Philippines, which

originated in *encomiendas,* or royal bequests, resemble other Asian estates in being tenancy estates, as are the great estates of Portugal, Spain, and Italy. In Portugal labor dues still exist, and they were only finally abolished in Italy in 1930. Tenants of these large estates live in conditions of extreme poverty, and from time to time dissatisfaction with their conditions erupts in violence, as it did in southern Italy in 1949. The estates in Latin America frequently include large areas of land that is unused because it is too rough, poor, or inaccessible, or occasionally because of the neglect or incompetence of the owner, who is often an absentee, or of his manager. Under these conditions the breakup and redistribution of estate land can produce very beneficial effects on production. Nevertheless, redistribution has not always proved successful; in the Philippines great estates which were broken up during the early years of the present century have reappeared.

The modern plantation differs from the traditional large estate in being much more heavily capitalized, in using a wage labor force whose remuneration and conditions of employment are determined by contract, and usually in having a nonindigenous ownership. It is treated more fully in Chapter 4.[9]

Another type of large estate is the state farm, or *sovkhoz,* of the U.S.S.R. These very large units have an average size of about 30,000 acres, twice that of the *kolkhoz,* and are common in the more scantily populated parts of Asiatic Russia, particularly in the pioneer lands of northern Kazakhstan and western Siberia. Unlike the collective farms, state farms have always possessed their own tractors and equipment. The cultivators are entirely wage laborers and possess no land of their own apart from gardens. For this reason the state farms are detested even more than the collectives.

[9] See p. 85–87.

Freeholds Freeholds, or owner-occupied farms, are probably the most numerous of all the world's farms, and to achieve ownership is the desire of most tenant farmers. But the great majority of freeholders own very little land indeed; even in Western Europe, with the notable exception of Great Britain and Denmark, the majority of the owner-occupied farms are below 50 acres. Most owner-occupied farms in Asia are very much smaller, and in most Asian countries a 10-acre holding would be considered large.

The freehold is often considered to be the ideal form of agrarian structure, but the small owner-occupier is all too frequently starved of capital. Freeholds are often the only form of holding on which it is possible to raise credit, but over large parts of the world the existing facilities for agricultural credit are entirely inadequate.

Tenancy There are three forms of tenancy—labor, share, and cash. Tenancies granted in return for labor dues occur in Latin America, but in the rest of the world they are now rare. In areas of permanent white settlement in Africa, native farm workers are occasionally permitted to cultivate plots on the owner's property. Tenants of this kind are virtually tenants at will, and it is difficult to conceive of a system less conducive to efficiency. The members of the *kolkhoz* are in a somewhat similar situation in that they are obliged to provide labor for the collective.

Share and cash tenancies occur almost wherever farming is carried on, though the former are perhaps the more widespread. Share tenancies are found in countries at all stages of economic development. Sharecropping is a distinctive feature of the southern United States (Fig. 3-6), and "share farming" is common in southeast Australia. In southern Europe *métayage* is still common, although it

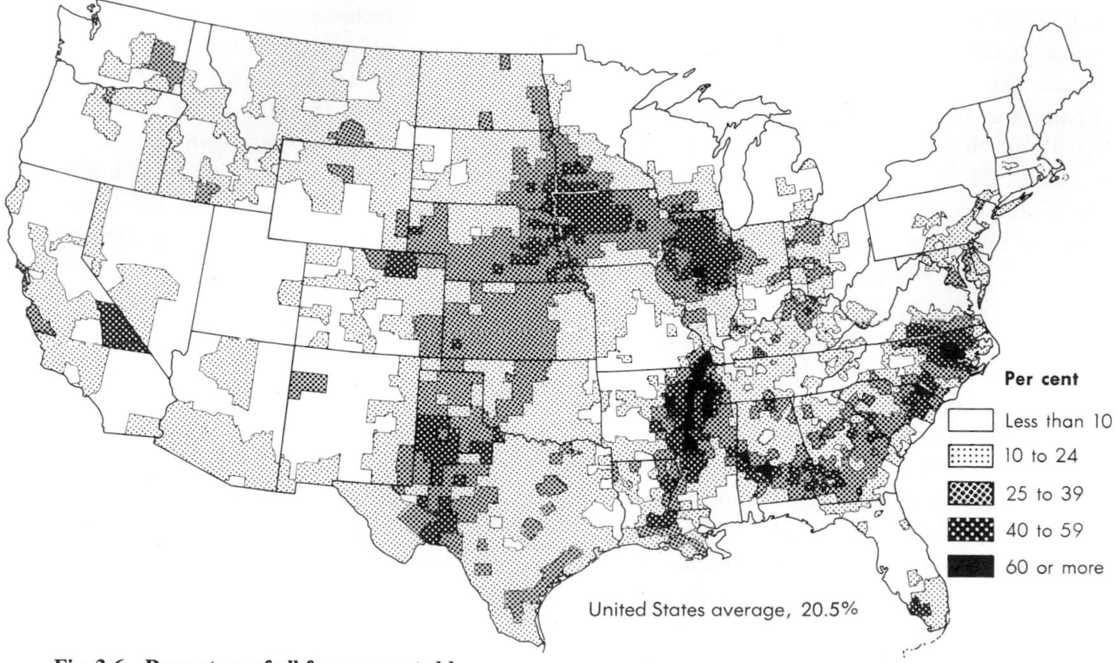

Fig. 3-6 Percentage of all farms operated by tenants in the United States.
Tenancy in the United States is most common in the Mississippi Valley and in certain parts of the South, where sharecropping is still widely practiced. Over large parts of the best-farmed areas of the country, tenancy is of limited importance. (USDA, 1959.)

has now largely disappeared in Western Europe. The great majority of Asian and Latin American tenants are share-tenants.

In the congested parts of Asia, the incidence of tenancy is very high. Thus, although the national average of tenancy in the Philippines Republic was only 35 per cent of all holdings in 1950, in 7 provinces it was more than 50 per cent, and in 4 provinces more than 60 per cent.[10] All of these provinces lie in the most densely populated parts of the country (Fig. 3-7). But the highest incidence of tenancy in the world occurs in Great Britain; more than 60 per cent of all farm occupiers in England and Wales are tenants, and over much of northern England tenancies account for more than 75 per cent of all holdings (Fig. 3-8).

Tenancy is not an inherently unsatisfactory type of tenure, although it often leaves much to be desired. In general, cash tenancies are preferable to share tenancies, for the cultivator himself reaps the benefit of any increased yields and thus has a greater incentive to improve his efficiency. Where such tenants enjoy security (as in Britain, where a tenant cannot be ejected without the permission of the Ministry of Agriculture) and where rents and conditions of the tenancy are determined by contract, tenant

[10] **Mutual Security Agency,** *Philippine Land Tenure Reform,* **Manila, 1952, p. 2.**

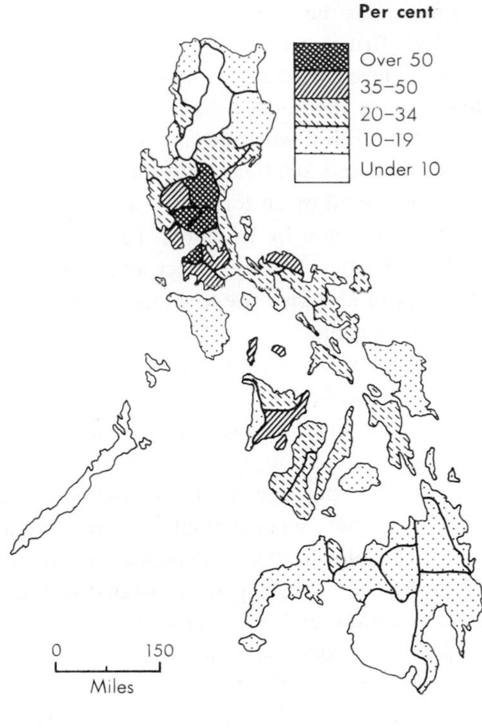

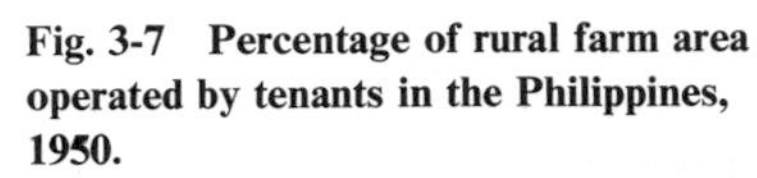

Fig. 3-7 Percentage of rural farm area operated by tenants in the Philippines, 1950.

Tenancy in the Philippines is not extreme, but in lowlands where agriculture is most favored, its incidence is great and has given rise to pressing social problems. (Mutual Security Agency.)

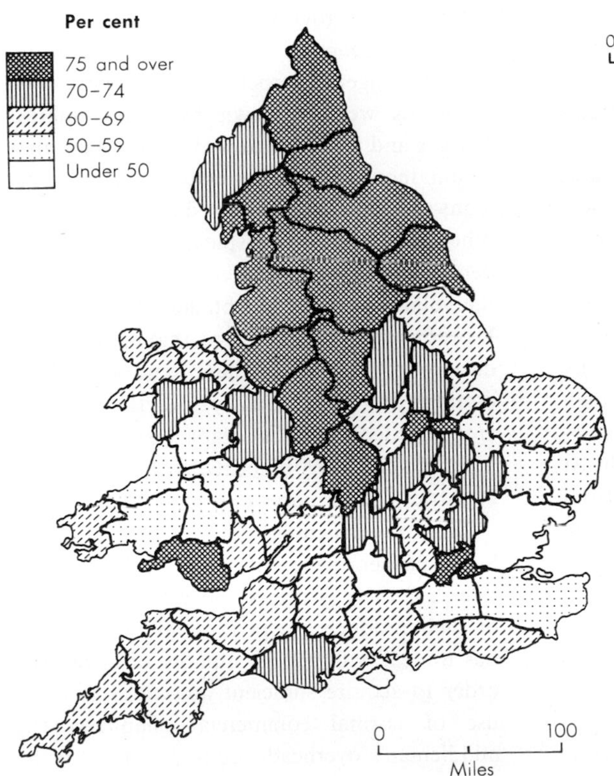

Fig. 3-8 Proportion of area (crops and grass) occupied by tenants in each county of England and Wales.

Great Britain has the highest incidence of tenancy in the world. In contrast to the Philippines, however, tenancy is most common in upland areas of poor soil; in eastern England, where physical factors provide near optimum conditions for plow agriculture, the incidence of tenancy is well below the national average. (National Farm Survey, 1946.)

farmers may be more prosperous than freeholders. British tenancies are invariably cash, and the level of rents has long been held too low to give landlords an adequate return on their capital. But where tenants enjoy no legal protection and relations with the landowner are determined by custom, the way is open for their exploitation by landlords. Lack of registration of titles, a consequence of inadequate survey, can also give rise to endless arguments about ownership.

Generally, rents tend to be high in underdeveloped economies, and with a rapidly increasing population there is an inexorable tendency for them to go higher. To be without land is to risk possible starvation, and the rural population bids against itself for the limited land available. In share tenancies a common division is for the crop to be shared equally by the tenant and the landlord. Where the landlord provides more, his share is proportionately greater; two-thirds or more of the crop may go to the lord if he provides animals and equipment as well as the land.

Occasionally, shares may be fixed by law. In the Philippines the landlord's share was limited to 30 per cent, and in Nationalist China to 32.5 per cent; but there was widespread evasion, and no serious attempt was ever made to enforce the legal maximum in either country. But high and often exorbitant shares levied by landlords, are less oppressive to tenants than insecurity of tenure. Under the conditions obtaining over large parts of South and Southeast Asia at present, tenants try to get as much from the soil as they can while the tenancy lasts. The result is a high tenancy turnover, damaging to both soil and social structure.

Credit, Cooperation, and Marketing

Agriculture by its very nature is an occupation which is singularly dependent upon credit, yet it is probably the worst served of all. During the period that his crop is maturing the farmer must have recourse to credit, and if he wishes to make improvements, credit is usually essential. But few farmers possess much in the way of collateral, and the vast majority are outside the scope of existing commercial banking systems and credit agencies.

Most farmers in underdeveloped economies have, therefore, to resort to special sources of credit. In China the main recourse of the credit-seeking farmer was to some member of the family or clan. In other parts of Asia credit is usually sought from the local shopkeeper or trader, who is often an alien. Alternatively, a tenant may apply to his landlord for credit. Credit of this kind is obtainable only at very high interest rates, and up to 300 per cent may be charged for unsecured loans, as the risk of default is extreme.

While the provision of such credit facilities is a consequence of rural poverty, it is also a powerful agent perpetuating poverty. The farmer is weighed down by heavy interest charges and is unable to make investment that would increase his productive efficiency. As loans are often sought for weddings, feasts, and other occasions of conspicuous consumption demanded by custom, there is a tendency for the volume of rural indebtedness to augment. It is not surprising, therefore, that many underdeveloped economies have endeavored to establish state machinery for provision of rural credit; indeed, without improved credit, any attempt at land reform or redistribution in such countries cannot hope to succeed.

Similar difficulties occur in marketing. Small farmers have only a limited output for sale, and there is usually no way of disposing of their produce except to a middleman who has to deal with a large number of farmers in order to acquire sufficient quantities to make use of normal commercial channels. The middleman's overheads are high, and so is the charge he makes for his services. Not infrequently he is the same person as the moneylender, and the fact that the farmer is dependent upon him for the disposal of his crop is security for an advance. This was the situation in the lower Menam plain of Thailand, where Thai tenant farmers traditionally disposed of their rice to Chinese middlemen, and in prewar lower Burma, where Chettyar moneylenders operated in similar fashion.

Farmers of countries at a high level of economic development are often able to improve their credit and marketing facilities through concerted action in cooperative organizations. Cooperatives also engage in processing and packing and purchase implements and fertilizers at bulk rates for their members. Dairying in Europe has been very closely connected with cooperation; cooperatives dominate the marketing of agricultural produce in the Netherlands and Denmark, and are well developed in Norway, Sweden, and Finland. In Britain they have made little headway, though they have been very successful in Ireland. In New Zealand, in Australia, and in the United States dairy cooperatives are very important, and in the latter two countries they are also very prominent in fruit packing and canning. However, certain products appear less suitable for cooperative marketing. In Australia and New Zealand attempts to market stock by cooperatives have been unsuccessful, and there has been no serious challenge to the present system of wool auctioning.

The success achieved by cooperatives in certain parts of the world has stimulated many governments of newly independent countries to encourage the development of cooperatives, especially where there is a strong tradition of mutual help at the village level. In many cases the initial impetus came from the former colonial power, as in most ex-British territories in Africa and Asia. The Indian Congress party adopted a program of nationwide village cooperatives in 1959, and in Indonesia cooperatives have been assigned a major role in national economic development by the constitution. But such platforms are largely emotional in appeal, and in both countries it does not appear likely that cooperatives will enlarge their proportionate contribution to national product.

It is not difficult to see why cooperatives have often failed to realize the hopes of their founders. The task of organizing such an association is far beyond the capabilities of the average Asian or African peasant; the initiative and direction have to come from above, at least in the early stages. Moreover, most farmers are engaged in subsistence production, they have little to sell individually, and the costs of collection are high. The absence of large local markets limits opportunities for economies of scale. It is not unusual, therefore, for the government to make cooperatives a part of its own marketing agency, as in Ghana and Thailand. One of the most remarkable and successful examples of state assistance is found in the Gezira area of the Sudan, where a unique tripartite scheme involving the state, private capital, and a growers' cooperative was established for the development of a new irrigation area devoted to cotton cultivation.[11]

Commodity Agreements One aspect of marketing needs a further general comment. This is the commodity agreement, of which a number of examples are discussed in later chapters. Commodity agreements are not confined to agricultural products, for they are also to be found in several branches of nonferrous-metal production. They may be "gentlemen's agreements," but more often they are negotiated by governments and, in theory at least, are binding on all signatories.

Commodity agreements arise from the desire of producers to hedge against fluctuations of commodity prices, to cope with the problem

[11] See p. 175.

of surpluses, and to isolate themselves as much as possible from competition. Their official aims are frequently vague, with references to "orderly development" or to "the necessity of ensuring a fair and stable price to producers." Economic development is more often a series of fits and starts than an orderly progression, but the concept of a fair price is medieval. Is the fair price to reward the *efficient* producer with an adequate return, or is it to apply to all producers? In practice, agreements are usually designed to raise prices rather than to stabilize them, and endeavor to exploit a monopoly or supposed monopoly position through restricting output. Their success so far has been minimal. It has proved impossible to get all producers to become parties to an agreement, for there is an irresistible temptation for some producers to remain outside and to raise output under its price umbrella; as the signatories' share of total production falls, defections become certain. The United States in the past has generally refused to support commodity agreements, although it has underwritten the International Coffee Agreement in order to assist the economic development of Latin America. Action to stabilize commodity prices (and the export income of underdeveloped countries) has much to commend it,[12] but it seems very doubtful if such ends are furthered by most commodity agreements, which in the main have failed either to raise prices or to stabilize them.

[12] **See Chapter 23.**

SELECTED REFERENCES

Bennett, M. K.: *The World's Food,* Harper & Row, Publishers, Incorporated, New York, 1954, part 3.

Clausson, Gerhard: *Communal Land Tenure,* Food and Agriculture Organization Agricultural Studies, no. 17, Rome, 1953.

Dickinson, R. E.: "Land Reform in Southern Italy," *Economic Geography,* vol. 30, pp. 157–176, 1954.

Food and Agriculture Organization: *Consolidation of Fragmented Holdings,* Agricultural Studies, no. 11, Rome, 1950.

———: *An Enquiry into Problems of Agricultural Price Stabilization and Support Policies,* Rome, 1960.

———: "Land Reform and Institutional Change," *State of Food and Agriculture,* Rome, 1961, pp. 86–113.

———: *Land Reform in Italy,* Rome, 1961.

Jacoby, Eric H.: *Agrarian Unrest in Southeast Asia,* 2d ed., Asian Publishing House, London, 1961.

———: *The Inter-relation between Agrarian Reform and Agrarian Development,* Food and Agriculture Organization Agricultural Studies, no. 26, Rome, 1953.

Lambert, Audrey M.: "Farm Consolidation and Improvement in the Netherlands: An Example from the Land van Maas en Waal," *Economic Geography,* vol. 37, pp. 115–123, 1961.

Nove, Alec: "Soviet Agriculture Marks Time," *Foreign Affairs,* vol. 40, pp. 576–594, 1962.

Organisation for European Economic Co-operation: *Land Consolidation: Cheaper and More Simplified Methods,* Paris, 1957.

Pelzer, Karl J.: *Pioneer Settlement in the Asiatic Tropics,* The American Geographical Society, New York, 1948, pp. 88–114.

Sakoff, A. N.: "The Private Sector in Soviet Agriculture," *FAO Monthly Bulletin of Agricultural Economics and Statistics,* vol. 11, no. 9, pp. 1–12, 1962.

Stamp, L. Dudley: *The Land of Britain,* Longmans, Green & Co., Ltd., London, 1950, pp. 298–334.

Trewartha, Glenn T.: "Land Reform and Reclamation in Japan," *Geographical Review,* vol. 40, pp. 376–396, 1950.

Zimmermann, Erich W.: *World Resources and Industries,* rev. ed., Harper & Row, Publishers, Incorporated, New York, 1951, pp. 156–175.

Chapter 4

TYPES OF AGRICULTURE AND THEIR DISTRIBUTION

Agriculture is not a single occupation in the real world but embraces an enormous variety of activities of every degree of economic complexity which have in common but one thing; that is, they all make use of land to promote the biological processes of plant and animal life for the satisfaction of man's wants.[1] The great Australian ranch, or "station," which runs thousands of animals over many square miles of country could hardly differ more from the plantation of the humid tropics, and neither resembles the dairy farm of Western Europe or eastern North America. It would be a very perceptive dairy farmer who could recognize the apparent chaos of vegetable growth in an African or Southeast Asian *swidden*[2] as an agricultural system that is as well defined and in some ways as elaborately organized as his own, and even he could hardly appreciate that the swidden has no owner in the Western sense. Yet the great plantation and the large ranch can also have an anonymous ownership, for when operated by joint stock companies, they are legally the property of shareholders who may number thousands; it is doubtful if more than a handful of the legal owners ever see their properties, which may be many thousands of miles removed from their places of residence. Nor, of course, is there any reason why they should wish to do so; what they expect from their boards is a reasonable return on their investment.

What has been said of the nature of agriculture needs to be interpreted in the light of these great diversities. Agriculture does, in general, offer lower incomes to those engaged in it than are received by workers in nonagricultural activities, but one of the largest and most famous plantation companies paid an annual dividend of more than 30 per cent for

[1] See E. W. Zimmermann, *World Resources and Industries,* rev. ed., Harper & Row, Publishers, Incorporated, New York, 1951, pp. 147–148, for a discussion of the definition of agriculture.

[2] See p. 71.

Fig. 4-1 **Major agricultural regions of the world.**

A classification at a world level must, of necessity, be highly generalized. (After Whittlesey, with modifications.)

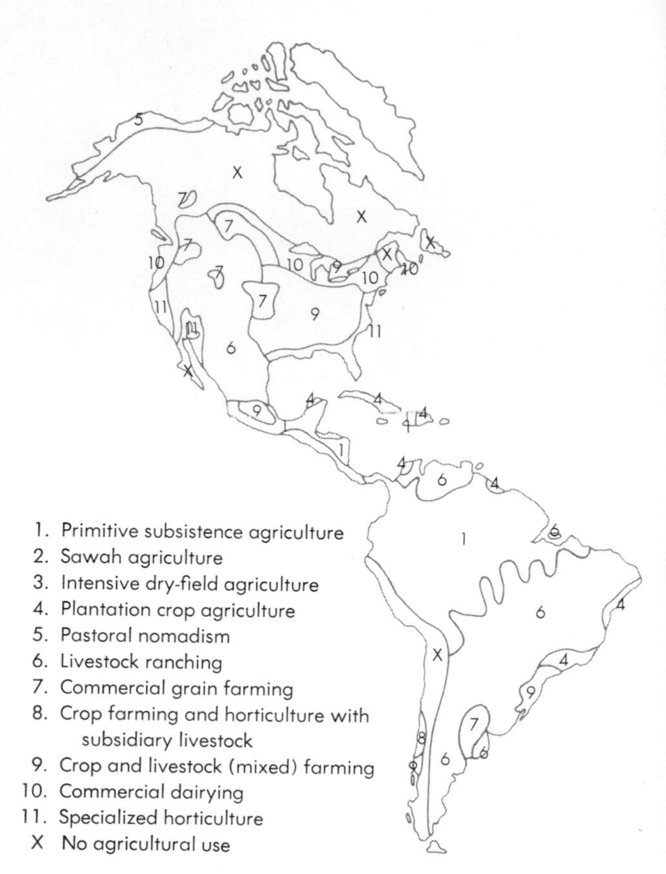

over seventy years.[3] Some system of classifying the many-sided nature of agriculture is required for a world view, and an analysis of the interactions between the various categories; wheat produced on the specialized wheat farms of Canada competes with wheat grown on the wheat-sheep farms of Australia and the wheat-cattle-alfalfa farms of Argentina and with the produce of every other farmer who is trying to sell wheat on the world market. All wheats thus compete not only with each other but also with all other foodstuffs for a share of the consumer's food expenditure.

Agriculture, of course, can no more be classified than climate; but classification is essential to understanding, and the validity of any system of classification depends on how well it serves the purpose intended. For a review of the whole world a system with about a dozen major divisions is perfectly adequate (Fig. 4-1); for individual countries, clearly, more detailed classifications are required (Fig. 4-2).

Most classifications of world agriculture now in use are modifications of a scheme devised by Derwent Whittlesey,[4] who based his classification on five criteria, as follows:

1. The crop and livestock association
2. The methods employed to produce the crop and livestock products

[3] **The** *Deli Maatschappij,* **a Dutch estate company with many interests in east Sumatra.**

[4] **Derwent Whittlesey, "Major Agricultural Regions of the Earth,"** *Annals of the Association of American Geographers,* **vol. 26, pp. 199–240, 1936.**

3. The intensity of application of capital and labor to the land and the productivity of the factors of production
4. The fate of the farm produce, that is, whether it is for farm subsistence or for sale
5. The farm buildings and other fixed equipment needed for production

The analysis, however, has tended to direct attention to farm output and farming techniques, and agrarian organization has been overlooked. A feature of the Whittlesey system is that it envisages economic development as the evolution of traditional agricultural systems into new types through the application of Western technology and managerial and financial skills. "Nomadic herding" gives place to "livestock ranching"; "shifting cultivation" in the tropics is displaced and modified by "commercial plantation crop tillage," and "subsistence crop and livestock farming" in higher latitudes gradually becomes commercialized.

Some of these types have a much greater degree of unity than others, and several writers have suggested modifications of Whittlesey's scheme. The system adopted here distinguishes eleven types as follows:

1. Primitive subsistence agriculture
2. Sawah agriculture
3. Intensive dry-field agriculture
4. Plantation-crop agriculture
5. Pastoral nomadism
6. Commercial grazing
7. Commercial grain farming

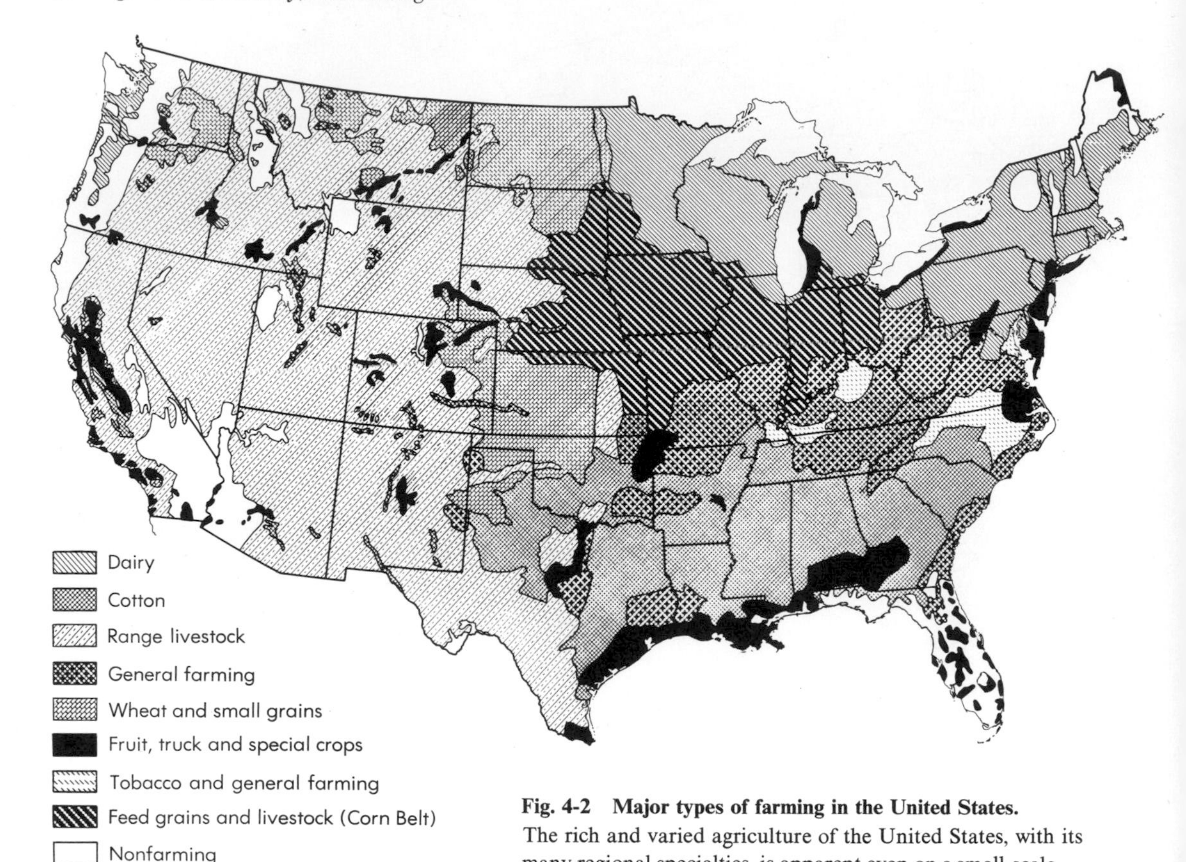

Fig. 4-2 Major types of farming in the United States. The rich and varied agriculture of the United States, with its many regional specialties, is apparent even on a small-scale map. (U.S. Department of Agriculture.)

8. Crop farming and horticulture, with subsidiary livestock
9. Commercial crop and livestock farming (mixed farming)
10. Dairy farming
11. Specialized horticulture

The world distribution of these types of agriculture is shown in Fig. 4-1.

PRIMITIVE SUBSISTENCE AGRICULTURE

Primitive subsistence agriculture is one of the least commercialized of all types of agriculture and is one of the most extensive. It is widespread throughout the humid tropics with the exception of Australia, and in Africa it extends over considerable areas of the dry tropics. In the latter continent it is, perhaps, the dominant form of agricultural activity.

Despite the enormous area over which it is practiced, primitive subsistence agriculture supports only a very small proportion of the world's population and exerts a negligible influence on the world market. Yet it cannot be dismissed in a few lines. Rational land policies for the humid tropics are being discussed by many international organizations in view of the rapid growth of world population and the very limited contribution to food supply provided by large parts of the tropical world; moreover, the rapid progress being made by Africans towards political independence and their desire for higher living standards make a higher level of agricultural productivity imperative.

The most widespread form of primitive subsistence agriculture is *shifting cultivation,* an agricultural technique which has many local names—*ladang* in Malaya and Indonesia, *caiñgin* in the Philippines, *chena* in Ceylon, *milpa* in Rhodesia, and *ngasu* in the southern Sudan. The Anglo-Saxon word "swidden" (fire-field) has recently been revived for this system of agriculture. The swidden was common in Europe in Neolithic times and is still found in Korea, far removed from the humid tropics.

The Rhythm of the Swidden

Two forms of swidden farming can be distinguished. True swidden farming is practiced by peoples whose material culture is so firmly intertwined with the swidden system that they cannot be permanently divorced from it without complete social collapse. When forced to take up other kinds of farming they revert as soon as possible to the traditional system, as the Moi people of the Annamite Chain have done with the withdrawal of the French from Indochina. True swidden farming, for all its apparent chaos, has been shown by many investigators to be a highly organized and intricate system of agriculture that operates in harmony with a humid tropical environment. Attempts to modify it by the introduction of European methods based on the experience of the very different temperate mid-latitudes generally fail. True swidden farming is essentially conservative of resources.

"False" swidden farming, on the other hand, such as the *chena* of Ceylon or the fire-field of Korea, is practiced as a supplement to the cultivator's permanent fields; the cultivator is essentially a sedentary farmer. His swidden is a temporary addition to the farm, and the crops grown and methods employed are essentially similar to those of the permanent fields.

Swidden agriculture has been described as a rotation of fields in contrast to a rotation of crops, but it is best to avoid the word "field" and substitute "clearing." The true swidden farmer never plants his clearing to one crop, as is the usual practice in fields. Instead, he sows a multiplicity of crops, and at different times, on the same clearing. By this means he prolongs his harvest period, secures a better-balanced diet, and reduces the possibility of crop loss through unfavorable weather conditions or pests. It is this confusion of crops, a minimum of clean weeding, and the apparently scattered and haphazard distribution of the clearings themselves that combine to give to the European a false impression of chaos and laziness. Nor is it strictly permissible to use the term "rotation," as this suggests a definite and regular annual succession. The true swidden farmer practices no set rotation of his clearings, nor does he keep any records. He uses his profound ecological knowledge, judging by the floral and faunal association when and whether an area is suitable for cultivation and what crops can best be grown.

In the swidden system sites for clearings are selected at the end of the rainy season, occasionally in primeval but more often in secondary forest, with a view to avoiding as far as possible the felling of really large trees (Fig. 4-3). The forest is then cleared, and the debris is allowed to dry out during the ensuing dry season, when the new clearings and the piled-up debris are fired. In the combustion the greater part of the chemical substances essential to plant life and locked up in the original forest material disappear, but enough remain to afford the swidden crops modest prospects of success. With the onset of the rains the

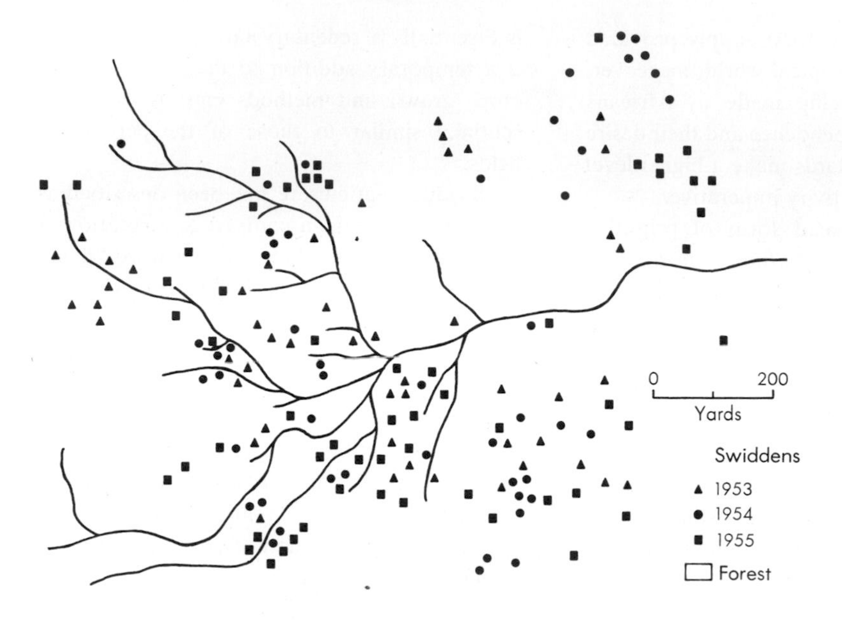

Fig. 4-3 Swiddens in Mindoro, Philippines.
Swiddens of the Hanunoo cultivators of Mindoro in the Philippines average about an acre in size, although some may be more than twice as large; the swidden cycle extends over about a dozen years, of which ten are fallow. Dispersal of swiddens assists natural regeneration, but recultivated swiddens seldom have the same boundaries or the same dimensions as earlier clearings. (H. Conklin, *Hanunoo Agriculture in the Philippines,* FAO, 1957.)

clearing is hoed or tilled with the digging stick; plow cultivation is unknown to the true swidden cultivator. The first crops are then sown, usually broadcast or dibbled, and often sown in association. The crops and the time of sowing vary widely, but are determined by knowledge born of immemorial local experience. Successive plantings are made, each crop being sown in the local environment that has been found to suit it best—on new clearings or swiddens that have borne a crop for one or more seasons, on ridges or refuse heaps, on termite mounds or on hearth ashes. Herbaceous perennials such as bananas and pineapples are also often planted. But few domestic animals are kept, and attempts to introduce them seldom succeed.

In the Asian tropics swidden farmers always grow "dry rice," that is, rice that receives no supplementary water and is entirely dependent upon rainfall. Rice occupies a fundamental position in the culture of Asian swidden farmers, even though it may not be the most important food crop in terms of total production. Corn, a wide variety of pulses, leafy green vegetables, and occasionally fruits are also planted. In African swiddens rice is at present little grown, corn and millets being the chief cereals, frequently grown in association with groundnuts. Where there is no real dry season, roots and tubers are especially important. Corn, manioc (cassava or tapioca), sweet potatoes, and yams are the commonest crops in tropical America; roots and tubers, including tuberous aroids, predominate in Melanesian swiddens.

The cultivation of a swidden produces a marked change in soil properties, and after the initial sowing different crops or crop associations are usually grown. There may be as many as three or more crop changes, but in time the abandonment of the clearing becomes inevitable. It grows progressively more difficult to prevent the encroachment and spread of weeds, particularly spear grass (*Imperata cylindrica*); yields decline, and soil exhaustion is frequently indicated by increases in pestiferous soil fauna. The labor of cultivation is no longer justified by the return. Often the land is abandoned to perennials interplanted in the later years of the swidden, and these continue to yield for a few years before being engulfed by the regenerating bush and forest.

Modifications of the Swidden

Some swidden cultivators shift their places of abode as well as their clearings, but this is a feature of cultural, not agricultural significance. Particular groups or tribes occupy areas which by agreement with their neighbors are regarded as their own particular territory, but there is no concept of land ownership in the Western sense—all families in the group have the right to *use* of land.

It follows that where a long fallow is required for the sequence of vegetational changes to restore the soil to its original condition—periods of up to twenty years or more commonly precede the reoccupation of old swiddens—a very large area is necessary to support even a modest population. European administrators ignorant of this fact have often, in the interests of forest conservation, pursued land policies which have tended to deny shifting cultivators access to their reserves.

It is now generally known that the luxuriance of the primeval forest of the humid tropics has little to do with the quality of the soil, which in general tends to have low reserves of humus and soluble minerals. The forest contains within itself all that is required for its survival. Under a climate with extreme insolation and heavy torrential rainfall and with the powerful assistance of the soil flora and fauna, decay and decomposition of leaf fall and other woody material proceeds extremely rapidly. Clearing, burning, and cultivation break this cycle. The slender reserves of soil fertility are speedily exhausted, and with the removal of forest cover there is the danger of heavy soil erosion. It is essential, therefore, that deforestation and cultivation should not continue to the point of serious soil damage and that sufficient time should elapse before the reoccupance of swiddens to allow nature to reverse the soil changes wrought by man. With a light population density, which affords time for soil restoration to take place, many investigators now conclude that on balance the swidden is a satisfactory form of land use.

The mode of life of true swidden cultivators makes a high population density impossible; this can only come about where there are external influences hindering the practice of the traditional mode of life, such as pressure from other groups, or where access to forest is denied by forest-conservation legislation. It is the false swidden cultivator who is the menace, for his swidden is not an integral part of his culture but is a manifestation of his land hunger. When the peasant has insufficient land to satisfy the needs of his family, he will, wherever he is able, encroach on forest land. He is seldom deterred by the possible illegality of his action; forest conservation and all that it implies in the prevention of rapid runoff, soil erosion, excessive silting, flooding, and damage to irrigation equipment has little significance to the land-hungry Asian peasant. Forest conservation has become progressively less effective as successive Asian nations have achieved independence, for leaders are unwilling to court political disfavor through the support of policies identified with former colonial regimes. Using the techniques of the sedentary cultivator, the false swidden farmer can speedily cause soil damage which may take great effort over many years to make good.

The realization, however, that under certain conditions swidden agriculture can constitute sound land-use practice has led to modifications aimed at making it suitable for a more commercialized economy. In the former Belgian Congo the "corridor" system has been introduced, which has aimed not only at raising agricultural productivity but also at increasing the production of *cash* crops, particularly cotton (Fig. 4-4). Cotton cultivation is also expanding in several former African dependencies of Britain, and by this means the shifting cultivator is slowly becoming more commercial-minded.

Another improvement is the "slash-mulch" technique that is being employed for the cultivation of abaca in the Philippines. Instead of being burned, the felled material is simply cleared to allow planting to take place and is then left to decompose. Under the climatic conditions of the humid tropics, decay and decomposition of the woody material takes place extremely rapidly, and the retention of the mulch accelerates decay through the activities of the soil flora and fauna. In two years even quite large trunks disappear, and almost the whole of the material contained within the original forest is made available for the continuance of the life cycle. A similar system is

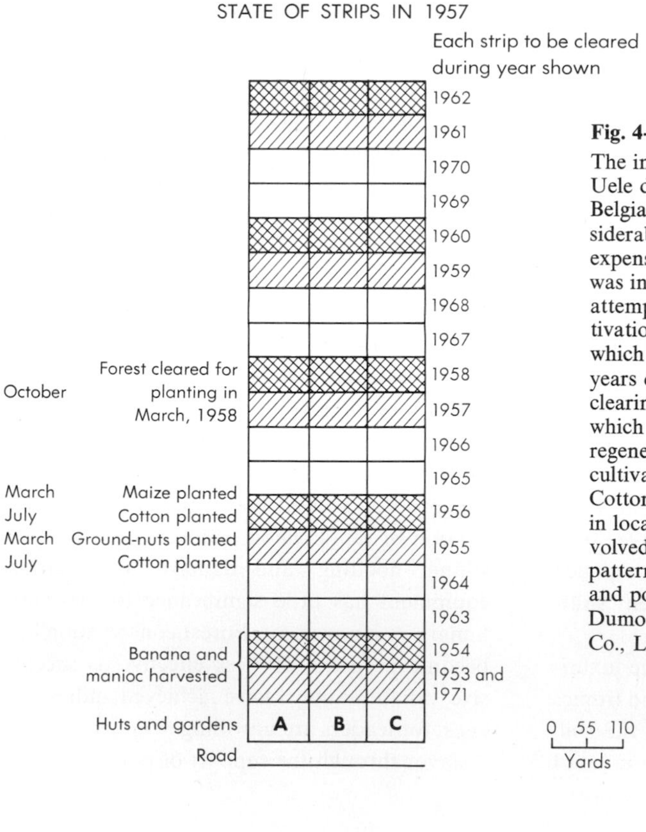

Fig. 4-4 The corridor systems in the Congo. The introduction of cotton cultivation into the Uele district of the northern Congo by a large Belgian ginning company resulted in a considerable extension of savanna land at the expense of the forest. The "corridor" system was introduced by the administration in an attempt to incorporate commercial cotton cultivation into traditional agricultural practices, which permitted forest regeneration. After two years of cropping cotton with food crops the clearings were planted to bananas and manioc, which were harvested until overgrown by the regenerating forest; the cycle of clearing and cultivation was to extend over eighteen years. Cotton cultivation produced some improvement in local living standards, but the system involved much arduous labor and its rigid field pattern made no allowance for irregular terrain and poor soils. (By permission from René Dumont, *Types of Rural Economy,* Methuen & Co., Ltd., London, 1957.)

also practiced by shifting cultivators in the Pacific coastlands of Colombia, where a continuously heavy precipitation prevents the slash from ever drying out enough to burn. It is likely that in the future the slash-mulch technique will become more widely practiced.

Fixation of the Swidden

Swidden agriculture yields a low return to those who practice it and provides limited opportunity for earning a cash income. Nevertheless some cash income is necessary for all swidden cultivators, and this has encouraged the cultivation of cash crops wherever possible. Rubber, pepper, and coffee are planted on *ladangs* in Sumatra. Such cash crop production inevitably makes for more sedentary cultivation. Over considerable parts of the world, however, the fixation of shifting cultivation was achieved long before commercial pressures began to make themselves felt; and it is a matter of considerable difficulty to explain how or why such a transition was made.

The fixation of shifting cultivation came about, but it must have been a gradual process, and the distinction between shifting and sedentary agriculture is by no means clear-cut. Shifting to contiguous plots instead of shifting to clearings some distance removed is commonly found. The key discovery to intensive land use in the humid tropics was the *sawah* (an Indonesian word for a flooded rice field), in which water, derived either from precipitation or from an external source, is retained by impounding walls. The origin of the sawah is obscure, but it was probably preceded by the cultivation of tuberous crops using some form of water control, much as taro is cultivated in parts of Polynesia today. With a more assured food supply than the swidden farmer, the sedentary cultivator could also undertake the cultivation of tree crops and could more easily incorporate domestic animals into the farm economy. Opportunities for commercial contacts also increased.

It is likely, then, that some form of water control in valleys where downwash provided partial replenishment of the minerals removed from the soil by cultivation was instrumental in the development of sedentary tillage. Primitive dams and distribution channels are used by many of the upland peoples who inhabit the headstreams of the rivers draining peninsular Southeast Asia. But often the sedentary subsistence farmer remains in part a shifting cultivator as well; the scattered groups of primitive sedentary cultivators in Southeast Asia have probably been influenced by the techniques of sawah cultivators of the floodplains and deltas, and may not represent an earlier phase of agricultural evolution. The dominant position of rice in the economy of swidden farmer, sedentary cultivator, and sawah farmer alike is a remarkable feature of the Asian tropics.

In the American tropics the existence of high mountains with numerous intermontane basins offered an escape from the humid lowlands, and an independent line of agricultural evolution was followed which produced a sedentary cultivation based on corn, beans, and squash. Several Indian peoples developed advanced techniques of water control. In the *tierra templada,* the temperate zone, wheat and barley can be grown, and towards the margin of the zone, the millet-like quinoa is important. Potatoes are an extremely important source of food at high elevations in South America, and are preserved for future consumption by repeated freezing and thawing, producing a foodstuff known in Peru as *chuño.* In these temperate highlands the hoe and the digging stick of the swidden farmer are replaced by the foot plow or even by the introduced European plow, which inverts the soil. Domestic animals are much more important than they are to the sedentary cultivator of the lowlands.

SAWAH AGRICULTURE

Sawah agriculture is one of the most successful types of land use in the world; already it supports between a third and a half of the world's population, and it will have to support an even greater proportion in the future. Sawah agriculture reaches its apogee in the humid tropics with marked wet and dry seasons, but it has a considerable climate tolerance, pressing closely towards the equator in one direction and in the other extending to the very margins of the warm temperate climates. It is a type of agriculture which is so closely identified with Asia that relatively few Americans or Europeans are aware that many millions of Asians support themselves by other agricultural systems.

This association with the teeming millions of Asia has obscured the many merits of the sawah system; the impression given by most writers is of a human anthill whose inhabitants are condemned to unremitting toil.[5] What is misleading about the anthill concept is that it suggests that the shortcomings of the sawah system are the consequence of exacting technical requirements which necessitate an enormous labor input.[6] The number of man-hours required to produce a ton of rice in some Asian countries is as much as 40 times that required in rice cultivation in the United States or Australia. Yet sawah agriculture actually cannot provide regular and continuous employment for all those who are nourished by it; *the teeming millions of Asia are the product of a population explosion resulting from European contact and influence which has affected sawah agriculture and other agricultural systems in Asia alike.*

The sawah system is a remarkable technical achievement, making possible a permanent sedentary agriculture in an environment where the rate of erosion can be as much as a thousand times that of cool temperate lands and where the general level of fertility is considerably lower. Moreover, it produces yields per unit area greatly exceeding those of any alternative method of food-producing agriculture in the humid tropics, and it has demonstrated an ability to maintain these yields for an immense period of time. Not the least of the merits of the sawah system is the manner in which it has been able to support an enormous increase in population in the last 300 years. In many of those areas which passed under European administration, the sawah system performed this feat in spite of the tremendous damage done to the indigenous social and agriculture structure through the failure of Europeans to understand Asian concepts of land tenure and their insistence on the introduction of Western ideas of land ownership. Many of the present grave shortcomings of Asian agrarian organization have in large part resulted from this European interference and the failure to replace the old order by a completely commercialized economy. Yet there is plenty of evidence that sawah productivity can be raised very considerably, and in view of the great anticipated increase in Asia's population, this is imperative.

The gentle slope of the sawah with its water-retaining embankments greatly reduces the dangers of soil erosion; under its water cover the soil is protected from even the most torrential downpour. In some areas, such as the Irrawaddy delta or peninsular Thailand, rainfall may be sufficient to provide all the water required for the rice crop. Where it is not,

[5] For example, see the excellent account of the system in Pierre Gourou, *Land Utilisation in French Indo-China,* Institute of Pacific Relations, New York, 1945, originally published as *L'Utilisation du sol en Indochine Française,* Centre d'Études de Politique Étrangère, Paris, 1940.

[6] The deployment of a large work force in the construction and maintenance of water control works has been closely associated by some writers with the development of centralized absolute government. See Wittfogel, Karl A., *Oriental Despotism,* Yale University Press, New Haven, Conn., 1957.

Young banana and manioc plants grown on a newly cleared corridor in the forest of the Congo near Leopoldville.

A few sawahs on this terraced hillside in Japan await final preparation before receiving the young plants from the nursery beds visible in the upper center of the photograph.

sufficient extra water for a good crop may be provided by flooding of rivers. There is often a large element of hazard, however, for there are few rivers whose regimes are so regular that a good crop is assured in every season; nevertheless, this is the manner in which rice is grown in much of the Menam plain of Thailand and in the lower Mekong plain of Cambodia and Vietnam. As the regimes of most rivers of East, South, and Southeast Asia are often capricious, it has become necessary to construct elaborate dams and distribution channels and to protect sawahs from excessive flooding by embanking the main watercourses. With the use of irrigation, as is also the case with natural flooding, some of the minerals removed from the soil by cropping are replaced from material in suspension.

The use of irrigation not only ensures a certain crop but, because the magnitude of harvest is closely related to the amount of water available in the growing season, also results in a heavier yield. With an elaborate and well-regulated irrigation system, multiple cropping is possible; as many as three crops a year may be taken in certain parts of Java or in south China.

The construction and maintenance of these elaborate embanking and irrigation systems, as already noted, demands a high degree of social organization and a strong and effective administration. The highest development of irrigation, however, was achieved by irrigation departments of former Asian dependent territories. By the use of new materials such as steel and reinforced concrete, the irrigation departments produced major works of engineering which resulted in an enormous extension of the sawah area. It was hardly the fault of the engineers that most of these great capital investments did little to provide permanent relief to the problem of land hunger and underemployment. It is worth comment that most of the great water-control and conservation schemes now in course of construction in Asia are multipurpose projects, which in addition to extending the sawah area will make a valuable contribution to industrial development.

Improved water control has permitted an extension of sawahs from the valley floors to the slopes by means of terracing. But terracing is by no means typical of all the rice lands of Asia; it is the exception rather than the rule. The most spectacular terraces rising tier upon tier for many hundreds of feet up steep mountainsides, such as those of the pagan Ifugao and Igorot peoples of the Mountain Province of Luzon in the Philippines Republic, cover only a very small area. Impressive terraces are also to be seen in south China, Japan, Tonkin, west Java, and Bali, but they are almost entirely absent in the rest of Southeast Asia and in the greater part of the Indian subcontinent. Most of the terraces are of long standing, and with the possible exception of China there appears little likelihood of any substantial extension; the return would not repay the cost involved.

The seasonal rhythm of sawah farming is closely related to the oscillations of wind systems over eastern and southern Asia, or monsoons. But great local climatic variations, the extensive employment of irrigation, and the existence of over 3,000 different varieties of cultivated rice combine to produce many variations of the system; descriptions based on the practices of south China are far from appropriate to Southeast Asia or to India.

The alternation of wet and dry seasons in monsoonal and monsoon-influenced climates well suits the life cycle of the rice plant. The dry season is the time for preparation and maintenance—the renewal and repair of the banks, or bunds, and of the irrigation and drainage channels. The first rains soften the soil ready for plowing, in which the slow but powerful water buffalo is indispensable over much of South and Southeast Asia. Meanwhile, work is pressed forward with the seedbed, often the only land receiving any fertilizer whatsoever, and the seed is sown, usually after having been germinated by steeping in water. With the increasing rains the seedlings grow rapidly, and the preparation of the sawahs to receive the young plants is carried to completion. The soil is gradually worked to the consistency of a thin cream, and water to the requisite depth for planting out is run onto the field or is allowed to accumulate. Transplanting is women's work; in the Far East plants are set out individually in rows to permit the use of a simple weeding push hoe, but this practice is by no means typical of India or of the whole of Southeast Asia, where plants are often set out indiscriminately. In China a system of double transplanting has been claimed by the Peking government to produce a large increase in yield, but this practice is also common in parts of Indonesia, Vietnam, and Cambodia.

With increasing precipitation the rice plants grow rapidly, but it may be necessary to run off the water from the fields at certain stages of growth in order to help restore the depleted oxygen content of the soil. When the heads have set, the water is run off for the last time, and the ripened grain is harvested either with a sickle or, frequently, with a knife, each individual head being separately severed.

In areas practicing multiple cropping there is heavy increase in labor input, as it is then a matter of urgency to get the harvest in and the fields prepared for the second crop. In southern Japan, where because of lower temperatures the second crop is wheat or some cereal other than rice, elaborate ridging is necessary to improve soil aeration during the winter. Rice followed by a rice substitute or vegetable crop is at least as common as two rice crops. Multiple rice cropping requires temperature conditions which restrict the practice to the tropics and necessitates considerable supplementary water during the drier season. The practice is therefore restricted to a few areas where these conditions can be met and where high population densities are found. The more important multiple-cropping areas are the alluvial plains of Kwantung and Tonkin, the north Java plain, and certain other parts of central and east Java and Bali. But the crop of the lower-sun season (the dry or drier season) is always much less than that of the higher-sun season (wet season) and is always of a different variety—usually a quick-maturing one.[7] Over much of Southeast Asia and a large part of India the sawahs produce only one crop, furnishing in the dry season only a poor grazing for the animals. Regular crop rotations are seldom encountered, but green manuring is practiced in some areas.

There is little place for animals in the sawah system except for those necessary for work purposes, and even the nourishment of these is a perpetual problem in the absence of any pasture. There is seldom enough grazing on the waste patches alongside roads, embankments, streams, and irrigation channels for the draft animals, and feed has often to be cut by hand and carried considerable distances. In the most congested parts of China and Tonkin even draft animals are replaced by human labor.

The high cost of keeping animals results in a very limited contribution to diet from animal products, and this is frequently reinforced by religious and social prejudices. The principal source of animal protein in the diet of sawah cultivators is fish, sometimes consumed fresh but often in the form of preserved or fermented sauces. Virtually every sawah produces a modest fish crop, and commercial freshwater fish-

[7] The dry season, of course, can occur at different periods of the year even within individual countries. See p. 133.

eries and pisciculture may assume considerable local importance. The rearing of carp species in ponds is a specialty of the Chinese, who have carried their techniques into other countries to which they have emigrated. North Java also has extensive commercial fishponds. Poultry, which need little land for their keep, also make a substantial contribution to diet; ducks are kept in large numbers, particularly by Chinese.

Holdings are very small, seldom exceeding an average of 2 acres, but this has to be viewed in relation to yield, which varies considerably, and the incidence of double cropping. This very small farm size arises from recent rapid increase in population, the absence of a law of primogeniture, and a social structure which over considerable areas is still in the process of adaptation to a monetary economy. Equally striking is the fragmentation of the holding into several minute noncontiguous plots, though a farm structure of this type is by no means confined to sawah agriculture. In some areas these obstacles to improvement are compounded with a high incidence of tenancy and tenancy turnover, but this situation is by no means typical of sawah agriculture. Even in the most congested regions of Java most families own some land, though it must be conceded that the area is very small.

Sawah agriculture is much more commercialized than is often supposed. In the Irrawaddy delta, in the lower Menam plain, and throughout Japan, it is in fact a highly commercialized activity. It is true that the rice-growing peasant is frequently a subsistence farmer by Western standards, but for him the rice crop is equivalent to a cash income. It is always salable, and save that it is less portable and more difficult to store, it is a ready substitute for cash.

Sawah techniques are most efficient in Japan, which has both the highest yield and the highest productivity per worker. There is a gradual decline in efficiency through Taiwan and China to Southeast Asia and a substantial further decline to the levels of Pakistan and India.

Japan's high level of efficiency arises from the use of selected seed and the liberal application of fertilizers, the latter being greatly facilitated by the existence of a large domestic chemical and fertilizer industry. The use of electric motors to power irrigation pumps and small threshing machines is almost universal in Japan, a consequence of the extensive rural electrification which has followed the harnessing of Japan's hydroelectric resources. Since 1950 there has been a rapid increase in the use of small two-wheeled tractors.

China at present lacks a large domestic fertilizer industry; its high yields are achieved by the extensive employment of organic manures of all kinds, including night soil, a practice that exacts a heavy toll in bacterial infection and helminthic infestation. The Peking government claimed very substantial increases in yields in the years following the Chinese agricultural revolution, increases which it attributed to deep-plowing extensions and improvements in irrigation and to double transplanting.

If the general level of efficiency of sawah agriculture could be raised to approach that of Japan, an enormous step forward would be made in meeting Asia's food problems. Climatic considerations alone make this feat unlikely of accomplishment, but the introduction of Japanese methods into other countries is slowly proceeding, and has already produced beneficial effects in India and Indonesia. Elsewhere in Southeast and South Asia little or no fertilizer is used, although the sawahs rented by the sugar companies in Java receive considerable benefit from the heavy application of fertilizer for cane production (Fig. 4-5).

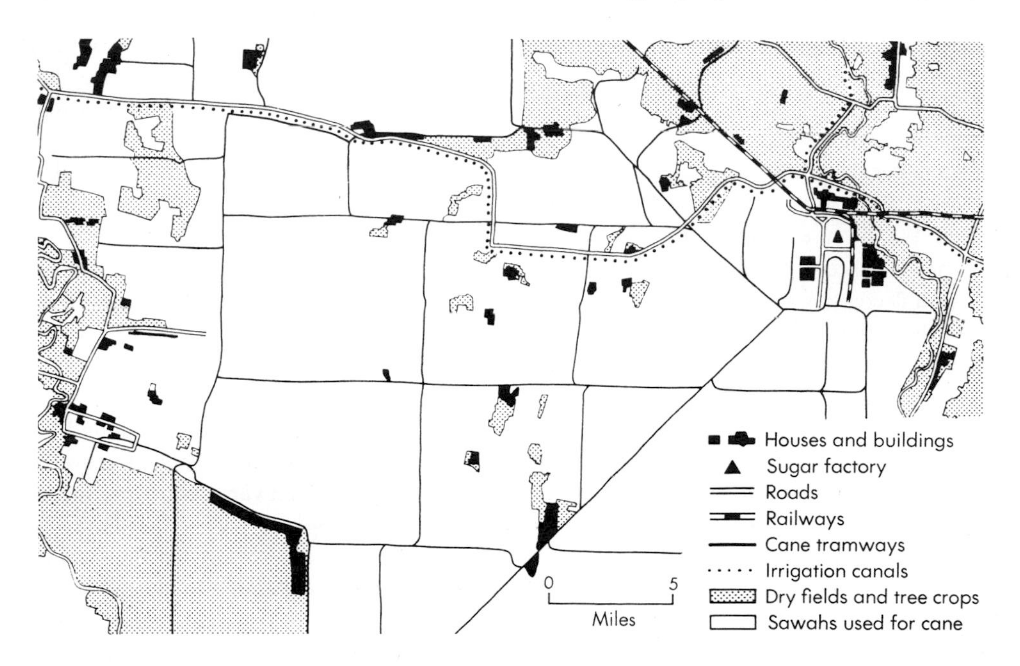

Fig. 4-5 Sawahs and sugar in Java.
All level land in Java capable of being irrigated is used for sawahs, but extension of irrigation was greatly encouraged by the sugar companies, which rented village rice land. The companies were not permitted to utilize more than one-third of the village sawahs in any one year, so that mills such as this at Djatiroto, the largest in the country, required access to extensive areas of sawahs. In the Twenties sugar cultivation involved all the best sawah land in central and in east Java, and heavy fertilizer application for sugar greatly benefited the ensuing rice crop. (*Atlas of the Netherlands Indies.*)

INTENSIVE DRY-FIELD AGRICULTURE

Within the large area devoted to sawah agriculture there are many districts which lie at too high an elevation to be periodically flooded or which for one reason or another cannot be irrigated; these cannot be used for sawahs, but they may nevertheless be intensively cultivated. Crops depending entirely on rainfall may be said to be grown on dry fields. Intensively cultivated dry fields are called *tegalan* in Indonesia, but no regional term has yet obtained wide recognition.

Though scattered throughout the area practicing sawah agriculture, dry-field agriculture becomes the dominant system in the drier portions of the Asian tropics and in north China; even within these areas, however, there are numerous localities in which hydraulic conditions favor sawah cultivation. The two systems thus interlock over a considerable portion of the Asian continent.

Over much of the area of dry-field cultivation precipitation seldom exceeds 40 inches and is often much less. Where precipitation is less than 15 inches, irrigation becomes essential for permanent agriculture; wherever such areas passed under British control, major irrigation works were constructed, as in the Punjab, Sind, Iraq, and Egypt. But this has not resulted in the appearance of the sawah system, although rice is grown in considerable quantities.

In intensive dry-field agriculture no crop is dominant in the farm economy. In moister areas dry rice and corn (maize) are almost universal; with decreasing precipitation corn is replaced by wheat and, in still drier and scorching environments, by many varieties of millets and sorghums. But none of these crops ever constitute a monoculture, as is the case with rice in sawah agriculture; they may all be found growing in close proximity to, and rotated with, many noncereal crops such as the Indian *gram* (chick-pea), grown both as a food and as green manure, and many kinds of oilseeds such as soybeans, groundnuts, sesame, and rape. Crop diversity helps provide a balanced diet, but its main purpose is to safeguard the farmer from climatic hazard; some crops will succeed whatever happens, and a failure can be partially made good by resowing with a quick-maturing crop.

As with sawah agriculture, intensive dry-field agriculture is capable of a high degree of commercialization, and industrial cash crops are occasionally of considerable importance. The greater part of the oilseed production is intended for local consumption, but large quantities of groundnuts, rape, sesame, and soybeans may be exported. Another important crop, particularly in former British dependent territories, is cotton.[8] This crop is grown both as a dry-field crop and with the aid of irrigation, but the better varieties are restricted to irrigated areas. Both India and China are major producers of cotton. The cultivation of the American upland types of cotton in India is restricted to the northern portion of the country, production being first undertaken during the cotton famine arising from the American Civil War. The cultivation of cotton and other cash crops in the Punjab was encouraged by the British practice of exacting payment for irrigation water, whereas in the Netherlands Indies it was provided without charge, the costs of irrigation being recovered from the land tax. Cotton grown on the black soils of the Deccan as a dry-field crop consists of short-staple and coarse local varieties.

A somewhat similar situation is found in China. Cotton is grown throughout the north China plain, but the best varieties are produced with the aid of irrigation in the loesslands to the west, the Wei valley being an important area. The cultivation of cotton has been greatly encouraged by the Peking regime, and its importance in the rural economy is now much greater than in the Thirties.

In sawah agriculture, irrigation makes multiple cropping possible; occasionally this can also be done on dry fields, a quick-maturing crop grown with the rains being followed by a drought-resistant crop such as one of the millets or sorghums. In India and Pakistan the crops harvested at the end of the rainy season or grown during the rains are called *kharif* crops; those grown during drier months and harvested before the onset of the rains are termed *rabi* crops. *Kharif* crops vary greatly between the irrigated valleys and the doabs (interfluves) of northern India and between northern India and the peninsula. Cotton is one of the principal *kharif* crops both of the Punjab and of the Deccan; others are sesame, groundnuts, and corn. In unirrigated areas of the doabs, *jowar* (great millet) is the principal crop; other millets and sorghums, such as *bajrah* and *ragi,* are grown in the Deccan, where millets may be grown both as *kharif* and *rabi* crops. The principal *rabi* crop of the Punjab

[8] By some curious historical accident, Egypt never officially become a dependent territory but remained nominally independent.

is wheat; this combination of cotton and wheat is also characteristic of Egypt.

Multiple cropping, however, demands favorable temperature conditions, and in China opportunities for this practice become rapidly reduced in the north China plain. The long winters are one of the principal reasons for the depressed condition of this part of the country, and aggravate the effects of a scanty and capricious rainfall and a marked susceptibility to flooding which make summer crop production hazardous.

As in sawah agriculture, animals occupy only a minor role; for plowing, water buffalo are replaced by oxen, horses, or asses, and in northern India and Egypt, by camels. India's enormous half-starved and disease-ridden cattle population consumes an amount of food that would keep a smaller national herd at a high level of productivity. The extensive use of dung as a fuel also deprives the fields of the only widespread source of organic manure. The reduction of the cattle population by retiring surplus animals to rest farms is now a part of official Indian agricultural policy, but religious opposition is still strong enough to prevent any large-scale slaughtering.

The general level of efficiency of intensive dry-field farming is low, largely as a result of a meager and unreliable rainfall; the enormous area under millets is striking testimony to India's agricultural backwardness. In Java opportunities for converting *tegalan* into sawahs are now very limited, but in India and China there is still abundant scope for the extension of irrigation, which is given very substantial priority in investment in the agricultural sector of both countries' national development plans. China's scheme for the regulation of the Hwang Ho, to be completed by 1975, will constitute one of the major civil engineering achievements in the world. The development will almost certainly produce a further extension of rice growing in north China at the expense of wheat, which has a lower yield per unit area (Fig. 4-6).

One method of ensuring a higher productivity per worker, now the subject of extensive experiments by the FAO and many governments in South and Southeast Asia, is the production of dry rice on large holdings with mechanical equipment; this would in effect be a type of commercial grain farming. At present mechanical dry-rice cultivation is still in the experimental stage. It would have to be carried out in virgin areas and would require extensive preliminary soil surveys; it is, however, a method of cultivation which might well become more important in the future.

PLANTATION-CROP AGRICULTURE

Plantation-crop agriculture, an intensely commercialized form of agriculture, has an importance to the world market out of all proportion to the limited area it occupies. Originating in the humid tropics, it represents the introduction into an alien environment of an agricultural system reflecting the techniques and attitudes of European capitalism. It is hardly surprising that this process has encountered many physical and social obstacles, not all of which have been successfully surmounted.

Historical Derivation

A plantation was originally any European planting of export-oriented cash crops under unitary management in the new lands made known through the "Geographical Discoveries." It was applied both to small plantings and large; for the latter, the term "estate" was inappropriate as the contemporary European estate was typically a collection of tenancies

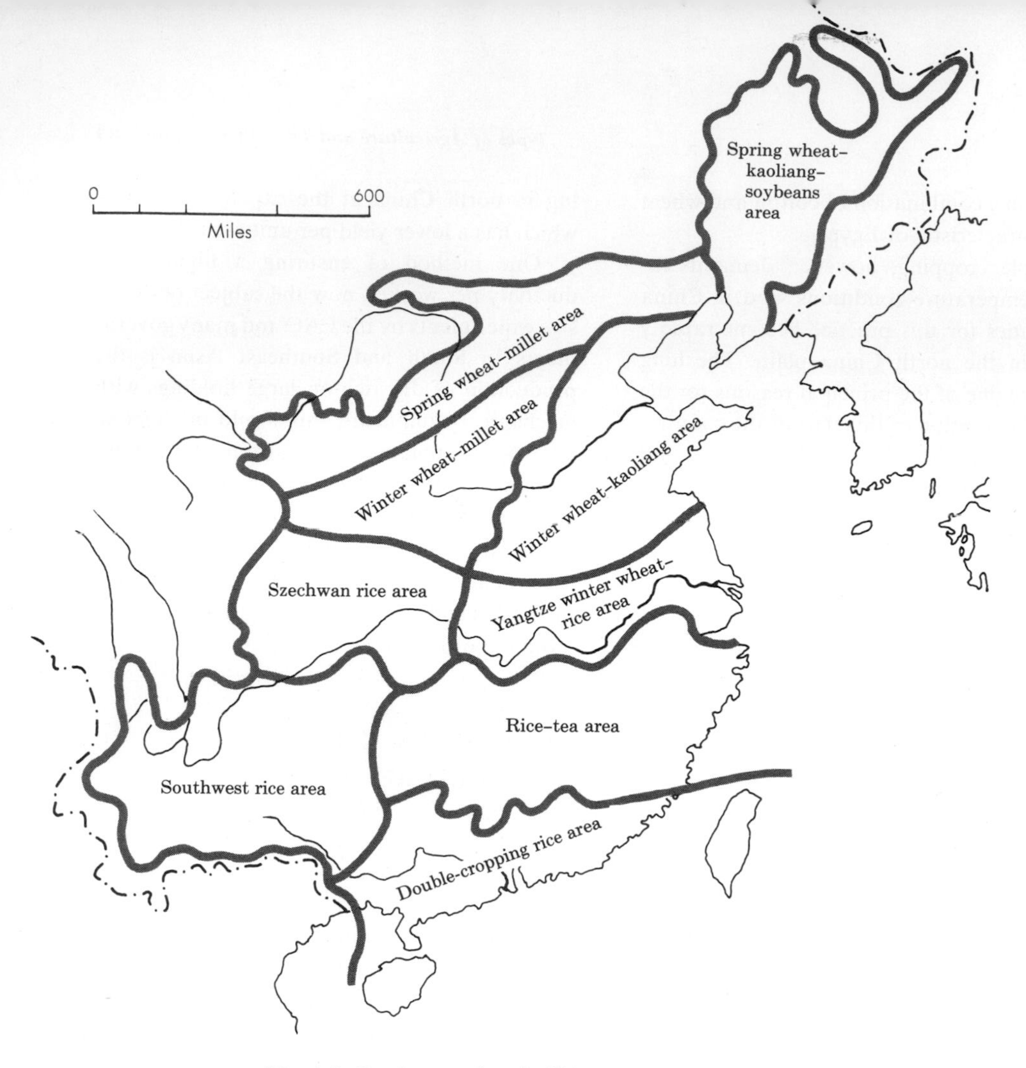

Fig. 4-6 Land-use regions in China.
The paucity of statistical information renders a regional differentiation of Chinese agriculture difficult. This map of land-use regions was based on sample surveys in those parts of China accessible to research workers in the early Thirties, and appears to require considerable modification. As a result of the extension of irrigation, the line dividing the rice region from the wheat region should now be further north. The extension of cotton cultivation in central and north China (and particularly in Hopeh, Honan, and Shantung), which provided the country with perhaps a 12-million bale crop in 1962, should also receive recognition in a map of land-use regions in the Sixties. (After Buck.)

and therefore under multiple rather than unitary management. The first plantations appeared in the islands of the Gulf of Guinea, but it was the Portuguese sugar plantations of northeast Brazil that set the pattern for the new type of agriculture; from Brazil the plantation system spread to the Caribbean islands and to the mainland of North America. Not until a second era of colonization in the late nineteenth century did the system again flourish in the Old World, and it was in Asia, not Africa, that it first reestablished itself. The initial impetus was given by the abolition of slavery in the British West Indies (1833) which led to the establishment of plantations in India and Ceylon by former slave owners.

A central feature of the old plantation system was the large unit operated by an alien labor force; indigenes were unable or unwilling either to engage in production on a scale sufficient to satisfy Europeans or to labor in enterprises operated by them. The labor problem was solved by the African slave trade, and from sugar the system spread to the cultivation of rice, indigo, cotton, and tobacco.

The modern estate industry still makes extensive use of alien labor, the introduction of which into some territories has created many difficult social problems, but free contract labor has replaced slave and indentured labor, both of which are no longer acceptable to civilized societies. However, indigenous peoples are now both willing and able to produce crops which were formerly the prerogative of estates, and so effectively do they compete that in some territories restrictions have been placed upon their operations. Native farmers, or smallholders, now produce a large proportion of many former estate crops, and there is reason for believing that their share of production will increase further in the future.

In view of the importance of the small farmer it is better to focus attention on the crops themselves and to use the term "plantation-crop agriculture" to describe the production of crops which were formerly grown by plantations but which may now be grown either by large units, or estates, or by smallholders. Some plantation crops have always been grown by local people for their own consumption, but many are European introductions. The techniques of growing and processing the latter have been learned from Europeans, and in one instance at least, smallholders have been able to improve upon European methods; close planting and the abandonment of clean weeding were practiced by rubber smallholders long before they were adopted by estates.

Plantation-crop agriculture presents a complex pattern of estate and smallholder production, and what holds in one part of the world is by no means the case in others. For some crops, such as tea, estates dominate production; for others, such as natural rubber, estates and smallholders divide production almost equally; in coconut production smallholders are by far the more important. Oil palm cultivation is exclusively an estate occupation in Southeast Asia, but in West Africa it is a smallholder activity. It is by no means a simple matter to determine why production in one area is a prerogative of estates and in another of smallholders; a factor of the greatest importance, however, is how former colonial regimes considered the interests of the indigenous peoples could best be furthered. The policies of newly independent countries in Asia and Africa now operate strongly in favor of the smallholder, and in some countries, of which Indonesia is an outstanding example, estate industries have been subjected to heavy disabilities.

The Estate

The main advantage that is claimed for the estate is that it produces a uniform product of high and standard quality. It enjoys economies of scale, an advantage that is particularly important for crops that require elaborate and costly machinery to process, such as sisal, sugar, and palm oil. Lowest unit costs are achieved when the machinery can be kept operating at full capacity for as long as possible. In the Hawaiian Islands, where labor costs are extremely high by world standards, this consideration has determined the whole structure of the sugar industry. Six large companies control the entire production; by the use of long-term cane and by irrigating the drier leeward southwestern slopes, harvesting is maintained throughout the year, so that apart from a brief annual shutdown for maintenance, mills are kept continuously in operation.

Apart from Latin America, where the

privately owned estate is common, there is a high degree of concentration in estate industries sometimes achieved through control rather than ownership, as is the case with the British "agency houses." Estate companies have access to the central technical and financial services of their parent organization, and thus can take advantage of any new technological development or market opportunities. The production of natural-rubber latices is almost entirely an estate prerogative, as smallholders lack the resources to acquire the special tank vehicles and equipment to handle this product. Hawaiian sugar producers make use of aerial color photography to detect backward or disease-affected areas of cane, a technique that is out of the question for small farmers.

Yet the estate has serious handicaps. Labor costs and fixed costs make up a large part of total expenses and are incurred whatever the level of production. Estates find it difficult to reduce production when prices are low; moreover, they cannot afford to dismiss labor at such times because they must ensure that they have an adequate labor force when prices are high. But it is just when prices are high that the attractions of alternative employment are greatest for estate workers; rubber tappers are apt to leave to work for smallholders, for at such times the latter can often outbid the estate. Estate production thus tends to be relatively inflexible; estates continue producing even in periods of very low prices so long as they cover their day-to-day expenses, nor do they expand production rapidly as prices increase.

Estates are overwhelmingly monocultural, as this permits the best deployment of a specialized labor force. The need to keep the labor force fully employed throughout the year is a principal reason for the concentration on perennials, and the cultivation of annuals under estate conditions is now distinctly uncommon. Tree crops with a year-round yield such as rubber and oil palm greatly assist the optimum utilization of labor and keep machinery operating at a high capacity factor.

Fungoid and virus diseases, which in a humid tropical climate are far more serious than in temperate latitudes, are a perpetual danger to estates. Pure stands, which never occur naturally in the equatorial forest, encourage the spread of infection, and constant vigilance and early remedial action are essential to good estate management. Some of these diseases have been overcome through scientific research, but some, such as Panama disease, have so far eluded control. This infection has compelled the abandonment of much land planted to bananas in the Central American republics; abandoned land can be used for other crops, but none are as profitable as bananas, and its effective utilization continues to present many problems.[9] Cacao is also particularly susceptible to disease when cultivated under estate conditions.

The political vulnerability of the estate is far more serious than its economic shortcomings. To most peoples of the humid tropics the estate is entirely alien, with no basis in, and few contacts with, local culture. Its importation of a nonindigenous labor force has hindered the development of national unity, and the history of indenture is not easily forgiven. Its produce is shipped out of the country, frequently to return in the form of manufactured articles which nationalists believe should be produced at home. These nationalistic complaints have more substance in some territories than in others; the *hoofdadministratoer* of a great estate company in the east Sumatra of the Netherlands East Indies was the law for most practical

[9] The United Fruit Company has made strenuous efforts to encourage the production of food crops by small farmers on abandoned land, but with comparatively little success. See Galo Plaza and Stacey May, ***United States Business Performance Abroad: The Case Study of United Fruit in Central America,*** **National Planning Association, Washington, 1958.**

purposes and a figure of major political importance. The obvious beneficial achievements of estates—employment conditions markedly superior to those obtainable outside, and the provision of schools, health services, and other social facilities which in countries at a higher level of economic development are provided by government—frequently count for little with nationalist leaders.

Thus, though they are often irrational, there is a kernel of truth in nationalist arguments; indeed, it is conceded by some economists that the type of investment made by Europeans in dependent territories did not lead, and could not have led, to an increase in real incomes per head and that it may well have depressed them.[10] Now, unless the estate can come to terms with indigenous peoples and convince them that its operations are an equal partnership between local and foreign interests, it can have little future in much of Asia and Africa.

Nowhere has the impact of nationalism on estate operations been severer than in Indonesia, before World War II one of the most important areas in the world for estate production. Difficulties over the renewal of leases and the issue of import licenses for capital equipment, an embargo on the discharge of redundant labor, penal taxation, and severe limitation on the remission of profits have forced many companies to the point of abandoning their operations. In 1958 all Dutch-owned estates were nationalized without compensation, a fate that also befell British-owned properties in 1964.

The widespread interests of the various estate controlling corporations, however, give them some protection against both economic and political vicissitudes, and there is a general tendency towards still greater concentration in estate industries. One of the largest organizations is the British-owned Harrisons and Crosfield Ltd., which controls nearly 2 million acres under rubber, oil palm, coconuts, tea, coffee, cacao, and abaca, with estates in Malaya, Sabah (North Borneo), Indonesia, India, Ceylon, and East Africa. Several other British organizations are almost as large, as is also the Franco-Belgian giant Socfin, which operates the world's largest oil palm estate and has properties in Vietnam, Cambodia, Malaya, Cameroun, and both Congo republics.[11]

The Small Holding

The growth of smallholder production is one of the greatest economic changes that have taken place in the agriculture of the humid tropics in the present century. British West African governments consistently discouraged the establishment of foreign-owned plantations, and held that the expansion and upgrading of native production provided the best prospects of economic development. Thus palm-oil estates sanctioned in Nigeria also had to provide planting material for native growers.[12]

Economically and socially, smallholder production has much to commend it. A small holding requires little capital investment, and it is usually easier for the smallholder to interplant or to take a cash crop while waiting for his holding to come into bearing. Largely because of these facts, smallholder production

[10] The following remark of Lewis is significant. "In actual fact, the record of every imperial power in Africa in modern times is one of impoverishing the subsistence economy, either by taking away peoples' land, or by demanding forced labor in the capitalist sector, or by imposing taxes to drive people to work." W. A. Lewis, "Economic Development with Unlimited Supplies of Labour," *The Manchester School of Economic and Social Studies,* vol. 22, p. 159, 1954.

[11] The two states calling themselves Congo republics are the former Belgian Congo, with its capital at Léopoldville, and the former French Congo, with its capital at Brazzaville.

[12] Alan Pim, *Colonial Agricultural Production,* Royal Institute of International Affairs, Oxford University Press, London, 1946, p. 135.

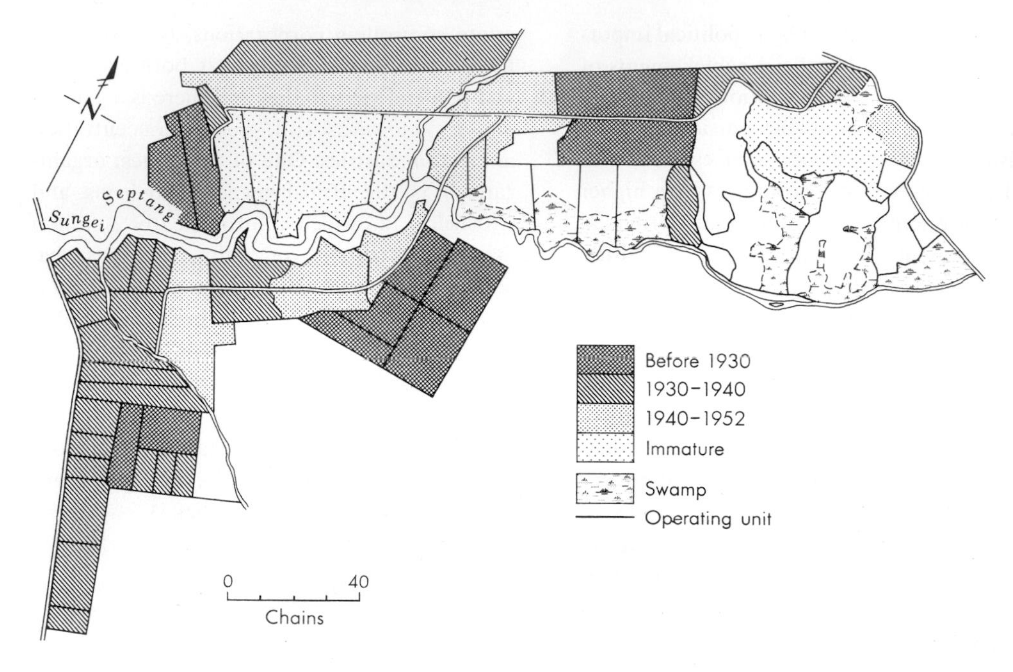

Fig. 4-7 Subdivided rubber estate, Malaya.
This rubber estate of some 2,300 acres produced 800,000 pounds of smoked sheet annually. It was sold off in 1958 and divided into 117 pieces, shared between 56 operating units; the great majority of the new owners were town dwellers who made their purchases for speculative purposes. The great majority of the new units were around 10 acres in size, in order to qualify for the maximum government replanting grants available to smallholders. Subdivision has been attended by a marked decline in the quality of rubber produced on the former estate area, although total output appears little affected, largely because of heavier tapping by the new small owner-operators. Estates purchased for speculative subdivision have largely consisted of properties that suffered damage or neglect during the Japanese occupation or during the postwar communist insurrection, or which possessed a high proportion of old rubber and other land of low productivity, so that they did not fit in with estate company policy of concentrating effort on properties with the lowest production costs. Subdivision, however, has affected only about 10 per cent of the estate area of Malaya. (By permission from Ungku Aziz, *Subdivision of Estates in Malaya,* University of Malaya, Kuala Lumpur, copyright, 1963.)

possesses a considerable degree of supply elasticity, responding promptly to price fluctuations (Fig. 4-7). Small holdings also are excellent training grounds for the acquisition of financial and managerial skills, which are in such short supply in underdeveloped countries. The ideal smallholder crop is perhaps rubber, which gives a year-round return with complete absence of labor peaks. The processing of rubber is simple and inexpensive, and smallholders can produce smoked sheet which commands a price only slightly inferior to that of estates. But even crops with greater seasonality can be successfully grown by smallholders. An outstanding example from Africa is the cultivation of *arabica* coffee on the slopes of Kilimanjaro by the Wachagga people of Tanganyika. In neighboring Kenya, the cultivation of *arabica* coffee by Africans was long forbidden in order to protect the interests of the white estates; Africans could grow only the less remunerative *robusta* variety.

The smallholder suffers the greatest disadvantage in the cultivation of crops which require marked seasonal labor inputs with lengthy intervening slack periods and which need elaborate and costly processing. Frequently the smallholder can only get his output treated at an estate factory. Sugar, tea, and sisal are crops of this kind; but abaca, palm oil, and copra are crops which also present difficulties to smallholders, at least for the production of the best qualities. Yet marked seasonality of labor requirements also operates against estates; some sugar estates therefore have found it expedient to use tenants to produce part or all of their cane, and do not farm their property directly. This is the system employed in Fiji, where the Colonial Sugar Refining Company of Australia now leases all its land to tenants, who agree to accept the advice of the company's technologists.[13] Tenants are also used to produce cane on estate land in the Philippines and in several Caribbean islands. But these producers are hardly independent smallholders, and their economic position is always weak; they carry, in fact, a disproportionate share of the real costs of the system.

There are, however, some striking examples of the successful cultivation by smallholders' cooperatives of crops which are relatively difficult to process. Cooperative associations overcome the limitations of small individual outputs; and with the aid of relatively inexpensive equipment such as hot-air copra driers, cacao-fermentation sheds, and mechanical presses for palm oil, cooperatives can effect a marked improvement in the quality of smallholder output. Among examples of successful cooperatives may be cited the oil palm cooperatives of southern Nigeria, the Kilimanjaro Native Coffee Growers Union, the most flourishing cooperative in the whole of Africa, and the cacao cooperatives of the Tolai people of New Britain in Australian-administered New Guinea.

[13] **The tenants are all Indian, descendants of indentured estate laborers.**

The Overall Situation

On the whole, estate and smallholder production should not be mutually exclusive. There are, perhaps, a few crops for which estate production appears more suitable and others for which smallholders are admirably fitted. But there are many in which the two can compete and in the production of which there is no clear balance of advantage. In countries where for one reason or another estates were especially favored by the colonial government, it would seem that estate production will account for a smaller proportion of total output. But this does not mean that there should be no place for the large estate; the well-managed large unit can hold its own in any kind of economic enterprise. What these countries need is an agricultural policy in which both estates and smallholders are assigned their part in economic development. For better or worse, the estates of Southeast Asia and Africa exist; no country can afford to allow such an economic asset to wither away.

In countries in which there has been no struggle for independence, the estate appears to have better prospects. Companies operating in Latin America now have much greater respect for national feelings than in the past and take every care to avoid giving offense. Even so, they have not escaped considerable censure. However, the large estate is still a prominent part of the Latin American cultural pattern, and despite the Cuban revolution, its disappearance in the near future appears unlikely.

It is incontestable that the level of incomes in plantation-crop agriculture is substantially higher than that in other forms of agriculture in the humid tropics. Increasing world population and the industrialization of underdeveloped economies suggest that demand for the products of plantation-crop agriculture will continue to grow. Some, it is true, are threatened by the development of synthetic products, and the present level of output of others will not be sustained without considerable new planting. But there are substantial opportunities for improving productive efficiency and it is up to the newly independent governments of the humid tropics to realize them.

PASTORAL NOMADISM

Pastoral nomadism has many characteristics which recall shifting cultivation. It requires access to very large areas of land, only a small portion of which is utilized at any time. It supports only a very low population density, and, like the true swidden farmer, the nomad is the prisoner of his environment—his way of living is so closely interwoven with his pastoral activities that the two cannot be separated. The life of the sedentary cultivator is entirely alien and repulsive to the true nomad, who seldom if ever makes a good plow farmer.

Pastoral nomadism is confined to the arid and semiarid continental interiors of the Old World. It is found in the savanna lands and desert margins of intertropical Africa and in the semideserts and steppelands of Asia, even reaching into the sub-Arctic grasslands of the tundra. This great latitudinal range inevitably produces considerable variations in the mode of living of nomad peoples, and the grazing animals that support the nomadic pattern of land use—cattle, sheep, goats, camels, yaks, reindeer, and horses—vary considerably in relative importance from one region to another according to climate, terrain, and the cultural tradition. But the basis of the system is always the same, whatever combination of livestock is kept. The nomad is entirely dependent upon his animals and their products for his livelihood. The animals in turn are dependent upon the natural forage, whose availability is closely determined by climatic considerations. When the local forage is exhausted, the nomad must strike his camp and move on.

The extremely mobile nomadic life with its sense of freedom is, perhaps, more attractive to Western eyes than the spirit-haunted life of the swidden cultivator in the rain forest. The sense of freedom is largely illusory; the nomad moves from necessity, following an annual cycle from winter (or, according to latitude, dry-season) quarters to summer (or wet-season) grazing. Moreover, the nomad's freedom of movement is more restricted than is usually thought. Apart from the necessity of keeping within range of potable water, the nomadic group cannot progress very far without coming into contact with a neighboring clan. Boundaries of clan territories are vague and determined by the varying pressures of custom and tradition. Endless opportunities thus arise for disputes over grazing or access to water, and quarrels once started tend to be perpetuated long after the initial point at issue has ceased to have any practical significance, by a social structure that demands blood for blood. In years when good spring and summer rains bring widespread and copious grass, territories are less likely to be rigorously defended, but in a year of deficient rainfall and consequent shortage of feed, any incursion into the clan territory is likely to be hotly resisted. Occasionally, a succession of bad years may force many clans to move, their traditional mistrust and hostility overcome by common misfortune. Mass migrations of this kind create opportunities for the appearance of new leadership and the formation of new social contacts and allegiances.

Such circumstances in large part explain the ephemeral empires of the nomads and the periodic incursions of Tartar, Mongol, and Kurd into the domain of the sedentary cultivators of China, Eastern Europe, and southwest Asia. In the past, these troublesome tribesmen, of extreme mobility and warlike disposition, have always been a menace to the sedentary farmers of the margins of the semiarid lands, to be contained if possible or else placated. The nomad's diet, with its relatively large intake of animal protein, played its part along with the advantages of social organization in the establishment of a general military superiority over the sedentary agriculturists. But social and technological change has undermined the old basis of nomad military strength, and disposal of the resources of the Asian "Heartland"[14] now rests firmly in Moscow and Peking. Changes initiated by the railroad and telegraph have been accelerated by the motor vehicle, radio, and formal education and indoctrination, and the nomadic way of life and the lack of a common language or religion have retarded the development of indigenous nationalism among nomad peoples. Part of Mongolia possesses the title of "People's Republic," but the direction of affairs in the nomad lands is entirely in conformity with development plans formulated by outsiders, which envisage little future for nomadism. There is some limited possibility for the extension of crop cultivation through further irrigation; the spectacular Turkmen canal, planned to extend from the Amu Dar'ya almost to the Caspian, is an example, but this grandiose project of the late Stalin era for "changing the face of the nation" now appears unlikely to be completed. A greater impact on the nomadic way of life is being made through the development of secondary industries and rapid urbanization; Buryat Mongols have been found to make capable factory workers in Irkutsk and Ulan Ude. The increase in population consequent upon the introduction of modern medical services must enhance the movement to the cities and mining centers, and new railway links between China and the U.S.S.R. will hasten the passing of the old order.

It is quite probable that these changes may have resulted in an increase in productivity in the nomad lands of Asia. In the old feudal order social standing depended, as it still does in some African societies, on the number of beasts possessed by the family, irrespective of quality. Little control over breeding produces herds of poor quality, capable of withstanding considerable privation but of low productivity.

Far-reaching changes are also taking place in the nomad lands of southwest Asia and Africa. Repelled by pressure on the traditional grazing lands and attracted by the high wages to be earned in the petroleum industry of the Persian Gulf, former nomads of the Arabian Peninsula and Kurdistan are acquiring new skills and outlooks whose ultimate effect must be completely to disrupt the old social and economic order. Lacking any such powerful agent as the petroleum industry, the pace of change has been somewhat slower in Africa, but the widespread achievement of African independence will give control over the destinies of the nomadic cattle keepers to the more numerous sedentary cultivators. Only in the Somaliland Republic do the African nomad peoples constitute a self-governing country. But however the passing of the nomadic way of life is viewed, it offers to the peoples themselves opportunities for achieving higher living standards.

[14] The term used by political geographers to describe the north central core of the Eurasian landmass, long inaccessible to sea power. It has been associated with the English geographer Mackinder and his followers, who claimed that control of the Heartland is the key to world power. See Halford J. Mackinder, ***Demographic Ideals and Reality,*** **Constable & Co., Ltd., London, 1919, chap. 6.**

COMMERCIAL GRAZING

Commercial grazing, or livestock ranching, is a highly capitalized form of agriculture with a markedly corporate structure; it constitutes a very extensive type of land use in which the land area per worker is very great. Over large areas of the interior of North America and of the southern continents where precipitation is too low to support cultivation, it is the only type of commercial agriculture possible. It may, however, penetrate into areas where precipitation appears high enough for plow agriculture, as on the Coastal Plain of Texas or on the western slopes of the Great Dividing Range in Australia, and it is also to be found in mountainous or upland areas where the growing season is too short or the terrain unsuitable for crop production. That it is poorly developed in Eastern Europe and the U.S.S.R. is largely because the institutional environment is unfavorable; socialized agriculture on the Russian model offers minimal rewards for the exercise of the care and attention so necessary in livestock management.

The basis of commercial grazing is the natural grasslands of the continental interiors, either of the prairie and steppe or of the savanna type, according to latitude. These are almost entirely unimproved, and the carrying capacity is low; in western New South Wales and Queensland more than 15 acres are necessary to support one sheep. It may seem something of a paradox that land of such low productivity can form the basis of a profitable agriculture that, almost uniquely, is seldom plagued with surpluses. The explanation, of course, is that the capital investment per worker is extremely high. The large ranch, or *estancia,* needs fencing, bores, wind pumps, dams, watering facilities, feed stores, dipping troughs, and shearing and wool sheds, as well as the ranch buildings themselves. For considerable periods of the year the large ranch may have to be virtually self-supporting, and has to carry the stores and equipment to make it so. Over much of northern Australia, where "station" properties are entirely unfenced, the main link with the outside world in the wet season is provided by the radio networks of the Flying Doctor service.[15]

The capital requirements of the commercial grazing industries have largely been met from overseas, mainly from countries which are large markets for livestock products. As in estate agriculture, British capital has taken a prominent part in the development of grazing industries. It was as important as domestic capital in the early development of ranching in the United States, and still has large grazing interests in Canada, Argentina, Uruguay, South Africa, and Australia. Ranching companies not infrequently form units of integrated organizations, as is the case with those owned by the great meat-packing and meat-extract companies, most of which operate ranches in many parts of the world. Before World War II one large British company, in addition to its *estancias* in Argentina, operated freezing works, its own refrigerated fleet, and a chain of meat outlets in Britain.

Commercial grazing has two main activities —the running of sheep and the running of beef cattle. Every other activity is entirely subordinate to these main interests, though in west Texas and in the Cape Province of South Africa Angora goats assume minor importance. It is not often that the two main types of livestock production can be combined; climate, terrain,

[15] A medical service now largely financed by the Australian government. By means of radio networks cattle stations can obtain medical advice or summon a doctor by air from their network base. The system also serves for general communications and is extensively used for educational purposes. It is a unique and highly successful method of providing a sparse population scattered over an enormous area with some of the social services deemed essential to modern society.

and the natural feed usually favor one kind of production against the other. But in some areas of commercial grazing a choice is possible; in these circumstances it is the relative profitability of the two kinds of production and expectations of future profitability that determines the selection. In North America and in Argentina there is a strong tendency for beef cattle to replace sheep, but in South Africa, Australia, and New Zealand sheep have more than held their own. A similar trend towards beef cattle could, however, be established in the latter countries if wool were to be severely affected by the competition of synthetic fibers.

In commercial grazing sheep are mainly kept for wool production; meat is a by-product. The best-quality wool is produced from merino sheep, which do well in semiarid conditions but which have a wider climatic tolerance than is often supposed. Mutton and lamb production, on the other hand, is better suited to higher-rainfall areas, and can be integrated into a mixed type of farming. In mountainous and rough country sheep are liable to attack by predators from which cattle are relatively safe; sheep, however, can crop closer to the ground than cattle and can make use of pastures which cattle cannot graze. The severe winters of the continental interiors in the Northern Hemisphere operate against fine-wool production, and the inability of North America to compete with wool produced in the southern continents partially explains the decline of sheep rearing in favor of cattle keeping, a transfer of interest which is also encouraged by the existence of other types of farming at close hand which can profitably fatten up lean range cattle.

In tropical savanna lands grazing faces many problems. Animals are susceptible to many diseases and parasites, which are much more difficult to control than in temperate climates. Indian zebu cattle, which have a better heat tolerance, have been crossed with European breeds, but breeding is poorly controlled as fencing is rare. More serious is the inadequacy of transport facilities; when beasts have to walk hundreds of miles to railheads, perhaps taking months on the journey, they suffer a substantial loss in weight. In the tropical grasslands of South America a feudal social structure is also a major obstacle to improvements in efficiency. Nor can Australia escape some censure, for the cattle industry of the north could not exist without its aboriginal stockmen, whose relations with the station owner or operator do not greatly differ from those between *vaquero* and *patron*.

As in most other forms of agriculture, commercial grazing has a strong seasonal rhythm; mustering, or rounding up, branding, dipping, and shearing follow the same cycle throughout the world. In exposed areas and where winters are severe, animals are driven down into sheltered valleys or transported to other districts for feeding during the winter. Much of the rangeland in North America is summer-grazing land only, which would be difficult to utilize without the diversified agriculture of the valleys. But animal production under such conditions is a higher-cost operation than in areas where winters are mild enough to permit animals being left out all year round. In northern Australia, cattle may pass from station to station on their trek to eastern railheads, many companies maintaining chains of stations for this purpose. The "channel country" of southwest Queensland, an area subject to periodic flooding, is a vital area for the resting of stock moving overland, and its importance to the Australian cattle industry may increase in the future.

It is not unusual for properties to possess some cultivated land, located near the main buildings or in some valley flat, or to keep a small dairy herd for the needs of the homestead. In the United States, grazing is closely integrated with the diversified agriculture of the irrigated river valleys of the High Plains, and many ranches themselves produce some supplementary feed from cultivated land. But in other parts of the world there may be no cultivated land at all; most Australian cattle stations possess only a vegetable garden. In southern Brazil and in Uruguay ranching is the dominant activity, although rainfall is quite high enough for the cultivation of a variety of crops. On the humid Pampa of Argentina commercial grazing and crop production are usually integrated; wheat and alfalfa pastures replace each other according to the varying profitability of wheat and beef. In Patagonia the irrigated valleys have a similar function to those of the High Plains of the United States, providing shelter and winter feed to animals driven down from the plateau. In the United States, the multiplicity of irrigation projects in the High Plains and intermontane plateaus and the existence of large areas of public domain which are let for summer grazing give rise to a more complex organization of grazing, with considerable movements of stock between irrigated land and the range and between mountain and forest summer grazing and the desert.

In more humid areas in temperate latitudes or where supplementary water can be made available, carrying capacity can be greatly increased by the sowing of temporary pastures such as alfalfa (lucerne) and other leguminous crops or by permanent improved pastures of ryegrass and medics (clovers). Where temporary pastures can be established, commercial grazing may merge imperceptibly with crop production, as is the case in much of the Argentine Pampa. Pasture improvement has been widely carried on in Australia and New Zealand, and in both countries much land with sufficient precipitation to support crop farming is used for sheep runs.

On the whole, however, commercial grazing is a means of making profitable use of enormous areas of relatively poor land where rainfall is insufficient for plow agriculture or where the combination of climate, lack of transport, and limited markets renders crop production impossible on a commercial scale, as is the case in much of the tropical grasslands. It is exceedingly difficult to see any alternative land use for much of the area now occupied by commercial grazing. Nevertheless, such enormous increases in efficiency have been achieved in livestock production in other types of agriculture that the future of commercial grazing in some parts of the world is questionable. Range livestock fed on natural pastures grow slowly and do not satisfy a general public preference for quality meat and for small joints. In the United States livestock ranching in the western grazing lands is in part kept alive by high tariffs on imported livestock products, but the proportion of the nation's cattle found in these areas is small. In the temperate lands of the southern continents, on the other hand, there is little prospect of any decline in grazing industries; climatic considerations give to these areas a substantial competitive advantage in the production of many kinds of livestock products. The tropical savanna lands are poorly equipped in every way to take advantage of technological improvements in livestock production, but with improved transportation much could be done to improve the efficiency of the cattle industry of northern Australia; by itself, however, the industry could not support the capital cost and recurrent charges of such improvements.

COMMERCIAL GRAIN FARMING

Commercial grain farming is practiced in the mid-latitude interiors of every continent, close to the margins of plow cultivation. Its most specialized development is to be found in the newly settled lands of the Americas and Australia, where it is a very capital-intensive type of farming; nevertheless, it lacks on the whole the corporate structure common in commercial grazing or in estate plantation crop agriculture, and is still largely practiced by privately owned, family farm units. A pale reflection of commercial grain farming is found in certain parts of Eastern Europe, such as the plains of Hungary, Moldavia, and Walachia, in the Ukraine, and in Kazakhstan in Asian Russia. Grain farming in the Soviet bloc differs in many particulars from that in the noncommunist world; in some of the areas mentioned concentration on cereal production is indicative of agricultural backwardness.

As its name implies, commercial grain farming is a type of agriculture in which cereals sold off the farm are the main source of farm income. It is a specialized form of agriculture, created by the needs of the industrially developing countries of the latter half of the nineteenth century in the face of a mounting shortfall of domestic grain and a substantial cost disadvantage in its production. It has proved a hazardous specialization. Few types of agriculture operate in such trying climatic conditions, and prosperity and disaster succeed each other as cereal prices fluctuate with cyclical movements of business activity. It is doubtful that any other type of farming has done so much damage to the soil, and in so short a period, or has experienced such territorial advances and retreats.

But for all its fluctuations of fortune, commercial grain farming is far from an ephemeral type of land use. It was the growth of vast urban agglomerations that brought this system of farming into existence, and as the whole tenor of economic development is to promote urbanization and to extend the range of nonagricultural occupations, its future appears to be assured. It is, however, most desirable that this system of farming should conform to the European tradition of "keeping the land in good heart." Fortunately, there is evidence that this is happening; it is highly improbable that wheat will ever again be grown in areas with a rainfall of barely 10 inches, as was the case in parts of Australia during the period between the two world wars. The tremendous improvements in yield per acre that have been achieved in this type of farming since 1939 have made the cultivation of such climatically marginal areas uneconomic, as well as undesirable.

Large units are a distinctive feature of commercial grain farming; farms of 1,000 acres are common, and large farms may be many times this size. Such units are essential for the economic deployment of the extensive variety of mechanical equipment needed by this type of farming and for the earning of an income large enough to pay for their purchase and upkeep. The development of labor-saving machinery was just as much a necessity for the appearance of commercial grain farming as improved transport, for its rationale is a prodigious local surplus. Thus commercial grain farming achieves a remarkably high productivity per worker; in the Palouse area of Washington a farmer needs only two hired hands to cultivate a wheat farm of 3,000 acres.

Larger and still more powerful tractors, together with a host of new machines for performing cheaply and expeditiously every conceivable kind of farm operation, have enabled this type of farming to record tremendous increases in productivity over the past two decades almost everywhere in the world. The use of such equipment has permitted the farmer to complete plowing, sowing, and harvesting in the minimum time when climatic and soil conditions are favorable and, in conjunction with a greatly enhanced use of fertilizer, has helped bring about a remarkable increase in yields per acre. Wheat yields in this type of farming are, it is true, still less than those recorded in areas practicing mixed farming in more humid environments, but the disparity is now much less than before World War II. Costs of cereal production, moreover, are very much lower in commercial grain farming, and this competitive advantage has increased with the passage of time.

Although in the world market wheat is by far the most important cereal produced by commercial grain farming, it is now seldom a monoculture, as rice typically is in sawah agriculture; depending on soil and climate, other cereals such as oats, rye, barley, corn, sorghums, sown grasses, and legumes may have a part in the rotation, and there are a few areas where rice, corn, or barley displaces wheat as the most important cash crop (Fig. 4-8). The closest approach to a wheat monoculture is perhaps found in the Palouse area of Washington, but even here a crop is not taken every year on the same land.

The relative importance of the various crops in the farm economy only in part reflects considerations of soil and climate; even more important are such state regulations as acreage allotments and marketing schemes. But collectively, grain crops provide the greater proportion of the farm income; animals are kept principally to supply the needs of the farm itself or such restricted local markets as may exist. In the commercial grain farming areas of the southern continents, however, it is quite possible for livestock products to produce a higher farm income than cereals in some years.

The North American continent is unique in having a number of discontinuous areas of commercial grain farming, each with its own particular crop combination or specialty. The largest is the spring-wheat region which extends from the southern portions of Alberta, Saskatchewan, and Manitoba in Montana, North and South Dakota, and Minnesota. Farming here has replaced natural grasslands developed on deep, black or dark brown soils, inheriting a great reserve of fertility which encouraged a continuous wheat monoculture. Crop rotations and fertilizers are now much more used than in the past; in fact, acreage restrictions have made their use essential. Climatic conditions are such that considerable fluctuations in output are inevitable from year to year; winters are long and severe, and much depends on the depth of the snow cover. Unfavorable conditions in spring and early summer can easily set back a crop that has successfully germinated, and there is considerable risk of damage by late-summer storms. Farm buildings are large and substantial, and at selected intervals along the railroads grain elevators tower over the generally flat or gently undulating countryside. At one time it was uneconomic to grow wheat more than 30 miles from a railroad, but with the development of trucking this has long ceased to be true.[16]

Occupying most of Kansas and western Oklahoma, with marginal extensions into neighboring states, is the winter-wheat belt, by far the most productive single wheat region of the United States and accounting for nearly 30 per cent of the national wheat output. The hotter summers discourage the cultivation of other temperate cereals such as oats, so important in the spring-wheat region, while in the scorching conditions of the southwestern portion of the belt even wheat tends to be replaced by sorghums, a changeover that has also been encouraged by acreage restrictions on wheat.

Most specialized of all wheat regions of North America is that of the Columbia plateau, or Palouse area, perhaps the apogee of commercial grain farming, with large, highly mechanized farms producing hard winter and

[16] See Chapter 22, p. 547.

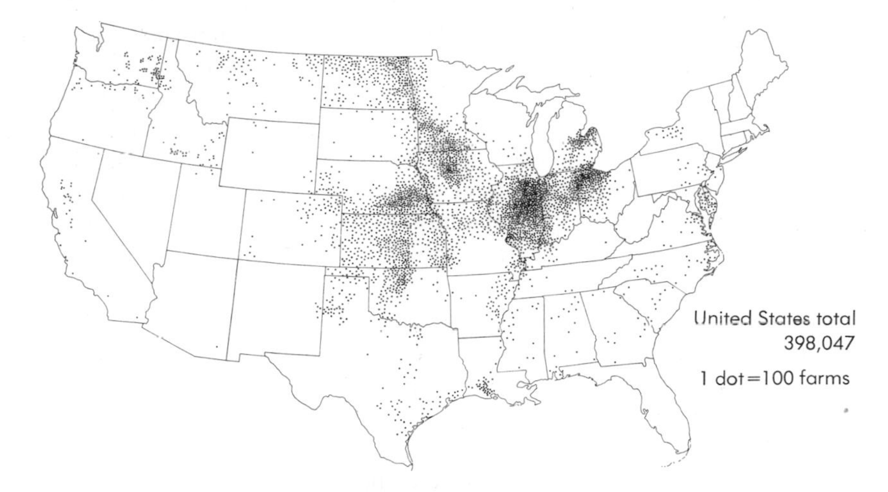

Fig. 4-8 Cash grain farms in the United States.
Farms deriving 50 per cent or more of the farm income from the sale of cereals, peas, and beans are most numerous in the central and eastern portions of the corn belt, where corn and soybeans find ready markets for stockfeed, and in the winter wheat region; they are, however, relatively most important in North Dakota, hub of the spring-wheat region. Some cash grain farms in Texas, Louisiana, and California are producers of rice. (U.S. Department of Agriculture, 1959.)

spring wheat and little else. This area, which has a rainfall of little more than 10 inches, was noted in the past for its "dry farming"—a technique of conserving soil moisture over two or even three years by plowed fallows.

Over large areas of the American wheat belts unsatisfactory farm practices with little attention to soil conservation have greatly reduced the original reserve of humus and soluble minerals. This "soil mining," in conjunction with a cycle of drier years, created vast dust bowls, or man-made deserts, which aggravated the low prices of the Great Depression and compelled the exodus of large numbers of farmers from the Great Plains. Fortunately, the damage to the soil has not proved irreparable; better farm practices such as contour plowing and the heavy application of fertilizer have revitalized areas of commercial grain farming. So successful have American farmers been at raising productivity that considerable areas have been thrown idle through government acreage restrictions on land for which it is not always easy to find an alternative use.

The extensive steppes of the Ukraine, southern Siberia, and Kazakhstan offer almost ideal conditions for large-scale cereal cultivation with mechanical equipment, but in comparison with North America the degree of success obtained is very modest. The Kazakhstan steppes were the scene of a great pioneering development in the Fifties, involving large *sovkhozy* and a considerable range of mechanical equipment; young persons were recruited or impressed to provide labor for the new farms, and the whole movement formed part of a highly publicized plan for equaling United States per capita consumption of farm products by the mid-Sixties. The newly plowed-up lands made a substantial contribution to total grain output in the early years, but yields were not sustained, and the movement has now been soft-pedaled.[17] In the Ukraine, where the collective is the dominant farm unit, some improvements in output were effected through post-1957 reforms. As already noted, collectives now possess their own machinery, but methods of production are still extremely crude by American or Australian standards; bulk handling and storage facilities are almost nonexistent, and much of the machinery itself is antiquated and underpowered. Though spring wheat is the most important crop, strenuous attempts have been made to popularize the cultivation of corn, which is really unsuitable for the drier lands of Kazakhstan and south Siberia. Large quantities of corn are grown in the Ukraine, and in Romania it is the principal food crop. In Romania and the Ukraine sunflowers, an oilseed crop, are also of considerable significance and are often a striking feature of the landscape. Only in Argentina among other areas of commercial grain farming is this crop of any importance.

The wheat belts of Argentina and Australia have more in common with each other than with the commercial grain farming regions of the Northern Hemisphere. Argentina and Australia are normally the lowest-cost wheat producers in the world, yet in both countries wheat cultivation is combined with livestock production.

In Argentina, wheat and beef-cattle production are interlocked in a unique wheat—alfalfa—cattle combination which in the pre-Perón period depended on the *patron*-tenant agrarian organization. Tenants of the large *estancias* established alfalfa, a crop whose deep rooting system makes it ideal for the Pampa, with its absence of surface water but copious underground supplies. Alfalfa is fed to high-grade beef breeds and greatly improves the chemical and physical properties of the soil, building up a reserve of fertility that is cashed in a wheat crop. So successful is this system that sheep, formerly numerous on the margins of the humid Pampa, have been pushed into Patagonia and Entre Ríos. In the warmer and wetter northeast Pampa wheat is replaced by corn, which, because of the extensive domestic use of alfalfa as feed, is principally grown for the export market. Before World War II, this area, centered on Rosario, was the world's leading corn-exporting region, a position it could regain with an improved domestic economic climate. Flaxseed, the source of an important drying oil, is another crop produced in large quantities in this area, as it is also in the spring-wheat region of North America.

Argentina's great rival in wheat production is Australia, which combines wheat growing with sheep raising; no less than one-third of the country's enormous sheep population of 150 million is kept on wheat farms (Fig. 4-9). During the postwar period of generally high wool prices, many farmers have derived a larger proportion of their income from wool than from wheat.

The Australian wheat belt forms a great crescent inland of the Divide, extending from southern Queensland to the Eyre Peninsula of south Australia. Though interrupted by the Great Australian Bight, it is continued in western Australia, where production has tended to increase in the postwar period. Large farms of 1,000 acres or more are the rule, though the average size in western Australia is greater than in the east, and all are highly mechanized. A further peculiarity of the Australian commercial grain farming belt is that

[17] It has been pointed out that from the climatic standpoint the plowing up of the Kazakhstan steppes is equivalent to plowing the grasslands in south central Montana. See Chauncey D. Harris, "Soviet Agricultural Resources Reappraised," *Journal of Farm Economy,* **vol. 38, p. 263, 1956.**

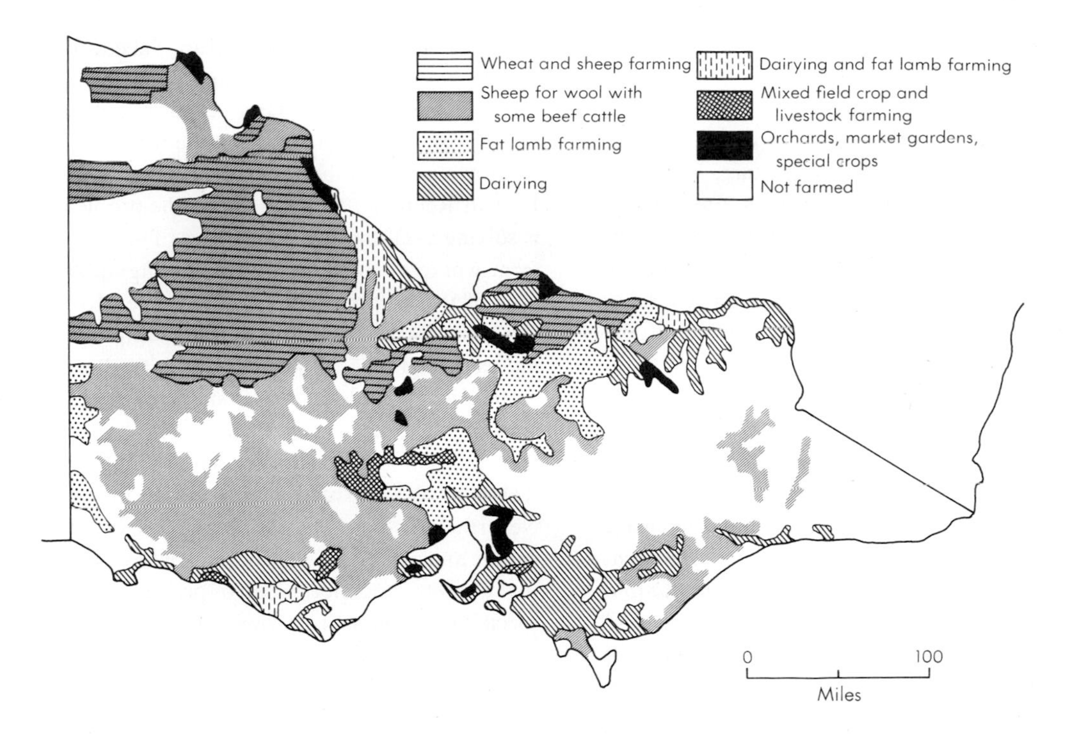

Fig. 4-9 Types of farming in Victoria, Australia.
Australian farming is even more specialized towards the production of livestock products than that of the United States, but in temperate Australia, livestock farming can assume many forms, as is indicated by this map of types of farming in Victoria. The wheat-sheep type of farming, found in the Mallee and Wimmera regions in the northwest of the state, offers perhaps the closest approach to traditional European mixed farming. (After R. Kent Wilson.)

it extends into winter-rainfall Mediterranean areas which elsewhere in the world have a more diversified agriculture. The extreme specialization in wheat in the northerly portions of the wheat belt in New South Wales and western Australia is a result of the high temperatures experienced in spring and summer, which do not favor oats and barley and which produce conditions too dry for corn. In the cooler climate of south Australia, however, the combined acreage of oats and barley now exceeds that of wheat as a result of the postwar growth of the European market for feed grains.

The dovetailing of animals and grain production in the farm economy of the Australian and Argentine regions reflects climatic advantages which do not occur in northern continents. Animal production is more economic in other types of farming in North America, and in Eastern Europe and the U.S.S.R. collectivization acts as a strong disincentive. The best prospects for commercial grain farming would appear to lie in the progressive abandonment of climatically marginal areas and in concerted efforts to free the channels of world trade in agriculture products.

CROP FARMING AND HORTICULTURE, WITH SUBSIDIARY LIVESTOCK

Crop farming and horticulture, with subsidiary livestock, corresponds to the "Mediterranean agriculture" of Whittlesey and other writers. While "Mediterranean" is acceptable in climatic terminology, it is much less satisfactory from the agricultural viewpoint; the agricultural systems of the Mediterranean basin are very diverse, and the differences between the agricultural systems of areas of similar climate in other parts of the world are also very striking indeed.

In North Africa the large, capital-intensive farms of the *colons* of Algeria and Tunisia occupied nearly all the best soils; highly mechanized low-cost producers of wheat, barley, wine, and livestock products, these large farms stood out in sharp contrast to the small fragmented holdings of the indigenous Muslim population, whose agriculture is better described as of the intensive dry-field type. After the achievement of Algerian independence, however, many of the large European farms were abandoned, and, despite the Evian agreement which safeguarded European interests, a decree of 1963 announced that all such properties would be socialized. They have since been farmed by cooperatives of former workers; efficiency has sharply declined, but the lot of the new occupants has made them the envy of the rest of the Algerian peasantry.

On the European side of the basin two systems of farming reflect a dichotomy that has persisted largely unchanged since classical times. One consists of the *latifundia,* or large estates, worked by tenants; the other comprises the small peasant-proprietors struggling to make a living from a poor, thin, and rocky soil, whose animals for centuries have been converting the once forested uplands into a waste of stunted thorn and scrub. Successive Italian governments have grappled with the twin problems of the large estates and an impoverished peasantry, but on the whole with as little success as the Gracchi brothers of the Roman Republic; to some extent the problem is solving itself through the exodus of southern farm workers to the rapidly expanding industries of the northern cities. Finally, the Mediterranean basin possesses several examples of modern highly commercialized agriculture, among which the north Italian plain is outstanding. This area receives considerable summer rainfall and so strictly lies outside the region of the Mediterranean climate proper. Nevertheless, it makes considerable use of irrigation and is a large producer of wheat, rice, sugar beets, tomatoes, dairy products, and specialties dependent on rapid rail connection with the industrial cities of Western and central Europe.

Of the other areas of a Mediterranean-type climate only central Chile has an agriculture which closely resembles that of the Mediterranean lands of Europe, a consequence of its Latin cultural origin. The large mechanized farms of the Cape region of South Africa resemble those of the former *colons* of the Maghreb, and in western Australia and south Australia a wheat-sheep agriculture, with intensive dairying in the moister coastal areas, is the rule. Californian agriculture is so highly specialized and capital-intensive that it cannot really be compared with that of any other part of the world.

The term "crop farming and horticulture, with subsidiary livestock" emphasizes the essential features of much of the agriculture of the Mediterranean basin and, with qualification, is a fair description of the agriculture of other areas with a Mediterranean type of climate. It indicates that, except in the neighborhood of great cities and in bordering mountain

The difficulties of farming the limestone margins of the Mediterranean basin are clearly visible; here Greek peasants make use of the mule to plow the larger patches of soil, but the many smaller ones between the rocks have to be cultivated with the mattock.

ranges, livestock are essentially subsidiary to the main farming operations of crop and horticultural production. It is not difficult to see why this is so in the Mediterranean basin; over most of the basin, the provision of animal fodder presents considerable difficulties. The natural vegetation of forest and xerophytic scrub has been debased by clearing and by close grazing, particularly by goats. The impoverishment of the vegetation, in conjunction with the widespread occurrence of limestones, is largely responsible for the parched and barren appearance of many upland areas. Hot, dry summers are unfavorable for the growth of grass, so that animal numbers are restricted to the limited carrying capacity of odd lots, waste, stubble, and the hillsides. Good summer grass can be produced from water meadows or where irrigation water is available; but only in the vicinity of great industrial cities, such as those of northern Italy, is dairying an important activity. Animals therefore tend to be kept for work purposes, though in the remoter parts of the eastern basin and in parts of the Spanish Meseta, the seminomadic shepherd still survives. In the more exposed and wetter uplands, where there are good forests of oak, beech, and chestnut to provide good seasonal feed, the keeping of pigs is still, as it was in classical times, an important subsidiary activity.

The greatest difficulty confronting the farmer is how to combat summer aridity, which grows progressively more severe from west to east in the Mediterranean basin. The most important crop by far is wheat; sown in autumn, it grows with the rains of winter and spring when evaporation is low, and is ready for harvesting at the onset of the hottest and driest period of the year. Dry-farming techniques of fallow plowing were well known in classical times and are still practiced. But if climate is favorable to wheat production, little else is; soils are generally of low fertility except in the vicinity of active volcanoes, and the shortage of animal manure is a further difficulty. Despite the payment of substantial subsidies by all governments, the Mediterranean lands of Europe have seldom been self-sufficient in wheat; under the Mussolini regime Italy's struggle to achieve self-sufficiency, an autarchic policy dictated by military reasons, became known as the *battaglio del grano* (battle of the grain). Costs of wheat production are high, as methods of cultivation, little changed from those of medieval times, are primitive by the standards of Western and central Europe. Absentee landlordism and *mezzadria* (share tenancy) have still not been eliminated in southern Italy, and the equivalent *métayage* of the French Midi has only disappeared in the present century. Concentration of land ownership has been confirmed and accelerated in Spain during the Franco regime.

Viticulture is an important feature of the farming of Mediterranean lands. The vine is cultivated wherever possible, and is an excellent way in which to make use of sloping land unsuitable for crop production; the vine, however, requires considerable labor to coax it through the long, dry summer, for it is usually grown without irrigation. The Mediterranean area produces comparatively few specialty wines; even the best of the Italian wines have not the world reputation of the great French vintages. The port wine of the Douro (an area with summer rainfall) and the sherry of the Jerez area of Andalucía have, however, long been popular with British peoples. The great bulk of the wine production is cheap red wine such as the *vin ordinaire* of France, produced in tremendous quantities in the Midi and in Algeria. Certain areas in the eastern basin, with its hot, dry summers, have specialized in the production of dried vine fruits, such as the Patras area in the Peloponnisos, famous for its currants, and the Izmir district of Turkey, which produces raisins.

Horticulture has always been an important activity in the Mediterranean region, although the proportion of the cultivated area under fruit, vegetables, etc., is very small. In Western and central Europe fruit growing is a specialized activity, little practiced by the average farmer, but in the Mediterranean area it is widespread; on hilly, undulating land it is a rational form of land use. Although individual farm production may be very small, horticulture can account for a substantial proportion of the farm income. Even on the poorest soils and under the most difficult conditions, the olive can usually be grown, but citrus and stone fruits are importations from summer-rainfall climates, and usually require additional water. Among the better-known specialty areas are the *huertas* of southern Spain, the lemon groves encircling Mount Etna in Sicily, and the citriculture area of Israel; among nonirrigated specialties may be mentioned the olive cultivation of the Guadalquiver valley of southern Spain (Fig. 4-10).

In every other area with a Mediterranean type of climate livestock play a substantially greater part in the farm economy. Perhaps the closest resemblance to the agriculture of Mediterranean Europe is found in central Chile, where the concentration of land ownership is even more extreme than in southern Europe. Chilean agricultural techniques are so primitive

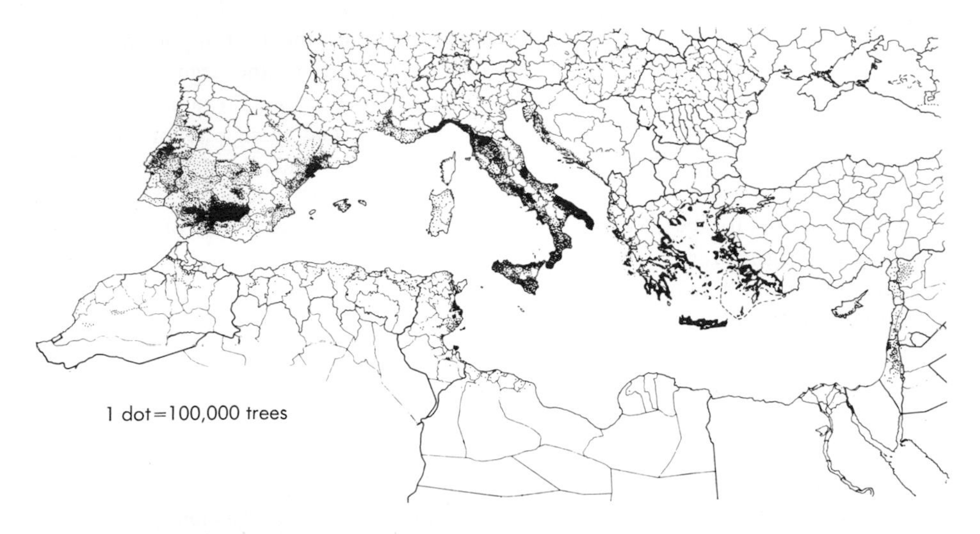

Fig. 4-10 Olive production in Europe and adjacent countries.
The olive's ability to withstand summer drought and to grow on very poor soils has made it of fundamental importance in Mediterranean agriculture since classical times. Although Spain is by far the largest producer, accounting for about one-third of world olive oil production, it is in Greece, which has the world's highest per capita consumption, that the olive is of greatest significance in national life. The olive is notoriously prone to biennial cropping, and a poor harvest exerts a depressing influence on the Greek economy. Italy is a substantial net importer of olive oil despite a level of output exceeded only by that of Spain, and as in Greece, close official control is exercised over production and marketing. (William Van Royen, *Atlas of the World's Resources,* vol. 1: *The Agricultural Resources of the World.* © 1954, by permission of Prentice-Hall, Inc., Englewood Cliffs, N.J.)

that crop yields are lower than in any part of southern Europe, and living standards of the rural population as a result of a *patron*-tenant organization, are probably below those of even the most isolated and backward portions of the eastern Mediterranean basin. Central Chile lacks the hot summers of the Mediterranean proper, and it is mainly in the dominance of wheat, which occupies over half the cultivated area, and the vine that agriculture most closely resembles that of the Mediterranean proper. There is no specialized horticulture apart from that necessary for the local market, and in the drier and unirrigated areas grazing is the principal activity; even in irrigated areas, pastoral activities use much more land than crop production. There is no shortage of opportunities for irrigation from the snow-fed Andean streams, but the limited local market and an outmoded agrarian structure stifle all initiative.

The southwestern Cape region of South Africa has a climate which more closely resembles that of the Mediterranean basin. Farms are large by European standards, though in comparison with the Chilean *haciendas,* concentration of ownership is modest. Horticulture, viticulture, and livestock production are the main sources of farm income, the former two being assisted by preferences in the British market. Viticulture owes much to the influence of Huguenot immigrants, but Afrikaner farmers dislike all crop production, and they remain primarily pastoralists.

The future of this type of farming, particularly in Europe, would appear to lie along the direction of greater specialization, a development that might well have progressed faster were it not for the autarchic policies pursued by most governments and the political pressures of the landlord class. The winters of the north Italian plain are too cold for the development of a specialized agriculture on the Californian pattern, but given a reduction in European agricultural tariffs and the abolition of landlord privileges, parts of Mediterranean Europe could begin to follow the example of California. The European Economic Community (EEC), or Common Market, has scarcely begun to tackle the former vexing problem of agricultural protection in Europe.

COMMERCIAL CROP AND LIVESTOCK FARMING (MIXED FARMING)

For Europeans, commercial crop and livestock farming is virtually synonymous with agriculture. It is a farming system that permits high productivity both of the land and the worker and also ensures the preservation of what Ricardo called the "original and indestructible properties of the soil." It is a flexible system of farming that leaves considerable scope for the skill of the farmer and for his judgment of market conditions.

Commercial crop and livestock farming, or mixed farming, as it is commonly called in Europe, achieves a high degree of interdependence between crops and livestock, and each makes a substantial contribution to the farm income. Farming in central Europe has involved both crop and livestock production from remotest times, but the complete interlocking of these two branches is a consequence of the technical innovations of the agricultural revolution of the seventeenth and eighteenth centuries, of which the most important was the introduction of roots and leguminous crops into the arable rotation. Previously it was always difficult to find enough animal feed from the meadow, woodland, waste, and stubble, so that medieval farm practice was to kill off many animals with the onset of the winter; those that were retained were always in very poor condition by spring. The limited fodder meant that livestock were never numerous enough to make possible the application of manure to all the fields, so that only a small area, the "infield," was cropped every year. On the "outfield," which received no manure, fallowing was essential.

The introduction of roots and legumes not only eliminated fallowing but also produced sufficient feed to keep animals well nourished throughout the winter. The old two- or three-course rotation (wheat and fallow, or wheat, barley or oats, and fallow) was thus replaced by the four-course, or Norfolk, system, so named after the English county in which it originated. By following wheat and barley with turnips, the land was cleaned, and the roots could be fed to livestock; in the following year, clover also provided forage and built up soil fertility for the ensuing cereal crops. As a result the stock-carrying capacity of the land was greatly increased, and the additional manure helped to ensure higher cereal yields. The desire to introduce these improvements stimulated the English country gentry to promote enclosure and consolidation, for on the old open fields with their innumerable strips such technical innovations were difficult to implement.[18] But in Continental Europe peasant resistance was greater, and unconsolidated strips still re-

[18] **One example of the old pattern of strip cultivation still survives in Britain, however. This is the famous village of Laxton in Nottinghamshire. Laxton is described by C. S. Orwin in *The Open Fields,* Cambridge University Press, London, 1938.**

main to this day a major obstacle to greater productivity over considerable areas.

The introduction of new crops such as corn, mangolds, potatoes, and newer grasses and legumes, together with the extension of the mixed-farming system to areas outside Europe, has resulted in many variations on the Norfolk rotation. Essentially, however, these are modifications aimed at further increasing the livestock-carrying capacity. In several areas the greater profitability of dairy cattle has led to the abandonment of plowed land and to the extension of permanent pasture in its place; many mixed farms now possess a dairy herd.

Both in Europe and North America the average farm size in commercial crop and livestock farming is about 150 to 200 acres, though considerably larger farms are of course found. In many areas there is a high incidence of tenancy. In Britain tenancy is preferred by many of the most able farmers, as they avoid capital expenditure on buildings, drainage, and fixtures, which are the responsibility of the landlord, and reserve their own capital for productive purposes. In the United States, tenancy has not the stability or social standing that it possesses in Britain, and most tenants hope ultimately to buy properties of their own. Nevertheless, average farm size (and inevitably capital equipment) tends continually to increase, and it may well be doubted how long the family farm, which is still the dominant unit of production, can survive.[19] It becomes steadily more difficult for newcomers to effect an entry if they have no farm to inherit.

Western Europe's mixed-farming system is a prodigious producer of wheat; its continued large-scale cultivation, however, depends not so much on advantages of soil and climate as on the heavy subsidies that all European governments pay to growers. In many parts of Western Europe fragmented fields and small farms hinder the deployment of mechanized equipment. In some areas, particularly in Britain, mechanization is far advanced, but much mechanical equipment is in fact underemployed,[20] and despite the fact that Western Europe achieves the highest wheat yields in the world, costs of production are high. The preoccupation with cereal production for direct human consumption is one of the principal differences between European commercial crop and livestock farming and that in North America, where large quantities of wheat are utilized for stock feed. Other cereals such as oats and barley are also extremely widely grown in Europe, but the emphasis on wheat results in a considerable shortfall in the production of these feed grains, and Europe regularly makes heavy imports.

The greater force of tradition in Europe, as compared with North America, expresses itself in many ways. European mixed farming has a polish that is very striking to an Australian or American visitor; many activities produce little return, but are regularly carried out to keep the countryside neat and tidy or because of local tradition. It is obvious that even the best of farmers cannot be equally efficient in all lines of production; this spread of interests is a relic of a former self-sufficiency that no longer exists. But concentration on the most profitable lines is not easy; the farm buildings and layout, designed for a multiplicity of purposes, often require drastic reconstruction to permit greater specialization. Substantial investment is usu-

[19] Since 1940, average investment per farm in the United States has increased eightfold, from $6,000 to $48,000. *Time,* Apr. 5, 1963, p. 9.

[20] Britain's largest field, situated on the Sussex downs, is some 400 acres in extent, but average field size is much smaller. Also, field access is often too poor to permit the use of the largest types of equipment. Few of Britain's tractors work more than the 500 hours per year that are considered necessary for economic operation.

ally necessary, and in Britain, where such undertakings are the responsibility of the landlord, it is exceptional to find a landowner who is able to afford such a large capital outlay.

Tradition and autarchic policies which promote a high level of production of crops for human consumption such as wheat and sugar beets are the principal obstacles to the improvement of European mixed farming; both of these, of course, reflect the social and political standing of farmers, of whom Europe still has far too many. The best opportunities for raising farm incomes in Western and central Europe lie in further concentration on livestock production, as in mixed farming in eastern North America, where the great bulk of farm crops is converted into livestock products of one kind or another. Climatic considerations do not favor low-cost corn cultivation over much of Western Europe, but they do encourage good grass growth. The use of improved permanent pastures could raise productivity very greatly, as could a more extended use of the long-term ley—a sown-grass–legume mixture plowed at the end of a period of years.

The great advantages of low-cost feed-grain production are most strikingly demonstrated in the corn belt of the United States, the apogee of commercial crop and livestock farming. The corn belt extends westward from central Ohio to Nebraska, and at these extremities is topographically clearly defined. North and south, however, its boundaries are set by factors of soil and climate, and the corn belt as a whole is more a statistical region than a physical one. Within it, however, topography, soil, and climate are close to the optimum for the production of several cereal and leguminous crops, and these advantages have been capitalized by an agrarian organization which has encouraged the maximum use of mechanical equipment on compact, consolidated farm units. The glacially derived soils are deep and easy to work; over large areas they were developed under a grassland cover and possess a considerable degree of natural fertility.

Cold, dry winters and hot, moist summers provide ideal conditions for the cultivation of corn, which is the mainstay of the farm economy. The use of hybrid corn has raised yields to prodigious levels; returns of more than 100 bushels per acre are now by no means uncommon within the region. Although a small area of north central Illinois is devoted to corn production for sale off the farm (and therefore more appropriately allocated to the commercial grain type of farming), the bulk of the corn produced within the belt is fed to animals on the farm itself, particularly cattle, hogs, and poultry. Corn is primarily converted into fat by the animal, however, so that the American hog is essentially a lard hog. Corn is generally followed either by oats, in the northerly portions of the region, or by winter wheat, in the south, and in turn by a variety of hay and pasture crops. A comparatively new crop of great significance is soybeans, valuable both for stock feed and as a source of oil.[21]

Although all farm operations are highly mechanized, crop rotations in the corn belt are usually contrived to reduce plowing to a minimum. In contrast to European mixed farming, corn belt agriculture has comparatively little permanent pasture, and, although cattle are kept in increasing numbers, there is little place for sheep. Cattle are typically feeders, either imported from western range land or, increasingly, bred on corn belt farms themselves; their mixed diet of corn, oats, and hay enables them to put on weight rapidly.

In the middle latitudes of the southern continents, mixed farming is much less well developed than in the Northern Hemisphere, and the proportion of the farmland in perma-

[21] See p. 142.

nent pasture is almost everywhere much higher than in the commercial crop and livestock farming of Europe and North America. In South America, Africa, and Australia physical and cultural conditions alike hindered the establishment of mixed farming. In none of these continents was it possible for European immigrants to acquire holdings of their own at little or no capital cost, as was the case in the United States, and almost from the beginnings of European settlement holdings tended to be of large size.

Such holdings could not be profitably operated on mixed-farming lines, as this would have required far too much labor; it was therefore necessary for them to be farmed in some other way than in the European mixed-farming tradition. Moreover, in the benign winters of the southern continents, crop production was often unnecessary; animals could be kept through the winter on natural grass growth supplemented by hay. Over the past three decades the advantages of a more pastoral type of farming have been confirmed by the establishment of improved pastures of high carrying capacity and by the substantial reduction in the cost of haymaking made possible with the introduction of the pickup baler.

Thus in those parts of Australia where rainfall is apparently high enough to support a mixed-farming type of economy, it never appeared, and only in a few restricted areas with better soils, principally on river flats, is a pale replica of corn belt agriculture to be seen. The comparative absence of cropping may appear evidence of backwardness, but such an impression is the reverse of the truth; the productivity of the New Zealand and Australian farm worker is the highest in the world.

The closest approach to the European mixed-farming system in the southern continents is perhaps found in the Canterbury plains of South Island, New Zealand, where low rainfall and low winter temperatures by New Zealand standards present far from optimum conditions for grass growth. Scottish settlers used to such a climate in their homeland reproduced their ancestral mixed-farming system, which has largely persisted down to the present.

Mixed farming has deep historical roots in Europe, and has been successfully adapted to the needs of a modern urbanized and industrialized economy. But overproduction has reached serious proportions in many areas, and the proportion of farmland under permanent pasture or sown grasses may increase if yields on plowed land continue to rise. Despite cultural difficulties, there is considerable scope for extension of mixed farming in East Asia, and in Hokkaido considerable progress has been made in this direction since the end of World War II. It is likely, however, that the essentially pastoral character of farming in the temperate lands of the southern continents will remain unchanged.

DAIRY FARMING

In commercial crop and livestock farming, dairy cattle may occasionally make a significant contribution to farm income, but in the cool and moist maritime climates of middle latitudes with a copious year-round precipitation and considerable cloud cover, dairying becomes the principal agricultural activity. Such climatic conditions are far from optimum for cereal cultivation, particularly wheat, and are frequently reinforced by unfavorable soils and terrain. Except in a few geologically favored areas in northern Europe, in eastern Canada, and in the northeast United States, thin and podzolized soils encumbered with glacial debris discourage plow cultivation. Forest and pasture represent the most rational land use under such

Types of agriculture previously unknown in Japan have been introduced in Hokkaido. Here, a farmer seeds land newly cleared for dairying in the Ishikari valley.

conditions, but in favored spots hay crops, potatoes, and roots are cultivated to provide feed during the long winter months when dairy cattle have to be kept indoors.

Farming of this type is widespread in the Baltic lands and parts of Scandinavia and is essentially peasant farming; its capital requirements are low, and the principal source of farm income is butter or cheese. But in much of northwest Europe and in eastern North America, dairy farming is more capital-intensive, and is carried on in areas that once supported crop and livestock farming. The existence of large urban markets and good transport facilities has encouraged the development of dairying even when physical conditions are not particularly favorable. Liquid milk is perishable and cannot be transported far; thus in the vicinity of great cities even thin, poor soils, or heavy clays can be utilized for dairying. In Britain much heavy clay land formerly supporting a system of mixed farming has been given over to dairying, and a similar change in land use has occurred in New England, once a significant producer of cereals.

In areas which are situated at more than overnight trucking distance from urban markets liquid-milk production is not feasible, and butter and cheese production takes its place. As these products can be transported thousands of miles under refrigeration, their production can become a highly specialized activity. Differential costs of production are thus of great significance in this section of the dairying industry, in contrast to liquid milk, in which international trade is negligible.

Costs of production of conserved milk products are closely related to the possibilities of reducing supplementary feeding. Areas possessing mild climates with good grass growth throughout the year have a substantial competitive advantage over areas in which animals have to be kept indoors during the winter and fed on a ration of hay, roots, and other cultivated feeds. Danish experience, however, shows that under certain conditions low-cost dairy production is not incompatible with intensive plow cultivation.

The average size of farms in specialized dairy regions is small, partly a consequence of the continuous care and attention required by a dairy herd. In Western Europe, the United States, Australia, and New Zealand, farms of about 100 acres are common in dairying districts, though such a farm would be distinctly large for Denmark. World dairy production is thus mainly derived from a multiplicity of small producers whose labor input is substantial. In highly developed economies, dairying is the only way open to a small farmer with limited capital to make a satisfactory income with year-round returns, but this is much more difficult if he is not producing for the liquid-milk market, in which he has a substantial degree of local protection. Small-sized units suffer from the usual disadvantages of shortage of capital and a weak marketing position, but these can be overcome by cooperation, which has been more successful in dairying than in any other branch of agriculture.

The effects of a favorable physical environment are best seen in the case of New Zealand, which successfully surmounts its 12,000-mile separation from its main market, Britain, through the lowest costs of dairy production in the world. Adequate precipitation at all seasons and winters which are mild enough to permit good grass growth largely account for the con-

Dairy cattle graze the summer pasture or "alp" high above Pontresina, in Switzerland. The dairy cow enables effective use to be made of alpine summer grazing, but in view of the problems of transport milk cannot be marketed in liquid form and the costs of producing preserved products are high.

centration of 90 per cent of the country's dairy cattle in North Island. In Taranaki, the Thames-Waikato plain, and North Auckland, the principal dairying areas, little or no supplementary feed is required save hay conserved from spring or summer flush growth; animals remain in the open throughout the year and even in winter can obtain most of their nourishment from pastures. This climatic advantage has been capitalized by extensive pasture improvements, in which New Zealand is indisputably the world leader. In much of North Island dairying has been a pioneer activity; land cleared of indigenous bush is seeded direct to high-quality pastures of ryegrass, cocksfoot, and clover mixtures. Strong cooperative organizations and rigorous state control ensure production of uniformly high-quality butter and cheese.

Even the most favored portion of Australia cannot match the climatic advantages of the dairying districts of New Zealand. Gippsland in eastern Victoria has mild winters and a year-round rainfall, but the latter is not as high as in North Island, and pastures can suffer from rainfall deficiency in summer. In the coastal districts of northern New South Wales and of southern Queensland physical conditions are far from favorable for dairying; the hot and humid summers produce rank grass of low nutritional value, and corn is given as a supplement.

Denmark, New Zealand's principal competitor in the world market for butter and cheese, is even more specialized in dairying, a development which arose from the decision to transform the traditional mixed-farming economy into one which would escape competition from low-cost foreign grains. This changeover, accomplished in the last quarter of the nineteenth century, was facilitated by the rural social and economic structure, which consisted of a community of small peasant-proprietors with a strong tradition of mutual self-help. A further powerful inducement was the existence of large urban markets in Germany and Britain. This favorable social and economic background was exploited by a series of technical and social innovations such as the cream separator, a basic machine in modern dairying, and the establishment of the world's first cooperative creamery and bacon factory. In every way Denmark thus played a pioneer role in modern dairying, and Danish techniques have been widely copied.

Danish dairy farming is essentially arable farming; permanent pasture is almost entirely eliminated in the most specialized dairying areas, most farms in the southeastern islands having so little that animals are tethered when in the open. Most Danish soils are light and easily worked, and are cultivated with the object of producing almost the entire stock ration from the farm itself. Fodder beets, mangolds, cabbage, and kale are produced in large quantities, and comparatively little feed is imported. The skim milk returned to the farm after the butter fat has been removed is one of the principal props of the remarkably efficient Danish bacon industry; on a diet of skim milk and barley the long and lean Landrace pig is delivered to the bacon cooperative within a pound or two of the optimum weight. No corn-fed animal can match the delicacy of flavor of Danish bacon, and in their small red cattle the Danes have solved a problem that continues to defeat many other dairy producers —how to produce quality beef from a dairy breed. An exacting system of state inspection ensures that the Danish "Lur" symbol of approval is a guarantee of the highest quality.

Yet Danish farming, for all its remarkable technical efficiency, is really only a prosperous type of peasant farming; it is increasingly difficult to obtain good tenants prepared to work the long hours at all seasons that the system entails. Young people particularly are leaving the family farm for Copenhagen, and there is some concern that the traditional 50-acre farm may not be able to offer the standard of living or amenities sufficient to maintain itself in the future.

No such difficulty occurs in the Netherlands, another major butter and cheese exporter and long dominant in the production of dried and condensed milk. For many years the Netherlands has experienced considerable population pressure, and the average farm is substantially smaller than in Denmark. Low wage costs, a consequence of population pressure, enable Dutch dairy products to be strongly competitive in world markets. The Netherlands has a large area of good polder grazing on which arable farming is not possible because of a high water table, but the severity of the winters makes supplementary feed essential.

In other parts of Western Europe, particularly in Britain, dairying is usually a processing activity; except for the period of World War II, when the reduction in imported feeds made a greater domestic fodder production imperative, the British dairy cow has been a converter of imported cake or meal into liquid milk for the urban market. In the moist and mild climate of Britain grass grows well, but most of Britain's grass is of very poor quality. Use of the ley, long a feature of Scottish farming, overcomes the deterioration which is inevitable in the British climate, even with the best grassland management, through its periodic plowing at intervals of five to seven years. In comparison with those of the Netherlands or Denmark, Britain's dairy herds are of generally poor quality, and although milk yields per cow are very high, the effective life of the dairy cow is very short. These unsatisfactory conditions largely result from a multiplicity of small producers with little capital, who have long been pampered by government. There are, however, some large and extremely efficient units, particularly on the chalklands of southern England; animals here may be kept in the open all year round and milked by portable milking machines, or bails, which make permanent milking sheds superfluous.

In North America as in Europe, dairying tends to displace most other types of farming in the vicinity of large cities. The growth of population on the Pacific Coast, above all in California, has been accompanied by one of the most remarkable developments in dairying in the world. Almost 60 per cent of the dairy cattle of the United States, however, are located in the main dairy belt which extends westwards from New York through Pennsylvania to the Great Lakes, and is continued beyond in Michigan, Wisconsin, and eastern Minnesota (Fig. 4-11). Areas of highland, rougher topography, and swampy and sandy tracts support few dairy cattle; northern Maine, the Adirondacks, and northern Michigan, Wisconsin, and Minnesota are largely negative areas for agriculture. The dairy belt of the United States extends onto the adjacent Lake Peninsula and the St. Lawrence lowlands of eastern Canada, but there are a number of selected districts in the Maritime Provinces which are also of importance in dairying.

The long, cool summers and a well-distributed adequate rainfall of the American dairy belt are very favorable for the growth of pastures and forage crops. The winters are long and severe, however, and the necessity for lengthy indoor feeding requires substantial buildings and storage provision for large quantities of hay and silage. Fodder production is highly mechanized and the investment per farm worker is considerably greater than in Europe; the use of automatic, self-recording milking machines is almost universal. This higher capitalization, however, does not offset the

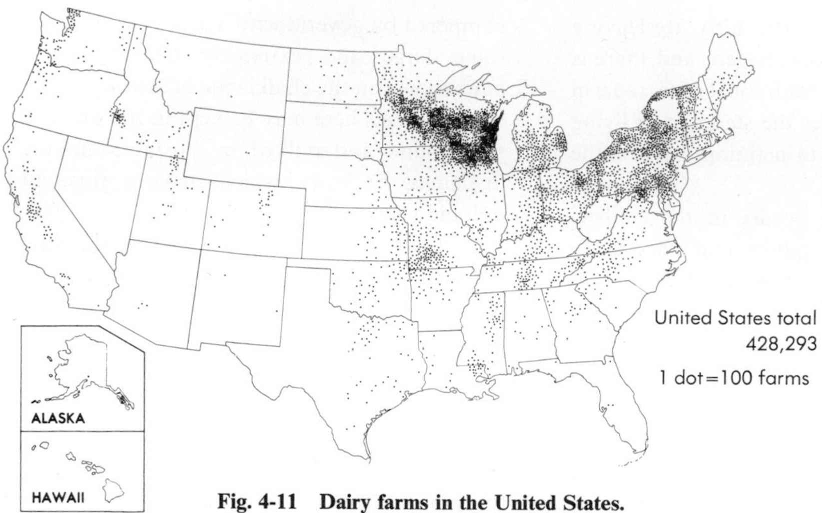

Fig. 4-11 Dairy farms in the United States.
Although there is a marked concentration in New England and in the Mid-Atlantic and Lake states, the distribution of dairy farms is also clearly related to that of urban markets. (U.S. Department of Agriculture, 1959.)

climatic advantages of New Zealand and the specialist dairying countries of Europe, and American costs of dairy production are relatively high.

The intense urbanization of the northeastern United States has encouraged a concentration on liquid-milk production in the eastern section of the dairy belt; the western section, despite the existence of some very large urban markets, is mainly devoted to the production of butter and cheese.[22] Most farmers are owner-occupiers, and although there are some very large and extremely efficient units, there are far too many small dairy farmers, particularly in the western section, for each to achieve a socially acceptable standard of living.

Dairy farming has many pressing problems. Liquid milk has to be produced in close proximity to its market, and technical considerations have encouraged a multiplicity of small producers. But modern techniques, such as the use of large, specialized vehicles for milk transport, the portable milking machine, and such devices as the "Rotolactor," a continuous milking machine capable of handling 2,500 cows per day, are rendering small units increasingly less competitive. The political pressure of the small farmers is, however, great enough to ensure that most governments pay prices to dairy farmers which cover the costs of the least efficient producers, so that the larger units make windfall profits. Almost everywhere in the world dairy farming is overpopulated, mainly because it requires less capital to enter than almost any other type of farming and produces a steady income throughout the year. It should be the object of policy to encourage the small inefficient producers to move out of the dairy industry.

[22] **The cause and consequences of the relationship between liquid-milk production and butter and cheese production are discussed in Chap. 7.**

SPECIALIZED HORTICULTURE

Although horticulture occupies a smaller area than any other type of farming, it is widely distributed; as with dairying, it is closely associated with urbanization, for the production of fresh fruit and vegetables occurs around, or in close proximity to, the peripheries of most of the world's great cities. These foodstuffs contain the vitamins and minerals necessary for the preservation of good health, and under the joint impetus of a growing public awareness of the value of such protective foods in diet and rising living standards, their production is mounting rapidly in many parts of the world. As with liquid milk, perishability of fruit and vegetables encourages production as close as possible to the market. There is a rapid loss of palatability with the passage of time, and the vitamin C content is oxidized and the folic acid in leafy green vegetables destroyed; rapid access to market while the produce is at its best, therefore, gives to local producers a high degree of natural protection. Improved methods of preparation and packing together with rapid-transport facilities have broken down local monopoly in the present century, however, and have opened the way to specialization on a very considerable scale. Distant areas with especially favorable soils or climate are now able to compete on almost equal terms with local growers, and the production of early or out-of-season lines has become an extremely lucrative, if highly speculative, activity.

Horticulture can be capital-intensive or labor-intensive; the former is the situation in the truck farming of the eastern United States, while the latter is suggested by the English term "market gardening." Also, it may be generalized, that is, devoted to the production of fruit or vegetables in season, or it may be specialized, concentrating on a particular line for which local conditions of soil or climate or established skill and tradition are especially advantageous; horticulture of the latter kind is mainly the preserve of large growers, whose capital investment is often very great. In general, fruit production requires a heavier capital investment than vegetable production, but the apogee of horticulture is greenhouse cultivation, which enables the grower to overcome shortcomings of local climate and weather and to establish the highest degree of control over the volume of output; the house grower is less embarrassed by the gluts which periodically plague most other growers of fruits and vegetables, nor does he suffer loss of output through inclement weather. The area under house cultivation is extremely small, but there are some districts which achieve a high degree of concentration on house cultivation, such as the Lea valley and the west Sussex coast of southern England, the coastal districts of North and South Holland in the Netherlands, parts of Brabant in Belgium, and selected areas bordering the lower lakes in North America. Specializing in luxuries and out-of-season delicacies, the house cultivator must be in close proximity to his market. But the peripheries of great industrial cities with their smoke-laden atmosphere are far from ideal environments, as a smoky atmosphere reduces the amount of daylight, and the *ejactamenta* from the power stations, refineries, and industrial plants may occasionally cause serious damage to crops.

Other horticultural specializations have arisen from the ability of modern methods of transport to convey perishable products over long distances at low cost. The development of canning and preserving industries has also stimulated horticultural production and helps to offset surpluses resulting from the biennial fruiting that characterizes many tree crops. But the opportunities for intensive specialization presented by the large urban markets of Western Europe have not been fully realized owing to the jungle of duties, quotas, and other restrictions imposed by European governments to protect their respective domestic producers. Thus Europe has no equivalent of the Central Valley of California; even truck farming has no European parallel, although perhaps the large vegetable farms of the English Fenlands are close. In the United States large, highly mechanized holdings are characteristic of truck farming, but in Europe numerous scattered small patches of intensive vegetable production predominate. There are some well-known specialty areas, such as the Brittany coast with its *primeurs* (early vegetables), but political and economic considerations have prevented the development of an agriculture such as is found in the Salinas valley, one of the principal "salad bowls" of the United States.

Europe's most famous specialty is its viticulture, particularly the production of *vins d'appellations controlées,*[23] an activity largely located outside the Mediterranean region. Specialty wines are each closely limited to particular districts, and even within them aspect and soil conditions further restrict the area suitable for planting. Each district thus tends to have a local monopoly for a particular wine, and the accumulation of skills in every stage of production renders this position almost unassailable; attempts to produce European-type wines outside the Continent have never succeeded, although some excellent wines are, in fact, produced in every Mediterranean climatic region of the world.

The most remarkable horticultural specialization in the world is found in California. The agriculture of this state demonstrates great variety, nor is it constant even in the short period, conditions which make generalized description difficult. There is, in fact, a little of everything, including intensive dairying, commercial grain farming, and commercial grazing. But specialized horticulture is dominant over large parts of the Central Valley, in the Napa, Sonoma, and Santa Rosa valleys north of San Francisco Bay, in the Santa Clara and Salinas valleys to the south, in the southern California basin, and in Imperial Valley—in short, in almost every portion of the state where conditions make cropping possible (Fig. 4-12). The many horticultural specialties, both annual and perennial, have a distribution pattern which is closely related to soil conditions. The inherent suitability of certain soils for particular crops only gradually became recognized, so that the state's agricultural development has tended to follow a hit-or-miss pattern. Some of the larger properties invite comparison with estate production in the intertropical zone, particularly in their dependence on a nonindigenous labor force, whose miserable and ramshackle quarters closely resemble the labor lines of a great estate and testify to their inhabitants' social and physical impermanence.

But Californian horticulture is not so uniformly monocultural as plantation-crop agriculture. One of the most remarkable features of the remarkable Californian agricultural economy is the manner in which growers switch from one line of production to another; new crops appear, spread, and are in turn replaced by others. There is a strong speculative element in Californian farming, for growers' returns depend in large part on getting their produce to eastern markets at a time when that from competing areas, for one reason or another, is in short supply. A lettuce crop may not cover its costs of harvesting, or it may earn

[23] Wines of registered nomenclature. The use of the famous regional names (Champagne, Médoc, Beaujolais, Port, etc.) is restricted to those wines produced within the appropriate legally defined region.

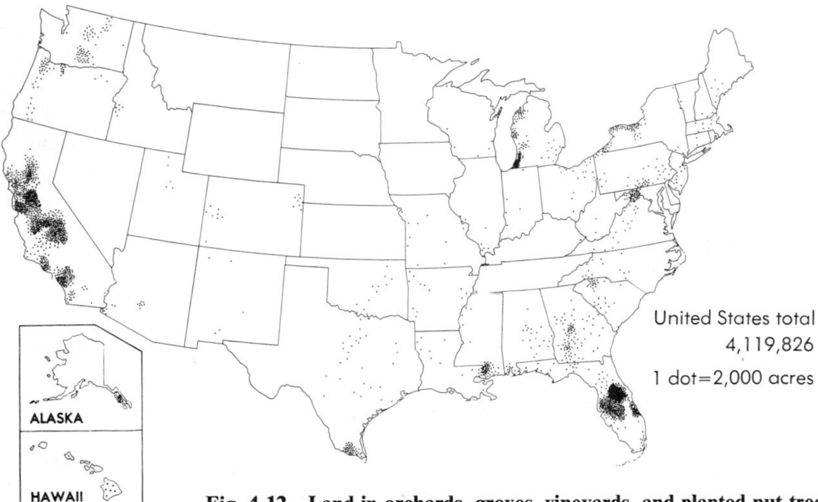

Fig. 4-12 Land in orchards, groves, vineyards, and planted nut trees in the United States. Fruit production is now overwhelmingly a prerogative of the specialist with large capital resources, and is closely confined to limited areas of suitable soil and climate, such as parts of California, central Florida, the Willamette valley of Oregon, southwest Michigan, and the Erie lakeshore. (U.S. Department of Agriculture, 1959.)

for its grower a small fortune. This speculative background in large part explains the frequent changes in growers' interests.

Numerous changes in the *location* of production result from the mounting demand for housing and other types of urban land. Orchardists in the Los Angeles basin are selling out as the urban sprawl advances and are replanting in the Central Valley, and in the face of the relentless population growth of the state it seems only a matter of time before the valleys of the San Francisco Bay area also are engulfed. Population growth, however, appears certain to confirm the present trend towards still more intensive specialization.

This development would, of course, have been impossible without the extensive use of irrigation and a heavy investment in packing and processing plants, in the development of which cooperative associations have played a prominent role. As in dairying, cooperatives have made great progress in horticulture, and some cooperative brand names have become world-famous. Improved transport and the development of the refrigerated railroad car have also been indispensable. Despite a progressively greater mechanization, however, Californian agriculture has not succeeded in reducing its dependence upon temporary labor, which has always been provided by immigrants. Japanese, Filipinos, and "Okies" and "Arkies" have been used in turn; in the period since World War II, Mexicans, imported under an agreement between the United States and Mexican governments, have been employed in increasing numbers. At times this labor force has been grievously exploited, and the Californian grower has less excuse than any, for the distinction between agriculture and industry is more blurred in California than in any other part of the world.

In comparison with California the eastern

areas along the Atlantic and Gulf Coastal Plains serve mainly local rather than national markets. With the exception of southern Florida, horticulture in these Coastal Plains is more generalized, truck farming being restricted to a series of discontinuous patches determined by local soil conditions and markets and devoted mainly to the production of vegetables in season. Southern Florida's growing vegetable and citrus production has become a strong rival to California produce on the national market, but even Florida's agriculture appears to lack the aggressive acquisitiveness, flexibility, and variety of that of California. Florida's summer rainfall and its lower price and income structure should, however, offer the possibility of lower costs of production in many lines; the state has greatly expanded its orange production *pari passu* with the loss of orchard land in southern California and has specialized in the production of quick-frozen orange juice. California's urban transgressions on orchard land have also stimulated a considerable expansion of citriculture in irrigated areas in the Southwest, particularly in Arizona.

THE AGRICULTURAL TYPES AND ECONOMIC DEVELOPMENT

This survey of the major types of world agriculture invites comparison with the types of economies analyzed in Chapter 1. As the boundaries of the major types of farming are never coincident with national frontiers and large countries may possess several types of agriculture, it is only to be expected that the correlation is not very close. Nevertheless, the comparison is instructive.

In the underdeveloped economies the lowest real incomes are found in areas practicing primitive subsistence agriculture and pastoral nomadism. Sawah cultivation and intensive dry-field agriculture have lent themselves to the support of high population density, but the cultivator is frequently not far from the margin of subsistence; they are the dominant agricultural types in the most populous, and therefore the most politically significant, parts of the underdeveloped world. Only Japan is anomalous; its sawah agriculture has attained a level of investment per rural worker unmatched elsewhere, and the country has succeeded in reducing the proportion of the total working population engaged in agriculture to less than 40 per cent.

Areas practicing plantation-crop agriculture have real incomes that stand out as markedly higher than those in indigenous agriculture in neighboring districts, but only in Malaya and in certain island groups has this type of farming become the dominant agricultural activity over the greater part of the national territory.

The remaining types of agriculture are of less significance in their respective national economies. Commercial grain farming and commercial grazing are almost exclusively confined to highly developed economies, the anomalies occurring in South America and in the U.S.S.R. So long as the latter refuses to duplicate the techniques of North America and the southern continents in these types of farming, productivity and real income of the rural worker in these types will remain markedly lower than in these other areas. Over large parts of South America, grazing industries are only partially commercialized, but in Argentina and Uruguay, highly competitive livestock industries have carried their respective economies to appear on the threshold of attaining the status of highly developed economies.

Crop farming and horticulture, with subsidiary livestock, is mainly restricted to semideveloped economies. Commercial crop and livestock farming, dairy farming, and specialized horticulture are all types of farming which are closely associated with highly developed economies and are often heavily subsidized by other sections of the national economies of which they form part.

SELECTED REFERENCES

Allen, G. C., and A. Donnithorne: *Western Enterprise in Indonesia and Malaya,* George Allen & Unwin, Ltd., London, 1957, pp. 67–148.

Andrus, J. R.: *Burmese Economic Life,* Stanford University Press, Stanford, Calif., 1947, pp. 42–88.

Bennett, M. K.: "Climate and Agriculture in California," *Economic Geography,* vol. 15, pp. 153–164, 1939.

Blake, D. J.: "The Estate Industries and Economic Development in Northeast Sumatra," *The Malayan Economic Review,* vol. 8, pp. 98–110, 1963.

Buck, J. Lossing: *Land Utilization in China,* The University of Chicago Press, Chicago, 1937.

Crawford, L. A., and E. B. Hurd: *Types of Farming in California Analysed by Enterprises,* University of California College of Agriculture, bulletin 654, Berkeley, Calif., 1941.

Cumberland, Kenneth B.: "The Agricultural Regions of New Zealand," *Geographical Journal,* vol. 112, pp. 43–63, 1948.

Dumont, René: *Types of Rural Economy,* Methuen & Co., Ltd., London, 1957.

Forde, C. Daryll: *Habitat, Economy and Society,* Methuen & Co., Ltd., London, 1954.

——— and R. Scott: *Native Economies of Nigeria,* Faber & Faber, Ltd., London, 1946, pp. 29–212.

Fryer, D. W.: "Estate Industries," in Wang Gungwu (ed.), *Malaysia: A Survey,* Frederick A. Praeger, Inc., New York, and The Pall Mall Press, London, 1964, pp. 227–245.

Gourou, P.: *The Tropical World,* 2d ed., Longmans, Green & Co., Ltd., London, 1958.

Higbee, E. C.: *American Agriculture—Geography, Resources and Conservation,* John Wiley & Sons, Inc., New York, 1958.

———: *Farms and Farmers in an Urban Age.* The Twentieth Century Fund, New York, 1963.

Higgins, B.: "Western Enterprises and the Economic Development of Southeast Asia—A Review Article," *Pacific Affairs,* Institute of Pacific Relations, vol. 21, pp. 74–87, 1958.

Jackson, J. C.: "The Smallholders," in Wang Gungwu (ed.), *Malaysia: A Survey,* Frederick A. Praeger, Inc., New York, and The Pall Mall Press, London, 1964, pp. 246–273.

Kannitkar, N. V.: *Dry Farming in India,* 2d ed., Indian Council of Agricultural Research, Delhi, 1960.

Kingdon, Ward F.: "Tibet as a Grazing Land," *Geographical Journal,* vol. 110, pp. 60–75, 1947.

Mohamed Awad: "The Assimilation of Nomads in Egypt," *Geographical Review,* vol. 44, pp. 240–252, 1954.

Mukerjee, P. K., and S. P. Gupta: *A Pilot Survey of Fourteen Villages in Uttar Pradesh and Punjab,* Asia Publishing House, Bombay, 1959.

Olmstead, Clarence W.: "American Orchard and Vineyard Regions," *Economic Geography,* vol. 32, pp. 187–236, 1956.

Pelzer, Karl J.: *Pioneer Settlement in the Asiatic Tropics,* The American Geographic Society, New York, 1948, pp. 47–78.

Pim, Alan: *Colonial Agricultural Production,* Oxford University Press, London, 1946.

Schlippe, Pierre de: *Shifting Cultivation in Africa: The Zande System of Agriculture,* Routledge & Kegan Paul, Ltd., London, 1956.

Stamp, L. Dudley: *The Land of Britain,* Longmans, Green & Co., Ltd., London, 1950.

U.S. Department of Agriculture. Department of Commerce, and Bureau of the Census: *Land Utilization in the United States,* 1947.

Van Royen, William: *The Agricultural Resources of the World,* Prentice-Hall, Inc., Englewood Cliffs, N.J., 1954.

Volin, Lazar: *A Survey of Soviet Russian Agriculture,* U.S. Department of Agriculture, 1957.

Wadham, Samuel, and R. Kent Wilson: *Land Utilization in Australia,* 4th ed., Melbourne University Press, Melbourne, 1964.

Whittlesey, Derwent S.: "Major Agricultural Regions of the Earth," *Annals of the Association of American Geographers,* vol. 26, pp. 199–240, 1936.

Wickizer, Vernon D., and M. K. Bennett: *Rice Economy of Monsoon Asia,* Stanford University Press, Stanford, Calif., 1941.

Yates, P. Lamartine: *Food, Land and Manpower in Western Europe,* Macmillan & Co., Ltd., London, 1960.

———: *Food Production in Western Europe,* Longmans, Green & Co., Ltd., London, 1940.

Chapter 5

FOOD CROPS

The survey of world agriculture in the preceding chapter was largely an organizational and regional one. But with two exceptions, all the major types of agriculture are involved in varying degrees in the operations of the world economy, and in many lines of production they may be strongly competitive; certain crops, of which sugar and tobacco are outstanding, can be produced under a variety of climatic conditions and under markedly different agricultural systems. This chapter and the two succeeding chapters focus attention on agricultural topics that require further consideration in relation to the world economy as a whole.

It is not easy to assess the relative contribution of the various agricultural products to the world market, but some broad indication can be obtained by examining the value of the more important products entering into world trade and comparing them with estimates for the gross value of agricultural production (Table 5-1). Many of the estimates given are little more than statistical exercises, but it can scarcely be doubted that among agricultural products the major cereals occupy an unchallenged position. Some agricultural commodities, such as rice, of major importance by value of output, contribute relatively little to world trade; others, such as natural rubber and cocoa, place virtually their entire output on world markets. Though commodity prices fluctuate considerably, wheat, cotton, wool, sugar, and natural rubber almost always rank in the leading half-dozen agricultural commodities by value of exports. Since 1950 coffee has assumed a position of major importance in world exports, but whether it will retain it is problematic.

It is convenient to divide crops between those intended for food and those destined for industrial use. The distinction is somewhat arbitrary, as there are few important food crops that do not require some preliminary processing before they are ready for consumption. Also, substantial quantities of nearly all food crops are used for industrial purposes, and the tendency for many to be in chronic oversupply has encouraged investigations to find further industrial uses for them. The distinction is, nevertheless, a real one; the demand for industrial products is more elastic than that for food, and in several parts of the world the fortunes of the industrial-crop producer have been markedly better than those of the food producer.

CEREALS

Among food crops the cereals are of unrivaled importance, and have apparently always been so since the dawn of agriculture. When prepared by traditional methods, the cereals go a long way towards providing most of the ingredients of diet necessary for a healthy and active life. But they are primarily energy foods, and the content of vitamins and first-class protein is not large. Moreover, a large proportion of these valuable constituents is lost in modern methods of preparation; the preference for white flour, produced by mills equipped with steel rollers, involves the expression of the wheat germ, and the demand for polished rice involves the removal of the outer layers which contain most of the vitamin content.

It is apparent from Tables 5-1 and 5-2 that wheat and rice are by far the most important cereals. In the environment of the humid tropics rice has many advantages both in cultivation and in preparation, but the reasons for dominance of wheat in temperate regions are

Table 5-1

Major Agricultural Commodities: Production and Trade by Value (Million dollars)

	PRODUCTION GROSS VALUE, 1950	EXPORTS, 1950	EXPORTS, 1961
Rice (milled)	11,200	480	560
Wheat	9,800	1,150	2,690
Corn	7,400	240	610
Cotton	4,300	2,240	2,060
Sugar	3,900	1,130	1,470
Tobacco	3,200	620	920
Butter	2,800	410	
Barley	2,700	150	290
Wool	2,500	1,920	1,620
Vegetable oils and oilseeds	2,500*	160*	1,410
Oats	2,400	50	
Coffee	2,200	1,690	1,800
Natural rubber	1,300	1,200	1,180
Rye	1,000	40	
Tea	500	390	550
Cocoa	400	420	470

* Groundnuts and soybeans only.

SOURCE: United Nations, *Commodity Trade and Economic Development*, New York, 1953. FAO, *State of Food and Agriculture*, 1962.

Table 5-2

Area, Production, and Yield of Major Cereals

	AREA (MILLION HECTARES)		PRODUCTION (MILLION METRIC TONS)		YIELD (100 kg PER HECTARE)	
	AVERAGE 1948–1953	1960–1961	AVERAGE 1948–1953	1960–1961	AVERAGE 1948–1953	1960–1961
Wheat	170	203	171	237	10.1	11.7
Rice (paddy)	103	119	165	242	16.0	20.3
Corn	87	103	138	214	15.8	20.8
Barley	52	66	59	86	11.3	13.7
Millet and sorghum	91	99	47	68	5.1	6.9
Oats	54	40	62	51	11.6	13.6
Rye	38	26	38	36	9.9	12.5

SOURCE: FAO, *Production Yearbook 1962,* Rome, 1963, Table 10A.

not so clear. The custom of consuming wheat in the form of bread is undoubtedly a factor of great importance, for while wheat bread has an attractive appearance, many cereals do not produce a good loaf. In north China, however, where wheat is a staple of diet, it is consumed largely in the form of alimentary pastes. Custom and tradition are factors of the greatest importance in the strong preference for wheat. The preference is well founded, however; both in food value and digestibility wheat justifies its premier position among the temperate cereals. The cultivation of other temperate grains is thus carried on either in areas where climate or soil is unsuitable for wheat production or as part of rotation systems in which wheat also has a prominent part.

The superiority of both wheat and rice is reflected by their substantially higher price levels. There is no doubt that rice is by far the most expensive cereal; since 1960 rice has stood at a little more than twice the price of wheat in the United States, and wheat prices in turn have varied between 50 and 100 per cent above those of corn. Rye on the whole has been priced slightly below corn, followed in descending order by sorghum, barley, and oats, the last being by far the cheapest of temperate cereals. While price levels in other countries have departed substantially from those in the United States, the relative prices of the various cereals have been broadly similar. In terms of value of output rice is the world's premier food crop,[1] although in terms of sown area and production it is surpassed by wheat.

Wheat

The origins of wheat reach far back into Neolithic times, and over the long period in which mankind has cultivated wheat, it has proved to have a very pliable genetic composition. Mutations, both natural and man-induced, have produced many varieties with a wide tolerance of soil and climatic conditions. Wheats have been bred to resist drought and scorching, to mature quickly, and to resist the attacks of fungoid and virus infection; without these new wheats the development of commercial grain farming would have been im-

[1] The arithmetical result of multiplying world rice output by a somewhat arbitrary world price is rather meaningless in view of the fact that a large proportion of world rice output is consumed on the farms where it is grown.

possible. Wheat is far from a homogeneous commodity; even when many producing countries are embarrassed by large wheat surpluses, certain wheat may nevertheless be in short supply.

Wheat can be grown at high elevation in equatorial latitudes, as in Kenya, and in the U.S.S.R. experimental plantings have occurred almost within the Arctic Circle. But these are extremes that involve heavy cost penalties, and optimum conditions are presented by temperate climates with moderate rainfall; a precipitation regime that encourages rapid germination and strong growth during the spring months, followed by hot, dry conditions once the ears have set, is especially advantageous. A comparatively level topography is essential for mechanized cultivation, but the plant is not particularly demanding in its soil requirements. The best are the loamy soils developed under grassland vegetation, such as the black earths and dark brown earths, but wheat does well even on heavy clays and on the finer sandy soils; excessively acid or coarse soils, however, are unsuitable. Soils, of course, are considerably modified by cultivation, and wheat growers in many parts of the world use large quantities of organic manures or artificial fertilizers.

The greatest demand for wheat in international trade is for the "hard," or "strong," varieties, that is, high-protein wheats, which in modern "gradual reduction" milling with fluted steel rollers produce good bread flours. To produce wheat of this kind requires hot, dry conditions, with just a little summer rainfall; the semiarid climates of continental interiors in middle latitudes are thus ideal for the production of wheats of this kind. Wheat grown in the more humid oceanic temperate climates is mainly "soft" wheat, better suited to pastry flour. Because it is grown under moister conditions (and usually with higher labor input), yields of soft wheat tend to exceed those of hard wheats, but the cultivation of soft wheats may be encouraged by the imposition of marketing schemes that place a premium on high yields, as is the case in Australia. Similarly winter wheat—wheat sown in the fall, remaining dormant through the winter, and growing rapidly in spring—has a higher yield than spring wheat. The cultivation of winter wheat is only possible in regions with mild winters, or where winters are severe if a snow cover protects the soil from frost action. The dry winters of continental interiors at best have only a light snow cover which is easily blown away; even where winter temperatures do not usually fall to very low levels, winter wheat may occasionally fail, so that resowing either with spring wheat or some other grain becomes necessary. In Western Europe wheat is almost always fall-sown (though spring wheat may occasionally be sown for stock feed), and in Mediterranean climates, where temperature and rainfall conditions encourage growth during the winter months, winter wheat is almost universal. Spring wheat is hard wheat, but winter wheat may be hard or soft, so that the world wheat trade uses such names as "soft white winter" and "hard red spring." A small but distinctive group is the amber wheats, or durums, used in the preparation of alimentary pastes such as spaghetti and macaroni. The durums are spring wheats and, despite immense overall wheat surpluses, have been in short supply over the past decade. There are only three major producers of both winter and spring wheat—the United States, the U.S.S.R., and China; only the United States is a major exporter of both types. In the United States winter wheat is by far the more important; the 1962 harvest of about 1.1 billion bushels included only about 300 million bushels of spring wheat.

Four major types of agriculture are involved in wheat production—commercial grain farming, commercial crop and livestock farming, crop farming and horticulture, with subsidiary livestock, and intensive dry-field farming. Only the first three are engaged in commercial production of major significance to international commerce; of these, the first has the lowest costs of production, and the third has the highest. The considerable number of types and grades of wheat and the existence of large producers in both hemispheres mean that the supply position is one of considerable complexity; there is, in fact, a wheat harvest in every month of the year in some part of the world. Western Europe, with its crop and livestock type of farming, easily leads in total output and in yield per acre (Table 5-3). Several European countries, particularly France, Italy, and West Germany, are occasionally large exporters, a consequence of the heavy subsidies paid to wheat growers; Sweden has been a significant exporter since 1954 (Fig. 5-1). The Continent is also a heavy importer, and unfavorable weather can create a very large Continental deficit; with favorable weather conditions, however, many European countries have wheat to sell.

Complexities of the World Wheat Market
The producers with very large surpluses for export every year are four in number—the United States, Canada, Argentina, and Australia. The U.S.S.R., though easily the world's largest producer, is largely concerned with providing enough wheat for its own domestic requirements.[2] But this country can at any time throw large quantities of wheat onto the world market when it can gain an important political or economic advantage from so doing; this interference, which is quite independent of price, naturally makes for instability. Before World War I Russia and India regularly were large exporters, but in both countries exports represented food which was needed at home. Since World War II the United States has resumed the position it occupied at the turn of the century as the world's leading wheat exporter, displacing Canada from the premier position it had held throughout the interwar period. The war greatly expanded national wheat production, and was followed by a period during which the disrupted state of European and Asian agriculture compelled the continuation of a high level of food exports. As world agriculture slowly recovered from the shocks of war, the need for these large exports progressively declined. But it is one thing to encourage farmers to produce more and to offer them incentives to do so, and quite another to persuade them that the need for their enhanced output no longer exists. Scaling down the immense domestic output of cereals is an enormous problem; the United States government has been obliged to acquire immense stocks which are a financial and political embarrassment alike to itself and to its allies, some of whom are heavily dependent upon primary products for the greater part of their export income.

Many countries of the British Commonwealth also achieved very large increases in wheat output during the war, and have retained their former competitive advantage. For low-cost wheat producers such as Canada, Australia, and Argentina, the immense wheat surpluses of the United States are very menacing. An American policy of dumping surplus wheat on the market for what it would fetch would result in a catastrophic fall in prices; on the other hand, the policy of disposing of American surpluses through relief and concessional schemes is, so these countries claim, attracting away their traditional customers.

[2] The shortage of meat, milk, dairy products, and fruits is responsible for a very high per capita consumption of bread in Russia. According to some observers, this is the reason for the podgy appearance of many Russian people.

Several conflicting pulls can thus be detected in the world wheat situation. Canada, Australia, and Argentina want a minimum of restriction so that they can reap the advantages of their low costs of production, but at the same time they want the immense United States surplus to be sealed off and want European countries to cease the export of wheat grown with high subsidies. Before World War II Australia and Argentina possessed the lowest costs of production in the world and were traditionally producers of semihard, or "filler," winter wheats, intermediate between the hard wheats of North America and the soft wheats of Europe. The composition of Argentina's wheat output has since changed substantially, more than half the total now consisting of hard wheats. Argentina's economy, however, has been heavily strained by the accelerated industrialization programs of its two five-year plans, and inflation has substantially reduced its former cost advantage. For many years trade in grains was reserved to the government, which paid producers substantially lower prices than those in the world market. Producers reacted to this exploitation by a sharp cut in

Table 5-3

Wheat Area, Production, and Yield

	AREA (MILLION HECTARES)		PRODUCTION (MILLION METRIC TONS)		YIELD (100 kg PER HECTARE)	
	AVERAGE 1948–1953	1961–1962	AVERAGE 1948–1953	1961–1962	AVERAGE 1948–1953	1961–1962
Europe	28.0	27.4	41.1	51.2	14.7	18.7
Western Europe*	17.7	17.6	28.2	36.5	15.0	19.1
Eastern Europe	10.3	9.8	12.9	14.7	14.4	18.3
U.S.S.R.	42.6	63.0	32.7	66.5	8.4	10.6
North and Central America	38.9	32.0	45.1	42.7	11.6	13.4
United States	27.8	20.9	31.1	33.6	11.2	16.1
Canada	10.5	10.2	13.5	7.7	12.8	7.5
South America	6.9	7.0	7.4	7.5	10.7	10.8
Argentina	4.5	4.2	5.2	5.1	11.5	11.1
Asia†	25.8	34.9	21.3	31.2	8.3	8.9
India	9.3	13.0	6.2	11.0	6.7	8.5
Pakistan	4.2	4.7	3.7	3.8	8.7	8.0
Turkey	4.8	7.9	4.8	7.1	10.0	9.1
Mainland China	23.0	26.5‡	15.9	31.3‡	6.9	13.0‡
Africa	6.0	6.5	4.3	4.2	7.1	7.7
Australia	4.6	6.0	5.2	6.7	11.2	11.3
WORLD TOTAL	169.8	202.8	171.2	236.7	10.1	11.7

* Noncommunist Europe.
† Excluding mainland China.
‡ 1959–1960.
SOURCE: FAO, *Production Yearbook 1962*, Rome, 1963, Table 11.

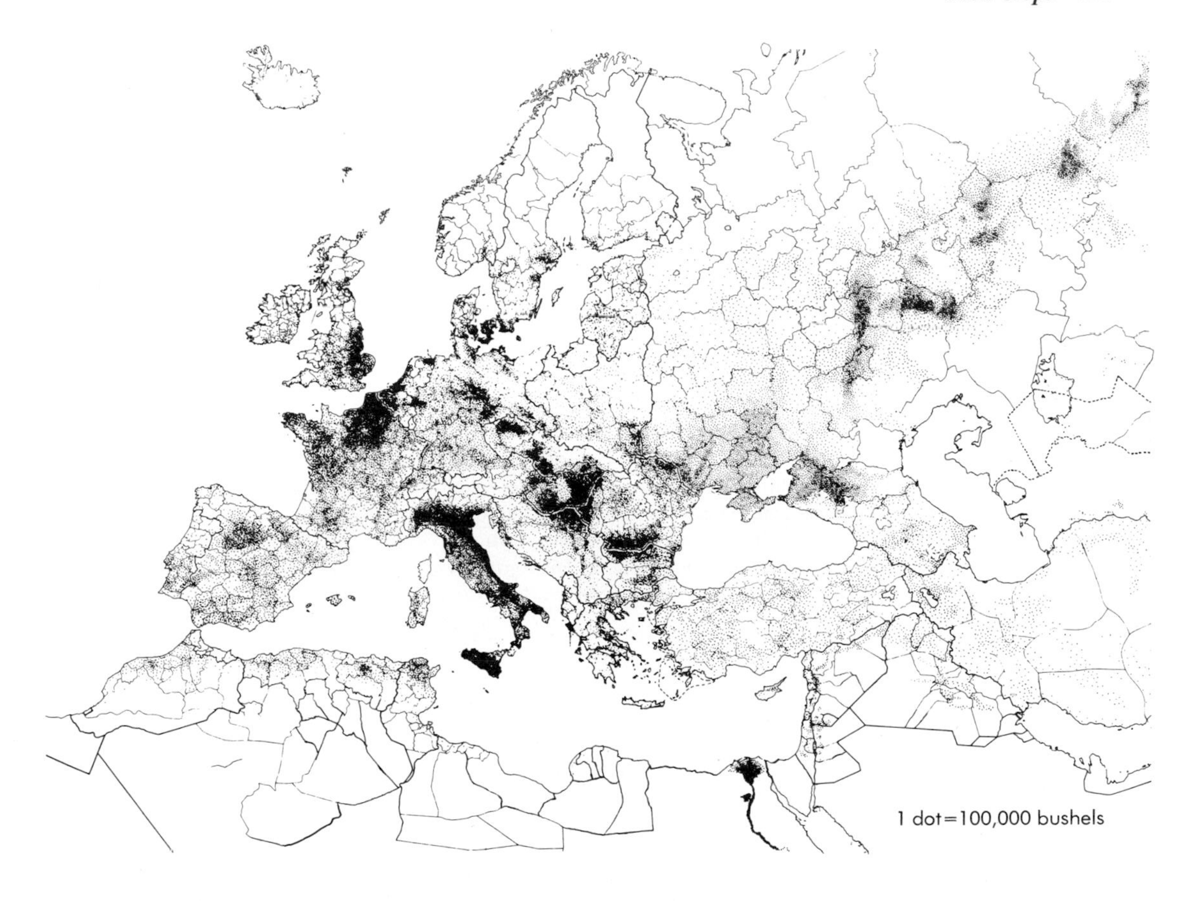

Fig. 5-1 Wheat production in Europe and adjacent countries.
Europe's enormous wheat output results not so much from a very large sown area but from high yields. Wheat production dominates the farm economy throughout the areas of best soil in western and central Europe, but wheat is also widely grown where climatic and soil conditions depart from optimum. In eastern and southern Europe, where techniques are considerably more primitive, wheat yields are substantially below the continental average. (William Van Royen, *Atlas of the World's Resources,* vol. 1: *The Agricultural Resources of the World.* © 1954, by permission of Prentice-Hall, Inc., Englewood Cliffs, N.J.)

output, and though there has been some improvement in prices paid to growers in the post-Perón period, the general situation of the country has continued to be one of considerable political and economic turmoil; both acreage and output of wheat have thus remained well below the pre-World War II level. More than 60 per cent of Argentina's wheat exports are directed to other Latin American countries, notably Brazil, about the same proportion as before the war; balance-of-payments difficulties, chronic in most Latin American countries, have resulted in much of Argentina's wheat trade being on a government-to-government barter basis.

On the other hand, Australia, by far the smallest of the major wheat exporters before World War II, has increased substantially in

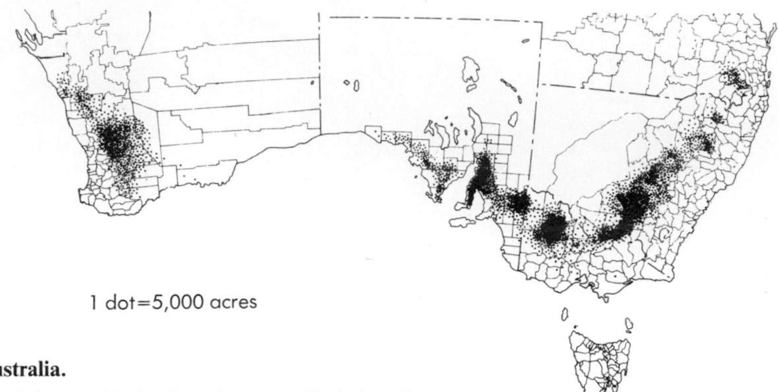

Fig. 5-2 Wheat acreage in Australia.
Except in New South Wales and Queensland, wheat in Australia is largely grown where the precipitation averages a little less than 15 inches annually. Victoria normally has the highest yields. In contrast to the situation in other major exporting countries, Australia's wheat acreage has shown a marked upward tendency, largely because of an expansion of the sown area in western Australia. (William Van Royen, *Atlas of the World's Resources,* vol. 1: *The Agricultural Resources of the World.* © 1954, by permission of Prentice-Hall, Inc., Englewood Cliffs, N.J.)

status (Fig. 5-2); Australian wheat exports have substantially exceeded those of Argentina since 1960, and the record level of 1961–1962 brought them to about two-thirds of those of Canada. Britain has traditionally been Australia's best customer, taking about half of its wheat exports before World War II, but Britain's share has progressively fallen in the postwar period and in 1961–1962 was less than one-eighth. Australia's new markets have been found in Asia, particularly Japan, but American concessional shipments to India and Pakistan have greatly reduced Australian wheat sales to these countries in some years. The most significant development, however, has been the great increase in trade with mainland China, a market which currently is denied to American exporters. China's large purchases of Australian wheat have resulted from the failure of its agricultural program and have been largely on credit; whether it will remain the leading buyer of Australian wheat is conjectural.

All European countries, including even the largest wheat producers such as Italy and France, must normally import some hard wheat, and the lowest-cost hard-wheat producer is Canada. Apart from a very small production of winter wheat in the east, Canada's output consists almost entirely of hard, high-protein wheats, for which physical conditions are near optimum in the southern Prairie Provinces; Saskatchewan alone accounts for about 60 per cent of the total national area sown to wheat and a somewhat smaller share of production. Intense mechanization and a rather lower price and income structure than the United States help account for Canada's low cost of production, but the country feels that American agricultural policy in the postwar period has prevented it from achieving the full benefits of its competitive advantage. Canada has vigorously opposed discrimination between export and domestic prices and other devices such as barter and concessional sales paid for in foreign currencies, by which its competitors have endeavored to offset higher production costs or to reduce stocks built up as a result of high price supports.

While Canada's wheat acreage has been consistently lower in the postwar period than in 1939, output has grown considerably, and on the whole, the country has managed to retain its share of a rising volume of world wheat exports.[3] Its principal market is still Britain, but it is one of slowly diminishing relative importance, and in Europe and Asia competition from subsidized American wheat exports has been severe.

In the United States also the present wheat area is substantially below that of before the war (Fig. 5-3). But so great has been the increase in the productivity of the American farmer that output has risen tremendously, and enormous surpluses of wheat and other grains have been accumulated, the storage of which alone costs the nation a staggering sum. The origin of these enormous surpluses (Table 5-4) lies in the attempts made to alleviate widespread rural distress in the Great Depression. The Agricultural Adjustment Act of 1933 established production controls over wheat, corn, cotton, rice, tobacco, hogs, and dairy products; the same year saw the creation of the Commodity Credit Corporation, empowered to deal in, and make loans on, agricultural produce, and the first price-support operations. Price support was gradually extended to a wider range of crops, and during World War II embraced all the more important agricultural products.

Price support has operated through the conception of parity;[4] a corollary has been the acceptance of overall acreage restrictions and individual farm allotments. High support prices and acreage allotments, however, have encouraged farmers to concentrate effort on their best land; through heavy fertilization and greater mechanization yields have been raised so greatly that the purpose of acreage restriction has been defeated. Under the pressure of mounting surpluses farmers have been asked to offset their greater efficiency by retiring land from production, as in the Soil Bank Program of 1956 to 1959, and to divert part of their acreage allotment. After 1955 price supports trended downwards as efforts were made to replace a rigid parity index by a more flexible system, and penalties were imposed for sowing in excess of the acreage allotment. Thus the 1962 wheat program provided for support at between 65 per cent and 90 per cent of parity; to qualify for support farmers had to divert a minimum of 10 per cent of their allotted acreage and were encouraged by compensatory payments voluntarily to divert a further 30 per cent.

Nevertheless, farm surpluses have continued to grow. The wheat carry-over for 1961–1962 amounted to over 1.3 billion bushels (36 million metric tons), about equivalent to the total volume of world trade in wheat in a year in which this had reached the highest figure then recorded. Determined to reduce the cost of storing such an astronomical quantity, the government has disposed of large quantities of wheat through the operations of Public Law 480 (the Agricultural Trade Development and Assistance Act of 1954), by which exports are made under barter transactions, or for famine relief and economic development, or against payment in local currencies. Public Law 480

[3] Canada's wheat acreage rose rapidly in the early Sixties. The 1963 sown area reached nearly 28 million acres, a figure only just surpassed by the 1940 peak.

[4] Parity is a measure of the exchange value of farm products in terms of general prices, calculated in relation to a given base period, originally the years 1910 to 1914. Modifications have been made since 1948 to bring the base period more up to date. In 1961 prices of twenty-one agricultural commodities were supported, and in sixteen of these support was mandatory.

Table 5-4

Wheat Situation in the Four Major Exporters, 1963–1964* (Million bushels)

	CARRY-OVER FROM PREVIOUS SEASON	NEW CROP	DOMESTIC REQUIREMENTS	AVAILABLE FOR EXPORT AND CARRY-OVER	EXPORTS FOR YEAR COMMENCING JULY 1, 1962
United States	1,195	1,138	598	1,735	638
Canada	489	723	145	1,067	331
Argentina	12	260	127	145	66
Australia	20	320	75	265	173

* Year commencing July 1, United States; August 1, Canada; December 1, Australia and Argentina.
SOURCE: *The Wheat Situation,* Economic Research Service, USDA, October 1963, March 1964, Washington.

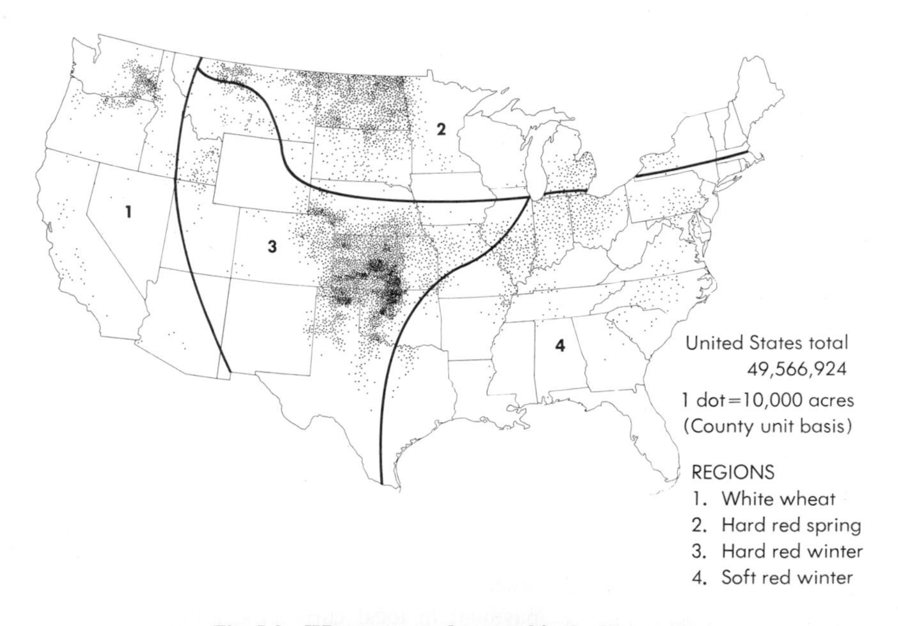

Fig. 5-3 Wheat acreage harvested in the United States.
Climatic considerations largely determine the distribution of the various wheat regions of the United States. Yields are highest in the Columbia Plateau district of Washington and in northeastern states, where they closely approach the levels of Europe; in the winter-wheat region of Kansas and adjacent states they attain only about half this magnitude, and in the spring-wheat region of the northern Great Plains States, only about one-third. (U.S. Department of Agriculture, 1959.)

wheat sales reached record levels in 1961–1962, accounting for some 70 per cent of total United States wheat exports; India and Pakistan have been by far the biggest recipients of concessional wheat sales since 1957, a development that has been particularly irritating to Australia. As commercial exports are also subsidized, every bushel of American wheat exported since 1953 has been subsidized in one way or other.

Every other major wheat exporter, however, also practices a form of price support, and Canada and Australia have enlarged their wheat exports by sales on extended credit; about 35 per cent of total world wheat exports is effected under concessional schemes of one kind or another (Fig. 5-4). Moreover, every major exporter has accumulated large surpluses, and the situation could well become worse through the system of import levies on foreign wheat to be adopted by the EEC if, as a result, the internal Community wheat price is forced up to levels that encourage a greatly expanded European wheat production.

Thus the prewar situation of large surpluses has reappeared, although there is a danger, according to the United Nations Economic Commission for Asia and the Far East (ECAFE), of world population outrunning food supplies. It is not easy to see a way out of the impasse; any substantial reduction in the support price of a major exporter would not

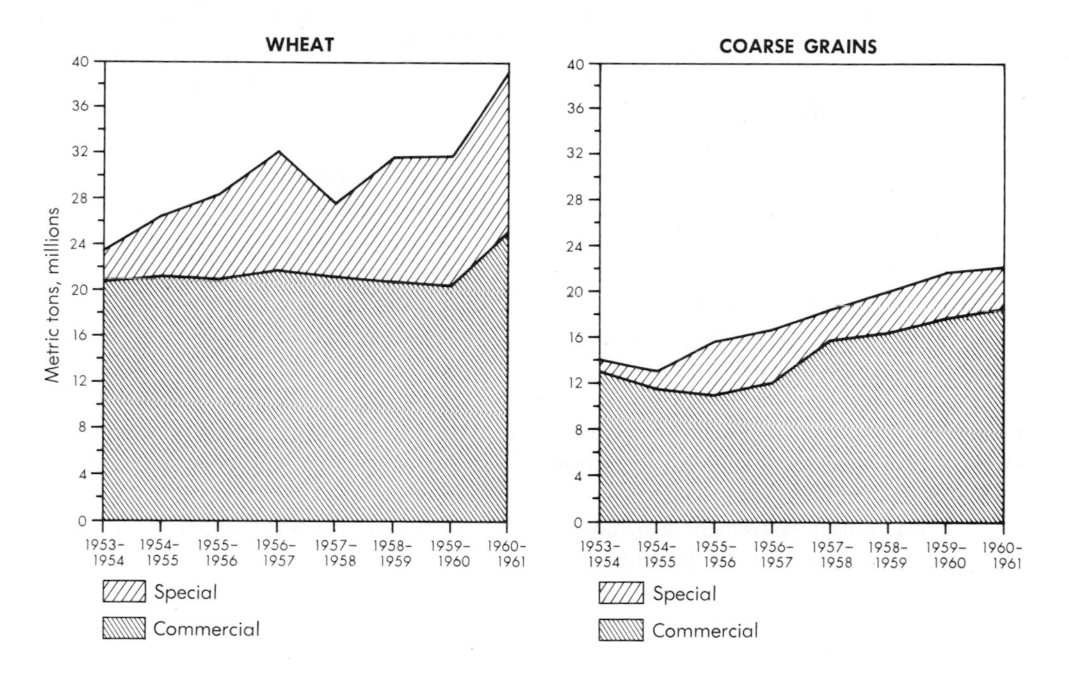

Fig. 5-4 Exports of wheat and coarse grains.
Sales on concessional terms have accounted for a substantial proportion of the postwar increase in wheat exports. Such sales have mainly concerned the United States, but Canada and Australia have also offered wheat on concessional terms, particularly by extending long-term credits to China. In contrast, world exports of coarse grains have mainly consisted of commercial sales. (FAO, *Commodity Survey,* 1962.)

only jeopardize the fortunes of its own farmers but, through its influence on the world price, would also affect those of all the other principal exporters.

The International Wheat Agreement The accumulation of surpluses and the necessity of avoiding a price war, together with the desire of importing countries for price stability, were the principal factors leading to the International Wheat Agreement of 1949 (IWA). The agreement fixed maximum and minimum prices in terms of Canadian currency and required participating importing countries to undertake to purchase fixed quotas at the minimum price and exporters to sell quotas at the maximum price when called upon to do so. Some two-thirds of the trade in wheat between participating members was conducted under the IWA in the first four years of operation, when world prices were considerably higher than the IWA maximum.

The IWA thus differed from earlier commodity agreements in representing consumer interests. The IWA, however, did not realize the high hopes expected of it. When it was renewed in 1953, Britain did not participate, for with the mounting pressure of surpluses, prices declined below the maximum, so that the advantages of trading under the agreement were substantially reduced. A three-year extension of the agreement in 1956 was largely nullified by growing United States Public Law 480 sales.

The new Wheat Agreement concluded in 1959 incorporated a number of departures from the original scheme. The quota system was replaced by an obligation on the part of importers to puchase a fixed proportion of their requirements from participating exporters, and Britain joined again by undertaking to buy not less than 80 per cent of its needs from exporting members of the agreement. A further Wheat Agreement to run until 1965 came into force in 1962. The new agreement followed the old in all essentials, but among importing countries Great Britain, West Germany, the Netherlands, and Japan increased their percentage-purchase undertakings, and the maximum and minimum prices were raised slightly above those of the old agreement.[5] Concessional sales still lie outside the scope of the agreement, and it is on the future of these that the success of the agreement will largely depend.

The Eastern Bloc Bombshell With a dramatic suddenness that has scarcely a parallel in the history of the world wheat trade, the international wheat situation was transformed in the fall of 1963. By the end of the year world wheat exports had been raised to the highest level ever recorded and there were strong indications that in 1964 wheat exports from the big three exporters, the United States, Canada, and Australia, would attain even higher levels than in the previous year. The immediate responsibility for the changed situation in the wheat market can be traced to the disastrous drought of 1963 in the U.S.S.R., which resulted in a decline in that country's wheat production of some 25 per cent.[6] An astonished world witnessed the unique spectacle of the two great powers of the Eastern bloc bidding against each other for wheat wherever it was available for sale to them, while Poland, Czechoslovakia, and Bulgaria stepped up their own purchases of Western wheat.

As the U.S.S.R., unlike China, was obviously far from the verge of starvation (although a mild form of bread rationing had, in fact, to be introduced), the magnitude of Soviet wheat purchases strongly suggested that

[5] The minimum has been set at $1.62½ (Canadian) and the maximum at $2.02½ (Canadian) per bushel for No. 1 Manitoba northern held in bulk store at Fort William and Port Arthur.

[6] USDA, *Foreign Agriculture*, vol. 2, March 23, 1964, p. 3.

the 1963 drought was merely the culminating disaster in a long succession of failures on the agricultural front, and further evidence was soon at hand. Large areas of the newly plowed virgin lands had been abandoned, the hog population had fallen catastrophically, and the *kolkhoznik,* whose living standards had been sharply trimmed from the peak level of 1958, had reacted in his usual way by stubbornly thwarting all attempts at increasing output. The Soviet government resorted to price rationing by sharply raising the price of the more desirable foods such as meat and butter, and as if itself weary of the unremitting agricultural struggle, allowed its own efforts in the agricultural sector to decline in 1963. In order to gain freedom of maneuver in the face of this latest disaster, the government needed large wheat stocks immediately, and it was determined to get them whatever the effect on Russia's balance of payments position. The magnitude of its purchases of Canadian and Australian wheat, in conjunction with China's growing purchases on credit, speedily threatened to reduce the large Canadian and Australian stocks to the vanishing point.

Although its own wheat stores remained firmly closed to China, faced with this additional bonanza for its rivals (and with mounting evidence of a Russian desire for an understanding with the West in view of its increasingly acrimonious dispute with China), the United States could no longer afford to turn a deaf ear to Russian overtures for the purchase of American surplus wheat. In October, 1963, President Kennedy authorized the first sales of surplus wheat to the U.S.S.R.; an order for 1 million tons of wheat worth nearly $80 million placed by Russia with the Continental Grain Co. represented the largest individual sale in the history of the world wheat trade. (The precise magnitude of Russian purchases of American wheat has still to be revealed.) By March, 1964, Russia had contracted for the supply of over 10 million tons of Western wheat, and had become by far the world's largest importer. This was in startling contrast to the general postwar situation, when in some years Russia had exported more than 5 million tons of wheat.

It is still too early to assess the full significance of these enormous wheat purchases by the Eastern bloc countries. However, Premier Khrushchev in an address to the Communist Party Plenary Session in December, 1963, revealed plans for a greatly expanded Russian chemical industry and commented on the great disparity in the use of chemical fertilizers between the United States and the U.S.S.R.; the United States, he claimed, applied 36.5 million tons of fertilizer to a cultivated area of 118 million hectares, whereas Russia used only 17 million tons on a cultivated area of 216 million hectares.[7] Until the planned fertilizer plants are in production and their output begins to reach Russia's fields, the country could still remain a significant wheat importer.

Rice

Rice shares with wheat the premier position among food crops. The area sown to rice is considerably smaller, and of this a substantial proportion represents multiple cropping; but rice yields are on the average much higher than those of wheat, although against this there is a heavier loss in milling. Whereas wheat is consumed as flour or a flour product, rice is mainly eaten as a grain, and the ease with which it can be rendered palatable through boiling is a great advantage to many peoples of the intertropical world.

As with wheat, there is a rice harvest in every month of the year in some part of the

[7] *Ibid.,* vol. 1, December 23, 1963, p. 8.

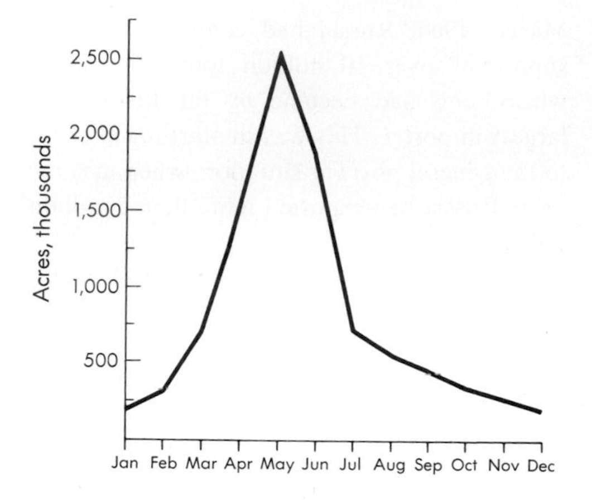

Fig. 5-5 Monthly average of rice harvested in Java.
Through the use of irrigation water in the dry season and rapidly maturing varieties, some Asian countries are able to take a rice harvest in every month. The most important harvest month, however, is at the end of the rainy season—April, in the case of Java.

Table 5-5

Area, Production, and Yield of Paddy Rice

	AREA (MILLION HECTARES)		PRODUCTION (MILLION METRIC TONS)		YIELD (100 kg PER HECTARE)	
	AVERAGE 1948–1953	1961–1962	AVERAGE 1948–1953	1961–1962	AVERAGE 1948–1953	1961–1962
Europe	0.3	0.3	1.3	1.6	42.6	48.2
North and Central America	1.1	1.4	2.5	3.7	22.1	27.4
United States	0.7	0.6	1.9	2.5	25.6	38.2
South America	2.4	3.8	4.1	7.0	17.1	18.6
Brazil	1.9	3.0	3.0	5.3	15.7	17.5
Asia*	69.2	78.6	97.1	137.4	14.0	17.5
India	30.1	33.6	34.0	51.2	11.3	15.1
Pakistan	9.0	9.7	12.4	16.1	13.8	16.6
Japan	3.0	3.3	12.0	15.5	40.0	47.0
Indonesia	5.9	6.8	9.4	12.5	16.1	18.4
Thailand	5.2	5.7	6.8	7.8	13.1	13.9
Burma	3.8	4.1	5.5	6.8	14.6	16.8
Mainland China	26.8	31.5†	58.2	85.0†	21.7	27.0†
Africa	2.7	2.8	3.4	4.1	12.3	13.9
WORLD TOTAL	102.5	119.4	164.6	242.2	16.0	20.3

* Excluding mainland China.
† 1960–1961.
SOURCE: FAO, *Production Yearbook 1962*, Rome, 1963, Table 18.

world; but in marked contrast to wheat production, many of the major producers themselves take a rice crop in every month, though the harvests are, of course, of unequal magnitude. The main harvest is always that at the end of the rainy or rainier season, but the relationship of landmasses to changes in atmospheric circulation results in some areas having main harvests that are out of phase with those of the remaining parts of the countries of which they form part. Thus the Madras area of India, eastern peninsular Thailand, and the Vietnam coast about Hué have an inblowing monsoon that brings substantial rains between September and April, when the Asian monsoon lands generally are experiencing dry conditions. Indonesia, which lies largely south of the equator, also has its main rice harvest in April, at the end of the rainy season in Java, instead of in October and November, which are the principal harvest months north of the line (Fig. 5-5).

The World Production Pattern The most striking feature of world rice production is its concentration in Asia (Table 5-5 and Fig. 5-6).

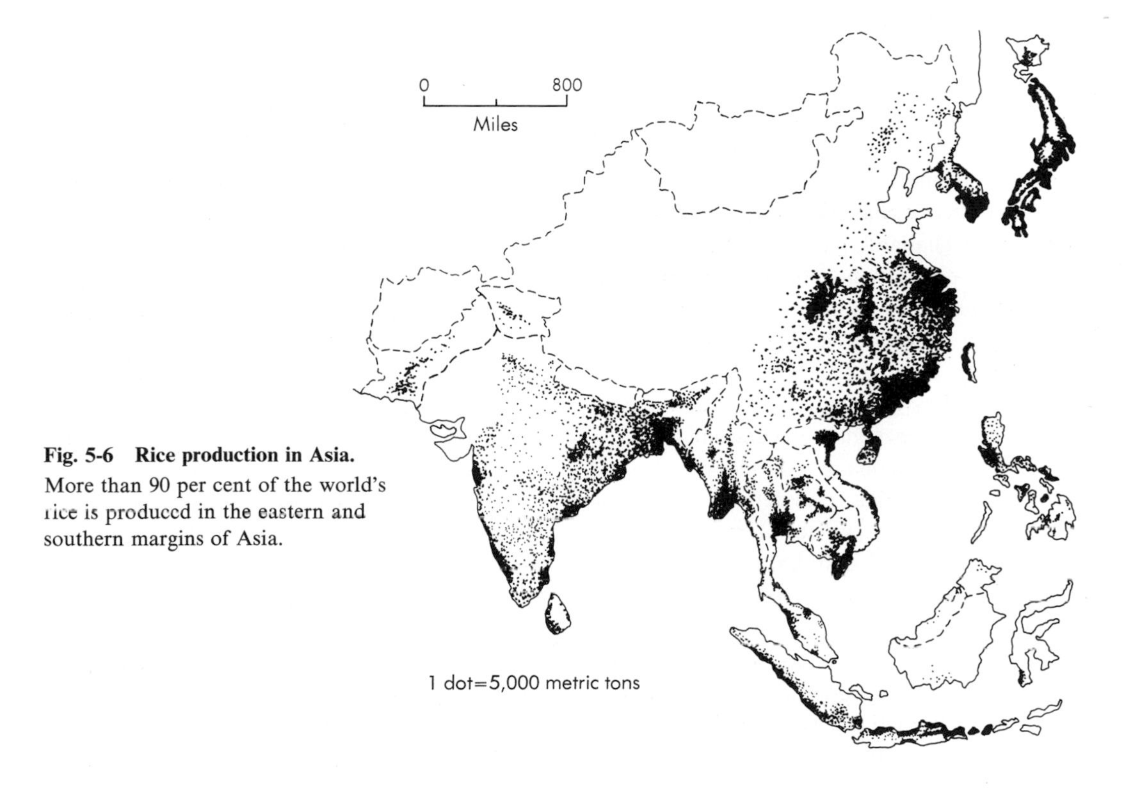

Fig. 5-6 Rice production in Asia. More than 90 per cent of the world's rice is produced in the eastern and southern margins of Asia.

Nevertheless, Asian production is relatively static, whereas in the rest of the world production is increasing rapidly; especially noteworthy is the rise of the United States to the position of the third-largest exporter, a role filled before World War II by French Indochina.

World War II resulted in enormous damage

to sawah agriculture; buffalo herds were drastically reduced, compelling the abandonment of much land, and forced deliveries in Japanese-occupied areas were further inducements to cut production. After the war, revolutionary and civil war raged through much of East and Southeast Asia, and India endured the agony of partition. But after 1952 there was a substantial improvement in the political situation, and Asian rice output took a considerable upturn.

Most Asian producers are endeavoring greatly to raise their present output. Their populations now stand at 25 to 30 per cent above the prewar level, and in Southeast Asia increases of more than 50 per cent have been recorded; per capita consumption, with the exception of Thailand, has everywhere declined. Moreover, population is still increasing rapidly. Only in the most favorable years do the largest producers—China, India, Japan, and Pakistan—normally approach a high degree of self-sufficiency. Lesser producers such as Malaysia and Ceylon are regularly deficient, and the Philippines occasionally so. Indonesia, once a large producer with a small deficiency, has now become by far the world's largest importer. Expanded output is also desirable because the periodic necessity to use large quantities of foreign exchange for food imports imperils national development plans, and there is uncertainty over the long-term availability of rice from the traditional rice exporters of the Southeast Asia mainland—Burma, Thailand, Vietnam, and Cambodia.

The best prospects of increasing rice output are in raising yields on the existing sawah area. Land reclamation and extensions of irrigation systems will permit of some extension of sawahs, but such schemes are expensive and take time to bring into operation.

The enormous discrepancy in yields between the Asian and non-Asian producers, and even between Asian producers themselves, testifies to the scope that exists for raising the general level of productivity of Asia's sawahs. Japan's yields are more than twice those of Indonesia and almost four times those of India, and Italy, Spain, California, and Australia achieve yields that are almost five times those of India.

In large part this technical superiority of the non-Asian producers is statistical; it is one thing to get a high yield on a few thousand acres, as in Australia or Spain, and quite another to obtain the same return on many million acres. All Asian producers would achieve higher yields if they could retire large areas of the poorest sawahs. Nevertheless, there is a good reason why these non-Asian producers do so very much better—they grow the *japonica* strains, which give a high response to fertilizer application. There is also evidence that the greater cloud cover of monsoonal climates during the rainy season is a further factor in depressing higher yields; the highest yields in the world are often obtained with the aid of irrigation in Mediterranean climates, which have clear and sunny summer skies.

The *indica* varieties of South and Southeast Asia are largely grown without fertilizer, nor in general do such strains show much response to its application. The mainly volcanic soils of Java produce an average rice yield lower than those of nonvolcanic Malaya, though it should be added that most Javanese sawahs are double-cropped. But the productivity of the best Javanese sawahs is more than four times the national average. Indonesia's pressing food problem would be solved if the national average could be raised to a figure approaching the yield of the best sawahs.

Japan's feat in raising its rice yield to around 25 hundredweight per acre (milled-rice equivalent) on a rice area of almost 8 million acres is remarkable, and will not be easy for other Asian countries to duplicate. There are few experimental and seed-testing stations, but

Fertilizer is applied on a rice experimental station in Malaya, a high-cost rice producer; note the rubber plants growing on a hill in the background.

Widespread use of light two-wheeled tractors has greatly enhanced the efficiency of Japanese farming. Japan remains a relatively high-cost rice producer, however, although for different reasons than those applicable to Malaya.

in every prefecture Japan has a seed station distributing proved seeds suitable for local conditions. Even when the best varieties become known, most countries face many years of work in making tested seeds available in quantity to their farmers. Most Asian countries now have some provision for the establishment of a heavy-chemicals and fertilizer industry in their development plans, but the fruits of these investments will also be some years in eventuating. Transport costs operate against a widespread use of fertilizers, and rural electrification, universal in Japan, is in the far distant future. However, a bullock-powered electric generator for pumping irrigation water has been tried out with success in India, and some such device might become widely adopted.

It appears unlikely that countries such as India and Indonesia or even Japan and China can ever dispense entirely with rice imports, although the world rice trade has declined substantially since 1939. The fall in exports (Fig. 5-7) largely reflects the decline in production in several traditional exporting countries—Burma, Vietnam, Cambodia, Korea, and Taiwan. Korea and Taiwan both possessed economies designed to function as "rice pumps" for Japan before World War II, and their substantial export surplus in large part necessitated the denial of supplies to the local population. Moreover, the rate of population increase in the large exporters of mainland Southeast Asia is about 3 per cent per annum. How long will these countries continue to have a surplus for sale, especially as their yields show a steady downward trend?

Nevertheless, the national development plans of Burma, Thailand, Cambodia, and Vietnam largely turn upon their respective abilities to maintain a high level of rice exports; in all, rice generates by far the largest proportion of the export income. Thailand, it is true, has succeeded both in raising its total rice exports and in reducing the proportion of its export income derived from rice, but Thailand's economy could not withstand a heavy fall in the foreign demand for its rice. This observation applies a fortiori to Burma, which has the lowest costs of production in the world; the Irrawaddy delta has a rainfall so heavy and reliable that, in contrast to the Menam plain of Thailand, irrigation is unnecessary. Even in spite of the payment of a subsidy for reclaimed land, Burma had still not regained its prewar rice area by 1962, so that there is abundant scope for a further increase in production. But in view of the high degree of political insecurity that prevails in much of mainland Southeast Asia, it would be folly to assume that supplies will always be available in large quantities.

In this changed postwar rice situation, two new major exporters have appeared—the United States and China. China has traditionally been a net importer, and it was always doubtful if the large exports made since 1955 could be maintained. In fact, China's rice exports fell away rapidly after 1958, when about 1.4 million tons were exported, and by 1962 had virtually disappeared with the failure of the agricultural program to reach its planned targets. Chinese rice has been sold under government-to-government barter deals, and with an improvement in domestic food supply China might well resume some rice exports; Indonesia appears to be a market in which Chinese rice exports might yield a handsome political dividend. The high level of United States rice exports has arisen partly from the immediate postwar rice scarcity in Asia and partly from the difficulty of scaling down domestic production once the need for a greatly expanded output passed. Since 1955 some 50 to 80 per cent of all American rice exports have consisted of concessional sales. This new Chinese and American competition greatly enhanced the difficulties of Bangkok and Ran-

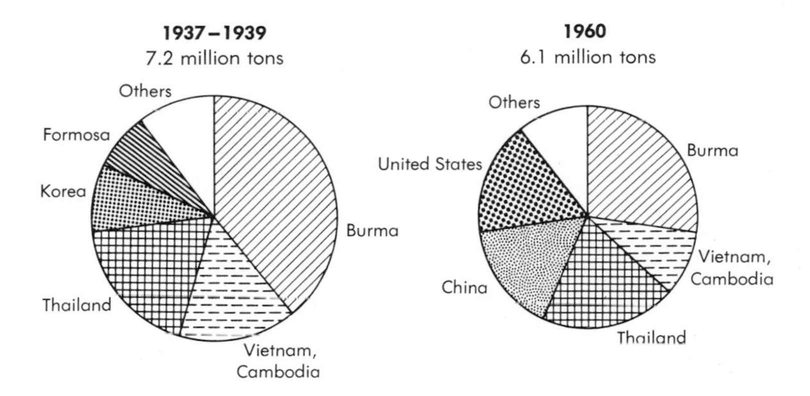

Fig. 5-7 Rice exports.
The world rice trade has not regained the levels of the immediate prewar years, and there have been considerable changes in the origin of exports.

goon in grappling with the new and unexpected problems of unsalable surpluses.

Until 1953 there was a considerable world rice shortage, and the price of rice in Asia was about six times that of the prewar years. The Burmese and Thai governments, which had established state monopolies over procurement for export, were thus able to make large profits by paying their producers less than the external price. By 1954, however, Asian agriculture had regained prewar production levels, and being unwilling to reduce their prices, both governments soon found themselves holding large surpluses. Thailand eventually abandoned state control over the rice trade, and Burma made several barter agreements with Eastern bloc countries. Meanwhile, the mounting wheat surplus and the availability of American cereals on concessional terms continued to exercise a depressing effect on the international demand for rice.

The rice-surplus situation also considerably affected the United States itself; by the end of 1956 it had piled up a rice stock of over 1 million tons, but by acreage restrictions and the maintenance of a high level of exports under the concessional terms of Public Law 480 rice stocks were reduced to a third of the peak level by 1961. The problems of enforcing acreage restrictions and ensuring a reasonable return to growers were heightened by the existence of two sharply contrasting producing regions with different cost levels. The greater part of the United States output comes from long-grain varieties grown in Texas, Louisiana, Mississippi, and Arkansas (Fig. 5-8). The minor producing area is the lower Sacramento valley of California, which produces round-seeded varieties. All American rice production is heavily mechanized; aircraft are used to drop germinated seed in flooded fields, and transplanting is never performed as in sawah agriculture. Nevertheless California yields are almost half as much again as those in the South, and costs of production are markedly lower. Californian rice has a high reputation in Asia, and the bulk of the output is normally exported; Californian growers feel that acreage restrictions discriminate against them in favor of the higher-cost southern areas, and many would be prepared to dispense with the whole apparatus of price support and restrictions, relying for

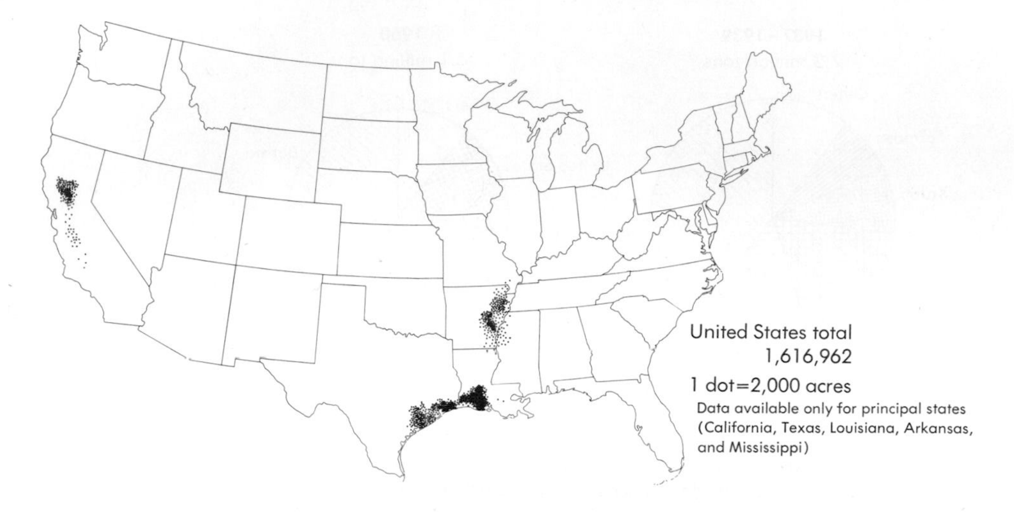

Fig. 5-8 Acreage of rice harvested in the United States.
Although a minor producer, the United States occupies a position of considerable importance in the world rice trade. Production occurs in two widely separated areas where rice is grown in rotation with other crops and never forms a monoculture as in much of Asia. (U.S. Department of Agriculture, 1959.)

markets on their competitive efficiency. The South, however, is by no means prepared to countenance what would probably amount to an expansion of production in a lower-cost region, and has used its considerable political influence to ensure that California makes a large contribution to acreage reductions.

The world rice surplus is considerably less of a problem than that of wheat. The rice surplus is very much smaller; rice is much more susceptible than wheat to inclement weather, and the concentration of production in a comparatively small part of the globe means that usually all the great rice producers share common fortunes or misfortunes. Moreover, whereas most wheat consumers tend to consume less wheat as their income rises, most rice consumers would probably eat more rice if they could purchase it—at least for some time to come.

Corn

Corn (maize) is the third great cereal used for human consumption. It occupies a considerably smaller area than rice, but against this it has the highest yield of any cereal. It also has a very considerable geographic range; though most productive in humid warm temperate climates, it is widely grown within the tropics.

However, corn as a food for human consumption is usually grown for want of something better. It is a staple of both swidden and intensive dry-field farming, but in Asia it is grown either because the preferred cereal, rice, does not succeed for one reason or another or because rice cannot be grown in sufficient quantities. Though of major importance as a staple food in Latin America, corn probably supports more people in Africa, the poorest of continents. In temperate latitudes corn is an important food only for peoples with very low income levels, such as the poorer rural folk of the southern United States, and the Portuguese and Romanians.

Low-grade wheat may be fed to stock in considerable quantities, but rice is always too valuable for human consumption to be used in this way. Corn, however, is primarily a stock feed; in addition to the grain, large quantities of green corn or corn chopped for silage are fed to animals. Although only a small proportion of the total consumption, more than 4 million tons have been consumed annually in the United States in most post-World War II years for the production of cornstarch, syrup, glucose, and alcohol, which are further synthesized into a wide variety of chemical and pharmaceutical products.

Corn is a native of the Americas, where its many varieties have long engaged the attentions of botanists and plant breeders (Fig. 5-9). Through their efforts came hybrid corn, which is one of the most outstanding achievements of modern agricultural research and which effected a revolution in American mixed-farming costs. Hybrid corn grown on the rich soils of the corn belt yields three to four times as much as corn grown in Mexico, South Africa, or Brazil, and its cultivation has lifted the modest prewar national average yield to the highest level in the world. On a harvested area of about 70 million acres the United States now accounts for about half the world's total output, though this proportion must decline as the cultivation of hybrid corn extends to other countries; it is already important in several European countries.

Though by far the world's largest producer before World War II, the United States was always outranked as an exporter by Argentina, where, because of the widespread use of alfalfa

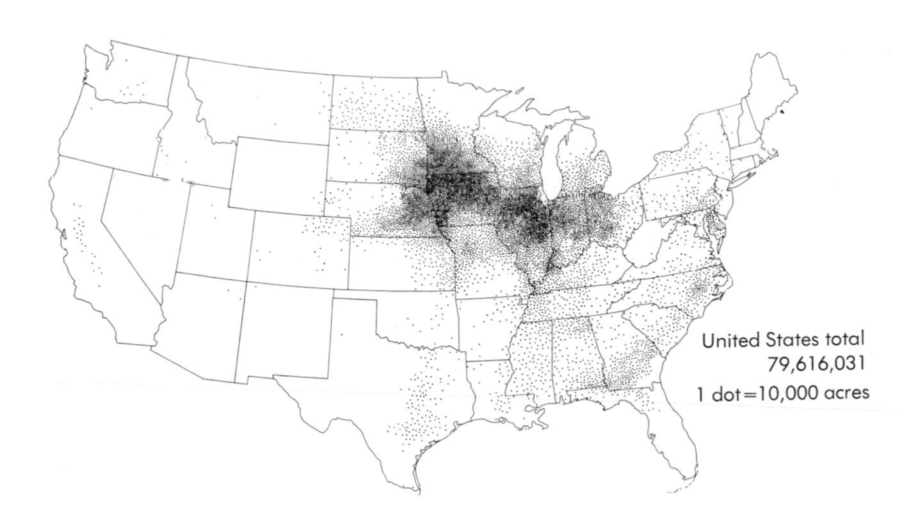

Fig. 5-9 Acreage of corn grown for all purposes in the United States.
The world's optimum conditions for corn cultivation are found in the Corn Belt of the United States. In the Corn Belt, however, corn is grown in a number of crop rotations, and the share of the total cropped area under corn is, in fact, higher in some southeastern states. (U.S. Department of Agriculture, 1959.)

as the principal fodder, a very large proportion of total output was available for shipment overseas. Corn then accounted for between a fifth and a quarter of the country's export income, a substantially higher contribution than that of wheat; since 1945, however, both production and exports have been adversely affected by the unfavorable internal political and economic climate, though there has been some improvement since 1957.

Argentina, however, faces an immense obstacle in any attempt to regain its prewar supremacy in the international market. Under the stimulus of high price supports and improved efficiency, United States corn output has become a flood. Since 1953 surplus stocks have climbed progressively higher; they surpassed those of wheat in 1956, and by 1961 had reached the staggering total of more than 50 million tons, equal to almost six years' world exports at the record level of that year. Though only a minute proportion of total production, United States corn exports have progressively increased, and by 1960 accounted for about half the world total.

This "crisis of abundance" is partly the result of a decision by American corn growers in 1958 to reject acreage allotments and to accept a lower level of price support. Since 1961, however, acreage controls have been reimposed, and the concept of a "normal production" (the average yield for the 1959 and 1960 crops) has been introduced to prevent attempts at defeating the purpose of acreage reduction by increased fertilizer application. All growers have had to accept a compulsory diversion of at least 20 per cent of their corn area to qualify for price support on any feed grain, and inducement payments enable additional diversions to be made. It remains to be seen how successful this new attempt to offset the mounting efficiency of the American farmer will prove in practice.

VEGETABLE OILS

The vegetable oils collectively form a very important group of agricultural products in world trade and are an important constituent of the diet of many subsistence farmers. Oils and the fats produced from them are highly concentrated energy foods, but oils also contain fat-soluble vitamins, and their consumption is necessary to make use of such vitamins occurring in other foods. Oils and fats are relatively expensive to produce and consumption per capita is closely related to income levels. With higher incomes in the advanced economies and a rapid increase in world population, production steadily enlarges.

The vegetable oils are very diverse; most are produced from annuals, but some are derived from tree crops. Over forty different varieties are regularly used for commercial purposes, and there are many more that are of purely local significance. The oilseeds and oils of major commercial importance are, however, few in number, and 90 per cent of the world trade in vegetable oils is accounted for by seven varieties; these are coconut, palm and palm-kernel, groundnut, linseed, soybean, and cottonseed oils. Six further varieties—rapeseed, sunflower, sesame, olive, tung, and castor oils—account for almost all of the balance.

The vegetable oils may be divided into three main categories as follows, the oils in each group being ranked in order of output:

Edible
- Soybean
- Groundnut
- Rapeseed
- Cottonseed
- Olive
- Sesame
- Sunflower
- Corn

Edible-industrial
- Coconut
- Palm
- Palm-kernel

Industrial
- Linseed
- Castor
- Tung

The edible oils are sometimes known as "soft" oils, in contrast to "hard" oils such as coconut oil and palm-kernel oil, according to the qualities which they impart to soap; hard oils are also quick-lathering. Some edible oils may not be so regarded in certain parts of the world; rapeseed oil, though a food in much of South Asia, is an industrial oil in Western Europe. The industrial oils are also known as drying or technical oils, and are principally used in the manufacture of paints and varnishes.

About 70 per cent of the total world production of vegetable oilseeds consists of edible oilseeds, the balance being divided almost equally between the edible-industrial and the industrial groups. But the greater part of edible-oilseed production is consumed where grown, so that about 45 per cent of world vegetable-oil exports is accounted for by the edible-industrial group as against as little over 40 per cent by the edible group.

The production of some oilseed crops is restricted by climatic conditions; palm and palm-kernel oils are both derived from the fruit of the African oil palm, the cultivation of which demands an essentially equatorial forest climate. Coconuts are restricted to intertropical areas, but groundnuts, soybeans, and cotton are extensively grown both in intertropical areas and in warm temperate climates, and linseed production can take place under either warm temperate or cool temperate conditions. Thus there can be sharp competition between a number of types of farming even in the commercial production of one major oilseed crop.

There are two further factors which greatly intensify this competition. Although each oil has particular advantages for one use, there are several uses for which one oil is readily substitutable for another. These opportunities for substitution have been widened by hydrogenation, that is, the injection of extra hydrogen into the oil molecule. In this way oils can be hardened into fats, improving their palatability and storage characteristics. A wide range of vegetable oils has thus been rendered competitive with edible fats of animal origin, particularly butter and lard, but by the same process the former have been subjected to competition from other oils such as whale oil, which can also be hydrogenated.

The effect of this intense competition is to produce a very narrow price range for most oils; normally only a few cents per pound separate the prices of the four leading edible oils and the three edible-industrial oils; whale oil and linseed oil also normally fall within this price range. The industrial tung and castor oils are much more expensive. At the head of the price range is the aristocrat of the vegetable oils, olive oil, normally twice as expensive as tung and castor oils. Olive oil is considered the finest of the vegetable oils and, in contrast to most other oils, is used for direct human consumption without further processing.

The rapid growth of synthetic-detergent production in the postwar period has markedly reduced the demand for the quick-lathering oils, for in detergent manufacture a little of these goes a long way. But as the production of many oilseeds fluctuates considerably from year to year as a result of the varying weather conditions experienced by the major producing regions from season to season, considerable short-term changes in the pattern of oil utilization are to be expected.

To some extent, however, substitutability is offset by the fact that the market for vegetable oils is far from a free one for there are particular consumption patterns in the great importing and consuming countries which cannot easily be changed. These arise either because there is a large domestic production of some oils, as in the United States, or because consuming countries have dependent or affiliated territories which receive preference in the oilseed market of the mother country. The supply situation is further complicated by the fact that several important oils (coconut, palm, palm-kernel, and linseed oils) are produced as joint products with other commodities, so that their availability is also affected by the price of the main or alternative product. The United States thus consumes large quantities of domestically produced cottonseed and soybean oils and, to satisfy other edible-oil requirements, relies mainly on imports of copra and coconut oil from the Philippines. Britain and France make large imports of groundnut and oil palm products from their former West African dependencies and of copra from their Pacific territories; Belgium imports oil palm products from the Congo. Britain also has in the past been a substantial producer of whale oil, a commodity of little significance in the United States, and imports substantial quantities of cottonseed oil from cotton producers within the British Commonwealth. A large proportion of commercial oilseed production thus enjoys a guaranteed or protected market.

The most remarkable development in vegetable-oil production and trade since the outbreak of World War II is the rise of the United States to the position of both world's largest producer and exporter; before the war it was by far the largest importer, a role now filled by the EEC. This greatly changed position is largely accounted for by the tremendous increase in the production of soybeans, of which the country is now the world's largest producer (Fig. 5-10). Soybeans fit well into the crop pattern of mechanized mixed farming; their cultivation has been encouraged by acreage restrictions on cereals, and by their recognition as a crop retarding soil erosion and depletion. Both soybean oil and cottonseed oil have found a large market in the manufacture of margarine, consumption of which has increased rapidly since Federal restrictions were removed in 1950. The export of these two oils, moreover, has been assisted through Public Law 480 concessional sales, so that the United States now outranks both Nigeria and the Philippines, normally among the largest exporters. In both these countries, however, oilseeds and oil account for a substantial proportion of export income; in Nigeria the figure is normally more than 40 per cent. Japan has been the principal buyer of American soybeans, the United States having replaced Manchuria as its chief supplier.

The principal vegetable oil of commerce is coconut oil; copra and coconut oil account for almost one-quarter of the total volume of world oil and oilseed exports. Coconuts are widely grown in coastal areas within the tropics. Although estates are dominant in the Pacific islands, coconuts have not on the whole proved a very attractive crop for large estates, and the great bulk of the world's copra is produced by smallholders. In the Philippines, the largest producer, there is a tendency for the share of estate production to enlarge at the expense of that of the smallholder. Smallholder copra production suffers from several disadvantages; prepared by traditional methods, the copra is of poorer quality than estate copra produced in hot-air driers. More serious is the high incidence of diseased and aged trees, and only accelerated replanting can save the smallholder coconut industry.

The oil palm produces the highest oil yield per acre of any oilseed crop and more than twice that from coconuts. It begins to yield after three years from planting, a much shorter gestation period than that of most other tree crops, and fruits continuously until it is too tall to be harvested economically. As oil palm cultivation thus makes possible a continuous labor input and gives the highest oil yields and quality with large and expensive hydraulic

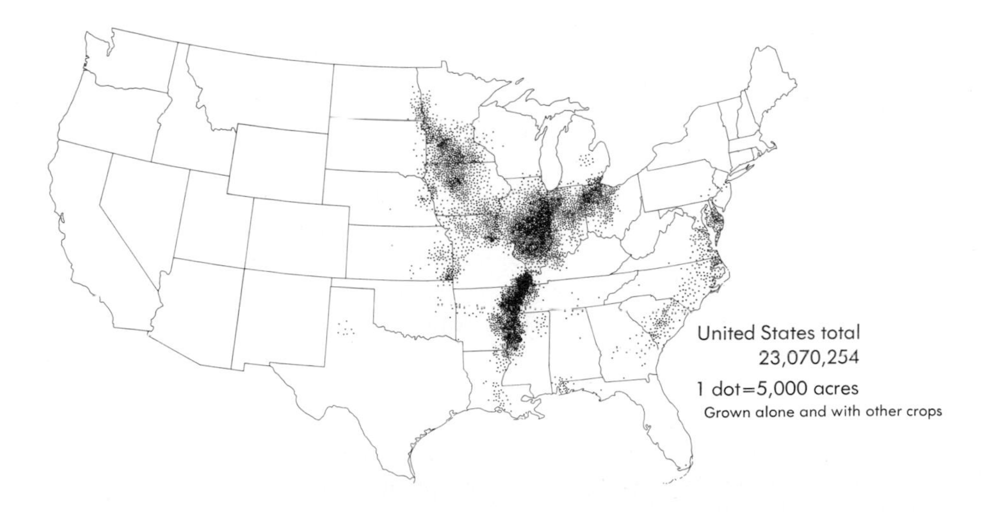

Fig. 5-10 Acreage of soybeans grown alone and with other crops in the United States. Soybeans have had an amazing rise to a position of major significance in American agriculture in the present century, and the country is the world's largest soybean producer, despite a sown acreage substantially below that of China. Soybeans may be treated as a green manure or as an intertilled crop for the production of beans, in which case they are equivalent to a cereal crop. Soybeans have taken over much land retired from other crops, particularly corn, and are most commonly grown in the Corn Belt and in the Mississippi Valley. (U.S. Department of Agriculture, 1959.)

presses, the crop invites estate production. Estate cultivation of oil palms is a very young industry indeed, dating only from just before World War I; in the Congo (Léopoldville) and Indonesia, the two most important areas for estate production, the future of the industry appears doubtful in the face of an often irrational nationalism. In Malaya, on the other hand, where the political climate is more favorable to the foreign-owned estate, oil palm cultivation has enjoyed a mild boom since 1957, and the planted area is increasing rapidly as rubber and coconut land is being diverted to oil palm production wherever soil conditions are suitable.

In Southeast Asia and in the Congo oil palm estates grow the "dura" variety, which has a moderately thick shell with a good oil-yielding pericarp. The indigenous West African producers, on the other hand, derive their output from thick-shelled types, more suitable for the production of palm kernels. While attempts to improve the quality of the Nigerian native producers' oil through a premium payment for special grade have been moderately successful, output has remained virtually static in the Fifties; moreover, throughout West Africa, where palm oil is a food, rising domestic consumption will limit the amount available for export. There is also a substantial production of palm oil from indigenous cultivators in the Congo, and this is the only geographical area in which both smallholders and estates participate in production; the Congo is also unique in possessing a kernel-crushing industry, this operation usually being performed at points of import as the residue provides a cattle feed which can find a wide market in the highly developed economies. Large plantings in the Congo are not yet in bearing, and though the industry has not been greatly disturbed by political troubles, it is difficult to have much faith in the ability of the shaky Congo government to maintain settled conditions necessary for such a capital-intensive industry.

SUGAR

The world sugar economy provides a rich field for the researcher into some of the more striking forms of economic lunacy. Very many nations produce sugar, either from beet or cane; only Japan among populous and important nations lacks a domestic sugar industry. With about twenty nations producing beet sugar and more than thirty producing cane sugar (and the numbers of both tend to increase), a wide range of cost levels is inevitable. But the high-cost producers show no tendency to reduce production, and the low-cost producers cannot enlarge their share of the market. There is a "world" price that bears no relation to that in all large and important sugar markets, and a "free" market that accounts for only about 15 per cent of world total consumption. Although there has been almost half a century of attempts at international control of world trade in sugar, there appears to be an irresistible tendency for overproduction. Nevertheless, every surplus has sooner or later been absorbed by expanding consumption, and the great disparity in per capita consumption between countries at various levels of economic development indicates very considerable scope for further expansion of world sugar production. The result of these periodic surpluses and shortfalls is to produce tremendous price fluctuations. At the beginning of 1962 the "free" market price of sugar had fallen to the lowest level for a quarter of a century; a year later the "free" market price had almost trebled and had regained the highest level of the postwar period.

There are several sugar-producing plants, some of which assume considerable local importance, but the great bulk of the world's sugar is derived from sugarcane, a tropical grass, and sugar beet, a temperate root crop. Both require deep, rich, well-drained soils and meticulous cultivation which involves much arduous labor; under certain conditions, however, the cultivation of both may be highly mechanized. Only the United States is a substantial producer of both beet and cane. Sugarcane is a herbaceous perennial, although in Java and Barbados it is treated as an annual; but beet is an annual crop. Both crops have

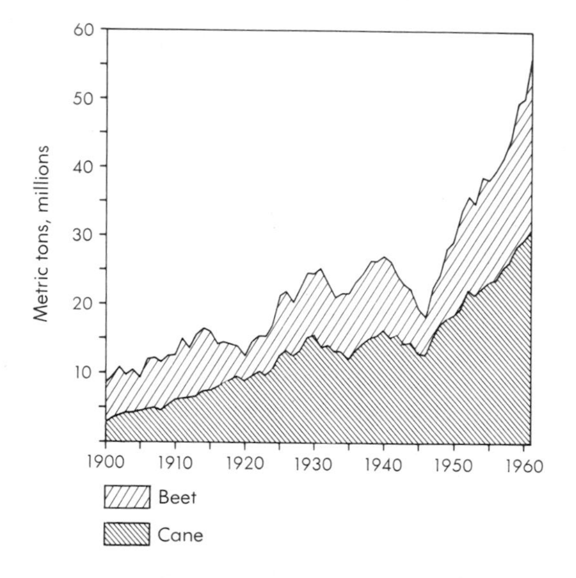

Fig. 5-11 Cane and beet sugar, 1900–1961. During the present century, sugar output has expanded tremendously, but the greater part of the increase has consisted of cane sugar. The U.S.S.R. has accounted for much of the postwar growth of beet sugar production. (FAO, *The World Sugar Economy in Figures, 1962.*)

Table 5-6

Production of Centrifugal Sugar (Million metric tons)

	AVERAGE 1948–1953		1961–1962	
	CANE	BEET	CANE	BEET
Europe		7.8		11.8
Western Europe		5.0		7.6
Eastern Europe		2.8		4.2
U.S.S.R.		2.6		6.6
North and Central America	10.6	1.6	11.6	2.3
Cuba	5.8		4.8	
Dominican Republic	0.5		0.9	
Mexico	0.7		1.6	
Jamaica	0.3		0.4	
United States				
Mainland	0.5	1.4	0.8	2.2
Hawaii	0.9		1.0	
South America	3.3		6.3	
Brazil	1.6		3.6	
Asia*	3.1		6.3	0.8
India	1.3		3.0	
Philippines	0.8		1.5	
Taiwan	0.6		0.7	
Indonesia	0.3		0.6	
Mainland China	0.3		0.9	0.3
Africa	1.5		2.8	
South Africa	0.6		1.0	
Australia	0.9		1.4	
WORLD TOTAL	20.0	12.3	29.6	21.9

* Excluding mainland China.
SOURCE: FAO, *Production Yearbook 1962,* Rome, 1963, Table 22.

experienced many fluctuations of fortune, but cane is now the more important in terms of total production, a position it is likely to retain in the future (Table 5-6 and Fig. 5-11).

Production and World Trade of Cane and Beet Sugar Costs of production for cane sugar are much lower than those for beet, for a number of reasons. As a perennial, cane is normally replanted only every three years. The yield of sugar from an acre of cane is very much greater than that from an acre of beet; under the most favorable conditions, it may be four or five times as much. It was the introduction of new high-yielding and disease-resistant varieties from the world's cane research stations that gave cane this tremendous advantage in the present century, and although sugar content and beet yield per acre have also been improved, an advance equivalent to that represented by the development of the famous Javanese cane variety P.O.J. 2878 appears unlikely. Cane is usually allowed fourteen to eighteen months in which to mature, but this period may be extended to two years when it is grown near the climatic margin. By planting two or three varieties a year with differing periods of growth, it is possible to extend the harvest season to keep the mills in operation for six months or more; Hawaii is unique in keeping its mills going throughout the year. The beet season, on the other hand, is very brief, for there is a marked reduction in the sugar content of beets if they are stored too long. Beet-sugar production thus has much higher overheads, and in order to help reduce these milling is frequently combined with refining, whereas most cane-producing areas export their sugar in the raw state. Labor costs too are generally lower in cane areas than in those producing sugar beet.

There is little doubt that in a freely competitive market, a great deal of the world's beet industry would be wiped out; some cane producers, such as Australia and the United States, would also disappear. But there are many reasons why governments assist the beet industry. It necessitates clean, open cultivation and heavy fertilizer application, thus keeping the land in top condition; it requires a large labor force, and a large rural population has been desired by many European governments in the interests of national military strength. Most of all, assistance to the beet industry has reflected the political power of the landowning class. On the best soils, such as the *limon* of northern France and the similar loess of central Europe, beet production does not involve a very heavy cost penalty (Fig. 5-12). On the whole, however, the beet-sugar industry is only kept in existence by a heavy subsidy. But cane sugar may also be subsidized, as in the United States and Australia; in the latter country cane cultivation is regarded as the only means of maintaining a large white population on the tropical coastlands of Queensland.

Most of the arguments put forward for the support of either beet or cane production can be seriously questioned, but in the conflict between beet and cane it is the cane farmer who is usually called upon to bear the cost of any imbalance between production and consumption. Cane sugar is a product of the monocultural plantation-crop type of agriculture, an agricultural system created to produce this very commodity; with two conspicuous exceptions, cane-sugar producers are at a low level of economic development. It is often the principal item in the export trade and the main prop of the economy; in Cuba, the British West Indies, Mauritius, Fiji, Hawaii, and Taiwan sugar accounts for over half of the export income. The cane farmer seldom has alternative sources of income. Beet, on the other hand, is a product of the crop and livestock type of farming in countries at a relatively high level of economic development. The beet farmer usually has many sources of income, and most other farm products are subsidized by the state. The beet farmer, in fact, has a guaranteed market, and his economic position is immensely more secure than that of the cane farmer.

In practice, most cane-producing countries have a foreign market in which they receive preference, in addition to the domestic one. But the market in which they receive special consideration is never large enough to dispose of the whole of the exportable surplus, and five large producers—Brazil, Taiwan, the Dominican Republic, Peru, and Indonesia—have no substantial protected market; their sugar, together with the portion of the output of other producers that cannot be sold in protected markets, has to find an outlet in the "free" market, which is considerably smaller

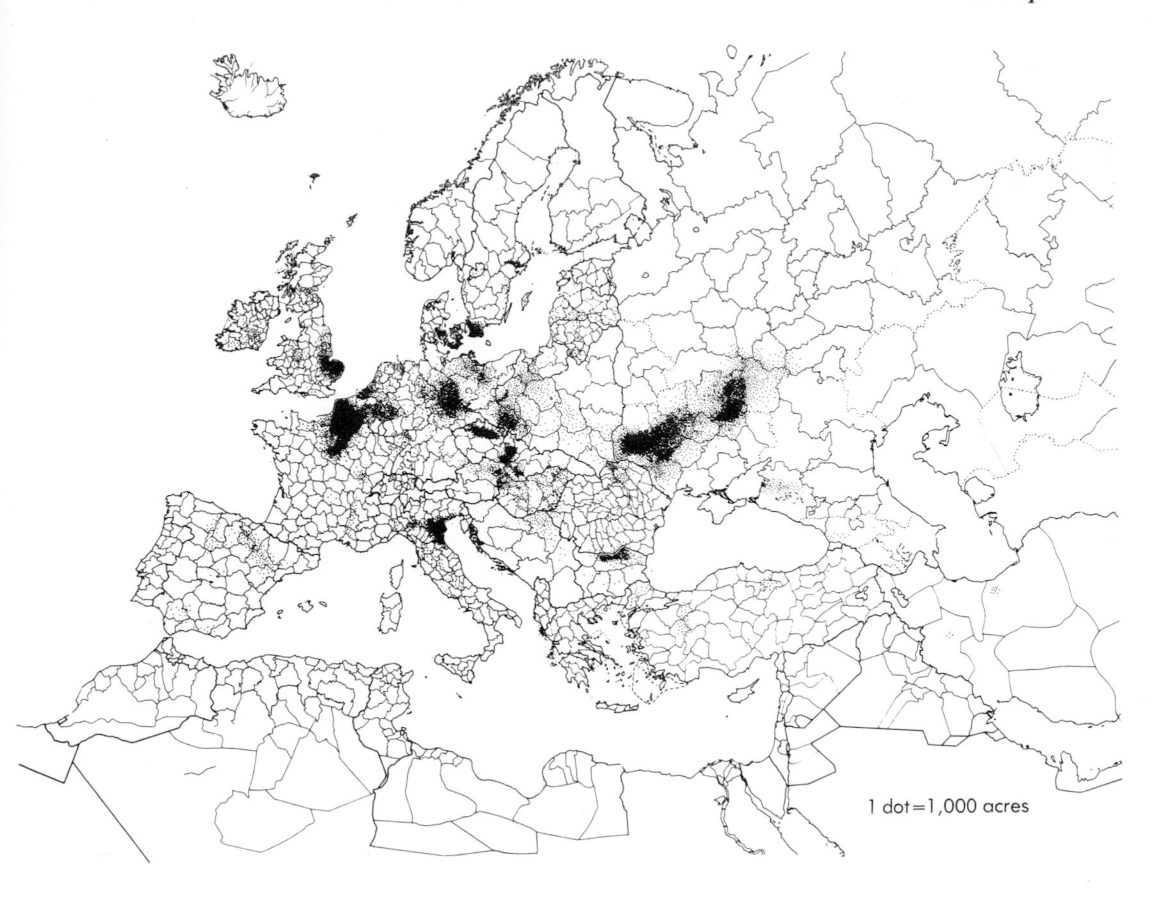

Fig. 5-12 Acreage of sugar beets in Europe and adjacent countries.
Europe produces more than 90 per cent of the world's sugar beets. Ideally, beets require a deep rich soil and a warm, moist climate; in the Ukraine, where much of Russian beet production is located, conditions are too dry for high yields. Beet cultivation, however, almost everywhere owes more to sociopolitical considerations than to physical ones. (William Van Royen, *Atlas of the World's Resouces,* vol. 1: *The Agricultural Resources of the World.* © 1954, by permission of Prentice-Hall, Inc., Englewood Cliffs, N.J.)

than that represented by the United States. The effect of this scramble is greatly to depress the world "free" market price.

Cane is grown under a variety of conditions, a reflection of the physical background and also of the fact that a large proportion of world output is grown for a protected market. Beet cultivation is confined to the Northern Hemisphere and shows much greater uniformity. The world's largest producer of sugar is probably India, but its production of both indigenous *gur* and centrifugal sugar is intended for domestic consumption; from the standpoint of the world market Cuba is by far the most important cane-sugar producer.[8] Cuba's rise

[8] **Centrifugal sugar is the crystalline sugar of commerce, produced in a high speed centrifuge which throws off the liquid molasses.**

to preeminence was the result of substantial United States investment in the industry following the Spanish-American War and the opening of the United States market to Cuban sugar. As a result output rose rapidly; from only about 1 million tons at the end of the Spanish occupation, sugar output rose to 3 million tons by the outbreak of World War I, and further rapid expansion occurred as a result of the destruction of the European beet industry. The first sugar boom collapsed in 1921; from then on, output oscillated considerably, and the country accumulated considerable surpluses. World War II and its aftermath provided further opportunities for expansion, Cuba's all-time record output of over 7 million tons being achieved in 1951–1952.

Under the impetus provided by an expanding American market, an advancing wave of sugar cultivation moved eastward from Las Villas, the original home of the industry in west central Cuba, into the undulating cattle country of Camaguey and Oriente provinces. This newer area is dominated by large modern *centrals* (mills), some of which, with an annual output of 150,000 tons, are giants by world standards. Both estates and smallholders participated in cane cultivation, but American interests before the Cuban revolution controlled estates totaling over 1 million acres and accounted for about one-third of the sugar output.

Since 1959, however, the Cuban revolution has dramatically transformed the world sugar situation. As the indigenous Cuban revolutionary movement lost its inertia, it was captured by the communists, and the island followed the familiar pattern of communist agricultural revolutions. Estate land was first redistributed to peasants, but this was followed in quick succession by cooperation and enforced collectivization, in the course of which the Cuban peasant failed even to retain the private plot of his Russian or Chinese counterpart. Relations with the United States deteriorated rapidly following wholesale expropriation of American property. In 1961 an embargo was placed on the import of Cuban sugar into the United States, and thereafter the island's economy moved completely within the Soviet orbit (Fig. 5-13). Exports continued to increase, but by 1962 the familiar effects of collectivization were beginning to show themselves; inadequate incentives had resulted in poor preparation of the land and inferior planting, and inexperienced workers drafted for harvesting caused great losses of cane. Cuba's sugar output for 1962–1963 fell precipitately, and the prerevolutionary output appears unlikely to be regained until the later Sixties. Food shortages, the usual accompaniment of communist agricultural planning, have also become more marked, and a substantial decline both in yields per acre and in sugar content seems inevitable. Despite a slump in production, however, Cuba's sugar income reached a record level in 1963, a result of the severe European winter of 1962–1963 which destroyed a large part of the beet crop and led to a dizzy rise in sugar prices.

Though outranked by Cuba, Brazil is still, as it has been since the seventeenth century, one of the very largest cane-sugar producers. Cane is grown in every state of Brazil, but it is particularly important in the coastal areas of the northeast. Until the early nineteenth century, with its development of a large beet industry in Europe, sugar was the mainstay of the Brazilian economy. However, Brazil appears to have been relatively little affected by the technical innovations that have revolutionized the industry in the present century; the primitive methods of cultivation—characterization that could be extended to the production of most Brazilian crops—are reflected in a yield of sugar per acre only barely superior to that of India.

Several geographic and economic peculiarities are demonstrated by other cane producers. In Australia, the largest producer in the British Commonwealth, the industry is subjected to a remarkable degree of state regulation. The cane areas extend in discontinuous patches along the coast from northern New South Wales to north Queensland, being restricted to those portions of the coast with a rainfall exceeding 40 inches. The present patchwork, however, which includes areas of both high and low productivity, reflects the history of the industry, which began near the climatic margin in northern New South Wales and gradually spread northward. Originally an estate industry using labor from the Pacific islands, sugar cultivation is now almost entirely a prerogative of small farmers, whose holdings average a little over 100 acres.[9] Mills, many of which are owned by growers' cooperatives, accept cane only from "assigned" land, a regulation aimed at avoiding overproduction; it is the assignment system—essentially a licensing system for sugar land—that accounts for the continuance of production in the southern areas. A unique feature of the Australian sugar industry is the use of white labor for field operations. Although Australia is a comparatively high-cost producer, on many counts the industry is a remarkably efficient one.

In Indonesia, now only a relatively minor producer, sugar is produced in a remarkable system which involved the renting of village sawah land by European or Chinese companies. Cultivation is restricted to central and east Java by climatic considerations, and in its heyday in the Twenties when almost 3 million

[9] There is one large estate, the property of a company with substantial interests in beef cattle and in wool production.

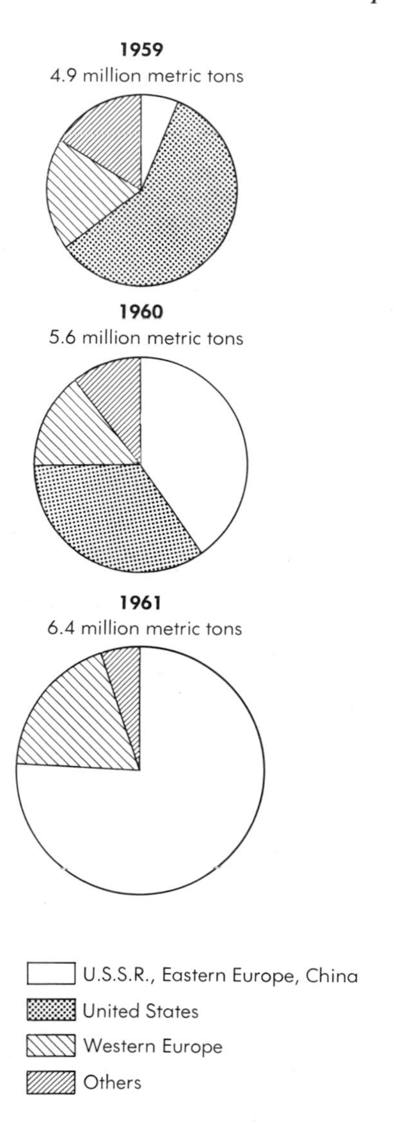

Fig. 5-13 Cuban sugar exports, 1959-1961. Cuba's increasing dependence on the U.S.S.R. is clear. As a result, Cuba failed to reap the maximum advantage from the tremendous rise in sugar prices on world markets in 1963, for much of its sugar was already pledged in advance to the U.S.S.R. Part of the windfall accrued to the U.S.S.R., which sold Cuban sugar in Western markets. (FAO, *Commodity Survey,* 1962.)

Fig. 5-14 Sugar beets harvested for sugar in the United States.
Sugar beets could be integrated into the mixed-farming economy of the eastern United States, but production is largely confined to the irrigated valleys of the West. The wide distribution of beet cultivation in an area of sparse and scattered population gives to the beet industry substantial political strength. (U.S. Department of Agriculture, 1959.)

tons of sugar were produced it affected all the best sawahs of these parts of the island. Under the Land Rents Ordinance the sale of land in Java to nonindigenes was forbidden, yet provision was made for renting land for export-crop production. Not more than one-third of the village sawah land could be planted, and the obligation to allow such land to revert to rice production for a subsequent wet season made the cultivation of perennials impossible. Thus cane was, and indeed still is, treated as an annual in Java, a feature that helps to account for the very high yields achieved, for with ratooning (that is, allowing a second and third crop to spring up from the rootstocks), yields progressively diminish. The industry, however, is only a shadow of its former self; once exporting over a million tons of sugar, the nationalized industry is now incapable of meeting even domestic requirements.

The highest yields of sugar per acre are achieved with the use of irrigation water, as in Hawaii, Peru, and Java, although the length of time the cane is in the ground has also to be considered, for the longer the term, the higher the yield. The best test of efficiency, man-hours per ton of sugar, gives a different ranking; Louisiana, Hawaii, and Australia all have very much lower figures than any other producer. In each of these areas cultivation is highly mechanized, for labor is expensive, and in the former two, mechanization is also extended to harvesting; though some 80 per cent of Australian cane is mechanically loaded, less than 5 per cent is mechanically cut. But mechanical harvesting has been forced on these producers by the scarcity of labor, for whenever alternative occupations are available, the sugar industry cannot retain its field work force; in Hawaii, each successive wave of immigrant labor has endeavored, for the most part successfully, to find other employment. High-yielding varieties

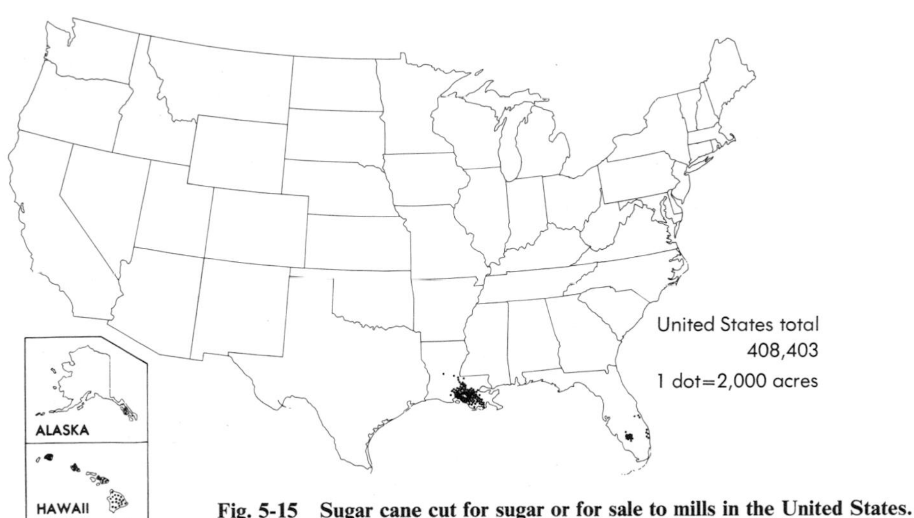

Fig. 5-15 Sugar cane cut for sugar or for sale to mills in the United States. Cane is grown in Louisiana and Florida; though the smaller producer, the latter state has the higher yields. (U.S. Department of Agriculture, 1959.)

and efficient transport to the mills are also important factors in achieving a high productivity per worker.

In contrast to the multiplicity of conditions under which cane is grown, beet cultivation is almost monotonously uniform throughout the world. In California and in the valleys of the High Plains in the United States beet is grown with the aid of irrigation water, a practice that is also followed in the north Italian plain. Some seventeen states produce beet, the largest producer being California, but many have only a very small production. Two, Louisiana and Florida, produce cane (Figs. 5-14 and 5-15). The effect of this is to secure a massive senatorial representation in any congressional discussion of the sugar industry and to ensure heavy support for what is probably the most costly sugar produced anywhere in the world.

Most beet-sugar producers are normally self-sufficient, but from time to time they may have surpluses for sale or may have to import some sugar to make good deficiencies resulting from a poor beet crop. The U.S.S.R., the world's largest beet producer, has contracted to take over 5 million tons of Cuban sugar between 1960 and 1964. But the most important sugar markets in the world are those of the United States and Britain; these two countries have a combined consumption exceeding 12 million tons per annum, of which domestic production supplies only about one-quarter and one-third, respectively. The balance is allocated between several suppliers, who receive a substantially higher price than that ruling on the "free" market. Britain also takes substantial quantities of sugar from nonprivileged suppliers; since the embargo on Cuban sugar the United States has also allowed nonprivileged suppliers a share in the American market.

The allocation of these two great sugar markets between their suppliers is shown in Fig. 5-16. The United States Sugar Act, to run until 1966, allocated 60 per cent of an estimated annual requirement of nearly 10 million tons to domestic producers. A quota of about one-half of that of 1957 to 1959 is re-

Fig. 5-16 Sugar allotments in Great Britain and the United States. Domestic sugar producers in the United States have been protected by import quotas since 1934. Since 1961, however, the United States has met much of its import requirements by "nonquota allocations," both from quota holders and other producers, and it is possible that a more flexible system of imports may replace the rigid quotas of the past. South Africa ceased to be a party to the Commonwealth Sugar Agreement in 1961, but it continues to receive a premium price in Britain for mutually agreed quotas.

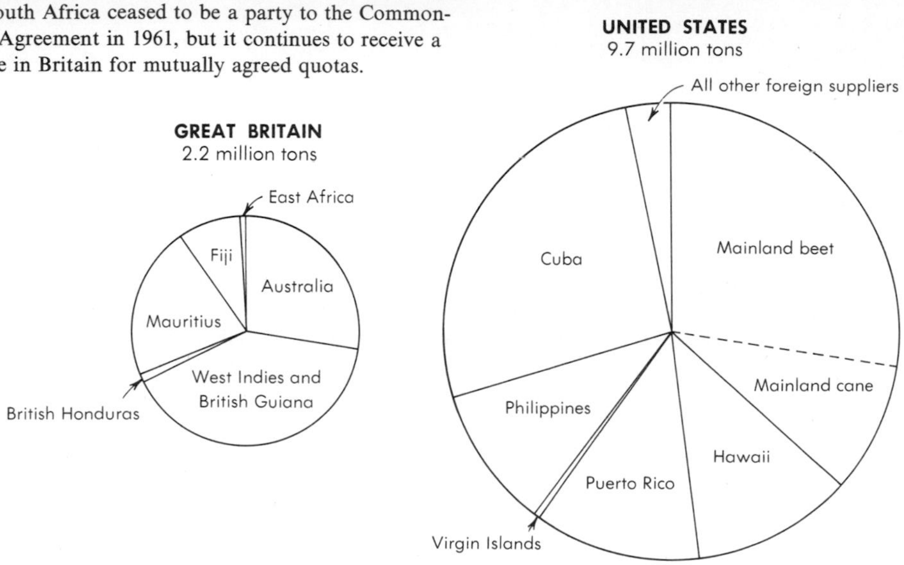

served to Cuba against the resumption of diplomatic relations despite the pressure of other suppliers to have it reallocated; this is to be temporarily filled mainly by purchases from other Latin American producers. The Philippines will continue to enjoy a premium price until 1966, but other suppliers will receive a gradual reduction in the premium over the "free" market price. Under the current act 65 per cent of any increase in consumption is reserved to domestic producers.

Under the British Commonwealth Sugar Agreement, Britain allots to Commonwealth suppliers overall quotas, which in 1963 totaled nearly 2.2 million tons. Part of the overall quota is purchased at a negotiated price, common to all suppliers and reviewed each year; the balance is paid for at the ruling world price. Other Commonwealth countries such as Canada and New Zealand are also linked with the agreement, and may take part of the overall-quota balance. After many years of severe sugar rationing during the war and postwar years Britain's consumption received a great fillip with the removal of restrictions, and the present agreement, concluded in 1951, permitted a considerable expansion in sugar production in many Commonwealth producers. The agreement has been renewed on a number of occasions, and is to run until 1965.

France and Portugal also import small quantities from their overseas possessions. Japan, an important prewar protected market, has now become "free" and satisfies its requirements mainly from Australia and Taiwan.

The International Sugar Agreements International action to regulate the supply of sugar on the world market dates back to the Brussels Convention of 1902, by which participating countries undertook not to subsidize the production or export of sugar. The convention, by limiting the export of cheap bounty-fed sugar from European beet producers, paved the way for the resuscitation of the cane industry in the present century. It resulted also in lower sugar prices in many European countries and an increased consumption.

Following World War I the speedy regeneration of European beet production precipitated a price collapse and large surpluses. Cuba was the first country to attempt to limit production, a policy that was doomed to failure as production increased in other countries. An agreement between private interests to limit production, the Chadbourne Scheme of 1931, failed for the same reasons—reductions in the output of participating countries were more than offset by increases in the output of nonparticipants. Nevertheless, in 1937, 1953, and 1958 international agreements were signed which progressively included more producing countries; virtually all sugar producers were parties to the 1958 agreement, whose export-control provisions expired in 1961.

The International Sugar Agreements of 1958 did not affect preferential sales, merely attempting to regulate trade in the "free" market. Quotas were allocated by an International Sugar Council in an attempt to balance supply and demand and to keep sugar prices stabilized between 3.15 and 4 cents per pound f.a.s. (free along side) Cuba. With the collapse of sugar prices in 1961 below the agreement floor price, however, the agreement virtually ceased to be operative. The history of successive sugar agreements is striking evidence of the failure of such agreements either to stabilize prices or to prevent periodic accumulation of surpluses.

BEVERAGES

The three beverages of greatest importance in the world economy are coffee, tea, and cocoa. Strictly speaking, coffee and tea are not food crops, but they occupy an important place in the consumption patterns of many peoples. Coffee and tea are mild stimulants and are broadly competitive, although each enjoys a marked preference in particular parts of the world. Cocoa is not really a competitor with coffee and tea, for the greater part of world cocoa consumption is accounted for by the chocolate and confectionery industries, cocoa as a beverage being essentially a by-product. All three beverages are products of plantation-crop agriculture. Geographically their production is markedly concentrated; coffee is mainly a crop of Latin America, tea production is almost entirely confined to Asia, and cocoa is particularly associated with West Africa (Fig. 5-17). But wherever produced, each of the beverages makes a substantial contribution to export income.

Coffee

Coffee is one of the most important commodities entering world trade; it has also produced perhaps the most spectacular surpluses. The production and consumption of coffee are heavily concentrated in the Western Hemisphere, but since the end of World War II there has been a marked increase in production in other parts of the world, particularly in the West African territories of the former Union Française.

Coffee of the *arabica* variety is by far the most important in world trade; the *robusta* and *liberica* varieties, widely cultivated in Africa by native peoples, are hardier and disease-resistant but produce coffee of inferior quality. Production of *robusta* and *liberica* coffee, however, has been given a considerable fillip by the popularity of soluble, or instant, coffees, for which these varieties are particularly suitable. The coffee tree is very susceptible to damage by frost and drought and

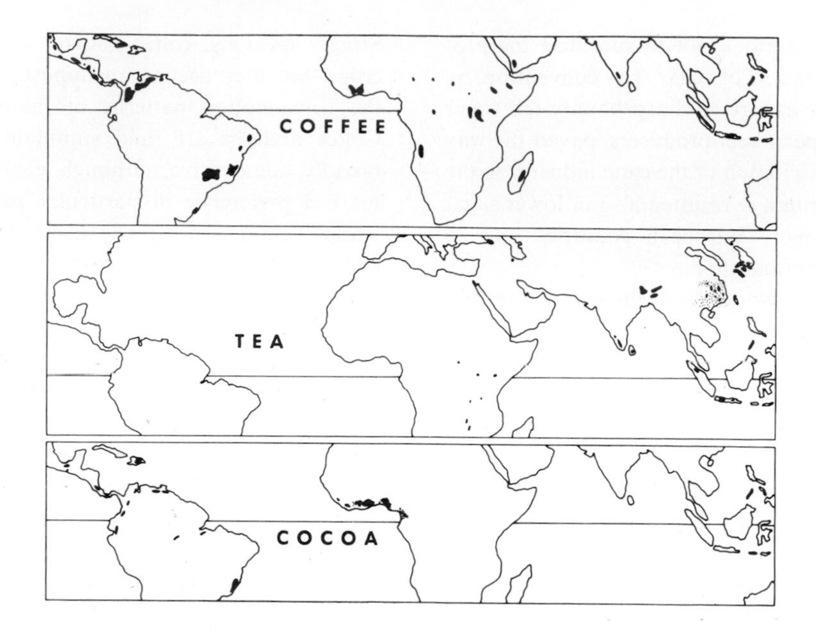

Fig. 5-17 World distribution of coffee, tea, and cocoa.
Both tea and coffee are crops of the tropical uplands; cocoa is more closely confined to equatorial lowlands.

requires a hot climate with an alternation of wet and dry seasons. Nevertheless, it can be grown in areas where rainfall is as little as 40 inches or in areas with 100 inches or more. Coffee is typically a crop of the intertropical uplands, for although the tree will grow in lowland situations, an elevated situation appears necessary for the production of beans of high quality. Generally, the lower the latitude, the greater the elevation at which coffee is grown. Shade trees are often employed, but this is not the practice in the largest producer, Brazil, where much coffee is grown at modest elevations of from 1,500 to 3,000 feet.

World coffee production has long been dominated by Brazil (Table 5-7). In world trade all Brazilian coffees are "Brazils," in contrast with the "milds" produced in other Latin American countries; except at times of very high prices, milds usually command a premium price. The growth of the beet-sugar industry in Europe first diverted Brazilian interest from sugar to coffee production, and from a negligible production at the beginning of the nineteenth century, coffee came to dominate the Brazilian economy and nation. By the end of the century Brazil produced three-quarters of the world's coffee, but its relative importance in the present century has declined considerably; since 1950 Brazil's share of world output has been about one-half (Fig. 5-18).

Expansion of coffee cultivation in Brazil was the result of a favorable combination of geographic and economic conditions, which offered the opportunity for huge speculative profits in a manner perfectly attuned to the Brazilian ethos; the elimination of potential competitors such as Ceylon and Java through disease was, from Brazil's viewpoint, little more than a fortunate accident. This speculative character of the industry is discernible in almost every particular of its organization.

Brazilian coffee has never really been cultivated; it is merely planted, and even this is carried out in a wasteful and inefficient manner.[10] After planting the trees receive the minimum of attention, and harvesting and processing of the beans are performed in an unscientific and haphazard manner. From the vast profits made by coffee planting in Brazil nothing has ever been plowed back in scientific research or even in the provision of a much-needed statistical service. The tremendous export surpluses generated by coffee could have been used to lift the Brazilian economy from an underdeveloped stage to a higher level of development. But given the Brazilian social structure, this was out of the question.

Brazil's greatest assets for coffee cultivation were an apparently unlimited area of suitable soil and cheap immigrant labor. Under such conditions Brazil could remain a low-cost producer despite a yield per tree of only about 1 pound of beans per annum, only a fraction of what is known to be possible. Erosion and exhaustion of the soil were thus of no consequence; so long as virgin *terra roxa* soils were available for planting, there was no incentive to adopt improved methods of cultivation and harvesting, and the *patron-colono* system ensured that new *fazendas* were planted at low cost to the landowner.

From the old coffee areas of Rio de Janeiro and Espirito Santo, speculative waves of coffee planting rolled across São Paulo, which has long been the most important producing state; and with the depletion of the soils of São Paulo, new planting spread into Paraná. Many of the *fazendas* in the latter state have only come into bearing since the end of World War II. But Brazil no longer enjoys its traditional advantages. Large-scale immigration has virtually ceased, industrialization and urbanization have reduced the supply of labor in rural areas and markedly increased its cost, and labor productivity is lower than before the war. Runaway inflation is not only an economic disaster but a threat to the whole fabric of Brazilian society; fortunately for Brazil, some of its competitors are in little better economic shape.

These grave shortcomings have been underlined by the repeated accumulation of huge surpluses. These surpluses, which also originated in the speculative character of the coffee industry, have been peculiarly a Brazilian problem, for other producers found no difficulty in disposing of all their output.

The coffee tree is notoriously an erratic cropper; a 30 to 50 per cent variability from year to year is by no means unusual. Favorable conditions can produce a very heavy crop which takes such toll of the tree that a rest

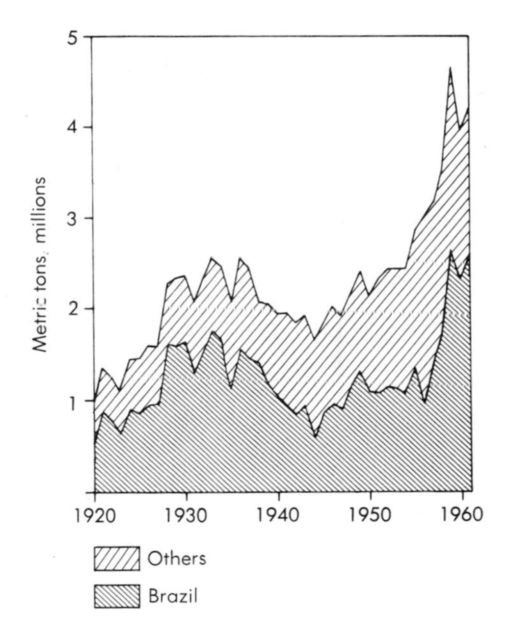

Fig. 5-18 World coffee production, 1920–1961. World coffee production has fluctuated widely from year to year, but under the stimulus of higher prices, output has increased rapidly since 1945. Brazil's share of world production, however, has tended to decline.

[10] Vernon D. Wickizer, *Coffee, Tea and Cocoa,* Stanford University Press, Stanford, Calif., 1951, p. 46.

period of light yields appears to be necessary before it can bear well again. Frost and drought can greatly reduce output and kill off many trees, but these checks may subsequently be followed by heavy yields from trees that survive. Coffee production can thus fluctuate in completely unpredictable fashion, and given the short-term inflexibility in the demand for coffee, prices can swing widely from year to year. These fluctuations in price have had profound consequence in Brazil, for high prices have invariably produced new speculative plantings; preventive regulations such as those enacted in 1902 and 1931 have always been allowed to lapse. The maturation of new plantings made at a time of high prices has repeatedly caused production to outstrip demand. Ultimately the Brazilian industry has recovered from recurrent surpluses and periods of price depression through the growth of world demand and through fortuitous reduction of output by frosts, drought, and fire. In 1963 widespread fires in Paraná wiped out enormous areas of new plantings.

Brazil's difficulties, however, were exacerbated by the adoption of coffee "defense" policies which themselves reflect the speculative nature of Brazilian economic life. A policy aimed at ironing out the inevitable yearly fluctuations in production had much to com-

Table 5-7

Coffee Production (Thousand metric tons)

	AVERAGE 1948–1953	1961–1962
North and Central America	370	595
Mexico	70	122
El Salvador	74	106
Guatemala	58	97
South America	1,510	2,700
Brazil	1,077	2,085
Colombia	359	468
Venezuela	47	48
Ecuador	19	53
Asia	75	220
Indonesia	51	117
India	22	46
Africa	280	755
Former French West Africa (Dahomey, Ivory Coast, Guinea)	52	176
Former British East Africa (Kenya, Uganda, Tanganyika)	59	147
Angola	56	159
Congo (Léopoldville)	20	54
Malagasy Republic	31	40
WORLD TOTAL	2,240	4,280

SOURCE: FAO, *Production Yearbook 1962*, Rome, 1963, Table 57A.

mend it, but the success of Brazil's first valorization schemes led the government to attempt something more far-reaching—to force up prices by withholding supplies from the market, essentially an attempt to exploit a supposed monopoly position. But under the shelter of the Brazilian price umbrella, other producers were able to expand their output of the preferred mild coffees, so that the immense stocks of coffee accumulated during the Thirties by the Brazilian government, and the millions of bags that were burned to prevent those stocks from becoming still more mountainous, availed nothing. Failing to get other producers to agree to limit production, Brazil abandoned its attempts at artificial price control in 1937, but crop burning continued until well into World War II; between 1931 and 1944 almost 40 million bags of coffee were destroyed.

Thus, while Brazil's share of the world coffee market declined, the national economy became more firmly shackled to coffee than ever. Any success achieved in raising prices was nullified by new plantings; diversification was retarded, and the economy remained at a low level of development. The transport system, with railroads aligned along ridgetops, avoiding the valleys, and focusing on the ports of Santos and Rio de Janeiro, was designed to further the development of the coffee industry. Eventually the administrative bureaucracy threatened to strangle the coffee industry itself; in the opinion of some observers, the pervasive influence of the government has been a greater obstacle to improvement of the industry than any other factor.[11]

In Colombia, Brazil's principal competitor, the whole organization of the industry is markedly different. Coffee is grown at much higher elevations, from 3,000 to 6,000 feet, and the average size of the *finca,* or estate, is much smaller than in Brazil. Shading and erosion control are practiced, and harvesting is carried out by progressively gathering the coffee berries as they ripen, instead of stripping the tree at one operation as in Brazil. Processing of the beans is also superior, most Colombian coffee being prepared by the "wet" process, in contrast to the "dry" process common in Brazil. Colombia has now established a position in the production of mild coffee comparable with that of Brazil in lower-quality coffees, and while its share of total world production is only about 15 per cent, it accounts for almost 60 per cent of mild-coffee production. In Central American states such as Costa Rica, the organization of production is broadly similar to that in Colombia.

Brazil's lack of success with unilateral control prompted it in the late Thirties to approach other Latin American producers with a view to a limitation of planting. These saw little reason why they should help Brazil to reduce its surpluses at their expense, and negotiations proved fruitless; however, an agreement was precipitated by World War II and the loss of the European market. This Inter-American Coffee Agreement of 1941 was the first international control scheme in which a consuming nation, the United States, took a leading part; although it helped the wartime position of growers it offered no solution to the basic problems of coffee production. After the initial postwar period of high prices, however, the mild-coffee producers showed a greater interest in regulation, and an unofficial agreement to withhold stocks was reached in 1957 by the members of the so-called "Mexico club," which included Brazil, Colombia, and most Central American producers.

Nevertheless, it was becoming clear that as a result of rapidly expanding production in Africa, Latin American producers could no longer expect to exert any appreciable influence on the market. Outside the highlands of Kenya,

[11] Wickizer, *op. cit.,* pp. 134–135.

Angola, and Rwanda-Burundi where the *arabica* variety is grown, coffee production in Africa is a smallholder activity carried on in the lowlands where *robusta* and *liberica* types are more suitable. Development of native coffee growing in French, Belgian, and Portuguese territories was greatly assisted from the Depression onwards by the granting of high-tariff protection in the home market. Though small, Africa's share of coffee exports is steadily growing, and its participation is vital to the success of any international agreement.

In 1960 the African producers decided to join the Latin American voluntary agreement, and in the following year it was made binding. Though long opposed to commodity agreements (where it was concerned as a consumer), the United States decided in 1961 to support an International Coffee Agreement as a means as assisting the economic development of Latin America, just as twenty years previously it had come to the rescue of the Latin American producers during the war emergency.

Nevertheless, opportunities for expanding coffee consumption do not appear to be very considerable; per capita consumption in the United States, though high, shows no tendency to grow, and coffee has in fact lost ground to other beverages. Per capita consumption in Scandinavia is even higher than in the United States, but in Germany and Italy it is substantially lower than before World War II. It seems inevitable, however, that the greater part of any increase in the EEC consumption will go to those African states that have been granted the status of association with the Common Market. In the long term there seems to be no alternative to a greater diversification of land use in the major producers. But while the success of the new agreement depends on the willingness of importers to buy from participating producers, the great fire in Brazil resulted in that country sharply reducing its stocks by the end of 1963. A year that produced substantial simultaneous reductions in world surpluses of wheat, sugar, and coffee must be judged unique.

Tea

Tea is a competitor with coffee for land and capital in upland areas in the intertropical world and for a share of the beverage market. It needs considerably more labor to harvest than coffee, and largely for this reason more than 95 per cent of world output is produced in Asia. Tea also requires elaborate processing, involving withering, fermentation, and rolling, and as there is a considerable weight loss in manufacture, this takes place in close proximity to the place of cultivation. For these reasons much of the world's production of black teas, which are by far the most important in world commerce, is organized on an estate basis; smallholders usually have their tea processed at an estate factory. In Indonesia and Ceylon, however, smallholder production has always been more important than in India, the largest black-tea producer, and green-tea production in China, Japan, and Taiwan is overwhelmingly a small-farmer activity. Green teas are comparatively simple to process, and are mainly used in domestic consumption.

Tea can be grown in both tropical and warm temperate climates, but it cannot withstand frost or dry conditions. Ideally, tea requires heavy rainfall throughout the year, and in low latitudes plucking of the new shoots can take place at intervals of a fortnight; cheap labor and continuous "flushing" gave to the Netherlands Indies the lowest costs of production before World War II. The finest qualities of tea are grown at high elevations, estates occurring up to 7,000 feet in the Darjeeling area of India, but fine quality depends as much on careful manufacture as on soil or climate.

As with coffee, tea is blended to produce an

Table 5-8

Tea Production (Thousand metric tons)

	AVERAGE 1948–1953	1961–1962
U.S.S.R	n.a.	37
South America	1	10
Argentina	n.a.	8
Asia	530	750
India	273	353
Ceylon	140	206
Japan	40	81
Indonesia	22	39
Pakistan	22	27
Taiwan	9	18
Mainland China	63	166
Africa	20	55
Kenya	6	16
Nyasaland	7	14
Mozambique	3	10
WORLD TOTAL	630	1,010

SOURCE: FAO, *Production Yearbook 1962,* Rome, 1963, Table 59.

acceptable and uniform product, so that fine-quality Darjeelings or Ceylons fulfill a similar function to that of the milds in coffee blending. Tea production, however, has a greater flexibility than coffee, for it is possible to raise output by coarse plucking or to reduce it by fine plucking if the market so demands. The speculative character of the Brazilian coffee industry is entirely absent from the efficient estate industry of India, the largest tea exporter. On the whole the tea industry shows considerable stability, as there is a broad identity between producers and consumers, a large share of production and consumption being in British hands.

China was long the principal producer and exporter, but with the expansion of tea cultivation in India it gradually sank to a minor role in world trade. Tea production in China was greatly affected by World War II, but the Peking government has expanded exports considerably since 1950, and a further substantial increase in both production and exports appears likely.

India is by far the largest producer (Table 5-8) and exporter, tea generating about 20 per cent of the export income. Tea cultivation is not widespread, as in south China, but is highly concentrated in two distinct and widely separated regions where it is the dominant economic activity. The major producing area is Assam, to which the tea plant is indigenous, a discovery that laid the basis of the tea industry in India, for earlier attempts to introduce Chinese teas had failed. In contrast to other tea-growing areas, estates in Assam are situated on the plains, heavy erosion having defeated the earlier attempts at cultivation at higher elevations. Assam produces neutral, or "filler," teas, which are blended with quality teas produced at high elevations, such as those of the nearby Darjeeling area. The minor area is the Nilgiri Hills of Kerala in south India, another producer of quality teas.

Though the tea industry of Ceylon is of

much smaller size than that of India, it is of considerably greater importance in the national economy, tea accounting for about two-thirds of the export income. Ceylon is the largest producer of quality tea, all of its output coming from upland areas of the south central portion of the island, where the number of rainy days per year exceeds 100. Though by far the greater part of Ceylon's output comes from British-owned estates, which use immigrant Tamil workers from southern India, there is a small production from Sinhalese smallholders, and this has tended to increase.

Indonesia is also primarily a producer of quality tea, and the distribution of tea cultivation, as in Ceylon, is closely related to those upland areas with more than 100 rainy days per year; the principal tea-producing area is in the Priangan uplands of west Java, with a lesser area in the Batak highlands of north Sumatra. Before World War II tea earned some 10 per cent of the Netherlands Indies export income, but its contribution to the Indonesian foreign exchange position is now much smaller, in part a consequence of a considerable decline in output.

The organization of production is quite different in the green-tea producers, where tea cultivation is often combined with other farming activities; there are considerably fewer pickings per year than in the black-tea-producing countries, and alternative occupations are thus essential. Green tea is not fermented, so that elaborate factory processing is unnecessary, and relatively little of the output is exported. As a result estate organization conveys no advantage.

Production and exports of tea now stand at a much higher level than before World War II, but the nationalist revolution in Asia has greatly increased costs. The large estates of north Sumatra have been forced to divide up their land between native producers, while in most estates in Java replanting is long overdue; there is no incentive to European companies to undertake this task in the face of Indonesia's uncertain political and economic future. In Ceylon, British estates have been forced to employ a larger proportion of Sinhalese workers, of generally lower productivity than former Tamil workers, while the Tamil population itself has been subjected to many socioeconomic disabilities. These difficulties have resulted in the sale of many estates to local speculators, who have cut up their purchases for small holdings. This has in almost every case resulted in a marked drop in output and a decline in quality; so serious did this problem become that in 1959 legislation was introduced to prevent the further breakup of Ceylon's estates.

The Indian government, on the other hand, has steadfastly opposed any actions that threaten the country's export earnings by hindering estate operations. In 1957 the State of Kerala acquired a communist government, and the tea estates of the peninsula were threatened with nationalization; but the local government was removed by the central government, and the danger was averted. Far more serious was the invasion of Assam by Chinese forces in 1962, which clearly demonstrated the vulnerability of India's most important export-producing area.

In some ways, tea has a more promising future than any other crop grown under estate conditions. In marked contrast to coffee, tea has a long history of scientific research; fertilizers and erosion control have long been employed on estates, and there has been considerable investigation into the problem of cost reduction, both in the field and in the factory. It is possible that some kind of mechanical harvesting may be employed in the future. This would necessitate considerable changes in present methods of planting, cultivation, and harvesting; hedge planting appears to offer the greatest scope for the use of mechanical equipment.

Partly because of the greatly enhanced labor costs of producing tea in Asia, there has been a marked expansion of tea cultivation in former British East Africa since the end of World War II, but the area is still only a minor producer, and the possibilities for further expansion appear limited in view of the restricted extent of areas of high rainfall and uncertainty about the intentions of the new leaders of Kenya, Tanganyika, and Malawi. The British African territories were not parties to the International Tea Agreement, which expired in 1955, under which the principal Commonwealth producers and Indonesia agreed to adopt export quotas. Tea production has increased in certain other countries since the war, e.g., Turkey, Iran, and the U.S.S.R., but in these countries tea cultivation is restricted to a few favorable areas, and production falls short of consumption.

Nevertheless, the sharp upward trend in world production gives rise to some concern for future price stability. Tea consumption is perhaps more closely associated with custom than with income level, and the prospects for expansion in British Commonwealth markets do not appear very great; but the U.S.S.R., which also has a long tradition of tea drinking, is a potential market of considerable magnitude.

Cocoa

The modern cocoa is essentially a comparatively unimportant by-product arising in the production of chocolate, a confection first produced by Van Houten in the early nineteenth century. Cocoa and chocolate are produced from beans extracted from the pods of the cacao tree, a native plant of the coastlands of Central America; the term "cocoa" is often used, however, to indicate both the beverage and the tree itself. In contrast to coffee and tea, cacao is a tree of the equatorial lowlands, though the plant seems able to tolerate a short dry season. Moreover, the great bulk of world output is derived from peasant farmers; estate production is largely confined to the Western Hemisphere, and in general is poorly organized in comparison with that of either coffee or tea.

The rise of cacao cultivation to a position of major importance in the world economy has occurred in the present century, and has been accompanied by a remarkable changes in the location and organization of production. At the beginning of the century the bulk of the world's cocoa came from estates in South and Central America, but smallholders in the coastlands of West Africa now account for about 70 per cent of world exports. The rapid expansion of cocoa cultivation in various West African territories suggests that cocoa is an ideal crop for the smallholder. Cacao is a tree of the equatorial forest, and smallholder techniques of close planting and a minimum of weeding reproduce a forest environment better than do the wider planting, clean weeding, and shade planting of estates. The West African farmer also usually practices a form of shifting cultivation, and his planting is made at very low cost. It was, almost certainly, the ease and rapidity with which smallholder production could be expanded, compared with the difficulty and expense of raising output on Western Hemisphere estates, that was responsible for the rapid growth of the industry in the Guinea coastlands.

Cocoa beans are classified into "ordinary" and "fine" grades, but the distinction has less significance than that between Brazils and milds in the case of coffee, or between fillers and quality teas. The largest producers supply mainly ordinary beans, the finer grades coming from small Caribbean producers. The Gold Coast, Ghana since 1957, became the leading producer shortly after World War I, a position the country has held ever since (Table 5-9). Ghana and Nigeria together provide about half of world exports. Since World War II,

Table 5-9

Production of Cocoa Beans (Thousand metric tons)

	AVERAGE 1948–1953	1961–1962
North and Central America	65	80
Dominican Republic	30	33
Mexico	8	16
South America	190	235
Brazil	125	156
Ecuador	28	44
Colombia	11	17
Asia	4	7
Africa	500	825
Ghana	253	415
Nigeria	109	202
Cameroun	49	70
Oceania (New Guinea, New Hebrides, Samoa)	4	16
WORLD TOTAL	760	1,160

SOURCE: FAO, *Production Yearbook 1962,* Rome, 1963, Table 58A.

production has greatly expanded in the West African States of the French currency area, a development that may be expected to continue in the future. The war, however, coincided with the spread of a serious virus infection, swollen shoot, which between 1939 and 1945 is estimated to have killed more than 5 million trees each year in Ghana.[12] This disease became so serious that it threatened the whole future of the Ghana industry; the only known treatment is to cut out infected trees, and as a result of strenuous efforts on the part of the government, growers had cut out more than 50 million trees by 1956. Capsid bug infestation has also assumed serious proportions in both Ghana and Nigeria. Fortunately, high postwar prices encouraged new planting with higher-yielding varieties, and this, together with rigorous spraying and improved agricultural practices, helped to push output steadily upwards.

[12] *Ibid.,* p. 295.

In Ecuador, the largest producer at the beginning of the century, cocoa cultivation suffered a considerable decline as a result of the fungoid disease "witch's broom," but production in Brazil increased steadily, and until the middle Fifties, when it was overtaken by Nigeria, Brazil was the second-largest exporter. Brazil has the great advantage of being the only major producer relatively free from serious disease problems, but the industry possesses many of the speculative traits common to almost all Brazilian commercial enterprise. The cocoa areas of Brazil are almost entirely confined to the coastlands of the State of Bahia, in which it is the dominant economic activity. Cocoa's contribution to Brazil's export income, however, is normally only around 5 per cent, as compared to around 60 per cent in the case of Ghana.

Since World War II the marketing of cocoa in Ghana and Nigeria has been in the hands of state cocoa-marketing boards, which accumulated large sums from the difference between the price paid to producers and that realized on the world market. Though strongly criticized, marketing boards have made considerable contributions to economic and social development, and it is doubtful if equivalent sums could have been reclaimed from growers through taxation. In Brazil, cocoa exports, as with almost every agricultural product, were reserved to a government agency and subject to "defense" policies; in 1961, however, trade was largely returned to private interests.

Cocoa has never been a crop with a surplus problem except during wartime, but rapid expansion of output in the late Fifties, a result of a period of high prices, and the large area not yet in bearing make this appear a possibility in the near future. The demand for chocolate, however, appears to possess considerable elasticity; since World War II Western Europe has absorbed increased quantities of cocoa beans, and the EEC now exceeds the United States as the principal importer. Japan also has appeared as an importer of considerable significance. Chocolate manufacturers, fearing that demand might exceed supply, have even investigated opening up new areas of cocoa production, such as Malaya, Sabah (North Borneo), and Australian New Guinea. Observers who forecast considerable opportunities for further expansion in the leading producers, however, have been proved correct, and an international cocoa agreement appears probable in the near future.

SELECTED REFERENCES

Callaghan, A. R., and A. J. Millington: *The Wheat Industry in Australia,* Angus and Robertson, Sydney, 1956.

Commonwealth Economic Committee: *Grain Crops,* H. M. Stationery Office, London, annually.

———: *Plantation Crops,* H. M. Stationery Office, London, annually.

———: *Vegetable Oils and Oilseeds,* H. M. Stationery Office, London, annually.

Dyer, Donald R.: "Sugar Regions of Cuba," *Economic Geography,* vol. 32, pp. 177–184, 1956.

Eckey, E. W.: *Vegetable Fats and Oils,* Reinhold Publishing Corporation, New York, 1954, pp. 302–377.

Food and Agriculture Organization: *Commodity Survey 1962,* Rome, 1962.

———: *Tea: Trends and Prospects,* Commodity Bulletin Series, no. 30, Rome, 1960.

———: *The World Coffee Economy,* Commodity Bulletin Series, no. 33, Rome, 1961.

———: *The World Sugar Economy in Figures, 1880–1959,* Rome, undated.

Forde, C. Daryll, and R. Scott: *Native Economies of Nigeria,* Faber & Faber, Ltd., London, 1946, pp. 217–291.

Fryer, Donald W.: "The Recovery of the Sugar Industry in Indonesia," *Economic Geography,* vol. 33, pp. 171–181, 1957.

Galletti, R., et al.: *Nigerian Cocoa Farmers,* Oxford University Press, London, 1956.

Grist, Donald H.: *Rice,* Longmans, Green & Co., Ltd., London, 1953.

Haarrer, A. E.: *Modern Coffee Production,* Leonard Hill, London, 1956.

Jackson, W. A. D.: "The Virgin and Idle Lands of Western Siberia and Northern Kazakhstan: A Geographical Appraisal," *Geographical Review,* vol. 46, pp. 1–19, 1956.

James, Preston E.: *Latin America,* The Odyssey Press, Inc., New York, 1959.

Jarrett, H. R.: "The Present Setting of the Oil-palm Industry," *The Journal of Tropical Geography,* vol. 11, pp. 59–69, 1958.

Kelley, Tim K., and Alan D. Tweedie: "The Expanding Queensland Sugar Industry," *The Malayan Journal of Tropical Geography,* vol. 5, pp. 44–56, 1955.

Mann, Alvin A.: "Production and Utilization of the Soybean in the United States," *Economic Geography,* vol. 26, pp. 223–234, 1950.

Music, D. A.: "Sugar: A Review of the Industry in the U.S.S.R.," *FAO Monthly Bulletin of*

Agricultural Economics and Statistics, vol. 9, no. 9, pp. 13–20, 1962.

Shen, T. H.: *Agricultural Resources of China,* Cornell University Press, Ithaca, N.Y., 1951.

United Nations: *Coffee in Latin America: 1. Colombia and El Salvador,* New York, 1958.

Urquhart, D. H.: *Cocoa,* 2d ed., Longmans, Green & Co., Ltd., London, 1961.

Van Royen, William: *Atlas of the World's Resources,* vol. 1: *The Agricultural Resources of the World,* Prentice-Hall, Inc., Englewood Cliffs, N.J., 1954.

Wadham, Samuel, and R. K. Wilson: *Land Utilization in Australia,* 4th ed., Melbourne University Press, Melbourne, 1964, pp. 107–132, 174–182, and 207–212.

Ward, Ralph E.: "Northern Great Plains as Producers of Wheat," *Economic Geography,* vol. 22, pp. 231–244, 1946.

Wickizer, Vernon D.: *Coffee, Tea and Cocoa,* Stanford University Press (for Food Research Institute), Stanford, Calif., 1951.

———: *Rice and Wheat in World Agriculture and Consumption,* Stanford University Press (for Food Research Institute), Stanford, Calif., 1941.

Woytinsky, W. S., and E. S. Woytinsky: *World Population and Production,* The Twentieth Century Fund, New York, 1953, pp. 583–594.

Zimmermann, Erich W.: *World Resources and Industries,* rev. ed., Harper & Row Publishers, Incorporated, New York, 1951, pp. 260–287.

Chapter 6

INDUSTRIAL CROPS

Although the area planted to industrial crops is only a fraction of that under food crops, over considerable areas of countries at all levels of economic development industrial-crop production is a dominant agricultural activity. Either such crops may be grown because of local tradition and long experience of their cultivation, as is the case with jute and abaca, or their cultivation may reflect a general unsuitability of soil for food crops. Usually, however, the cultivator has a choice of growing either food or industrial crops, and his decision turns on their respective profitability. The jute area of Bengal fluctuates with changes in the relative prices of jute and rice. Cotton is not grown in either Japan or Java, although it would be quite possible to do so; it is cheaper for these countries to import raw cotton and to grow as much rice as they can. The conflict may, nevertheless, be a serious one; in Egypt cotton occupies land that is also urgently needed for food production.

Industrial crops comprise a great range of products, but the most important are the vegetable fibers, natural rubber, and tobacco; crops of lesser importance include those producing essential (or volatile) oils and many of pharmaceutical interest. Several of the latter have experienced heavy competition from synthetic products, quinine and camphor having been almost entirely displaced by man-made substitutes. Almost all industrial crops are subject to some such competition, and their prospects of retaining a market depend as much on their ability to remain competitive in price as on their physical properties. Considerable possibilities of cost reduction do in fact exist, though this is not to imply, of course, that they will be realized. Nevertheless, the complete extinction of industrial-crop production as a result of competition from synthesized substitutes, of which indigo cultivation is perhaps the most striking example, is a rare occurrence. Hindrances to efficient operation of the Java cinchona estates are as great a handicap to the quinine industry as competition from newer synthetic drugs; silk, which suffered severely from the competition of man-made fibers, has regained favor since World War II, and the obstacles to further expansion lie mainly in the markedly increased labor costs of the principal producing countries.

COTTON

Although the vegetable fibers are by far the most important division of industrial crops by any criterion, this situation is almost entirely accounted for by cotton, one of the world's great crops for over a century, and before World War II often the leading agricultural commodity in world trade. Cotton is likely to remain by far the most important of all fibers for a considerable time to come (Table 6-1); nevertheless, it has shown a chronic tendency to be in considerable oversupply. Partly through technological progress and partly through economic policies that have encouraged cotton cultivation, the world's cotton supply has greatly enlarged over the past three decades. Consumption, however, has not kept pace; the world per capita consumption in 1960 of nearly 7.5 pounds per head did not represent much of an advance over the 6.3 pounds of 1938, and most of this increase took place in the late Fifties at a time when boom conditions were being experienced in many highly developed economies. Thus the rate of growth of cotton consumption has done little more than reflect the increase in world population. It has failed to grow more rapidly partly because of the continued low income levels in the tropical parts of the world, where cotton is by far the most suitable fiber for apparel purposes, and partly because of the competition from other fibers in countries at a high level of economic development; between 1938 and 1960 world per capita consumption of rayon more than doubled.

Table 6-1

Estimated World Production of Industrial Fibers

	PRODUCTION (MILLION LB)		PERCENTAGE OF TOTAL FIBER PRODUCTION	
	AVERAGE 1946–1951	1961–1962	AVERAGE 1946–1951	1961–1962
Cotton	13,393	23,110	54.5	50.8
Wool	2,186	3,277	8.9	7.2
Rayon filament	1,507	2,545	6.1	5.6
Rayon staple fiber	998	3,383	4.1	7.5
Noncellulose man-made fibers	96	1,832	0.4	4.0
Flax	986	1,386	4.1	3.0
Silk	38	71	0.2	0.1
Jute and allied fibers	3,465	7,726	13.9	17.0
Hemp (all types)	1,944	2,583	7.8	5.8
TOTAL	24,613	45,913	100.0	100.0

SOURCE: CEC, *Industrial Fibres*, London, 1963.

While the consumption of food crops takes place continuously, that of industrial crops can be deferred if business conditions deteriorate. Cotton prices can therefore swing wildly, but downswings produce little reduction in supply because the great majority of cotton growers can do little but market as much cotton as they can. Most cotton cultivators are short of cash, and their crop is often mortgaged in advance of the harvest.

In Brazil cotton may be left to develop into a tall, woody shrub, but it is generally treated as an annual crop, a procedure that helps to destroy insect pests. Cotton is widely cultivated between latitudes 30°N and 30°S approximately, but in parts of the intertropical world the rainy season is too long and too wet for the production of quality cotton (Fig. 6-1). Cotton of this type is mainly produced in humid warm temperate climates, although the finest qualities and the highest yields are obtained when the plant is grown with the aid of irrigation in semiarid or desert areas.

Cotton is usually classified according to the fiber length, or staple, for this determines the quality of the spun yarn. Short-staple cottons are those with a fiber length of less than ⅞ inch, and are grown mainly in India and Southeast Asia. Medium, or "middling," kinds, the upland cottons of the United States, have a staple length varying from ⅞ to 1⅛ inches, and are the principal kinds grown in the Americas, in the U.S.S.R., and in parts of intertropical Africa; cottons of this type account for about 85 per cent of world cotton output. The long-staple cottons have fibers exceeding 1⅛ inches in length and produce the finest yarns. The most famous cotton of all is the Sea Island, with fibers up to 2½ inches in length, grown along the Georgia and Florida coasts before the advent of the boll weevil but now cultivated only in certain West Indian islands. Long-staple cottons, however, tend to be confined to arid and semiarid areas, and attempts to grow such types in more humid regions usually result in degeneration. The world's largest producer of long-staple cottons is Egypt, which has developed many famous varieties, such as the Ashmouni, Sakel, and Karnak types. Similar cottons are produced in the irrigated valleys of the Peruvian coast (Tanguis) and in the Sudan. About 3 per cent of United States cotton production consists of long-staple American-Egyptian types, grown in irrigated valleys of the Southwest. The major types of cotton are largely noncompetitive with each other, and long-staple kinds usually command a premium price.

Cotton cultivation requires immense quantities of labor, with marked seasonal peaks at planting, chopping (hoeing), and picking. Cotton would thus appear to be a crop which is best suited to peasant agriculture in the less developed parts of the world. But it is a crop which levies a heavy toll on the soil and on its cultivators, and in most parts of the world cotton farmers are among the poorest of people. In a few areas, however, cotton cultivation is a highly mechanized activity carried on by large-scale corporate enterprises.

The United States

The dominant position of the United States in world cotton production is in some ways anomalous (Table 6-2); it is the legacy of the historical and cultural influences which permitted the continuation, in debased form, of the antebellum nineteenth-century plantation agriculture. Right up to the outbreak of World War II cotton cultivation confirmed in existence a large and poverty-stricken labor force for whom no alternative employment existed and whose level of material welfare was lower than that of any other group in the country.

The expanding textile industries of Western

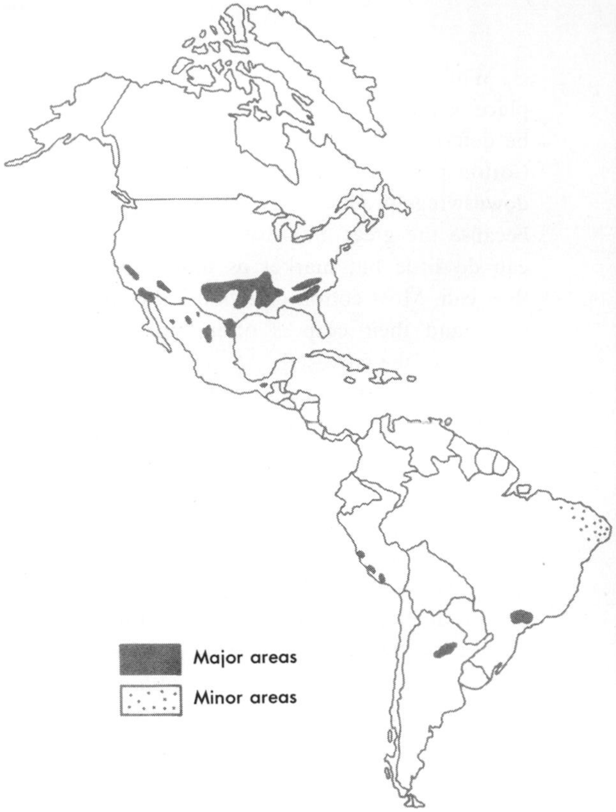

Fig. 6-1 Cotton-producing areas of the world. Much of the world's cotton is still produced in areas with a warm temperate climate, but intertropical producers are slowly enlarging their share of total output.

Major areas

Minor areas

Europe laid the basis of the cotton economy of the old South; with pressure on traditional sources of supply, the cultivation of cotton in the southern United States became extremely profitable, and the invention of the cotton gin opened the way for large-scale production. The labor-supply problem was solved by resurrecting the institution of slavery, which had been on the point of expiring from its sheer economic inefficiency, and rapid depletion of the soil resulting from cotton cultivation was offset by the progressive clearing of new land. The westward march of this speculative development, in many ways similar to that of coffee cultivation in Brazil a few decades later, was arrested partly by increasing aridity but mainly by its polarization as a *casus belli.*

With the abolition of slavery and the end of free virgin land, the old speculative industry disappeared; cotton cultivation could no longer be organized in large units, and it became primarily an occupation of small farmers, the majority of whom were share-tenants. The area under cotton continued to expand, reaching a maximum in 1925, when almost 46 million acres were planted.

Originally a region of mixed farming in which cotton, although the most important cash crop, never occupied more than a very small proportion of the total farmland, the South by the twentieth century had become the cotton belt—a region of small farms overwhelmingly dependent upon cotton and with an agrarian structure that reproduced many of the worst features found in the underdeveloped countries of Asia and Latin America. Even in 1937, by which time there had been a substantial decline in the cotton acreage, almost

three-quarters of American cotton farmers were share-tenants, of whom the majority were colored and produced less than 10 bales each. Of this amount, which represented the limit that one tenant family could pick, one-third was usually turned over to the landowner, but the proportion could reach one-half if the landowner provided seed and mules as well as the land. Moreover, the great majority of such farmers were deeply in debt to local storekeepers and moneylenders (Fig. 6-2).

In certain areas, however, the large holding survived the Civil War and continued to be the dominant form of enterprise. These were areas of deep, rich soils—the bottomlands of the Mississippi, Yazoo, Red, Arkansas, and Tennessee Rivers—where high yields justified the investment in drainage and reclamation that was necessary to bring them under cultivation. In newer areas of cotton cultivation the small-tenant-farmer system never appeared, for here, too, considerable capital was required. This was the situation in much of Texas, long the most important producing state and normally accounting for about 25 to 30 per cent of national output, in irrigated areas of the Southwest, and in the San Joaquin Valley of California. In all of these areas the organization of cotton cultivation has been quite different from that of the old cotton belt of the South (Fig. 6-3).

The decline in the area planted to cotton in the United States from the mid-Twenties has had many causes. One was the growing depredations of the boll weevil, which within three decades of its arrival from Mexico in 1892 had spread across the entire cotton belt. The Great Depression was another powerful cause, and the ensuing price-support legislation which was to introduce the principle of parity linked to

Table 6-2

Cotton Area and Production

	AREA (THOUSAND HECTARES)		COTTON LINT PRODUCTION (THOUSAND METRIC TONS)	
	AVERAGE 1948–1953	1961–1962	AVERAGE 1948–1953	1961–1962
Europe	400	655	60	220
Spain	47	319	8	106
U.S.S.R.	2,274	2,335	970	1,528
North and Central America	10,540	7,320	3,340	3,700
United States	9,798	6,327	3,105	3,117
Mexico	676	793	220	436
South America	3,380	4,290	620	950
Brazil	2,603	3,223	395	606
Peru	151	244	76	134
Asia*	8,020	10,740	1,090	1,750
India	5,659	7,572	485	800
Pakistan	1,245	1,412	245	327
Turkey	474	649	119	200
Mainland China	4,406	n.a.	868	2,410†
Africa	3,210	3,860	700	770
United Arab Republic	761	734	396	336
Sudan	207	477	74	201
WORLD TOTAL	31,900	34,900	7,600	10,900

* Excluding mainland China.
† 1959–1960.
SOURCE: FAO, *Production Yearbook 1962*, Rome, 1963, Table 62.

acreage reductions also had the effect of stimulating production in other parts of the world. By the outbreak of World War II the cotton area had fallen to almost half the 1925 peak, and by 1961 to about a third.

Side by side with reduction in the cotton area a considerable exodus of labor to the North occurred. This migration was accelerated by World War II, which also brought alternative employment into the old cotton area through expanding industrial activity. Increased mechanization both in cultivation and picking, the abandonment of marginal land, and the liberal use of fertilizers have raised cotton yields in the United States, distinctly modest before the war, to among the highest in the world. The mechanization of picking in turn has further stimulated labor emigration, and new crops such as soybeans, peanuts, and forage crops of many kinds have become increasingly important in the older parts of the cotton belt.

While the cotton area in the old South was contracting and a type of mixed farming with increasing attention to livestock was emerging, the cotton area in west Texas, New Mexico, Arizona, and California grew rapidly from 1925 onwards. Texas possessed the advantage of a level topography that encouraged mechanical cultivation, and the drier conditions of the

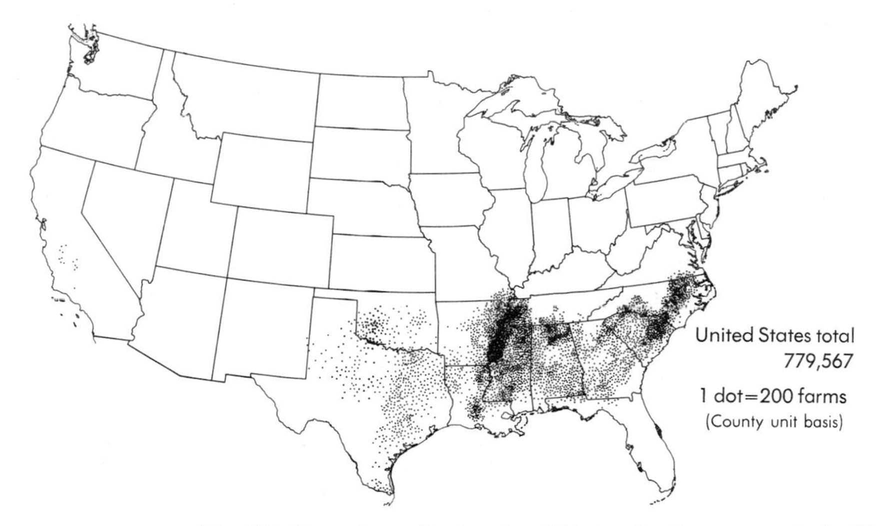

Fig. 6-2 Farms harvesting less than 25 bales of cotton per year in the United States. Farms producing less than 25 bales of cotton annually are widely distributed throughout the "old South," (U.S. Department of Agriculture, 1954.)

western plains provided a check to the boll weevil. Cotton in the Southwestern states is restricted to the irrigated areas of the middle Pecos, Rio Grande, and lower Colorado Valleys, and in California, to the San Joaquin and Imperial Valleys. Yields in the Southwest and in the San Joaquin Valley are three or more times the national average, and the drier con-

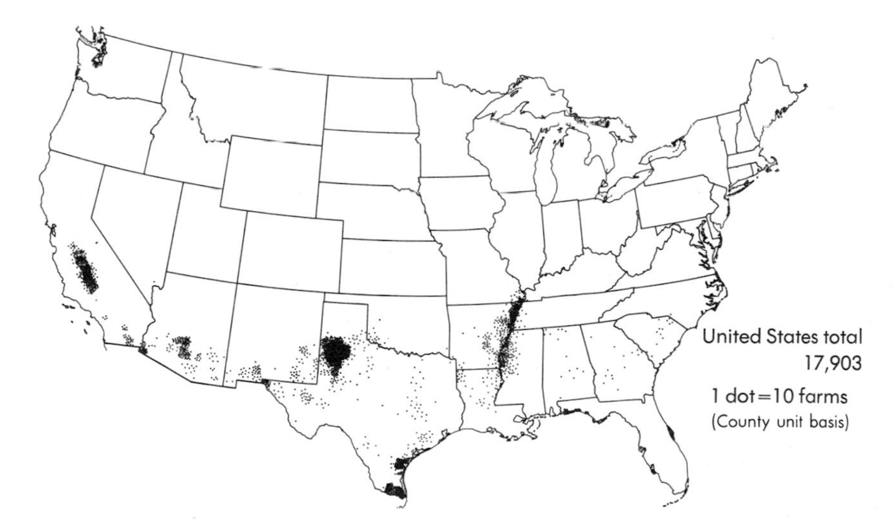

Fig. 6-3 Farms harvesting 100 or more bales of cotton per year in the United States. The large farm units producing 100 or more bales annually are mainly located in California and the Southwest. (U.S. Department of Agriculture, 1954.)

ditions permit the cultivation of some long-staple American-Egyptian varieties; California's production, however, is almost entirely of the medium-staple Acala variety. Large farm units, the use of migrant or Mexican labor, and the extensive employment of mechanical cotton pickers are distinctive features of cotton cultivation in the West. Since 1945 cotton has become California's most important crop by value of output, and the state is exceeded in total production only by Texas and Mississippi.

These changes, however, did not help to redress the imbalance between supply and demand which has existed since the Great Depression, and by the outbreak of World War II, a total of 12 million bales had been accumulated by the United States government under its price-support program. In large measure this surplus stock reflected the loss of export markets to foreign producers, who had been able to expand their output as a result of the pressure exerted by the higher American price level on the world market. In the immediate postwar period world consumption was at a high level, but from 1951 onwards the failure of demand to expand at a rate commensurate with the increase in production again produced an acute surplus problem. Continuous reductions in the American cotton acreage failed to produce any appreciable contraction of output in the face of the higher technical efficiency of American growers. The high internal price level continued to encourage expansion of foreign production, a remarkable growth taking place in Mexico, which by 1960 had raised production to about six times the prewar level to become the third-largest producer of the free world.

In order to help reduce stocks the United States began to make substantial sales under the concessional terms of Public Law 480 from 1956 onwards, but almost 5 million bales were still held by the Commodity Credit Corporation by the end of 1960. This attempt at maintaining a "fair historical share" of about 40 per cent of world cotton exports provoked Mexico and Egypt to make use of barter transactions to protect their trading position. Cotton, although the largest United States export until 1920, now accounts for less than 5 per cent of export earnings; for other producers, however, notably Egypt and other African territories, Mexico, and Peru, the proportion is very much higher, and the price drop resulting from the injection of large quantities of surplus American cotton into the world market meant a substantial loss of foreign exchange.

Egypt

Egypt occupies a distinctive position among world cotton producers. It has long been the largest producer of long-staple cotton, which, apart from being much in demand for quality fabrics, is exclusively utilized for such purposes as sewing cotton. The development of a cotton economy in Egypt, as in the old South, has been mainly responsible for pressing social and economic problems, which are fully the equal of those encountered in the most congested parts of East or South Asia.

Cotton has long been grown in Egypt, but its appearance as a major crop dates from the rule of Mehemet Ali in the first half of the nineteenth century. As Egypt is virtually rainless, all agriculture is dependent upon irrigation, but the traditional irrigation by natural flooding of the Nile is useless for cotton, which, being a summer crop, requires an assured supply of water just when the Nile is at its lowest (April to June). The extension of cotton cultivation thus required the development of perennial irrigation, in which the river level is raised to permit its discharge into distribution canals. Dams and distribution canals were constructed in Upper Egypt (the country upstream from the delta), and in the middle nineteenth century, cultivation spread also into Lower Egypt. This development was greatly accelerated by the American Civil War.

The great extension of irrigation, however, came as a result of the British occupation of 1882 with the construction of regulating dams, such as the Delta barrage and the Asyūt, Isnā, and Naj 'Hammādi dams, and the great storage dams of Aswān and Jebel Aulia, the latter being situated in the Sudan. Another consequence of the British occupation—though it is probable that it merely confirmed a trend which had existed before—was a rapid increase in population. Hence most of the benefits of irrigation flowed to the large landowners, for whom cotton became the most profitable crop. It could not be stolen by hungry *fellaheen* and could always be pledged in advance to a bank. Cotton became, in fact, the basis of the country's credit system, and in Upper Egypt, where large landowners are most powerful, serious food shortages have repeatedly occurred through preoccupation with cotton cultivation.

Most large landowners were absentees, the work of cultivation being performed by tenants. The majority of small owners were also obliged to work on neighboring estates, as their holdings were not large enough to provide for their subsistence throughout the year. The increasing pressure of population inevitably tended to push the level of rents higher, and the shortness and insecurity of tenancies resulted in a high rate of tenancy turnover and rapid exhaustion of the soil. The latter was further accelerated by a rotation system which involved the cultivation of three soil-depleting crops, wheat, corn, and cotton, in two years. Because of the use of irrigation, Egyptian cotton yields are among the highest in the world but the long-term trend shows little evidence of increase; and in view of the primitive methods of cultivation and the limited use of fertilizer, it is hardly surprising that the national average yield of about 450 pounds per acre is only half that realized in California.

Egypt can supply up to two-thirds of the world's fine long-staple cotton, and cottons of this kind (1⅜ inches or longer) normally account for about half the total output of the country. Such cottons are the Gizas, Sakels, and Karnaks, but there is still a substantial production of the medium long-staple kinds (1⅛ to 1⅜ inches) such as the Ashmounis, which have been grown in Egypt for nearly a century. This concentration on long-staple cottons, however, has had two serious consequences. It has been a considerable handicap to the Egyptian cotton-textile industry and to local cloth consumers, for Egyptian cotton is expensive and the import of cheap medium-staple cotton and foreign textiles has long been subject to close regulation. More importantly, the supreme position of the country among long-staple-cotton producers has encouraged government on a number of occasions to attempt to exploit a monopoly position which did not in fact exist. As cotton normally accounts for between 60 and 70 per cent of the export income, it is understandable that government should desire to maximize cotton export earnings; but, as Brazil found with its attempts to influence the world price of coffee, Egypt's acreage restrictions and government cotton purchases in the Twenties and early Thirties merely resulted in an expansion in the output of other producers. These operations particularly benefited the Sudan.[1]

Egypt shares with the United States a recurrent surplus problem, and the price of American cotton has a profound influence on the price of Egyptian cotton. Since 1951, when world cotton supply resumed its prewar tend-

[1] **Charles Issawi,** *Egypt: An Economic and Social Analysis,* **Oxford University Press, London, 1947, p. 66.**

ency to be in excess of demand, Egypt has found considerable difficulty in marketing its cotton at a satisfactory price. This difficulty was enhanced by the estrangement between the Nasser regime which came to power with the revolution of 1954 and the countries of Western Europe that had always constituted the main market for Egyptian cotton. Egypt's reaction to this situation was to make barter deals with the Eastern bloc countries, in exchange for military equipment and other manufactures. On the whole, however, Egypt has not found the experiment a profitable one; the effective "price" paid by the Eastern bloc countries has proved distinctly unfavorable, for they have been unable or unwilling to supply the goods required by Egypt in the quantities contracted for. But despite the signing of financial agreements with Britain and France, which finally disposed of the aftermath of the Suez crisis, Egypt's cotton trade is still largely conducted with the Sino-Soviet bloc.

Cotton and perennial irrigation have created modern Egypt, but the country faces a much more difficult problem than the old South in escaping from a labor-intensive cotton economy. For the *fellaheen* ". . . perennial irrigation has spelt two things: bilharzia and incessant work."[2] Even the South never possessed a situation in which over 90 per cent of all holdings were less than 5 acres and more than 70 per cent were less than 1 acre, as was the case in Egypt in 1939.[3] But improvement in the abysmally low living conditions of the rural population will require far-reaching land reform and the diversion of land from cotton to other crops; improved cotton yields would make this possible and would free land without reducing the country's export income. Whether the Nasser regime's new land reforms, which limit holdings to 100 acres, can accomplish this remains to be seen. In 1961 the cotton export trade was entirely taken over by the state, and it has since acquired all private cotton gins. The Egyptian government, in fact, now has complete control over production, prices, and exports and is, moreover, increasing its share of cotton manufacture. A disastrous 1962 season saw Egypt outranked for the first time as a long-staple-cotton producer by the Sudan, not an auspicious start for the nationalized cotton industry.

[2] *Ibid.*, p. 158.
[3] *Ibid.*, p. 73.

Other Producers

The three largest producers of cotton after the United States are the U.S.S.R., China, and India. Production in the U.S.S.R., now twice that of 1939, is almost entirely confined to Uzbekistan, where cotton is grown under irrigation; both medium- and long-staple varieties are grown. China and India grow mainly short-staple native cottons with some medium-staple American types; both countries make some use of irrigation, although the great bulk of their cotton is grown without supplementary water. India has long endeavored to raise the proportion of middling varieties grown in the country, but cottons of this kind still account for less than 10 per cent of total output. In West Pakistan, where cotton cultivation is entirely dependent on irrigation water, the proportion of medium-staple varieties is much higher.

In the past India has been an important exporter of raw cotton, but the great growth of the domestic cotton-textile industry has led the country to become on balance an importer. The United States, Egypt, and India no longer dominate the world trade in cotton, for there has been a remarkable increase in the number of countries that have become substantial producers of cotton since 1940; Mexico, Argentina, Turkey, many Central American republics,

Spain, and many African countries have all achieved large increases in output. These countries, with the important exception of Mexico and the African countries, produce mainly for the domestic market however, and their increases in raw-cotton production have been linked with the growing tendency for cotton-textile manufacture to gravitate towards areas of cotton cultivation.

The Gezira irrigation scheme of the Sudan, located between the White Nile and the Blue Nile, has an importance out of all relation to its size or to its cotton production. Though it covers only about 1 million acres, about half of which is cultivated every year, the scheme is regarded by many as a model of how economic development in underdeveloped areas should be undertaken.

The Gezira scheme, which came into existence with the completion of the Sennār Dam on the Blue Nile in 1925, involved a tripartite agreement between the state, tenant cultivators, and private capital, but the functions discharged by private capital passed to the control of a public body in 1950. Both the state and the tenant possess a 40 per cent share of the proceeds of the cotton crop, and the nationalized managing agency has 20 per cent. Fertility is preserved by fallows both before and after the cotton crop, but the food crops (principally millets) grown in rotation with cotton by the tenant are entirely his own. Through the use of tractor plowing, selected seed, and scientific research, all provided by the Gezira Board, the yield of cotton is almost a third higher than in Egypt.

This unique scheme eliminates most of the social and economic shortcomings that flow from the fact that there is a strong tendency for the benefits of irrigation and other improvements to pass to the landlords. The Gezira tenants have security of tenure, the benefits of scientific research and competent marketing, and an annual income per head estimated in 1949 at $560 from their holdings of 30 acres or so.[4] Few other farmers of the Middle East or of intertropical Africa enjoy such a standard of living, and it is doubtful if any other crop but cotton, given the geographic and economic environment of the Sudan, could have created it.

In other parts of Africa also, especially in Uganda, commercial cotton cultivation is proving that it can support a standard of living distinctly above that of the average for the continent. Cotton, integrated into a sound peasant agriculture, can be a good servant of economic development; as a cash crop on which the tenant is entirely dependent for his livelihood, it has usually been an obstacle to economic and social well-being.

OTHER VEGETABLE FIBERS

In comparison with cotton all other vegetable fibers are of minor importance; world jute output only equals about 20 per cent by weight of the world's cotton crop and probably only about 5 per cent by value. In the past silk has been one of the most important fibers in world trade, and its price reached fantastic levels during the boom of the Twenties; it seems improbable, however, that either the output or price level of that era can be regained. Silk is, strictly, an animal product, but all economic and social considerations compel its grouping with the vegetable fibers.

Nevertheless, in relation to national and regional economies the minor vegetable fibers can assume considerable importance, and in emergencies shortages are not easily overcome. Jute provides almost 50 per cent of the export income of Pakistan and manufactured jute 20

[4] **Lord Hailey,** *An African Survey,* **rev. ed., Oxford University Press, London, 1957, p. 101.**

per cent of that of India; sisal provides almost 25 per cent of the foreign exchange earnings of Tanganyika and abaca about 10 per cent of those of the Philippines. The production of most minor vegetable fibers is highly localized, and attempts to promote cultivation in other areas have met with little success. But while it is true that the production of a particular type of fiber is usually a marked regional specialty and that each fiber has special advantages for a particular use, many minor fibers compete strongly with each other and almost all face increasing competition from man-made fibers.

Some fibers are used both for apparel and industrial purposes, but most find their main market in only one of these fields. Flax, silk, and Italian hemp are apparel fibers; jute and kenaf constitute the sacking fibers; and abaca and sisal are used for cordage (all cordage fibers are termed "hemps" in the cordage trade). Fiber production involves many types of farming. Sisal, henequen, and abaca production may be regarded as examples of plantation-crop agriculture; jute cultivation is closely associated with sawah agriculture, as is sericulture. Flax and true hemp are produced in a mixed, or crop and livestock, type of farming. Fiber production is thus greatly influenced by the competitive demands made upon the land and labor of the farmer by other crops. Jute production fluctuates in accordance with the relative prices of rice and jute; the heavy labor input required by flax cultivation and fiber preparation, together with the greater profitability of livestock, have driven the crop from much of Western Europe. Flax cultivation for fiber, as distinct from linseed, is increasingly restricted to the lower-labor-cost areas of Eastern Europe and the U.S.S.R., and this is also the case with true hemp.

Most vegetable fibers need immense amounts of labor to produce, and labor with a skill that is born of long experience. It is largely this consideration that is responsible for the fact that the production of many fibers is highly localized. Many regions of the world possess the physical conditions necessary for jute or abaca production, but attempts to develop these industries outside their traditional areas have achieved only meager success; this was the case during World War II, which severely curtailed production of certain fibers. Jute production only regained its prewar level in 1954, and abaca was still below its 1939 level in 1960, so that substitutes have had to be increasingly employed for both.

These exacting labor requirements arise from the nature of the crops themselves. The minor vegetable fibers are either bast, that is, inner-bark, fibers or leaf fibers. Bast fibers such as flax and jute are long and therefore are easily spun, but being annuals their cultivation entails much labor. The production of flax for fiber and true hemp requires meticulous cultivation, close planting, and repeated weeding; jute requires successive thinning as well as weeding. Preparation of bast fibers is also very demanding of labor; it involves retting, that is, steeping in water to remove the gummy material, and stripping, or scutching. Flax can be mechanically scutched, a development rendered mandatory in Western Europe by rising labor costs, but the existence of large quantities of cheap labor has been an obstacle to the development of stripping machinery for jute.

The leaf fibers, on the other hand, which are known in the cordage trade as "hard hemps" to distinguish them from the bast "soft hemp" fibers, are mostly herbaceous perennials whose cultivation does not entail so much labor as the production of bast-fiber crops. Mechanization has made greater progress in separating, or decorticating, leaf fibers, but machinery for the leaf fibers sisal and abaca (the latter usually known in the cordage trade as manila) is expensive, so that its employment is only possible to the large unit, or estate. Thus the cultivation of sisal, henequen, and maguey, leaf fibers which are eminently suitable for low-cost production nonmarine cordage and binder and baler twine, is entirely an estate industry, but the abaca industry of the eastern Philippines is comprised of a smallholder and an estate section. Competition from nylon cordage, which though considerably dearer is more durable, and rising costs of production have resulted in abaca losing ground to its cheaper rival, sisal.

A remarkable feature of the pre-World War II Philippine abaca industry was the existence of a large Japanese colony in the Davao area of Mindanao, which operated the largest unit in the industry (Fig. 6-4). At the end of the war the colonists were repatriated, and the estate, which represented the largest Japanese investment in plantation-crop agriculture outside Taiwan, was broken up and divided among war veterans. Production fell heavily, and the abaca industry continued to suffer from disturbed political conditions.

Sisal production, on the other hand, has continued to expand; this xerophytic plant makes use of land that is generally unsuitable for food production and, once planted, requires comparatively little attention. Labor requirements are limited to periodic harvesting of the leaves, as the process of decortication is highly mechanized. Sisal production is mainly confined to East Africa, particularly Tanganyika and Kenya; cultivation of the closely related henequen is confined to the Yucatan Peninsula of Mexico.

Silk is more exacting in its labor requirements than any other fiber, and its production is only possible to a country that has very large quantities of cheap and highly skilled labor. For this reason and also because the cultivation of mulberries makes good use of sloping land unsuitable for sawah cultivation, more than 95 per cent of the world's production of raw silk is produced in East Asia. The tending of silkworms is traditionally a means whereby the womenfolk of the cultivator's family can enlarge the meager farm income; only a depressed peasantry can provide the low-cost labor force necessary for silk production, and this obstacle has ultimately defeated attempts to perpetuate the industry in other parts of the world. In the nineteenth century France and Italy became substantial producers of finished silk textiles based on locally produced raw silk, but although Lyon and Milan still possess some importance in the manufacture of silk textiles, raw-silk production in France has virtually

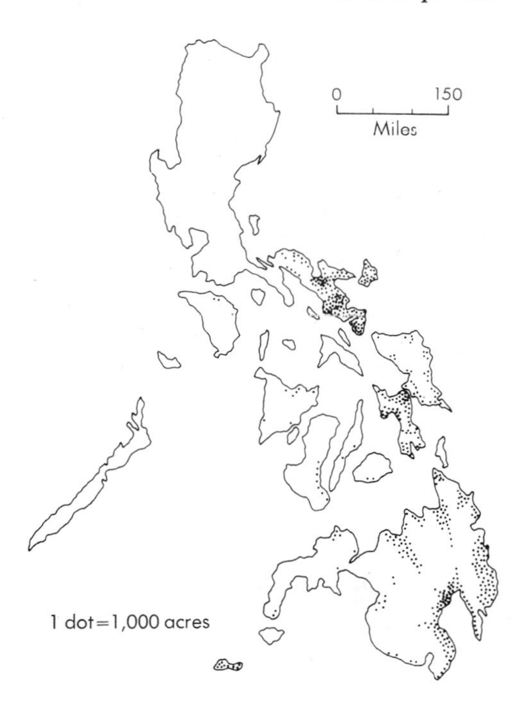

Fig. 6-4 Abaca producing areas in the Philippines. Philippine abaca production is restricted to the eastern portion of the country where there is no dry season; the main focus of production has moved from southeast Luzon to Mindanao, where typhoon damage is less likely. Since the winding up in 1960 of the war-time United States plantations in Guatemala and in Costa Rica, abaca production has been confined to the Philippines and to Sabah (North Borneo).

disappeared and that of Italy trends steadily downwards despite substantial government assistance in both countries. Moreover, European climatic conditions make it impossible to produce more than one crop of mulberry leaves and silkworms per year in contrast to the multiple cropping in the Far East, a disadvantage which further enlarged the cost disparity with the low-labor-cost producers, Japan and China.

The decline of European production was more than offset by expansion in Japan, which between World War I and the Great Depression accounted for almost the entire increase in world output. At the height of the fortunes of the raw-silk industry in 1929, about 2¼ million Japanese peasants were directly engaged in sericulture, and the total employment given by the industry was considerably higher. During World War II the area devoted to mulberries in the Far East was drastically reduced, and in 1946 world raw-silk output was only a quarter of that of the immediate prewar years. Silk production has made a remarkable recovery in Japan since 1950, however, with practically no increase in the mulberry area, which still remains at less than half of the prewar level. This expansion has been achieved through higher-yielding varieties of silkworms and through technical improvements in rearing. Sericulture is still practiced in about 15 per cent of all farmhouses, and in the highland basins of central Honshu it is still carried on in almost every household.

But Japan is no longer a low-labor-cost country, and in Japan's booming post-1950 economy exports of raw silk have been relatively unimportant; in 1961 raw silk accounted for only about 1 per cent of the export income, compared with 12 per cent in 1938 and almost 40 per cent in 1929. The greater part of Japan's production is now consumed at home, and in export markets competition from China, which has markedly lower labor costs, is becoming severe. In China, expansion of the silk industry offers many possibilities of employment for the one factor of production, i.e., labor, that the country possesses in prodigious quantities. China's development plans have contained provision for the extension of the mulberry area, for the training of technicians in sericulture, and for an enhanced output of wild silk.

NATURAL RUBBER

There are many plants that produce the natural plastic termed rubber—*balata, castilloa, ficus elastica,* and *gutta percha.* Some of these are natives of the rain forest of tropical Africa and some occur in the forests of the tropical America—and all had their advocates in the early days of the rubber industry. Also, certain temperate-latitude dandelions figured prominently in experimental rubber production in the interwar years, such as the Mexican *guayule* and the Russian *kok-saghyz*. But the natural rubber of commerce is entirely derived from the latex of *Hevea brasiliensis,* a tree native to the Amazon region, which was planted in large numbers on estates in Southeast Asia from the beginning of the present century.

The growth of the natural-rubber industry that ensued is, perhaps, the most outstanding agricultural success story of the present century; only a little over two decades were necessary to elevate natural rubber to a position of major importance in the world economy. Yet even this short period was enough to create a problem, or what was imagined to be a problem, of surplus production.

Growth and Spread of the Southeast Asia Industry

It is true that the foundations of the natural-rubber industry were laid by Wickham's successful transport of rubber seeds from Brazil in

1876, but in itself this was of little significance. The real founder of the natural-rubber industry was H. N. Ridley of the Singapore Botanic Gardens, whose tapping experiments showed that sustained and continuous latex production was possible from cultivated trees. So long as tapping seriously injured or even killed the tree, rubber had to remain a forest industry; Ridley, however, showed that rubber could be produced as a cultivated crop. The first commercial plantings of rubber in Malaya occurred in 1895, and thereafter development was rapid.

The Europeans who established the estate industry were naturally anxious to undertake production in areas that were under their political control, and as the cost of tapping forms a large part of total costs and the operation requires a certain degree of skill, a cheap and tractable labor force is essential. These two considerations were mainly responsible for the establishment of the industry in dependent territories in Southeast Asia, where a large area with the necessary climatic conditions of year-round high temperature and humidity was under the control of European powers and where a large labor force was either locally available or could easily be imported from India or China.[5] Estate production was already well established in this area before the coming of rubber, particularly on the rich volcanic soils of east Sumatra, where tobacco and coffee estates were planted from 1866 onwards. In Malaya estate production had achieved only moderate success, in part because of unfavorable soil conditions, but rubber's minimal requirements of plant minerals especially suited it to the Malayan environment.

Ridley's work thus enabled Malaya to take full advantage of the rapid growth of the motor-vehicle industry after 1905, which greatly stimulated natural-rubber production; once rubber had proved a success, large numbers of indentured Tamil laborers were brought in to provide the tapping force for the expanding estate area. From Malaya rubber cultivation spread into the Netherlands Indies. Apart from west Java, where large areas had passed into nonindigenous ownership in the early nineteenth century (the famous "P & T" lands), the Agrarian Law limited the possibility of cultivating tree crops in Java, so that attention was turned towards those parts of Sumatra where estate industries were already firmly established.

Other territories in Southeast and South Asia also came to participate in natural-rubber production; large estates were established in Ceylon, Cochin China, and Cambodia; few, however, were prepared to invest in estate production in independent Thailand, and the industry here was largely a creation of Chinese smallholders. One area in which rubber cultivation was not established, somewhat surprisingly, was the Philippines. This was the result of pressure brought by Filipinos on the new American administration not to subject a primitive and little-populated part of the country to the strains resulting from the injection of large amounts of foreign capital. It is possible, however, that the integration of Mindanao into the Philippine nation might have been accelerated by the development of natural-rubber industry.

The five- to seven-year gestation period for rubber initially gave a decided advantage to European companies. The Chinese of Southeast Asia, however, some of whom had considerable experience in large-scale agricultural enterprise, also took up rubber cultivation, eventually on a large scale, and have long occupied a key position as rubber buyers, shippers, and producers, particularly of small-

[5] The Dutch planters of Deli in east Sumatra, who may be said to have initiated large-scale estate production in Southeast Asia, and their British counterparts in Malaya would have preferred to use Chinese labor. The use of Javanese and Indian laborers, respectively, was largely the result of pressure by the Netherlands Indies and Indian governments.

A fortunate few of the world's cotton farmers are able to enjoy very large incomes, but most, as these in Egypt, earn only a meager return for their back-breaking labor.

In processing rubber on an estate in Cambodia, the coagulated rubber is passed through a battery of rollers and sliced into sheets, which are then placed on a trolley for transport to the smokehouse in the background. After a few days the rubber is stabilized, and may be stored indefinitely.

Processing latex to produce sheet is a very simple operation. This Malayan smallholder's coagulating pans are made, as usual, from cut-down kerosene tins. Half an hour after treatment with weak formic acid, the coagulum will be turned out of the pan and mangled, producing sheet ready for treatment in the smokehouse.

Table 6-3

Production of Natural Rubber (Thousand metric tons)

	AVERAGE 1948–1952	1961
North, Central, and South America	30	25
Brazil	22	23
Asia	1,650	1,950
Cambodia	16	40
Ceylon	101	97
Federation of Malaysia	725	820
Malaya and Singapore	661	748
Sarawak and Sabah	64	72
Indonesia	635	682
Thailand	103	186
Vietnamese Republic	36	79
Africa	60	145
Congo (Léopoldville)	10	38
Liberia	31	43
Nigeria	14	56
WORLD TOTAL	1,740	2,120

SOURCE: FAO, *Production Yearbook 1962*, Rome, 1963, Table 67.

holder rubber. Estate workers who had completed their period of service were the first to commence planting rubber on small holdings. Smallholders now account for about 45 per cent of the rubber production of Malaya and about 55 per cent of that of Indonesia. Almost all of Thailand's rapidly growing production is produced by "Chinese" smallholders in peninsular Thailand.[6]

Smallholder production has many advantages, as was indicated in Chapter 4. Smallholders in Malaya and Ceylon, however, now carry a considerable burden as a result of the restriction schemes of the interwar years, which in effect banned new planting. After 1922 new smallholder planting was only possible between the ending of the Stevenson restriction scheme (1922 to 1928) and the International Rubber Agreement (1934 to 1941); as a result the age composition of smallholders' trees is very unfavorable, a very large proportion being over forty years old and of low productivity. These restriction schemes, largely introduced as a result of pressure from estate industries in two British dependencies, were quite unavailing, moreover; their effect was to stimulate production in the Netherlands Indies and, when that area itself became a party to a restriction, in Borneo, Thailand, Indochina, and African countries (Table 6-3).

The Present Situation and Future Prospects

World War II transformed the rubber industry, for within four years a new industry capable of producing nearly a million tons of

[6] **From the legal standpoint they are Thais, as only Thais can own land in Thailand. But most rubber smallholders are of Chinese or of mixed Chinese ancestry.**

synthetic rubber was created.[7] Even without the war, however, a synthetic-rubber industry would have appeared sooner or later; world natural-rubber production is now unable to supply the total demand for rubber, and it is clear that an expanding share of total consumption will be met by synthetic.

Nevertheless, there is reason for believing that natural rubber will never lack a market if it can match the price of synthetic. For most prewar years the price of natural rubber not only has been well above that of synthetic but also has fluctuated considerably. This high degree of price instability encourages manufacturers to substitute the comparatively stable-priced synthetic rubber for natural rubber wherever possible. The reasons for the violent swings in natural-rubber prices are largely to be traced to the cyclical demand for rubber by the motor-vehicle industry, the largest single user of natural rubber, and a short-term inflexibility of supply common to all tree crops. As the contribution of natural rubber to total supply diminishes the amplitude of these oscillations should decline.

Opportunities for cost reduction in the natural-rubber industry are very considerable. With high-yielding clones[8] it is possible to get more than a ton of rubber to the acre, whereas the national average in Malaya, the largest producer of natural rubber, is only about 600 pounds; replanting or new planting with high-yielding clones produces a remarkable reduction in unit costs. Since 1952 one of the most remarkable efforts in the history of tropical agriculture has taken place in Malaya as the country has endeavored to replace its stock of aged, low-yielding trees. Through government-assisted replanting schemes, financed by a cess on exports, Malaya between 1952 and 1961 replanted or new-planted a total of nearly 1.1 million acres of rubber, nearly a third of the total rubber acreage in the earlier year (Fig. 6-5). As new high-yielding trees come into bearing, output per tapped acre must progressively rise; by 1963 the yield per tapped acre for high-yielding material on European estates was nearly 1,100 pounds.

Malaya's rubber area remained virtually stationary for many years, but after the achievement of independence in 1957 the planted area began to grow rapidly as government pursued policies favorable to the smallholders (Fig. 6-6). Land was made available for new planting, though much of this has taken place on large planned smallholder settlement schemes whose management rests with a state authority. Considerable smallholder replanting has also taken place, though the fact that smallholders cannot forgo income while waiting for their new planting to come to maturity has kept the rate of replanting below that planned. At the same time, the political climate has not been unfavorable to estates, and European companies have raised their proportion of high-yielding rubber to over 70 per cent of their total planted area.

This immense Malayan effort in new planting and replanting has been accompanied by considerable research into methods of producing rubber with special technical characteristics, into improved packing and grading, and into finding new markets for natural rubber. While it is true that proportionate expenditure on research is still less than in the synthetic industry, there is abundant evidence of the determination of the Malayan natural-rubber industry to maintain a high level of competitive efficiency. Since 1957 Malaya has regained the position of world's largest rubber producer and it appears likely to retain it in the future.

In Indonesia, on the other hand, replanting and new planting have not been carried out on a scale sufficient to maintain competitive

[7] See Chap. 19, pp. 514–516.

[8] A clone is a race of plants with a common genetic inheritance, so that every individual, therefore, has identical characteristics.

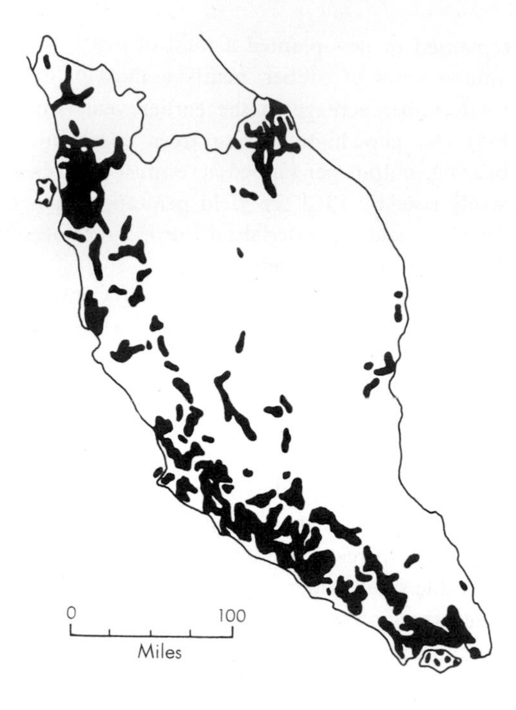

Fig. 6-5 Area alienated for rubber in Malaya. Greater accessibility and improved transport facilities resulting from the growth of tin mining have been responsible for the location of much of Malaya's rubber land in the western portion of the country. In the east, primitive transport and the sterilization of large areas in "Malay Reservations" acted as strong deterrents to rubber planting.

efficiency. Restrictions of all kinds have been placed on the operations of estates, and difficulties over renewal of land leases have discouraged new investment. All Dutch-owned estates were taken over by the state in 1958, and British-owned properties were also seized in 1963 as a result of British military support for the new state of Malaysia in meeting Indonesia's policy of armed "confrontation." Smallholders in Sumatra and Borneo have been exploited by government marketing schemes, and although a replanting scheme has been established on paper, there is an acute shortage of selected planting material to implement it. With an increasingly unfavorable age composition a reduction in the productivity of Indonesia's rubber trees is inevitable, and output must decline in the near future. Considerable new planting with high-yielding material, however, has also taken place in formerly British Borneo (now Sarawak and Sabah, both included within the Federation of Malaysia) and in several African countries, particularly Nigeria.

This expansion of rubber cultivation has much to commend it, for in many ways the rubber tree is unique among tropical crops. It produces a regular income with a modest and continuous labor input, so that seasonal un-

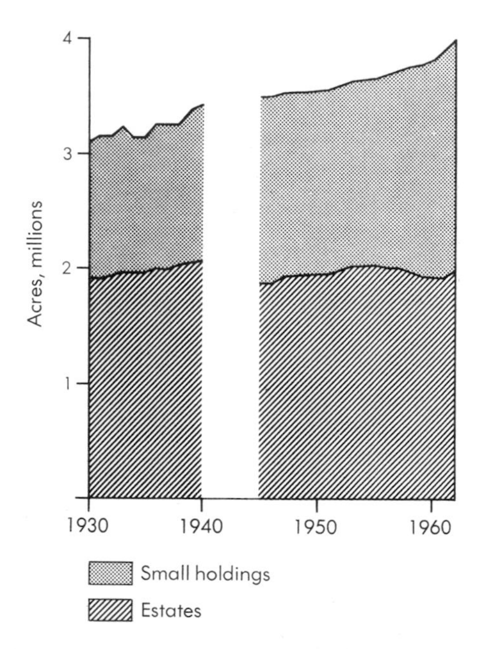

Fig. 6-6 Area planted to rubber in Malaya. After a long period of restriction, the area of smallholder rubber in Malaya began to grow rapidly after the achievement of independence in 1957.

employment is unknown; it tolerates a wide variety of soils and is in no way soil-depleting; it can withstand considerable neglect and so is not injured if low prices make tapping uneconomic. If the motor-vehicle industry can maintain a high rate of growth—and the opportunities for further expansion are still enormous—the natural-rubber industry has an assured future. Nevertheless, it is largely to the expansion of commercial vehicle production that the natural rubber industry must pin its hopes, for the automobile tire market has largely been lost to synthetics.

TOBACCO

Tobacco is one of the great crops of the world; it is grown in almost every country in middle and low latitudes and, with the exception of corn, is more widely cultivated than any other major crop. Moreover, the world area sown to tobacco and world output are both increasing very rapidly; in 1961 world tobacco output was some 80 per cent above that of the years preceding World War II (Table 6-4). Although tobacco is here regarded as an industrial crop in that it supports a large manufac-

Table 6-4 *Tobacco Area and Production*

	AREA (THOUSAND HECTARES)		PRODUCTION (THOUSAND METRIC TONS)	
	AVERAGE 1948–1953	1961–1962	AVERAGE 1948–1953	1961–1962
Europe	390	425	380	350
Greece	84	102	49	74
Bulgaria	74	96	45	56
U.S.S.R.	213	150	157	175
North and Central America	855	690	1,130	1,200
Canada	43	56	62	95
Cuba	55	55	34	47
United States	674	475	958	935
South America	225	310	195	270
Brazil	149	227	113	167
Asia	895	1,185	720	975
India	331	400	247	311
Indonesia	n.a.	200	n.a.	79
Pakistan	69	80	70	86
Philippines	37	100	22	70
Turkey	122	140	91	102
Mainland China	186	n.a.	220	n.a.
Africa	255	285	140	205
Southern Rhodesia	67	91	44	111
WORLD TOTAL	2,940	3,360	2,830	3,600

SOURCE: FAO, *Production Yearbook 1962,* Rome, 1963, Table 61.

turing industry, tremendous quantities of tobacco are grown for local consumption, and only a small proportion enters world trade.

Tobacco consumption is closely related to income levels, and the postwar increase in consumption in part reflects the higher living standards in many parts of the world. The pattern of consumption is also closely influenced by the various fiscal policies pursued by governments, for tobacco is universally regarded as a major source of revenue. Thus tobacco is subject to more regulation than any other crop; cultivation, curing, manufacture, and trade may all be closely controlled or even organized as a state monopoly.

The remarkably widespread distribution of tobacco cultivation arises from the fact that virtually every society has adopted the habit of smoking. As an annual crop with a short growing season, it can be cultivated even at such comparatively high latitudes as that of southern Sweden, and it can also be grown during relatively dry periods in the humid tropics. Despite this wide climatic tolerance, however, the greater part of the world's tobacco is produced in temperate latitudes.

The properties of tobacco are closely affected by the soil and climatic conditions under which it is grown, and in the production of the highest-quality tobaccos attempts are made to modify both. Certain restricted areas possess such favorable conditions of soil and climate that they are world-renowned for their production of high-quality tobaccos; such are the Vuelta Abajo district of Pinar del Rio Province in western Cuba, the Deli area of east Sumatra, and the Connecticut Valley in the United States, all producers of cigar tobaccos. The quality of tobacco is also affected by the curing treatment, which may be carried out by exposing the leaf to sun and air or by means of heat, as in fire or flue curing. A modern technique is homogenization, which enables inferior leaf to be upgraded, but the process is largely restricted to the higher-priced specialty tobaccos.

The Four Types of Tobacco

Although every major producing country grows many kinds of tobacco, it is possible to classify tobaccos into four major types. These are light flue-cured tobaccos (known in the trade as Virginia tobaccos), Oriental tobaccos, cigar tobaccos (which include fillers, binders, and wrappers), and all other tobaccos;[9] the last type consists mainly of dark air- and fire-cured tobaccos, grown in Asia for local use.

Of these four major types the first two are by far the most important, as they are principally used in the manufacture of cigarettes. The continued and worldwide growth in the popularity of cigarettes as against other forms of tobacco consumption is by far the most significant trend in the tobacco industry, and the great postwar increase in tobacco production is almost entirely accounted for by expansion in the output of tobaccos of this kind; light flue-cured tobaccos account for almost a third of the world's total production, and the proportion is increasing steadily. The production of such tobaccos is heavily concentrated in North America and accounts for almost two-thirds of total United States production, but it is expanding in many other continents, particularly in Africa, where it has already assumed a position of major importance in the economies of Southern Rhodesia and of certain other ex-British territories.

Oriental, or Turkish, tobaccos are grown widely in those parts of southeast Europe that once formed part of the Ottoman Empire and in the Levant. There are many famous specialty tobaccos in this class, such as Sobranje and Latakia. While Turkish tobaccos have never

[9] **Food and Agriculture Organization,** *Tobacco,* **Commodity Bulletin Series, no. 20, Rome, 1952, pp. 4–6.**

been popular in the British market, traditionally they have appealed to the central European countries. However, this preference for Turkish tobaccos has been greatly influenced by political and economic considerations; Nazi Germany attempted to use its position as the largest buyer of these tobaccos to bring southeast Europe within its political and economic orbit. The two world wars greatly reduced the production of Turkish tobaccos, but there has been a substantial increase in output since 1950. As a result of the increased American influence in central Europe born of World War II, American-type cigarettes have become very popular in West Germany, and it is unlikely that the 1939 consumption pattern will be restored. Nevertheless, Turkish tobaccos have succeeded in making some limited appeal in the British market, and exports to the United States and to other non-European countries are at a much higher level than before World War II.

The cigar tobaccos are predominantly dark tobaccos. Their production is declining, partly because of the increasing preference for cigarettes and partly because of political and economic difficulties in the countries in which they are grown. Much cigar tobacco is produced by foreign estates in the tropics, and in both Cuba and Indonesia, which produce the finest filler and wrapper tobaccos, respectively, it is not possible to foresee any changes in the near future that would make estate production more attractive.

World Production, Trade, and Consumption

Many types of farming are involved in tobacco cultivation. Very large quantities are produced both in sawah and intensive dry-field agriculture, China and India being the second- and third-largest producers, respectively, in the world. In central and east Java tobacco was produced by European companies on sawah land in a manner similar to that of sugar, although the cultivation was carried out by local farmers under contract to the "estate" companies. Since 1950, however, the production of dark filler tobaccos has been displaced by the cultivation of flue-cured types for domestic consumption, and the role of the former "estate" companies has been taken over by cooperatives. The tobacco planters of the Deli area of the east Sumatra, where tobacco was grown under estate conditions, early evolved a unique method of cultivation, in effect a refinement of shifting cultivation, in which tobacco was grown only once in eight years, the land being then allowed to revert to secondary forest; experience had shown that more frequent cropping produced a deterioration in quality. Large areas of land were therefore necessary, and the local population was allowed to take a dry-rice crop after the tobacco harvest. Since the Japanese occupation of the Netherlands Indies during World War II, the tobacco estates have been invaded by squatters, and successive Indonesian governments have made no attempt to dislodge them. With the nationalization of the great Dutch companies in 1958, there has been little prospect of rehabilitating the Deli tobacco industry.

In the United States and in Western Europe, tobacco is grown as a crop in a system of mixed farming involving carefully selected crop rotations which may also include fallows. Yields under this mixed-farming type of production are very much higher than those achieved elsewhere, and, largely through the extended use of fertilizers, are continuing to increase. The production of many specialty tobaccos, however, appears to require soils of low productivity, and the application of fertilizer merely results in a deterioration of quality.

Irrespective of the type of farming, tobacco

cultivation makes great demands on both labor and land. More than 400 man-hours may be required to cultivate an acre under tobacco, and although some operations can now be performed by mechanical equipment, there are many, including harvesting and grading, that have to be performed by hand. Tobacco is sown in a specially prepared seedbed, and the seedlings require transplanting in the field. The growing plants also need frequent cultivation and regular inspection for pest damage; in the case of cigar wrapper tobaccos, which must be free of holes, the latter operation is of fundamental importance.

The United States is the world's largest producer, consumer, and exporter of tobacco (Fig. 6-7). Before World War II it produced almost half the world's tobacco (excluding those countries now within the Eastern bloc), but in the postwar period its share of world output has tended to decline in the face of a more rapid increase in production elsewhere. Though American output is substantially above the prewar level, this has been achieved, as in the case of cotton, on a greatly reduced area. Yields of all tobaccos have been raised above the prewar level, but the increase has been most striking in cigarette tobaccos, that is, in the light flue-cured tobaccos and burley, a light air-cured type which has been much in demand for cigarette blending with the increasing popularity of filter-tipped cigarettes. The average yield for these types of tobaccos in the late Fifties was half as much again as in the prewar years, an increase achieved largely through better knowledge of fertilizer techniques. Flue-cured and burley tobaccos account for almost 90 per cent of national tobacco output, the balance consisting largely of dark fire-cured and cigar tobaccos. The production of cigar wrappers and binder tobaccos is a specialty which was already at a high level of technical efficiency before World War II, so that the postwar increase in yields has been only modest. In the middle Connecticut Valley and in the Quincy district of Florida, high-quality wrapper tobaccos are grown under a protective covering of cheesecloth, which helps to reduce moisture losses from evaporation and transpiration. This practice is also employed in several tropical areas specializing in high-quality cigar tobaccos.

Of the principal tobacco-growing districts of the United States the inner Coastal Plain and the Piedmont are the principal producing areas (Fig. 6-8); North Carolina alone accounts for over 40 per cent of the national output. West of the Appalachians, Kentucky and Tennessee constitute the only important producing areas. The greater part of American tobacco has traditionally been produced by very small farmers, the majority of whom are tenants; except in limited specialty areas the development of large-scale highly mechanized production has been much slower than in the case of cotton. But tobacco cultivation depends not only on soil and climate but also on the relative profitability of other crops. Tobacco is one of the major crops supported at a high level of parity, and this support is conditional upon the acceptance of acreage allotments. In the postwar period tobacco has been relatively more profitable than most other crops, and growers have been able to defeat the purpose of acreage restriction by raising yields. As with wheat, corn, cotton, and rice, large surpluses have been created.

World trade in unmanufactured tobacco is only a small proportion of total production; the United States normally exports about one-quarter of its output, almost all in the form of cigarette tobaccos. Although tobacco exports in most postwar years have been substantially above the 1939 level, the dollar shortage and trade restrictions have prevented the United States from reaping the fullest benefit from the increasing preference for Virginia-type tobaccos and American-style

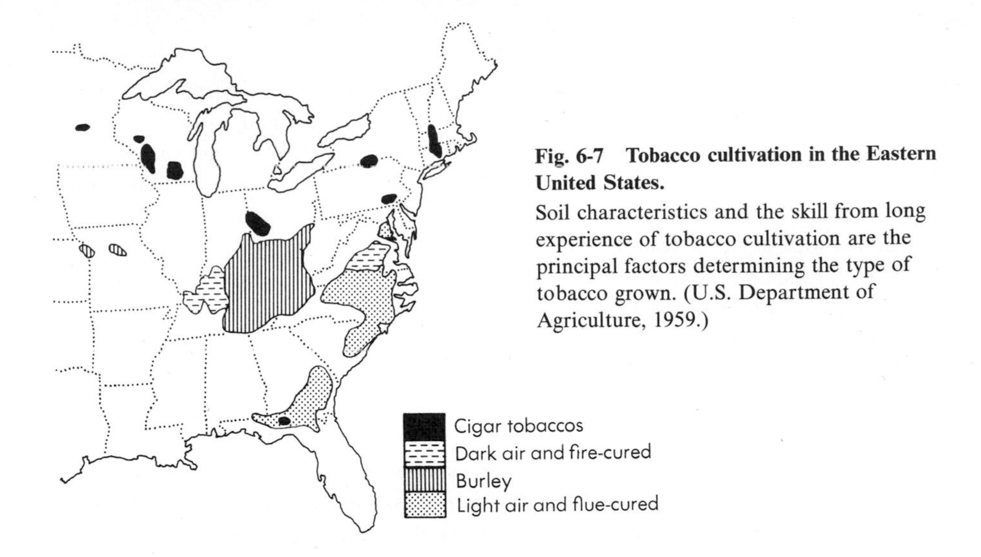

Fig. 6-7 Tobacco cultivation in the Eastern United States.
Soil characteristics and the skill from long experience of tobacco cultivation are the principal factors determining the type of tobacco grown. (U.S. Department of Agriculture, 1959.)

cigarettes. In order to reduce surplus stocks large Public Law 480 sales have been made, although since 1959 the volume of concessional exports has diminished. The world preference for American tobaccos has led most American cigarette manufacturers to invest heavily in overseas plants; Britain, however, largely because of balance-of-payments difficulties, has purchased less American tobacco in most postwar years than formerly, and its consumption of Commonwealth Virginia-type tobaccos, produced mainly in the Rhodesias, has expanded greatly. Only in Greece, Turkey, and Southern Rhodesia does tobacco account for a large proportion of the export income.

Increasing world population and indus-

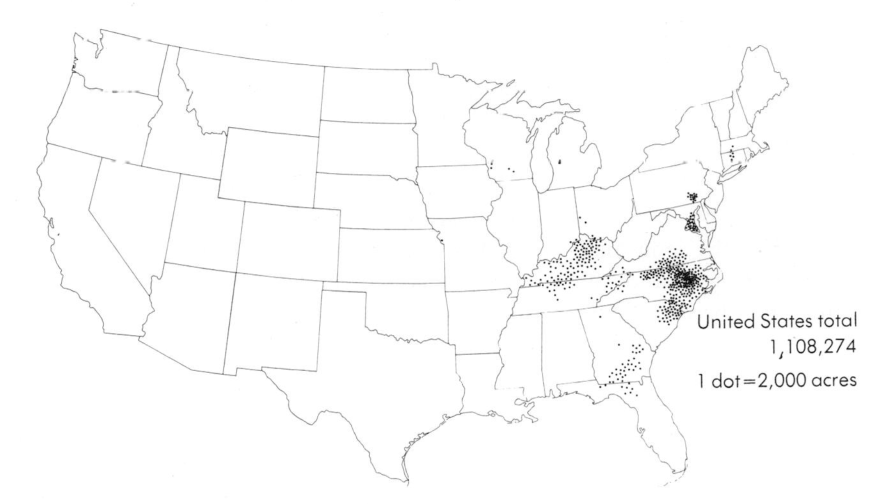

Fig. 6-8 Tobacco harvested in the United States.
Tobacco cultivation occurs in many Eastern states, but North Carolina accounts for more than 40 per cent of the United States output. (U.S. Department of Agriculture, 1959.)

trialization in semideveloped and underdeveloped economies make it highly likely that the present rate of increase in world consumption will continue for some time to come. There is no direct substitute for tobacco; its competitors are really other semiluxuries such as confectionery or alcoholic beverages, and the habit of smoking, once acquired, is hard to give up. Even heavy taxation may make little difference to consumption, apart from driving consumers to cheaper types of tobacco. So far the evidence of a possible connection between lung cancer and tobacco consumption has failed to effect any significant decline in consumption, although in several countries there was a temporary drop during the middle Fifties. If the evidence for a strong connection becomes overwhelming, and already there are organizations that are entirely convinced on existing evidence, governments would find themselves placed in a difficult position.[10] It is highly likely, however, that further research into possible tobacco carcinogens will indicate ways of overcoming this problem, and a substantial decline in consumption in any country where the present per capita consumption is high appears improbable in the near future.

THE PROSPECTS FOR INDUSTRIAL CROPS

Our common theme links the industrial crops. Nearly all require large quantities of labor to produce and this labor, because of its generally low productivity, earns a poor reward. Natural rubber and some perennial vegetable-oil crops, however, are outstanding in offering to the cultivator the possibility of a considerable income with a modest labor input.

Largely through increased labor costs since the end of World War II, industrial-crop production in many countries has remained fairly static. There is no reason for believing that the world is prepared to pay substantially higher prices for its industrial raw materials to meet these enhanced costs. The evidence suggests that the reverse is more likely to be the case, for it is fairly certain that man-made synthetic products will continue to set the price pattern; it was correctly remarked that "Malaya can do nothing to alter the cost of synthetic rubber; she can only conform to it."[11] A somewhat similar observation might well be made about the vegetable-fiber-producing countries. Rayon-staple fiber has been the cheapest textile fiber for some years; its share of world fiber consumption trends continually upwards, and newer noncellulose synthetic fibers show a similar growth pattern. With expanding output and improved technology, unit costs of most synthetic raw materials will continue to fall. In the case of natural rubber there is scope for a parallel reduction of unit costs, but it is not easy to see any comparable opportunity for the more labor-intensive industrial crops. That it is occasionally possible, however, even in underdeveloped economics, to reduce labor requirements for industrial-crop production by substituting capital equipment, is shown by the Gezira scheme in the Sudan.

In highly developed economics, on the other hand, industrial-crop production had long been overpopulated before World War II, and in the postwar period intense mechanization led to a

[10] As a result of pressure from the British Medical Association, the Ministry of Health in 1963 began a national campaign to bring to the notice of the public the great hazard to health of heavy smoking. A survey conducted by the association in 1962 to ascertain the smoking habits of doctors revealed a very substantial decline in tobacco consumption since the first evidence of a causal connection between smoking and lung cancer appeared. In several European countries, restrictions have been placed on advertisements for cigarettes.

[11] *Report of the Mission of Enquiry into the Rubber Industry of Malaya* (Mudie report), Government Printer, Kuala Lumpur, 1954, p. 6.

rapid exodus of workers. The survival of industrial crop production in such economies will demand still higher levels of mechanization in the future.

SELECTED REFERENCES

Bauer, Peter T.: *The Rubber Industry: A Study in Competition and Monopoly,* Longmans, Green & Co., Ltd., London, 1948.

Brown, C. H.: *Egyptian Cotton,* Leonard Hill, London, 1955.

Commonwealth Economic Committee: *Industrial Fibres,* H. M. Stationery Office, London, annually.

———: *Plantation Crops,* H. M. Stationery Office, London, annually.

Durand, Loyal, Jr., and E. T. Bird: "The Burley Tobacco Region of the Mountain South," *Economic Geography,* vol. 26, pp. 263–282, 1950.

Food and Agriculture Organization: *Commodity Survey 1962,* Rome, 1962.

———: *Jute,* Commodity Bulletin Series, no. 28, Rome, 1960.

———: *Per Caput Fiber Consumption Levels,* Commodity Bulletin Series, no. 31, Rome, 1960.

———: *Tobacco,* Commodity Series Bulletin, no. 20, Rome, 1952.

Garner, Wightman W.: *The Production of Tobacco,* McGraw-Hill Book Company, New York, 1951.

Hance, William A.: "The Gezira: An Example in Development," *Geographical Review,* vol. 44, pp. 253–270, 1954.

Indian Central Jute Committee: *Jute in India,* Calcutta, 1959.

Large, David C.: "Cotton in the San Joaquin Valley: A Study of Government in Agriculture," *Geographical Review,* vol. 47, pp. 365–380, July, 1957.

Ooi Jin Bee: "The Rubber Industry of Malaya," *The Journal of Tropical Geography,* vol. 15, pp. 46–65, 1961.

Prunty, Merle C., Jr.: "Recent Quantitative Changes in the Cotton Belt of the Southeastern States," *Economic Geography,* vol. 27, pp. 189–208, 1951.

Silcock, T. H. (ed.): *Readings in Malayan Economics,* Eastern University Press, Singapore, 1961, pp. 233–316.

Spencer, J. E.: "Abacá and the Philippines," *Economic Geography,* vol. 27, pp. 95–106, 1951.

Woytinsky, W. S., and E. S. Woytinsky: *World Population and Production,* The Twentieth Century Fund, New York, 1953, pp. 595–629.

Chapter 7

LIVESTOCK AND LIVESTOCK PRODUCTS

Man makes use of animals for food, as beasts of burden and for work purposes, as providers of industrial raw materials, and for recreation. The total number of animal species that serve these ends is larger than is often supposed, but very few are of major importance in the world economy.

MAN'S CHOICE AND DEVELOPMENT OF LIVESTOCK

With the same genius that characterized his selection of the cereals as his main food crops, man unerringly chose the bovoids as the principal providers of the livestock products that he needed. The bovoids and the horses are grazing animals with a specialized diet, both groups of animals being capable of digesting cellulose.[1] The keeping of these animals necessitates access to large areas of grazing or, where this is not possible, the cultivation of supplementary feeds; thus they cannot find a place in all types of farming. The real costs of keeping bovoids are relatively high, and this is reflected in the prices realized by cattle and sheep products. Nations at a low level of economic development with high population densities cannot afford either to maintain large areas of pasture or to permit the large calorie loss incidental to animal production dependent on fodder crops.

In contrast to the bovoids, the swine and the fowl are found almost wherever agriculture is practiced. These animals were originally forest dwellers with a generalized diet and in large measure can be left to forage for themselves; they reproduce easily and quickly and demand so little care that they can be kept as a part-time activity. In many types of farming,

[1] **A new machine capable of producing protein suitable for human consumption from miscellaneous vegetation has now been perfected, and could have far-reaching consequences in underdeveloped economies.**

therefore, the real cost of keeping these animals can be very low. Nevertheless, in advanced economies pig and poultry farming can also constitute highly specialized and capital-intensive activities, and in such economies small pig and poultry keepers tend to be high-cost producers.

One bovoid, the goat, does possess some of the economic characteristics of the swine and the fowl. The goat is a browsing as well as a grazing animal; indeed, the most important characteristic of the goat is its ability to pick up a living from a sparse and stunted vegetation, particularly in hilly terrain where no other domestic animal could survive. Under such conditions the productivity of the animal is very low, but it is achieved at little real cost; hence the attractiveness of the goat to the peasants of the Mediterranean region and of the Old World deserts. The goat is a dual-purpose animal, but it is a very good dairy goat indeed that can produce 400 gallons of milk per year, whereas a prize dairy cow can yield five or more times this quantity. In the highly developed economies of middle latitudes goats cannot normally compete with cattle for dairy purposes, for the latter permit a much higher productivity per worker; for this reason the keeping of dairy goats is usually either a smallholder or a specialist activity.

Man's principal domesticated animals have proved just as pliable as his crops. New varieties have been bred to fit into different environments and to meet new needs or supply existing needs more efficiently. Sheep, originally inhabitants of the mountainous zones of the Northern Hemisphere, now range the interior plains and plateaus of the southern continents in vast numbers. Zoologically, the difference between an animal from a Bantu herd and an Aberdeen Angus, or between a potbellied Chinese pig and a Landrace, may not amount to very much; from the economic standpoint, however, it is profound. But it has not been possible to achieve a successful adaptation of the more important domesticated animals to every type of climate and terrain even with selective breeding, and there are a number of species, such as the camel, llama, water buffalo, and yak, which, though of fundamental importance in the economic life of considerable portions of the earth's surface, are of minor significance in the world as a whole.

By means of selective breeding and modifications of the environment, such as the provision of bores and watering facilities in arid and semiarid areas and the use of buildings to house animals through long and severe winters, man has greatly extended the geographic range of his animals. Nevertheless, for most livestock products there are optimum physical conditions which make for low-cost production. Dairying can be carried on within the humid tropics; but under such conditions it can never hope to equal the low costs of production in areas with moist temperate climates, where grass growth is possible through much of the year and where there are few obstacles to the establishment and maintenance of good pastures.

The production of one kind of livestock product often involves others. Hides and tallow are joint products with beef, and substantial quantities of beef and veal are produced in dairy farming. Wool is associated with mutton and lamb, and lard with pig meat. It is often possible to effect some variation in the output of such joint products, either by changes in the management of the stock or by the use of different breeds. Multipurpose animals provide some insurance against price movements; dairy cattle that will produce acceptable beef, or sheep that will yield wool and drop lambs that will quickly fatten to marketable size, are often preferred to animals whose profitability is dependent upon only one product. Such multipurpose breeds are common in the commercial crop and livestock type of farming, particularly in Europe. On the other hand, physical and economic considerations may be so favorable to one line of production that there is no question of switching production. Under such conditions farmers have to rely on periods of high prices to compensate them for losses sustained when times are bad.

Many complex factors influence the size and composition of the world's livestock population. Natural and man-made calamities, particularly droughts and wars, periodically result in great losses. Droughts are a major hazard in the commercial grazing type of farming, which presses closely upon the arid regions of continental interiors. Tremendous losses were inflicted on livestock in Europe and Asia during World War II, but despite continued political disturbances in much of Asia, these were largely made good by 1955. World livestock numbers trend steadily upwards under the pressure of increasing population, and although there are several important disparities, the world distribution of livestock is closely related to the distribution of population. In highly developed economies, however, pig and poultry numbers appear to be susceptible to short-period cyclical fluctuations which arise from excessive optimism or pessimism by producers over future prospects.

Any discussion of livestock numbers must take into consideration the enormous disparities in the productivity of animals over space and time. In highly developed economies the productivity of livestock has been raised prodigiously over the past few decades by improved methods of breeding and feeding.[2] Animals mature more quickly and hence consume less food; their proportion of waste or inedible products has also been reduced. The rate of reproduction has been accelerated, particularly by the use of artificial insemination. An enormous livestock population of low productivity such as exists in India, which has almost one-fifth of the world's cattle, can be of less economic significance than a very much smaller number of highly productive animals.

[2] **This improved productivity is strikingly illustrated by New Zealand, the world's lowest-cost producer of many livestock products. Between 1921 and 1960 the average butterfat yield per dairy cow increased by 37 per cent, the average annual lamb production for each 100 breeding ewes rose from 83 to 97, and annual wool production per sheep rose by almost 25 per cent.**

Work Animals

So great has been the decline in the number of work animals in Western countries over the past three or four decades through the increased employment of the automobile, truck, and farm tractor that the fundamental importance of work animals in the world as a whole is apt to be overlooked. It is, for example, only through the employment of some 90 million buffaloes that sawah agriculture is able to support more than one-third of the world's population. The correlation between the distribution of buffaloes and sawah agriculture is striking, for no other domesticated animal is so closely associated with a single type of agriculture. India, China, and Pakistan together possess more than two-thirds of the world's buffalo numbers, and the balance is almost entirely accounted for by Southeast Asia.

There is no means of ascertaining how many of the world's 900 million cattle are employed for work purposes, but the number must be very large. Oxen are the principal draft animals in the intensive dry-field type of agriculture; in southern Europe and in many parts of Latin America the plow is more likely to be drawn by oxen than by any other animal, and indeed, oxen were extensively used for plowing in western and central Europe until quite modern times. Over much of Asia and Latin America the creaking oxcart is still an

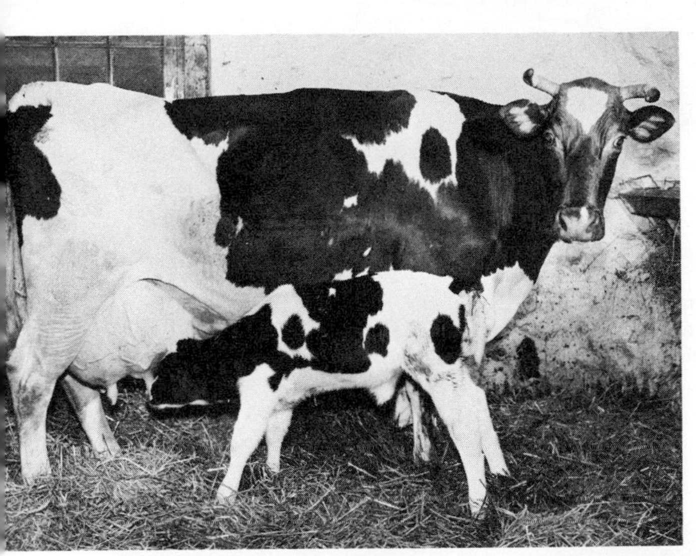

The enormous disparities in the productivity of the world's livestock are strikingly suggested by comparison of an African cow with a pedigree animal.

Improvements effected by over 150 years of selective breeding are apparent in this juxtaposition of a prize merino with a descendant of McArthur's original merino flock, introduced in Australia in 1796.

This American dairy farm and battery house illustrate modern methods of livestock production. Through ample, automatic feeding, and close confinement, the bodily activity of the animal is reduced; its energies are directed to putting on weight rapidly or to producing more milk, eggs, or other products.

important means of transport in the rural areas. As a draft animal the ox has many virtues; it is strong, does not need to be shod, and is easily yoked by the horns. Its principal disadvantage is that its work rate is slow in comparison with that of the horse.

For speed and tractability the horse is unsurpassed among draft animals. The horse was used from very early times for riding and as a pack animal, but its use for farm and general draft purposes had to await the invention of the hard collar, a discovery that was not made until the Middle Ages. With the aid of this invention horses were able to supplant ox teams for plowing in Western and central Europe, an operation in which their superior speed was a decided advantage. Outside Europe, however, and other temperate latitudes to which Europeans have emigrated, the use of horses for farm purposes has never been widespread, although mules and asses are much used in North Africa and the Middle East.

In the past three decades the number of horses employed on farms has fallen dramatically in Europe and North America, and the decline has also been marked in other parts of the world populated by peoples of predominantly European stock, such as Australia, New Zealand, and Argentina. In the United States the horse and mule population on farms in 1960 was only one-fifth that of 1920, making possible the release of over 70 million acres of cropland for the production of food and other livestock products. In temperate latitudes the size of the horse and mule population is almost a direct index of agricultural inefficiency; thus the U.S.S.R. has about six times as many horses and mules as the United States for an agricultural area that is only about 15 per cent larger. The very large horse population in Eastern Europe is an important contributory factor in the shortage of foodstuffs for human consumption; Poland, with more than 2.5 million, has the largest number of horses in Europe outside the U.S.S.R. In the U.S.S.R. and in Eastern Europe horses are still extensively employed for nonfarm draft purposes, a reflection of the unwillingness of the centrally planned economies to make substantial investment in road construction and in the motor-vehicle industry.

It is unlikely that the number of work animals can be greatly reduced in underdeveloped economies through the employment of machinery, and there are many weighty social and economic reasons for resisting such a change in the near future. Improvements in breeding and in rearing livestock are likely to have more beneficial effects on Asian and African agriculture than attempts to introduce tractors and other farm machinery.

CATTLE

Most of the world's cattle serve a multiplicity of purposes; they provide milk, meat, and other products and, occasionally, power for draft purposes. In the more highly developed economies, however, herds usually show a marked differentiation of function, and there are often pronounced regional specializations. These generally arise from combinations of physical and economic factors which encourage concentration on either milk or meat production; but these advantages derive much of their validity from the agricultural policies pursued by governments, and changes in official policy can result in substantial alterations in the composition of the cattle population. Since World War II governments in most highly developed economies have sought to encourage beef production, with the result that in such economies the proportion of beef cattle is now higher than before the war. In the later Fifties beef cattle in the United States were almost twice as numerous as dairy cattle, although in 1938 the latter were more numerous.

World Distribution

The most striking feature of the world distribution of cattle is the enormous size of the cattle population of India, but a large proportion of India's cattle are not "kept"—they are merely allowed to exist. In total numbers the United States holds second position with almost 100 million animals in 1960, followed in order by the U.S.S.R., Brazil, and Argentina (Table 7-1). In 1928 the U.S.S.R. occupied second position, but subsequent collectivization and war greatly reduced cattle numbers.

Such a national approach, however, obscures the fact that the world's *most productive* cattle are heavily concentrated in the humid temperate mid-latitudes of the Northern Hemisphere, where commercial crop and livestock farming and commercial dairying are practiced. In the temperate and tropical grasslands, where commercial grazing and pastoral nomadism are found, cattle not only are less numerous but in general are of markedly lower productivity. In the tropics natural pastures are of low nutritional value, and their improvement presents many difficult problems; cattle pests and

Table 7-1 *Cattle Numbers (Millions)*

	AVERAGE 1947–1952		1960–1961	
	CATTLE	COWS	CATTLE	COWS
Europe	99.6	47.3	117.1	53.8
Western Europe	75.9	32.5	86.2	36.9
West Germany	10.8	12.9	6.0	6.5
France	15.6	19.6	7.9	10.3
Italy	8.3	9.8	4.0	4.9
Britain	10.2	11.9	4.5	6.0
Eastern Europe	23.7	14.8	30.9	16.9
U.S.S.R.	55.8	24.4	75.8	34.9
North and Central America	114.7	144.1		
Canada	7.9	4.0	10.9	5.3
United States	80.4	41.4	97.3	46.4
South America	136.7		161.2	
Argentina	45.0		43.2	17.2
Brazil	51.3		74.0	
Uruguay	8.1		8.7	
Asia	212.5		251.0	
India	155.3		175.7	
Mainland China	32.8		44.5*	
Africa	91.6		114.1	
Australia	14.5	8.4	17.3	10.1
New Zealand	4.9	2.7	6.4	3.2
WORLD TOTAL	763.3		932.2	

* 1959–1960.

SOURCE: FAO, *Production Yearbook 1962*, Rome, 1963, Tables 70 and 71.

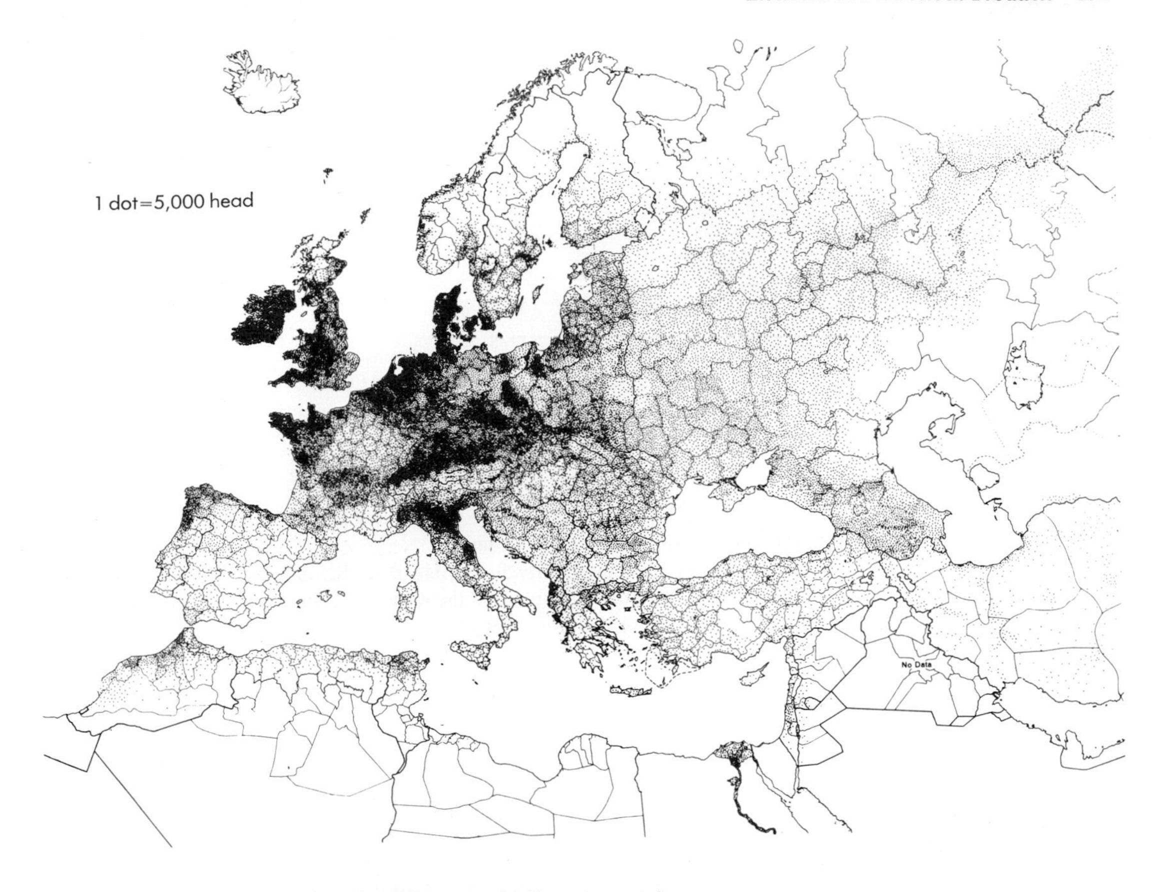

Fig. 7-1 Distribution of cattle in Europe and adjacent countries.
The concentration of cattle in northwest Europe is clearly visible, although high densities also occur in several parts of central Europe. (William Van Royen, *Atlas of the World's Resources,* vol. 1: *The Agricultural Resources of the World.* © 1954, by permission of Prentice-Hall, Inc., Englewood Cliffs, N.J.)

diseases are widespread, and European breeds do not do well. Indian, or zebu, cattle withstand high temperatures and high humidity better, but much work remains to be done to develop animals of superior productivity under such conditions.

In the value of both beef and milk output Europe still outranks all other continents, despite the fact that agricultural policies in Eastern Europe greatly hinder livestock production; Europe's margin over Anglo-America, however, is relatively less than before World War II. Cattle are thickly distributed throughout Western, central, and Eastern Europe, but with the exception of the north Italian plain, which on both climatic and economic grounds can justifiably be regarded as an extension of central Europe, their numbers are markedly fewer on the southern margins of the Continent (Fig. 7-1). The greatest concentrations are on the lowlands of northwest Europe, where a humid cloudy climate with cool summers and the large areas of heavy soils provide conditions which are best suited to permanent pasture.

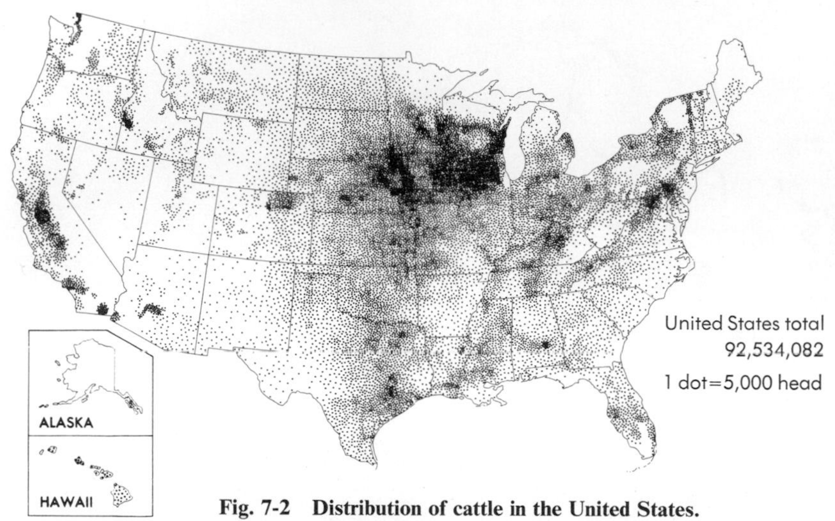

Fig. 7-2 Distribution of cattle in the United States.
Areas of rugged terrain and desert are clearly discernible in the distribution pattern of the nation's cattle, but the concentration of animals in the western section of the corn belt is striking. (U.S. Department of Agriculture, 1959.)

Climate and good management have resulted in pastures of high carrying capacity, yielding prodigious crops of hay; in parts of the Netherlands 1 acre of permanent grass can support a cow for most of the year, and the famous pastures of Leicestershire in the English Midlands can fatten a bullock without supplementary feed. There are secondary concentrations of cattle on the hill-lands and uplands of central Europe, but the areas of fertile loess soils, such as the *limon* of the Paris basin and the *boerde* lands of Germany and central Europe, have markedly fewer cattle, a situation that might be considered overdue for change. The hill-lands of Europe and the wetter western margins breed more animals than they can support, and these areas supply "stores," that is, cattle purchased off the farm for fattening. Ireland normally supplies more than half a million stores each year to Britain, a trade that provides more than one-third of the country's export income. In Britain cattle are, in large measure, processors of imported feeds and fodders, and to a lesser extent this is also true of Denmark and Switzerland. Given the economic situation of these countries in relation to the world at large, such policies make good sense.

The distribution of cattle in the United States reflects the large proportion of arid and semiarid land in the country, although all but a small proportion of such country can be grazed (Fig. 7-2). But aridity has been reinforced by past mismanagement; much of the range in the Mountain states, both public and private, is of very low or negligible productivity, and the present carrying capacity depends essentially on the hay and feed crops from the irrigated valleys. Together the Pacific and the Mountain states support only about one-sixth of the nation's cattle, although in the former there are important local concentrations serving nearby urban markets. On the Great Plains, where crop farming and ranching grade imperceptibly into each other, cattle are more numerous.

In contrast to Europe, the highest cattle

densities are found, not where conditions encourage permanent grass, but where soil and climate are most favorable for feed-grain production; areas of comparable soils in Europe are largely devoted to wheat, sugar beets, and potatoes for human consumption. But even in the focus of concentration, in Iowa and southwest Wisconsin, the cattle density is well below that of many parts of Western Europe. One important reason for this situation is that other livestock, particularly hogs, are strongly competitive with cattle for feed grains, a situation that does not exist in Western Europe. Throughout the East cattle are both numerous and widespread.

The most remarkable expansion of cattle numbers during the past two decades has occurred in the South. From South Carolina to central Texas, lands formerly exhausted by cotton cultivation have been rehabilitated through the use of chemical fertilizers and the establishment of improved pastures of crimson clover, Bermuda grass, and lespedeza. Particularly outstanding has been the transformation of the black belt of Alabama, whose originally fertile black loams once supported one of the most prosperous plantation areas of the old South; for its size the black belt is one of the most productive beef-cattle areas in the country.

South America's huge cattle population has a marked peripheral distribution, for the extensive hot and humid interior lowlands can support relatively few animals. But only on the plains bordering the Rio de la Plata does either the density or the productivity of cattle approach levels found in the humid temperate latitudes of the Northern Hemisphere. Argentina's cattle population shows regional and functional specializations that recall those of the United States. Beef cattle are grazed on the dry Pampa and move east for fattening; in the humid Pampa beef cattle are fattened either on pasture alone or with supplementary feed, and in the moistest eastern portions of the Pampa dairying is of considerable significance. In Uruguay and in Rio Grande do Sul, Brazil's southernmost state, cattle depend almost exclusively on pastures. Elsewhere in Brazil cattle are mainly found along the eastern portion of the Brazilian plateau; already there are large numbers in the coffee-producing areas, and it is quite possible that a new type of farming, based on corn and cattle, could ultimately displace the old coffee economy.

In South Africa, Australia, and New Zealand, physical and economic conditions make for strong competition between cattle and sheep rearing. In South Africa cattle are displaced from western Cape Province and are most numerous in the higher and more humid eastern Cape region. A somewhat similar pattern is presented in Australia, where the most productive cattle are largely confined to the humid temperate southeastern and southern margins. Inland from the Divide sheep are generally so much more profitable that cattle are pushed to the north. Although tropical Australia contains rather more beef cattle than the southern portion of the continent, the productivity of stock in the south is very much greater. In New Zealand conditions in North Island are so suitable for dairying that cattle have become the dominant livestock almost everywhere except in portions of the drier east coast (Fig. 7-3).

Beef

Beef is the most important meat product, normally accounting for about half of the world's meat output. Its consumption is highest in countries with high per capita incomes and where the ratio of the cattle population to the human population is high; Argentina, Uruguay, Australia, and New Zealand thus have a per capita consumption exceeding that of the

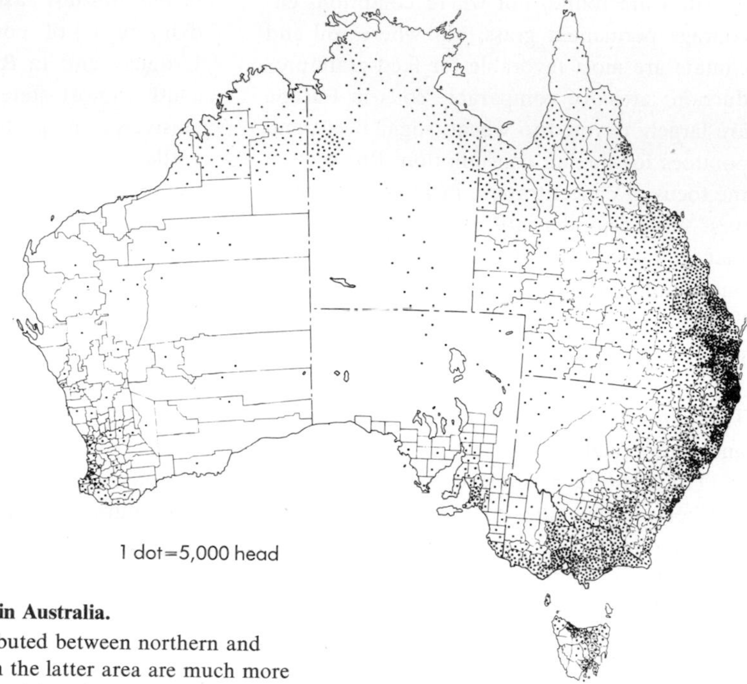

Fig. 7-3 Distribution of cattle in Australia.
Cattle are almost equally distributed between northern and southern Australia, but those in the latter area are much more productive. (William Van Royen, *Atlas of the World's Resources,* vol. 1: *The Agricultural Resources of the World.* © 1954, by permission of Prentice-Hall, Inc., Englewood Cliffs, N.J.)

United States and that of Britain. Beef production may constitute the major farm activity, as is often the case in the commercial grazing type of agriculture, or it may be but one of many farm activities, as in the commercial crop and livestock type. Consumer preference for lean and tender meat and small joints ("baby beef") has increased the advantages of the latter type of farming for beef production, for with cheap feed grains animals can be quickly brought to maturity. In total production the United States easily leads, followed by Argentina and the U.S.S.R., although in the U.S.S.R. per capita consumption is still very low. The United States, once a major beef exporter, is now on balance an importer, although in relation to domestic production imports are still small. The late Fifties witnessed a great growth in boneless-beef imports from New Zealand and Australia, but the continuance of this trade largely depends on the willingness of domestic producers to tolerate meat imports.

Despite a per capita beef consumption that is enormous even by the standards of the other leading consumers, Argentina is easily the world's largest exporter of beef, accounting for between a third and a half of world exports. The large landowners, or *estancieros,* have been able to pay very high prices for pedigree English bulls in order to build up the quality of their herds. Quality beef produced with low-cost feed and a short transit time to Britain that makes it possible for beef to be shipped in a chilled instead of a frozen state have given to the Argentine beef industry a considerable competitive advantage. The post-World War II social and economic situation in Argentina, however, has been unfavorable to a high level of beef exports; relatively low prices to producers and the maintenance of a high level of domestic consumption in the face of declining cattle numbers have reduced the volume of exports to well below the prewar level.

In Britain, which has always been the leading beef importer, there has been a marked preference in the postwar period for quality baby beef produced at home, and lower-grade imported beef has been more difficult to sell than before World War II. Partly for this reason, and partly because of a marked reduction in exports from Argentina, Britain's beef imports have not yet regained their prewar level.

Dairy Products

Dairying is a very widespread activity, but it is only in economies at a high level of development that commercial dairying assumes a position of major importance in the agricultural sector (Fig. 7-4). Many of the most famous beef breeds originated in Britain, but in dairy breeds the Netherlands and north Germany, with their Friesians and Holsteins, have made perhaps the greatest contribution. In the production of milk with a high butterfat content, however, the Channel Islands breeds are unsurpassed.

Over the past two decades scientific breeding and improved livestock management have so increased the efficiency of the dairy cow that in many countries an expanding milk output has been achieved with a stationary or declining national dairy herd. This enhanced efficiency has often resulted in overproduction, however, as consumers have failed to expand their consumption of dairy products fast enough; after years of wartime austerity, British people have had to accept the spectacle of surplus milk being poured into disused quarries and coal mines.

Dairying may supply milk either for direct human consumption or for manufacture into butter, cheese, or condensed products. For many purposes, there is no real substitute for fresh milk; it is highly perishable, and cannot economically be transported far. Thus international trade in fresh milk is virtually nil, and fresh-milk producers usually enjoy a high degree of natural protection. Butter, cheese, and condensed products, on the other hand, can be transported over great distances, and interregional and international competition may be severe. This competition is intensified by the existence of dairy substitutes, of which margarine is the most important. Thus the prices received by the dairy farmer for fresh milk are always higher than those he obtains for milk intended for manufacture, and farmers whose output is largely destined for the liquid-milk market have a considerable financial advantage over those who mainly supply butter and

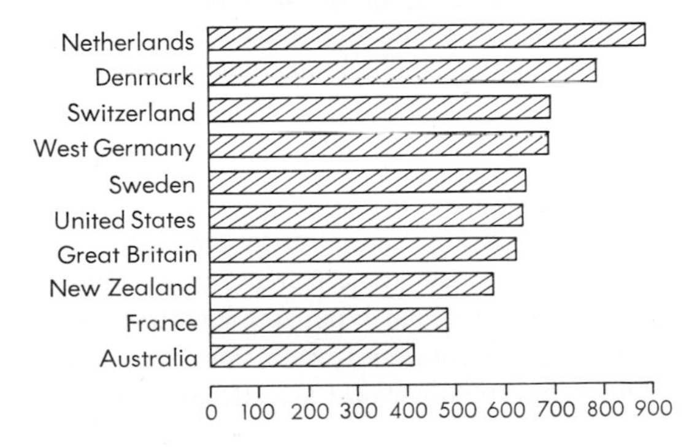

Fig. 7-4 Average annual milk output per cow in gallons, 1956–1960.
The productivity of the dairy cow is highest in the specialized dairying countries of northwest Europe. (Commonwealth Economic Committee, *Dairy Produce,* 1962.)

cheese factories. There may also be a wide gap between domestic and export prices of dairy products.

Commercial dairying is subject to a high degree of official control, and access to the profitable liquid-milk market is closely restricted. This is partly to maintain sanitary standards in the industry and to ensure uniform high quality. Its more important purpose, however, is to achieve a socially equitable distribution of income between the two main types of dairy farmers and between dairy farmers and the rest of the community. As a result patterns of milk production and utilization are often very complex, and there are numerous anomalies that cannot be explained in terms of environmental factors.

Large urban agglomerations always encourage the development of dairying in their immediate vicinity. In northwest Europe and in much of eastern North America a high degree of urbanization and climates that are particularly suitable for the production of nutritious pastures combine to create conditions that are particularly favorable for dairying. The most favorable conditions of all from the standpoint of the dairy farmer are found in England and in New England, for in both areas the relationship between supply and demand is such that a very large proportion of the total milk output can be consigned to the liquid-milk market, leaving little over for manufacture; more than two-thirds of Britain's milk output is consumed as liquid milk. Both areas are large enough, of course, to show considerable regional variations in efficiency of production, and the highest returns are obtained by those farmers whose holdings are large enough to realize the economies made possible by new techniques and increased mechanization.

But elsewhere in the dairy belts of Europe and North America, of which England and New England are, respectively, the western and eastern extremities, milk output is far in excess of the liquid-milk demand, and a large proportion has to be consigned to factories and condenseries. In the three Lake states of Minnesota, Wisconsin, and Michigan (which with adjacent portions of Illinois and Iowa are the focus of the dairy industry of the United States) and in Belgium, the Netherlands, northern Germany, and Denmark, two-thirds or more of the total milk output has to be processed. The Lake states dairyman has to contend with a climate that is rather less favorable for the production of the cheapest feed (pastures and hay) than that enjoyed by his New England counterpart, and has proportionately more of his land under feed crops. The same is also true of the Continental European dairy farmer in relation to the English dairyman; moreover, the Continental dairy farmer's holding is likely to be considerably smaller than the English dairyman's, and this also compels a relatively greater fodder-crop production. In both England and New England the farmer is able to afford to buy concentrates and feeds; his own time and capital can be much more profitably employed in other tasks than in raising feed crops. The Lake states dairyman also has to meet the competition of such a wide variety of domestically produced fats that Americans consume less than half as much butter per head as do the British; since 1950, when Federal restrictions on margarine production were lifted as a result of pressure from Southern producers of cottonseed, he has had to meet a challenge long known to the European dairy farmer.

Outside Europe and Anglo-America only Argentina and the British southern Dominions are important producers of butter (Table 7-2). Despite a considerable increase in population in all the principal producing countries, total world production and trade stand at a lower level than before World War II, and consider-

Table 7-2

Butter and Cheese Production, 1961
(Thousand metric tons)

	BUTTER	CHEESE
West Germany	456	311
France	272	339
Italy	62	345
Belgium	88	21
Netherlands	97	213
Britain	54	116
Denmark	172	122
Sweden	84	58
Switzerland	32	70
Ireland	66	6
U.S.S.R.	894	268*
Canada	165	59
United States	696	740
Argentina	54	130
Brazil	26	36
Australia	185	48
New Zealand	213	101

* 1960.
SOURCE: FAO, *Production Yearbook 1962,* Rome, 1963, Table 85.

able butter surpluses have repeatedly occurred. Competition from margarine and vegetable cooking fats and a fall in the per capita consumption of bread consequent upon higher living standards have been the main reasons for the depression that has fallen over most butter-producing areas.

The lower per capita consumption of butter has resulted in demands for further government assistance to the dairy industry in most producing countries. In the United States the decline in the proportion of milk production utilized for butter has been partly offset by increases in the offtake by cheese, ice-cream, and dried-milk manufacture, but unless dairy farmers can realize the economies made possible by larger productive units, the upper Lakes dairy area, which produces one-half of the nation's butter, will continue to be depressed.

Outside the United States, the world butter situation is dominated by the huge British market. Britain is, in fact, the only large market in which all butter producers can compete, and it normally absorbs more than three-quarters of the half a million tons of butter entering world trade each year. There are two principal groups of competitors, the more important consisting of Australia, New Zealand, and Denmark. In all three countries dairying owes its present dimensions largely to its access to the British market; both Denmark and New Zealand export more than two-thirds of their total butter output to Britain, and Australia about one-third. In the two British southern Dominions dairying has expanded into every area where physical conditions were suitable. It now seems that this process was carried too far; the physically less well-endowed areas, South Island in New Zealand and the southern Queensland coastlands in Australia, have considerable cost penalties, and retrenchment in these areas is proceeding. In the face of the external tariff of the Common Market, Danish butter, which has always commanded a substantial premium, will become more dependent on the British market than before.[3]

The second group of butter suppliers on the British market comprises a varying assembly of countries which can include the Netherlands, Finland, Poland, Sweden, Argentina, and, before World War II, the Baltic States. These countries have a much lower degree of dependence on Britain, and for some the German market is more important. But in favorable seasons they may have for sale large surpluses which have a depressing effect on butter prices in Britain; at such times charges of dumping are commonly made by aggrieved competitors. Only Denmark is really free from this censure; all other producers, in effect, subsidize butter exports to Britain.

By leaving this intense competition largely to others the British dairy farmer prospers, and the British housewife normally enjoys the cheapest butter in the world. Yet even in Britain margarine consumption has gained at the expense of butter. British experience strongly suggests that butter is preferred when the price margin over margarine is small; the high per capita consumption of margarine in many European countries is a consequence of high internal butter prices in order to subsidize butter exports.

Only through further rationalization can dairy farmers meet the challenge of the vegetable oils; in both Europe and North America, however, it is not easy to see how this can be done without causing hardship to many small dairy farmers. Dairying gives a year-round return and needs relatively little capital to enter; the demand for small dairy farms, however, has greatly pushed up land values, and saddles the industry with an inflated cost structure.

[3]The European Free Trade Association (EFTA), or Outer Seven, of which Britain and Denmark are members, does not aim at the establishment of free trade in agricultural products. It is clear, however, that Britain will have to provide some compensation for any losses sustained by Denmark in butter sales to the Common Market.

SHEEP

In consequence of their mountain ancestry and their covering of the natural protein fiber, wool, sheep are among the hardiest of livestock. All sheep produce wool of some kind, but the best wools come from special wool breeds. These include the old long-haired breeds from the highlands of Britain, but the most important is the merino, originally developed on the Spanish Meseta but now mainly kept in the southern continents. Other breeds provide both wool and meat, such as the short-haired breeds of the chalk and limestone areas of southern England. Many sheep are crosses between these two major groups, and some of these crosses have become stabilized breeds, for example, the Border Leicester and the Corriedale, a New Zealand breed. A few special French and Italian breeds provide milk in addition to meat and wool, thus serving a triple purpose. For more than six hundred years sheep have been of great importance in British farming, and in the long process of developing breeds which combine the maximum number of desirable characteristics, Britain has played a major part. This tradition has been followed by British emigrants to new lands, both Australia and New Zealand having made great contributions to breeding and to sheep management.

Though sheep are almost synonymous with wool, only in Australia and South Africa does wool make a greater contribution to total agricultural income than mutton and lamb. Nevertheless, from the standpoint of world trade, wool is by far the most important sheep product, and it is usually one of the six major commodities, by value, entering world commerce. This situation is accounted for by the high price of fine wools and the very large export of such wools from a few specialized producers.

Sheep can make use of pastures unsuitable for cattle, both in elevated cold and humid environments and in semiarid lands. In very rugged or forested country cattle are usually the preferred stock, for under such conditions wool is easily damaged and sheep are liable to attack from predators. High temperatures in conjunction with high humidity are usually considered inimical to sheep breeding, but the issue is a complex one, and the main deterrent to sheep running in such environments is more often unsuitable feed. Sheep fit well into arable farming in the commercial crop and livestock type of agriculture, particularly on light or porous soils. Over considerable areas sheep and cattle may be strongly competitive. However, sheep generally require more skilled attention than cattle, and the shepherd must exercise constant vigilance.

World Distribution and Meat and Wool Production

The world's sheep and cattle populations are approximately equal (Table 7-3), but the distribution of the two kinds of livestock is very different. Both Europe and Africa have more sheep than cattle, and in these continents the two kinds of livestock have almost complementary distribution patterns. Europe's sheep are most numerous along its southern margins; northwestern and central Europe, which have a heavy concentration of cattle, possess comparatively few (Fig. 7-5). The British Isles, however, are exceptional. The hardy mountain breeds still provide the best and often the only way of utilizing the extensive areas of poor upland grazing in Britain, although it is doubtful if numbers could be maintained without the payment of the substantial hill-sheep subsidy. An explanation of the prolonged dominance of sheep farming in many parts of the British Isles, however, lies in the economic history of Britain, with the early development of enclosure and the rise of the woolen industry.

In Africa sheep are most numerous in the northern and southern margins, so that the whole of the Mediterranean basin appears as a major area of sheep concentration. Asia's sheep are mainly located in the uplands and semiarid plateaus of southwest Asia, although there is increasing interest in sheep rearing in western China. The U.S.S.R. has a large and rapidly expanding sheep population, located mainly in Soviet Asia; second in sheep numbers on a national basis, the U.S.S.R. plans through the widespread use of artificial insemination to attain the premier position in the near future. Both North and South America possess considerably fewer sheep than cattle, and in the former the disparity is very great.

Sheep numbers in the United States have been declining for almost three-quarters of a century, but since World War II the fall has been rapid; the population of 33 million sheep recorded in 1961 was only some 60 per cent as large as that of 1939.

Some 60 per cent of American sheep are in the flocks of the western range states, the greatest concentration being located on the Edwards Plateau of Texas. Even in the western states, however, the sale of sheep and lambs is the principal source of the sheep rancher's

Table 7-3

Sheep Numbers and Wool Production

	SHEEP (MILLIONS)		WOOL (THOUSAND METRIC TONS, GREASY BASIS)
	AVERAGE 1947–1952	1960–1961	1960–1961
Europe	120.5	135.2	146
Western Europe	84.7	95.1	95
Britain	19.9	29.0	39
Spain	25.4	22.6	14
Eastern Europe	35.8	40.1	51
U.S.S.R.	76.9	133.0	220
North and Central America	39.0	41.0	65
United States	31.5	33.0	59
South America	121.7	121.0	191
Argentina	51.1	49.0	104
Uruguay	23.1	n.a.	50
Asia	123.5	159.9	90
Mainland China	31.1	60.8*	42*
Africa	120.1	134.9	84
South Africa	33.2	n.a.	63
Australia	141.5	152.7	440
New Zealand	33.9	48.5	190
WORLD TOTAL	776.4	987.1	1,465

* 1959–1960.

SOURCE: FAO, *Production Yearbook 1962*, Rome, 1963, Tables 73 and 93.

income. Large flocks of a thousand or more animals graze the open range for part of the year, often on leases held by grazing cooperatives; when on the range, the animals have usually to be folded at night for protection from coyotes. As with cattle, winter management necessitates access to the feed of the irrigated valleys. In the East, sheep are unimportant livestock; they tend to be kept largely from custom, and except in the bluegrass region of Kentucky, are limited to small flocks to graze odd patches or to check weed growth.

During the nineteenth century there was a strong emphasis on the merino and other fine-wool breeds in the United States, but with increasing competition from more physically favored producers overseas, these have now disappeared, and dual-purpose, short-wool breeds predominate. The importation of Basque shepherds has helped relieve the labor shortage in the West, but the mechanized techniques that have produced such great increases in the productivity of labor and land in other farming enterprises are largely inapplicable to sheep rearing, and the greater profitability of other livestock has been largely responsible for the long decline of sheep numbers. Nevertheless, there is considerable scope for the introduction of techniques that have proved so successful in sheep rearing in Australia and

New Zealand. Perhaps the greatest obstacle in the way of their introduction has been the prolonged and high level of tariff protection granted to the American grower of wool. High domestic costs of production are clearly suggested by a per capita consumption of mutton and lamb that is only one-quarter of that of Britain and not much more than one-twentieth of that of Australia and New Zealand. A further consequence of high-tariff protection for the American wool grower has been to encourage competition from synthetic fibers.

Australia, New Zealand, Argentina, Uruguay, and South Africa dominate world trade in sheep products. Though collectively they possess less than one-third of the world's sheep, they account for almost 60 per cent of total wool production and for a considerably higher proportion of the fine-wool output; and the first four countries together provide more than 90 per cent of the world exports of mutton and lamb, New Zealand alone supplying almost three-quarters of the total. It is clear that exceptionally advantageous physical and eco-

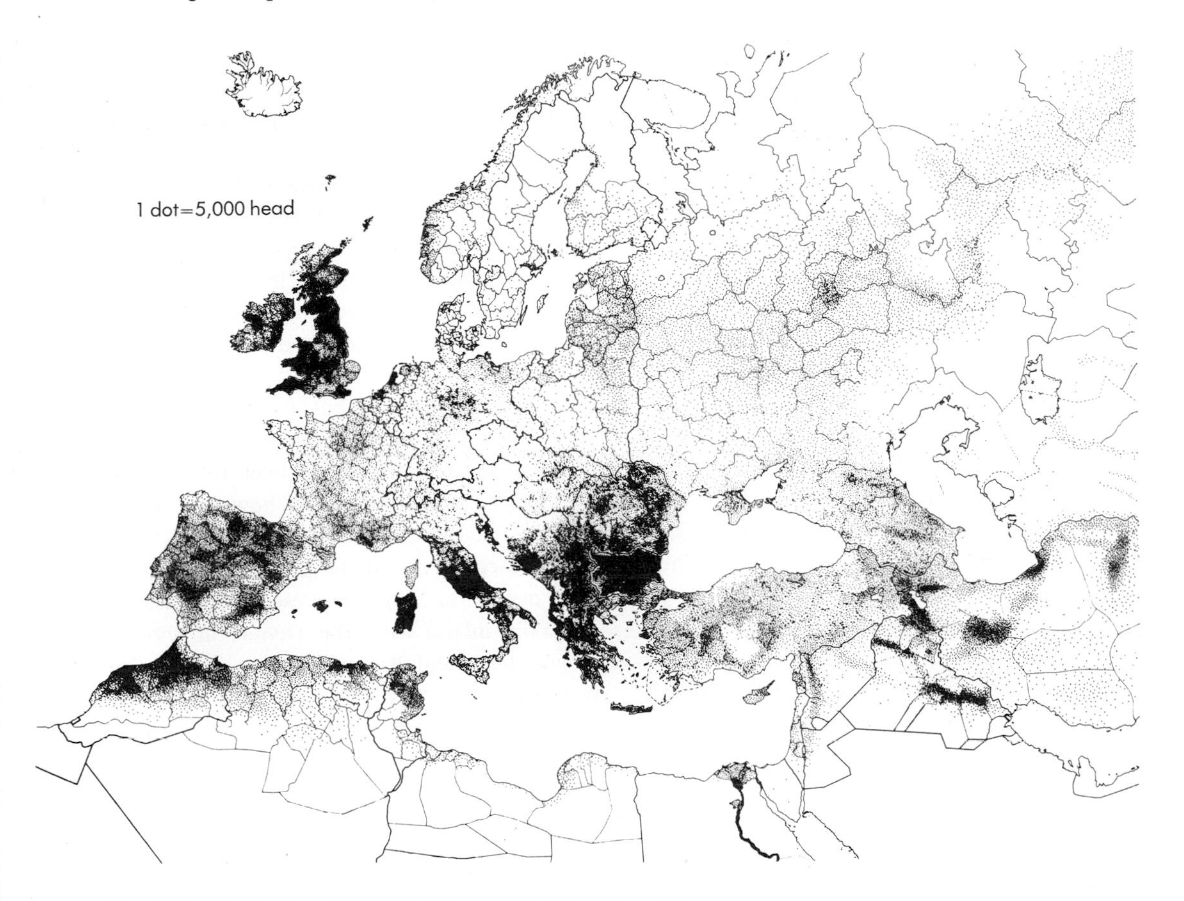

Fig. 7-5 Distribution of sheep in Europe and adjacent countries.
Sheep are most numerous in southern and southeastern Europe, but the highlands of Britain also possess very large numbers. (William Van Royen, *Atlas of the World's Resources,* vol. 1: *The Agricultural Resources of the World.* © 1954, by permission of Prentice-Hall, Inc., Englewood Cliffs, N.J.)

nomic conditions for sheep raising are enjoyed by these countries, and over considerable areas of each, sheep dominate the rural economy.

Sheep are found in all parts of Argentina, but the greatest concentrations are in the moister portion of the Pampa, in Entre Ríos, and in Patagonia; in Uruguay they occur in large numbers throughout the country with the exception of the La Plata littoral. In both the Pampa and Entre Ríos cattle are strongly competitive with sheep, and the greater profitability of beef production and dairying has led to a long decline in the importance of sheep in these parts of Argentina.[4] The dry, windswept Patagonian plateau has almost 40 per cent of Argentina's sheep and is the only area in which the merino breed is important; less than one-fifth of Argentina's wool output consists of fine merino wool. In the warmer and moister Pampa the merino breed has virtually disappeared; the availability of more nutritious pastures and the necessity of achieving returns per unit area comparable with those of other forms of livestock production have resulted in a concentration on fat-lamb production and a change to such breeds as the Romney Marsh and Corriedale.

Sheep raising reaches its apogee in Australia and New Zealand, both countries having almost eight times as many sheep as cattle. The development of sheep industries in the two Dominions has been greatly influenced by access to the large British market, but as producers they are complementary rather than competitive, and both are now endeavoring, with considerable success, to widen the market for their traditional exports.

Merino sheep were introduced into New South Wales very early in the nineteenth century while it was still a penal colony, but it was in the years from 1860 to 1890 that Australia fully realized its great advantages for fine-wool production. During this period sheep raising was pushed to its furthest physical limits and even beyond, venturing into areas such as the far west of New South Wales and interior Queensland, where 20 or more acres were necessary to support one animal. Physical, economic, and social conditions at this time combined to make wool production extremely attractive. Wool was a commodity of high value, ideally suited to the primitive transport of a pioneer society; though natural pastures and other feed were only of modest or low nutritional value, very large areas of land could be utilized with little or no preparation, and the social organization finally confirmed the rights of the "squatter"—the large grazier who occupied Crown (public) land to which he had no legal title. Wool production in Australia has never been an occupation open to the small farmer, and large units were, and indeed still are, an economic necessity in a continental interior with light and very variable rainfall.

Sheep numbers fluctuated violently from 1890 onwards in response to climatic and economic vicissitudes, but from the end of World War II continuous growth has carried flocks to the record level of over 155 million in 1960. In the drier areas, however, sheep numbers have been declining steadily over the past half-century, and the greatest concentration occurs in a great crescent in eastern Australia inland from the Divide, in a zone where the rainfall varies from 15 to 25 inches or more (Fig. 7-6). This is a considerable rainfall by Australian standards, and the reason for the continued dominance of wool production in this area is largely to be found in the achievement of extraordinary increases in the productivity of animal, land, and worker, which have maintained the profitability of wool production against all other enterprises. Bores and pumps for watering stock, mechanical shearing, protective fencing from predators (particularly the dingo), improved breeding

[4] **Maximum sheep numbers in Argentina were attained in 1879, almost contemporaneously with the United States.**

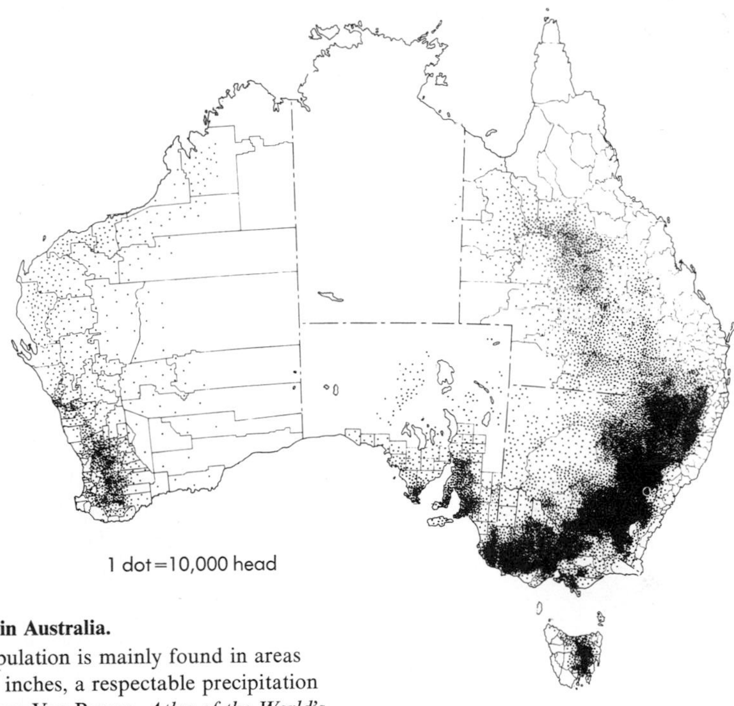

Fig. 7-6 Distribution of sheep in Australia.
Australia's enormous sheep population is mainly found in areas with a rainfall of from 15 to 25 inches, a respectable precipitation by Australian standards. (William Van Royen, *Atlas of the World's Resources*, vol. 1: *The Agricultural Resources of the World.* © 1954, by permission of Prentice-Hall, Inc., Englewood Cliffs, N.J.)

and stock management, and, above all, pasture improvement have lifted the productivity of the Australian merino and the sheep worker to among the highest levels in the world. In the postwar period widespread use of the virus disease myxomatosis has gone far to eliminate the rabbit menace, and the reduced competition for feed has greatly lifted both the quality and weight of fleeces. As already noted, one-third of all sheep are found on wheat farms; these are mainly crossbreds, producing meat as well as wool. In irrigation areas and on the coastal margins, fat-lamb production replaces fine-wool production, but Australia's sheep are overwhelmingly merinos, this breed accounting for more than three-quarters of the total. Almost half of all sheep are found in New South Wales alone. In view of the great technical efficiency of sheep running in Australia the limited attention so far given to artificial insemination appears a striking omission.

With nearly 48 million sheep in 1961, New Zealand had by far the highest number of sheep per capita of any country in the world. In the early years of settlement merinos were introduced from Australia, but in the warm and humid environment of North Island English breeds were found to be more suitable, particularly the Romney Marsh (Fig. 7-7); this breed now accounts for almost three-quarters of the national total. In South Island merinos have continued to be of importance on the "high country" of Otago, where a type of ranching based on native tussock grass is found, but they only account for about 2 per cent of the national total. The development of the re-

Fig. 7-7 Distribution of sheep in New Zealand. Sheep are particularly numerous in the relatively drier east of New Zealand and in rough country; on lowlands with higher rainfall they tend to be replaced by dairy cattle. (William Van Royen, *Atlas of the World's Resources,* vol. 1: *The Agricultural Resources of the World.* © 1954, by permission of Prentice-Hall, Inc., Englewood Cliffs, N.J.)

frigerated ship from 1880 onwards hastened the change towards breeds primarily suited to fat-lamb production, and from then on wool production really became a sideline. Nevertheless, in consequence of its high productivity per animal, New Zealand is second only to Australia as a producer and exporter of wool, producing very large quantities of medium-quality wools that are more suited to the woolen than the worsted industry.

Just as the country has no equal in low-cost dairying, it is without a peer in prime-fat-lamb production; more than 15 million lambs are slaughtered every year, principally for export to Britain. About three-fifths of the total lamb output is derived from the lowland areas of South Island, where fat-lamb production is the principal farm activity, although the famous Canterbury lamb is produced in other parts of the island as well as on the Canterbury plains. In North Island, which has rather more than half the total sheep numbers, sheep farming as a specialist activity is largely confined to the drier eastern portion of the country, although there are considerable numbers of sheep in all the principal dairying districts. From the Wairarapa through Hawke Bay to Gisborne, the principal area of sheep concentration in North Island, sheep farming is mainly carried on in hilly country, and the sale of store sheep is an important source of farm income.

As in Australia, sheep farming has shown very substantial technical advances over the past three decades, New Zealand flocks now having the heaviest fleeces in the world. Tremendous increases in productivity have been achieved through pasture improvement, a development pioneered in New Zealand and one in which the country is still the world leader. Improved grasses and clovers developed in New Zealand are now eagerly sought abroad, and the widespread practice of topdressing with superphosphate by means of mechanical blowers or by aircraft has enormously increased carrying capacity. In hilly country, which comprises a substantial proportion of the national territory, the use of aircraft has revolutionized sheep farming. It is, in fact, increasingly common for pasture improvement to be carried out entirely by aircraft, with little or no preliminary preparation on the ground; pesticides, general supplies, and fencing materials are also dropped from aircraft.

With an assured and low-cost labor supply, South Africa has remained comparatively unaffected by the technical progress made in Australia and New Zealand. The distribution of sheep in South Africa is broadly similar to that of Australia; they are most numerous in the better-watered eastern Cape, in the high veld of the Orange Free State, and in southern Transvaal, all areas where the rainfall varies from 20 to 30 inches. In the drier western Cape Province sheep running is the dominant rural activity everywhere save in the extreme southwest, but there are fewer animals than in the east. South Africa is the second-largest producer of fine wool, after Australia, and except for a very small proportion of nonwooled sheep, the country's 38 million animals consist entirely of merinos.

Wool in the World Economy Apart from the coarsest wools, which are mainly of Asian origin and used in carpet weaving, wool is almost exclusively employed as an apparel fiber. Broadly, there are three main classes of wool: merino, or fine, wool; crossbred wool (not necessarily produced from crossbred sheep), which is coarser than merino but suitable for apparel purposes; and carpet wool, consisting of the coarsest kinds. Merino wool commands a premium over crossbred wool, but the margin varies constantly according to the state of the world market and the level of business activity; it tends to be lowest in boom conditions when merino wools are very highly priced, for at such times manufacturers endeavor to substitute crossbred wools for fine wools, thus bidding up the price of the former. World wool production increases only slowly, for a considerable period of time must elapse before any decision to increase flocks is fully implemented, and in the short period the supply of raw wool is relatively inflexible.

This inflexibility of supply, in conjunction with a demand that fluctuates according to the level of business activity or to future expectations of activity, produces a highly unstable price level. This instability of price is a powerful inducement to textile manufacturers to employ substitutes of relatively constant cost wherever possible. But it is worth noting that wool is one of the very few major commodities in world trade that has never experienced a surplus problem except in time of war, and the dangers of a high level of wool prices which would encourage manufacturers to switch to synthetic fibers, are fully realized by the more discerning producers.

Any means by which the cost of raw wool can be reduced will greatly assist wool in its struggle with synthetic fibers. Abundant opportunities for cost reduction certainly exist; even in Australia there are too many farmers who, content with the generally high level of wool prices since World War II, have failed to press on with pasture improvement or to make every effort to eliminate rabbits. Not enough is known about the processes by which the sheep converts feed into the protein fiber known as wool or about the best feed for wool production. In both Australia and New Zealand official organizations for the prosecution of scientific research are vigorously pursuing these problems, and a levy is made on producers to finance such research. Nevertheless, in view of the enormous resources of the giant chemical companies engaged in synthetic-fiber production, the present level of effort might well be judged inadequate.

HOGS AND POULTRY

Of other livestock, hogs and poultry are by far the most important; just how important they are in the world economy is a matter of some conjecture, as their numbers are only imperfectly known. The most important geographic characteristic of these forms of live-

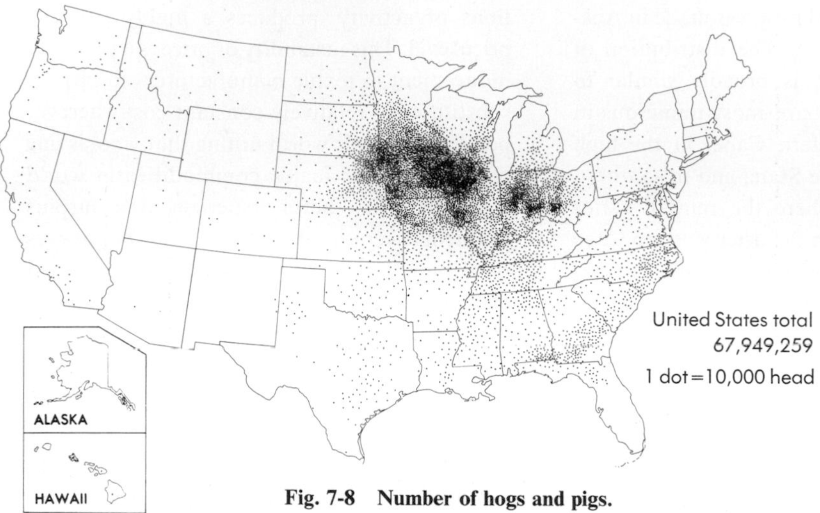

Fig. 7-8 Number of hogs and pigs.
The close coincidence of hog and corn production is obvious. (U.S. Department of Agriculture, 1959.)

stock, their ubiquity, has already been mentioned. The facility with which they can be accommodated to different types of agriculture is strikingly evidenced by the fact that in both hog and poultry numbers China and the United States vie with each other for the premier position among the nations of the world. The fact that hogs and poultry can be reared almost anywhere gives to most countries a high degree of self-sufficiency in pig and poultry products, so that in comparison with other livestock products, world trade in these commodities is small. Nevertheless, Britain, the world's largest buyer of foreign foodstuffs, imports very substantial quantities of all types of pig and poultry products.

Hogs and poultry can both find their own keep, but when they do the productivity per animal is low. The average American hen produces more than 200 eggs per year; it is doubtful if the Chinese hen produces as many as 100. High productivity per animal is achieved through cheap and plentiful feed, so that the animal's energy is expended in bodily growth and reproduction rather than in keeping itself alive. Over the past two decades a revolution in egg and poultry production has been effected by specialization, and although the majority of fowls in the United States are still found in comparatively small farm flocks, the future clearly lies with the large-scale specialist producer. It is quite likely that somewhat similar techniques will prove equally successful in hog production.

The distribution of hogs in the United States is closely related to the availability of cheap feed grains, particularly corn (Fig. 7-8). The American hog is principally a lard hog, converting starchy foods into fat, and the introduction of hybrid corn greatly confirmed the advantages of the corn belt for this type of production. Since World War II, however, competition from margarine, vegetable shortening, and cooking fats has adversely affected the demand for lard, and there has been a swing of consumer preference towards leaner, firmer pork and bacon. This has resulted in changes in the traditional method of feeding hogs and the use of protein supplements in the diet such as soybean meal, and has been one cause of an increased interest in the leaner breeds popular in Canada and Europe. In these areas hogs are fed a mixed diet of barley or rye, potatoes, and roots, occasionally supplemented by skim milk; in Denmark and the Netherlands particularly, skim milk is a major item of diet. Animals so nourished are eminently suitable for the production of bacon and hams. As a bacon hog, the Danish Landrace is unsurpassed, maturing on a diet with a minimum of starchy constituents to produce bacon commanding a substantial premium. As with Danish butter and eggs, rigid maintenance of quality by the Danish cooperatives has helped build up a marked consumer preference for Danish bacon in the British market. Almost 14 per cent of Denmark's export income is gained through the sale of bacon and hams, principally to Britain.

Poultry keeping is subject to even fewer physical limitations than hog raising. Within broad limits it is capable of being carried on anywhere; modern scientifically designed poultry houses and vitamin-enriched feed encourage farmers to produce eggs and table birds in semidarkness. The increases in the productivity of both hen and rooster as a result of scientific breeding in conjunction with highly mechanized house layouts in which eggs, feed, and droppings are all moved by conveyors have few parallels in other branches of farming; a 3-pound chicken can now be produced in a little less than nine weeks. The development of a specialized "broiler bird" weighing from 2 to 3 pounds is perhaps the most remarkable development of a remarkable industry in the United States. Within a few years the broiler industry has reached a high degree of organization, with specialists producing roosters and hens for breeding stock, others concentrating on chicks for sale, and broiler producers rearing chicks in automated houses that can turn out 2,000 or more broilers a week for the packing plants (Fig. 7-9).

This great industry, now producing more than 2 billion table birds a year, virtually came

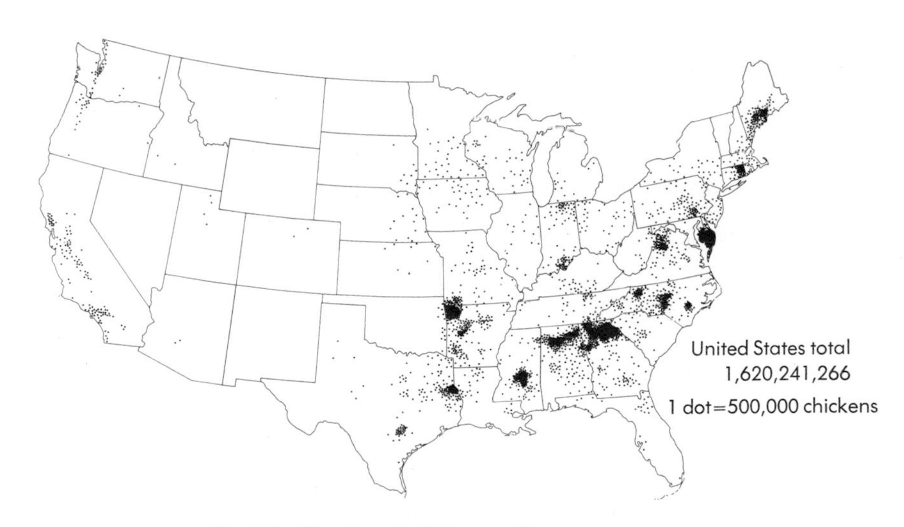

Fig. 7-9 Number of chickens sold.
The broiler industry is well established in the middle Atlantic region, but Georgia is the largest producer on a state basis. (U.S. Department of Agriculture, 1959.)

into existence only a few years before World War II; Sussex County in the Delaware peninsula, the Shenandoah valley, and northeast Georgia were the first to take up the industry on a large scale, but at present it shows little evidence of any strong control in its location pattern save proximity to urban markets. The new methods pioneered in the United States are now being successfully employed in Britain and in Continental Europe, and appear certain to extend further afield in the near future.

SELECTED REFERENCES

Bidwell, Percy W.: *Raw Materials: A Study of American Policy,* Harper & Row, Publishers, Incorporated, New York, 1958, pp. 213–243.

Commonwealth Economic Committee: *Dairy Produce,* H. M. Stationery Office, London, annually.

———: *Industrial Fibres,* H. M. Stationery Office, London, annually.

———: *Meat,* H. M. Stationery Office, London, annually.

Commonwealth of Australia, Bureau of Agricultural Economics: *Statistical Handbook of the Sheep and Wool Industry,* Canberra, 1961.

Cumberland, Kenneth B.: "The Agricultural Regions of New Zealand," *Geographical Journal,* vol. 112, pp. 43–63, 1948.

Durand, Loyal, Jr.: "The Lower Peninsula of Michigan and the Western Michigan Dairy Regions," *Economic Geography,* vol. 27, pp. 163–183, 1951.

———: "Major Milksheds of the Northeast Quarter of the United States," *Economic Geography,* vol. 40, pp. 9–33, 1964.

Food and Agriculture Organization: *Commodity Review, 1962,* Rome, 1962.

Henderson, David A.: "'Corn Belt' Cattle Feeding in Eastern Colorado's Irrigated Valleys," *Economic Geography,* vol. 34, pp. 364–372, 1954.

James, Preston E.: "The Process of Pastoral and Agricultural Settlement on the Argentine Humid Pampas," *Geographical Review,* vol. 40, pp. 121–137, 1950.

Lewthwaite, Gordon R.: "Wisconsin and the Waikato: A Comparison of Dairy Farming in the United States and New Zealand," *Annals of the Association of American Geographers,* vol. 53, pp. 59–87, 1964.

McConnell, H. G.: "The Livestock Industry in Uruguay," *Quarterly Review of Agricultural Economics,* vol. 15, pp. 110–113, Bureau of Agricultural Economics, Canberra, 1962.

Organisation for European Economic Cooperation: *Problems in Dairy Policy,* Paris, 1958, vol. 1; Paris, 1960, vol. 2.

Van Royen, William: *Atlas of the World's Resources,* vol. 1: *The Agricultural Resources of the World,* Prentice-Hall, Inc., Englewood Cliffs, N.J., 1954.

Wadham, Samuel, and R. Kent Wilson: *Land Utilization in Australia,* 4th ed., Melbourne University Press, Melbourne, 1964, pp. 54–173.

Woytinsky, W. S., and E. S. Woytinsky: *World Population and Production,* The Twentieth Century Fund, New York, 1953, pp. 630–681.

Chapter 8

FORESTRY AND FOREST INDUSTRIES

Forestry and fishing are only minor occupations of mankind. Total world employment in timber felling is estimated by the FAO at about 5 million, and employment in primary forest industries, that is, sawmilling, pulp and paper, plywood, and hardboard, at a further 5 million. Another 5 million are estimated to be employed in secondary forest industries, that is, woodworking and furniture, and about 1½ million in scientific forestry and reforestation. Directly and indirectly, therefore, forests provide employment for probably less than 17 million people, an insignificant proportion of those engaged in agriculture. However, an enormous number of part-time workers are also engaged in timber or wood getting in addition to their normal occupations.

The distribution of commercial forest industries of major significance in the world economy is closely restricted, but where they are practiced, they are of major local importance. In Sweden and Canada forest products are the largest source of foreign exchange earnings, an observation which also holds for Finland and usually for the U.S.S.R. among countries at a lower level of economic development.

Forestry is merely one method of using land to serve human ends, but its organization, like that of agriculture, can assume forms of a wide degree of economic complexity. It is a type of land use which has experienced, and continues to experience, strong competition from alternative uses, particularly agriculture; it has been estimated that since 1947 some 60 million acres of forest land have been lost, mainly to agricultural uses.[1] Yet the distinction between these two methods of using land can be tenuous, for very many countries practice a form of silviculture that is virtually timber cropping. Seeds of selected species are sown in specially prepared beds, the seedlings transplanted to nursery plots, and the young trees eventually planted out in their permanent quarters. There they are periodically thinned

[1] Food and Agriculture Organization, *World Forest Resources,* Rome, 1957, p. 17.

out, and finally, after many years, the timber is felled. However, forestry of this kind still provides only a small portion of the total output of forest products, the great bulk of which is derived from natural forests.

The population explosion and the increase in per capita timber consumption which is likely to accompany the achievement of a higher level of economic development in underdeveloped countries have given rise to concern about stocks of natural timber. But ultimately it is the capacity of land to produce forest that will determine how future needs for forest products will be met. If the world wishes to have enough of these to meet all its requirements in perpetuity, and at a reasonable price, it must live within its forest income and endeavor to enlarge that income. The capacity of land to produce forest varies widely over the face of the world and is primarily a reflection of climate and terrain, but it can be greatly increased or reduced by the intervention of man. In the past man's activities have mainly exerted the latter effect, and this is still the situation over much of the world.

FOREST UTILIZATION

From earliest times one of the most important uses of forests has been as a source of fuel, and at least half the present world output of forest products consists of fuel wood.[2] Wherever it has been available wood has always been a preferred building material, and this is still so at the present despite the existence of many alternative materials. Shipbuilding exerts a large demand for timber and has been a major cause of extensive deforestation in the past, while the demand for "naval stores" such as turpentine, rosin, masts, and spars also enlarged the drain on forests. Prodigious quantities of timber have been used in mining and smelting metalliferous ores and in coal mining. In all of these traditional employments the relative share of timber has been very greatly reduced over the past century, but the total demand for timber has continued to increase rapidly. Important new uses for forest products have appeared, which will continue to exert a far-reaching influence in forest exploitation; these include the manufacture of wood pulp and paper, wood cellulose, veneers and plywood, and many kinds of fiberboard and hardboard. Many of these new forest industries have demonstrated a remarkable capacity for growth, and it is likely that this will be maintained in the future. In fact, it appears that every advance in the level of development produces new demands for wood and wood products; in the hands of the scientist wood has become a remarkably versatile material, capable of a wide variety of applications.

The principal industrial use of timber is for structural purposes; in terms of the roundwood, or unsawn, equivalent, sawmills consume about two-thirds of the volume of world wood output (Table 8-1). Wood-pulp and paper manufacture absorbs a little more than one-quarter, and plywood about 4 per cent. In terms of value of output, however, it is certain that in the near future the paper and pulp industry will assume the premier position among forest industries. World wood-pulp production has expanded by about 5 per cent per annum over the past two decades, a rate of growth that is equaled by few manufacturing industries.

The indirect uses of forests are scarcely less important than the direct uses. Forests are essential to check rapid runoff and soil erosion in hilly country, and in many parts of the world their removal has had the gravest consequences. Without its forest cover the way is open for

[2] Food and Agriculture Organization, *State of Food and Agriculture*, Rome, 1958, p. 163.

Table 8-1

World Primary Forest Industries, 1960

	ROUNDWOOD EQUIVALENT OF OUTPUT (MILLION CUBIC METERS)	GROSS VALUE OF OUTPUT (MILLION $)	INVESTMENT (MILLION $)
Sawmilling	561	15,400	8,400
Pulp and Paper	252	14,300	36,000
Plywood	38	1,500	1,700
Board	10	573	740
TOTAL	861	31,773	46,840

SOURCE: FAO, *State of Food and Agriculture*, 1961, p. 98.

great physical and chemical impoverishment of the soil; under extreme conditions, as in certain parts of the tropics where laterization has proceeded to the point where all soluble minerals have been removed, deforestation has produced man-made deserts on which nothing can grow. The effect of forests on climate is still not entirely clear, but the planting of belts of trees as windbreaks can have markedly beneficial effects on agriculture. Finally, forests and the wildlife they support possess great recreational value.

For these reasons it is common to find that the state often has a large interest in forest exploitation. Moreover, sound forest management may require such lengthy production cycles that it is unattractive to private capital. Strategic considerations may also reinforce the interest of government in scientific forestry. A notable example of this is provided by Britain, where the timber shortages of World War I resulted in the establishment of the Forestry Commission, which since the early Twenties has made large plantings in many areas unsuitable for agriculture. This policy paid considerable dividends during World War II, when Britain was again largely deprived of foreign timber supplies.

World Forest Distribution and Productivity

Perhaps as much as half the land surface of the earth was occupied by forest in Paleolithic times, before the spread of agriculture. At the present, this proportion has been reduced to about 30 per cent. The remaining forest area is, nevertheless, enormous, amounting to some 15 million square miles, but over half this area is too remote and inaccessible for commercial exploitation (Table 8-2). The greatest areas of unexploited forest lie in Latin America, in Africa, and in Soviet Asia, and are poorly located even in relation to the new markets that can be expected with a higher general level of world economic development.

Of greater immediate significance, however, is the very low productivity of much of the area at present exploited; over enormous areas the output of forest products per square mile is only a fraction of what is known to be possible with good management. Much of the responsibility for this situation rests with the extravagant methods of cutting used in the past; failure to leave sufficient mature trees to provide seed for regeneration and the damage to growing stock through preventable fires and through

Table 8-2

Distribution of the World's Forests (Million hectares)

	FOREST			
	ACCESSIBLE	INACCESSIBLE	TOTAL	TOTAL LAND AREA
Europe	138.2	2.8	141.0	473.0
U.S.S.R	1,131.1	11.9	1,131.1	2,233.8
North America	400.3	333.2	733.5	1,874.7
Central America	54.5	19.5	74.0	271.9
South America	276.7	679.9	956.6	1,774.8
Africa	380.2	372.6	752.8	2,977.4
Asia*	325.8	194.2	520.0	2,717.6
Pacific Area	25.5	70.4	95.4	854.4
WORLD TOTAL	2,732.3	1,672.6	4,404.9	13,177.6

* Includes China.
SOURCE: FAO, *Yearbook of Forest Product Statistics, 1962*, Rome, 1962.

the introduction of diseases and insect pests have converted vast tracts of forests into scrubland and waste of minimal productivity. This impoverishment of the forest has been accompanied by a progressive diminution in the quality of timber, as the supply of large-diameter logs from the virgin forest has declined. Sound forest policy must endeavor not only to remedy both these shortcomings but also to adapt the supply of forest products to meet the changing pattern of timber consumption that is being brought about by the rapid growth of modern forest-product industries.

Forests are the climax vegetational form wherever precipitation is heavy and year-round. Such areas comprise much of both the equatorial region and the western margins of continents in middle latitudes (Fig. 8-1). Forests also occur in many areas of markedly seasonal precipitation; indeed, they occur wherever it is possible for trees to extract enough moisture from the soil to offset the transpiration losses inseparable from an arborescent form of life. Many species have specializations designed to reduce such losses; seasonally low temperatures by themselves are little check to forest growth, constituting, in effect, a physiological drought for which the very important group of the conifers is well adapted.

Commercially the enormous botanical variety of the world's forests can be allocated to two main divisions, the coniferous forests and the broad-leaved, or hardwood, forests. The *coniferous forests* account for only about one-third of the world's forest area, but they provide half the exploited forest area and produce four-fifths of the output of sawnwood. They are largely confined to high latitudes in the Northern Hemisphere, where the taiga, a forest composed mainly of various species of spruce, fir, pine, and larch, interspersed with the broad-leaved birch and aspen, extends from coast to coast in the North American and Eurasian continents. Over enormous areas, however, the severity of the climate results in a very low productivity, particularly towards the northern margin, and the forest is frequently interrupted by great expanses of swamp and bog. In lower latitudes coniferous forests occur in mountainous regions and in lowlands of poorly sandy soil; normally at such latitudes they cannot compete with broad-leaved forests. With a warm and humid climate the growth rate of the pine forests of the southeast United States is many times that of even the most productive parts of the taiga.

Less than 10 per cent of the world's coniferous forest area is located in the Southern Hemisphere. To help remedy this shortcoming, more than 2 million acres of conifers have been planted in parts of the Southern Hemisphere, the preferred species being the Monterey pine (*Pinus radiata*), which in the mild climates of temperate portions of the southern continents grows very rapidly. About half of all such plantings have occurred on the central volcanic plateau of North Island, New Zealand.

The *broad-leaved,* or *hardwood, forests* can be subdivided into the temperate deciduous forests, and the evergreen broad-leaved forests of the intertropical world; however, some commercially important tropical timbers such as teak are derived from monsoon forests that drop their leaves in the dry season. The timbers of the broad-leaved forests compete with each other rather than with those of the coniferous forests. Much of the original temperate deciduous forest has been cleared for agriculture, but the tropical hardwood forests constitute the largest area of unexploited forest in the world, covering almost half of South America and a similar proportion of central Africa.

In relation to their weight coniferous timbers are strong and are easily worked; hence they are often known as softwoods. Of greater commercial importance, however, is their low cost of extraction, as coniferous forests have a simple age and species structure and have a very limited subsidiary vegetation which is no obstacle to logging. A log of coniferous timber is much lighter than a hardwood log of comparable size, and its transport is often aided by the frozen ground and snow cover of winter. Coniferous timbers also offer advantages in the manufacture of wood pulp and paper, although almost all timbers can now be used for pulping. The close proximity of vast areas of coniferous forest to the main consuming centers of Western Europe and eastern North America is also a factor of the utmost importance in the greater utilization of such forests.

In contrast, the broad-leaved forests possess a variety of species that make for high extraction costs; individuals of the same species may be widely separated and dispersed among other species of limited or negligible value. In the evergreen rain forest this handicap is augmented by the massive buttresses of many species and the extreme toughness of the timber, and innumerable woody scramblers and the richness of the understory vegetation often render it difficult to extract felled logs without doing considerable damage to the forest. Powerful socioeconomic obstacles often reinforce the physical hindrances to commercial exploitation. The difficulties confronting exploitation of these forests are so formidable that although South America possesses the largest continuous area of hardwood forest in the world, the bulk of the continent's production of industrial wood consists of softwood from the limited area of the so-called "Paraná pine forest" in southern Brazil and from the Chilean pine forests of southern Chile.

Thus, the commercial exploitation of tropical hardwood forests has largely been confined to the extraction of the most valuable cabinet woods, such as the mahoganies, rosewood, and greenheart, in a limited number of relatively accessible areas; many underdeveloped countries make considerable imports of forest products from the Northern Hemisphere even though they possess great areas of forest land. However, it is reasonably certain that the

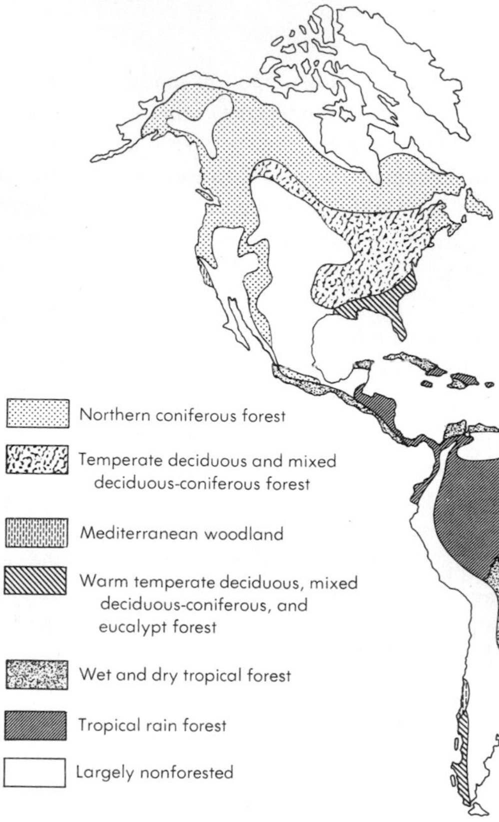

Fig. 8-1 Principal forest types of the world. Much of the original forest of temperate latitudes has been removed through extension of agriculture, but the greatest forest losses are now occurring within the tropics.

Northern coniferous forest
Temperate deciduous and mixed deciduous-coniferous forest
Mediterranean woodland
Warm temperate deciduous, mixed deciduous-coniferous, and eucalypt forest
Wet and dry tropical forest
Tropical rain forest
Largely nonforested

rapidly increasing population of the underdeveloped economies will compel a greater exploitation of the present enormous area of tropical hardwoods, and the relative contribution of the conifers to the world's supply of forest products is likely to decline in the future.

Products of Forest Industries

Three major producing areas dominate the world supply of forest products—Anglo-America, Europe, and the U.S.S.R. Together these areas account for some 70 per cent of total removals of forest products and about 85 per cent of sawnwood production. The U.S.S.R. alone has about half the total world area of softwoods, but its share of the softwood cut is considerably lower; however, over the past half-century the output of sawnwood in the U.S.S.R. has increased very rapidly, while that of the other two major producing regions has remained comparatively stable (Table 8-3). On the other hand, output of the new forest industries, particularly pulp and paper, has grown enormously in both Europe and North America (Table 8-4).

Changes in the location of the lumbering industry which have been such a feature of past forest exploitation have continued in the present century, but the old "timber mining" type of exploitation is fast disappearing with the necessity for greater competitive efficiency. All forest industries show a tendency towards a progressively higher capital-labor ratio; the small, portable sawmill which followed the

advancing axmen is giving way to the large mill with an annual output of 20,000 standards[3] or more. Such a mill represents a very considerable capital investment, which must be safeguarded, and requires some three-quarters of a million acres of well-managed forest land to sustain it in northern Europe.

Concentration has proceeded furthest in the pulp and paper industry, for an integrated pulp and newsprint mill permits substantial savings in fuel costs, and there are considerable economies of scale. Even a medium-sized modern integrated mill requires a capital investment of up to 20 million dollars. Pulping utilizes small-diameter logs, so that it can make use of second growth and other material unsuitable for sawmilling; it can also consume some of the waste material from sawmilling, which can amount to as much as 40 per cent of the original timber volume. As board industries can consume even shavings and sawdust, integration of forest industries permits the fullest use of forest resources.

[3] 1 standard = 4.67 cords; 1 cord = 128 cubic feet

Pulp and Paper Paper is composed of cellulose fibrous material, various fillers being added to impart desired properties. Cellulose is found in all plants, and a wide variety of materials are still used in papermaking. Over the last century, however, wood pulp has risen to a position of preeminence in papermaking; it now provides more than 60 per cent of all fibrous materials used in the paper industry of the United States and more than 70 per cent of

Table 8-3

Sawnwood Production (Million cubic meters)

	1913	1937–1938	1961	
			SOFTWOODS	HARDWOODS
Europe	45.9	56.7	55.2	13.5
U.S.S.R.*	11.9	33.9	88.7	15.6
North America	112.8	72.7	81.6	11.8
Canada			17.7	0.9
United States			63.9	10.9
Central America			1.4	0.6
South America			3.3	5.5
Africa			0.6	1.7
Asia†			30.5	13.5
Pacific Area			2.9	2.6
WORLD TOTAL			264.2	64.8

* Boundaries at date stated.
† Including mainland China.
One standard = 4.672 cubic meters.
SOURCE: FAO, *Yearbook of Forest Product Statistics, 1962; State of Food and Agriculture, 1957.*

Table 8-4

Wood-pulp Production (Million metric tons)

	1913	1937	1961	
			MECHANICAL	CHEMICAL
Europe	4.6	11.4	6.3	11.9
Norway, Sweden, and Finland		6.8	3.2	7.5
U.S.S.R.*	0.2		1.0	2.4
North America	3.4	10.5	9.6	23.1
Canada			5.5	5.1
United States			4.1	17.9
Central and South America			0.3	0.5
Asia†			1.2	3.6
Pacific Area			0.3	0.3
WORLD TOTAL			18.8	41.8

* Boundaries at date stated.
† Includes China.
SOURCE: FAO, *Yearbook of Forest Product Statistics, 1962*, Rome, 1962.

those used in the European paper industry.[4] To produce a ton of newsprint in a modern integrated mill, which must have a minimum output of 150,000 tons per year for economic operation, requires 100 tons of water and 2,000 kilowatt-hours of electric power. The requirements for the manufacture of pulp and paper are therefore a copious and assured supply of raw materials, cheap power, chemicals, capital, and unlimited water. These requirements, in fact, largely restrict the manufacture of pulp and paper to countries at a high level of economic development; Canada and the United States together produce more than half the world's pulp, and Europe about one-quarter.

There are two main methods of producing wood pulp, the mechanical and the chemical, but the semichemical process, which is particularly suitable for pulping hardwoods, is rapidly increasing in importance. Approximately one-third of world pulp output is produced by the *mechanical,* or *groundwood, process,* which is very suitable for the production of newsprint. Although relatively cheap and simple, this process is selective in its raw materials, requiring woods with little gum and resin; thus spruce and fir are the most sought-after species. The groundwood process is most important in Canada, where it accounts for more than half the output, and in Europe, where a little more than one-third of all pulp is produced by this process; the limited supplies of suitable raw materials make mechanical pulp of small significance in the United States. The power and capital requirements of groundwood pulp and newsprint production are much larger than those of other forest industries, for the economies of scale make large units mandatory.

In *chemical processes,* the lignin in wood is dissolved by acids or alkalis, leaving pure cellulose. All chemical processes are more expensive and give a lower yield than the mechanical method, but they produce finer papers and can make use of a wide variety of timbers. The sulfite process, which uses calcium bisulfite at high temperature and pressure, is mainly used for the production of book and fine paper, and also requires wood of low resin content. The sulfate process employs sodium sulfate and caustic soda, and is very suitable for use with resinous timbers such as pines; it produces strong kraft papers for wrapping and for containers. Again, the United States and Europe differ considerably in the employment of the two principal chemical processes. Sulfite pulp accounts for only one-third of chemical pulp output in the United States and is of declining importance, but that of the sulfate process progressively increases. In Europe, however, sulfite pulp still accounts for over 70 per cent of chemical pulp output. The reasons for the greater importance of the sulfate process in the United States are to be found in its suitability for the enormous area of pine forest in the South and in the great importance of packaging materials in the United States economy, in which high-speed wrapping and packing have become an integral part of mass production. The sulfate process has the further advantage that the chemicals used can be easily recovered, thus lowering costs and avoiding the stream pollution that is often associated with the sulfite process; with a large supply of suitable raw materials, it appears probable that the sulfate process will also be of increasing importance in Europe in the future. Chemical processes are less demanding in their power requirements than groundwood; on the other hand, water requirements for bleached pulp are about five times as great, and chemical consumption may amount to half the total weight of bleached-pulp output. It is to be expected, therefore, that the two principal pulp-making industries show

[4] The lower figure for the United States reflects the greater use of wastepaper, which is of particular importance in the paperboard industry. The collection and use of wastepaper in the United States is facilitated by a per capita paper consumption which is more than twice that of Western Europe.

These digesters separate cellulose from lignin in chemical pulping; the photograph was taken before the building housing the equipment was fully completed.

"**Log dozers**" manipulate logs on this British Columbia river (below, left).

Control of insect pests is greatly facilitated by aerial spraying (below, right).

considerable differences in their respective location patterns.

The *semichemical process* employs two stages, wood chips being first cooked to remove sufficient lignin to permit subsequent mechanical extraction of the cellulose. At present chiefly used for the manufacture of roofing felt and corrugated board, the process lends itself well to the use of hardwoods, and its use in the United States has been greatly stimulated by the growing scarcity of softwood pulp; already hardwood pulp amounts to 15 per cent of total output, and by 1975 it may amount to as much as one-quarter. This process would appear to have a bright future in the European industry, which also derives about 15 per cent of its pulp output from hardwoods.

Papermaking originally grew up near its markets, which also provided much of the raw materials in the form of rags. Some old paper mills, whose siting was often determined by the availability of water, have sought refuge from competition through specialization. In centers with inadequate or negligible supplies of local pulpwood large modern mills have been erected at tidewater locations using imported pulp, such as on the lower Thames and Medway in Britain.[5] With a small domestic pulp production but a very large paper consumption, Britain has acquired large interests in pulp and paper manufacture in Scandinavia, Canada, and the United States. Throughout the world there is a growing tendency for integrated mills producing both wood pulp and paper to enlarge their share of output, so that papermaking is becoming more and more an industry that is raw-material oriented.

Board Products The manufacture of various types of fiberboard and hardboard is a twentieth-century industry that has shown an even more rapid rate of growth than that of pulp and paper. Fiberboard is manufactured mainly from groundwood pulp, but many broadleaved species can be used, either by themselves or in blends with coniferous pulp, and the industry can also use sawmill residues; in Sweden about half the board output is produced from sawmill waste. Even more spectacular has been the growth of the particle-board industry, which dates only from World War II. Developed in Germany as a timber substitute during the wartime shortage, particle board is a sheet material of lignocellulose bonded with a thermosetting resin of phenol or urea. Many raw materials can be used in its manufacture, but forest-product waste is mainly utilized in Europe, which produces two-thirds of the present world output; about half of Europe's output is accounted for by West Germany alone. As the capital investment for a particle-board mill is only half that of a fiberboard mill of comparable output and water is not needed and power requirements are extremely modest, the location of particle-board mills is subject to fewer restrictions than those of other forest industries; moreover, resin costs may amount to more than the cost of wood materials. As economic operation does not require large units, the particle-board industry could be of profound importance in achieving a much fuller utilization of forest products. Its manufacture has also been taken up on a considerable scale in Japan, which, despite some magnificent and well-managed forests, experiences a chronic timber shortage.

[5] **Such mills have higher costs than integrated mills, as pulp for export must be dried. The lowering of tariffs in the EFTA will thus expose them to increasingly severe competition from integrated Scandinavian mills.**

FOREST INDUSTRIES OF THE UNITED STATES AND OTHER LANDS

Timber production and industries connected with timber generate about 5 per cent of the United States national product, that is,

Fig. 8-2 The United States possesses a rich variety of forest types. (U.S. Forest Service.)

about the same proportion as produced by agriculture. The United States has over 660 million acres of forest land,[6] about one-third of the total area, but almost 200 million acres, mainly situated in the Rockies and the Southwest, are noncommercial forests, withheld from timber production for protective and other purposes (Fig. 8-2). The commercial forest area is almost equally divided between softwoods and hardwoods, but almost three-quarters of the timber cut consists of softwoods. In general, hardwoods are underutilized, for growth exceeds cut, but in respect of the more valuable species the situation is much less favorable.

Timber production in the United States has shown marked shifts in location in the past, and further changes are inevitable in the future.

[6] Including coastal Alaska. Interior Alaska possesses a further 120 million acres of forest, of which one-third is regarded as commercial forest.

The effect of these changes has been substantially to raise the costs of lumber, as the principal centers of production have moved further and further from the main markets, which lie in the Northeast. The diminishing stands of quality virgin timber have also resulted in substantially higher prices for large-diameter logs, which for purposes such as veneer manufacture have become in short supply. Until 1860 the principal lumbering area was the spruce and fir forests of northern New England. After the Civil War the white, red, and jack pine forests of the Lake states took over the premier position, to be displaced about the turn of the century by the longleaf and slash yellow pine forests of the South. In the late Twenties, the West became the leading producing region, a position that it will hold for some time to come. But since 1906 and despite an increasing utilization of the magnificent forests of the Pacific Northwest, total lumber production has slowly declined; at one time a major exporter of timber products, the United States since 1940 has become a substantial net importer.

The West (that is, the Pacific and Mountain states, to which the United States Forest Service also attaches the Black Hills of South Dakota) has only a quarter of the total forest area, but it produces about half the sawnwood and possesses no less than 70 per cent of the standing-timber volume (Fig. 8-3). This is because it contains the last remaining stands of virgin forest, some of which, such as the Douglas fir forests of the wetter western slopes of the Coast Ranges and of the Cascades of Washington and Oregon and the redwood forests of the Coast Ranges of northern California, produce a tremendous volume of timber from one mature stem. With the felling of these mature forests the main center of timber production must return to the East, where all forests are second growth; at the present the mature stands of the West necessarily result in a low volume of growth in comparison with the East. In marked contrast to other parts of the country, much of the western forest area has been retained in public ownership; national forests account for 52 per cent of the commercial forest area of the West but for only 17 per cent of the national commercial forest area. Until World War II timber cut from national forests supplied only a very small proportion of the total domestic cut, but from then on the importance of public timber increased rapidly; by 1960 about a fifth of the total timber production originated in national forests, and this share must enlarge in the future as the more accessible forests, which are largely in private hands, are depleted.

Washington and Oregon constitute by far the most important lumbering area in the West; these two states alone account for about a

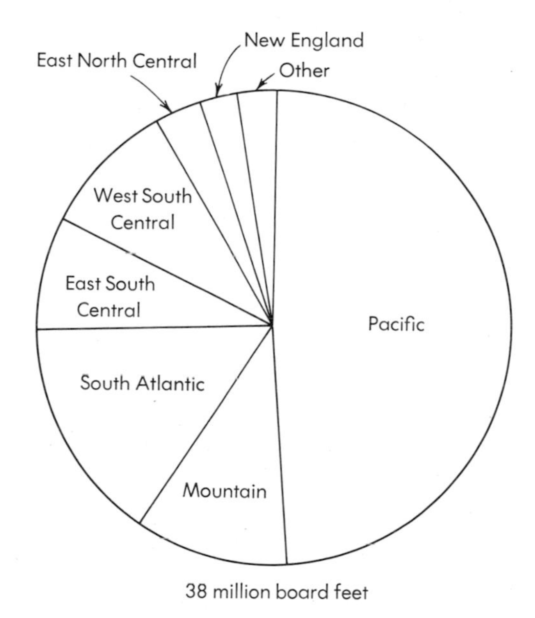

Fig. 8-3 Lumber production by census regions in the United States, 1960.
The most populous portions of the United States provide only a fraction of their timber requirements; the three Pacific states produce nearly half the United States timber output.

third of the national sawnwood production. About half the western cut consists of Douglas fir, which, because of its quality and suitability for many purposes, has become the most widely used timber in the United States. The balance of the western cut largely consists of ponderosa pine and Jeffrey pine and western hemlock, the two former occurring in association over much of the drier eastern mountain slopes of the Cascades and northern Sierras of California and over much of the Rockies; but there are a number of other species of commercial importance, such as western red cedar, western white pine, Sitka spruce, and various western firs. Transport of the enormous logs from the forest has been greatly facilitated by the use of large crawler tractors and specialized handling equipment; logs may be lifted on to powerful diesel trucks by power shovels equipped with heel booms or may be picked up by giant grabs, and redwood logs too large for transport can now be split instead of being sawn.

Though it accounts for only about 15 per cent of the national pulpwood production, the Pacific Northwest is becoming of increasing importance as a pulp producer as the virgin timber is depleted (Fig. 8-4). The pulp industry in this part of the country was originally based on cheap western hemlock, which occurred in association with Douglas fir and was also removed in logging operations. Other materials are now used as well, and production has been given a substantial impetus by the acquisition of large areas of forest by paper manufacturers, who operate their properties on a sustained-yield basis. There is a growing tendency for large sawmills to possess or to cooperate with pulp mills. Nevertheless, the forest industries of the Pacific slope are a striking example of a common American problem—how to reconcile large-scale units which achieve low-cost production and the elimination of waste, on the one hand, with opportunities for the small producer, on the other. Despite its large modern mills the area still possesses an enormous

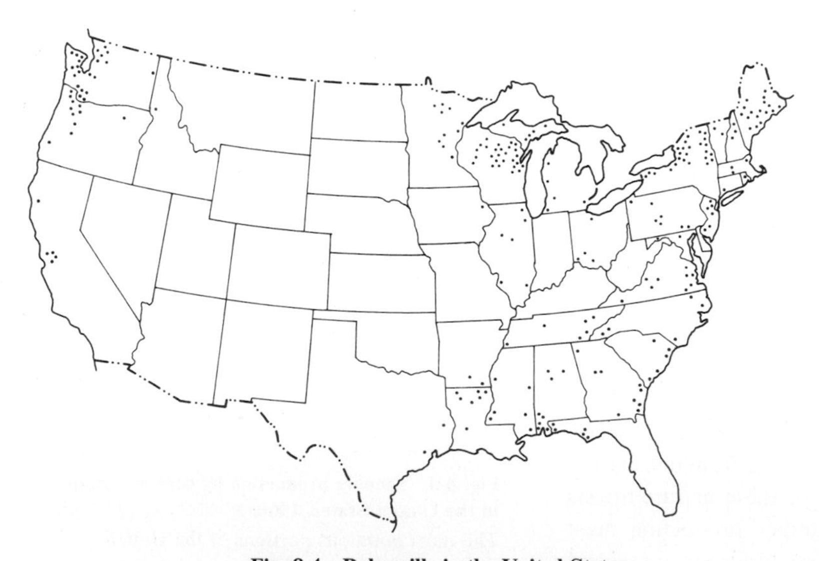

Fig. 8-4 Pulp mills in the United States.
The location of pulp mills in the United States appears more closely related to markets than to raw materials. (After Thoman.)

number of small portable sawmills whose felling practices leave much to be desired and in whose operations a large proportion of the original timber volume is wasted.

Though outranked by the West, the yellow pine forests of the South still produce about 40 per cent of the total output of sawnwood and not far short of half the national pulpwood production. In contrast to the West, the area of publicly owned forest in the South is very small, but the large privately owned property is relatively more important. More than half of all the large privately owned forest properties (that is, exceeding 50,000 acres) in the country are located in the South, and there is a pronounced tendency for this concentration to grow. The dominant position of the large private forest property in the South is the result of the great growth of the pulp and paper industry since the Twenties, and the economies of scale. To ensure that they operate near capacity, most large pulp mills prefer to meet at least half of their pulpwood requirements from their own forests. Many of the largest-sized mills own sufficient forest land to be independent of outside suppliers, although others purchase pulpwood from farmers and landowners. The main paper products of the South are kraft paper and newsprint; as in other parts of the country (but in contrast to the general situation in Canada and in Scandinavia), many of the largest newsprint mills are owned by newspapers themselves. One of the largest newsprint mills in the South is that operated by the Bowater Company, a largely British-owned concern, at Calhoun, Tennessee.

Although no longer of importance in sawnwood production save in isolated areas serving mainly local markets, the East and the North are of considerable significance in pulp production, accounting for about 40 per cent of the national output. Pulping provides a market for inferior second-growth logs and, increasingly for many hardwoods. With its longer industrial history, the pulp and paper industry in this section of the country possesses a much greater diversity than the industry in the West and South; all types of paper are manufactured, but the area produces a high proportion of the finest types of paper. Many old, established centers of papermaking, originally based on local materials, have succumbed in the face of competition from newer areas, but there are many survivals in Wisconsin, Michigan, and New York where the paper industry has found refuge from competition through specialization or has successfully adopted newer methods by importing raw materials from other parts of the country or from abroad. Production of groundwood pulp in the United States is largely confined to Maine.

The problems confronting forestry in the Northeast are severe. Indiscriminate cutting has led to the extension of hardwoods at the expense of the softwoods and to the debasement of the hardwoods themselves through a reduction in the proportion of the more valuable species. Similar problems occur in other parts of the country, but their solution in the Northeast is retarded by the great dissemination of ownership; a very large proportion of the forest land consists of small lots, so that the application of modern forestry methods is rendered difficult and expensive.

Canada

As a producer of forest products Canada is surpassed only by the United States and the U.S.S.R. Forest industries are of greater relative importance in the Canadian economy, however, and normally three-quarters or more of the total output of forest products is exported. Forests cover over 40 per cent of the area of the Dominion and over 60 per cent of that of the ten provinces; the proportion of the total forest area that consists of softwoods is also higher than in the United States. About

95 per cent of Canada's forest land is in public ownership.

Save for Prince Edward Island, where the original mixed forest cover has been largely cleared, all provinces participate in forest exploitation. In sawnwood, British Columbia, with its forests of Douglas fir, hemlock, spruce, and cedar, is of major importance. Douglas fir is Canada's principal timber in terms of value of output, but in volume it is exceeded by spruce. As in the lumber industry of the adjacent portion of the United States, sawmilling in British Columbia is characterized by units of very large size, many working in conjunction with pulping plants; pulp production, though only some 15 per cent of the national total, is expanding rapidly, and substantial areas of forest have been leased to American paper and rayon companies. Possessing no less than 70 per cent of the country's stocks of sawnwood on accessible forest lands, British Columbia will probably remain a major sawnwood producer for some time to come.

Eastern Canada lacks the high-quality timber of the Pacific Coast, but its extensive areas of spruce, balsam fir, and pine forest and its tremendous water resources provide the basis for an industry that accounts for about 40 per cent of world pulp output. In terms both of employment and a value of output, the pulp and paper industry is Canada's principal manufacturing industry, producing some 15 per cent of export earnings. Its growth has stimulated, and been conditional upon, the expansion of hydroelectric power, of which the industry is the country's largest consumer.

Through eastern Canada as a whole, almost 90 per cent of forest licenses or leases are held by pulpwood producers. Large pulp mills are located in every province of eastern Canada except Prince Edward Island, but the greatest concentration occurs along the margins of the St. Lawrence lowlands in Quebec and along the margin of the Laurentian Shield in Ontario. Integrated mills number about half the total establishments and account for an increasing share of total paper production; eastern Canada produces all types of paper, but its specialty is newsprint, of which Canada is by far the world's largest producer, with an output over four times that of the United States. The world's largest integrated newsprint mill is claimed to be that of the Bowater Company at Corner Brook, Newfoundland. Logging is traditionally a seasonal occupation, but the increased use of mechanical equipment is gradually transforming it into a year-round activity, and the temporary logging camp is giving way to more permanent communities.

Canada's importance as a supplier of forest products to the United States is profound and is likely to grow with the passage of time. The United States takes about two-thirds of Canada's exports of lumber and about 90 per cent of its exports of pulpwood, wood pulp, paper, and veneers. The export of newsprint is facilitated by the absence of American tariffs on imported newsprint, but for other types of paper the American tariff barriers are severe. Canada would like to reduce its chronic adverse trade balance with the United States by exporting more of its forest products in processed form and to discontinue supplying large quantities of raw materials for processing across the frontier. A similar situation, however, applies in the case of most other Canadian raw materials, and this is becoming a major issue in Canada's relations with the United States.

Europe and the U.S.S.R.

Scientific forestry began in Europe,[7] as did most of the modern forest-product industries. Two world wars, population growth, and a very

[7] As discussed in this section Europe is noncommunist Europe, that is, excluding the U.S.S.R. and its satellites.

high rate of economic growth since 1950 have placed a very severe strain on Europe's forest resources. Although Europe is still an exporter of forest products, its surplus must disappear in the near future if its present rate of economic growth is maintained. This deficiency could, it is true, be easily made good from the U.S.S.R.; however, the U.S.S.R. is certain to experience increasing demands for timber arising from its own economic development and from that of satellite countries.

As a producer of forest products, Europe falls into two major divisions. All of west, central, and southern Europe is a marked deficiency area, in which the proportion of forest land is very low. Forests cover less than 10 per cent of the surface area of Britain, Ireland, and the Netherlands and barely reach this figure in Denmark. Forests originally covered three-quarters of France and Italy but now amount to no more than one-fifth despite a very large area of mountains and hill-land which offers limited opportunities for agriculture. In order to expand the forest area, many European countries have made extensive new plantings of conifers, such as those on the sandy heathlands of the Landes of southwest France, the geest of northwest Germany, and Breckland in East Anglia; large areas of uplands, most of which probably carried a coniferous forest cover in the past, have also been replanted. Conifers have also been planted in areas that were formerly under a hardwood forest, an operation that, on the whole, has achieved only modest success. Strict control over cutting is enforced in most European countries, even though a high proportion of forest land is generally in private hands.

In Norway, Sweden, and Finland, on the other hand, a large proportion of the original forest cover still remains. Almost 60 per cent of the land area in Sweden and nearly 70 per cent of that of Finland are forested; in Norway, with its very extensive area of mountains, the proportion falls to a quarter, but there is, nevertheless, a substantial surplus of forest products available for export.

The coniferous forest of Scots pine (the principal conifer of Western and central Europe), Norway spruce, fir, and larch which has developed on the thin, poor soils of the lake- and rock-strewn wilderness of the Baltic Shield is the basis of one of the most important sawnwood- and pulp-producing areas in the world. The development of this forest wealth was largely a consequence of nineteenth-century economic expansion; before this time the area north of approximately 60°N exercised a negligible influence in the economic life of Europe. The forest industries of northern Europe have thus always been largely directed towards an export market, but their development has inevitably resulted in a very high per capita lumber consumption, that of Finland being by far the highest in the world.

In contrast to the situation in the rest of Europe, logging and sawmilling in northern Europe are large-scale activities; many mills along the coasts of the Gulf of Bothnia and the Gulf of Finland rival in size those of the Pacific Northwest and of British Columbia. More than 20,000 of these sawmills exist in Norway, Sweden, and Finland, but a relatively few large mills account for the greater portion of sawnwood production; Sweden, the largest sawnwood producer, has an output of more than 1.5 million standards annually. As elsewhere in the world, the location of sawmills is closely determined by the facilities for transporting logs from the forest to the mill and from the mill to the market. In the pioneer areas of northern Sweden and Finland, where most of the large modern mills are located, mills are situated on the coast so that logs can be floated downriver and the sawn products loaded directly into freighters specially designed for the lumber trade. In southern Finland and in central and southern Sweden, where sawmilling is an older established industry, mills are smaller and tend to be located inland in close proximity to their log supply, moving their sawn products by truck or rail. As the northern portion of the Gulf of Bothnia is frozen for six months of the year, the lumber export trade is markedly seasonal. In marked contrast to the Canadian ownership pattern, the forests of northern Europe are largely in private hands, but the distinction between private and public ownership has little practical significance in view of the stringent laws regulating cutting and replanting; in Sweden cuttings in privately owned forests are determined by a Forest Conservation Board.

Norway, Sweden, and Finland produce some two-thirds of Europe's wood pulp and one-third of its newsprint (Fig. 8-5). Again in contrast to Canada, the output of chemical pulp (chiefly sulfite) substantially exceeds that of groundwood pulp, and considerable progress has been made in modifying the standard sulfite process to avoid stream pollution, through the replacement of calcium bisulfite by recoverable ammonium bisulfite. Substantial exports of groundwood pulp are also made to countries of Western and central Europe for conversion into newsprint; Britain usually slightly outranks Finland for the premier position among European newsprint producers. Norway, Sweden, and Finland are also the principal suppliers of high-quality cellulose sheet for the European rayon industry.

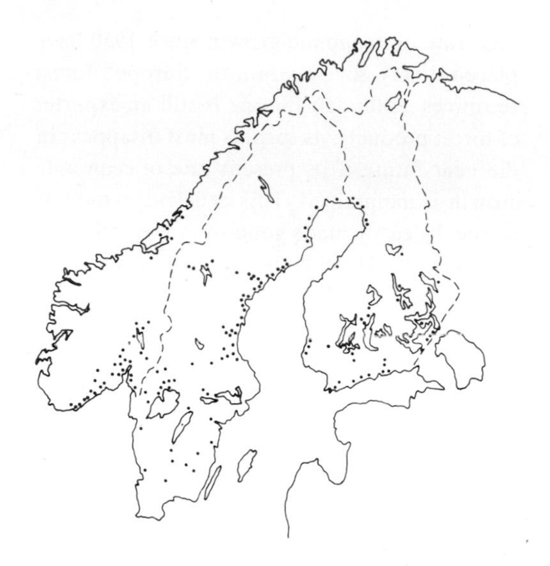

Fig. 8-5 Pulp mills in northern Europe. These mills are largely raw-material oriented. (A. Somme [ed.], *A Geography of Norden.*)

The taiga of the U.S.S.R. closely resembles the forest of northern Europe, although Siberian species of spruce, fir, and larch become increasingly important towards the east. Its development, however, has so far been relatively little affected by the modern forest-product industries, and the U.S.S.R. is mainly a producer of sawnwood. Since the end of World War II Russian sawnwood output has overtaken that of both Europe and the United States, and in 1960 accounted for a third of total world production. From Finno-Karelia and the Kola Peninsula the main center of activity has moved eastwards to the basin of the Northern Divina, down which logs are floated to Archangel, the foremost center of the sawmilling industry in the European Continent and the principal port for the export of Russian timber. Technically very primitive before World War II, the Russian timber industry has received considerable investment in postwar development plans; crawler tractors and mechanical saws have been introduced, and many large modern sawmills have been constructed. Timber exports have always been a major source of foreign exchange to the U.S.S.R., but much trade takes place on a government-to-government basis. Britain is usually the largest buyer of Russian timber.

Forest-product industries, in consequence of the nature of the Soviet economy, have not matched the rate of growth of sawnwood production, and per capita paper consumption is very much lower than that of Europe. The forest-product industries have not followed the northward and eastward march of timber production, being located in the southern margin of the taiga; southern Finno-Karelia, essentially tributary to the Leningrad industrial region, has the greatest concentration.

SELECTED REFERENCES

Alderfer, E. B., and H. E. Michl: *Economics of American Industry,* McGraw-Hill Book Company, New York, 1957, pp. 284–303.

Food and Agriculture Organization: *State of Food and Agriculture,* Rome, 1962, pp. 88–128.

———: *World Forest Inventory, 1958,* Rome, 1960.

———: *World Forest Resources,* Rome, 1957.

———: *Yearbook of Forest Product Statistics,* Rome, annually.

Haden-Guest, Stephen, et al.: *World Geography of Forest Resources,* The American Geographical Society, Special Publication no. 33, The Ronald Press Company, New York, 1956.

Organisation for European Economic Cooperation: *The Pulp and Paper Industry in Europe,* Paris, 1959.

———: *The Pulp and Paper Industry in the U.S.A.,* Paris, 1961.

Prunty, Merle C., Jr.: "Recent Expansion in the Southern Pulp-Paper Industries," *Economic Geography,* vol. 32, pp. 51–57, 1956.

Rodgers, Allan: "Changing Locational Patterns in the Soviet Pulp and Paper Industry," *Annals of the Association of American Geographers,* vol. 45, pp. 85–109, 1955.

Royal Commission on Canada's Economic Prospects, Forestry Study Group: *The Outlook for Canadian Forest Industries,* Ottawa, 1957.

Somme, Axel (ed.): *A Geography of Norden,* J. W. Cappelens, Oslo, 1960, pp. 181–191, 248–251, 311–318.

Stafford, Howard A., Jr.: "Factors in the Location of the Paperbound Container Industry," *Economic Geography,* vol. 36, pp. 260–266, 1960.

United Nations and Food and Agriculture Organization: *Timber Trends and Prospects in the Asia-Pacific Region,* Geneva, 1961.

Chapter 9

FISHING AND FISHERIES

The term "fishing" may be interpreted as the landing of all types of marine and freshwater products, of which there is a very great variety. Whaling, because of its many special features, is customarily regarded as a separate activity, but the distinction is one of convenience only. Certain practices of the whaling industry, such as the use of factory, or processing, ships, have already been adopted in other types of marine production, and it is greatly to be hoped that the international cooperation which is perhaps whaling's most distinctive feature will ultimately embrace all the world's major commercial fisheries. Total employment in fishing is estimated at about 5 million, but as with forestry, there is an enormous number of part-time fishermen, and the influence of fisheries in national life extends far beyond the numbers employed and the value of output.

The total output of the world's fisheries, excluding the products of the whaling industry, was estimated by the FAO as amounting to some 41 million tons in 1961, almost double the output of 1948 but still substantially below the world meat output (Fig. 9-1). If the present rate of growth of the world fishing catch is maintained, however, it will exceed total meat output within a very few years. About 90 per cent of the total fisheries output consisted of fish, the balance being largely made up of shellfish and crustaceans. Freshwater fisheries supply only a little over 10 per cent of the total output, so that marine products are clearly of overwhelming importance in the world's fisheries.

The principal use for fish is as food, either fresh or in some preserved form; less than 10 per cent of the world output is absorbed in nonfood uses, principally the manufacture of foodstuffs for animals and fertilizers. In densely populated parts of the world with poorly developed animal industries fish usually provide the principal source of animal protein in diet; in all underdeveloped countries the scarcity and high price of meat is a strong stimulus to fishing. On the other hand, those Southern Hemisphere countries with a high

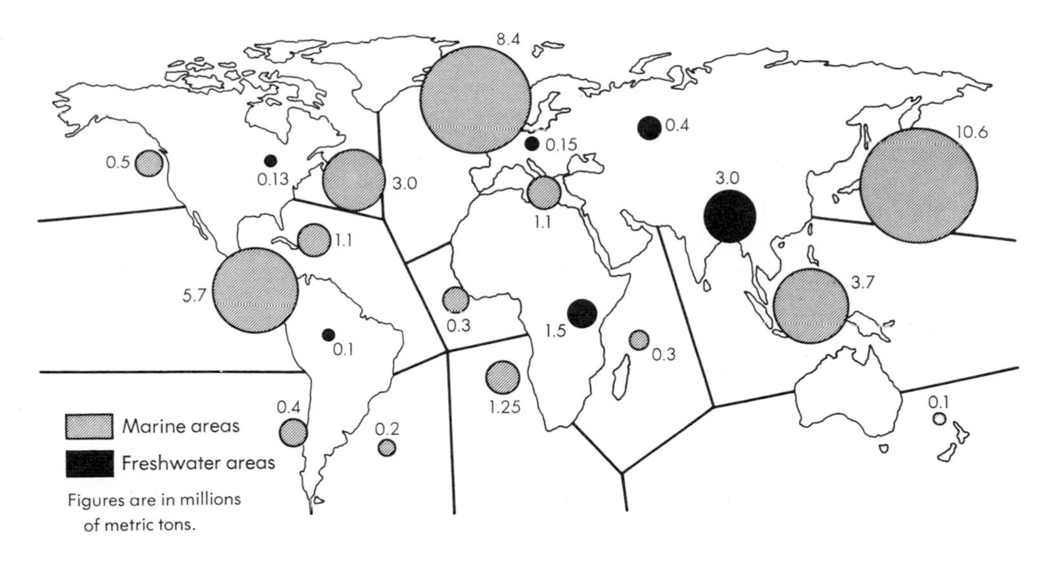

Fig. 9-1 World fishery production by regions, 1961.
Rapid expansion of landings in China and Japan has carried the northwest Pacific to the premier position among world fishing grounds. (FAO, *Yearbook of Fishery Statistics,* 1961.)

meat consumption per head have poorly developed fisheries. But whereas some underdeveloped economies have a very high per capita fish consumption, Thailand, Burma, and the Philippines having the highest levels in the world, the great majority consume considerably less per head than do the highly developed economies, and it is in the latter alone that the use of fish for purposes other than for direct human consumption assumes considerable importance. Generally, underdeveloped countries overutilize their freshwater fisheries but underutilize their sea fisheries; the former are generally of very minor significance in highly developed economies. The limited capital equipment at the disposal of the fisherman and the physical difficulties encountered in sea fishing in low latitudes, such as the widespread occurrence of coral and of large predators which damage nets, are considerable limitations to sea fishing in many countries at a low level of economic development. However, cultural factors are also important; unlike the Japanese, the Chinese have never been deep-sea fishermen, despite their long history of seafaring.

Although in certain areas, such as south China, Japan, and north Java, pisculture is an important activity in the local economy, for the world at large fishing is essentially "marine hunting." It is a form of hunting in which the quarry possesses habits which are imperfectly known and little understood. The present century has witnessed a quickening of interest in oceanography and marine biology, but knowledge of the life cycles of many important commercial species is so incomplete as to constitute a profound obstacle to the maintenance of a high level of productivity. Only a great increase in research expenditure can fill these gaps, but as fish know no frontiers whatever mankind may propose, a close degree of international cooperation is also vital in implementing the results of scientific research.

This limited knowledge of marine biology

is a principal cause of the speculative character of much of the fishing industry. Catches may be so tremendous in one season as to produce a sharp decline in prices, and in another they may be meager in the extreme. Species formerly plentiful off certain coasts may suddenly disappear, impoverishing whole communities. Sea fishing is at the mercy of wind and weather, so that short-term fluctuations in supply are also considerable; bad weather can make windfall profits for those vessels fortunate enough to secure good catches while their competitors are forced either to cease fishing and run for shelter or to lie idly in harbor. By its very nature fishing is an enterprise that offers only modest returns to those engaged in it. Under certain conditions, however, a favorable capital-labor ratio may result in a very high productivity per worker; thus the crew of a tuna clipper or a large Hull trawler, remunerated by a share of the proceeds of the catch, may be persons of substance in comparison with the majority of fishermen. But fishing, even at best, is a hard and unattractive occupation and frequently a dangerous one. Throughout history the development of fishing has often resulted from limited opportunities of making a livelihood on land.

As in agriculture, it is clear that very modest technical improvements could often produce a marked increase in the productivity of many of the world's fishermen; but the limitations to such an increase are likely to be sharply defined. It may be true that there are as many fish in the sea as there ever were, but what fishermen really desire is the maintenance of numbers in the species of interest to them, in areas which it is convenient for them to fish. Many fishing grounds show definite evidence of overfishing; both world wars provided relief from regular trawling in the North Sea, which resulted in a considerable increase in the average size of many species when intensive fishing was resumed. Fishing apparatus of high productivity, such as traps and fish wheels, has been prohibited in certain areas in the interests of conservation.

How far man can enlarge the size of the fish population of commercial importance in the seas is an extremely controversial question, but there is no question that in the comparatively limited areas of intensive fishing, the natural replacement of the commercial fish population may be seriously impaired. This problem again focuses attention on the necessity of international cooperation; it is not possible to expect any nation to limit its fishing activities if its abstinence is exploited by commercial rivals.

DISTRIBUTION OF FISH AND FISHERIES

The enormous extent of the oceans and the remarkable response of fish life to the great variety of environments open to it have resulted in a tremendous proliferation of forms; alone among the vertebrates, fish rival the insects in numbers[1] and in variety. It is possible that the total number of fish species may amount to more than 50,000; nevertheless only a few hundred of these are of economic importance, and the number of those of major significance is even more restricted. The molluscs and the crustaceans, two other great divisions of animal life that support valuable fisheries, occur in even greater numbers and diversity; but only a few score species of these also are of direct commercial importance.

Sea fish are customarily divided into pelagic, or free-swimming, species inhabiting the surface layers and demersal, or benthonic,

[1] **There may be as many as 500 million herring in a shoal; many millions of such shoals occur each year in the main herring fisheries.**

forms, the bottom-dwelling varieties; however, the distinction is somewhat arbitrary. In total catch, pelagic fisheries are the more important. The clupeoids (herring family), which include many varieties of herring, shad, menhaden, sprats, sardines, pilchards, and anchovies, constitute the largest share of the pelagic catch and are by far the most important of all fish species, but the scombroids (mackerel family), which include mackerel, tuna (tunny), albacores, bonitos, jacks, and other related species, are very important in warmer waters (Fig. 9-2).

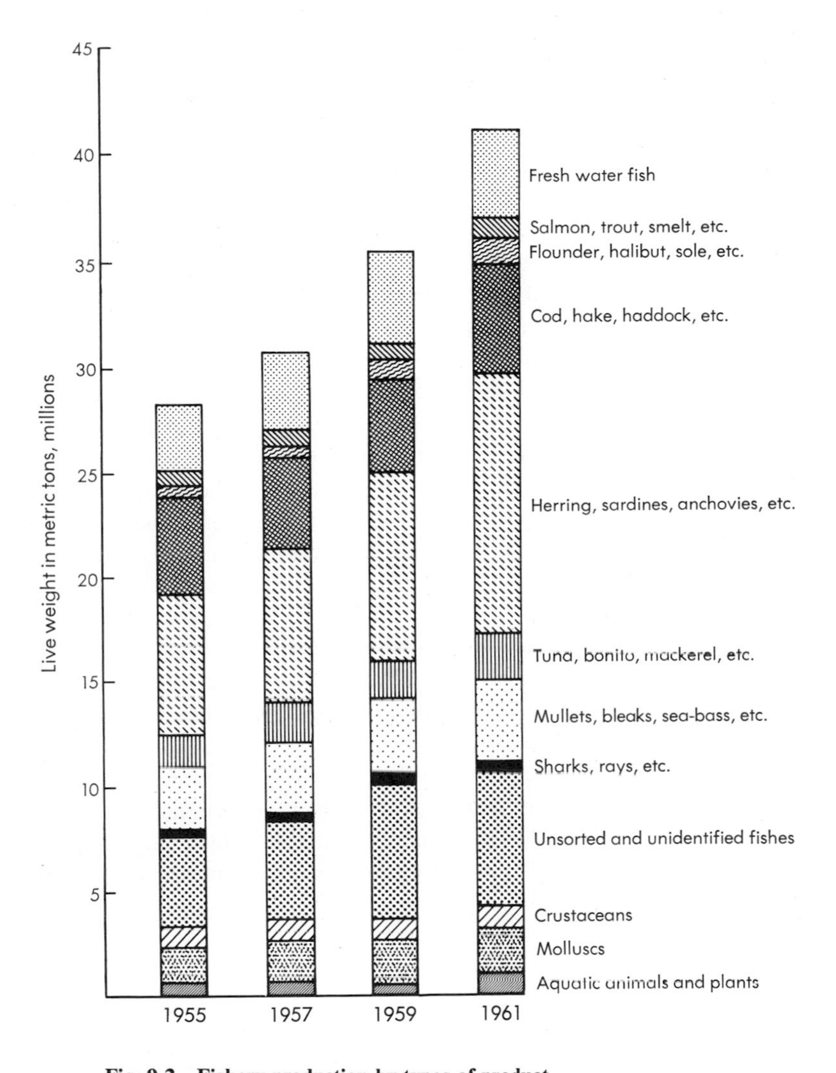

Fig. 9-2 Fishery production by types of product.
World fishery production has increased rapidly, but there has been little change in the composition of the catch. (FAO, *Yearbook of Fishery Statistics,* 1961.)

Many pelagic species are caught by nets; if correctly chosen, nets allow young and immature individuals to escape through the meshes. Most pelagic fish undertake considerable migrations which, though familiar for centuries, are still imperfectly understood; the spawning grounds of some of the most valuable species, such as tuna, are still unknown. Fishing for pelagic species, therefore, tends to be a seasonal occupation.

Demersal fish include cod, haddock, hake, and other species of the cod family and many kinds of flatfish such as halibut, plaice, and sole; in British fisheries these species are collectively known as "whitefish." Demersal species are mainly caught by means of long lines or by trawling, practices which do not distinguish between mature and immature individuals.[2] On the whole they demand more labor to catch than pelagic species, so that they command a higher price. In most countries for which statistics are available, the value of the demersal catch exceeds that of the pelagic.

The distribution of fish, as of all marine life, is directly affected by water temperature and salinity and by oceanic currents, for these factors profoundly influence the availability of food supplies. In the sea as on land, all animal life is fundamentally dependent upon plants, which form the basis of elaborate food chains. Apart from the larger algae, or seaweeds, the plant life of the sea is microscopic and provides food for many minute forms of animal life. Directly or indirectly, all fish are dependent upon this assemblage of minute plant and animal life, collectively known as plankton.[3] Plankton occurs throughout the upper layers of the oceans, but it is most plentiful in the cold surface waters of high latitudes in proximity to the continental landmasses, where the supply of plant nutrients is greatest. Coastal waters and epicontinental seas provide by far the largest share of the world catch, the fisheries of the open oceans being at present of limited importance. Tuna and related species move in large shoals over considerable stretches of ocean, but for the most part the species of the open oceans do not occur in concentrations which make for low costs of production.

The Northern Hemisphere, with its extensive continental shelves, accounts for some 98 per cent of the world's catch, but this primarily reflects the great concentration of population in this hemisphere. Five countries—China, Japan, the United States, the U.S.S.R., and Peru—produce more than 50 per cent of the total catch (Table 9-1). Nevertheless, fish have no nationality until caught; two-thirds of the total world catch originates in four great fishing areas—the northwest Pacific, the northeast Atlantic, the east central Pacific, and the northwest Atlantic. No one country fishes all four areas, but the U.S.S.R. fishes three. In comparison, the production of fish from the extensive tropical seas is very small, although the shallow seas of the large submarine extension of Southeast Asia may be considered an important exception. Tropical seas lack the convectional overturn of temperate waters by which nutrients derived from decaying organic material are returned to the surface, although in some areas cold currents and the upwelling of cold water may result in an enriched supply of plankton. There is some evidence, however, that the effects of the lower plankton production of the tropical seas have been overstated, and it is reasonable to assume that the world

[2] It had long been considered that the pressure of fish in the trawlnet made it impossible for immature specimens to escape. However, it now appears that such fish can pass through the mesh.

[3] They appear to get relatively little, however. The Danish biologist Thorson estimates that fish consume only 1 to 2 per cent of the total available fish food; the rest is consumed by invertebrates. It would therefore appear that reduction in the number of invertebrate predators would open up the possibilities of a greatly expanded fish population. See Alistair Hardy, *Fish and Fisheries,* Collins, London, 1959, p. 137.

Handling the large nets used in the Mediterranean tunny fishing requires much labor.

Table 9-1

Fish Catch, 1962

	METRIC TONS, THOUSANDS
Africa	2,640
North America	4,400
Canada	1,115
United States	2,905
South America	8,070
Peru	6,830
Asia	17,520
Japan	6,864
Mainland China*	5,020
India	974
Indonesia	943
Europe	8,350
Denmark	785
Britain	944
Iceland	832
Norway	1,338
Portugal	578
Spain	1,006
France	737
West Germany	633
U.S.S.R.	3,620
Pacific Area	130
WORLD TOTAL	44,720

* In 1959.
SOURCE: FAO, *Yearbook of Fishery Statistics, 1962*, Rome, 1963.

will have increasingly to look to the lower latitudes for much of its needed rise in fish production. More attention to species of little importance at present and the adoption of new fishing methods rather than the importation of those now used in temperate areas will be necessary, however, to make fuller utilization of what must be in total an astronomical fish population. The fisheries of the temperate waters of the Southern Hemisphere are also capable of considerable expansion; here limited markets and competition from other foodstuffs are the major obstacles.

Many nations subsidize their fishing industries, for reasons much the same as those for which they subsidize agriculture. Strategic considerations are very important, for the fishing fleet is traditionally the adjunct of the navy, providing both men and ships in times of emergency; the U.S.S.R. uses its large fishing fleet for intelligence purposes, as did Japan in the interwar period. In the late Fifties many European nations paid substantial subsidies to their fishing industries, partly to help them reequip with new vessels and more efficient fishing gear and partly to offset reductions in fishermen's incomes resulting from the extension of territorial waters by a number of nations; this effectively closed many valuable fishing grounds to all but the nationals concerned.

Northeast Atlantic Fisheries

Until 1957 the northeast Atlantic was, and had long been, the leading fishing area in the world. The area is shared by many nations, most of which also fish in the northwest Atlantic area, for the oceans are open to all, and those from distant places can often compete on better than equal terms with locals if their equipment is modern and efficient. All nations restrict the right to fish territorial waters to their own nationals (except where specific fishing treaties exist), but it is by no means clear how far these territorial waters extend offshore. In the northeast Atlantic the extent of territorial rights has become a major issue, for the offshore banks and shallow grounds are the breeding grounds of many varieties. A few nations, particularly Britain and the United States, both of which traditionally support the freedom of the seas, recognize only the 3-mile line as the boundary of territorial waters, but others claim 6 or 12 miles, and some up to 200 miles or more.[4] Of crucial importance are the Icelandic fishing grounds; by claiming, in company with certain other nations, territorial limits which extend offshore "from headland to headland," Iceland has converted many formerly *de facto* international waters into its exclusive fishing property. Britain has refused to accept this situation, and a long and confused struggle has followed, in the course of which Icelandic fish was for a time shut out from its former British market. An international conference held at Geneva in 1960 narrowly failed to obtain approval for a joint British-American proposal recognizing a 6-mile limit for territorial waters, plus a further 6 miles of exclusive fishing rights for a decade. Four years later most European nations agreed to accept such limits, but Iceland, Norway, and Denmark still refused to be parties.

The northeast Atlantic fisheries extend from the Barents Sea to the Moroccan coast and as far west as Greenland; some countries restrict their operations to particular fishing grounds, but Britain's fishing fleets range over the entire area. Of outstanding importance are the fisheries of the North Sea; this small area only one-quarter the size of the Gulf of Mexico produces almost half as much fish as the entire North American continent and its bordering seas.[5]

Many methods of fishing are employed; there is the simple equipment of the Portuguese "brotherhoods" (cooperatives) fishing from the shore or the great permanent tunny traps off the Iberian coasts, and there are the powerful diesel trawlers from Hull and Grimsby equipped with echo-sounding equipment and every electronic device operating in the frozen darkness of the Arctic winters of the Barents Sea. By weight of catch, herring are the most important species, and the fishery long exerted an important influence on European history. Herring are caught either in static nets, hung in great curtains by "drifters," or in various types of moving nets, such as purse seines and ring nets. Before World War I Britain was the principal herring producer and exported tremendous quantities of salted fish to Europe; Britain's former customers, however, now have large herring fleets of their own, and its present interest in herring fishing is quite minor. A new development, and one that has caused considerable concern for future stocks, is the trawling for young herring in areas east of the Dogger Bank by Dutch, Danish, and German fishermen, using a light trawl operating close to the bottom. These fish are not suitable for food and are converted into fish meal for livestock. Other clupeoid species of major importance are the pilchard (sardine) and, in more southern waters, the anchovy; these waters are also the principal areas for mackerel and related species.

The demersal catch is only slightly inferior in total weight to that of the clupeoids, but its value is very much higher. Cod and other species are caught by the trawl, by long lines, or by seining. Trawling was greatly stimulated by the application of steam power to fishing vessels, a development which was pioneered by Britain from about 1880 onwards and which revitalized the British industry after a long period of stagnation. British fishing vessels gradually penetrated further and further from their home ports, and by the first decade of the present century were fishing for cod in the Barents Sea and for hake off the Moroccan coast. Trawling is the principal British method of catching demersal species; the modern

[4] The most extreme case is that of Indonesia, which has claimed all the seas enclosed by the many Indonesian islands as territorial waters.

[5] United Nations, *Scientific Conference on the Conservation and Utilization of Resources,* vol. 7: *Wildlife and Fish Resources,* New York, 1951, p. 116.

otter trawl, a great bag measuring 80 feet across and held open by the kite-like action of the otter boards, is dragged across the sea floor for some three to four hours. Trawling requires smooth bottoms, which occur widely on the European continental shelf, but on rocky bottoms the trawl is replaced by long lines. A long-liner operating off the west coast of Scotland may lay up to 15 miles of line carrying nearly four-thousand hooks. An alternative to the trawl is the seine, a small version of the trawl; this is much used by Scandinavian fishermen. In seining the vessel steams on a triangular course, dropping its seine on the middle leg, which constitutes the base of the triangle; on regaining its starting point the seiner winches the net towards it. Seining can be carried out very quickly, and the operation is repeated many times; it employs smaller vessels and crews than are required for trawling, so that it is not suitable for use on more distant fishing grounds.

Norway is the largest European producer of fish and normally makes the world's largest herring catch; this accounts for about half the national landings. Norway has a substantial export trade in salted herring and dried cod, mainly with countries of southern Europe. In value of catch, however, Britain usually occupies the premier position; Britain has by far the largest catch of cod and similar species in the world, and in flatfish production it is exceeded only by Japan. The foremost British flatfish is the plaice, trawled in immense quantities from the North Sea. However, Britain's fish production is insufficient to meet the demand, and normally the country receives considerable landings of "whitefish" from Icelandic vessels; Iceland's large production, about half that of Britain, is almost entirely available for export. Other European countries making large catches are West Germany, Spain, France, Portugal, and Denmark (Table 9-1, p. 242).

Among the more important developments in the European fishing industry since the end of World War II is the continued expansion of the traditional processing industries, such as those producing dried and salted fish, canned products, fish oils, and fish meal, but the most rapid growth has been in the production of packaged, quick-frozen fish fillets, which have now become an important competitor with fresh fish. Norway was long the leading producer both of oils and of meal, and until 1957 it normally produced about one-third of the world output of fish body oils; since then, however, it has been surpassed by both the United States and Peru. Britain's processing industries are of relatively minor importance, for over three-quarters of the British catch is consumed as fresh fish; the country is, however, a substantial producer of cod-liver oil and white fish meal. The postwar period has also witnessed considerable replacement of steam-powered vessels by diesel-engined craft,[6] a trend of major significance in all fishing countries, and a concentration of activity on the major fishing ports; the latter, however, was already far advanced in Britain before the war.

Fisheries of the Northwest Atlantic and North America

European fishermen were operating on the banks off the northeast coast of the North American continent long before there were any permanent European settlements, and they still come in large numbers to the fogbound waters off Newfoundland for cod. Local production, however, is much greater, for the cold waters of the shallow grounds of the northwest Atlantic provide about one-third of the catch of the United States and almost two-thirds of that of

[6] In 1960 Britain placed in service the first of a series of very large trawlers with a large stern port, in the style of whaling factory ships, for handling the trawl.

Canada. Though less extensive than the European continental shelf, that of eastern North America contains a number of shallow banks from Long Island to Newfoundland which support a tremendous population of demersal species; on the average, each of the quarter of a million square miles of the banks produces more than 1 ton of such fish for the United States each year. The Grand Bank southeast of Newfoundland is the most important single area for cod in the world, and may well be capable of still higher production.[7]

Although the banks are eminently suitable for trawling operations, this type of fishing was slow to develop in the northwest Atlantic, and the traditional method of catching cod and similar species by means of long lines set by dories is by no means entirely displaced. Cod are so prolific that herring and other pelagic species are, probably, considerably underfished. The rocky coasts of northern New England and of the Maritime Provinces produce a large lobster catch, which, in both Canada and the United States, almost equals in value that of the cod, hake, and haddock fishery. Although of major significance in the fishing industry of eastern Canada, cod is relatively unimportant to the New England fishermen, for whom haddock is the main interest. Of increasing importance, however, is the rosefish; this fish, which had a limited market before World War II, has since become greatly in demand for the production of quick-frozen fillets and fish sticks, and in value of output it is now little inferior to haddock.

The warmer waters of the middle and southern Atlantic coasts and of the Gulf produce a large variety of species, but particularly noteworthy is the very high value of the shrimp catch, which easily exceeds that of any other species taken by United States fishermen. This shrimp fishery, now the largest in the world, has greatly expanded in the postwar period; more than 100,000 tons are taken in most years by otter trawling off the southern and southeastern coasts. Also remarkable for its very high value of output is the oyster fishery of the middle Atlantic states, in which Chesapeake Bay is outstanding. Indeed, the very important position held by crustacean and shellfish production is a distinctive feature of the fisheries of the United States, for in most postwar years crustaceans and shellfish have accounted for 40 per cent or more of the total value of all fishery production. This situation has no parallel in any other major fishing nation.

By comparison, the value of the menhaden catch is distinctly modest, but the fishery is remarkable for its enormous output; menhaden now account for almost one-third of the weight of the total United States catch, production first attaining 1 million tons in 1956. The menhaden, a clupeoid, occurs in shoals containing astronomical numbers of individuals. Caught in purse seines or ring nets, menhaden are too oleaginous for direct human consumption and are mainly utilized for conversion into fish meal and fertilizers. Although the menhaden supports an industry of substantial importance, remarkably little is known about the life cycle of this fish. Other species caught in large quantities by the fisheries of the states are the herring-like shad and alewife, formerly more important than at the present, mullet, and a considerable number of perch-like fish—red snapper, croaker, porgy (or scup), bass, and weakfish.

The fisheries of the Pacific Coast of the United States and of Canada account for about one-quarter of their respective national catches by weight, and about one-third by value. In the cold northerly waters salmon and halibut are the most important species, but in warmer waters sardines and tuna make up the largest

[7] **United Nations, *op. cit.*, p. 29.**

An experimental winch developed by FAO helps to beach fishing craft in Ceylon.

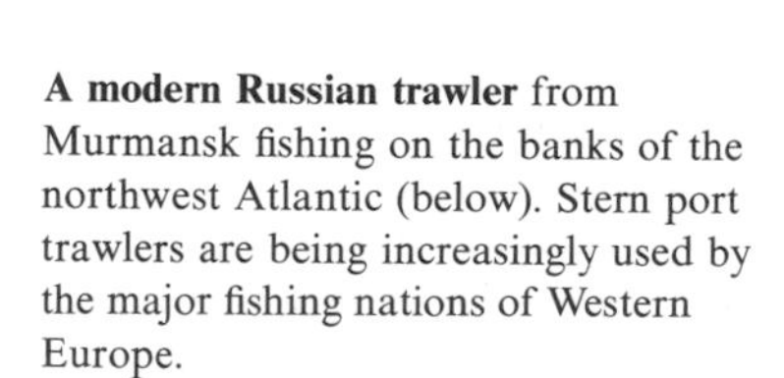

A modern Russian trawler from Murmansk fishing on the banks of the northwest Atlantic (below). Stern port trawlers are being increasingly used by the major fishing nations of Western Europe.

catch. Before World War II Japanese fleets also fished for salmon and halibut off Alaskan waters, and the postwar reappearance of Japanese vessels in this area has been the subject of a number of diplomatic exchanges between the Japanese and American governments.

All the major commercial fisheries of the Pacific Coast have experienced considerable fluctuations of fortune. The salmon catch, long the most valuable of all catches of North American fisheries, suffered a tremendous decline in the present century in consequence of overfishing, stream pollution, and the construction of high dams which seriously affected both the upstream run of fish making their way to spawning grounds in the headwaters and the seaward migration of young fish. However, the salmon fishery may regain its former stature as the conservation methods employed over many years finally begin to take effect. Methods designed to trap fish migrating upstream have been outlawed, and most salmon are now caught in purse seines or in ring nets, offshore. Pollution of streams has been reduced, many blocked tributaries on the major river systems have been cleared, and there is a tendency for modern hydroelectricity dams to have fish ladders incorporated in the design, as the addition of these structures after construction has not proved very successful. Ingenious methods of transporting fish around high dams by means of road tankers have also been employed. Another major difficulty of the salmon fishery has arisen since World War II from the prolonged dollar shortage which has greatly affected the export trade in canned salmon, a matter of considerable concern for Canada; since 1958, however, Britain has once again become a very large buyer of Pacific Coast salmon, and the outlook for the industry is now brighter than for some considerable time. Somewhat similar vicissitudes have been experienced by the halibut fishery, in which agreement between the United States and Canada has considerably helped to ameliorate the effects of a long period of overfishing.

The changes in the composition of the Californian catches have been even more pronounced than those of the Pacific Northwest, British Columbia, and Alaska. Before World War II sardines constituted the principal catch, both by weight and by value; but for some reason pilchards ceased to frequent the Californian coasts, and by 1956 the catch had fallen to barely one-twentieth of the prewar level. On the other hand, the postwar period witnessed a rapid expansion in the tuna fishery, which now has a value of output exceeding that of the United States salmon fishery.

Tuna fishing is quite unlike any other, for tuna appear in shoals far from the shore, and are caught by fast diesel vessels. Tuna fishing first involves catching bait, usually pilchards, which are kept alive on board in special tanks. The pilchards are thrown overboard on encountering a tuna shoal, and the tuna are caught on barbless hooks attached to poles. This method of fishing gives very high productivity per worker, and the capital equipment per worker in tuna fishing is very high by the standards of most fishing enterprises; e.g., light aircraft or helicopters are extensively used in tuna spotting. Tuna clippers range further from their home ports (Los Angeles or San Diego) than any other American fishing vessels, venturing as far south as the coast of Peru. By the mid-Fifties the industry was suffering severely from the competition of Japanese tuna fleets, whose labor and operating costs were substantially lower than those of American vessels. American tuna production was revived, however, by import quotas and by a remarkable venture into foreign production on the part of the largest canning company, the Van Camp Corporation. Packing plants have been established at Samoa, Puerto Rico, and Ecuador, and fish-receiving stations have been erected in Sierra Leone, Senegal, and the Ivory Coast. In 1962 only about half the American output of canned tuna was produced from fish landed by American boats; apart from operating their own boats with local crews, the canning companies have also advanced loans to independent indigenous fishermen and have provided training in modern fishing techniques.

Japanese Fisheries

Japan has been the world's principal fishing nation for almost half a century, and during much of this time it has enjoyed an almost complete monopoly of fishing in some of the most productive waters in the world. It is exceedingly unlikely that Japan's good fortune will hold for very much longer; since 1950 China's fish catch has expanded remarkably, and it is highly likely that the country had displaced Japan as the world's foremost producer of fish by 1961. But Japan still catches the greatest variety of species, ranging from the bottom dwellers of the Arctic waters of the North Pacific to the fast pelagic species of the warm seas of low latitudes, and no other country can show such a variety of fishing methods. Japan's fishing industry, in keeping with the rest of the Japanese economy, consists of a complex blend of ancient and modern; labor-intensive and capital-intensive methods of operating in rivers and estuaries, close inshore, and in the open ocean are encountered in an industry which has in general kept pace with the remarkable postwar advance of the Japanese economy.

This diversity of fishing methods originates in part from the contrasting water masses around the Japanese islands; the cold waters of the Oya and Chishima currents which encircle Hokkaido and the warmer waters of the Kuroshio off southern and eastern Honshu encourage a great variety of species within a comparatively restricted area. More importantly, however, this diversity reflects the nature of Japanese society, with its traditional rural basis now almost balanced by the superstructure of a modern industrialized economy. All the traditional fishing methods employed in other parts of Asia, such as cast nets, lift nets, and fish traps, are encountered in Japan, but the industry also possesses well-equipped vessels which travel further and keep at sea longer than any other fishing craft in the world. Japanese tuna vessels range the whole of the warmer waters of the Pacific; they also operate in the Indian Ocean, and since 1960 have ventured into the Atlantic on fishing expeditions that keep them at sea for six months at a time. Only in whaling, among other fisheries, are such lengthy, long-range operations encountered.

Japanese fishermen take species which are closely allied to all the major commercial species of other major fishing areas, as well as many which are unknown or insignificant elsewhere. Before World War II sardines accounted for almost one-third of the total catch, but the sardine fishery has since greatly declined, both absolutely and relatively. This decline has been attributed to changes in water temperature and circulation off the coast of Wakayama Prefecture in southernmost Honshu; it has been partially offset by a greatly increased anchovy catch. Much the most important species in the Japanese fisheries at the present are the scombroids (mackerel family), which account for about 15 per cent of the total catch by weight; mackerel are taken everywhere off Japan save in northern and northeast Honshu, but the larger tunny-like species are confined to the warmer waters of the south and southeast. Japan makes by far the largest tuna catch in the world. The largest quantities of tuna are taken in areas situated at no great distance from the

Japanese islands by pole-fishing methods, but in the increasingly important long-range Pacific tuna fishery, pole fishing is supplemented by the use of long lines which may total more than 60 miles in length; both methods are pursued by large, specially equipped vessels usually assisted by "mother," or factory, ships. Japanese fishing companies have also erected receiving stations or processing plants in several Pacific islands. Other important mackerel-like fish taken in the warmer waters of Japan are the saury pike, yellowtail, and jack, or horse, mackerel.

The colder waters of northern Japan are much less important than the warmer waters, but they produce large quantities of herring, Alaskan pollack (a cod-like species), halibut, and other flatfish. The most valuable cold-water catch, however, consists of salmon, which are caught off the northern coasts and in more distant North Pacific waters by catchers serving factory ships.

The output of the Japanese fisheries has continued to expand in the postwar period, no mean achievement in view of the serious limitations under which the industry has operated. Many important fishing grounds were lost as a result of the war; these included those around the Kuril Islands, the Siberian inshore waters which Japan fished through its prewar fishing treaty with the U.S.S.R., the waters around Korea, Taiwan, and the Chinese mainland, and the extensive fisheries of Southeast Asia. Also, the Japanese were for some years restricted to only a comparatively small section of the open Pacific by the Allied Supreme Command. Of all these losses those in northern waters were the most serious, and Japan has since 1950 been involved in spasmodic and fruitless negotiations with the U.S.S.R. over the salmon fishery of the North Pacific.

The increase in Japanese fisheries output has been achieved by broadening the range of species taken, by increasing the size of vessels and fishing more distant seas, and by the development of new methods of fishing. Coastal fisheries, always the most important part of the industry,[8] now appear to be incapable of further expansion, and additional increases will largely have to come from more distant operations. All considerations prompt the Japanese to press forward with the discovery of new fisheries, and no country in the world has such an active fishery research program.

Some of Japan's former fisheries are now worked by China, which probably makes the largest fish catch in the world. Perhaps about one-third of China's fisheries output is derived from freshwater fisheries and from pisciculture, but most of the post-1950 increase in catch probably came from inshore fisheries. It is highly unlikely that in view of China's annual population increase of about 15 million Peking has neglected such an obvious source of additional food supply as the country's extensive sea fisheries. China, however, lacks the resources to equip its fishing fleets with modern vessels and fishing gear, and for some time to come will probably limit itself to inshore operations.

The East Central Pacific

Within less than a decade the east central Pacific has become one of the world's most important fisheries by weight of catch, though the wealth of the cold Humboldt current in fish has long been obvious from the guano deposits of innumerable seabirds. Between 1957 and 1961 Peru's fish catch increased so rapidly that

[8] Before World War II about 80 per cent of the catch came from areas within 20 miles of the shore. Supreme Command of the Allies in the Pacific, ***Japanese Natural Resources,*** **Tokyo, 1949, p. 97.**

the country surpassed in weight of catch such long established major fishing nations as the United States and the U.S.S.R. As the catch is almost entirely composed of clupeoids such as herring, sardines, and anchovies, the value of Peru's catch is still only modest.

WHALING

Whaling has many characteristics that sharply distinguish it from other fishing activities. It is the most capital-intensive of all fishery enterprises; the few survivals of the primitive methods of the past have no relevance to the world economy. World fishery output trends steadily upwards, but whaling is a declining industry. Fish is a low-cost protein food competing with other animal protein foods, but whaling's principal interest is whale oil, which has to compete with a wide range of low-cost vegetable oils. World vegetable-oil production has increased considerably in the postwar period, and there is abundant opportunity for further expansion of output. It is possible that improved methods of catching whales, such as the use of electric charges for killing and the increased employment of aircraft, may temporarily improve the competitive position of whaling, but there is definite evidence that the present level of whaling is seriously affecting whale stocks. A rate of killing that exceeds the rate of reproduction must result in increased costs in the whaling industry, and unless reversed will ultimately lead to its extinction.

Since the eclipse of the sperm whale industry in the late nineteenth century as a result of the growth of the petroleum industry, whaling has concentrated on baleen whales and in particular on the giant rorquals, whose capture only became possible with the introduction of steam-powered catching vessels and the Foyn harpoon gun. These creatures feed upon small crustaceans, or "krill," which occur in enormous numbers in Antarctic waters during the summer. About 60 per cent of all whales caught each year are processed in some twenty factory ships operating in Antarctic waters, and a further 5 per cent are handled by three shore stations on the island of South Georgia and one in the Falkland Islands. The balance of the baleen catch is largely derived from shore stations which capture whales migrating between Antarctic feeding grounds and breeding areas in warmer waters.

Since the end of World War II, however, there has been a considerable revival of the sperm whale industry, in which the Japanese have taken a leading part. This toothed whale generally frequents warmer waters than the baleen species; also, its oil is incompatible with that from baleen whales, so that the capture of both types presents considerable difficulties to the processing factory or factory ship. It has been largely in consequence of the renewed interest in sperm whaling, which is not subject to international regulation, that the level of the whale catch has been maintained at about fifty-five-thousand to sixty-thousand whales a year, for the baleen catch has shown a sharp decline; particularly noteworthy has been the decline in the catch of blue whales, the world's largest animals and long the most sought-after species.[9] The revival of sperm whaling has led to some decline in the relative importance of the Antarctic, which in the recent past has usually accounted for 95 per cent of the total catch, Japanese sperm whalers being most successful in the Bering Sea and off the Japanese islands.

The modern whaling industry was pioneered by the Norwegians, who were the first to concentrate on the Antarctic waters and to

[9] The catch of blue whales is limited by the International Whaling Commission to around 5 per cent of the total catch.

employ floating-factory ships, which are now dominant in the industry. Other participants in the industry include Britain (long the second-largest producer of whale oil, after Norway), Japan, Germany, the U.S.S.R., Argentina, South Africa, and the Netherlands; Germany, however, has not reentered the industry since 1945. Japan and the U.S.S.R. are comparative newcomers, the latter having entered the whaling industry only since the end of World War II; whaling has great advantages for these two technically advanced countries, which lack large domestic supplies of vegetable oils and do not wish to use foreign exchange in their purchase. In 1956 Japan supplanted Britain as the second-largest producer of whale oil and in 1960 displaced Norway from the premier position. In 1963 however, Britain withdrew completely from the whaling industry.

World output of whale oil in the postwar period has oscillated about a level of 400,000 tons per annum, only two-thirds of the peak output of 1930. The factory ship, the basis of the modern industry, is a large vessel of up to 30,000 tons, and may have as many as eight catchers to serve it; tank vessels are also necessary to transport the oil after it has been extracted. Until 1955, whaling from factory ships between 70 and 160°W was forbidden in the interests of conservation by the International Whaling Commission, which was established in 1946 with fourteen members.

Table 9-2 *Whale Oil and Sperm Oil Production, 1961–1962 (Thousand metric tons)*

	WHALE OIL	SPERM OIL
Japan	130.1	35.6
Norway	85.8	13.0
Britain	32.7	3.5
Netherlands	12.4	3.0
Iceland	2.1	1.4
Canada	2.0	0.8
United States	1.0	0.2
Brazil	1.9	0.4
Australia	5.3	4.1
New Zealand	0.2	
South Africa	6.0	10.5
U.S.S.R.	73.9	27.9
Total Antarctic Pelagic	305.3	34.8
Total South Georgia	7.7	0.8
Total Outside Antarctic	40.6	85.8
WORLD TOTAL	354.0	121.0

Totals show rounded figures.
SOURCE: FAO, *Yearbook of Fishery Statistics, 1962*, Rome, 1963.

Whaling is a seasonal activity, the season lasting about 70 to 120 days, depending on the progress of catching. The total catch is also regulated by the International Whaling Commission; there were attempts before World War II to reach an international agreement on the conduct of the whaling industry, but none of these succeeded in establishing a global quota. The Commission fixes the total number of baleen whales to be caught in each season in terms of "blue whale units,"[10] and when the quota has been attained the season is declared closed. For most postwar years the quota remained at 16,000 units; in 1957 it was reduced to 14,500, and in 1964 it was fixed at 8,000 units. There can be little doubt that but for some effective regulation, the modern industry would ultimately destroy itself, just as did the Arctic right whale industry of the seventeenth and eighteenth centuries, and as the sperm whale industry nearly did in the nineteenth. Nevertheless, the powers of the Commission are severely limited, and it is doubtful whether they are entirely adequate to safeguard the long-term interests of the industry. Since 1960, in fact, and largely because of the attitude of the Soviet Union, the Commission has been ineffective, and the rate of catching has exceeded that considered advisable for the maintenance of stocks.

THE OUTLOOK FOR THE WORLD'S FISHERIES

World fishery output trends steadily upwards, but many experts find the fishing industry something of a paradox. Fish is a wholesome and nourishing food, and can be produced at very much lower cost than other animal protein foodstuffs; nevertheless, fisheries account for less than 1 per cent of the world's food supply.[11] Economic rather than physical considerations prevent this proportion from being substantially enlarged. For the most part the populations of countries at a high level of economic development eat as much fish as they desire; it would be comparatively easy for such countries to expand their fishery output if demand justified it. The people of underdeveloped areas would certainly consume more fish if they could get it at a price they could afford, but such a price is seldom high enough to justify investment in modern methods of fishing. Against this background the vision of an enormously expanded fishery production with submarine tractors busily eradicating unwanted invertebrates[12] seems to relate to the very distant future. Undoubtedly there are many ways of reducing fishing costs still awaiting discovery, but it is doubtful if these will enable fish to account for a greatly enhanced share of total food consumption.

However, the relative unimportance of fisheries in world alimentation has not made it any easier to achieve international agreements regulating the major fishing areas. There are agreements covering the northwest Atlantic area and there are agreements for certain fisheries in the North Pacific, such as the halibut agreement between the United States and Canada, which has been very successful in rebuilding depleted stocks. But agreements inevitably tend to be regarded suspiciously by smaller producers, as attempts by those already in control of production to maintain their privileged positions. The rapid rise to positions of major importance of such erstwhile minor producers as China, Peru, and Spain, however, indicates how rapidly fishery output can be augmented.

[10] 1 blue whale = 2 fin whales = 2.5 humpback whales = 6 sei whales

[11] United Nations, *op. cit.*, p. 116.

[12] Alistair Hardy, *Fish and Fisheries*, Collins, London, 1959, p. 303.

SELECTED REFERENCES

Ackerman, Edward A.: *Japan's Natural Resources,* The University of Chicago Press, Chicago, 1953, pp. 109–152.

Commonwealth Economic Committee: *Vegetable Oils and Oilseeds,* appendix on whale oil, H. M. Stationery Office, London, annually.

Dewhurst, J. Frederic, et al.: *Europe's Needs and Resources,* The Twentieth Century Fund, New York, 1961, pp. 546–560.

Food and Agriculture Organization: *Yearbook of Fishery Statistics,* Rome, annually.

Grierson, J.: "Whaling from the Air," *Geographical Journal,* vol. 110, pp. 33–47, 1947.

Hardy, Alistair: *Fish and Fisheries,* Collins, London, 1959.

Marts, M. E., and W. R. D. Sewell: "Conflict between Fish and Power Resources in the Pacific North West," *Annals of the Association of American Geographers,* vol. 50, pp. 42–50, 1960.

Morgan, Robert: *World Sea Fisheries,* Methuen & Co., Ltd., London, 1956.

Royal Commission on Canada's Economic Prospects: *Commercial Fisheries of Canada,* Department of Fisheries, Ottawa, 1956.

Schlipjer, E. J.: *Whales,* Hutchinson & Co. (Publishers) Ltd., London, 1962.

Walford, Lionel A.: *Living Resources of the Sea,* The Ronald Press Company, New York, 1958.

While, Donald J.: *The New England Fishing Industry,* Harvard University Press, Cambridge, Mass., 1957.

Woytinsky, W. S., and E. S. Woytinsky: *World Population and Production,* The Twentieth Century Fund, New York, 1953, pp. 715–748.

PART III

Mining and manufacturing industries

Chapter 10

INDUSTRY AND POWER IN THE WORLD ECONOMY

The economic history of the highly developed economies clearly shows that the growth of manufacturing industries has been an important part of the process by which they have been able to attain their present high income levels. It is true that not all economists believe that to place a heavy emphasis on industrialization is the only or indeed the best way of bringing about a higher level of economic development in economically backward countries. However, it is highly significant that no country has achieved the transition from the underdeveloped level without greatly expanding its manufacturing industries, and industrialization is an integral part of the nationalist movement throughout the underdeveloped world. Burmese, Egyptians, and Indonesians are determined to have steel mills and other complex and capital-intensive industries; any suggestion that such activities might be economically ill-advised is likely to provoke the retort that the real purpose of such arguments is to retard Asian or African modernization in the interests of a disguised, economic neocolonialism.

INDUSTRY AND LEVEL OF DEVELOPMENT

Governments, of course, have always encouraged manufacturing industries, if only for reasons of military strength. In fact, however, the share of the planned investment allocated to manufacturing industry in most Asian countries is distinctly modest; only China has devoted a large share of development expenditure to industry.[1] Many Asian countries urgently need to raise domestic food production, which necessitates the allocation of large

[1] China's First Five Year Plan, published in 1955, allocated 41 per cent of development expenditure to industry, as against only 8 per cent for agriculture. Since the disasters of 1959 and 1960, however, relatively larger resources have been allocated for raising agricultural production.

funds to agricultural development. Thus, while it is certain that manufacturing industries, at present heavily concentrated on either side of the North Atlantic, will eventually become more widely distributed through the world, this dispersal is likely to be protracted.

The Small Industries of Underdeveloped Economies

The divorce between industry and agriculture is of comparatively recent origin, and has arisen from the application of machinery and inanimate energy to the processes of manufacture, which made a shift of production from the home and small workshop to the factory mandatory. In Western Europe the old domestic system of manufacturing disappeared with the Industrial Revolution, but in other parts of the world handicraft and cottage industries still survive, and may provide more employment, even if of a somewhat intermittent kind, than modern factory industries. Partly because of this fact, figures of the occupational distribution in underdeveloped countries underestimate the extent of industrial activity, which may employ many families when there is little or no work to be done in the fields. Cottage industries, however, are sometimes carried on by specialists who have no other occupation.

Another type of industrial activity found in many Asian countries is small-scale industry.[2] Industries of this type are usually carried on in special workshops; they employ considerable skilled labor, and occasionally they may also use power. The principal stimulus to this kind of activity in the past was the existence of a princely court, which provided a high degree of protection to the industry and constituted its main market. With the decline of the power and prestige of the royal or baronial houses, some of these traditional industries have adapted themselves to a broader market; but other small-scale industries have grown up through the activity of small entrepreneurs that developed with the establishment of national economies. Occasionally whole villages may be supported by cottage or small-scale industrial enterprises; in Java, villages situated near suitable deposits of clay are often more dependent on tile making than on agriculture.

However, because of the comparative crudity of their finished products and their inability to achieve the economies of large-scale production, cottage and small-scale industries are seldom competitive with factory industries. Cheap and speedy links between town and country provided by bus and truck services have added to their difficulties, but the desirability of maintaining employment at the highest possible level has prompted several governments to protect small-scale industries from factory competition. India has placed quotas on the output of cotton cloth and certain other goods from large factories, and other factory-produced articles competing with handicraft products are subjected to a tax.

Many experts believe that the present low level of efficiency of nonfactory industry could be considerably improved. Even simple technical innovations could greatly increase the output per worker; the flying shuttle, invented by Kay in 1733, is still unknown to a very large number of Indian handloom weavers. Very substantial improvements in productivity are possible through the use of electric power, but the almost complete absence of generating stations over large parts of Asia is an insuperable obstacle to such development.

[2] This is variously defined in national statistics, and it seems best to follow the definition of such an industry by the United Nations Economic Commission for Asia and the Far East (ECAFE) as "one which is operated mainly with hired labour usually not exceeding 50 workers in any establishment or unit not using any motive power in any operation, or 20 workers in an establishment or unit using such power." See *Economic Survey of Asia and the Far East, 1958,* Bangkok, 1959, p. 100.

The low level of efficiency of small industries tends to be preserved through state protection, and that they are not a suitable vehicle for a massive all-around industrial advance is clearly demonstrated by the "great leap forward" of China. Under the policy known as "walking on two legs" (that is, making use of modern and traditional industrial technologies), the expansion of indigenous small-scale production became a national hysteria; every village with access to coal or iron deposits experienced a mushroom growth of crude blast furnaces, while in the cities, furnaces fed with scrap metal sprang up in backyards and vacant lots. A great expansion also took place in village production of copper, coal, cement, and mineral fertilizers. However, much of the iron from the village furnaces proved to be unusable, and it is difficult to see how the enormous claimed output of coal could have been utilized. Since 1959 the attempt to force up the output by small-scale methods of commodities that elsewhere require large-scale capital-intensive technologies has been quietly dropped.

Small-scale industries could, however, conserve foreign exchange by reducing the volume of consumer-good imports and by economizing on the import of capital equipment necessary for large-scale production. It is hardly surprising, therefore, that some countries have tried to provide the means by which small-scale industries could achieve economies of scale. The Indian Second Five Year Plan provided for the construction of industrial estates on which small industries could obtain cheap gas, water, power, and other services; arrangements were also made for the supply of improved tools, machines, and raw materials at reasonable rates. Other services planned for small industries included hire-purchase and marketing facilities. The Netherlands Indies government erected a number of central finishing and processing stations for village industries which handled the more difficult stages of manufacture and final finishing. This policy has been continued by the Indonesian government in the *perusahaan induk,* a machine-equipped processing plant intended to serve producer cooperatives. Nevertheless, the results of such policies are not encouraging; the share of small-scale industry in India's total industrial output continually declines, and a similar fall appears to have taken place in China.[3] In Indonesia, *induks* have not infrequently been sited in locations which make economic operation impossible.

In Japan, a unique combination of physical and cultural circumstances has enabled some small industries to remain competitive with large-scale factory production. The manner in which small industries adapted themselves to new methods and to new products is one of the most remarkable features of the country's industrial development; in effect, the smaller industries of Japan are extensions of large-scale factory industry, to which they are attached through the practice of commissioned production, or subcontracting. The division of labor, the use of machinery and electric power, and the role in export production of Japanese small industries sharply contrast with the situation of small industries in other parts of Asia. However, the special circumstances that have permitted small establishments to account for over half the total production of many Japanese industries do not appear likely to occur elsewhere.

Large-scale factory industry in underdeveloped economies is very restricted and employs only a small fraction of the total work force; India has only some 3 million factory workers, as against 18 million in nonfactory industry. Only rarely do factory industries represent the fruit of indigenous enterprise and capital; in

[3] *Ibid.*, p. 101.

the past they have typically resulted from the activities of aliens or immigrants, and are still largely owned and managed by foreigners. Increasingly, however, they represent the direct investment of the state.

Industrial Growth and Economic Advance

Although the share of the work force engaged in manufacturing industry increases as a country progresses from the underdeveloped level, it does not increase indefinitely; in some of the highly developed economies there has been a tendency for the relative size of the industrial labor force to decline. The reason for this is simply that more and more complex and expensive machinery is substituted for labor, which thus becomes available for deployment in other activities. It is only in the centrally planned economies, with their deliberate restriction of service industries, that employment in manufacturing reaches very high proportions; figures of from 40 to 50 per cent are attained in some Eastern European satellites. Such high figures do not, of course, indicate a high level of material welfare; a highly developed economy, in which one worker controlling a fully automated line of transfer machines can produce a thousand fully machined automobile cylinder blocks in a shift, simply does not need to use its labor in such a fashion.

While the proportion of the work force engaged in manufacturing is increasing, considerable changes also take place in the distribution of employment between manufacturing industries themselves (Table 10-1). Despite statistical imperfections which make any international comparisons difficult, the general course of industrial evolution is not seriously in doubt. In underdeveloped economies the greatest industrial employment is found in industries that have relatively simple technologies and modest capital requirements, utilize local raw materials, and produce goods for which there is a wide and stable local demand.

Table 10-1

*Percentage Distribution of Industrial Employment in Selected Categories**

	U.S.A.	U.K.	W. GERMANY	JAPAN	INDIA†
Metal Products	14	12	19	12	4
Machinery	28	36	26	19	6
Textiles	6	9	11	21	39
Food, Drink, and Tobacco	10	10	9	11	18
Paper, Printing, and Publishing	8	6	5	8	3
Chemicals	6	6	9	7	4
Timber and Wood Products	6	3	5	9	3‡
Clothing	7	6	6	3	n.a.
Other Industries	15	12	10	10	23
TOTAL	100	100	100	100	100

* Figures are averages for the mid-Fifties.
† Average daily employment in factories only.
‡ Also includes stone and glass.
SOURCE: Statistical abstracts of U.K., U.S.A., India, and Japan.

Foremost among such industries are cotton textiles and food and drink products; in India these two categories account for almost 60 per cent of total factory employment, and their share of industrial employment would be even higher with the inclusion of nonfactory industrial activity.

As economic development proceeds, textile industries become progressively less important in the industrial sector of the economy, even though the output of textile industries continues to increase; technologically more complex and capital-intensive industries come to command a larger share of the labor force. The metal industries become of increasing importance; in highly developed economies metal fabricating, metalworking, and machinery production may account for almost half of the total employment in manufacturing industry. Table 10-1 strikingly illustrates the great strides made by the Japanese economy, whose pattern of industrial employment is much closer to that of the highly developed economies than to the underdeveloped pattern of India.

Some industries such as chemicals, however, appear to show little proportionate increase in employment with a higher level of economic development. This is because industrial expansion largely involves an increase on the capital-labor ratio; most chemical products necessitate the use of large, capital-intensive plants if they are to be produced at all. Modern chemical plants operate almost automatically and require only a very small labor force in relation to their floor space. Thus investment per worker is very high; it exceeds 1 million dollars in the case of carbon-black plants.

That such changes in the distribution of the industrial labor force accompany a rising level of economic development is confirmed by the industrial history of the present highly developed economies. In Western Europe and the United States, cotton-textile industries were the first industries to be affected by the application of power and new mechanical techniques. As industrialization proceeded, mining, metalmaking, and metalworking industries became of increasing importance. Of course, not all the highly developed economies have followed the same evolutionary pattern; cotton textiles have always been of very minor significance in Australia and New Zealand, and it cannot be expected that all economies at low levels of development will experience the same industrial evolution as Western Europe. Nevertheless, Japan appears broadly to be doing so; there has been a marked fall in the share of cotton textiles in total industrial employment since 1930, when the cotton industry attained its maximum importance in the Japanese economy. In countries that have centrally planned economies such as China, such shifts in industrial emphasis are likely to take place even more rapidly.

THE LOCATION OF MODERN INDUSTRY

The growth of mechanical techniques of production and the increasing use of power result in as far-reaching changes in industrial location as in industrial organization. Industries previously widespread became concentrated in particular areas, and new and highly localized industries come into existence. Certain modern industries, of which the automobile industry is perhaps the most striking example, appear to demonstrate some degree of fortuity in their location. Great changes in the distribution of population accompany the growth of manufacturing industries.

Apart from a few classic studies, such as that of the German economist Weber, who held that industries would be located at the point

This Indian shoemaker typifies cottage industry, an early stage of industrial evolution (above left). The tendency of the cotton-textile industry to adopt a factory organization even at a low level of national economic development is illustrated by these spinning frames in a Bolivian mill (above, right).

Metalworking and metal making gradually increase in importance; this small-scale Indian establishment manufactures bicycle parts.

The replacement of labor-intensive by capital-intensive methods is strikingly suggested by the contrast between a Chinese steel mill and a battery of transfer-type machines at an American auto plant.

that resulted in lowest transport costs,[4] the theoretical study of industrial location has on the whole been unattractive to economists. Recent years, however, have seen a considerable renewal of interest in the study of general location theory, which has been associated with regional "input-output" analysis and examination of "central place" tendencies; these studies seek to determine intraregional and interregional causes and consequences of additional investment and to examine the factors that make for agglomeration of human activity. Yet it may be doubted that a general theory of industrial location could have any more validity than a general theory of population; deductive studies do not usually shed much light on the location pattern of particular industries.[5] The present location pattern of any industry can only be comprehended in the light of the preexisting pattern of industrial location at the time of its establishment; indeed, the complex and constantly changing pattern of industrial activity has been likened to a living organism.

Manufacturing industry consists of either *processing* or *assembly*.[6] The former consists of the working up of raw materials, an operation which may have several stages, as in the manufacture of cotton textiles; the latter covers those operations which piece together the processed materials. These two activities may be integrated and carried on in the same plant, or they may be separated either structurally or geographically. But the structure and location of industry are the outcome of decision making by manufacturers in which each aspect profoundly influences the other; it is not possible to give a coherent analysis of the location of any industry without some reference to its structure.

A study of industrial location necessarily involves examination of the factors influencing the cost conditions under which the industry in question operates. Generally, industries will select locations that offer the lowest costs of production, and those that select locations that result in high costs will be forced out of business. However, manufacturers make decisions on the basis of the best information available at the time and have no greater powers of clairvoyance than other citizens. On the other hand, the established industries in particular areas tend to perpetuate themselves, and put up a vigorous fight when threatened by rivals in newer areas. Many industries possess examples of units whose locations are anomalous; by specializing in a particular line, they can often survive even though new centers of production prove better placed to take advantage of technological and economic change.

Although it may well be doubted if any general theory of industrial location has exerted influence on the location of a single plant, Weber's analysis has helped to illuminate the broad principles that govern industrial location, and has been followed in many geographic and economic studies. These factors include raw materials, fuel and power, labor, transport, and markets. However, even in countries which have basically laissez-faire economies, social and political considerations are often of great significance in influencing industrial location.

[4] Weber's *The Location of Industries,* published in 1909, gained a wide measure of acceptance and is the basis of most general studies of industrial location. One writer even urged the removal of the Upper Silesian iron and steel industry to Breslau in order to comply with Weber's condition.

[5] See, for example, E. M. Hoover, *Location Theory and the Shoe and Leather Industries,* Harvard University Press, Cambridge, Mass., 1937.

[6] P. Sargant Florence, *Logic of British and American Industry,* Routledge & Kegan Paul, Ltd., London, 1953, p. 8. The Statistical Office of the United Nations defines manufacturing as the "mechanical or chemical transformation of inorganic or organic substances into new products, whether the work is performed by power driven machinery or by hand, whether it is done in a factory or in the worker's home, and whether the products are sold at wholesale or retail." The definition also includes the assembly of component parts of manufactured products and repair.

Raw Materials Raw materials can assume a wide variety of forms; their influence on location will depend on their number and on whether processing or assembly is involved. The attraction of raw materials will clearly be greatest in those processing industries using a few bulky and heavy raw materials that are of low unit value and that do not add much value in manufacture. Under such conditions this factor may well be decisive, particularly where processing results in a substantial loss in weight. Every increase in the number of raw materials, however, reduces the locational influence of any particular one, and in the location of complex assembling industries, such as automobiles, the influence of raw-material supplies may be minimal. Where processing involves a substantial gain in weight, as in the manufacture of rubber products, the influence of raw materials is also reduced; the manufacture of tires is poorly developed in areas of natural-rubber production.

Some industries are definitely tied, or "rooted," to their raw-material supplies; but some raw materials may be very widely distributed, as is the case in cement manufacture, so that a considerable choice of location may in fact be possible. On the whole, raw materials appear of only minor significance in industrial location; most industries which are so tied have only modest growth rates. From the manufacturer's standpoint, the necessity of having to establish plants in close proximity to raw materials is an irksome restriction that hinders him in exploiting new markets which arise as a result of changes in the distribution of population; in a country such as the United States, this is a consideration of supreme importance. It is hardly surprising, therefore, that considerable effort is being directed towards the development of technologies that will free manufacturers from dependence on geographically restricted raw materials.

Of greater importance than proximity to raw materials is access to them. It need be no handicap to possess limited local raw materials if funds are available for their purchase and transport from elsewhere. Japan's post-1950 rate of industrial growth is one of the highest ever recorded in the world, but it has been largely based on imported raw materials. Hong Kong's industrial history illustrates even more strikingly how little is the significance of local raw materials when all other essentials for industrialization are present. The shortage of certain raw materials, particularly those for the metal-making and metalworking industries, is certainly an obstacle to the industrialization of many underdeveloped economies, but it is, perhaps, the least of their difficulties. However, it is extremely important in such economies that new industries should not be burdened with high costs in consequence of locations which have paid too little attention to the question of raw-material supplies; several Asian countries possess large modern plants which are poorly related to their supplies of raw materials or which were established to use local raw materials that subsequently proved unsatisfactory. That such situations arise is usually the result of political pressures exerted on behalf of the selected areas, but these, of course, can occur in all types of economies.

Fuel and Power In the early stages of industrialization the availability of power is a factor of considerable importance; in Lancashire and in southern New England the cotton industry gravitated to sites where waterpower was available. With the application of the steam engine to industrial production the coalfields and areas in close proximity to them came to possess substantial advantages, for when the only means of transmitting steam power was by means of belts and shafting, every manufacturer had to be a power producer. This is no longer the case, for although the largest manufacturers still find it necessary to be in the power business (if only to meet emergencies), the development of electric power produced in large central generating stations has made possible a divorce of power production and manufacture and has greatly widened the choice of locations open to industrialists. Such power stations can operate on imported coal or oil and the absence of local fuels is only a minor impediment to industrialization.

Moreover, as a result of improvements in technology, a ton of coal at present is immensely more productive than in the early days of the Industrial Revolution; in the eighteenth century 8 tons of coal were needed to smelt 1 ton of pig iron, but a modern blast furnace needs only ¾ ton of coke to produce this amount. But while these developments have somewhat reduced the attraction of the coalfields for manufacturing industries, most coalfields remain important manufacturing areas, for their concentrations of population created as a result of past industrial development constitute an important market for new industry, which may have little demand for coal itself. In contrast, the industrial development associated with areas of petroleum production is limited and of a specialized kind.

Certain industries are particularly attracted to locations where cheap and plentiful electric power is available; prominent among these are pulp and paper, electrochemical and electrometallurgical industries, reduction of aluminum, production of calcium carbide, synthetic fertilizers, and activities associated with production of nuclear energy, such as the extraction of heavy water. All of these activities have long been associated with areas of cheap hydroelectricity, but they are also increasingly located in areas where electric power can be generated cheaply from mineral fuels such as coal and lignite.

Transport Facilities The availability of transport facilities and the costs of transporting raw materials and finished products to and from manufacturing areas have assumed a central position in many treatments of industrial location. Certain heavy industries[7] are exacting in their transport requirements, and may need waterside facilities as well as rail connections. Among industries that commonly seek waterside locations are petroleum refining, grain milling, oilseed crushing, sugar refining, paper and paperboard manufacture, heavy chemicals,[8] iron and steel, marine engineering, and the manufacture of heavy electric and submarine cables; some of these industries also need waterside locations because of their water requirements and for effluent disposal. Many of these industries are found in great port cities, where they can make use of imported raw materials, and are thus among the most rooted of all industrial activities.

While other industries may have specific transport requirements, these can often be provided at relatively low cost; iron and steel plants must have rail transport, but the selection of suitable locations is made on other grounds. Yet the continuous improvements in roads and in the motor vehicle have made many industries virtually independent of other forms of transport and, in conjunction with the wider use of electric power, have operated to produce a considerable degree of indeterminacy in the location of some industries. The question of transport costs is very complex. Transport

[7] This term is seldom defined, but is a convenient one nevertheless. The following criteria have been used to determine the heaviness of an industry: weight of raw materials per worker, loss of weight in manufacture, cost of raw materials in relation to total costs, proportion of male to total workers, floor space per worker, and horsepower per worker. See P. Sargant Florence, *Investment, Location and Size of Plant,* Cambridge University Press, Cambridge, 1948, appendix 1; and Wilfred Smith, *Distribution of Population and Location of Industry on Merseyside,* Liverpool University Press, Liverpool, 1948, p. 112.

[8] See p. 505 for a definition of this term.

costs may be far from proportional to the distances or quantities involved. It does not cost twice as much to ship goods through double the distance, as the initial loading and unloading may make up a large part of total transport costs; moreover, differential rating policies may mean that lower rates per ton-mile are charged for long hauls than for short. In the United States such differential freight rates have long been attacked by Western states as retarding their industrialization in the interests of Eastern manufacturers.

Labor Supply The existence of a skilled labor supply can be a factor of considerable importance in industrial location, particularly in the craft industries, such as jewelry, gun making, and optical, scientific, and musical instruments, and in luxury industries such as fur and *haute couture.* The location of such industries may be closely circumscribed within a small district, as in the case with the British jewelry and silverware industry of London and Birmingham; however, extreme localization often owes as much to other considerations as to a restricted labor supply. Many industries prefer to recruit labor that has little special skill and to train it on the job; in fact, the existence of a particular pattern of labor skills in an area may even repel new industry, as was the case in south Lancashire during the period between the two world wars. For several industries the question of labor supply is of only minor significance in location, for the whole tenor of industrial development in highly developed economies is to replace skilled operatives by automatic machines set by technicians. In a highly developed economy the industrialist is usually able to assume that he will be able to obtain an adequate supply of labor wherever other conditions are favorable for production, for in an economy of this kind a large number of vacant employment opportunities will inevitably encourage population movements to fill them. As a number of industries at the present can have a wide choice of locations without incurring substantial cost penalties, many experts in regional planning have urged the adoption of a policy of taking work to the workers; this point, however, raises the whole issue of public control over industrial location.

Markets Markets may be specific and localized or diverse and widespread. Industries producing goods for further processing or for assembly in other industries tend to be situated in close proximity to them, and interlocking markets may produce what Weber termed an agglomeration of industries. Industries producing consumer goods, however, find the increasing concentration of population in large cities that is such a marked feature of countries at a high level of economic development an irresistible magnet. The great metropolitan centers of such economies invariably possess a wide range of industrial activities, but are particularly attractive locations to new consumer-goods industries; hence the rate of industrial expansion in the metropolitan areas has come to exceed that of their respective countries. The self-generating expansion of population and industry in such cities has given rise to much concern, but it has proved impossible to arrest. However, the continental extent of the United States has enabled it to develop a number of major metropolitan centers, in contrast to the situation in Europe, where the national capitals are usually of overwhelming importance.[9]

Nowhere in the world is this cumulative

[9] Western Germany is anomalous here; its division of industrial, financial, and administrative functions between Hamburg, Frankfurt, the North Rhine–Westphalia conurbation, and Bonn is faintly reminiscent of the situation in the United States. However, should unification of the two Germanies prove possible, it is likely that the supremacy of Berlin would be speedily reestablished.

process of growth better illustrated than in the metropolitan area of southern California, which has now moved far beyond an industrial specialization in consumer goods; already the nation's principal producer of aircraft by World War II, it is now one of the major centers of the electronics industries, and in missile and rocket technology it is without a rival. This simultaneous expansion of population and industry has been sometimes criticized as unsound and lacking a rational basis—but yet it goes on from strength to strength.

Structural Factors Forces arising in the industrial structure may also exercise a strong influence on location; these relate to the size of plants, the degree of their internal integration, and the extent of linkages between plants. In the United States, the smaller the plants in an industry, the less its localization; conversely, highly localized industries tend to have large plants. However, the latter tendency may be modified by the "external economies" that arise from having a concentration of producers in one locality. Under such conditions, specialist plants can serve a number of factories in related manufacturing processes, and thus an overall level of efficiency comparable with that possessed by large integrated plants can be obtained. On the basis of such linked functions an agglomeration of mainly small plants can give rise to a major industrial area, even on a limited local resource base. Thus, with its coal and iron industries largely things of the past, the Birmingham and Black Country conurbation is second only to Greater London among Britain's industrial regions, and alone among them can match the capital's rate of industrial growth; it is, as Florence puts it, "an object lesson in the economic advantages of localization in and for itself, without reference to nature."[10]

[10] **Florence,** *Logic of British and American Industry,* **p. 88.**

The effect of vertical and horizontal integration on industrial location is clearly visible in certain modern industries with high growth rates, such as automobiles, rayon, and chemicals. Enterprises with a very high degree of vertical integration, such as Ford and Fiat, have different location patterns from the both horizontally and vertically integrated General Motors and British Motor Corporation. In semideveloped countries the vital necessity of achieving the economies of scale that come from large-scale operations often compels extreme vertical integration, so that in effect there is only room for one manufacturer. Success in one line of activity invites attention to others, so that giant corporations such as Fiat or Mitsui, though modest enough by the standards of General Motors or Royal Dutch–Shell, come to occupy a dominant role in the industrial sector of their respective national economies.[11] Under such conditions corporation policy is of decisive influence in industrial location.

Social and Political Factors As technical change has made possible a greater degree of indeterminacy in industrial location, social and political considerations have become progressively more important. The old industrial areas of the "palaeotechnic" era, based on coal, iron, and steam power, are grimy, unattractive places, dear to the native but seldom attractive to a manufacturer seeking a location for a new pharmaceuticals or electronics plant. Proximity to a favorite golf course or to a great metropolis to "please the wife" may exert considerable influence on a manufacturer in selecting a location for a new plant. Cities competing for new industrial establishments flourish their social or educational advantages before the manufac-

[11] **It has been claimed that Fiat accounts for about 10 per cent of the total Italian industrial production.**

turer as well as their economic assets. Politicians and lobbyists work to influence the state to erect new government establishments in areas they represent or to award contracts to enterprises in their constituencies. On the other hand, city authorities faced with the problem of providing social facilities of all kinds for rapidly expanding populations or government departments endeavoring to prevent acute labor shortages in a particular area from becoming worse may strenuously resist the incursion of new industrial development. The location of new plants may thus present a complex problem of the conflict of interests; it can well happen that the industrialist's estimate of the potential profitability of his site is outweighed by the additional social costs which have to be borne by the community as a whole. Polluted atmospheres and streams, increasing congestion, lengthening journeys to work which in effect produce a longer working day, and inadequate housing, schooling, open space, and other facilities are the inevitable consequences of rapid and uncoordinated industrial expansion.

The Regulation of Industrial Location

Official action to regulate the location of industry may arise from the kind of conflict outlined above, a solution of which is the aim of most schemes of city planning. Many city or regional authorities possess special powers to regulate industrial location in conformity with their physical planning schemes, and can direct new industrial activity into specially designated zones. More far-reaching control, however, may be exercised by the national government in discharge of its responsibilities for the health of the national economy, an obligation which is now accepted by all democratic governments. The state is also under heavy pressure to ensure that the number of employment opportunities in the various parts of the country is kept at a socially equitable level and to take action to redress any great disparity.

In Britain the laissez-faire economy of the nineteenth century produced a remarkable pattern of industrial localization, in which certain areas, such as South Wales, Lancashire, Clydeside, and Northumberland and Durham, had become mainly specialized in capital-goods industries largely serving an export market. In these districts clogging of the channels of world trade through the interwar growth of economic autarchy and the shattering blow of the Great Depression produced levels of unemployment that amounted to 50 per cent or more of all male workers. The industrial decline of these districts was arrested, however, by the intervention of World War II, and under the postwar Distribution of Industry Act the British government assumed responsibility for achieving their more balanced industrial development, with the encouragement of consumer-goods industries and others that afford employment for women. The act empowers the government to prevent further industrial expansion in London, the west Midlands, and certain other areas of extremely rapid industrial growth, such as Oxford, and authorizes the expenditure of public money for assisting the expansion of industrial enterprise in designated "development areas." Thus the British government has advanced capital for modernizing the Scottish steel industry; also, it has prevented certain automobile manufacturers from making further extensions to capacity on their present sites and has obliged them to seek sites in development areas on Merseyside and in Scotland. Nevertheless, rates of unemployment in these areas have remained well above the national average.

The United States has not proceeded as far

as Britain in regulating the location of new industry,[12] although the Federal government can award contracts for public works or for defense purposes to designated areas of unduly high unemployment. The French government has endeavored to restrict the expansion of existing industry and the establishment of new industry in the Paris region and to direct such development to the west and south, and in the Netherlands similar machinery exists for encouraging industrial development in the northeastern provinces. In Italy the *Cassa per il Mezzogiorno* has been established since the war to accelerate economic development in the south, in order to reduce the disparity in employment and living standards with the heavily industrialized north.

Such action can have much to recommend it, especially when there is a reasonable chance that it can bring areas to the point of "takeoff," at which further economic growth becomes self-sustaining. Nevertheless, the economic advantages of localization are considerable; they are in fact part of that increasing specialization which is the key to economic development. As the level of economic development rises, industrial activity tends to become more concentrated in specific localities; the divorce between agriculture and industry becomes pronounced, and the domestic craftsman is replaced by the factory operative. It may well be that the extreme regional specialization of Britain during the nineteenth century was possible only while Britain was the "workshop of the world." But the concentration of industrial activities in the great metropolitan areas is unlikely to be arrested. Six centuries of attempts at controlling the spread of London and the concentration of economic activity in the capital have proved abortive; the work of the *Cassa per il Mezzogiorno* appears to have been of greater benefit to the northern cities that have supplied the new capital equipment than to the south itself, which is making use of it. The built-in advantages of the expanding metropolitan conurbations have been aptly summarized thus by a British royal commision: "Nothing succeeds like success."[13]

INDUSTRIALIZATION AND POWER

Although proximity to sources of fuel and power may no longer be so important a factor in industrial location as in the past, access to such supplies is essential if industrialization is to take place at all. The transition from an economy in which industrial activity is limited and confined to technologically simple industries to one in which manufacturing plays a major role and in which there is an increasing emphasis on complex and capital-intensive industries involves an enormous increase in the consumption of energy. Nor does the demand for power, or strictly speaking, energy, slacken once the economy attains the highly developed stage; in fact, the contrary is the case.

International comparisons of energy consumption are difficult because the differing patterns of energy consumption from nation to nation necessitate the use of somewhat arbitrary conversion factors, but there is a close correlation between energy consumption per capita and the per capita income and per capita

[12] The Area Redevelopment Act of 1962 provides for the granting of loans to public or private applicants for the purchase of land and for the provision of facilities for factory construction. Loans are also available to public bodies for improving facilities, for technical assistance, and for job retraining. All in all, 148 urban areas, mainly in old industrial districts, and 753 rural areas, all with more than 6 per cent unemployment rates, were designated under the act. Besides the fifty states, Puerto Rico, Guam, and Samoa are eligible for assistance.

[13] *Report of the Royal Commission on the Distribution of the Industrial Population (Barlow Report),* H. M. Stationery Office, London, 1940, p. 170.

Table 10-2

Energy Consumption in Selected Countries, 1957

	TOTAL ENERGY CONSUMPTION (MILLION METRIC TONS OF COAL EQUIVALENT)	ENERGY CONSUMPTION PER CAPITA (TONS OF COAL EQUIVALENT)
Turkey	8.4	0.3
Greece	3.5	0.4
Portugal	4.1	0.5
Italy	59.1	1.2
Switzerland	13.9	2.7
France	125.3	2.8
W. Germany	190.7	3.8
Belgium	35.9	4.0
Britain	253.0	4.9
United States	1,400.0	9.0

SOURCE: OEEC, *Europe's Needs for Oil,* Paris, 1958.

industrial production (Table 10-2). The high level of energy consumption in the United States and in Western Europe results from intense industrialization and a low cost of energy per unit. In both areas there are large and easily won sources of fuel, but the low cost of energy arises from the economies of scale that are achieved when technological progress and increased energy consumption go hand in hand. Thus it is not possible to mine coal or to produce or refine oil without the use of steel; but to produce steel, large quantities of coal and oil have to be used, so that in a sense, coal and oil produce themselves. The low cost of energy in highly developed countries is essentially a result of a tremendous capital investment in energy production and in associated industrial activities that help to produce energy.

Any action that can produce a reduction in the cost of energy will be of material benefit to countries at a lower level of economic development in their industrialization programs. At present such countries have to economize in their use of energy; unable to afford the high capital investment necessary for the production of cheap inanimate energy, they use types of energy that require minimal investment, such as animal power or even human energy. The cost per unit of such animate energy, however, is fantastically high; the real costs of erecting a modern multistory block, which can be put up by a few hundred men in ten months, are negligible in comparison with those involved in the construction of a pyramid of ancient Egypt, an operation which required the labor of tens of thousands over decades. The Peking government, it is true, is making full use of its enormous supply of human energy in transforming the face of China, but a centrally planned economy does not obey market forces.

In underdeveloped economies, therefore, the principal use of energy is for heating, lighting, and transport; manufacturing industry probably accounts for less than 10 per cent of total energy consumption, whereas in highly developed economies it may account for as much as 50 per cent or more.

In the United States manufacturing industry accounts for a somewhat lower share, a result of the great consumption of energy by private automobiles[14] and a very heavily mechanized agriculture; in some highly developed economies at high latitudes, such as Sweden and Canada, heating and lighting also account for a substantial proportion of energy consumption; and in all highly developed economies outside Anglo-America the automobile is accounting for an increasing share of energy consumption. Indeed, it is possible that it is in Eastern Europe and the U.S.S.R. that manufacturing industries absorb the largest share of total national energy consumption, despite the fact that it is in the highly developed economies that production per capita of the "energy-intensive" industries—chemicals, petroleum products, coal, iron and steel, and nonferrous metals—reaches its highest levels. However, all estimates of future energy needs indicate that manufacturing industries will account for an increasing share of energy consumption. By 1975 manufacturing industry in the Organisation for European Economic Cooperation (OEEC) area is expected to generate 47 per cent of the total energy demand, as compared with 41 per cent in 1955.[15]

The Changing Pattern of Energy Consumption

Since 1860 or thereabouts, when statistics of energy production first became reliable, world energy production has increased about thirty times.[16] The greater part of this increase, however, has been accounted for by the few countries that have attained a high level of economic development; almost half of total energy production is accounted for by Anglo-America alone. The insatiable demands for additional energy supplies on the part of the highly developed economies and the certainty that in the not distant future the underdeveloped economies will also begin to make considerable demands on world energy sources have given rise to some speculation about the adequacy of such resources to support a high level of material well-being for all the world's population, especially in view of the magnitude of population increase.[17] But side by side with this increased energy output have occurred considerable changes in the pattern of energy consumption.

Energy supplies may be regarded as either *primary* or *secondary*. The former represent new increments of energy, whereas the latter are merely transformed primary energy, that is, primary energy rendered into a more convenient and usable form; the great growth of secondary energy consumption in the form of electric power is one of the most important economic characteristics of the present century.

Primary energy resources are either of the perpetual or accumulated (fund) type. The former originate from solar radiation, and the total energy so received by the earth is prodigious; but perpetual resources are difficult and expensive to harness, for the energy is lost or dissipated almost as fast as it is received. Most of the solar energy received by the earth is expended in the hydrologic cycle; an infinitesimally small proportion is utilized by

[14] Some three-quarters of the installed horsepower in the United States is located in the automobiles of its citizens.

[15] Organisation for European Economic Cooperation, *Towards a New Energy Pattern in Europe,* Paris, 1960, p. 25. The OEEC area includes all the countries of Europe except Spain, Yugoslavia, and the Soviet satellites, together with Greece and Turkey. In 1960 the OEEC became the Organisation for Economic Cooperation and Development (OECD) and also included Canada and the United States.

[16] *Ibid.*, p. 15. Total world consumption of all forms of energy in 1960 was estimated by the Sixth World Power Conference, Melbourne, 1962, as 32.7×10^{12} kilowatt-hours.

[17] A number of writers have examined the adequacy of world resources in the light of present demographic trends; among the most stimulating is Harrison Brown, *The Challenge of Man's Future,* The Viking Press, Inc., New York, 1954.

hydroelectric power installations. Hydroelectricity is of great importance in certain countries, but for physical and economic reasons is unlikely ever to be a major significance in the world as a whole. Tidal energy may become of importance in certain areas, and is utilized by two plants on the Channel coast of France. In low latitudes, solar furnaces or batteries of photoelectric cells may also become of substantial local significance. Greater opportunities for harnessing perpetual energy may, however, arise through further research into photosynthesis, the process by which green plants, using the energy of light, convert carbon dioxide and water into sugar and starch.

The solar sources of energy are, for the most part, diffuse and discontinuous; to be economically valuable energy supplies must be concentrated and continuously available. Thus the resources of accumulated energy, the fossil fuels, are of outstanding importance in the world at present. All expert investigations agree that in the foreseeable future these energy sources will continue to be of the greatest significance in the world economy; in fact, their proportionate contribution to world energy production is likely to expand over the next twenty-five years. Insofar as atomic energy is derived from finite deposits of radioactive minerals, it too must be regarded as a fund energy source; "breeder" reactors, which generate their own fuel, can be regarded as a perpetual energy source, but expert opinion throughout the world is unanimous that they are not likely to make a major contribution to total energy production until the last quarter of the century.

The past half-century has witnessed great changes in the relative contributions made by the various fund energies to total energy sup-

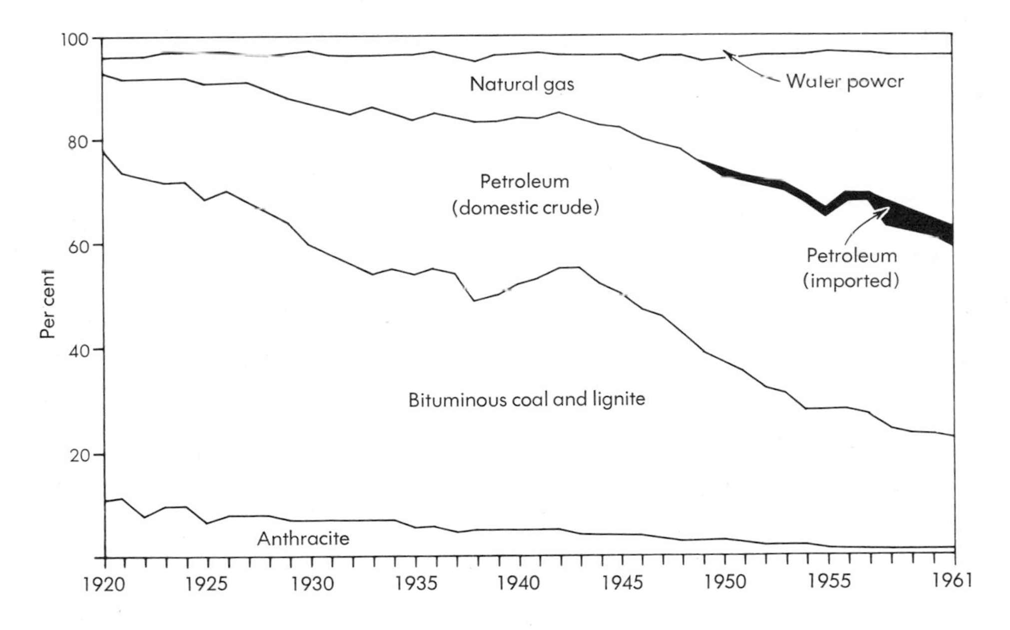

Fig. 10-1 Energy consumption in the United States.
The most significant change since 1945 has been the increasing importance of natural gas. (U.S. Bureau of Mines.)

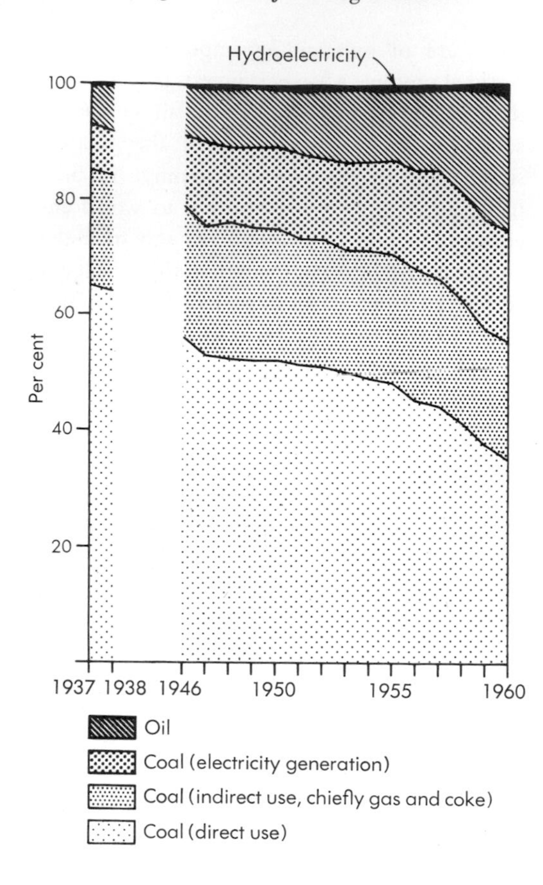

Fig. 10-2 Sources of power in the United Kingdom.
Britain has derived an increasing proportion of its total energy consumption from Middle East oil since 1945. Since 1957, nuclear energy has also made a contribution to total energy supply.

plies. These changes have all involved the replacement of relatively high-cost energy by low-cost forms of energy; essentially, *labor-intensive energy sources have been supplemented and in part displaced by capital-intensive sources.*

The great changes in energy consumption in the United States are strikingly illustrated in Fig. 10-1. Even as late as 1920 bituminous coal still accounted for nearly 70 per cent of energy consumption, but thereafter its share fell rapidly. Most remarkable of all perhaps has been the growth in the importance of natural gas; of as little importance as petroleum as a source of energy at the beginning of the century, by 1930 it still accounted for less than 10 per cent of total energy consumption. In the following two decades, however, its share more than trebled, and it now holds almost equal rank with petroleum as a major source of energy.

Precisely similar changes have taken place in Europe, the second great energy-producing area in the world. In 1938 coal accounted for over 80 per cent of total energy supplies in the OEEC area and for more than 90 per cent in some coal-rich countries. By 1960 this share had fallen to only 55 per cent, although coal production in the OEEC area remained virtually unchanged over this period; by 1975 the contribution of coal to total energy supplies is unlikely to be more than 37 per cent. This change is all the more remarkable in that, while in the United States the extra energy supplies which have operated to reduce the relative importance of coal have largely originated in domestic sources, in Europe they have been imported (Fig. 10-2). By 1975 it is possible that as much as 45 per cent of Europe's energy requirements may have to be met by imports,[18] largely in the form of petroleum from the Middle East and North Africa. Such a heavy reliance on nonindigenous sources of energy certainly raises many questions of national security, as was painfully obvious in the Suez crisis of 1956. However, these have to be seen in their right perspective, and there is reason for believing that they are not of such importance as was imagined only a few years ago. Certainly, without additional supplies of low-cost energy derived from Middle East petroleum, the remarkable industrial expansion and the high

[18] **Organisation for European Economic Cooperation, *op. cit.*, p. 60.**

rate of economic growth in postwar Europe would have been impossible.

SELECTED REFERENCES

Alexandersson, Gunnar: *The Industrial Structure of American Cities,* University of Nebraska Press, Lincoln, Nebr., 1956.

Dennison, S. R.: *Location of Industry and the Depressed Areas,* Oxford University Press, London, 1939.

Estall, R. C.: "The Problem of Power in the United Kingdom," *Economic Geography,* vol. 34, pp. 80–89, 1958.

——— and R. O. Buchanan: *Industrial Activity and Economic Geography,* Hutchinson & Co. (Publishers), Ltd., London, 1961.

Florence, P. Sargant: *Investment, Location and Size of Plant,* Cambridge University Press, Cambridge, 1948.

———: *Logic of British and American Industry,* Routledge & Kegan Paul, Ltd., London, 1953.

———: *Postwar Investment, Location and Size of Plant,* Cambridge University Press, Cambridge, 1962.

Fuchs, Victor R.: *Changes in the Location of Manufacturing in the United States since 1929,* Yale University Press, New Haven, Conn., and London, 1962.

Guyol, Nathaniel B.: "Energy Consumption and Economic Development," in Norton Ginsburg (ed.), *Geography and Economic Development,* The University of Chicago Press, Chicago, 1960.

Harris, Chauncy D.: "The Market Factor in the Localization of Industry in the United States," *Annals of the Association of American Geographers,* vol. 44, pp. 315–348, 1954.

Herman, T.: "The Role of Cottage and Small Scale Industries in Asian Economic Development," *Economic Development and Cultural Change,* vol. 4, pp. 356–370, 1956.

Hoffman, W. G.: *The Growth of Industrial Economies,* University of Manchester Press, Manchester, 1958.

Isard, Walter: *Location and the Space-economy,* The Technology Press of the Massachusetts Institute of Technology, Cambridge, Mass., and John Wiley & Sons, Inc., New York, 1956.

———: *Methods of Regional Analysis,* The M.I.T. Press, Cambridge, Mass., and John Wiley & Sons, Inc., New York, 1960, pp. 232–308.

Loesch, August: *The Economics of Location,* Yale University Press, New Haven, Conn., 1954.

Manners, Gerald: "Regional Protection: A Factor in Economic Development," *Economic Geography,* vol. 38, pp. 122–129, 1962.

"Modernization of Small Industries in Asia," *Economic Bulletin for Asia and the Far East,* vol. 11, pp. 24–40, 1961.

Organisation for European Economic Cooperation: *Europe's Growing Needs of Energy: How Can They Be Met?* Paris, 1956.

———: *Europe's Needs for Oil: Implications and Lessons of the Suez Crisis,* Paris, 1958.

———: *Towards a New Energy Pattern in Europe,* Paris, 1960.

Parsons, J. J.: "California Manufacturing," *Geographical Review,* vol. 39, pp. 229–241, 1949.

Political and Economic Planning: *Location of Industry in Great Britain,* London, 1939.

Report of the Royal Commission on the Distribution of the Industrial Population, Cmd. 6153, H. M. Stationery Office, London, rep. 1964.

Rodgers, Allan L.: "Regional Industrial Development with Reference to Southern Italy," in Norton Ginsburg (ed.), *Geography and Economic Development,* The University of Chicago Press, Chicago, 1960.

The Smaller Industry in Japan, Asia Kyokai, Tokyo, 1957.

Thompson, John H.: "A New Method for Measuring Manufacturing," *Annals of the Association of American Geographers,* vol. 45, pp. 416–436, 1955.

Ullman, Edward L.: "Amenities as a Factor in Regional Growth," *Geographical Review,* vol. 44., pp. 119–132, 1954.

United Nations, Department of Economic and Social Affairs: *New Sources of Energy and Economic Development: Solar Energy, Wind Energy, Tidal Energy and Thermal Energy of the Seas,* New York, 1957.

Zelinsky, Wilbur: "Has American Industry Been Decentralizing?" *Economic Geography,* vol. 38, pp. 251–269, 1962.

Chapter 11

THE PETROLEUM INDUSTRY

The petroleum industry has no peer in the world economy: its every aspect requires the use of superlatives. Certain other industries, such as pharmaceuticals, aluminum, and electronics show an equally high growth rate, and the giants of the automobile and the chemical industries can match the largest corporations of the petroleum industry in many tests. But petroleum is the most international of all industries; oil exploration, production, transportation, refining, and marketing form integrated operations embracing countries at all levels of economic development. The familiar signs of the seven great "majors" are to be seen in more than one-hundred countries of the free world; their combined gross receipts comfortably exceed the national income of several countries at a high level of economic development. It has been estimated that between 1950 and 1960 the free world oil industry spent some 90 billion dollars in extending its capacity; this investment probably represented about one-sixth of total private fixed-capital formation in the United States and nearly one-third of that of the rest of the free world.[1] Petroleum products are the most important commodity entering world trade by any criteria, and account, in fact, for about 10 per cent of its total value. The transport of crude oil and refined products employs a specialized fleet which accounts for more than one-third of the entire world shipping tonnage.

[1] **Chase Manhattan Bank,** *Capital Investments by the World Petroleum Industry,* **New York, 1961.**

THE GROWTH OF PRODUCTION

The petroleum industry celebrated its first centenary in 1959, in which year world output attained a figure of almost 1 billion metric tons for the first time. The industry that began with Drake's well at Titusville, Pennsylvania, a century earlier had indeed come a very long way. World output first attained a level of 10 million tons per annum in 1890 and virtually doubled every decade thereafter. This geometric increase, a phenomenal performance, shows little sign of slackening; between 1949 and 1962 the average annual increase in output was around 7 per cent. Assuming—and it is a big assumption—that generally amicable relations between producing companies and host governments are maintained, the annual rate of growth of oil output is expected to amount to at least 5 per cent until 1975, at which time world output would attain some 2 billion tons. Even if a lower rate of increase is envisaged, however, the additional world requirements of oil over the next two decades appear prodigious.

Marked changes in the location pattern of production have accompanied this rapid increase in output. No country that has once attained a position of importance in the industry has ceased to be a significant producer (that is, a producer of more than 1 per cent of world output per annum), but the number of major producers has steadily augmented as the search for oil has been pushed to every corner of the globe. Except for a few brief years around the turn of the century when it was temporarily eclipsed by Imperial Russia, the United States has always been by far the world's largest producer, and as late as 1939 it still accounted for about two-thirds of world output. By 1962, however, the share of the United States in world production had fallen below one-third (Table 11-1), and it is certain that this proportion will continue to decline; although the United States will still be the largest individual petroleum producer, its output will be exceeded by that of the Middle East within a few years if the political climate in the Middle East continues to be generally favorable to Western enterprise. In no sense, however, does this relative decline of the United States reflect the approaching exhaustion of its petroleum resources; on the contrary, *proved* reserves (that is, those known to be in the ground and recoverable by existing techniques) have never stood higher. The decline rather is the result of a complex interaction of conflicting political and economic interests that largely originate in the United States itself.

By World War I Mexico had become the second-largest producer, after the United States, and the beginnings of the industry had appeared in the Middle East. The first successful oil strike in Venezuela occurred in 1917, and during the interwar period production grew rapidly, the country becoming the world's second-largest producer and the largest exporter. The great oil discoveries of Saudi Arabia and Kuwait came in the Thirties, but development was delayed by World War II; thereafter, however, expansion was tremendous, and in the late Fifties came the discovery of large petroleum sources in Libya, North Africa, and West Africa. Once the leading world producer, the Russian petroleum industry suffered a long period of stagnation and neglect through two foreign wars, revolution, and civil war; not until 1927 was the level of output of 1902 regained. Since the end of World War II, however, expansion of the petroleum output has been particularly rapid; at its planned rate of increase, the U.S.S.R. could become the world's leading producer in the Seventies.

It is not difficult to account for the tremendous growth of the world petroleum

Table 11-1

Petroleum Production (Million metric tons)

	1948	1960	1963
North America	274.7	373.6	405.0
Canada	1.7	25.6	33.0*
United States	273.0	348.0	372.0
Latin America and the Caribbean	91.7	197.5	232.0
Venezuela	71.7	152.4	169.9
Mexico	8.4	14.2	16.4
Argentina	3.3	9.1	13.9
Colombia	3.3	7.7	8.3
Trinidad	3.0	6.0	6.7
Western Europe	3.5	14.9	16.4
West Germany	0.9	5.5	7.3
Middle East	57.7	265.3	338.5
Kuwait	6.4	81.9	97.1
Saudi Arabia	19.0	62.1	81.0
Iran	25.3	52.2	71.6
Iraq	3.4	47.5	55.4
Kuwait Neutral Zone		7.3	16.8
Qatar		8.2	9.1
Bahrein	1.5	2.6	2.2
United Arab Republic	2.1	3.5	4.7*
Africa		10.3	51.7
Algeria		8.6	24.0*
Libya			22.1
Nigeria			3.8
Far East	7.0	26.9	29.5
Indonesia	4.3	20.6	22.8*
Brunei	2.7	4.6	3.8
Eastern Bloc	34.0	168.2	227.8
U.S.S.R.	29.2	147.9	206.0
Romania	4.1	11.5	12.2
Mainland China†		5.5	5.5
WORLD TOTAL	468.6	1,056.7	1,295.0

* 1962.

† Estimated.

SOURCE: United Nations, *Statistical Yearbook*, 1962; *Monthly Bulletin of Statistics*, May, 1964.

industry. In production, transportation, storage, and utilization, oil offers tremendous advantages over most other forms of energy; moreover, it compounds these advantages with two others of supreme importance: low cost and price stability. All of these advantages arise from the physical nature of petroleum; being a liquid, it is much easier to handle than coal, and it can often be lifted to the surface by the natural energy present in the underground reservoir. Its production always involves highly mechanized, capital-intensive methods and is continuous; or more precisely, production is controlled by the turn of a valve and the throw of a switch. Weight for weight, petroleum has a higher calorific value than coal, a consequence of a more favorable hydrogen-carbon ratio; 1 ton of petroleum is approximately equivalent to 1.4 tons of coal in energy output. Finally, improvements in refining techniques have made it possible to alter the relative proportions of refined products produced from particular crudes to meet differing patterns of demand or to meet shifts in the pattern of demand resulting from economic growth.

The Nature, Occurrence, and Recovery of Petroleum

Petroleum is a thick, dark green, brown, or yellow liquid composed of a complex mixture of hydrocarbons. It may be so waxy that it will not flow without special treatment, and it may contain a number of other substances such as sulfur, which it is necessary to remove. Two main classes of crude oil are usually distinguished: the light oils, with a paraffinic base and a relatively high hydrogen-carbon ratio, and the heavy, asphaltic-base crudes, with a higher carbon content. Each type of oil has advantages for particular uses, but improvements in refining technology have greatly extended the range of use of all crudes.

Oil occurs in the interstices of porous rocks, particularly sandstones and limestones, and in the joints and bedding planes of permeable rocks. There is still a considerable range of opinion among geologists regarding the method of formation of oil, but an organic origin is now widely accepted. There is considerable support for the hypothesis that *the creation of oil is an integral part of the cycle of sedimentation,* or in other words, that petroleum is inevitably produced in the complex process by which material is removed from the continental landmasses and deposited in the epicontinental seas, a process which has continued throughout geologic time. According to this theory, the formation of petroleum takes place through the decomposition of organic material in the absence of oxygen, on the margins of the continental shelves at some depth below the seabed; it has always occurred, and presumably is still taking place at the present.

Certain economically important consequences follow from this theory, consequences which go far to explain the behavior of the petroleum industry. The most important is that the occurrence of oil is not a restricted and rather special phenomenon; on the contrary, it is likely to be found wherever sedimentary rocks occur. Hence the chances of discovering oil should bear an approximate relationship to the effort expended in seeking it. The United States is not the world's largest producer because it has been best endowed by nature with oil resources, for its reserves are now known to be distinctly modest in comparison with those of the Middle East; it rather owes its position to the almost feverish search for oil in the country, a search which has involved the drilling of considerably more than a million wells in all and which adds about 50,000 new wells per year on the average.

The petroleum geologist confines his search for oil deposits to areas possessing great thicknesses of sedimentary rocks; in particular, he tries to trace shorelines of old continental masses. But petroleum, once formed, will not remain *in situ;* as its specific gravity is lower than that of water, which is inevitably present in sedimentary rocks during their formation, it will tend to move laterally or vertically, displacing water. The migrating oil may traverse many layers of rock, moving upwards through the joints, perhaps to appear at the surface as a "show," there slowly to evaporate away. It is necessary, therefore, to look for traps in which migrating oil is prevented from further movement. Such traps not only entomb petroleum but also, in effect, concentrate it; the oil in a trap may have reached it from a very extensive and originally horizontal source rock.

Oil traps are of two kinds, structural and stratigraphic. *Structural traps* arise from various deformations of originally horizontal sedimentary strata; the essential condition is that in some way, permeable and impermeable beds must be brought into contact so that further oil migration is impossible (Fig. 11-1). By far the most important kind of structural trap is the anticlinal structure, and traps of this kind account for almost the entire enormous output of the Middle East. In anticlinal structures it is common for oil to be under considerable gaseous and hydrostatic pressure, so that once the reservoir is pierced, the oil (and gas) will rise to the surface in a gusher; such a natural flow may continue with undiminished vigor for many years, and is a pronounced feature of the industry in the Middle East. Other structural traps arise from faulting; this type is numerous in the western portion of the

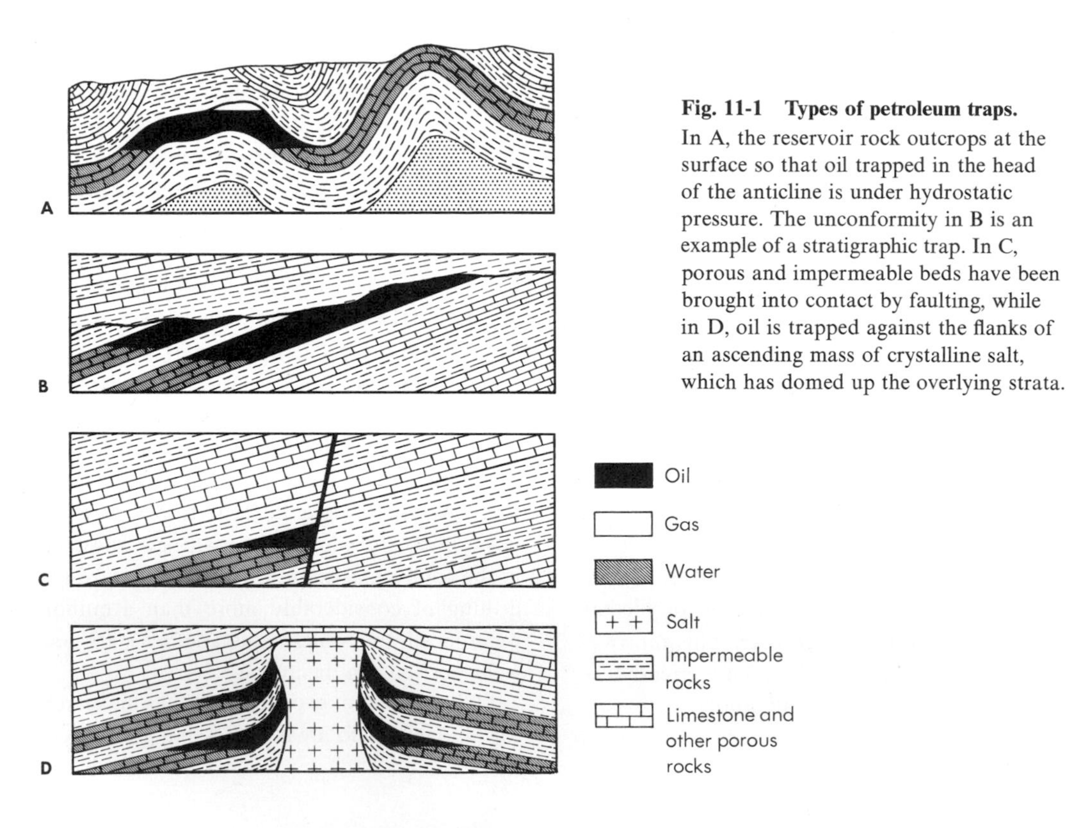

Fig. 11-1 Types of petroleum traps. In A, the reservoir rock outcrops at the surface so that oil trapped in the head of the anticline is under hydrostatic pressure. The unconformity in B is an example of a stratigraphic trap. In C, porous and impermeable beds have been brought into contact by faulting, while in D, oil is trapped against the flanks of an ascending mass of crystalline salt, which has domed up the overlying strata.

Gulf Coast fields of the United States. Still others arise through igneous intrusions or from the intrusion of salt domes; salt domes are very numerous in the eastern portion of the Gulf Coast fields of Texas and Louisiana and have been detected in drillings offshore, and they also occur in West Germany.

Stratigraphic traps, on the other hand, arise from changes in the conditions of sedimentation. They may result from discontinuities in the porosity or permeability of the rocks or from unconformities (Fig. 11-1). Although they undoubtedly occur elsewhere, such traps are of major significance only in the United States, where they occur in large numbers in certain fields and notably that in east Texas, and in Venezuela. But while structural traps can be detected by geologic or by geophysical methods, there is no means at present of detecting the existence of stratigraphic traps. These are only discovered by speculative exploratory drilling.

In the United States, such speculative drilling, or wildcatting, has been greatly encouraged by the taxation structure. In the rest of the world, however, the search for oil is much more concentrated on the large structural traps, and the proportion of dry, that is, unproductive, holes is very much lower. The enormous reserves of the Middle East have been proved with the drilling of but some 3,000 wells, and a dry hole is something of a rarity. In the United States only about one in ten of the 16,000 exploratory wells drilled each year (that is, wells put down in areas never before productive) is successful in finding oil. Among wells that do encounter oil, the proportion of those that find it in commercially exploitable quantities is smaller still. All petroleum exploration, of course, involves an element of chance, but the heavier the investment necessary for exploration and development, the greater the necessity to concentrate on the most promising structures.

But while it is generally true that, as the oilman says, "Oil is where you find it," the world industry has had no difficulty in meeting every increase in demand. In fact it has done considerably better, for the rate of proving new reserves in recent years has substantially exceeded that of the increase in consumption. It is certainly true that world petroleum resources are not infinite, but the gloomy predictions made from time to time of an early end to the industry have proved quite unfounded. Important new fields have continually been discovered; improved techniques have greatly lifted the recovery rate, and under favorable conditions as much as 85 per cent of the oil present in the ground can be recovered. By "secondary recovery," that is, techniques involving the injection of water or of gas, or by combustion of petroleum *in situ* with the simultaneous injection of air, the output from many old fields has been raised very considerably. Drilling has proceeded deeper and deeper, so that wells exceeding 20,000 feet in depth are now possible; directional drilling has enabled wells to penetrate beneath the seabed, and offshore drilling platforms permit the production of oil from the continental shelves. Further development of the turbodrill, a technique much used in the U.S.S.R., is likely to result in a substantial reduction in the costs of drilling. But even with existing techniques, it is clear that the world is in no danger of an oil shortage in the foreseeable future; the American geologist Weeks has estimated that the world's resources of petroleum recoverable in the light of existing technical and economic conditions are some sixteen times the oil already produced and that a further quantity may ultimately be recoverable through secondary methods[2] (Table 11-2). All such estimates are highly speculative of course, but it may

[2] Lewis G. Weeks, "Fuel Reserves of the Future," *Bulletin of the Association of American Petroleum Geologists,* vol. 42, p. 434, 1958.

Table 11-2

Potential Reserves of Crude Petroleum (Billions of barrels)	
World ultimate potential reserves	1,500
Already produced	93
Already proved	325
Possible reserves (land)	882
Possible submarine reserves	200
Ultimate potential reserves of the U.S.A.	240
Ultimate potential reserves of the U.S.S.R.	250

SOURCE: Lewis G. Weeks, "Fuel Reserves of the Future," *Bulletin of the Association of American Petroleum Geologists*, vol. 42, 1958.

safely be assumed that long before the world's petroleum resources are on the verge of exhaustion, petroleum will be greatly supplemented by other forms of energy.

STRUCTURE AND MAJOR LOCATIONS OF THE INDUSTRY

Some preliminary knowledge of the structure of the petroleum industry is essential for an understanding of the pattern of world oil production and of the many complex problems that have emerged in areas in which production takes place. The unceasing search for new oil supplies throughout the free world despite a substantial surplus capacity (world oil output could probably be raised by 40 per cent without drilling many more wells) also originates from the structure of the industry.

Outside the countries of the Eastern bloc, the world petroleum industry is dominated by seven giant petroleum companies, usually known as the "majors." Five are American-controlled and largely American-owned, and among them is the world's largest petroleum company, Standard Oil of New Jersey. Of the two remaining majors one, British Petroleum, is a British concern in which the British government is the majority stockholder. The other, Royal Dutch–Shell, is a joint British-Dutch enterprise; the "group," as Royal Dutch–Shell is known in the industry, is the world's second-largest producer, after Jersey Standard, and has the most widespread geographic interests of any of the majors.

The majors are completely integrated organizations engaged in every aspect of the industry. Operating through subsidiaries in almost every country of the free world, the majors have a grip on world oil production that is unappreciated by most Americans, accustomed as they are to a multiplicity of producers, refiners, and marketing organizations; the seven companies between them account for almost three-quarters of free world total production (Table 11-3).

Although they are among the largest individual producers, the majors are primarily engaged in the production of foreign oil, which, for reasons that will become apparent, can be produced at very much lower cost than that of producing oil in the United States. All but a very small proportion of the output of Venezuela and of the Middle East, the most important producing areas in the free world after the United States, is solidly in their hands. The great bulk of United States production, on the other hand, comes from a large number of independent producers. The reason for this difference between the structure of the industry in the United States and that in the rest of the world is largely to be found in the very different conditions that existed in the two areas in the early days of the industry.

Petroleum production and refining is a capital-intensive industry; every technological development makes it more so. But in the early years of the industry in the United States, when much easily accessible oil awaited discovery, entry into production was relatively easy. It was Rockefeller who saw that the key to control lay in the more capital-intensive refining section, and by the turn of the century his Standard Oil Trust had come to control almost 90 per cent of marketing and refining in the country. With the breakup of the trust in 1911, increasing competition among its successors, from which the present American majors are descended, gradually brought about more integrated operations, for by this means the refiner enjoyed both an assured supply of crude and outlets for his products. Nevertheless, public opinion continued to demand a place for the small operator, and despite the growth of giant integrated concerns, production in the United States is still widely disseminated among a multiplicity of producers.

Outside the United States, however, integrated operations were necessary from the beginning. Oil in the Netherlands Indies, in Mexico, and in Persia was situated far from its market; the companies engaged in its production had necessarily also to be engaged in transportation, in refining, and in marketing. Large units were also necessary to negotiate concessions from governments, for in the world at large, mineral rights are the property, not of the landowner, but of the state.

Though active in Mexico and in the Nether-

Table 11-3

The Structure of the Petroleum Industry, 1960 (Crude petroleum production, million metric tons)

	U.S.A.	OTHER WESTERN HEMISPHERE COUNTRIES	EASTERN HEMISPHERE	WORLD TOTAL
Standard of New Jersey	25.3	66.9	33.6	125.8
Royal Dutch–Shell	19.8	47.4	33.8	101.0
Gulf	20.1	10.7	47.7	78.5
British Petroleum		0.1	75.9	76.0
Texaco	27.8	11.7	28.1	67.6
Standard of California	16.8	4.5	28.1	49.4
Socony Mobil	12.9	8.5	19.8	41.2
Compagnie Française des Pétroles		0.1	18.9	19.0
TOTAL, 8 COMPANIES	122.7	149.9	285.9	558.5
Other Free World Producers	225.2	69.7	35.1	330.0
Eastern Bloc			168.2	168.2
GRAND TOTAL	347.9	219.6	489.2	1,056.7

SOURCE: Petroleum Press Service; United Nations, *Statistical Yearbook*, 1962.

The great range of capital equipment employed by the petroleum industry is suggested by the portable drilling rigs operating along the French coast, and a view of part of a west Texas plant producing natural gasoline and liquefied petroleum gases from well head gas.

The striking changes produced by the petroleum industry on the landscape are clearly visible in these photographs of an offshore oilfield in the Caspian Sea, and of pipelines and a permanent settlement in the desert, near Dahran, Saudi Arabia.

lands Indies, American producers lagged behind Europeans in moving into what were to prove the free world's most productive oil fields outside the United States, those in the Middle East and Venezuela. Although Jersey Standard has been involved in production outside the United States almost since the beginning of the industry, other American majors were comparative latecomers to foreign production; California Standard's venture into foreign production came only in the middle Thirties. Since World War II, however, companies from nations such as Japan and Italy which were left out of the world oil scramble or which lost former interests through military defeat have begun to bid above the majors for exploratory and developmental concessions, particularly in Venezuela and in the Middle East. This pressure has forced the majors to step up their own exploratory and developmental activities in order to protect their share of the market.

As a result world oil supplies have risen rapidly; in the late Fifties a large "shut-in" surplus was created which lacked a market. Concessions in the Sahara and in North Africa multiplied rapidly, and in the space of a few years, the area gave every promise of ultimately becoming a major producing area. Despite their intense activity, however, it is abundantly clear that the majors cannot expect to retain their present large share of free world output outside the United States; they are under increasing pressure from American independents, from aggressive foreign companies such as Italy's state-owned Ente Nazionale Idrocarburi (ENI) and Japan's Arabian Oil Company, and from state-owned companies established by the governments of producing nations.

The two non-American majors represent the extremes of geographic concentration and dispersal. British Petroleum, which traces its origin from the establishment of the Anglo-Persian Oil Company in 1909, is mainly concerned with production in the Middle East; alone of the majors it has no production in the United States or in Venezuela, although it has important interests in Canada. Its concentration of effort on the area with the lowest costs of production in the world gives to the company tremendous competitive strength, but at the same time has made it very vulnerable to the more irrational manifestations of nationalism. On the other hand, the Royal Dutch–Shell group, which from humble beginnings in north Sumatra in the last quarter of the nineteenth century has grown to the position of the world's second-largest producer, has production interests which extend to every continent and is extremely strong in all three principal producing areas of the noncommunist world. All the American majors have interests in the Middle East and in Venezuela, although for some the latter is of relatively minor significance; these companies, however, have interests in other areas of Latin America.

Fiercely competitive though the world oil industry appears, there is a considerable degree of cooperation between the majors. They combine in various groupings for the purposes of production and in yet other groupings for the purposes of refining and marketing. These groupings may extend over several continents, as in the cases of the former Standard Vacuum Oil Company (Stanvac), a subsidiary of Jersey Standard and Socony-Mobil which operated throughout Africa, Asia, and Australia,[3] and Caltex, a subsidiary of California Standard and Texaco which still operates in the same areas. Yet all the majors cooperate in one way or another in production in the Middle East, and several majors are linked by long-term purchasing contracts, mainly from British Petro-

[3] **The Standard Vacuum Oil Company was dissolved in 1960 under American antitrust laws, and its properties were divided between its parent organizations.**

leum. It is hardly surprising that from time to time the general public believes that the competition is more apparent than real.

The Petroleum Industry in the United States

Although strictly speaking the commercial production of petroleum did not begin in the United States, the country may justly be regarded as the founder of the modern petroleum industry. Only since the end of World War II has production in the United States failed to keep pace with that of the rest of the world. Without drilling another well, the country could raise its annual petroleum output by perhaps as much as 100 million tons (almost 750 million barrels), and its declining share of world production is closely related to the fact that American interests now produce so much oil outside the United States; American interests now control some 55 per cent of the petroleum production in the free world. In refining and in consumption the United States is in an even more commanding position than in production, though here again its share is declining. In 1939 the United States possessed about 70 per cent of the free world's refining capacity and accounted for about the same proportion of world consumption; by 1962, however, these proportions had fallen to some 45 per cent and a little less than 60 per cent, respectively. Nevertheless, even despite the more rapid growth of consumption in Western Europe, the world's second most important consuming area, it is estimated that in 1965 consumption per head in the United States will still be twice that of the former.

The Oil Fields From its beginnings in the Appalachian plateau, the center of oil production in the United States has moved westwards and southwards, but Texas, where oil was first produced commercially in 1889, has been the leading state for more than half a century, and currently accounts for about 30 per cent of total national production. Production in the United States is derived from many thousands of individual oil pools (Fig. 11-2). Though the grouping of the pools into fields is somewhat arbitrary, the following major producing fields may be recognized in order of output:

The *Mid-continent* fields, extending in a

Fig. 11-2 Oil and gas fields in the United States.
The two types closely coincide, but there are some important "nonassociated" gas fields. (U.S. Geological Survey.)

broad arc through central Texas, Oklahoma, and Kansas, to which the fields of east Texas, northern Louisiana, and Arkansas may conveniently be attached.

The *Gulf Coast* fields of Texas and Louisiana, which extend offshore into the Gulf itself. The ownership of offshore oil has long been disputed by the Federal and the state governments. Texas and Florida have been awarded all oil up to 10.5 miles from the shore by virtue of "their traditional and historic boundaries," but elsewhere the Federal government retains the ownership of all oil on the continental shelf beyond the customary 3-mile limit.

The *Californian* fields, situated in the southern San Joaquin Valley and within the Los Angeles metropolitan area. California was long the second-largest producing state and remained so until the late Fifties. The state is, however, a substantial oil importer.

The *Rocky Mountain* fields, a name usually applied to several fields that lie either within the Great Plains or in the intermontane plateaus. The principal producing areas are in Wyoming, but others are located in Colorado, in Montana, and in North Dakota. Since the end of World War II an important new producing area has emerged in the Four Corners district, Utah's production having climbed steeply. The fields of the Canadian Prairie Provinces can also be regarded as part of the Rocky Mountain fields, and may expand production greatly if marketing difficulties can be resolved. The Rocky Mountain fields also contain vast deposits of oil shale and tar sands; at the present these are uneconomic to process, but a number of projects currently under investigation may lead to a fuller utilization in the future.

The *Lower Lakes* fields of Illinois, Indiana, Ohio, and Michigan. The most important producing areas are in Illinois, where production first began in 1889. After many years of relatively low output, production in Illinois rocketed during World War II, only to fall again in the postwar period.

The *Appalachian* fields. These consist of many hundreds of fields extending from New York to Kentucky; production in all, however, is very low. Apart from their historical importance, the Appalachian fields are chiefly noted for their suitability for producing high-grade lubricating oils.

Additionally, Alaska has been proved to contain large deposits of petroleum, and the state may become a large producer if transport difficulties can be overcome. Offshore production from the coasts of southern California, the Gulf, and the south Atlantic states can also be expected to increase considerably.

The Overproduction Problem Mineral rights in the United States are the property of the landowner; petroleum, however, is fugitive and is subject to the "law of capture." The very large number of oil pools, in contrast to the limited number of enormous fields of the Middle East and of Venezuela, would inevitably have made for higher costs, but the operation of the law of capture, which encourages a landowner to drill in order to prevent neighbors from taking his oil by default, has encouraged drilling far in excess of that necessary or even desirable. This unregulated drilling has led to loss of pressure in reservoirs and to a reduction in the recovery rate.

The drilling of more wells than are necessary for economic operation has also been encouraged by the "depletion allowance," a concession which allows producers to reduce their tax liability, ostensibly to encourage a high rate of oil discovery, and by "prorationing." Prorationing is the imposition by individual states of physical restrictions on petroleum production, partly in the interests of conservation but mainly to prevent overproduction. The Connally Act of 1935, which prohibits the sale across state boundaries of oil produced in excess of state quotas, in effect ensures Federal support for restriction. Originally spurred by the great fall in the price of crude consequent upon the discovery of the great east Texas field shortly before the Great Depression, all the important producing states —Texas, Louisiana, Oklahoma, and California —now make monthly adjustments in quotas. Many minor producing states do the same, and others have voluntary agreements restricting production. There has also been a tendency for oil pools to be operated as units; such measures have been arranged by producers themselves, however, and are largely voluntary.

Ironically, although prorationing has materially reduced waste and has brought about a higher recovery rate from reservoirs, it has in effect acted as a price-support system for oil, enlarging the disparity in cost between domestic and foreign oil resulting from generally more favorable physical conditions overseas. Prorationing and the depletion allowance have been largely responsible for the drilling of an enormous number of unnecessary wells in *proved* oil fields, for their effect is to reward successful drilling by a share in the market. Nearly half of the wells in Texas are marginal wells exempt from restriction; as a result, efficient wells operate at considerably less than capacity. Hence output per well in the United States is the lowest in the world, lower even than in Europe, and diminutive in comparison with the situation in the Middle East.

Industry Structure and Politics The petroleum industry in the United States has a structure of considerable complexity. There are the domestic subsidiaries of the great majors such as Shell Oil and Jersey Standard's Humble; there are other integrated descendants of the Standard Oil Trust with limited overseas interests, such as Standard of Indiana; there are great integrated companies such as Cities Service, Phillips, Tidewater, Union, and Sinclair; and there are pipeline operators and refiners. While some thirty-five large companies dominate the industry, *production* is shared by many thousands of operators and small enterprises. Little capital equipment is needed to enter the industry, for all drilling expenses can be met by granting a share of the lease, and landowners are only too eager to allow drilling on their properties. Small operators produce as much as two-fifths of total petroleum output and make a substantial proportion of the new discoveries; most of these, however, ultimately pass into the hands of the great companies. There is, inevitably, a high mortality among speculative small producers, but their ranks are continually augmented by new entrants, and their political strength is very substantial. Pressure from the independents was originally responsible for the imposition of a tariff on imported oil and later for the imposition of import quotas.

The majors and the larger independents that have succeeded in getting a foothold in foreign production are convinced that rising costs of domestic production and mounting demand will compel the import of more and more foreign oil; this the smaller independents emphatically deny. The west coast, a substantial oil-deficit area despite California's large production, is exempt from quota restrictions, but east of the Rockies these have become steadily more severe, a development that has been of particular concern to Venezuela. The frantic scramble into foreign oil production of all large independents strongly suggests that from the economic standpoint, the majors have much truth on their side. It does appear highly likely that the United States will have to import increasing quantities of foreign oil in the future, if only to honor its obligations to assist economic development in the underdeveloped world.

Oil Transport From field storage tanks crude oil moves mainly by pipeline towards refineries and to bulk terminals at the ports. More than 100,000 miles of oil and gas lines were in existence before the Great Depression, and the total mileage now exceeds 500,000, of which about half represents trunk lines. Progressively larger lines have been employed with the continual increase in production, for the capacity, or throughput, of a line increases with the square of its radius. Refined products also are increasingly moved by pipeline; although crude and refined products cannot be interchanged in a line, a special products line can easily handle a variety of products.

Although pipelines represent the cheapest method of moving oil overland, they only justify their cost when they can be used continuously at maximum capacity; moreover, their destination cannot be changed. Water transport by large tanker is still substantially cheaper and is thus preferred wherever possible. Much oil, therefore, reaches eastern markets by sea, and a network of lines connects the Mid-continent fields with the Gulf ports, which contain the largest concentration of refining capacity in the country. Transcontinental lines are nevertheless very important; linking Texas and Louisiana with Northeast are the Big Inch and Little Inch lines (now respectively a crude and a products line after a variety of employments since their construction during World War II); the Mid Valley line links Texas and Ohio, and the Plantation line connects Louisiana with North Carolina; these four lines have a combined throughput of over 1 million barrels per day (50 million tons per annum). Other transcontinental lines extend between Texas and southern California and between the Four Corners and Los Angeles.

Venezuela and its Competitors

Although the existence of oil in what is now Venezuela was known to the conquistadores, the great petroleum wealth of the Maracaibo basin remained unknown until 1917, and not until 1923 was the first really big strike made. From then on expansion was extremely rapid, and by the Thirties Venezuela had become the world's second-largest producer and the largest exporter.

About 70 per cent of Venezuela's oil production comes from the fields around Lake Maracaibo; the balance is produced in a number of small scattered fields in the eastern llanos (Fig. 11-3). The Bolivar field extends along the northeast borders of the lake, many wells have been drilled in the shallow lake itself, and the concession of the largest producer, Creole, a subsidiary of Jersey Standard, is entirely lacustrine. Other important fields are located northwest of the lake. Two small offshore islands of the Netherlands West Indies, Curaçao and Aruba, have played an important part in the development of the petroleum industry in western Venezuela; for many years they have operated two of the world's largest refineries, to which crude is conveyed by a fleet of barges, as tankers are unable to operate in the shallow waters of the lake. Pressure from the Venezuelan government, however, has led producing companies greatly to enlarge refining facilities in the country, and these now possess a larger capacity than those on the Dutch islands.

Venezuela's costs of crude production are substantially lower than those of the United States. Yet output per well is still small in comparison with that in the Middle East, and the costs of exploration, drilling, and transportation on the thickly forested coasts and in the eastern llanos, where large tracts are regularly flooded during the wet season, are very high. Subsidiaries of Jersey Standard,

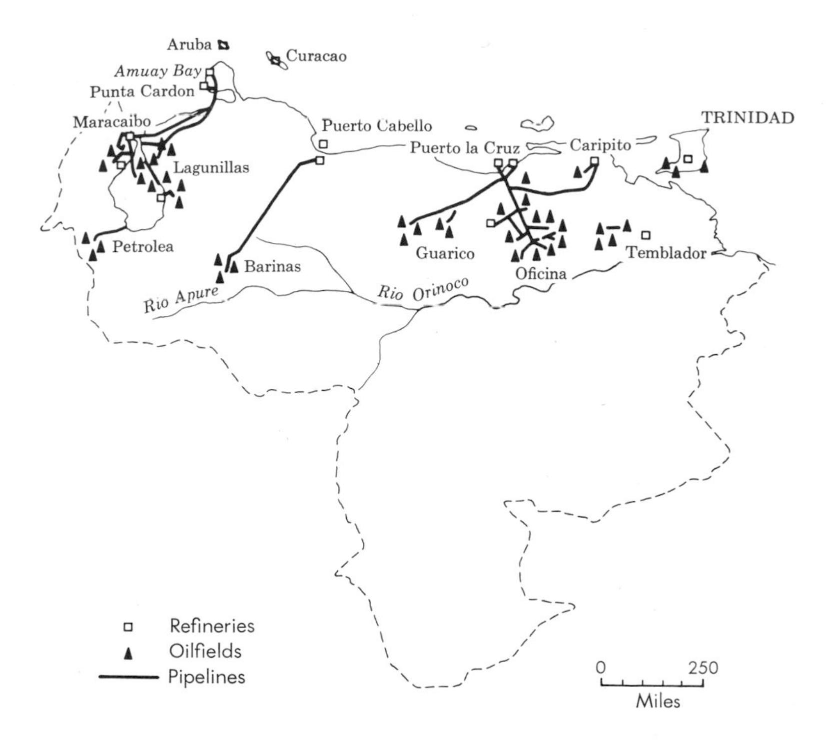

Fig. 11-3 Oil fields in Venezuela.
Venezuela's most important oil fields are situated in the Maracaibo basin, but those of the Apure basin and in eastern states are increasing their share of total national production.

Gulf, and Royal Dutch–Shell produce more than half the total crude output, but their share is slowly declining as other producers acquire concessions. Venezuela's crudes vary considerably in composition, but the country is noted for its asphaltic and specialty crudes.

The destination of Venezuelan oil exports has changed greatly since World War II. Western Europe was formerly the main purchaser, but its increased consumption of "sterling" Middle East oil and the restrictions placed on the purchase of "dollar" oil by many European countries led to a substantial diversion of oil exports to Canada, the United States, and other countries of Latin America.

In 1950 Venezuela adopted a "50-50" profit-sharing agreement between operating companies and the state, which soon spread into the Middle East and other producing areas;[4] in 1959 Venezuela again set a precedent by raising its oil royalties to increase its share to 60 per cent. This move was rendered abortive through a marked drop in the crude prices, but as Venezuela has generally followed a policy of cooperating closely with the companies, the government's unilateral action suggested the possibility of difficulties for the operating companies similar to those they have experienced in other Latin American producers. With the increasing hostility of Cuba

[4] Royalties paid by producing companies on all oil produced, plus taxes paid by them to government, were to amount to 50 per cent of the estimated profits of local production.

towards the Venezuelan government, however, this danger appears to have been averted.

Mexico Mexico's production grew tremendously following the first big strike in 1901. Spurred on by the demands of World War I, Mexico in 1921 reached an all-time peak output of over 190 million barrels (27 million tons) and became the world's largest producer. Mexico's most important fields lie in two groups, the northern fields west of Tampico and the southern fields to the south; the extreme narrowness of the latter and the enormous productivity achieved by some wells led to their designation as the "Golden Lane." From 1921 onwards, however, the social and economic environment resulting from the still simmering national revolution of a decade earlier rendered the position of the British and American oil companies increasingly difficult. Production sagged, exploratory activities were reduced, and salt water began to invade the more productive fields. In 1938 the oil companies' properties were expropriated by the Mexican government, since which time the industry has been operated as a state monopoly. Production dropped still lower, and the country ceased to be a major exporter.

Despite some improvement since 1945, the country's oil production in 1962 was only two-thirds of the peak rate. Mexico has, it is true, enjoyed the advantage of substantially cheaper internal oil prices than those in the rest of the world, but there is little evidence that this has stimulated a high rate of economic growth and the country has forfeited the greatly expanded export income which would have resulted from a continued growth of production. Broadly similar difficulties have arisen in the industry in Colombia, Brazil, Peru, and Argentina, where, after promising beginnings, rapid growth has been hindered by increasing state regulation. The losses of all of these countries have been Venezuela's gain.

The Petroleum Industry of the Middle East

In an industry in which rapid growth has come to be taken for granted, the development of the oil resources of the Middle East has nevertheless been phenomenal (Fig. 11-4). Nowhere else in the world do such colossal oil reservoirs occur, and in such limited areas. Tiny Kuwait, a barren sheikdom of but some 5,800 square miles, was estimated in 1958 to possess virtually one-quarter of the free world's proved petroleum reserves (as compared with only 15 per cent for the entire United States), and the Middle East as a whole was credited with over 71 per cent of the total.[5] Nowhere else in the world are the costs of producing petroleum so low, and in no other part of the world do such intractable social and political problems beset the industry; a scantily populated area of negligible significance as recently as 1930, the Middle East now stands in the very forefront of world political and economic affairs.

Growth of the Industry Widespread seepages have been known in the Middle East since classical times, and a desultory commercial production of bitumen and other crudely refined products was carried on over many centuries; thus it may appear surprising that the development of petroleum resources was so protracted. In the last quarter of the nineteenth century European interests began to seek concessions in Persia and in the Ottoman Empire, but corrupt and inefficient administrations, the mutual jealousies of the Great Powers, the distance from consuming markets, poor transport facilities, and the desolate and barren nature of the terrain constituted immense obstacles to development.

Apart from the small fields flanking the

[5] These estimates may need to be written down as the magnitude of Africa's reserves becomes apparent.

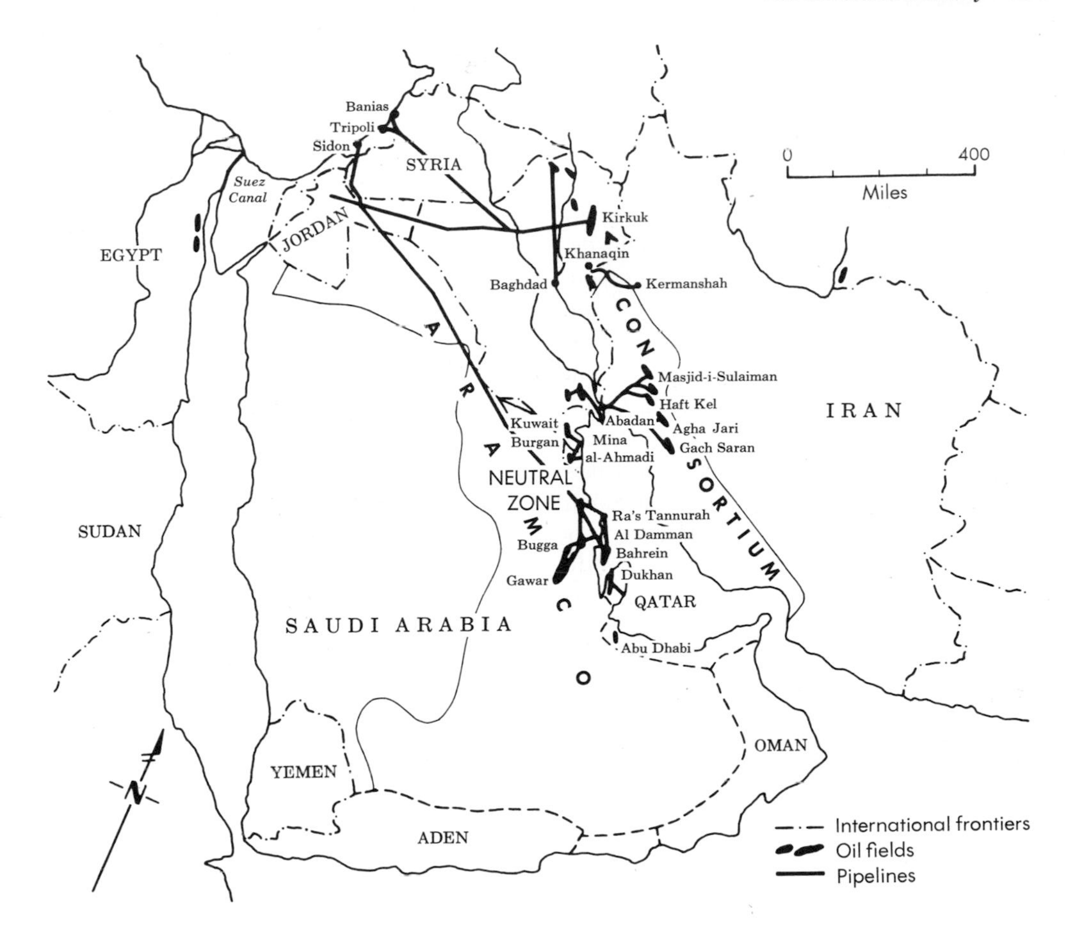

Fig. 11-4 Oil fields of the Middle East.
The map shows producing concessions as they were in 1962. Since that date negotiations for the surrender of unproductive areas have taken place; these will be reallocated to new producing companies, in which host governments are likely to hold a substantial interest.

Gulf of Suez in Egypt and the recent discoveries in Israel and in central Iran, all the Middle East fields lie within a great triangle with its apex on the Iraq-Turkey frontier, in the broad downfold between the Zagros Mountain system and the old rocks of the Arabian plateau. The fields of Iran and of the Al Mawsil (Mosul)-Kirkūk area in Iraq occur in the highly folded foothill zone of the Zagros, but the southern Iraqi fields and those of the western margins of the Persian Gulf in Kuwait, Saudi Arabia, and Qatar are of the broad, anticlinal type. Both types have demonstrated an ability to support a rate of expansion of petroleum output unmatched elsewhere in the world.

The foothill fields were the first to be developed; the discovery of the Masjid-i-Sulaiman (Solomon's Mosque) field in 1908 in Khuzistan, southern Persia, by an English company formed by William D'Arcy may justly be said to mark the beginning of the modern Middle

East oil industry, and led to the establishment of the Anglo-Persian Oil Company in the following year.[6] Exploration in what is now Iraq was long delayed by political difficulties, and not until 1927 was the Kirkūk oil field discovered. Transport difficulties, the onset of the Great Depression, and World War II long delayed development of the fields of northern Iraq, and their full potentialities were not realized until after 1950. The Fifties also witnessed the development of the great fields of Damman in Saudi Arabia, Dukhan in Qatar, and Burgan in Kuwait, all discovered shortly before the war, and a succession of new strikes —Qatif, Abqaiq, Ghawar, and others in Saudi Arabia, Ahmadi, and the northern fields near the Iraqi border in Kuwait—which clearly demonstrated the enormous reserves of the Middle East. Within a dozen years production in Saudi Arabia jumped from the trickle that had been produced throughout the war to over 50 million tons; production in Kuwait, which began in 1946, was closely approaching 100 million tons by 1962.

Until 1950 Iran was by far the largest producer in the Middle East. The nationalization of the property of the Anglo-Iranian Oil Company in the following year, however, resulted in a fall in production to the level of three decades before, and provided a great stimulus to production in both Saudi Arabia and in Kuwait. With the successful settlement of the dispute in the establishment of the "Consortium" (Iranian Exploration and Development Company) in 1954, Iranian output expanded rapidly, and by 1962 exceeded 65 million tons, double that of 1950. No important new fields have come into production in Iran since the end of the war, but the Agha Jari field, discovered in 1937, has expanded its output very greatly and now accounts for over 70 per cent of the country's total output.

[6] The ancient name of Iran was adopted by Persia in 1935, whereupon the Anglo-Persian Oil Company became the Anglo-Iranian Oil Company. The company took the name British Petroleum in 1954, following the settlement of the dispute over the nationalization of its properties.

Locational Advantages A unique combination of geologic and geographic circumstances has given to the Middle East the lowest costs of petroleum production in the world, costs which are probably only one-quarter those of the United States and a little over half those of Venezuela. The reasons for this enormous competitive advantage are partly to be found in the great size of the oil reservoirs, a consequence of a history of sedimentation and of folding that was extraordinarily favorable to the formation and to the trapping of oil, and in the occurrence of such reservoirs at no great distance below the surface. Only the fields of southern Iraq have required drilling below 10,000 feet, and the great fields of Kuwait produce from wells descending less than 5,000 feet. But as each field has been developed from the outset under a single management operating under a concession from the state which usually embraced the whole of the national territory, it has been possible to eliminate waste and to drill just the number of wells necessary to produce an output of the size required. Thus individual wells have an enormous output; in Kuwait the average per well is over 6,000 barrels per day, almost five hundred times that of the average for wells in the United States.

Additionally, nearly all the major fields lie at no great distance from the coast, so that only short pipelines are required; only the fields of northern Iraq have not enjoyed this advantage, a main reason for their late development. The construction of the first pipeline across the desert linking Kirkūk with Haifa and Tripoli, completed in 1934, enabled production to rise to 3 million tons; but not until the completion in 1949 of new 16-inch lines and in 1952 of the

30- to 32-inch line from Kirkūk to Banias in Syria, laid parallel to the 1934 lines, could Iraq take its place as a major producer. Similar lines would be necessary to develop the central Iran fields of Qom, which is not yet in commercial production.

Nevertheless, enormous capital expenditure has been necessary to exploit these geographic advantages. Iran and Iraq have long suffered from the restrictions on navigation at the head of the Persian Gulf caused by a network of swamps, mud flats, and sandbanks, and the ever increasing size of tankers and particularly the employment of the so-called "supertankers" of upwards of 80,000 deadweight tons have aggravated these difficulties. Two completely new terminals, one serving the fields of southern Iraq and the other the little developed Gach Saran field of Iran, have been built to handle a considerable expansion of output. Neither Saudi Arabia nor Kuwait possessed harbors capable of taking large modern vessels, and they have had to be provided with such facilities. Ra's Tannūrah on the Saudi coast has been developed as the main loading point. Since 1950 Saudi crude has been provided with another major outlet in the 1,100-mile Trans-Arabia pipeline (Tapline), linking the Saudi fields with Sayda in Lebanon, but the increasing size of tankers has robbed this 31-inch line of much of the anticipated savings in transport costs, and its principal effect has been to reduce congestion in the Suez Canal.[7] Kuwait, on the other hand, has concentrated on improving its oceanic terminals to accommodate the very largest size of vessels, and the two piers of Mina-al-Ahmadi, capable of handling several supertankers simultaneously, form by far the largest crude-loading terminal in the world. Since mid-1961 laden tankers of 50,000 deadweight tons have been able to pass through the Suez Canal; larger vessels have to be "topped up" at Mediterranean ports. Laden vessels of 80,000 tons and over cannot pass through at all, and have to travel via the Cape. But so great is the anticipated expansion of Middle East oil production that every outlet will need to be improved; almost certainly, there will have to be new pipelines, new terminals, and further improvements to and perhaps even a duplication of the Suez canal.

[7] See p. 561 for a discussion of the role of supertankers.

The Western Operators It is in the Middle East that the fortunes of the majors are most closely interwoven (Fig. 11-5). In part this is because the capital costs of producing oil in the Middle East and transporting it to distant markets have been so great that they have exceeded the resources even of the largest companies; moreover, concessions have generally embraced the whole national territory, and by joint operations the risks involved in the explorations of these large areas are shared among the participants. But the close relations among the majors also reflect political pressures.

One of the most significant features of the development of Middle East oil industry, once an almost exclusive preserve of British, French, and Dutch interests, is the steady increase since 1930 of American participation; by 1962 American companies accounted for considerably more than half the total output, though British Petroleum remained the largest individual producer. This remarkable change occurred in an area over which Britain long exercised political control; Britain was largely responsible for the delineation of the present boundaries of the Arab states, many of whose rulers, in fact, have retained their positions by virtue of treaties with the former government of British India.

The expansion of American interest arose from State Department pressure for the tradi-

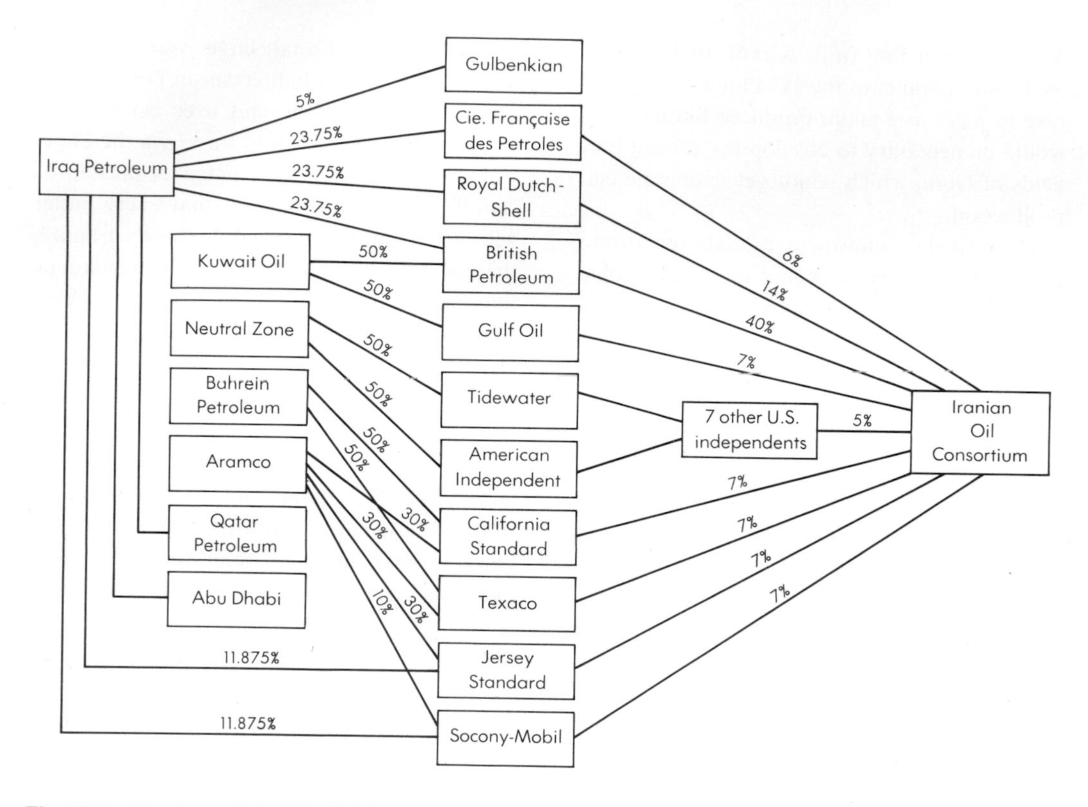

Fig. 11-5 Structure of the Middle East petroleum industry.
The close interlocking of the interests of the seven international majors is very apparent in this diagram of the structure of the Middle East oil industry; seven other United States independent companies share with Tidewater and Aminoil a 5 per cent interest in the Iranian Consortium. Not shown in the diagram is the interest of the Japanese Arabian Oil Company in offshore production in the Kuwait Neutral Zone, and that of Italy's ENI and Indiana Standard in Iranian offshore production. Note the interest of Gulbenkian, "Mr. Five Per Cent," one of the original concessionaires of the pre-1914 Turkish Empire.

tional open-door policy; American companies were thus given a share in the former Turkish Petroleum Company (now the Iraq Petroleum Company) when the former German interests were eliminated after World War I, and later were also successful in obtaining concessions from Arab rulers. In no part of the Middle East are American interests unrepresented, and in Saudi Arabia, the Bahrein Islands, and the Kuwait-Saudi Neutral Zone, production is exclusively in American hands. Since 1954 United States companies have shared an equal interest with the former concessionaire in southern Iran, British Petroleum, as a result of the establishment of the "Consortium."

That this massive American penetration into production is scarcely consistent with the restriction of Middle East oil imports into the United States is another of the many contradictions that ultimately result from the conflict between the majors and the independents. The independents already have a small interest in the Iran "Consortium," and have secured, though at a high price, the concession for the

Kuwait-Saudi Neutral Zone. In offshore areas and in other areas which have not yet been allotted or which the majors have been compelled to relinquish, independents are competing with Italian, Japanese, and German interests, all of which endeavor to offer more attractive terms. It is scarcely surprising that under these circumstances, it has been increasingly difficult to hold the established 50-50 profit-sharing agreements between governments and operating companies. These agreements however, relate to the *profits of local production only;* the majors are adamant in their refusal to allow host governments to share in the profits of their worldwide marketing operations. It was this issue that precipitated the Iran crisis and led to the temporary elimination of the country as a major producer. This pressure for a larger share in the industry for the oil-producing countries themselves, however, has helped to swell the world oil surplus, which is exerting strong downward pressure on prices and hence on national oil revenues.

Other Major Producers

Although the Gulf-Caribbean and the Middle East represent the two major concentrations of petroleum production in the world, certain other producers, either because of their past or potential importance or because of their geographic position, merit attention; these are the U.S.S.R., Canada, Indonesia, and Africa.

The U.S.S.R. Commercial production in Russia began only a little later than in the United States, and by the end of the nineteenth century, largely as the result of substantial injections of foreign capital, the country had become the world's largest producer and exporter. Two world wars, revolution, and ensuring internal disorder exacted a heavy toll; but from 1928 onwards production grew steadily. Since 1945 a very high rate of increase has been maintained as a result of the increasing emphasis placed in successive national development plans on the production of low-cost energy. In 1961 the U.S.S.R. displaced Venezuela as the world's second-largest producer, and long-range plans for the Soviet petroleum industry envisage an output of about 390 million tons or more by 1970, rather more than the present production of the United States. There is no reason to doubt the ability of the U.S.S.R. to attain such a target.

For a long period of time the ease of discovery and the high yields of the pools of the northern flanks of the Caucasus resulted in a concentration of effort in this area, which as late as 1940 still accounted for over 70 per cent of the total output. The main center of production was the Apsheron Peninsula near Baku, though the older fields at Groznyy and Maykop also made a small contribution. The occurrence of oil in the lower Volga basin, however, had been known in the Thirties, and the German invasion during World War II constituted a powerful incentive to develop alternative sources of supply; from 1950 onwards the growth of production in the area between the lower Volga and the Urals was rapid. At present about three-quarters of Russia's oil production originates in the Tatar and Bashkir Autonomous Republics and in the Kuybyshev district, which with the Saratov and Volgograd districts to the south constitute Russia's "second Baku" (Fig. 11-6). East of the Urals, however, production is confined to northern Sakhalin, and is insufficient for the needs of the Pacific coast region. It appears likely, therefore, that considerable efforts will be made to discover oil in the Far Eastern area, and to ease the problem of supplying the expanding industrial areas of Siberia a 2,500-mile pipeline between the "second Baku" and Irkutsk is under construction. A 3,500-mile

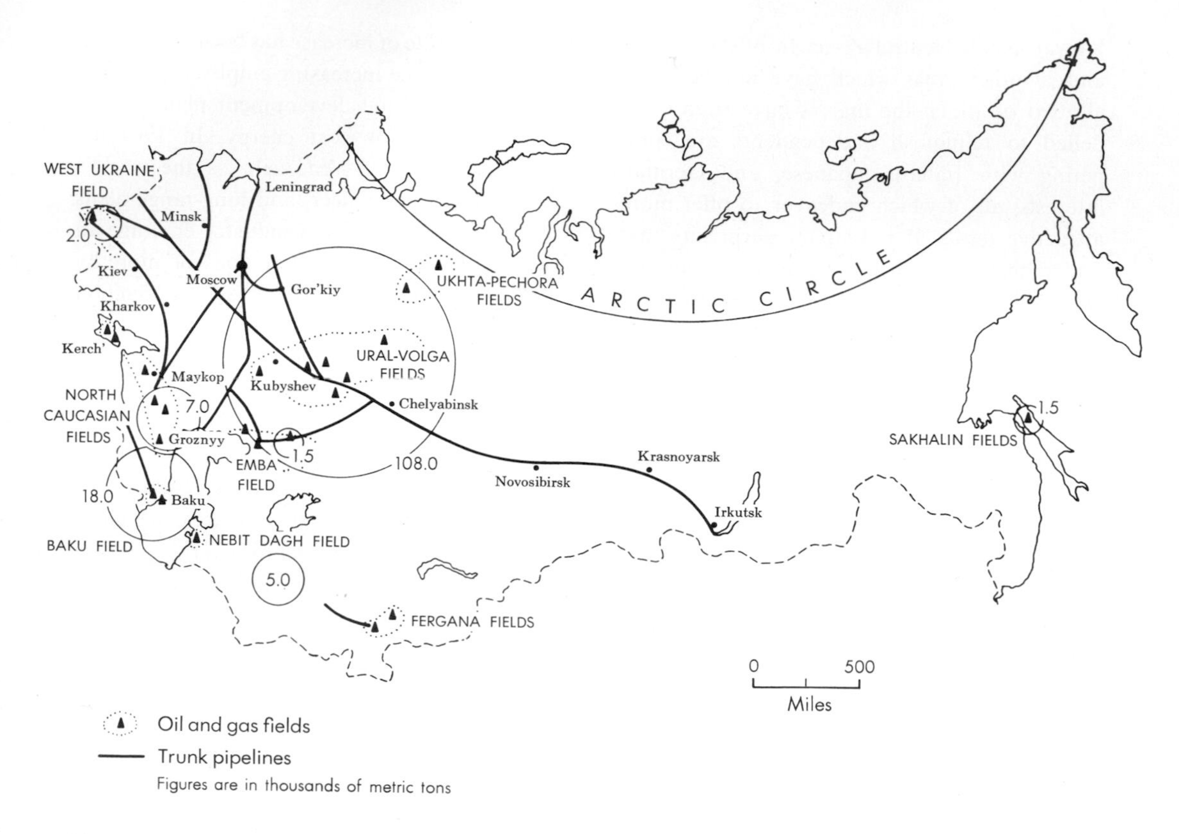

Fig. 11-6 Oil fields in the U.S.S.R.
Russia's principal oil fields lie in the Ural-Volga region, formerly called the "second Baku." Production, however, now greatly exceeds that of the Baku region.

trunk pipeline from the Ural-Volga area to Poland, East Germany, and Czechoslovakia is scheduled for completion in 1964 as part of the Soviet bloc's plans for a closer degree of economic cooperation.[8]

Since 1958 the U.S.S.R. has become an important exporter of oil, exporting more than 33 million tons in 1961, and its intervention in the world market has exerted a further depressing influence on prices. For various reasons, Egypt, Iceland, and Finland have taken more oil from the U.S.S.R. than from the free world in recent years, but Italy and West Germany have also taken substantial quantities, and Cuba has become entirely dependent on Russian oil. The costs of petroleum production in the U.S.S.R. are undoubtedly very low by world standards, and the country may very well become an embarrassing competitor in world markets. For political as well as economic reasons, Russia will probably strive to enlarge its sales to the underdeveloped countries. Russian oil, moreover, is mainly sold or bartered on a government-to-govern-

[8] **The Council for Mutual Economic Assistance (Comecon), the Russian equivalent of the Marshall Plan and the former OEEC, is the vehicle for such cooperation; it includes the U.S.S.R. and its Eastern European satellites.**

ment basis, and thus requires no costly distributive outlets; in some countries the refusal of the majors to handle Russian oil through their distributive channels led to serious political crises.

The only other producer of importance in the Soviet bloc is Romania, whose output, derived from the Carpathian foothills of the Ploeşti area, has been stable for several years. All of Romania's oil is refined internally, and there is a considerable export trade with other Eastern bloc countries.

Canada Before World War II Canada's small petroleum production was derived almost entirely from the Turner Valley field of Alberta. In 1947, however, the Leduc field south of Edmonton was discovered, and in the following year the Redwater field, also in the vicinity of Edmonton, was brought into production. These discoveries initiated a great boom in oil exploration in the western provinces, and it soon became clear that Canada possessed the resources to become a major world producer. Production expanded more than tenfold in a decade, reaching a level of nearly 700,000 barrels per day (34 million tons per annum) in 1962. But Canada could have produced double this quantity had markets been available, and many wells produced much below their capacity.

Canada's difficulties arise from the fact that the country's main centers of consumption lie some 2,000 miles to the east of the main producing region, and the fact that in Alberta, the largest producing province, excess capacity has been fostered by a system of prorationing on the United States model, which rewards successful drilling by a share in the market. The Interprovincial pipeline and the Transmountain pipeline link the Edmonton area with Ontario and with the Pacific Coast, but the large Montreal market remains inaccessible to domestic oil; this is supplied by imports of foreign oil, mainly from Venezuela. The natural market for Canadian oil would appear to be the adjacent portion of the United States, but tariff barriers, physical quotas, and expanding production in the Rocky Mountain fields has limited the entry of Canadian oil. There is thus strong pressure for the construction of pipeline facilities to tap the large market of the eastern provinces, and an acrimonious dispute has arisen in which economic and political considerations are inextricably interlocked; of basic significance is the fact that 90 per cent of Canada's oil production is in the hands of United States companies, some of which have considerable interests in the import of about 350,000 barrels per day (17.5 million tons per annum) of Venezuelan and Middle East oil into eastern Canada. On this issue of additional pipeline facilities, the Canadian subsidiaries of the majors and of the independents tend to take opposite viewpoints.

Indonesia Indonesia is only a minor producer by world standards; its importance arises from the fact that it is the only substantial producer in the Eastern Hemisphere east of the Persian Gulf and the fact that it is very favorably placed to supply the expanding markets of East Asia and the Australian region; it is, moreover, no newcomer to the industry, for petroleum production in what is now Indonesia began in the earliest years of the industry. No less than four of the seven majors are involved in petroleum production in Indonesia, but since the end of World War II, American companies have accounted for an increasing share of the total output.

Apart from a small output produced by east Java and by east Kalimantan (Indonesian Borneo), Indonesia's oil is derived from the foothill country between the east coast swamps and the mountainous backbone of Sumatra.

The old Atjeh fields in the north are now of minor importance, and the main producing area is the Minas field of central Sumatra operated by Caltex; this field has accounted for the greater part of the postwar increase in output. Other important fields lie in south Sumatra in the vicinity of Palembang, where the country's two largest refineries are located.

Indonesia, however, is yet another country in which the future of the petroleum industry has been rendered obscure by growing nationalist pressures. The present level of output cannot be long sustained without the granting of new concessions, and the postwar increase in output has been entirely derived from fields discovered before the war in concessions that are more than three decades old. Inflationary pressure in the country has greatly increased costs, and Indonesia's share of its traditional markets has greatly declined since 1945; only about one-third of Australia's oil requirements are now imported from Indonesia, as compared with almost two-thirds before the war. In 1958 Stanvac moved its exploratory personnel from the country in view of the refusal of the government to grant new concessions. The Indonesian government has since decided to restrict future private participation in the oil industry to the role of contractors to state entities. Japanese and independent American companies are at present acting in this capacity in north Sumatra, but it is doubtful whether the situation in Indonesia will prove sufficiently attractive to encourage the large investment necessary to maintain the country's position as a major producer. Hopes raised by a new *modus vivendi* concluded in 1963 between the foreign companies and the Indonesian government were immediately dashed by Indonesia's "confrontation" with the new state of Malaysia and the ensuing nationalization of British properties.

Africa Since 1960 African production has become very important, and substantial new developments can be expected in the future. Africa enjoys the advantage of close proximity to the very rapidly expanding European market, and costs of production in the main producing areas appear low even in comparison with those of the Middle East. The main producing area is Algeria, where output has expanded rapidly since the completion of pipelines from the Saharan fields of Hassi Messaoud and Edjelé to the Algerian port of Bougie and to the Tunisian port of Skirra. Algerian oil was discovered only in 1956, but by 1965 output is expected to reach 35 million tons. Under the Evian agreement the new Algerian Republic undertook to respect the considerable French interests in the industry; however, European and American companies are also actively prospecting in other parts of the Sahara.

Libya also has become a substantial exporter since the first discoveries were made in the mid-Fifties. Libya's output of nearly 10 million tons in 1962 came mainly from a group of fields close to the head of the Gulf of Sirte, of which the Zelten field of Jersey Standard is the most important. Libya thus enjoys a considerable advantage over Algeria, whose oil fields lie at considerably greater distance from the coast. The third African territory to show promise of rapid growth is Nigeria, where a multiplicity of American and European companies are operating in the Niger delta.

REFINING, CONSUMPTION, AND TRADE

Crude oil has to be subjected to an elaborate process of refining to make it usable, in marked contrast to coal, which is largely consumed raw. Refining operations have become progressively more complex as the range of employments for oil products has expanded; a modern refinery may produce as many as eighty distinct products and may represent a capital investment of more than 15 million dollars. Refining is an operation in which there are considerable economies of scale, at least up to a throughput of 100,000 barrels per day (5 million tons per annum), but the life of certain sections of a refining plant is short, and rapid technical change can bring on obsolescence before the expected working life has been realized. The size of a refinery and the nature and relative proportions of the various refined products are closely related to the general level of economic development in the area the refinery is designed to serve; they are also influenced by the type of crude used, but technological progress has given the refiner a considerable degree of flexibility, and market influences are more important.

The simplest type of refining operation is the "topping plant," which removes the lightest fractions, that is, those constituents that vaporize most easily. Such plants are usually "pioneers" designed to satisfy purely local markets; they often appear on oil fields in course of development, particularly where these occur in isolated areas. Essentially similar is the process of fractional distillation used in "straight run" operations; as crude oil may be regarded as a continuous gradation of boiling-point material, each particular fraction, or "cut," is collected from a fractioning tower in which vapors from heated crude are allowed to rise. The lightest fractions, gasoline and kerosine, are collected from the top of the tower, and the heavier fractions are condensed lower down, where the temperature of the vapors is higher. In fractional distillation, however, the yield of the lighter fractions, which have always provided the greater part of the total revenue from refining operations, is limited, and this has led to a premium on light, paraffin-based crudes, which have the highest gasoline content.

The increasing demand for gasoline, however, necessitated an improvement in the gasoline yield in refining operations, which was realized by the development of the cracking process. In cracking, the excess heavier fractions are converted into lighter ones by the application of heat and pressure; developed shortly after World War I, cracking received a great impetus after 1930 through the employment of catalysts. Further advances include catalytic reforming, that is, the conversion of saturated straight-chain hydrocarbons (paraffins) and saturated ring-chain hydrocarbons (napthenes) into saturated branching chains, thus increasing antiknock properties; polymerization, which enables waste gases from the cracking plant to be converted into gasolines; and alkylation, in which unsaturated hydrocarbons are converted into saturated hydrocarbons. Essentially, these processes improve both the quantity and the quality of gasolines obtainable from a given stock of crude.

The main products resulting from refinery operations are gasoline, kerosine, gas oil (so called from its use in the enrichment of town gas), diesel oil, residual, or fuel, oil (the residual oils from distillation and cracking), lubricating oils, and bitumen and other solid or semisolid residues. Large quantities of gas are also produced, some of which are used in the refinery itself; other products of increasing importance include the liquefied petroleum gases (propane and butane), jet fuel, and feedstocks for the petrochemical industry.

Consumption patterns for these products vary greatly from country to country; those of countries at a high level of development include a large proportion of gasoline, but in underdeveloped countries gasoline consumption is relatively low and kerosine is the most marketable item (Fig. 11-7). Western Europe, however, occupies a median position in its gasoline consumption; the most striking feature of its products consumption is the high proportion of fuel oil, which has been increasingly substituted for scarce and high-cost coal in many

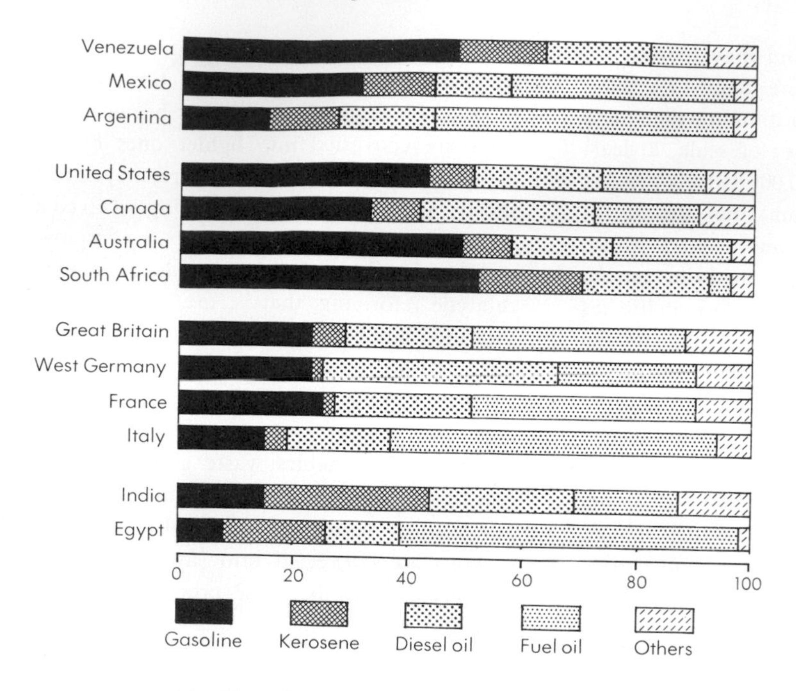

Fig. 11-7 Consumption of petroleum products in 1959–1960, in per cent. Highly developed economies such as that of the United States, Canada, and Australia have a consumption pattern of products that involves a high proportion of gasoline. Western Europe, however, is more notable for its large proportionate consumption of fuel oil, and crudes with a high gasoline content are of less value than they are to the United States. Underdeveloped economies are characterized by a relatively large proportionate consumption of kerosene, and Egypt's consumption pattern is somewhat anomalous.

industrial uses. Japan has a similar consumption pattern, but in the United States and Canada fuel oil finds natural gas a powerful competitor.

Great changes have occurred in the location of the world's refining capacity over the past two decades. Before World War II the United States possessed over 70 per cent of world refining capacity, but at present its share is only about one-third; over this period, however, its refining capacity has more than doubled (Fig. 11-8). This change in part reflects the relative decline of the United States as an exporter; before World War II the Gulf Coast possessed the greatest concentration of refining capacity in the world and exported tremendous quantities of refined products. The Gulf Coast still holds this distinction, but great concentrations of refining capacity have arisen in all major consuming areas, both within the United States itself, where the east and west coasts are the preferred sites for new construction, and in the world at large.

Several factors have combined to bring about the growth of refining at points of consumption. Technical improvements have reduced the wastage in refining, thus reducing the pull of the areas close to the site of production, and increased demand has enabled consuming areas to construct large refineries of economic size. The desire to conserve foreign exchange by switching from the import of refined products to cheaper crudes has been a powerful incentive in many countries with balance-of-payments difficulties, and new refining industries act as a general stimulus to the economy and permit the development of ancillary industries such as petrochemicals.

The greatest expansion in refining in consuming areas has occurred in Europe, whose share of world refining capacity rose from less than 5 per cent before World War II to more than 20 per cent in 1960. Owing to the greater importance of fuel oils in the European economy, European refineries operate with a products composition which includes only 20 per cent of gasoline in comparison with the 40 per cent gasoline content that is usual in the United States refineries; on the other hand, the proportion of fuel oils is correspondingly greater. Europe's largest refinery is the Pernis refinery of Shell at Rotterdam, but Southampton and Hamburg both have plants almost as large.

There has also been a considerable expansion of refining in producing countries that at present consume relatively little oil. This is largely the result of government pressure to enlarge the local stake in the industry and to increase the level of employment. But the construction of refineries in underdeveloped economies is substantially more costly than in those at a higher level of economic development, in large part because the operating company has to provide much of the infrastructure —housing, transport facilities, and social services—that elsewhere is the responsibility of the state. Of the total investment necessary for such a refinery, the earning assets may account for as little as 20 per cent. Moreover, such a refinery, in common with all enterprises in such economies, invariably has to employ

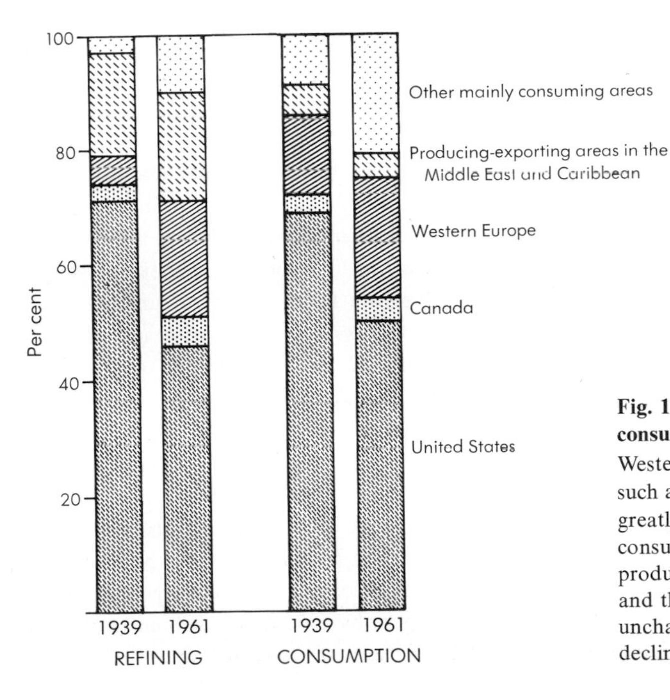

Fig. 11-8 Changes in petroleum refining and consumption.
Western Europe and other consuming areas such as Canada, Japan, and Australia have greatly enlarged their share of refining and consumption since 1939. The standing of the producing-exporting countries of the Caribbean and the Middle East has remained relatively unchanged, but that of the United States has declined considerably.

more workers than are necessary for efficient operation. Nevertheless, nearly every producing country has now obtained a substantial refining industry, and there is continual agitation to increase the proportion of production refined locally. Petroleum refining, in fact, is becoming one of the most widely distributed of all industries.

As a result of the growth of new producers and of the changes in the refining industry, the composition and direction of world trade in petroleum and products has altered considerably over the past three decades. Before World War II trade consisted largely of refined products, but in the postwar period crude has been of overwhelming importance. Once a major exporter, the United States has become the world's largest importer, taking over 2 million barrels per day (100 million tons) in 1962, and in the absence of restrictions, imports would probably continue to rise rapidly. From 1963 imports have been restricted to some 12.2 per cent of domestic crude production, except on the west coast, where an overall quota is set by the U.S. Bureau of Mines estimate of the deficiency between available domestic supplies and demand. The United States, which formerly exported large quantities of refined products to Europe, is now mainly an exporter of specialty products. The most remarkable change in the world trade pattern, of course, has been the expansion of Middle East exports; these have pushed out most of the former Venezuelan exports to Europe and in the United States market have expanded from virtually nothing at the end of World War II to account for a fifth of all oil imports. In the Far East and in the Australian region, Middle East oil has expanded its share of the market at the expense of Indonesian oil. In the booming European market Middle East oil may, however, have a serious competitor in North Africa, particularly as France has endeavored to persuade members of the EEC to grant preferences on Algerian oil.

NATURAL GAS

Although it may appear somewhat cavalier to treat natural gas, a fuel that already accounts for almost one-third of the total energy consumption of the United States, as an offshoot of the petroleum industry, such, in fact, is the case historically; some two-thirds of the natural-gas output of the United States, by far the world's largest producer, originates in oil companies. Much natural-gas production is incidental to that of petroleum, and many gas fields have been discovered in the search for oil. About two-thirds of the world's estimated gas reserves are not associated with oil deposits; this is the situation in North America, Algeria, and the U.S.S.R., but in the Middle East, Venezuela, and Indonesia oil and gas occur in association. In the latter areas much of the gas produced in petroleum production is flared or else is put back into the ground to conserve reservoir pressure.

Only in the United States, Canada, and the U.S.S.R. has the existence of a large market made it profitable to market gas in very large quantities, and in these countries the natural-gas industry is, to a considerable extent, structurally separate from the petroleum industry. But it is highly likely that with the passage of time natural gas will assume greater importance in many more countries. Italy's postwar economic growth has been greatly facilitated by the discovery of large quantities of natural gas in the northern part of the country. France has a considerable gas field in the Pyrenean foothills, and the Netherlands has recently discovered gas in large quantities in Groningen; by 1975 it is possible that within the EEC natural gas may account for as much as 15 per cent of energy consumption from indigenous sources.

The United States marketed about 13,000 billion cubic feet of natural gas in 1961 and accounted for about 90 per cent of the entire world commercial consumption; the only other large producer was Canada, with a production of about 700 billion cubic feet. Texas and Louisiana together account for nearly 70 per cent of United States production; California is relatively less important as a producer of gas than of petroleum, and the state has a large and mounting deficiency which has to be made good by imports from the principal producing areas of Texas and the Southwest and, since 1962, from Alberta also. California's natural-gas consumption has also sharply increased as a result of antismog legislation, which has caused a switch from the consumption of fuel oils.

Since World War II virtually every part of the United States has been provided with natural-gas supplies as a result of new pipeline construction; in 1960 there were almost 2 million miles of trunk pipelines. Natural gas not only has absorbed many markets formerly served by coal but also has cut into those served by petroleum. Physically gas has little advantage over petroleum distillates, and it is difficult to store and to transport; large-diameter welded pipelines are necessary to withstand the high pressures required for long-distance transport. Thus the rapid growth in consumption of natural gas largely results from the fact that on the basis of energy content it is substantially cheaper than fuel oil; this arises from the control exercised over wellhead prices and gas transmission by the Federal Power Commission (FPC). However, American refiners have so far made little attempt to expand markets for their heavier distillates because of their preoccupation with gasoline.

Canada's gas fields lie mainly in southern Alberta and in the Peace River area on the Alberta–British Columbia boundary; as in the United States, the postwar increase in marketed gas has been tremendous. The Canadian gas industry is subject to provincial control similar to that exercised by the FPC in the United States. In contrast to Canada's petroleum, its gas does not have to meet competition from imports in eastern markets, and transcontinental pipelines connect the Alberta fields with Toronto and Montreal, as well as with Vancouver. Canadian gas has also found entry into the United States considerably easier than has Canadian oil.

SOCIAL AND POLITICAL PROBLEMS

Rapid economic growth invariably creates pressing social and political problems; the tremendous expansion of the petroleum industry and its worldwide distribution have inevitably given rise to social and political problems of major importance. Some of these reflect fundamental issues that face all human societies but that have been polarized by the development of the industry.

How justifiable is the control of something like three-quarters of the free world's oil supplies by a handful of giant corporations? This problem, at least, is solving itself; there is little likelihood of the majors retaining their present very large share of world output in the face of pressure from independents and from companies owned by host governments. Linked in the Organization of Petroleum Exporting Countries (OPEC), producing countries are determined to enlarge their share of the industry and to prevent the price of oil from declining in relation to the prices of industrial products, a fate which has befallen almost every commodity in the postwar period.

Perhaps the greatest problems confronting

the industry in much of the world arise from irrational manifestations of nationalism. The majors have done their best to avoid entanglement in local politics, but their operations necessarily involve governments, and it cannot seriously be denied that their royalty payments have sometimes helped to prop up administrations that have become completely out of touch with popular political and social aspirations; often, of course, the petroleum industry has helped to make the local population aware of the shortcomings of the government. The record of the international oil companies in underdeveloped countries is nothing to be ashamed of;[9] they have made enormous contributions to education, social welfare, and economic development and have tried to be good citizens of the countries in which they operate. But these activities necessarily expose the local population to the winds of change from the outside world, and nowhere are these winds blowing more strongly than in the Middle East, where the regimes of all the territories of the Arabian Peninsula are overripe for reform.

Oil companies have to deal with the governments in existence; hence national upsurges invariably associate oil companies with former discredited regimes. Moreover, to most nationalists the great oil companies are agents of foreign governments; and, indeed, the British and French governments are the largest stockholders in British Petroleum and the Compagnie Française des Pétroles, respectively. Nationalist revolutions are thus frequently followed by the imposition of restrictions on operating companies which make profitable production increasingly difficult, and in extreme cases their property may be nationalized. Those governments that have made experiments in nationalization have not found the experience a very profitable one; and clearly, for countries in which technical and administrative skills are in exceedingly short supply, the operation of such a complex and dynamic industry as petroleum presents almost insoluble difficulties. Nevertheless, there are others that still appear willing to try, and the irrationality of many manifestations of nationalism is a source of danger. Iraqi oil workers were urged by Cairo to blow up the pipelines conveying oil to the Mediterranean during the Suez crisis of 1956, and did so, thus depriving themselves of employment.

The location of such a large proportion of the free world's oil production in close proximity to the southern margins of the U.S.S.R. provides the U.S.S.R. with numerous opportunities to work mischief through fanning the fire of nationalism. The situation is further complicated by the existence of Israel; to be nationalist in the Arab world is also to be anti-Israel, and in Arab eyes the West holds the major responsibility for the creation and the continued existence of the Israeli state. Palestine refugees are an active and vociferous element in all Arab oil-producing states, and in view of the close identification of the oil companies with Western governments by the population, the position of the oil companies is far from a strong one.

Nevertheless, oil is at present the only major resource of the Middle East; Kuwait possesses no surface water at all. There is no other market for Middle East oil than the industrialized countries of the West; the U.S.S.R. certainly cannot make use of it, and its own oil exports have reacted unfavorably on the incomes of oil-producing states. It is greatly to be hoped that self-interest will deter producing countries from prejudicing their chances of attaining higher living standards by discouraging further investment in the petroleum industry.

[9] **See, for example, Benjamin Higgins,** *United States Business Performance Abroad: The Case Study of Stanvac in Indonesia,* **National Planning Association, Washington, 1958.**

SELECTED REFERENCES

"Big Natural Gas Expansion in the U.S.S.R.," *Petroleum Press Service,* vol. 29, pp. 58–61, 1962.

Clarke, J. I.: "Oil in Libya: Some Implications," *Economic Geography,* vol. 39, pp. 40–59, 1963.

Duce, James Terry: "The Changing Oil Industry," *Foreign Affairs,* vol. 40, pp. 627–635, 1962.

Hartshorn, J. E.: *Oil Companies and Governments,* Faber & Faber, Ltd., London, 1962.

Hassmann, Heinrich: *Oil in the Soviet Union,* Princeton University Press, Princeton, N.J., 1953.

Higgins, Benjamin: *United States Business Performance Abroad: The Case Study of Stanvac in Indonesia,* National Planning Association, Washington, 1958.

Hodgkins, Jordan A.: *Soviet Power: Energy Resources, Production and Potentials,* Prentice-Hall, Inc., Englewood Cliffs, N.J., 1961.

Kamen-Kaye, N.: "Petroleum Development in Algeria," *Geographical Review,* vol. 48, pp. 463–473, 1958.

Leeman, Wayne A.: *The Price of Middle East Oil,* Cornell University Press, Ithaca, N.Y., 1962.

Longrigg, Stephen H.: *Oil in the Middle East,* rev. ed., Oxford University Press (for Royal Institute of International Affairs), London, 1961.

Lydolph, Paul E., and Theodore Shabad: "The Oil and Gas Industries in the U.S.S.R.," *Annals of the Association of American Geographers,* vol. 50, pp. 461–486, 1960.

McClean, J. G., and R. W. Haigh: *The Growth of Integrated Oil Companies,* Harvard University Press, Cambridge, Mass., 1954.

McNee, R. B.: "Functional Geography of the Firm, with an Illustrative Case Study from the Petroleum Industry," *Economic Geography,* vol. 34, pp. 321–337, 1958.

Manners, Gerald: "The Pipeline Revolution," *Geography,* vol. 47, pp. 154–163, 1962.

Melamid, Alexander: "Geographical Pattern of Iranian Oil Development," *Economic Geography,* vol. 35, pp. 199–218, 1959.

———: "Geography of World Petroleum Price Structure," *Economic Geography,* vol. 38, pp. 283–298, 1962.

Mission of the International Bank for Reconstruction and Development: *The Economic Development of Iraq,* The Johns Hopkins Press, Baltimore, 1952.

———: *The Economic Development of Venezuela,* The Johns Hopkins Press, Baltimore, 1961.

Nelson, J. R.: "Prices, Costs and Conservation in Petroleum," *American Economic Review,* vol. 48, pp. 502–515, 1958.

Netschert, Bruce C.: *The Future Supply of Oil and Gas: A Study of the Availability of Crude Oil, Natural Gas and Natural Gas Liquids in the United States in the Period thru 1975,* The Johns Hopkins Press (for Resources for the Future), Baltimore, 1958.

Organisation for European Economic Cooperation: *Long Distance Gas Transport in the United States,* Paris, 1958.

Parsons, James J.: "The Natural Gas Supply of California," *Land Economics,* vol. 34, pp. 19–36, 1958.

"Pioneer Survey of World Gas Resources," *Petroleum Press Service,* vol. 29, pp. 253-255, 1962.

Pratt, W. E., and Dorothy Good: *World Geography of Petroleum,* Princeton University Press (for The American Geographical Society), Princeton, N.J., 1950.

Taylor, Wayne C., and J. Lindeman: *United States Business Performance Abroad: The Case Study of the Creole Petroleum Corporation in Venezuela,* National Planning Association, Washington, 1955.

Weeks, Lewis G. [ed.]: *Habitat of Oil,* Association of American Petroleum Geologists, Tulsa, Okla., 1958.

"World Wide Oil Report," *Oil and Gas Journal,* December, annually.

Zimmermann, Erich W.: *Conservation in the Production of Petroleum: A Study in Independent Control,* Yale University Press, New Haven, Conn., 1957.

Chapter 12

THE COAL INDUSTRY

It is possible that, as in the case of oil, coal was known and used in classical times; it was certainly familiar to contemporaneous Chinese civilizations. The commercial production of coal first began in Britain and in other parts of Western Europe early in the thirteenth century, and by 1600 coal output in Britain had attained a level of about 1 million tons per year. The development of coal mining thus considerably predates the Industrial Revolution, but it was not until the discovery of a method of using coal to smelt iron that the mineral began to play a fundamental part in economic life. In the remarkable acceleration of the pace of economic growth in Europe from the mid-eighteenth century onwards, coal occupied a vital role; coal, iron, and the steam engine, first in Britain and later in Continental Western Europe and in North America, came to form the first triumvirate of modern, capital-intensive industrial society. Every development of the mechanical arts enlarged the demand for coal, and a higher coal output in turn made for further expansion of mechanized production. On the basis of its coal and iron Britain became the "workshop of the world"; not until coal production first in the United States and later in Germany began to approach that of Britain was Britain's economic supremacy seriously challenged. The rise of Russia, Japan, China, and India as major powers was also related to an increased coal production.

Despite the rise of other fuel and power industries in the twentieth century, coal is still vital in many industrial activities. Nevertheless, world coal output increases only very slowly; moreover, for some considerable time the whole of the increase has been accounted for by countries at low or modest levels of economic development—the U.S.S.R., South Africa, Japan, China, and India. In terms of calorific value there is little difference between the present world outputs of coal and petroleum; in value of output, however, petroleum is easily in the lead, and within little more than a decade it will also outrank coal in physical output. All the major coal producers of the Western world have long since passed their peak production; it is probable that at some time in the future coal production in the United States may again exceed 600 million tons per year, but that Britain might again produce almost 300 million tons and Germany some 250 million tons per year appears quite out of the question. The extreme sickness of the coal industry in the Western world has been patently obvious for decades; no other industry has had such a bitter history of labor relations, a fact that still hampers attempts to improve efficiency, and no other industry has found it so difficult to retain its labor force. The decline in coal production in many countries is in fact closely related to the exodus of labor from the industry.

The misfortunes of the coal industry since World War I have largely arisen from the rupture of the nineteenth-century "virtuous circle" of coal, iron, and the steam engine. Coal then represented low-cost energy, but through the process of economic development and the creation of capital equipment that has made alternative forms of energy available at lower cost, this has ceased to be true in the present century. But also, the coal industry must be held partly responsible for its own undoing; through its failure to make sufficient capital reinvestment to maintain competitive efficiency and through its inadequate attention to research into new and better ways of producing and consuming coal, it has conceded enormous markets to the petroleum and natural-gas industries by default. Since the end of World War II considerable strides have been taken to restore the coal industry to a high level of efficiency in the United States, Britain, and several other countries of Western Europe; nevertheless, the continued decline of coal in the pattern of world energy consumption appears inevitable.

NATURE AND OCCURRENCE OF COAL

Coal is a sedimentary rock occurring in seams varying from less than 1 inch to more than 100 feet in thickness. It is formed through the partial decomposition and subsequent petrifaction under heat and pressure of vegetable matter derived from ancient forests. The varying nature of the coal forests, the diverse conditions under which their remains were entombed, and the degree of heat and pressure to which these remains have been subjected have resulted in coals of very widely differing qualities. The earliest stage in the formation of coal is believed to be the accumulation of peat. With the passage of time and increasing pressure of overlying sediments, the moisture content and volatile constituents are progressively reduced. As in the formation of oil, formation of coal is, presumably, still taking place at the present; in contrast to petroleum, however, the world's greatest coal production and the most valuable coals are derived from Paleozoic rocks.

It is customary to classify coal into three principal types, but in practice there is no clear-cut distinction, for no two coal seams are exactly alike in composition. The three types are lignites and brown coals, bituminous coals, and anthracites (Fig. 12-1).

Lignites and brown coals are geologically young, dating from the Tertiary period; they are very soft and friable, and their moisture content may be as much as one-third by weight, so that they cannot be transported far without treatment. They are liable to spontaneous combustion when exposed to the air, and are thus kept moist in mining operations by sprays of water. They often occur in deposits of enormous thickness with little overburden, so that they can be extracted with modern earth-stripping and earth-moving machinery in great opencuts, or strip mines. Such coals are usually consumed on the spot, either for the generation of electricity or for the production of organic chemicals; or they are converted into briquettes. They are of great importance in Germany, which has worked chemical miracles with brown coal, using it in the Lurgi process for the production of methane, the principal constituent of natural gas. Other important producers of brown coal are the U.S.S.R., Czechoslovakia, and the State of Victoria in Australia. Immense deposits of brown coal exist in the United States; though little worked at present, they may become of great significance to the proliferating chemical industries.

Bituminous coals comprise the world's most valuable coals; most date from the Carboniferous period, but some subbituminous coals are of Jurassic or Cretaceous origin. The bituminous coals have a fixed carbon-volatile ratio that gives very high heat value and are suitable for a wide variety of purposes. Their most important use in the past has been for steam raising, and coals which are well fitted for this employment, that is, low-volatile coals, are often called steam coals. Some are capable of producing a massy coke that is ideal for use in the blast furnace, and such coking coals usually command a substantial premium; others on destructive distillation produce large quantities of gas, and have been widely used in the past for the manufacture of town gas. The bituminous coals have received the full weight of competition from petroleum and natural gas, but for certain uses, such as electricity generation and iron smelting, they are still of supreme importance. Bituminous coals

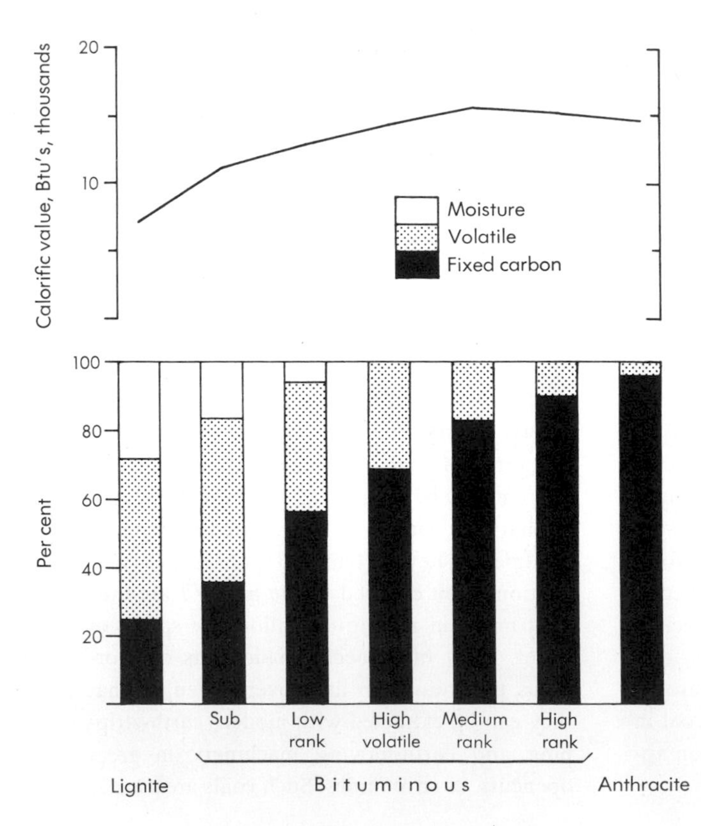

Fig. 12-1 Composition of coals. Coals of high rank have a high fixed carbon content, and an increase in carbon content is accompanied by an increasing calorific value; the highest calorific values, however, occur in medium-rank coals. In lignites and subbituminous coals, moisture and volatile content can vary considerably.

are produced in very varying conditions; the greater part of the world's bituminous coal, however, is won from underground mines.

Anthracite is a hard shiny coal. It has a fixed carbon content exceeding 90 per cent by weight and burns with a bluish flame producing great heat but little smoke and ash; it is ideal, therefore, for domestic space heating. Unfortunately, the geologic conditions which have combined to produce this remarkable fuel also make high extraction costs inevitable. Anthracite fields have fractured and faulted seams, in which a high productivity per worker is exceedingly difficult to attain; for this reason, much of anthracite's former market has been lost to lower-cost fuel oil and natural gas, and the hard-coal section has long been the most depressed division of the United States coal industry. While anthracites are by no means uncommon, there are only two important producing fields in the world; the larger of these lies in the Susquehanna and Schuylkill valleys of northeast Pennsylvania, and the other occurs in the Swansea Valley of South Wales.

Coal is thus far from a homogeneous commodity; despite the fact that it is often possible to substitute one kind of coal for another, certain types can be in short supply when others cannot find profitable markets. It is a measure of India's backwardness that the country is forced to use metallurgical coking coal for purposes for which ordinary coals would serve as well.

Coalfields usually consist of a large number of seams separated by intervening limestones, shales, and other rocks. Maps of coalfields usually indicate the outcrop of a particular series of rocks, such as the Pennsylvania series of the Carboniferous period in the United States or the contemporaneous Coal Measures in Britain. In some European fields the coal-bearing series dip away under a cover of younger rocks, constituting a "concealed field"; one British field is entirely concealed. Coal seams extend over wide areas, occasionally over hundreds of square miles, and may outcrop in a number of places. Hence, in great contrast to the petroleum industry, entry into the coal industry is very easy; moreover, no elaborate and expensive processing is necessary, for most coal is consumed raw.[1] The fact that the largest companies engaged in coal production cannot match the stature of the petroleum giants in large part arises from the great physical differences in the nature and occurrence of the two fuels.

COAL MINING TECHNOLOGY

All mining enterprises face essentially similar problems, and their organization has much in common; however, it is perhaps in coal mining that these problems are most sharply delineated. By its very nature mining is an operation in which there is a powerful tendency towards increasing costs; a large capital reinvestment is continually necessary merely to *maintain* output. Deposits at or near the surface may be won fairly easily and cheaply, but as these are exhausted it becomes necessary to dig deeper or to follow seams underground. The expense of removing overburden or of extending and supporting underground roadways increases sharply. The underground roadways, transport and ventilation systems, winding machinery, and surface installations all have to be maintained, whatever the level of production, so that fixed costs form a large part of total costs in all mining enterprises.

Some metalliferous mines may produce a number of associated metals such as lead, zinc, and silver, but little variation in the proportion of each produced is usually possible. Many

[1] Most mines, however, now have washing and grading plants.

mines, however, produce only one product, according to an elaborate operational plan extending over several years. Once committed to a plan of operations, management has little opportunity for making changes, and even minor variations can prove extremely expensive. A coal mine management has to decide how to extract as much coal as cheaply as possible from its concession and which seams it is to attack and in which order. By the time it has fully implemented its original plan, the market for its product may have altered considerably. In Britain a large modern pit takes four years or more to bring into full production; by the time that many post-World War II pits had come into operation, expansion of oil output in the Middle East had rendered them unnecessary. It is true that manufacturing industry also experiences time lags in creating new production, but if a decision subsequently proves to have been incorrect, a manufacturing plant can more easily cut production or switch to another line.

Coal mining is fundamentally a problem of handling enormous quantities of material, usually in extremely confined spaces; seams as thin as 18 inches have been successfully worked in underground mines in Britain. Where seams outcrop at the surface or lie at no great distance below ground the confined-space difficulty may be removed; extremely high productivity per worker can be attained with modern excavating and earth-moving machinery in strip mines, or opencast working, and the high proportion of the United States output that is derived from mines of this kind is a very material factor in the high productivity per worker achieved in the country. It is the necessity of operating in confined spaces that is largely responsible for the labor-intensive nature of the coal industry; coal is produced discontinuously, in an elaborate production cycle in which much time and labor is expended in preparation and maintenance. Intense efforts have been made in the United States since the end of World War II to develop methods of mining that will produce coal so that it flows continuously from the mine portal. These have achieved a large measure of success in some American mining districts; they have, in fact, constituted a technological revolution.

Underground mines, which account for nearly 70 per cent of the coal output of the United States and an even higher proportion of the world output, are of two main types. In the world coal industry vertical-shaft mines are by far the more important type, but in the United States such mines are something of a rarity. Where coal seams outcrop along the sides of valleys that have incised the coal-bearing series, they can be attacked from horizontal or sloping roadways, or "drifts." This second main type of mine has existed for centuries in Britain's Northeastern field, and is standard in many mining districts in the United States. Such drift mines, or "adit" mines as they are known in Britain, generally operate at much lower cost than shaft mines, for winding up the shaft (which may descend as much as 1,000 yards) is a time-consuming and expensive operation that constitutes a major bottleneck.

The two principal methods of mining coal underground in shaft and drift mines both originated in Britain. The older method, and that still in use in Britain's Northeastern and South Wales fields, is the "pillar and bord," or "pillar and room," method. In this system of mining a number of parallel roadways, or "headings," are driven into the seam, and these are connected by subsidiary roads at right angles. Some coal is removed in driving the headings and roadways, and the remainder is left in large rectangular blocks, which are gradually removed. Part of the coal, however, is left standing in pillars to support the roof; occasionally, these pillars may be partially ex-

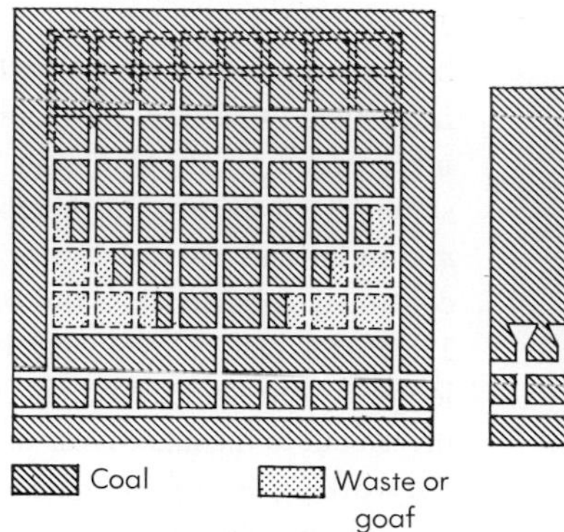

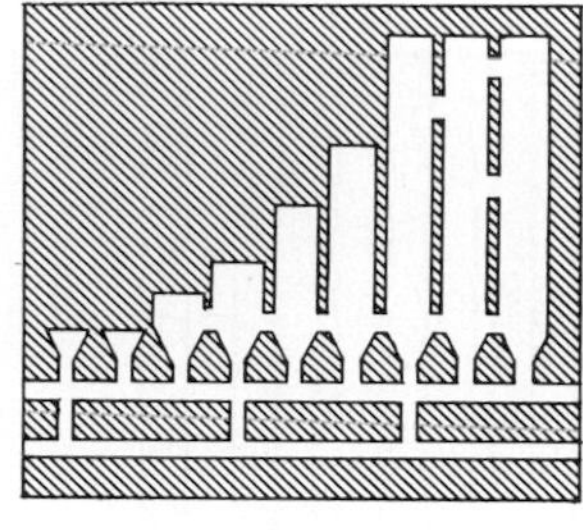

Fig. 12-2 Pillar and room working.
The left diagram is an example of pillar and room working in northern England; a little coal is produced in driving the roads (bords, or rooms), but very much more in the subsequent extraction of the pillars, which average about 30 to 40 yards square. In this example, roads indicated by pecked lines have still to be driven, but alternatively, the whole of the panel to be worked may be divided up before pillar extraction begins. Note that two main roads are required to provide continuous circulation of air through the workings. The diagram on the right is an example of mechanized pillar and room working in the United States, in which the pillars are greatly reduced in width; such a system is well suited to the use of continuous mining machines.

tracted at a later date (Fig. 12-2). The pillar and room method is excellent for working thick seams, and although as much as 50 per cent of the coal may not be recovered, roof control, the *sine qua non* of good coal-face management, is cheaply and easily assured. Another great advantage of the pillar and room method is that with appropriate equipment, it can give very high productivity per worker. A small team of skilled workers can cut, drill, load, and put up roof supports in one working day, and in Europe, where continuous shift working is the rule, it is possible to get two coal-getting shifts per day. The main disadvantage of the method is that it is very wasteful of coal; but wherever it is technically feasible, it is generally preferred, and it is the dominant method of underground mining in the United States.

The alternative "longwall" method, first developed in the thin seams of the Midlands fields of Britain, is the standard practice in Western Europe, the U.S.S.R. and most satellite countries, India, and many other countries. Its commonest form is the "longwall advance" system, the "longwall retreat" system being distinctly uncommon. In longwall mining roads are driven outwards from the shaft pillar (the area around the pit bottom from which no coal is removed in order to protect the shaft and surface buildings from subsidence) towards the margins of the mine concession. From these roads subsidiary roads are turned, and on either side of these roads, or "gates," coal faces, usually about 100 yards in length, are opened up. In longwall mining the whole of the coal is removed from the working face, the roof being shored up with timber, steel, or hydraulic props; these are later recovered, being replaced by strip-like stone packs built up from the floor to the roof at right angles to the face in the "gob," or "goaf" (the area from

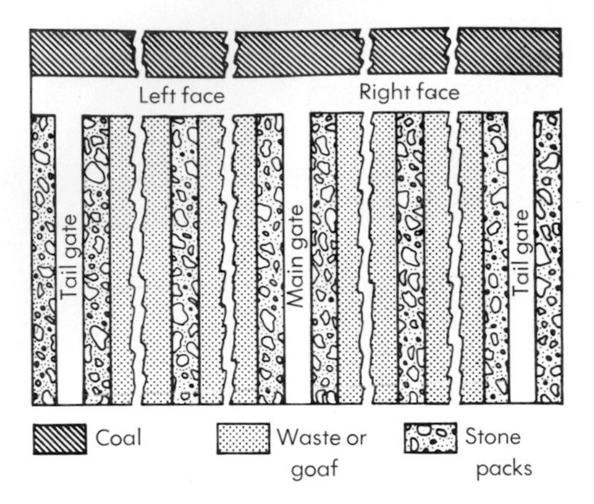

Fig. 12-3 Longwall advance working. Many variations on longwall mining are possible, but this mechanized double-face system is standard practice in many British fields. Two converging conveyors bring coal from the working faces, each about 100 yards long, to the main gate, while return airways lead backwards from the distant end of each face.

which the coal has been removed).[2] In the longwall advance method the working face moves forward every day by the depth of coal removed; where electric coal cutters are used, this distance is usually about 6 feet. At a safe distance behind the face the roof is allowed to subside. Thus the whole of the coal is removed in a series of great panels; when the working face reaches the concession boundary, its supply roads are abandoned, and a new working face is opened up from the initial line of advance.

The longwall system is an elegant system of mining, ideally suited to the days when cheap and skilled labor was plentiful, but it has great disadvantages, which have been intensified with the development of mechanized mining. The longwall advance system suffers from the obvious handicap of having to maintain and extend roads in areas where continual subsidence is to be expected (Fig. 12-3); this can be overcome by the use of the longwall retreat method, in which roads are driven out to the margins of the concession, and the working faces move backwards towards the pit bottom. The initial outlay for this system is considerably higher than for the advance method, and the latter has the advantage of producing a large quantity of coal almost as soon as the mine commences operations; and as coal producers have always tended to take a short-term view, the cheaper system has become almost universal. More serious is the fact that the longwall system commits the mine to an elaborate cycle of operations, in which failure to complete any particular task brings the whole of the mine to a standstill; in practice this means that coal production is usually confined to but one shift, two being necessary for preparation and for maintenance. But perhaps most important of all, mechanization of longwall mining has undermined the status of the collier, that is, the face worker; once a highly skilled worker, he has become a laborer, scarcely as important as the cutters, borers, flitters, packers, rippers, and other maintenance men.[3]

[2] **Mechanical or hydraulic methods of stowing material in the goaf may also be used; these practices which replace the traditional hand laid stone packing are more common in Continental Europe than in Britain. Packing, or stowing, uses material produced in extending the headings and roadways, but large quantities of stone have to be sent out of the mine.**

[3] **Every mining district has its own particular nomenclature; these terms are used in the Yorks, Derby, and Notts field, Britain's most important coalfield. Cutters operate the electric coal cutters; borers drill the shot holes in the face in which explosive charges are placed to blow down the undercut coal; flitters dismantle and reassemble the conveyor belts on the face as it moves forward and extend the gate belt; packers build up the strip stone packs in the goaf; rippers tear down the strata on the "lip" above the gate so that the main gate can advance with the face. In pillar and room working all these tasks can be performed while coal is being extracted.**

Of greater significance, however, than the method used to win coal from the face is what happens to it subsequently; the very high productivity per worker achieved in the coal industry in the United States owes as much to efficient methods of coal loading and transport as it does to the favorable geologic conditions which permit mechanized extraction from the face. The productivity per worker of European mines is held back not so much through low productivity at the face as through slow and inefficient haulage from the face to the pit bottom and from the pit bottom to the surface; in Britain, for every face worker there is approximately one other worker employed on coal transport. The recipe for high productivity per worker is power loading and locomotive haulage, unless, as is the case in certain mines in the United States and in South Africa, coal can be transported right out of the mine portal on conveyor belts. However, these things must be planned for at the beginning; it is both very difficult and very expensive to introduce them into established mines in full production.

As with all mining and manufacturing enterprises, the most efficient coal mine is the most recent one; but in general, entry into the industry is easy and departure is difficult, and in many countries of the free world overcapacity is a major problem. Labor finds it particularly difficult to leave the industry, for coal mining very often takes place in isolated areas in which there is little alternative employment. Dirty and dangerous though it may be, coal mining is, nevertheless, universally regarded in mining areas as "a man's job," while employment in factories or in offices is considered effeminate. The decline in the labor force in the industry in all the main producers of the Western world has come about not so much through an exodus of labor as through a failure to attract new entrants to replace losses due to wastage and retirement.

WORLD COAL PRODUCTION AND COAL RESERVES

The distribution of the world's major coalfields closely coincides with the outcrop of Upper Carboniferous rocks. In the past the two most important producing areas lay on either side of the North Atlantic, and in particular, in the United States, Britain, and Germany; these three producers accounted for more than two-thirds of world output before World War II.

This picture has since been greatly modified by the rapid increase in production in the U.S.S.R. and in certain other Asian countries, particularly China (Table 12-1). In the Fifties it appeared probable that the U.S.S.R. would displace the United States as the world's leading producer in the near future; however, the greater attention now paid by the Russian planners to lower-cost energy in the form of petroleum and natural gas now renders this unlikely. China's increased output has been phenomenal; inflated though the claimed output in 1960 of 400 million tons may have been, it is clear that China's labor force could easily produce a tremendous output even with a very low productivity per worker if the labor force were applied to the country's known coal resources.

With the exception of South Africa and Southern Rhodesia, Africa appears deficient in coal, as does much of South America; Australia, however, is well endowed with coals of all types, which through geographic good fortune occur in the moister eastern portion of the country.

Many attempts have been made to estimate

Table 12-1

Coal Production, 1963

	METRIC TONS, MILLIONS
United States	424.8
Canada	7.9
EEC	228.5
West Germany	142.0
France	48.0
Belgium	21.0
Netherlands	11.6
Italy	5.9
Britain	199.2
Japan	51.6
India	67.2
South Africa	42.0
Australia	25.2
U.S.S.R.*	534.9
Poland	112.8
Czechoslovakia	26.8
Mainland China†	420.0
WORLD TOTAL‡	1,942.0

* Including lignite.
† 1960.
‡ Including coal equivalent of brown coal and lignite, but excluding Mainland China.
SOURCE: United Nations, *Statistical Yearbook*, 1962; *Monthly Bulletin of Statistics*, May, 1964.

the magnitude of the world's coal reserves, and in the days before the petroleum industry had made any substantial contribution to world energy supplies such exercises appeared far from academic; the gloomy view of Britain's coal reserves taken by the economist Jevons prompted Gladstone to consider ways of discharging the national debt. At present the British National Coal Board can suggest with equanimity the eventual closing of all of Britain's mines.

What is important to know is not so much the total size of the reserves as the magnitude of the *recoverable* reserves, and this is far from clear. All that is certain is that in relation to current consumption, recoverable reserves are proportionately very much larger than proved reserves of petroleum, and it can be safely assumed that the world's recoverable coal reserves are sufficient to permit an expanding rate of consumption for more than a century. All the evidence suggests, however, that world production will decline rather than increase, and it is quite likely that within a century the coal industry will havc become extinct in most Western countries. None of the present major coal producers need, therefore, fear a shortage of coal in the near future; indeed, they are more likely to find it increasingly difficult to sell all the coal that they are capable of producing.

The Coal Industry of the United States

The United States supplanted Britain as the world's leading coal producer about the turn of the century and has held this position ever since.

Not until after the Civil War did United States coal production grow rapidly; by 1870 output had reached a level of about 50 million tons.[4] Until this year anthracite had mainly been produced, but thereafter bituminous coal forged rapidly ahead. From a level of about 200 million tons at the turn of the century, bituminous-coal production virtually doubled in the next decade. During World War I the demands of the national war effort pushed production up to a level of almost 600 million tons in 1917, the year in which anthracite production reached its all-time peak of almost 100 million tons. But the period of rapid growth ended with the war; only in three interwar years did bituminous production again exceed 550 million tons, and in the depths of the Great Depression it fell to only 310 million tons. This period of difficulty witnessed considerable changes in the location of production.

World War II provided another enormous stimulus; output climbed to over 600 million tons in 1944 and, with the impetus of aid programs to war-ravaged Europe and Asia, attained a level of over 630 million tons in 1947, the highest ever recorded (Fig. 12-4). The later postwar period brought further difficulties, but the reaction of the soft-coal industry was an all-out drive to improve competitive efficiency through further mechanization; anthracite production, however, which had limped along at a level often little more than one-half of its 1917 peak in the interwar period, declined sharply under increasingly severe competition from

[4] Short tons of 2,000 pounds; Britain's coal production is given in long tons of 2,240 pounds, and that of other producers in metric tons (2,204.6 pounds).

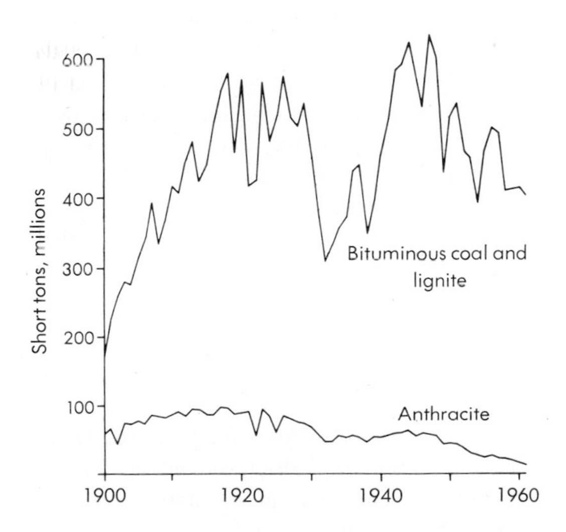

Fig. 12-4 Coal output in the United States, 1920–1961.

Coal production in the United States during the present century has experienced many fluctuations of fortune; the variations from year to year in bituminous production, however, are in large part a reflection of the incidence of labor disputes. The long-term decline of the anthracite industry since 1920 is striking.

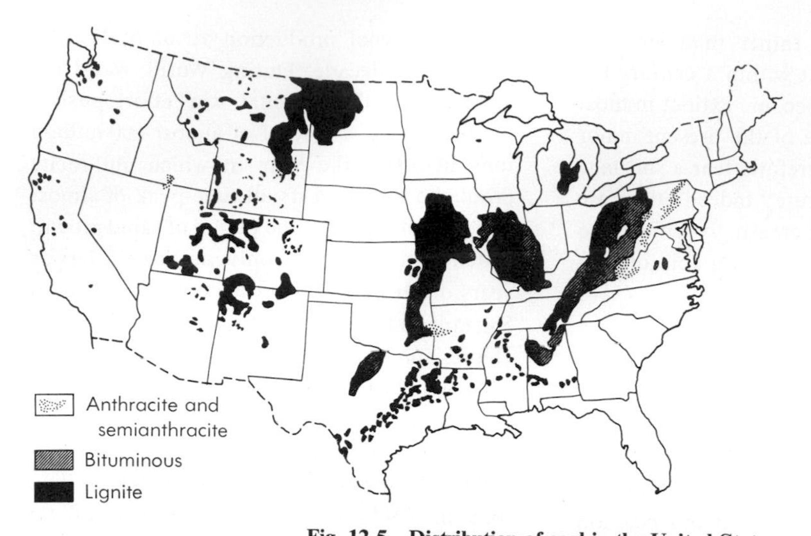

Fig. 12-5 Distribution of coal in the United States.
Though the occurrence of coal is widespread, production is localized in a limited number of areas. (U.S. Geological Survey.)

fuel oil and natural gas, and by 1960 output had fallen below 20 million tons.

Nevertheless, in the opinion of many experts, total coal output may attain even higher levels in the future than it has in the past; that the United States coal industry may run counter to a well-established trend largely arises from the intense effort that has been made to convert coal mining from a labor-intensive to a capital-intensive industry, and from the favorable physical conditions that have permitted the employment of progressively more labor-economizing machinery.

The Coalfields Coal of some kind is found in almost every state of the Union, but about 40 per cent of the estimated total recoverable reserves of about 1,000 billion tons[5] consists of subbituminous coals and lignites; these low-rank coals occur mainly in the sparsely populated High Plains and in the intermontane plateaus and are unlikely ever to be used on more than a minor scale. Bituminous coals occur widely (Fig. 12-5), but 95 per cent of output is derived from but two fields, which also contain almost two-thirds of the recoverable reserves.

The *Appalachian* field, which has dominated the coal industry since 1870, will in all probability continue to be the leading producing area for as long as coal mining is a major industry; it contains large reserves of easily won coals of all kinds, including coking coal. It extends south-southwest from western Pennsylvania for some 600 miles and underlies much of the Appalachian plateau, but mining is concentrated in a few districts where geologic conditions are particularly favorable, and there are large intervening areas where no mining takes place. The three principal producing districts are (*a*) the northern district, lying mainly in Pennsylvania but including adjacent portions of West Virginia and Ohio, (*b*) the southern district, including the remainder of West Virginia, eastern Kentucky, and small portions of Virginia and Tennessee,

[5] **U. S. Geological Survey,** ***Coal Resources of the United States,*** **Circular 293, 1954.**

and (*c*) the southeastern district[6] of Alabama. A marked feature of mining practice in this field which contrasts sharply with that of most European coalfields is the concentration in each producing district on one seam or on a relatively small number of seams.

The almost horizontal strata of the Appalachian plateau, the good roof and floor partings of the seams, and freedom from faults and fractures are immense advantages; moreover, the deep dissection of the plateau by numerous streams allows the maximum development of slope, or adit, mining. Even where shaft mines are necessary it is seldom that they descend below 400 feet, and a general freedom from water and gas permits the use of techniques which are not possible under European conditions.[7]

Until World War I the northern district, of which Pittsburgh is the center, was the chief producer; the Pittsburgh seam, about 5 feet in thickness, dominated the industry and, in the Connellsville area, produced the best coking coal in the country. After 1920, however, the southern district expanded production as that of the northern district contracted; for more than a quarter of a century West Virginia has outranked Pennsylvania in bituminous-coal production, and since 1951 its coal production has exceeded that of Pennsylvanian bituminous and anthracite coal combined. The reasons for the growth of the southern district are to be found in the lower costs of new mines, many of which were created by the demands of World War I, and in the absence, until the New Deal, of strong labor unions; the exodus of labor from Southern farms also helped in keeping wages low. The main producing area of West Virginia is the Pocahontas district in the south of the state, particularly famous for its high-grade steam coals, although coking coals are also mined. Production in Kentucky has also grown considerably since World War I, the state ranking third in order of production, after West Virginia and Pennsylvania. On the other hand, production in the Alabama district has remained relatively static. Here also only one seam, the Pratt seam, is extensively worked, and its excellent coking properties have encouraged the development of the iron and steel industry in the Birmingham area.

The *Eastern Interior* field lies mainly in Illinois, with extensions into Indiana and Kentucky; it produces soft coals of lower calorific value than those of the Appalachian field, and their use was largely responsible for the pall of smoke that hung over St. Louis and other midwestern cities before the enforcement of antismog legislation. A basin-like structure, the field is mainly worked around its margins where strip mining is possible, and shaft mines seldom descend more than 100 feet. This field, with its poorer-quality coals which do not make metallurgical coke, has suffered relatively more than the Appalachian field from the competition of other fuels.

The *Western Interior* field, lying mainly in Missouri, produces low-quality coals similar to those of the Eastern Interior field. There has been a marked drop in the number of mines in operation in this field since the end of World War II as competition from nearby sources of natural gas has become increasingly severe, and underground mining is entirely defunct. The scattered fields of the *High Plains* and *Rockies* are worked only in a few places, in proximity to mining centers or at selected spots on transcontinental railroad systems. The use of the diesel locomotive has resulted in a great decline in coal production in western states, but occasionally, where coking coals occur as in Utah and in Colorado, the development of an iron and steel industry has led to an increase in coal production.

The anthracite fields of eastern Pennsylvania present mining conditions which depart

[6] The term, used in the Bituminous Coal Act of 1937, relates to the national orientation.

[7] For example, the use of electric trolley locomotives, forbidden in Britain.

widely from the typical bituminous situation. These fields are situated in the Appalachian Valley zone of folding and compression, and mining conditions are more typically European than American; seams are generally thin, fractured, and seldom horizontal, and mines are deep. As a result productivity per worker is only about a third of that in bituminous-coal mining, although still substantially above the average for Western Europe. With the loss of its former large market in central heating, the anthracite districts of the Wyoming and Lackawanna Valleys are among the most depressed industrial areas in the country.

The Changing Pattern of Production and Consumption Since the end of World War II far-reaching changes in both production and consumption have taken place in the United States coal industry. Severe competition from other fuels has compelled a concentration of effort on the best and most easily worked areas, where the deployment of new laborsaving machinery enables the fullest economies of scale to be realized. There has been little reduction in the number of small mines—these will probably survive as long as the industry itself because of their great flexibility—but the large mines with an output of more than half a million tons per year have progressively increased their share of total output, and now account for almost half.

Strip mining has expanded greatly with the introduction of successively larger machines. Shovels capable of lifting 100 tons at a bite are now in use, making the removal of as much as 100 feet of overburden economically feasible, and still larger behemoths of almost double this capacity are shortly to go into operation. From about 10 per cent of the bituminous output before World War II strip mines had expanded their share of production to account for nearly 30 per cent by 1961; large strip mines have even come into production in Pennsylvania and in West Virginia, always the strongholds of underground mining in the past, and on the rich farmlands of Illinois and Indiana the great growth of strip mining has created some pressing problems of conflict of land use. Even higher productivity has been achieved in auger mines, in which batteries of Archimedean screws bore for as much as 200 feet into coal seams exposed along hillsides. Auger mines require rather special physical conditions, but by 1961 they were already accounting for nearly 3 per cent of total bituminous output, and were especially numerous in West Virginia.

Underground, the employment at the face of electric power-loading machines has been pushed up to match that of coal cutters; over 85 per cent of underground coal production is now mechanically cut and loaded. In many mines, 20-ton mechanical dinosaurs, continuous-mining machines which combine the functions of cutter and loader, chew into the seam and deliver coal continuously at the rate of 10 tons per minute. The employment of these new machines has been facilitated by the technique of roof bolting, that is, suspending the roof from the overlying strata by means of long steel expanding-bolts, thus freeing the working area from obstruction. The transport systems employed in American mines, superb by world standards before World War II, have been further improved by the extensive use of electric shuttle cars to deliver coal from the face to main loading stations or to main conveyors which move the coal out of the mine portal. Above ground, long-distance conveyors, coal pipelines in which pulverized coal is suspended in water, and increased use of water transport have helped to reduce the coal industry's thralldom to relatively high-cost rail transport.[8]

Through this technical revolution produc-

[8] The first coal pipeline, between Cadiz, Ohio, and Cleveland, designed to move 1.2 million tons of coal per annum, came into operation in 1958. Increased railroad efficiency, however, has made pipeline construction less attractive than it appeared in the late Fifties.

tivity per worker has more than doubled since 1945; output per man-day for all underground mines approached 12 tons in 1962, and for all mines it attained 15 tons. Without this increase in productivity the maintenance of a high level of output would have been impossible; with a labor force less than one-quarter the size of that of Britain, the United States produces about twice as much coal.

Before World War II about a quarter of total coal output was produced by "captive," that is, consumer-owned, mines; these were mainly the property of iron and steel companies, railroads, electric power utilities, gas and coke producers, and chemical corporations. At present captive mines produce only one-sixth of coal output, largely through the declining interest of railroads in direct coal production with the virtual elimination of the steam locomotive.

Railroads accounted for over 20 per cent of total coal consumption before World War II, but at present their share is virtually negligible. There have also been sharp reductions in consumption in steel mills and for domestic purposes, in both of which natural gas has been the principal competitor. To offset these losses there has been a very great increase in consumption by electric utilities, which now constitute the largest user and accounted for some 48 per cent of total consumption in 1961 (Fig. 12-6); power stations provide the best market for the poorer-grade, fragmented coals produced in strip mines and in highly mecha-

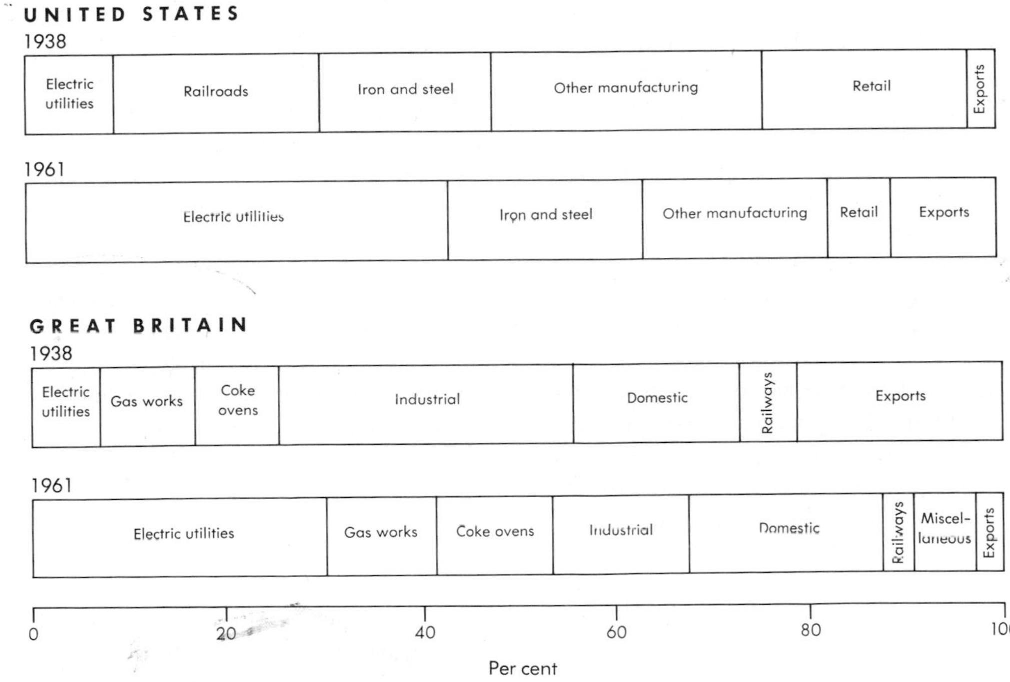

Fig. 12-6 Coal utilization in the United States and Great Britain, 1938 and 1961.
Broadly similar changes have occurred in the utilization of United States and British coal over the past two decades. Note, however, the differing coal export trades.

nized underground mines. The postwar growth of the iron and steel industry has also meant an increasing demand for coking coal, and about a quarter of total consumption is now accounted for by by-product coking plants and "beehive" units; now of only very minor significance, the old and outmoded beehive coking plant can nevertheless make a rapid and valuable contribution to coke production in an emergency, as was shown during World War II and again during the Korean conflict.

One of the most remarkable changes in the coal industry is the great increase in the export trade. The United States has long supplied Canada with coal, a trade that averaged around 20 million tons in the mid-Fifties, after which it showed a sharp decline, but the greatest demand has originated in Europe. Coal exports have fluctuated violently; they were very high in the immediate postwar years, with the European fuel crisis, and again following the Suez incident. In 1957 over 76 million tons were exported, almost 50 million of which went to Europe; in that year the United States almost attained a level of coal exports comparable with that of Britain before World War I. Japan has also been a regular, if selective, buyer of American coal for its booming iron and steel industry. In view of the distance of the coalfields of the United States from the coast, this export trade is a striking comment on the efficiency of both American coal producers and the coal-transporting railroads. West Virginia is the main supplier of coal for the export trade, the growth of which has made Norfolk the world's principal coal-exporting port, a role long held by Cardiff.

The Future of the Industry The future of the coal export trade largely depends on political considerations; low-cost American coal can easily undersell locally produced coal in the European market, and pressure from petroleum is also encouraging several European countries to take action to protect their domestic coal industries. Also, the coal industry can consider itself unfortunate that the enormous sums spent in modernizing American mines and in the development of new methods of mining have not resulted in the attainment of a substantially higher level of competitive efficiency; the deserts of the Middle East and North Africa have yielded up their treasures with unexpected ease. Nevertheless, the changed pattern of consumption offers real grounds for brighter prospects in the future; all long-range forecasts predict a continued rapid growth in electricity and steel production, and in neither of these can the United States afford to lag behind the corresponding rate of growth in the U.S.S.R. Still more capital-intensive methods of mining are under development; the Pittston Company's Moss No. 3 mine near Carbo, Virginia, will produce 6 million tons of coal per annum (almost 30,000 tons per day) in full operation, and is expected to have a productivity per worker four times the present national average. Underground gasification and hydrogenation have also been examined as means of expanding the market for coal, but the present surplus of petroleum has made these economically unattractive; the great growth of the petrochemical industry has also challenged coal in the production of organic chemicals. On the whole, it would appear that the coal industry will continue to depend upon a few major users.

The Coal Industry of Great Britain

Coal mining is still Britain's largest industry in terms of employment; in relation to its size and population, Britain produces more coal than any other country. But the industry has greatly declined from the position it held in 1913 when a peak output of almost 290 million (long) tons was attained and mine workers were over 1¼ million strong. In 1913 not far short of 80 million tons were exported, much to neighboring countries of Europe, including Germany, Britain's principal industrial competitor.

The problem of the British industry in the interwar period was essentially that of readjustment to a declining export trade; but in marked contrast to the situation in the United States, the postwar period was one of coal shortage and unsatisfied demand, a situation that was largely common to all countries of Western Europe. During World War II British coal output fell below 200 million tons, largely in consequence of the loss of manpower, and seriously prejudiced the British war effort. In desperation the British government introduced a measure without parallel in Britain's history —direct labor conscription for the coal-mining industry and transfer of personnel from the fighting services.[9] Following the nationalization of the coal industry in 1948 strenuous efforts were made by the National Coal Board to reorganize the industry on a more efficient basis, and with the addition of some 12 million tons of coal produced in opencast (strip) workings, production rose to almost 225 million tons in 1952. Unfortunately, the expansion of Middle East oil output soon removed the urgency; from 1958 onwards coal stocks became a considerable embarrassment, and by 1960 output had again fallen below 200 million tons.

British Coalfields Britain possesses more than twenty coalfields, including several that are not worked (Fig. 12-7). In the early Industrial Revolution some of the smaller fields, such as the South Staffordshire field and the Shropshire field, where the ironmaster Abraham Darby first made use of coke in the blast furnace, played an important part, but at present this multiplicity of fields is a handicap. If Britain had but one major field comparable to that of the Ruhr in West Germany on which it could concentrate its efforts, the task of revitalizing the industry would be very much simpler. In point of fact Britain has just such a field in its Yorks, Derby, and Notts (Yorkshire, Derbyshire, and Nottinghamshire) field, which would

Fig. 12-7 Coalfields in Great Britain.
This map shows concealed and exposed coalfields, as well as fields occurring in rocks other than the Coal Measures. The concealed field in the West Midlands lies at great depth, however, and mining is confined to the few exposed portions in Warwickshire and Staffordshire. Mining extends under the sea in a number of British fields. (National Coal Board.)

[9] **Largely owing to the opposition of the miners and of the general public, this measure was perhaps the only conspicuous failure of the war effort. The author speaks with experience, having served in a Nottinghamshire colliery under the scheme.**

well repay a concentration of effort; but unfortunately, postwar Britain was not able to forgo production from its many other fields, and in practice the transfer of labor and other factors of production from the poorer fields has proved very difficult. Since 1945 no British government has been prepared to pursue measures which would result in a marked decrease in employment in the coal mining industry.

Collectively the British fields possess coals of all types, and several fields have coastal locations which have encouraged the development of a coal export trade. Coalfields occur on either flank of the Pennine upland in northern England, in the Midlands, in a discontinuous belt across south Wales and southern England, and in the central lowlands of Scotland. The major fields are the following:

The *Yorks, Derby, and Notts* field, which is, and will continue to be, the mainstay of the industry. With an output of about 80 million tons in 1962, it accounted for some 40 per cent of British coal output; it produces coals of all types, but is best known for its domestic household coals, or "brights." This field has an important concealed eastern extension on which many of the modern mines are situated. The only major field which has always looked mainly to the home market, it enjoys good physical conditions and has an output per manshift (OPMS) almost twice the national average in the southern, or Notts and Derby, section of the field. It is the only major field to make a profit for the National Coal Board; all the others make substantial losses.

The *Northeastern,* or Northumberland and Durham, field also has a concealed section, in which workings penetrate beneath the seabed. The field produces all types of coal, Durham, the most productive portion, being famous for its high-quality gas and coking coals and Northumberland for its steam coals. The field was formerly a very large coal exporter, but in the interwar period it became perhaps the most depressed industrial area in Britain. Its present output of about 35 million tons is a little less than 20 per cent of the national total.

Though the *South Wales* field produces all types of coal including anthracite, its specialty is steam coal, which in the days of coal-fired merchant vessels was exported all over the world for bunkering purposes; a particularly large export trade was conducted with Europe and the Mediterranean. Productivity per worker, largely in consequence of poor physical conditions and the extreme age of many workings, is the lowest of any major field. The great decline of the export trade in the interwar period had tremendous consequences for the field, which degenerated into a chronically depressed area. Both absolutely and relatively, production has fallen dramatically, and the field now accounts for scarcely 10 per cent of the national output.

The *Scottish* fields collectively produce somewhat less than 10 per cent of total coal output. They present very varied conditions, the oldest worked field being in Lanarkshire, where physical conditions are very poor, and the newest in Fifeshire, where physical conditions are considerably better. The *Lancashire* field, which contains no coking coal, also has very poor physical conditions.

The remaining ten productive fields are all small; five produced less than 2 million tons each in 1961, and clearly have no future. In the Midlands fields physical conditions vary considerably, being best in the *Warwickshire* and the *Leicester and South Derbyshire* fields, where coal mining is a comparatively recent activity. The Leicester and South Derbyshire field is remarkable in that it is the only British field to have raised its output above that of 1913 and 1937; using fully mechanized pillar and room working with two coal-getting shifts, the field has the country's highest OPMS, almost twice the national average of 1.1 tons in 1961. Its operations and those of the nearby Warwickshire and South Staffordshire fields produce a profit for the National Coal Board.

In comparison with the coal industry of the United States, the British industry suffers from limited opportunities for strip working. Shaft mines are almost universal, and even the deepest mine in the United States does not approach the average depth of British mines. In many of the poorer fields of the west, mines are deep, hot, and wet and have much gas emission, and seams in general are considerably more fractured and inclined than in American fields. The average size of mine is much smaller, and in many British fields an output of 1,000 tons per day ranks a colliery as a large one. There is a marked increase in productivity per worker at the face with increasing size of mines, but in many fields this is lost through inefficient haulage.[10] Many mines work several seams concurrently, a practice that is very unusual in the American industry. Some fields, however, show a marked concentration on a particular seam; in the concealed portion of the Yorks, Derby, and Notts field the Barnsley, or Top Hard, seam, is often worked exclusively.

Problems and Prospects It is apparent that poor physical conditions were not primarily responsible for the long period of stagnation during which OPMS remained virtually stationary. Of the European fields only the Upper Silesian field enjoys physical conditions appreciably better than the average for Britain, yet most Continental producers were able to increase OPMS in the interwar period, and many have continued to perform better than Britain since the end of World War II.

Mechanization came late to the British industry; more than 90 per cent of coal was hand-cut in 1913. From then on, however, the use of electric coal cutters and face conveyors increased rapidly, and by the outbreak of World War II about 70 per cent of total output was mechanically cut and conveyed. But because of inadequate and antiquated haulage and winding systems, this mechanization at the face was largely rendered abortive; thus there was little attempt at power loading, nor, in general, did physical conditions permit the use of existing American equipment. Mechanization also brought new social problems—the erosion of the skill of the collier and the dangerous practice of passing responsibility from shift to shift. The technical and organizational shortcomings of the British industry were made abundantly clear by the *Reid Report,*[11] which frankly declared the existing organization of the industry incapable of carrying out the technical changes which alone could restore the industry to a high level of efficiency.

Following the nationalization of the industry in 1946, this task fell to the National Coal Board. The Board's long-term plan for revitalizing the industry included the cessation of mining in the poorer, high-cost fields which lie mainly in the west; thus, production has been terminated in the Bristol and Somerset field and in the Forest of Dean. Older, high-cost pits in all fields were to be closed, and labor was to be transferred to more efficient pits. These were to be equipped with power-loading machinery designed for British conditions and, wherever possible, with locomotive haulage. By 1961 about 40 per cent of Britain's coal production was power-loaded at the face. The Board also planned for the sinking of a considerable number of really large mines (that is,

[10] With endless rope haulage, a train of "tubs" may take one hour or more to travel from a distant face to the pit bottom.

[11] Ministry of Fuel and Power, *Coal Mining: Report of the Technical Advisory Committee (Reid Report),* Cmd. 6610, H. M. Stationery Office, London, 1945.

with a daily output of 4,000 tons or more) in the best fields, using fully mechanized pillar and room working.

With the advantage of hindsight, the Board's plan appears to have been too ambitious; impossible targets were assigned to some fields, particularly in Scotland, where work on a colliery designed to produce 8,000 tons per day at Glenrothes, Fifeshire, was finally abandoned in 1962. Recurrent balance-of-payments crises also interfered with the Board's plans, and with the growth of petroleum production in the Middle East the planned output of 240 million tons for 1960 to 1965 which was envisaged in 1950 could not be sold even if it were produced.[12] Political considerations also hampered the Board's operations; the production of opencast coal, a profitable operation that is performed by licensed private producers, is to be terminated by 1965 in order to maintain employment in underground mining.

Coal in Western Europe

The European Coal and Steel Community (ECSC), which was in a very real sense the parent of the broader EEC, has as its aim the establishment of a common pricing system for all coal, iron, and steel products within the six member nations. The High Authority of the Community at Brussels has, however, experienced very considerable difficulty in implementing this policy, partly because of varying wage structures and partly because of the widely differing physical conditions in the coalfields within the Community.

The ECSC produces about 10 per cent more bituminous coal than Britain, and of the total production of about 240 million (metric) tons, West Germany produced about one-half (Fig. 12-8). Germany's maximum coal production was attained in 1942, when almost 250 million tons were produced, together with some 255 million tons of lignite; in 1945, however, the coal and lignite fields of Saxony and Silesia passed to East Germany and to Poland. The balance of the Community's output is shared among France, Belgium, and the Netherlands, Italy producing less than a million tons. Coal production in Western Europe made a rapid recovery from the effects of World War II, and in contrast to Britain, output in most countries is above the level of 1913.

France, Belgium, and the Netherlands Apart from a small output from scattered fields in the Massif Central, the French output (almost 52 million tons in 1962) is derived from the northern coalfield of the departments of Nord and Pas-de-Calais, which extend across the frontier into Belgium, and from the comparatively newly developed Lorraine coalfield. Physical conditions in the northern field are poor; mines are deep, hot, and wet, and seams are thin and much fractured. Nevertheless, OPMS in France has risen continuously since 1945, and at present is only slightly inferior to that of Britain. Apart from a few small mines in the south, the French industry is under public ownership; the use of the longwall advance method with two coal-getting shifts is facilitated by the employment at the face of pneumatic picks instead of electric coal cutters as in Britain; this is one of the principal differences in face practice between Britain and Continental Europe.

In the Belgian portion of the shared field physical conditions are even poorer than in the French portion, and OPMS is the lowest in Western Europe; in the newer Campine field of the north, however, productivity per worker is higher. Belgium has produced almost 30 million tons in some postwar years, but since

[12] **The Board's** *Revised Plan for Coal, 1959* **forecast a total demand of 200 to 215 million tons by 1965.**

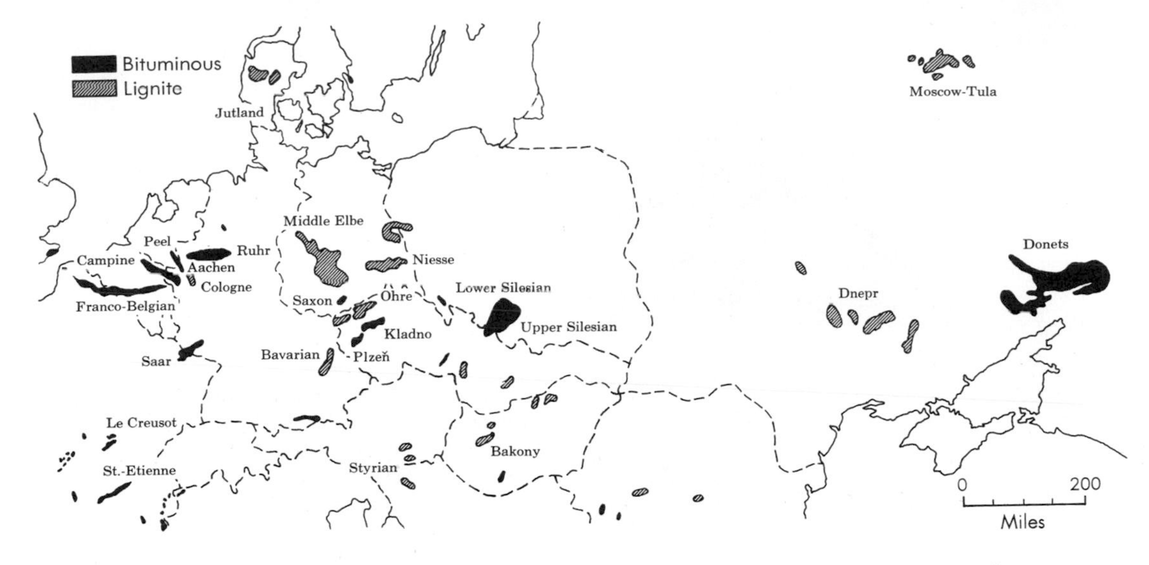

Fig. 12-8 Coalfields in Europe.
Relatively few of Europe's many bituminous and lignite fields are of major importance.

1958 production has fallen considerably, and it is clear the industry faces a difficult period of retrenchment.

Coal mining in the Netherlands is a modern industry that began only in this century and is entirely publicly owned. The Netherlands industry is confined to the south of Limburg Province, and is remarkable for its technical brilliance in attaining a very high OPMS under difficult conditions. Although output is small (about 12 million tons in 1962), there are only a dozen collieries; thus the industry is highly concentrated, and output per mine is the highest of any European field, even exceeding that of the Ruhr.

The Ruhr Apart from about 16 million tons from the Saar, returned to Germany in 1957, and about half that quantity from the small Aachen field, the whole of West Germany's coal output in 1962 was derived from the Ruhr, the most important field in the European continent; the Ruhr itself lies well south of the most productive portion of the field, which is situated between the Ruhr and Lippe Rivers. In many ways the Ruhr, or North Rhine–Westphalia field, resembles Britain's Yorks, Derby, and Notts field; coal-bearing rocks outcrop along the Ruhr Valley but dip away northwards under a cover of younger rocks for an indeterminate distance, and the old workings in the exposed field now account for only a very small proportion of the output. All types of coal, from anthracite to high-volatile bituminous coals, are produced, but the Ruhr's specialty is its high-quality coking coal, which has long accounted for the largest proportion of output, and reflects the remarkable domination of the industry by iron and steel producers.

The Ruhr has the highest OPMS in Western Europe after the Saar, which does not produce coking coal, but physical conditions are little if at all superior to those of Britain; the basins and saddles which are such a feature of the field's structure result in many seams being inclined far from the horizontal, and superior

Longwall advance working is accomplished with pneumatic picks in the Ruhr. This method of mining requires considerable strength and skill on the part of the worker.

The thickness of brown coal deposits has encouraged the use of highly mechanized methods of strip mining. This bucket wheel excavator, below, operates near Cologne, in West Germany.

organization and technology are the main reasons for the higher efficiency of the Ruhr industry.[13] In marked contrast to the multiplicity of producers in the United States and in prewar Britain, coal mining in the Ruhr has long been heavily concentrated; in 1938 twelve large companies produced three-quarters of the total output.[14] In comparison with most British mines the typical Ruhr colliery is very large, producing more than half a million tons per year; several produce more than 4,000 tons per day. Large concessions avoid the waste that has occurred in many British fields, where much coal has become sterilized between concession boundaries or has been lost through past failure to keep proper records of workings. Longwall advance mining with two coal-getting shifts and the use of pneumatic picks are standard practice, but of greater significance in the attainment of a high productivity per worker is the use of level roads driven through the strata in which locomotive haulage is possible and efficient winding.[15]

The advantages of the Ruhr, therefore, arise essentially from the economics of scale resulting from a concentration of production in large units. In addition, the high quality of Ruhr coking coal and the lack of alternative sources of supply encouraged the development of great vertical combinations that closely bound together coal, iron and steel, and chemical producers. Most of the great combinations date from before World War I, but further concentration was carried out following the French occupation of 1923 and 1924; and, although the breakup of the great coal and iron combines was declared part of Allied policy at the end of World War II, they have grown in strength in the postwar period. As in most other countries of Western Europe, the national government has a substantial share in the industry and, directly and indirectly, the state has always exercised a considerable degree of control over both the working and the marketing of coal.

The Ruhr has also benefited enormously from improvements in inland waterways and from the construction of canals which have facilitated coal transport to the coast and to other parts of the country. The German canals are very different from their narrow British counterparts excavated in the early days of the Industrial Revolution; the largest can accommodate barges carrying upwards of 1,000 tons. The Rhine-Herne Canal connects the most productive part of the field with the Rhine and with the Dortmund-Ems Canal, which gives access to the North Sea; the Mittelland Canal, completed shortly before World War II, connects with the Elbe and the Oder. Coal traffic up and down the Rhine rivals that on the upper Ohio and its tributaries, and Belgium and the Netherlands have constructed large new canals to attract the profitable Ruhr trade to Antwerp and to Rotterdam. After decades of discussion, agreement was finally reached in 1960 between the French and West German governments for the canalization of the Moselle River, thus providing a water link between the Ruhr and the iron-ore fields of Lorraine. The new waterway was completed in 1964.

The establishment of a common market for

[13] A direct comparison of OPMS for all workers between the two areas is not at present possible. The Reid Commission quotes OPMS for all workers in Britain as 1.148 long tons in 1938, as against 1.523 for the Ruhr. Underground OPMS in 1959 was estimated by the OEEC as 1.72 metric tons for Britain and 1.85 for West Germany.

[14] Chauncy D. Harris, "The Ruhr Coal Mining District," ***Geographical Review,*** **vol. 36, p. 211, 1946.**

[15] Norman J. G. Pounds in ***The Ruhr,*** **Faber & Faber, Ltd., London, 1952, p. 148, states that skip winding (that is, the use of a large bucket into which coal is tipped at the pit bottom) is little used. The Reid Commission, however, considered it a material factor in the Ruhr's high OPMS. The use of skips, in place of cages with tubs in which the coal has traveled to the pit bottom, is clearly a considerable economy, particularly in deep mines. The Koepe system of single-rope winding also has considerable advantages over British practice. See** ***Reid Report,*** **pp. 18, 93–94.**

coal and iron products and the abolition of quotas, tariffs, and restrictive practices should operate to the advantage of the low-cost Ruhr area. Each step taken in the achievement of this goal has been accompanied by an increase in trade in coal and iron products within the EEC, although it does not appear likely that Ruhr coal will displace that of the Franco-Belgian and Dutch fields from their traditional markets. Moreover, Western Europe's growing petroleum consumption is already creating considerable difficulties for the coal industry in the EEC; the maintenance of employment in the mining industry has become an important political issue in West Germany as in other countries.

Coal in the Soviet Bloc

Collectively, coal production in the satellite countries of Eastern Europe exceeds that of Britain in terms of bituminous-coal equivalent and is not greatly inferior to that of the EEC, which has a population almost twice as large. But this substantial output is partly accounted for by a large production of lignite, and recurrent shortages of fuel have been a major obstacle to the national development plans of the countries in the Soviet bloc. Among the satellites only Poland, with an output of over 100 million tons, can be considered a large producer of bituminous coal, and Czechoslovakia is the only other producer of any note. East Germany is particularly deficient in bituminous coal, possessing only the small fields of Saxony, and although bituminous coal is supplemented by enormous deposits of lignite (of which the country is the world's largest producer), the latter is unsuitable for many purposes.

If Eastern Europe were an economic unit, it is likely that its coal output would be higher than it is; in the great triangle-shaped Upper Silesian field, it has an asset quite comparable with the coal resources of the Ruhr. From the physical standpoint the Upper Silesian coal basin is Europe's most favored field, and before World War II OPMS was the highest in Europe; seams are thick, generally level, and little fractured and lie relatively close to the surface. Many features of the industry recall the Ruhr, with collieries operating extensive concessions, efficient haulage and winding, and a substantial direct state interest. Yet the Upper Silesian field has never realized its apparent potentialities, and its development has lagged far behind the Ruhr. In part this reflects the poor quality of coke made from much of the coalfield, but of greater importance has been divided political control and the marginal location of the field for the three powers that shared it before World War I. With the resurrection of the Polish nation after World War I, Poland's portion of the field was largely denied its former German market, and with the assistance of cheap freight rates to the coast, Polish coal began to find an outlet in other foreign markets, greatly to the disadvantage of Britain. After World War II Poland acquired control of the greater part of the field, and its coal resources were almost doubled; moreover, it also obtained the small Lower Silesian field, which produced excellent coking coal. Coal production from the Upper Silesian field has progressively increased since the end of World War II, and is now substantially above the prewar peak; but Poland, its economy strained to the utmost, has been unable to meet all domestic demands and has had relatively little available for export to its neighbors.

The Soviet bloc's Council for Mutual Economic Assistance (Comecon) has, however, planned for the coordinated development of the coal resources of Eastern Europe, and Czechoslovakia has made substantial investment in the Polish industry. Czechoslovakia inherited the Ostrava section of the Upper Silesian field after World War I, but the main centers of production have been the coal basins of Plzeň and Kladno in Bohemia, which still, as in the days of the Dual Monarchy, constitute the main forms of heavy industry. Nevertheless, the U.S.S.R. can have little real desire to see the formation of an integrated economy in Eastern Europe such as that envisaged in the Common Market; this, of course, could only lead to a diminution of its influence in the area. With the completion of the Soviet oil pipelines, the Silesian field may lose its last chance of exerting a major unifying effect on the economy of Eastern Europe.

The U.S.S.R. In 1958 the Soviet Union apparently became the world's largest producer of coal with an output of about 425 million tons (hard-coal equivalent), but as in Eastern Europe, this figure includes a large lignite output. So rapid has been the growth of coal production in the U.S.S.R. in recent years that it appeared highly likely that in the not distant future it would surpass that of the United States by a wide margin. This does not now appear so certain; planned output for 1960 was almost 600 million tons, but for 1965 only a small increase is envisaged. The great increase in production since 1928, when output first regained the 1913 level of about 30 million tons, has in large measure been achieved through a considerable increase in the labor force in the industry; in this respect, the coal industry of the U.S.S.R. stands in marked contrast to that of Western countries. However, the Soviet economy can now expect increasing difficulties in increasing the size of its nonagricultural labor force, and with increasing emphasis on oil and natural gas, the large reported reserves of coal in the scantily populated Tunguska basin of eastern Siberia may never be worked.

The coal resources of the U.S.S.R. appear to be at least as great as those of the United States, but they are less favorably distributed in relation to population, and the growth of production has been accompanied by long hauls to the main centers of consumption. The reduction of excessive coal-transport costs, however, was a feature of the Third Five Year Plan (1937 to 1942), which aimed at increasing production from resources nearer to the main areas of consumption.

In the Donets Coal Basin (Donbas) of the southern Ukraine, the Soviet Union possesses the third great coalfield of Continental Europe. The field produces all types of coal, from coking coal in the western extremity to anthracite in the eastern; physical conditions are markedly inferior to those of the fields of Upper Silesia and the Ruhr, for seams are thin and considerably faulted, and methods of working are very labor-intensive. The development of the Donbas came considerably later than that of the other great European fields, the great impetus to expansion coming with investment of considerable quantities of French capital from 1890 onwards. By 1913 output had risen to over 25 million tons, almost 90 per cent of the Russian total, and at the commencement of the First Five Year Plan (1928) the Donbas still provided over three-quarters of the national output. Thereafter, however, its share fell considerably, although output continued to grow and by the German invasion of 1941 was closely approaching 100 million tons.

The decline in the relative importance of the Donbas in coal and in metal production was a result of the planned development of the fuel resources of other parts of the country and particularly of western Siberia, where before the revolution coal mining was largely restricted to supplying the railroad system. The First and Second Five Year Plans saw a great increase in production in the Kuznetsk Basin

(Kuzbas) of western Siberia, which was closely bound up with the development of the high-grade iron ores of the southern Urals 1,100 miles distant. This joint development was controlled by the Ural-Kuznetsk *kombinat,* one of a number of large organizations with this name which in many ways resemble the large corporations of the highly developed economies. The Kuzbas field contains a higher proportion of coking coals than the Donbas, but the rapid growth of the iron and steel industry soon placed such burdens on the railroad system that a nearer supply of coking coal became imperative for the Ural industry. This problem was partially solved by the development of the Karaganda field of northern Kazakhstan, some 600 miles distant.

Coal production in Soviet Asia received a great stimulus with the occupation of the Ukraine during World War II, and has continued to grow in the postwar period with the planned decentralization of Soviet heavy industry. Certain other fields have also increased in relative importance, notably the Moscow-Tula field, which, though producing only subbituminous coal and lignite, lies within the central industrial region, still the most important single industrial complex in the country. Production has also expanded in the Ural fields, which produce coal suitable for general industrial purposes, and in a number of districts in eastern Siberia and in the Maritime province, or Far Eastern region. However, with the post-1960 confirmation of the principle of specialization and the growth of the internal oil-and-gas-line system, further opportunities for the expansion of coal production appear limited to iron and steel production and to electricity generation.

Other Producers

Several other producers show features of interest. Australia is almost unique among the highly developed countries in possessing a coal industry that has shown a slow but continuous growth of production over the past half-century; moreover, it has the highest output per man-day after the United States, and its 1961 figure of about 5 tons was easily capable of further improvement. Almost 80 per cent of Australia's black coal is produced in New South Wales, on the northern, western, and southern margins of a great coal basin of which Sydney is approximately the center. The Union of South Africa, where production is mainly confined to Natal and the Transvaal, has also enjoyed a continuous increase in production, and by virtue of very favorable physical conditions and low labor costs has the lowest costs of production in the world.

India and Japan have much less favorable physical conditions, but in both countries output has expanded considerably in the postwar period. India's principal coalfields are confined to the Damodar Valley at no great distance from Calcutta. Though these are favorably located in relation to the iron ores of northern Bihar, they are poorly placed in relation to the distribution of population; moreover, reserves of coking coal are slender. Japan's output of almost 50 million tons is derived from the extremities of the country. The principal producing area is northern Kyushu, but costs of production are higher than in the Ishikari area of Hokkaido, the other major producing area. Japanese coal is largely unsuitable for coking, and is mixed with imported coal for use in the iron and steel industry; before World War II coal suitable for this purpose was imported from Manchuria and from northern Indochina, but in the postwar period the United States and Australia have filled this deficiency. The decision to reduce high-cost coal production in Kyushu is in many ways indicative of the country's transition from the status of a semi-developed economy.

The Great Growth of the Chinese Industry The most remarkable development in world coal production in the postwar period has been the tremendous increase in production in China. China's enormous coal resources have long been known, the deposits of Shansi and Shensi being the largest in Asia outside the U.S.S.R., but the pre-World War II production of around 60 million tons was largely derived from Hopeh and from Manchuria. After China regained the prewar output in 1952, its coal production forged ahead at a very rapid rate; claimed production was 130 million tons in 1957, rising to 270 million tons in 1958, to 350 million tons in 1959, and to 425 million tons in 1960. This great increase in output was accompanied by considerable changes in the location of production.

Discount the figures how one will, it is nevertheless certain that China has moved into the very front rank of coal producers; China is already producing more than Britain or Germany ever did, and there seems no reason why it should not soon overtake and surpass both the United States and the Soviet Union. Indeed, this seems almost inevitable; China has not so far made any major petroleum strikes, and to develop any such resources would extend still further the country's critically short resources of capital. The labor-intensive nature of coal mining appears eminently suitable for the Chinese economy; the numerous small scattered deposits of the kind that are now so costly to work in countries at a high level of economic development present no problem to the country which has the world's largest supply of labor.

It is highly significant that indigenous small-scale methods have made a very substantial contribution to the increase in output; 40 per cent of the 1959 output was attributed to small- and medium-sized mines,[16] and it is largely to the small local mine that China must look for raising output in the more populous southern portion of the country and for reducing north-to-south coal traffic. A large number of new fields have been discovered south of the Yangtze River in areas previously considered as lacking in coal; north of the Yangtze it appears that, with the exception of the pioneer northwest, the large-scale mechanized mine will continue to account for the greater part of the output, and in Hopeh, Shansi, and Honan a considerable number of large new sinkings have been made. It is probable that in the near future coal production in north China will exceed that of the northeast region (Manchuria), which, by virtue of the progress made by its former Japanese occupiers and its dense railway network, has always been the principal producing area; T'ai-yüan in Shansi is being developed as a major center of heavy industry comparable with the Anshan-Shenyang (Mukden) complex in Manchuria, and another large iron and steel plant is to be erected at Pao-t'ou in Inner Mongolia.[17] Although the 400-foot seam of Fu-shun is worked in an enormous opencut, the majority of Chinese mines are shaft mines.

The pattern of consumption differs very markedly from that of the other major producers, for both the iron and steel industry and electricity generation are relatively poorly developed, although both are expanding rapidly. Large quantities of coal are consumed by China's growing railroad network and in rural cooperatives, and the great increase in consumption for domestic purposes has helped to banish forever the inactivity that descended over the north China countryside with the onset of winter.

[16] It appears, however, that the opening up of small mines was carried out to an excessive degree, for the following year also saw a considerable reduction in their number.

[17] T. J. Hughes and D. E. T. Luard, *The Economic Development of Communist China, 1949–1958,* Oxford University Press, London, 1959, p. 97.

SELECTED REFERENCES

Allen, G. C.: *British Industries and Their Organization,* Longmans, Green & Co., Ltd., London, 1959, pp. 49–91.

Deasy, George F., and Phyllis R. Griess: "Geographical Significance of Recent Changes in Mining in the Bituminous Coal Fields of Pennsylvania," *Economic Geography,* vol. 33, pp. 283–298, 1957.

——— and ———: "Some New Maps of the Underground Bituminous Coal Mining Industry of Pennsylvania," *Annals of the Association of American Geographers,* vol. 47, pp. 336–349, 1957.

Diebold, William: *The Schuman Plan: A Study in Economic Cooperation, 1950–59,* Frederick A. Praeger, Inc., New York, 1959.

Francis, Wilfrid: *Coal: Its Formation and Composition,* Edward Arnold (Publishers) Ltd., London, 1954.

Gebhardt, G. (ed.): *Ruhrbergbau: Geschichte, Aufbau und Verflechtung, seiner Gesellschaften und Organisationen,* Verlag Glueckauf, Essen, 1957.

Harris, Chauncy D.: "The Ruhr Coal Mining District," *Geographical Review,* vol. 36, pp. 194–221, 1946.

Lister, Louis: *Europe's Coal and Steel Community: An Experiment in Economic Union,* The Twentieth Century Fund, New York, 1960.

Miller, E. Willard: "The Southern Anthracite Region: A Problem Area," *Economic Geography,* vol. 31, pp. 331–350, 1955.

Ministry of Fuel and Power: *Coal Mining: Report of the Technical Advisory Committee (Reid Report),* Cmd. 6610, H. M. Stationery Office, London, 1945.

National Coal Association: *Bituminous Coal Facts, 1964,* Washington, 1964.

National Coal Board: *Revised Plan for Coal, 1959,* H. M. Stationery Office, London, 1959.

Organisation for European Economic Cooperation: *The Coal Industry in Europe,* Paris, 1960 and 1962.

Political and Economic Planning: *The British Fuel and Power Industries,* London, 1947, pp. 59–97.

Pounds, N. J. G.: *The Ruhr,* Indiana University Press, Bloomington, Ind., and Faber & Faber, Ltd., London, 1952.

———and W. N. Parker: *Coal and Steel in Western Europe: The Influence of Resources and Techniques on Production,* Indiana University Press, Bloomington, Ind., and Faber & Faber, Ltd., London, 1957.

Rodgers, Allan: "Coking Coal Supply: Its Role in the Expansion of the Soviet Steel Industry," *Economic Geography,* vol. 40, pp. 113–150, 1964.

Roepke, Howard G.: "Changing Patterns of Coal Production in the Eastern Interior Field," *Economic Geography,* vol. 31, pp. 234–247, 1955.

Shimkin, Demitri: *Minerals: A Key to Soviet Power,* Harvard University Press, Cambridge, Mass., 1953.

Thomas, Trevor M.: "Recent Trends and Developments in the British Coal Mining Industry," *Economic Geography,* vol. 34, pp. 19–41, 1958.

Trueman, Arthur (ed.): *The Coalfields of Great Britain,* Edward Arnold (Publishers) Ltd., London, 1954.

United Nations Economic Commission for Asia and the Far East: *Coal and Iron Ore Resources of Asia and the Far East,* Bangkok and New York, 1952.

Woytinsky, W. S., and E. S. Woytinsky: *World Population and Production,* The Twentieth Century Fund, New York, 1953, pp. 840–881.

Zimmermann, Erich W.: *World Resources and Industries,* rev. ed., Harper & Row, Publishers, Incorporated, New York, 1951, pp. 454–489.

Chapter 13

ELECTRIC ENERGY

Although electric forces constitute the bonds that hold together all the atoms making up the universe, *usable* electric energy is secondary energy, that is, energy derived from a primary source such as coal, oil, or natural gas, which can be made to release energy through combustion, from the mechanical energy of falling or moving water, from the internal heat of the earth, or from heat produced by the nuclear fission of elements refined from radioactive minerals. The potential energy locked up in all these sources is converted at the electric power station into a new form of energy, which is transmitted to the consumer and reconverted by him in a variety of employments such as heating and lighting or the production of mechanical energy to drive machines. Electricity is thus essentially a tool, or agent; yet its use makes available sources of energy which it would be difficult, inconvenient, or prohibitively expensive to harness in any other way, and in this sense it has greatly enlarged the energy sources at man's disposal.

THE PLACE OF ELECTRICITY IN THE WORLD ECONOMY

Electricity consumption per capita is closely related to the general level of development; the highly developed economies have by far the largest per capita consumption, and there is a fairly close correlation between per capita product and per capita electricity consumption as one descends the scale of economic development (Table 13-1). World electricity consumption trends sharply upwards, and the average annual increase in production of electric energy over the past decade has been very high even in countries at a low or modest level of economic development, such as India, Greece, and Turkey. In these countries, however, electricity production is still very small, so that the attainment of a relatively

Table 13-1

Installed Capacity and Production of Electric Energy, 1960

	INSTALLED CAPACITY (mw)	ENERGY PRODUCTION (MILLION kwhr)	PERCENTAGE OF PRODUCTION FROM HYDRO PLANTS	ENERGY PRODUCTION PER CAPITA (kwhr)
United States	185,900	841,000	18	4,650
Canada	21,100	114,000	92	6,330
Australia	6,000	23,100	18	2,240
New Zealand	1,600	6,800	81	2,830
Britain	37,200	136,700	2	2,610
West Germany	27,700	116,400	11	2,180
France	21,900	72,100	56	1,580
Sweden	9,000	34,800	89	4,650
Norway	6,200	31,300	99	8,720
Switzerland	5,900	19,100	97	3,570
Austria	4,100	16,000	74	2,280
Japan	23,600	115,500	51	1,660
Italy	16,500	56,200	82	1,140
Mexico	3,000	10,700	48	300
India	5,500	19,700	40	40
U.S.S.R.	67,000	292,300	18	1,360
WORLD TOTAL	2,294,000			77

SOURCE: United Nations, *Statistical Yearbook*, 1961.

large annual increase is not difficult. In countries at a high level of economic development such as those of Western Europe and of North America, the production of electricity increases at a much faster rate than the increase in national product, and often twice as fast. In several such countries, electricity production doubles every seven to ten years, a rate of growth roughly commensurate with that of the petroleum industry. To maintain such a high growth rate, which nevertheless is frequently insufficient to keep pace with mounting demand, very heavy capital investment is necessary. The electricity-supply industry is thus one of the most highly capitalized industries in the world; each year since 1948 investment in electricity supply in Britain has accounted for more than 7 per cent of total gross fixed investment,[1] and the situation in most other highly developed economies is essentially similar.

The huge and continuous world increase in electricity production reflects above all the tendency in economies at a high level of economic development for the power at the disposal of the worker to grow as both industry and agriculture become progressively more mechanized. In such economies, manufacturing industries usually account for one-half or more of total electricity consumption, the chemical and metal industries with their very high growth rates being particularly avid consumers.

[1] Broadly, investment in plant and other durable assets, including that made for depreciation.

However, the higher income levels resulting from economic growth have also greatly enlarged the range of electric appliances used in homes, and in highly developed economies domestic consumption can still make up a substantial proportion of total demand. In high latitudes, where winters are long and severe, domestic uses can amount to as much as one-quarter of total consumption.

It was to supply the domestic market with light that the electricity-supply industry first began in the last quarter of the nineteenth century, and this historical pattern is repeated in countries at a low level of economic development. In such countries, the electric power consumed by manufacturing industries may well be less than that lost in transmission. But if electricity can be brought into the home, it may also be applied to the cottage and small-scale industries to augment the productivity of the worker and thus importantly to raise real incomes in underdeveloped economies; the use of the electric motor gives to the worker in such industries the possibility of achieving a level of productivity more commensurate with that of the worker in large-scale industry and also permits a substantial degree of industrial diversification. The experience of Japan shows conclusively the great advantages obtainable through the wide extension of electricity supply; not only would the remarkable expansion of the Japanese small-scale industries have been impossible in its absence, but without the employment of electric motors for pumping irrigation water and for driving threshing machines, the Japanese farmer could not have attained a high level of productivity. It is hardly surprising, therefore, that most underdeveloped countries attach considerable importance to the production of electric power in national development plans.

Electricity is certainly not an ideal form of energy, but its advantages are very substantial, even if they are usually taken for granted. Perhaps its greatest assets are its flexibility and divisibility. It can easily be converted into a wide variety of manifestations of energy to serve a multiplicity of purposes; moreover, the consumer needs to take from his source of supply only as much as is necessary to serve his purpose. It can be transmitted instantaneously over considerable distances, direct to centers of consumption. This involves losses, it is true, but these can be kept within acceptable limits for distances of up to about 400 miles by the use of high-voltage transmission lines, and technological progress is steadily enlarging the distance over which economic transmission is possible.

Moreover, very considerable economies of scale are realized in electricity generation; costs per unit fall sharply with increased output, which in turn stimulates still larger consumption. As a result, electric power has made possible the development of industries which are prodigious consumers of power, particularly the electrochemical and electrometallurgical industries. Together with the pulp and paper industry, such industries are strongly attracted to areas where large quantities of electric energy can be made available at very low unit cost; thus they have become closely identified with the northern Pacific Coast and the southeastern margin of the Laurentian Shield in North America, the Alpine and Scandinavian regions in Europe, and certain other restricted parts of the world where physical and economic conditions have combined to favor greatly the generation of hydroelectricity.

Although not large consumers of electricity, the electronics and telecommunications industries are fundamentally dependent upon the availability of electric power. (For a further discussion, see chapter 16.) The importance of rapid and reliable communications to the world economy can scarcely be overstated; in countries at a high level of economic development they are essential in every economic activity.

The greatest disadvantage of electric energy is that it cannot easily be stored. Small quantities, it is true, can be stored in batteries or accumulators, and the field of employment for the fuel cell[2] is likely to expand considerably. But the storage of electricity on a large scale is not possible, and from this handicap arise some of the most fundamental problems of the electricity-supply industry.

POWER-SUPPLY SYSTEMS AND THEIR OPERATION

Electric power is mainly produced in central power stations, which serve a multiplicity of consumers. This is largely a consequence of the economies of scale mentioned above; one large station is less costly both to construct and to operate than a number of small stations of equivalent capacity. Central power stations may be either privately or publicly owned, but there is a strong tendency for the publicly owned share of the electricity-supply industry to augment, and in several highly developed economies the industry is entirely in public ownership. A limited number of consumers, however, may find it profitable to operate their own generating stations; such "autoproducers," as they are sometimes called, tend to be large manufacturing enterprises of the types already described or other enterprises which have access to very low-cost fuel. Among the latter may be included collieries; railroad or traction authorities or companies; iron and steel plants, which make use of blast-furnace gases for electricity generation; and sugar mills, which use crushed cane, or bagasse, as fuel. Many industrial establishments, of course, maintain emergency generating plants to avoid any production losses resulting from an interruption to the normal central supply.

The Load Factor Any generating system has to produce power for as many consumers as may wish to switch on, and a large number of considerations influence consumers' demands for power. The level of demand can vary very greatly from hour to hour, from day to day, and from season to season; there are pronounced peaks at morning and evening, and the winter load is usually heavier than the summer load (Fig. 13-1). If all requirements are to be met, therefore, sufficient generating capacity mush exist to cope with peak demands, but at other times some plant must remain idle or operate at only a fraction of its capacity. The capacity of generating plant to produce power[3] is measured in kilowatts (kw), or for certain purposes, in kilovolt-amperes (kva); the physical energy it produces, however, is measured in kilowatt-hours (kwhr).[4]

It is clearly desirable that plant should have some reserve capacity over and above the peak demand it has to meet, but for the most economic operation it is essential that plant be worked hard for as long as possible, that is, that a high load factor be achieved. The load factor is the ratio that the actual energy output of a station in a given period bears to the

[2] An electrochemical device that produces electricity by the reverse of electrolysis; oxygen and hydrogen under pressure are made to combine to form water, thus producing a flow of current in an external circuit.

[3] The reader may like to be reminded that the classic definition of power is the rate of doing work; a 50-horsepower engine can perform ten times the work of a 5-horsepower engine within a given period. 1 horsepower = 746 watts

[4] For convenience it is sometimes preferable to use larger units to measure both generating capacity and the production of electric energy. In ascending order of magnitude are the megawatt (10^3 kw) and the gigawatt (10^6 kw), the gigawatt-hour (10^6 kwhr), and the terawatt-hour (10^9 kwhr).

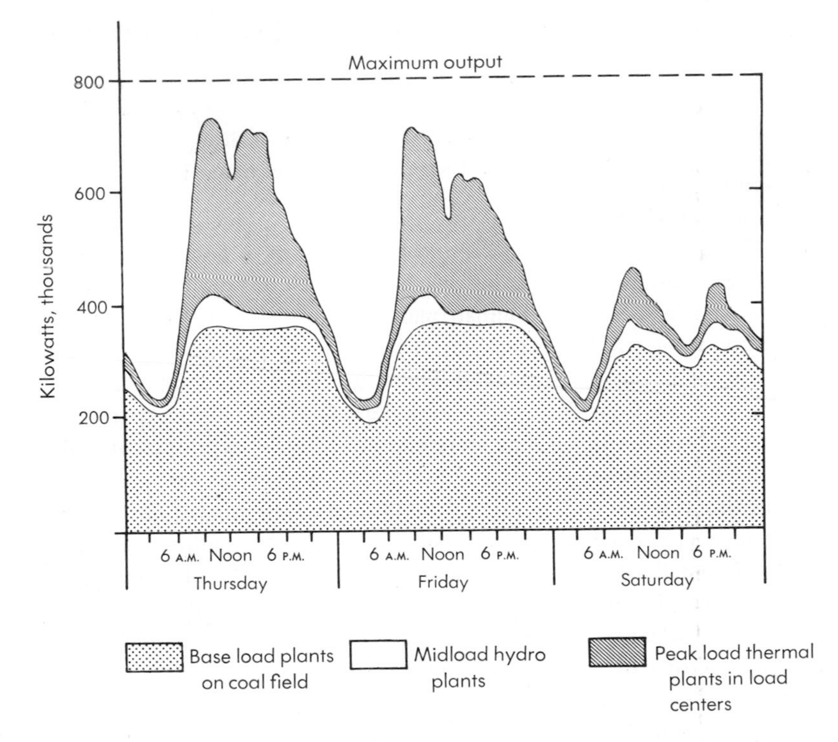

Fig. 13-1 Load on a power system.
Morning and evening business rushes, lunch hour and afternoon break, and the lower level of activity on Saturday (a half day in most highly developed economies), are all clearly discernible in the daily curve of electric power production. (State Electricity Commission of Victoria.)

output that would be produced if the peak load output were maintained over the whole of the given period; thus the attainment of a high load factor implies a substantial ironing out of inequalities of demand over the period under review. Since costs per kilowatt-hour fall sharply as the load factor rises, the attainment of a high load factor is a primary objective of supply undertakings.

Interconnection and the Plant Utilization Factor One way of achieving a higher load factor is to charge different rates for electric power at different periods of time; power may be offered at very low rates during the night or at other off-peak periods; rates for summer may be lower than those charged for winter. In this way it is sometimes possible to encourage electricity consumption at times when generating capacity is otherwise underemployed. But where only one class of consumer exists, the attainment of a really high load factor is usually impossible, with the result that the cost of power per unit remains high. A plant supplying a single town cannot, except under very special circumstances, achieve an annual load factor of much above 30 per cent. By interconnecting a large number of plants (or electricity-supply systems) and by broadening the range of demand patterns, however, the overall load factor can be pushed up very substantially. Such a diversified demand makes possible more efficient use of generating equipment and enables the best performance to be obtained from varying kinds of hydroelectric or thermal electric stations.

Interconnection confers other substantial advantages. Each individual station need carry less reserve capacity, for a temporary shortfall of power in one part of the system can be made good by transferring temporary surpluses from other parts of the system; in other words, the plant utilization factor is raised.[5] Emergencies are more easily overcome, and the temporary retirement of plant for maintenance is rendered easier. Interconnection also makes possible the use of very large turboalternator sets, the employment of which has effected a marked reduction in the costs of producing electric power in the post-World War II period.[6] The enormous new units now coming into service can only be employed in large interconnected systems; it is imperative, otherwise, that each station be equipped with a number of small units, in order to reduce the chances of interruption of supply in the event of a breakdown and to facilitate maintenance. Interconnection can also compensate for variations in streamflow in areas dependent on hydroelectricity. Finally, interconnection greatly assists the electricity-supply industry in meeting the ever expanding demand for power; plant originally designed for base-load employment may be progressively moved to midload and to peak-load duties as more modern and efficient plant becomes available to take over the higher base load.

High-voltage Transmission and Extended Interconnection

With their extensive interconnected networks and a wide range of power-demanding industries, highly developed economies achieve annual plant utilization factors that range typically from 50 to 60 per cent; that of the United States normally exceeds the average for Western Europe (Table 13-2). Apart from the more intense industrial development of the United States (the greater horsepower at the disposal of the American worker has already been noted), seasonal fluctuations in power consumption in the United States have been markedly reduced by a great increase in the use of air conditioning, which has resulted in the maintenance of a high level of domestic

Table 13-2 *Plant-utilization Factors for Selected Countries, 1960*

Country	Factor
Luxembourg	65.5
Canada	61.6
Norway	57.6
Japan	55.9
United States	51.6
U.S.S.R.	49.8
New Zealand	48.5
West Germany	48.0
India	46.2
Sweden	44.2
Australia	43.9
Britain	41.9
Italy	38.9
Switzerland	37.0
Belgium	36.3
Netherlands	35.8

SOURCE: Calculated from United Nations, *Statistical Yearbook*, 1961.

[5] **This is the ratio between the actual energy produced by a plant within a given period and the energy theoretically capable of production by using the generating plant at its *full rated capacity* for the whole of that period.**

[6] **A turboalternator combines the functions of a steam turbine and a generator in one unit, the turbine blades and the generator rotor being mounted on a common shaft.**

demand in summer. On the other hand, the limited and specialized demand for power resulting largely from the poor development of manufacturing and the limited opportunities for interconnection make electric power expensive in underdeveloped economies; this, in turn, discourages new industrial activity, so that load factors remain low. Hence it is necessary in such economies that the encouragement of manufacturing and the expansion of electricity generation proceed hand in hand.

Yet even in highly developed economies, there is still very substantial scope for reductions in the cost of electric energy through the fuller use of generating capacity; even in the United States, a national average plant factor of about 55 per cent implies a considerable underutilization of capacity, and in most Western European countries the national average plant factor is lower still. The remedy for this shortcoming is still more widespread interconnection in great continental networks that transcend national frontiers. This ideal is still some way off, but it is being steadily brought nearer by the development of transmission at increasingly higher voltages.

The extended use of very high-voltage transmission is encouraged by several factors. When the voltage at which power is transmitted is doubled, the capacity of the line to transmit power is squared; it is also very much cheaper to erect a high-voltage line than a number of smaller lines of equal total capacity, even if rights-of-way for the latter can be found, by no means an easy or inexpensive task. Thus, with the anticipated increase in the demand for power, substantial cost reductions per unit should be possible from the use of very high-voltage lines. Apart from economies of scale in transmission, very high-voltage lines make possible the interchange of large blocks of power in giant networks, for *in very large quantities,* transmission of power becomes feasible over distances greater than those normally regarded as the limit of economic transmission. For many years the longest and highest-voltage line in the United States was the 285-kilovolt line between Hoover Dam and Los Angeles, but Sweden has a 380-kilovolt line connecting the Härspranget hydroelectric station within the Arctic Circle with Halsberg in central Sweden, a distance of over 600 miles, and even higher voltages are employed in the U.S.S.R.

The technical and economic problems associated with such very high-voltage lines are considerable; apart from those involved in construction and maintenance, they include stability, interference with radio and television transmission, and severe line losses. However, the consensus of expert opinion in highly developed economies is that these problems can be overcome and still leave a net gain through reduced transmission costs, except where it is possible to convey fuel by water transport between the points concerned. This fact has had a considerable influence on the location of new large power stations. In the U.S.S.R., however, despite considerable experience with high-voltage lines, there still appears to be some doubt about the relative advantages of long-distance high-voltage transmission and long-distance coal transport by railroad. The electric power industry of the U.S.S.R., however, as is also the case with the Soviet iron and steel industry, receives a substantial subsidy from the railroads in the form of very low freight rates for coal, and so long as this situation continues, the U.S.S.R. will not reap the full benefit of its research into high-voltage transmission.

Western Europe is moving steadily towards a complete interconnection of national networks under the aegis of the plans for Continental economic integration. The six countries of the EEC are already linked and also

This control room coordinates a large interconnected system in the southern United States.

have connections with Switzerland and Austria, which are members of the EFTA, or Outer Seven. These linkages are mainly at relatively low voltages, but the nucleus of a 380-kilovolt system of interconnection already exists; since 1962 Britain has been linked with France via a 380-kilovolt dc submarine cable,[7] and the main links in Britain's own grid system are being modified to allow transmission at this higher voltage in the future.

At present West Germany, France, and the Netherlands are net importers of electric energy; West Germany imports power from Austria and from Switzerland, and Switzerland also supplies France. In northern Europe, Sweden exports power to Denmark via a submarine cable under the Öresund. Very substantial economies would result from an interconnection of the Scandinavian countries with those of central Europe, but this is still some way off; Norway still lacks a national interconnected network, although it has the highest national plant-utilization factor in Europe. As an example of the potential benefits available through long-distance interconnection, although Norway and Switzerland both derive all but a small proportion of their electric energy from hydroelectric stations, their respective peak loads occur six months out of phase, that of Norway occurring in the winter and that of Switzerland in the summer; interconnection, therefore, should enable both systems to operate more efficiently.

It must be emphasized that interconnection is a *continuous* two-way process of interchange, even though over a given period one part of an interconnected system may appear on balance as an exporter or an importer. Switzer-

[7] **The use of direct current in place of alternating current has considerable advantages for submarine transmission; direct current is also likely to become increasingly used for very long-distance high-voltage transmission.**

General Electric's experimental line at Pittsfield, Mass., operating at 750 kv, is the highest voltage line in the United States.

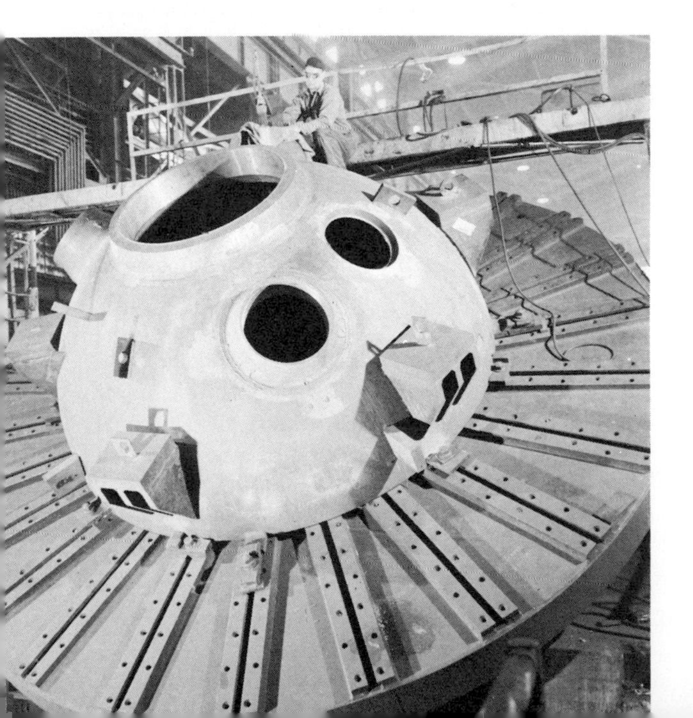

This head of a nuclear reactor vessel is under construction in a Milwaukee plant. The massive nature of the equipment, which weighs some 23 tons, is obvious.

land, for example, draws on West Germany's thermal power production when streamflow is low, as is frequently the case in winter. Similarly, the channel link between England and France will enable French hydroelectric power generated in the Alps, the Massif Central, and the Pyrenees to be interchanged with power generated on the Midland coalfields of Britain; moreover, because of climatic differences, variations in winter time zones and certain differences in work and living habits, peak demands on the two systems occur at different times of the day, so that a daily interchange should also benefit both systems. International interchange of power, of course, creates several administrative problems, but in Europe these have been greatly eased by the work of an international body[8] representing the eight countries with interconnected networks; foreign exchange to pay for purchases of power is granted automatically. As a result, power interchange between European countries has increased rapidly, trebling between 1950 and 1958—a period when there was only a twofold increase in power production.[9]

Extended interconnection has already made considerable progress in the United States; many of the supply systems of the eastern and central states are linked, and there are connections with adjacent parts of Canada. Chicago is the center of a seven-state interconnected system, but a complete coast-to-coast linkup is still some way off. At present more than three-quarters of all power-transmission lines in the United States operate at 138 kilovolts or less, but with higher-voltage transmission it should eventually be possible to connect the largely thermal-based systems of the eastern and central states with those of the Pacific Coast, where hydroelectricity is of paramount importance.[10] Such a spreading of peak loads over several time zones offers the possibility of substantial reductions in power costs.

The U.S.S.R. also has a considerable interconnected network, whose main links operate at among the world's highest voltages. These connect the thermal power stations of the central industrial region with those of the Donbas and with the hydroelectric stations of the Dnieper, Don, and Volga. The new Donbas-Volgograd line is designed to operate at 800 kilovolts. This is the highest voltage so far employed anywhere, although in 1962 an experimental line in Massachusetts began operating at 760 kilovolts.

METHODS OF GENERATING ELECTRICITY

Electric power stations may be expressedly designed to meet base, mid, or peak load and, as has already been indicated, may be either of the hydro or thermal type. Hydro stations use the energy of falling water to spin a water turbine, which is coupled to a generator; and whether large or small, all hydro stations have much in common. Thermal stations show greater diversity. The largest and commonest types make use of steam-driven turbines to drive generators, the two machines now usually being combined in the turboalternator, but thermal stations may also use diesel engines or gas turbines. Steam for thermal stations is most often raised by burning bituminous coal or brown coal, but natural gas or residual oil may also be used, or the heat may be generated by nuclear fission. Which of the two main types of station is employed, or which prime mover and fuel employed in the case of a thermal station, depends upon the relative cost and

[8] **The Union for the Coordination and Transmission of Electrical Energy (UCPTE).**

[9] **Organisation for European Economic Cooperation,** *The Electricity Supply Industry in Europe,* **Paris, 1960, p. 41.**

[10] **Katharine Hamill, "Cheaper Power through Higher Voltages,"** *Fortune,* **June, 1959, p. 140.**

availability of fuel supplies, the nature of the demand the station is to serve, and its role in the supply system. As already indicated, the two methods of electricity generation are not often directly competitive, for interconnection enables the advantages of both to be realized. Under certain physical and economic conditions, hydroelectricity can be of extreme importance, but the areas where such conditions obtain are closely restricted. For the world as a whole thermal stations are by far the more important, and they are becoming increasingly so with the passage of time.

Hydroelectricity

As a permanent, renewable resource, the generation of hydroelectricity appears extremely attractive, particularly to underdeveloped economies short of mineral fuels; the energy of a large mass of moving water is very impressive. But to harness that energy is usually an extremely expensive undertaking, costly not only in capital outlay but also in time. Some six to eight years are necessary for the construction of a large hydroelectricity station and its associated works, and even before the decision to construct it can be taken, much time has to be spent in preliminary hydrologic and geological surveys; thus much capital is locked up with no prospect of an early return. For underdeveloped countries such as India, where immediate increases in productivity are vital, it would seem, then, that massive programs of hydroelectricity development are ill-advised at present.

Even in highly developed economies, the share of hydroelectricity in total electric power production tends to decline; apart from the fact that it involves locking up much capital that would produce a higher return in other occupations, the expansion of hydroelectricity just cannot keep pace with the growth of demand. Since 1959, the Soviet Union has also greatly reduced the role of hydroelectric power in national development because it was absorbing a disproportionate amount of capital; new thermal stations were proving increasingly necessary to give a quicker return and to keep industrial productivity rising.

Moreover, sites for the generation of hydroelectricity are likely to be far removed from main centers of consumption, so that the problem of line losses and transmission costs assumes considerable importance. Mountainous terrain with its associated high precipitation, in which suitable sites are most likely to occur, can seldom support many people. Several of the world's most spectacular sites, theoretically capable of producing enormous quantities of power, are situated in areas so remote from present or potential load centers that their harnessing can be completely discounted; among such sites are the great bend of the Tsangpo (the upper Brahmaputra) in southern Tibet (theoretically capable of producing about one-quarter of the electric energy produced by all the world's present generating stations combined), the Victoria Falls of the Zambezi, and the Iguassú Falls of the Paraná.

Compounded with these disadvantages is a further one: water power is capricious. Streamflow varies from season to season and from year to year, and some regularization of flow is usually necessary. Glacier-fed streams have their peak discharge at the season of snowmelt, that is, spring and early summer, while rain-fed streams are highest in, or shortly following on, the season of maximum precipitation. Very heavy discharge may reduce the fall, or "head," by raising the level downstream, effectively drowning the fall; if extra power can be generated at such times, it must be sold at very low rates. Run-of-river plants, using ordinary streamflow, can usually be provided with capacity to make use of the greater water discharge that is available 30 to 40 per cent of the year, which may be three or more times the minimum flow. This usually requires the construction of regulating dams, although the size and cost of these can be reduced in so-called "pumping" generating stations, which use off-peak energy from thermal stations to lift water above the dam. Large stations may require storage dams, which regulate flow from year to year; these, however, are generally associated with multipurpose schemes of river development, of which the generation of hydroelectricity is only a part.

Yet despite these formidable disadvantages, which make it very unlikely that hydroelectricity will ever account for a large proportion of the world's total production of electric energy, under certain physical and economic conditions its generation offers great advantages. Hydro stations achieve a very high level of technical efficiency, delivering about 80 per cent of the theoretical energy input, a level of efficiency about three times that of most thermal stations. As there is no combustion, the plant is clean and there is no problem of corrosion. The plant has a long life and maintenance costs are low; moreover, less labor is needed to operate a hydro station than a thermal plant of equivalent capacity. Once installed, therefore, the main costs are interest payments[11] and depreciation charges; thermal stations have to meet large and, for the most part, continually increasing bills for fuel. Finally, the generators of a hydro station can be brought into service very quickly; this is very important in an interconnected system, for their power can be delivered within minutes and quickly synchronized with the rest of the supply system. This characteristic makes hydro stations very suitable for meeting peak loads.

[11] **Because of the large capital sums involved, the rate of interest has a profound influence on the construction and operation of power stations.**

The Distribution of Hydroelectricity Generation A general distinction can be made between hydroelectric schemes based on low or moderate falls of less than 200 feet in a large catchment area with a very great discharge and those based on limited catchments and high heads. The former are generally found in the middle courses of large river systems and are frequently associated with multipurpose schemes, while the latter are located on headstreams in mountainous areas. For both types, the best geographic conditions occur where streams are fed from a heavy, well-distributed rainfall, where runoff is slow, and where there is considerable natural storage. A heavy forest cover and the presence of lakes are therefore distinctly advantageous, but more importantly, sites must occur within economic transmission distance of main load centers. Hence the greatest development of hydroelectricity generation is found on the margins of those mountainous regions of the Northern Hemisphere experiencing humid temperate climates; here physical and economic conditions closely approach the optimum. Outside these areas only certain parts of the U.S.S.R. and Japan can show a comparable degree of development, although similar physical and climatic regions of the Southern Hemisphere such as Tasmania and New Zealand have also made considerable use of their resources for developing hydroelectricity. Where the national territory or the effectively occupied territory closely falls within such areas, the share of hydroelectricity in total power generation can rise to very high levels; in Norway over 95 per cent of all generating capacity is installed in hydro stations, and in Switzerland over 90 per cent. Other countries with a very large proportion of their total generating capacity in hydroelectric installations include Canada, Sweden, Italy, Austria, Japan, and France (Table 13-1). Several of these countries are deficient in mineral fuels, and hydroelectric stations have been developed to meet base-load duties; generation usually takes place within easy transmission distance of the main centers of demand, and in many of these countries the physical conditions that have encouraged the generation of hydroelectricity have also encouraged the development of large power-consuming industries, particularly pulp and paper.

In most Alpine countries, in Norway, and in Japan, development has typically taken the form of small stations with high or moderate heads. Such stations are relatively inexpensive to construct, and are very suitable for situations in which hydroelectric potential is disseminated among a large number of streams; this type of development is also found in the southeastern states of the United States. In Sweden, in Canada, and generally in the United States, development has more usually been based on large or very large discharges with low heads.

Nevertheless, even in countries in which hydroelectricity accounts for a very large part of total electric energy production, the share of hydroelectricity is tending to decline, and thermoelectric power is becoming increasingly important. This is partly because of the considerations mentioned above, but it also arises from the fact that the most accessible and most easily developed sites are already being used; further development of hydroelectricity will involve substantially higher costs. In Switzerland almost one-half of the total potential for hydroelectricity development is already harnessed, and the remainder will probably be developed within the next fifteen to twenty years.[12] In Norway the best sites in the most populous parts of the country (the southeast) are already harnessed, and although only about one-quarter of the total potential is at present utilized, the remaining sites lie on the scantily populated west coast. Similar conditions are found in Austria and in Sweden; in the latter country the main load centers lie in the central and southern parts of the country, while the best sites lie in the north, within the Arctic Circle. Japan also faces difficulties, for a considerable proportion of its total potential has already been developed, and new schemes are likely to prove extremely costly. In both Canada and the United States there has been a slow decline in the share of hydroelectricity in total power capacity over the past two decades, largely in consequence of the inordinate increase in the demand for power.

Multipurpose Projects

The generation of hydroelectricity is only one way of utilizing water resources; in the present century it has become increasingly realized that it is possible to combine several methods of utilizing water resources in large multipurpose projects. Most such projects represent a very substantial investment, and may include allocations for irrigation, navigation, afforestation, and even industrial development, as well as for power generation. It is frequently very difficult to assess the direct return from each separate section of such schemes, which have to be judged as a whole in the light of the social achievements desired; thus in some schemes the proceeds from the sale of electric power may be used to recover the costs of irrigation, as in Australia's Snowy Mountains scheme, or navigation may be subsidized, as in certain schemes in the North American continent. Political considerations assume a vital importance in decisions to implement multipurpose schemes and national prestige may also be an important factor.

Although the coordinated development of

[12] Organisation for European Economic Cooperation, *The Production, Transmission and Distribution of Electricity in Europe,* Paris, 1957, p. 66.

As Japan's more accessible sites for the generation of hydroelectricity have already been developed, the country has had to turn to the more remote parts of the Japanese alps to meet its expanding demands for electric power. This winter view is of the dam on the Kurobe River, a project financed by the World Bank.

the water resources of a major drainage basin was first undertaken in the United States—the Tennessee Valley Authority (TVA) may justly be regarded as the world's first great multipurpose river project—the centrally planned and the underdeveloped economies have become the most ardent supporters of the multipurpose project as a means of stimulating national economic development. Thus the Soviet Union has planned to convert the Volga into a chain of lakes; China has an ambitious scheme for controlling the Hwang Ho River; India has its Damodar valley and Bakhra Nangal schemes; Indonesia has its Asahan project in north Sumatra; Egypt has the High Aswān project; and Ghana has the Volta River scheme. It is by no means certain, however, that these grandiose projects, with their egregiously large demands on national resources of capital, skill, and foreign exchange, represent the best way of encouraging economic growth, and some now appear unlikely to be completed as originally planned.[13]

With the increasing popularity of multi-

[13] The International Bank for Reconstruction and Development (the World Bank) considered that the High Aswān project would absorb a disproportionately large

purpose schemes, the large single-purpose hydroelectric development is becoming rather uncommon;[14] at the same time this popularity has led to an increase in the interest of the state in electricity production, for the numerous conflicts of interest that inevitably arise in an economy in the implementation of such schemes can only be resolved by an official body. In the United States the rapidly increasing demand for water for all purposes, and in particular for further industrial expansion, exerts considerable pressure making for the extension of multipurpose projects. Indeed, so great is the present rate of increase in demand that the once seemingly inexhaustible water resources of the country will be severely taxed in the not distant future, and it appears inevitable that further large works will be necessary in most of the major drainage basins of the country in the future. Australia also, among highly developed economies, must undertake further multipurpose projects if it is to sustain its present high rate of population growth and economic development.

Largely in consequence of its multipurpose schemes, the United States has become the world's largest producer of hydroelectricity. The promotion of multipurpose schemes has been pursued by several American administrations in the present century, but such schemes received considerably enhanced emphasis during the Thirties, a development that was to prove of inestimable value during World War II.

The distribution of hydroelectric capacity over the country is very uneven, being concentrated in the West and particularly in the Pacific Northwest (see Fig. 13-2, p. 350). This reflects, of course, the comparative aridity of much of the area, the shortage of mineral fuels (although several Western states are now fast becoming important producers of petroleum), and, perhaps not least, the political power of the West, which has enabled it to obtain large Federal allocations. The humid East, however, possesses by far the world's best-known multipurpose project, despite the fact that the East contains no single engineering work comparable with the great dams on the Colorado and the Columbia. The international standing of this project, TVA, rests primarily on its deliberate creation as an agency for the rehabilitation of an area where per capita incomes were distinctly below the national level; given this genesis, it is hardly surprising that TVA has exerted a tremendous appeal for underdeveloped countries, several of which have attempted to establish comparable schemes.

The main features of TVA, now in its third decade of existence, have become so well known as to require little comment. Its main aims were to produce hydroelectric power, to improve navigation, and to alleviate flooding, by means of a number of generally small dams with low heads placed across the Tennessee River and its headstreams (Fig. 13-3). It has been conspicuously successful in realizing its goals. Commercial freight traffic on the Tennessee River has increased faster than on any other river, domestic consumption of power has risen substantially faster than in the country as a whole, and more than 6 billion dollars

share of Egypt's resources for the next twenty-five years; moreover, the increase in the irrigated area that will result from the high dam will barely keep pace with population increase. In the aftermath of the Suez crisis that speedily followed the withdrawal of the offer of American aid, Egypt announced its intention of proceeding with the project unaided; then, in 1959, Egypt and the U.S.S.R. signed a new agreement for the construction and finance of the dam. Work has been slow, however, and against Russian protests, much Swedish drilling equipment has been acquired by the Egyptians to speed up operations.

[14] The world's largest hydroelectricity station, a single-purpose scheme, is located at Bratsk on the Angara River in the U.S.S.R., and was to have a capacity of 4,500 megawatts. The plant took more than ten years to build, and work ceased when generating capacity reached 3,800 megawatts. Whether the extra generators to raise capacity to the planned figure will be installed now appears uncertain. The size of individual generating units in a large hydroelectric station is only about half of that now possible in thermal stations, because of the problem of "cavitation" in water turbines.

have been invested in riverside industrial plants and in terminals (between 1933, when TVA was created, and 1960).

A considerable change, however, has occurred in the pattern of energy production by TVA; once primarily a producer of hydroelectric power, in 1961 it had some 65 per cent of its generating capacity in thermoelectric plants. This change occurred as a result of the emergencies of World War II and the Korean conflict. The former produced a greatly enhanced demand for power, which could only be met in the short period by an extension of thermoelectric facilities. A second and considerably greater increase in thermal plant construction took place after 1951; this was closely associated with the enlarged activities of the Atomic Energy Commission at Oak Ridge and at its new plant at Paducah, Kentucky. Between 1951 and 1958 installed generating capacity more than trebled, reaching a level of over 10.2 million kilowatts in the latter year. Hand in hand with all this change in production has come a corresponding important change in the consumption of TVA power: although consumption by farms, residences, and industrial establishments has continued to increase, TVA has mainly become a supplier of power for defense industries, a development quite unforeseen at the time of its

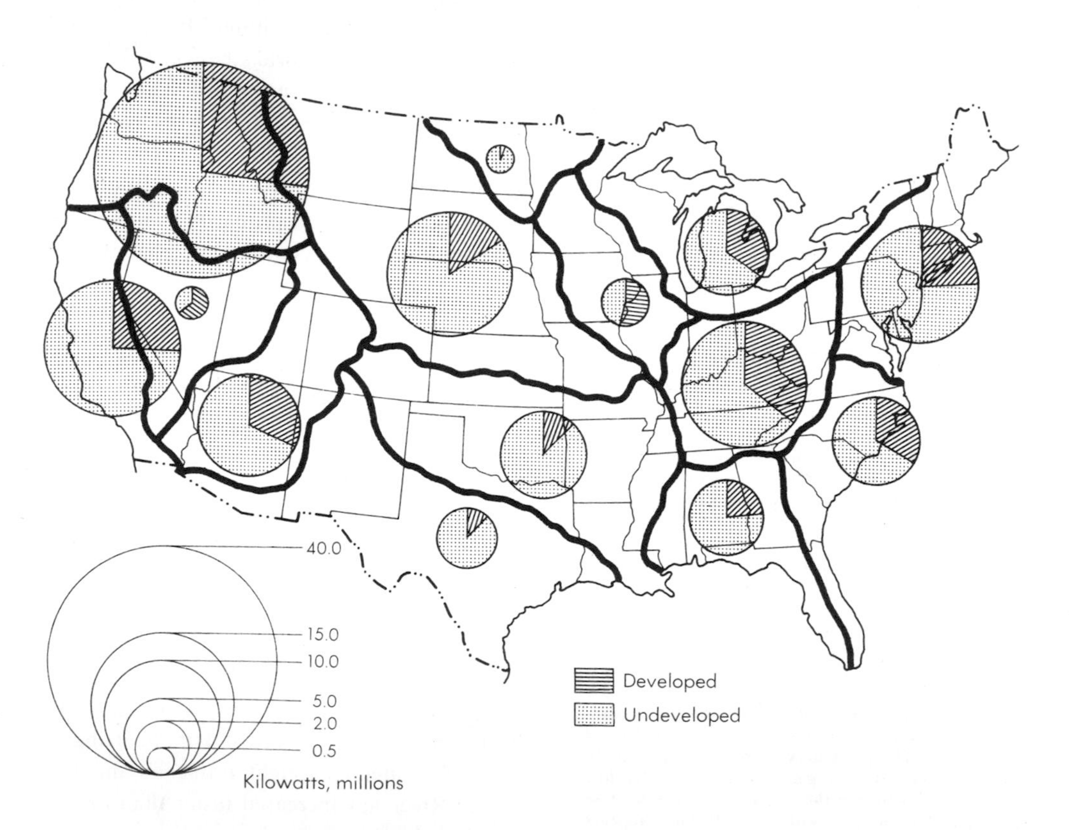

Fig. 13-2 Potential and developed hydroelectric capacity by regions. The great hydroelectric potential of the Pacific Northwest is obvious. (Federal Power Commission.)

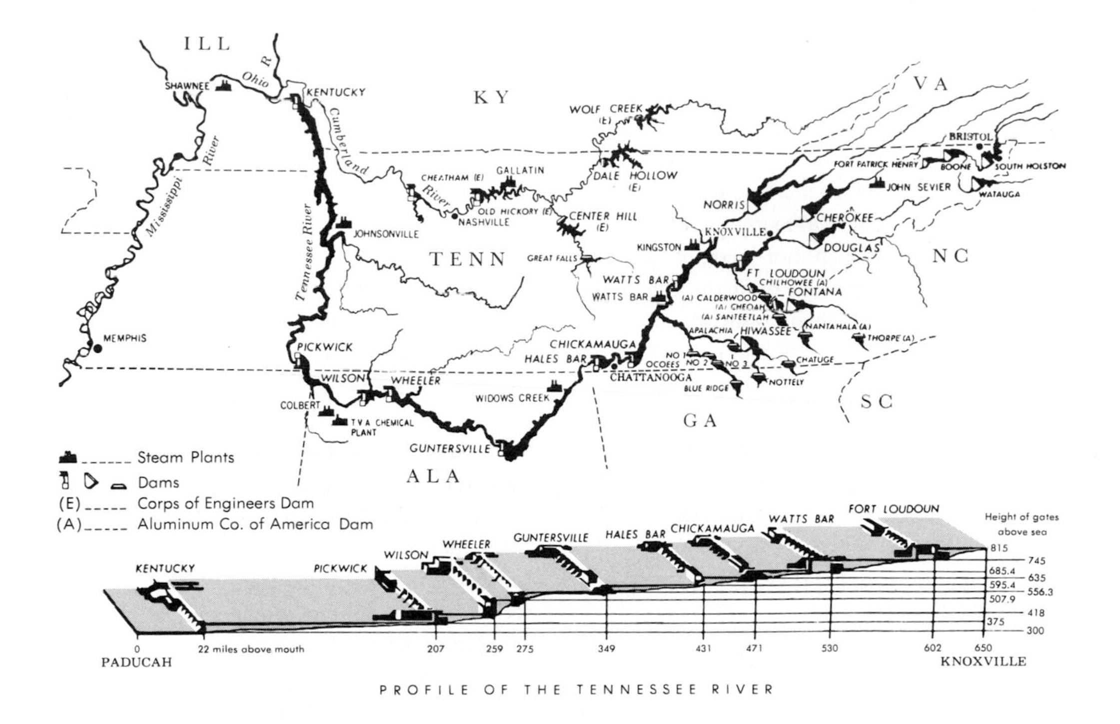

Fig. 13-3 Network of TVA dams and plants along the Tennessee River.
The Tennessee Valley Authority, born of the Great Depression, is still the world's best-known multipurpose water resources scheme. (Tennessee Valley Authority.)

creation. It has also become a completely self-financing organization, and is no longer dependent on Federal allocations.

The Columbia River possesses the greatest potential waterpower resources in the North American continent, only a small fraction of which are at present developed despite the existence of the great Grand Coulee, Chief Joseph, and Bonneville dams. The fuller harnessing of the Columbia is now possible, however, as result of an agreement with Canada in 1961; in return for constructing storage dams on the headwater of the Columbia and Kootenay Rivers, Canada is to be compensated by a share of the power that will be generated in new stations located on the American sections of these rivers.

Unlike the schemes of the Pacific Northwest, which are primarily for purposes of power production and irrigation, the St. Lawrence Seaway project, the second great example of cooperation, produces power incidentally; its primary purpose is to make the Great Lakes accessible to oceangoing vessels. The Iroquois, Long Sault, and St. Lawrence power dams are primarily intended to drown the International Rapids and to keep the level of the St. Lawrence in the "power pool" constant during the navigation season. A major multipurpose project that has long been debated but still has not come to fruition[15] is the creation of a Missouri Valley Authority. This has been the subject of

[15] **The long-discussed St. Lawrence Seaway project finally became reality only when the Canadian government made it clear that it was prepared to undertake the whole operation itself.**

a number of conflicting proposals. These, however, have mainly concerned the methods of flood control and the use of irrigation water rather than questions of power generation.

It appears inevitable that multipurpose schemes will continue to increase in the future, and it is almost certain that many will be undertaken in Africa, though not perhaps in the forms at present proposed. Both the U.S.S.R. and China have large schemes under construction or in advanced stages of planning; China's great Hwang Ho River control scheme is intended to be the precursor of the still more ambitious Yangtze scheme, which may well develop into the world's most stupendous multipurpose project. However, it is highly unlikely that such multipurpose schemes will enlarge the share of hydroelectricity in total electric energy production.

Thermoelectricity

Though less spectacular than hydro installations, thermal power plants are immensely more important in the world as a whole. When more power is needed in a hurry, as during a war emergency, the construction of new thermal plants is the only solution possible. A capital cost that is about half that of a hydro installation of comparable capacity, and sometimes less, and a short construction time are perhaps the greatest advantages of thermal power stations. Their location, moreover, is not subject to exacting physical controls as is the case with hydroelectric plants; they can be situated at main load centers and have their fuel carried to them.

Their main disadvantages are a low efficiency, only about one-quarter of the potential energy in the fuel finally being made available in the form of electric energy, and higher operating costs than for a hydroelectric station of comparable capacity. In practice, however, these disadvantages are largely discounted by the extreme suitability of thermal power stations for consuming the substantial quantities of small, broken coal and dust produced by modern mechanized mining. The "cyclone furnace," one of a number of technical innovations that have recently revolutionized the costs of producing electricity from thermal stations, burns pulverized fuel; it is also possible to consume the "slurry" from the coal-washing plants now installed at almost all modern collieries.

The New Technology of Thermoelectricity Production Throughout the present century, the cost of producing a unit of electric power from thermal stations has been progressively lowered as a result of improvements in fuel technology and in generating equipment. These economies have resulted essentially from increases in the scale of operations. Since the end of World War II new metallurgical techniques have permitted the construction of thermal stations that have carried this principle further.

Before World War II steam pressures of less than 500 pounds per square inch were common in boilers of thermal generating stations; at present, pressures of up to 2,000 pounds per square inch are quite usual. These advances in boiler design have been matched by increases in the size of generating sets. In many parts of the United States, the small size of the supply system limits the size of the generating set that can be employed, but in the national networks of some European countries such as Britain the size of units can be as large as technical considerations permit.[16] In the United States utilities are generally prepared to install units of up to 10 per cent of the total capacity of the system, and on this basis it

[16] In practice the limit in Britain is set by the maximum permissible single load on British roads, that is, 160 long tons.

would be possible for Britain to install units of 2,000 megawatts, that is, not greatly inferior to the installed capacity of the Grand Coulee. Units of this size are still some way off, but the increase in size of the average generating set in countries at a high level of development has been very large. Modern 100-megawatt turboalternators attain a thermal efficiency of almost 33 per cent, compared with 26 per cent or so realized by the 30-megawatt sets common before World War II; at High Marnham, Nottinghamshire, the British Central Electricity Board operates a 550-megawatt set, the largest single-shaft set in the world, an operation that attains an efficiency of almost 37 per cent.[17]

These enormous new turboalternator units have reduced the capital cost of producing a kilowatt of electric power to almost half of that in 1939; not only have they greatly improved the competitive position of thermoelectricity vis-à-vis hydroelectricity, but they have also been responsible for a considerably reduced emphasis on plans for the production of electric power from atomic plants. These new turboalternators have also had far-reaching consequences for the location of thermal stations.

The Siting and Location of Thermal Generating Stations In an analysis of industrial activity it is often convenient to distinguish between what might be called locational and what might be called siting factors. The former include those considerations that influence the general area preferred for such activity in relation to the economy as a whole. The latter include those that govern the choice of site within the area selected; occasionally siting requirements may be so exacting that if they cannot be met within the preferred area, they compel the examination of areas originally regarded as less attractive.

In practice the siting of thermal power stations, especially of the largest kind, is fairly closely circumscribed. It is possible to erect such stations near main load centers, and many are so located. It is, however, becoming increasingly difficult to find suitable sites at main load centers, and it is virtually certain that in any highly developed economy the proposed construction of a new station of the largest size in a thickly populated urban area will encounter considerable opposition from many interests. A large thermal station requires a considerable site area, whose magnitude is also closely affected by such considerations as the possibility of future extensions, whether or not use has to be made of cooling towers, the methods of transporting and handling fuel, and disposal of ashes.

For the operation of steam turbines a large and continuous supply of water is necessary; this may be withdrawn from a river or lake and is discharged at a higher temperature. As a station uses about 50 gallons of water per hour per kilowatt generated, total water requirements are prodigious. Thus there may be considerable conflict with other users of water; there is also a danger that the use of a small stream or water body where seasonal variations in flow or tidal influences are present may result in warmer discharge waters being recirculated, thus causing a loss of efficiency. Such difficulties can be overcome by the use of cooling towers down which warm water is sprayed against an ascending current of air; only a small evaporation loss has to be made good, and as water is used over and over again, a large power station can be adequately served by a mains-water reticulation system. A large power station dependent on mains water may require two or three such towers; reaching almost 300 feet in height and of a hyperbolic-

[17] **A 1,000-megawatt set is on order for a Philadelphia generating station at the time of writing; this however, is a two-shaft, or two-stage, plant.**

curved elevation, these towers have become very distinctive features of the landscape of many industrial areas in highly developed economies.

As a 250-megawatt station needs about 2,500 tons of coal per day, of which 10 to 20 per cent may be left as ashes after combustion, a considerable area is needed for coal handling and for ash disposal. Although certain uses have been found for treated ashes, such as topdressing for pastures, the main method of ash disposal at present is to dispose of it either in dumps or at sea. Elaborate precautions have to be taken to prevent the discharge of fine grit, soot, or sulfur into the atmosphere; nevertheless, such emissions can cause a considerable nuisance in urban areas and may damage crops in agricultural districts.[18]

For these reasons large thermal stations located near their load centers tend to be situated on alluvial marshland bordering a river or canal which can provide both water and a means of fuel and ash transport. Such land is largely unsuitable for residential purposes and is of limited agricultural value. However, the attraction of the load center has become considerably less since World War II. In the United States, Britain, West Germany, the U.S.S.R., and several other countries, the preferred location for new thermal stations is at, or in close proximity to, the source of fuel supply, that is, the coalfields.

This change of emphasis in location has followed from the two technological advances already examined—the development of long-distance high-voltage transmission and the substantial increase in the size of turboalternator sets; it is cheaper to transmit electric power in large quantities by high-voltage line than to move coal overland to load centers. In the United States the greatest proliferation of large new thermal plants has taken place along the Ohio valley, which enjoys the advantage of cheap coal transport from the Appalachian and Eastern Interior fields; this development has been closely linked with a remarkable expansion of chemical and metallurgical industries. In Britain the Trent valley plays a similar role, being situated in close proximity to the most productive and lowest-cost coal-producing district in the country. In West Germany the Ruhr and in the U.S.S.R. the Donbas and the Moscow-Tula fields exercise a similar attraction. In areas where coal can be produced very cheaply, and particularly in the United States, it would appear that there is still considerable room for further concentration of power stations in areas within easy reach of coalfields. Among countries at a high level of economic development the only conspicuous exception to the pattern of large new stations located on or near the coalfields appears in Belgium, which is meeting its increasing demand for electric power through the construction of a number of relatively small and lightly connected stations located at load centers. The small size of the country and the fact that electricity supply is in the hands of a number of companies may help account for this difference, but strategic considerations also may be involved.

Other types of thermal power plant require little comment. In areas where petroleum or natural gas is cheap and plentiful, one of these fuels may replace coal in the furnaces of large stations, and for small stations serving minor towns or country areas, the diesel unit has many advantages. A recent development is the use of gas turbines coupled to generators in "packaged" units; these can be conveniently distributed throughout the supply system to meet local peak loads, for they deliver power

[18] **The decline of the horticultural industry of the Lea valley in Greater London, once Britain's principal hothouse area, has been partly attributed to the crop losses caused by the expansion of power stations in the area.**

very quickly. Remote-controlled units of this kind have proved very successful in Britain, which has relatively very little hydroelectric capacity and limited opportunity for its installation.

ATOMIC ENERGY

The main use of atomic energy has been, and will probably long continue to be, for military purposes. Commercial uses have so far been very largely in the nature of by-products; these uses include the manufacture of radioactive isotopes for agriculture, industry, science, and medicine and the production of a small quantity of electric energy. It seems fairly clear that the contribution of atomic energy to the supply of electric energy will increase, even though considerable time may have to elapse before all the claims that have been made for this new source of power become fully justified.

It is possible that in the future electric energy may be generated directly by the periodic reversal of a stream of charged particles produced by an atomic reactor. However, it needs to be emphasized that at present all atomic power stations are essentially thermal plants; the turboalternators employed are largely standard equipment, and the sole purpose of the atomic reactor is to produce heat for steam raising. It follows, therefore, that many of the considerations that govern the employment and siting of other thermal power plants apply also in the case of atomic power plants.

All existing atomic power plants produce heat by the fission of U-235, one of the isotopes of uranium. Atomic reactors, however, may operate either on natural uranium, in which both U-235 and U-238 are present, or on enriched fuels, that is, pure U-235 or natural uranium with the addition of a substantial quantity of U-235. U-238 cannot sustain a chain reaction, the mechanism by which the fission process is sustained; it absorbs neutrons to produce plutonium, which, though employed in military uses, has not yet been found suitable for use by itself in commercial power plants. Another man-made element that may have future commercial application in atomic power plants is U-233, produced from thorium.

About a dozen types of atomic power plant were in use in 1961, and the number seems certain to increase; broadly, however, the main distinction is between those that operate on natural uranium, the so-called "slow" reactors, and the fast reactors and "breeder" reactors that operate on enriched fuels. The first type has received particular emphasis in Britain, where the commercial production of electricity from atomic plants has made greatest progress, while the United States has been more concerned with the development of technically more advanced fast-reactor types. This difference has arisen from the contrasting situation of the two countries in relation to supplies of fissionable material and to other sources of energy.

In Britain supplies of enriched material have been largely derived from the United States, a dependence that could prove hazardous, and, moreover, have been largely reserved for military purposes. In view of the importance of Middle East oil in meeting Britain's energy needs and the postwar difficulties encountered in raising coal output, a policy of pressing forward with the expansion of relatively simple atomic power plants operating on natural uranium produced within the British Commonwealth was considered essential (Fig. 13-4).[19] Although the first commercial production of electricity in Britain was that supplied to the

[19] **As already noted, the rapid expansion of petroleum production and the emergence of new low-cost producers removed much of the logic from this plan.**

Fig. 13-4 Atomic power stations in Great Britain. Coastal locations have been preferred for Britain's nuclear power electricity generating stations. Dounreay is an experimental fast "breeder" reactor, for which an isolated location in a region of sparse population was considered essential.

British grid system by the Windscale, Cumberland, plant, this was largely incidental to the production of plutonium for military purposes; the world's first atomic power station intended expressly for the production of electricity came into operation in 1957 at Calder Hall.

The United States, on the other hand, not only possesses a plentiful supply of enriched fuels from the diffusion plants of the Atomic Energy Commission, but also has an embarrassment of riches in the form of alternative sources of energy (Fig. 13-5). Thus there has been no urgency for the construction of atomic stations that would replace the conventional sources of fuel in thermal stations, and much of the expenditure in the United States on atomic power has been in research on, and construction of, advanced fast reactors, such as that employed at the Shippingport (Pittsburgh) plant.

Atomic power plants are extremely costly, and it can scarcely be doubted that considerations of national prestige have also been involved in their construction. Slow reactors require particularly massive works of civil engineering, and in fast reactors problems arising from corrosion and high temperatures become very formidable. Atomic power stations produce highly poisonous waste products whose disposal is not only difficult but very expensive, and elaborate precautions have to be taken to protect workers from toxic radiations; the inherent dangers in their operation were clearly demonstrated in the 1957 fire at the Windscale plant in Britain which necessitated the confiscation and destruction of milk supplies over a large area following the contamination of pastures with radioactive material. As noxious industries,[20] therefore, their siting has to be very carefully considered; in Britain, coastal situations well removed from any large centers of habitation have been preferred.

On the other hand, atomic stations allow a certain measure of latitude in their general location, for sites can be considered in relation to the main load centers of the supply system. Having no problem of fuel supply—only a few hundred pounds or so of uranium per year are necessary to keep them in operation, so that fuel-transport costs are negligible—Britain's atomic power plants have a marked peripheral distribution. This appears a comparatively

[20] **Industries which emit poisonous fumes or vapors or in which workers come into contact with poisonous or injurious substances. In most countries they are legally defined.**

Fig. 13-5 Atomic energy establishments.
The Ohio, Tennessee, and Columbia valleys—areas where cheap electric power is available from conventional sources—have been preferred for the location of atomic energy establishments in the United States.

small advantage to set against the very high capital costs and large interest burden; moreover, the disparity between conventional thermal stations and atomic plants in operational costs has tended to enlarge with the development of successively larger coal-fired stations. However, economies of scale should present themselves with larger atomic plants; existing plants are of small capacity compared with the largest coal-burning plants, but stations of 1,000 megawatts or 2,000 megawatts capacity are possible in the future and should deliver electric energy at a cost per unit roughly equivalent to that from the most efficient thermal stations at present.

Such stations would have to operate with a very high load factor, 75 per cent or more, and their employment might necessitate that existing thermal plants surrender part of their own base load to maintain the atomic giants at or near their optimum level of efficiency. Western European countries, in which coal stocks have become an economic and political embarrassment, can scarcely view this with equanimity, and so it is expected that development of large atomic plants will be protracted. The European Atomic Energy Committee (Euratom), the common nuclear organization of the six countries of the EEC, doubts that by 1965 more than 3,500 to 4,000 megawatts of nuclear capacity will exist in the Common Market countries, supplying perhaps about 3 to 5 per cent of total electricity requirements. Of this about half will probably be located in France, where for reasons of military and political prestige there has been a greater emphasis on the construction of atomic power stations than in other EEC countries. Britain's atomic program reflects the sense of urgency generated by the Suez crisis; by 1965 Britain may have about 5,000 to 6,000 megawatts of nuclear capacity, capable of supplying about 12 per cent of requirements of electric energy. In the United States, it is unlikely that even by this time nuclear power will supply as much as 1 per cent of the electricity output of the United States; in this regard it is significant that most of the existing establishments for the production of atomic material and for its utilization are situated in those parts of the country where electric power is relatively cheap, that is, in the Tennessee and Ohio valleys and the Pacific Northwest.

In view of the difficulties being encountered by countries at an advanced level of economic development in utilizing atomic energy for commercial purposes, the idea of rapid transformation of underdeveloped economies through the agency of atomic power appears a myth. Moreover, the failure of many of the advanced countries to implement plans for atomic power made a decade or so ago has led to a marked overproduction of uranium, and when contracts of the United States and British governments with their suppliers expire, a considerable drop in the price of natural uranium appears likely. In 1960, the OEEC doubted that even by 1975 atomic power plants would provide as much as 10 per cent of Europe's total energy requirements, on the most optimistic assumptions, and believed that a figure of about 5 per cent is much more probable. All the evidence suggests, therefore, that the rapid rise of atomic energy to a position of major importance in the world economy is likely to be deferred until the last quarter of the present century.

SELECTED REFERENCES

Barnea, J.: "Economic Implications of Electrification in Underdeveloped Economies," *Economic Development and Cultural Change,* vol. 2, pp. 371–379, 1954.

Bolton, D. J.: *Electrical Engineering Economics,* Chapman & Hall, Ltd., London, 1959.

Church, Martha: *Spatial Organization of Electric Power Territories in Massachusetts,* University of Chicago, Research Papers in Geography, no. 67, Chicago, 1960.

"Electric Power in Japan Today," *Oriental Economist,* vol. 26, pp. 191–203, 1958.

James, J. R., et al.: "Land Use and the Changing Power Industry in England and Wales," *Geographical Journal,* vol. 127, pp. 286–309, 1961.

Mounfield, P. R.: "The Location of Nuclear Power Stations in the United Kingdom," *Geography,* vol. 46, pp. 139–155, 1961.

Organisation for Economic Cooperation and Development: *Fifteenth Survey of Electric Power Equipment,* Paris, 1962.

Organisation for European Economic Cooperation: *The Electricity Supply Industry in Europe, 10th Enquiry,* Paris, 1960.

———: *The Electricity Supply Industry in Europe, 12th Enquiry,* Paris, 1962.

———: *The Production, Transmission and Distribution of Electricity in Europe,* Paris, 1957.

Political and Economic Planning: *British Fuel and Power Industries,* London, 1947, pp. 147–219.

Raitt, W. L.: "The Changing Pattern of Norwegian Hydroelectric Development," *Economic Geography,* vol. 34, pp. 127–144, 1958.

Rawstron, E. M.: "Distribution and Location of Steam Driven Power Stations in Great Britain," *Geography,* vol. 36, pp. 249–262, 1951.

United Kingdom, Central Office of Information: *Nuclear Energy in Britain,* H. M. Stationery Office, London, 1957.

United States Congress, Joint Committee on Atomic Energy: *Development, Growth and State of the Atomic Energy Industry,* 1958.

Chapter 14

THE IRON AND STEEL INDUSTRY

As an economy attains a higher level of development the metal-making and metal-working industries become progressively more important. The base of the complex superstructure of the metal industries is the iron and steel industry; not only does it account for by far the largest share of total metal production, but the fabrication and working of every other metal and the harnessing of every source of fuel and power are impossible without its aid. Despite the rapid growth of metal substitutes over the past two decades, it is still true that the higher the level of economic development, the greater the per capita consumption of iron and steel. Nothing exerts such an attraction to the politicians responsible for the national development programs of underdeveloped countries as a domestic iron and steel industry or some portion of one.

Nature of the World Industry The iron and steel industry is essentially a processing industry;[1] it does not include the assembly of finished products which form the province of a wide range of engineering industries, although certain of the larger iron- and steel-producing companies may have substantial interests in such related activities. Thus, the Bethlehem Steel Corporation is one of the largest shipbuilders of the United States, and the British steel company Dorman Long is well known for bridge building. Some of the products of the industry, such as wire or nails, enter directly into final consumption. Others enter consumption indirectly; strip is used in tremendous quantities by the food-canning industry, and sheet steel is one of the main raw materials of consumer-durable goods such as automobiles and electric appliances. A large proportion of the industry's output, however—girders, plates, rails, hoops, and angles—forms the raw material of the capital-goods industries. The industry thus occupies a key position in modern industrial society, and its

[1] See p. 264.

fortunes are closely related to the condition of the economy as a whole. The almost complete absence of the capital-goods industries and the consumer-durable industries in economies at a low level of development is a powerful obstacle to the establishment of an iron and steel industry.

Except during the occasional interruptions resulting from economic depression, and most noticeably during the interwar period, world steel output has climbed steadily over the past three-quarters of a century, and in 1961 closely approached a level of 400 million tons per annum (Fig. 14-1 and Table 14-1). This increase, however, has largely resulted from an expansion in output in economies already at a high level of development. Until about 1870 Britain dominated the industry, but after that date the rapid growth of the industry in the United States carried that country into the premier position, which it has held ever since. Nevertheless, for a time the United States was closely challenged by Imperial Germany, which reached its greatest relative importance as an iron and steel producer in 1900, and after World War II a new rival appeared in the U.S.S.R. Russian steel production grew rapidly during the period between the two world wars, and since 1945 has continued to expand at a very high rate. Perhaps even more remarkable, however, is the rapid growth of steel production in Japan, which by 1960 was producing more than three times its peak World War II output; since 1950 China has also appeared as a major producer.

Requirements of the Industry Although iron is comparatively plentiful in the earth's crust, commercially workable ore deposits are far from common. This is because iron is a cheap metal, so that the iron content of the ore must be high to make mining worthwhile. Generally, an iron content of 50 per cent or more is economically desirable, although in Western Europe ores with an iron content substantially below this figure are extensively employed, and

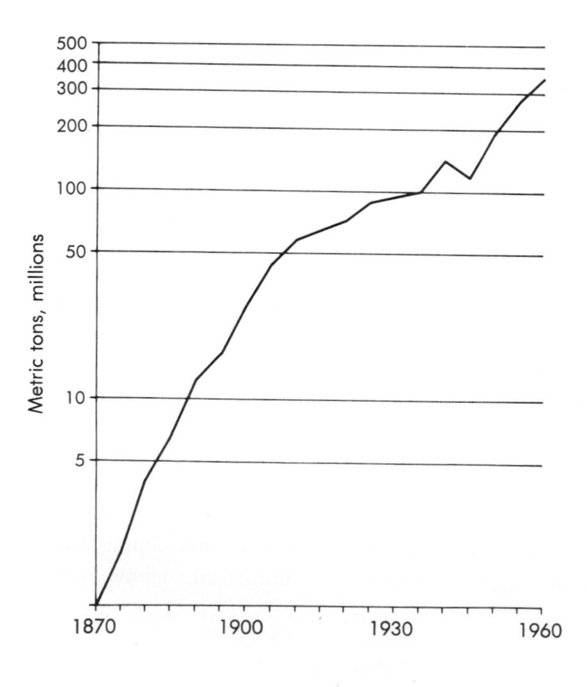

Fig. 14-1 World steel production, 1870–1960. Not until the eve of World War II was a world output of 100 million tons of steel attained, but a further 100 million tons was added in little more than a decade. The very high postwar rate of growth is striking. (British Iron and Steel Federation.)

Table 14-1

Production of Iron and Steel, 1963 (Million metric tons)

	PIG IRON AND FERROALLOYS	CRUDE STEEL*
United States†	63.4	100.1
Canada	5.6	7.4
EEC	53.5	73.7
West Germany	23.0	31.6
France	14.4	17.2
Italy	3.8	10.8
Belgium	7.0	7.6
Luxembourg	3.6	4.1
Netherlands	1.7	2.4
Britain	14.9	22.8
Austria	2.2	3.0
Sweden	1.9	3.8
Spain	1.9	1.9
Japan	20.4	31.5
India	6.7	6.0
Australia	3.6	4.3
South Africa	2.4	2.9
U.S.S.R.	58.8	80.3
Poland	5.4	8.0
Czechoslovakia	5.3	7.6
East Germany	2.2	3.6
Mainland China‡	22.0	15.0
WORLD TOTAL§	263.0	374.0

* Rolled steel output is usually about three-quarters that of crude steel; alloy, or special steels, normally account for less than 10 per cent of crude steel output except in time of emergency.

† The United States first produced over 100 million tons of crude steel in 1951, and again exceeded this figure between 1955 and 1957.

‡ Estimated 1961 figure.

§ Excluding mainland China.

SOURCE: United Nations, *Statistical Yearbook*, 1962; *Monthly Bulletin of Statistics*, May, 1964.

in Britain ores with an iron content as lean as 20 per cent are profitably worked. Moreover, the ore must occur in really large bodies; small high-grade deposits are now of little significance for the industry. Large high-grade ore deposits are eagerly sought after throughout the world; even if located in remote and difficult terrain, they well repay the provision of transport facilities to the coast, the erection of preliminary processing or beneficiation equipment, and the employment of specialized fleets of ore carriers. In their restless search for new sources of ore supply, the great iron and steel companies behave in a way reminiscent of the petroleum majors. In almost every major producing country of the noncommunist world the contribution of foreign ore to total ore consumption steadily enlarges; Africa and Latin America are of increasing importance as suppliers of ore both to the United States and to Europe.

The most desirable ores are those composed of magnetite (black iron oxide, or lodestone), which may possess an iron content exceeding 70 per cent, or of hematite (red iron oxide), in which 60 per cent may be exceeded. Large deposits of magnetite are not common; among the most important are those of northern Sweden and of the southern Urals in the U.S.S.R. Hematites are perhaps the most important of all the world's iron ores; they occur in large quantities in the upper lakes area of the United States, in eastern Canada and Labrador, in Venezuela, Brazil, and Chile, in the Ukraine, and in India (Table 14-2). In Europe ores of the yellow brown oxides, limonite and siderite, are of special importance, and in Britain iron carbonates were of vital significance in the early Industrial Revolution. Apart from possessing a satisfactory iron content, ores must also be physically suitable for use in the blast furnace, although it is increasingly common to subject ore to some preliminary treatment.

Of greater significance than a supply of iron ore is a source of fuel; at present the only way of smelting ores cheaply and in large quantities is by the use of coke. Coal capable of producing the massive coke needed in the blast furnace is by no means common, and many countries possessing large quantities of high-grade ore are hamstrung in their efforts to establish a domestic industry by lack of coking coal. Though also essential, limestone and a good water supply are so widely available that they are of little real significance.

But ultimately the most important requirement for the industry is not the availability of a source of fuel or of an ore supply. It can scarcely be overstressed that the iron and steel industry *is a capital-intensive industry;* the absence or scarcity of suitable domestic raw materials need not be an insuperable obstacle to its establishment, but a deficiency of capital certainly is. An iron and steel industry has to be organized in large enterprises if it is to exist at all, for only in this way is it possible to realize the economies of scale which make possible low-cost processing of tremendous quantities of raw materials of low value. Large-scale, low-cost production is only possible through a high investment per worker; China's millions of backyard workers could produce less than half the iron output of the country's limited number of modern blast furnaces. It is of course this fact, rather than a deficiency of suitable raw materials, which is proving such an obstacle to the development of the industry in underdeveloped economies. The size of unit that is necessary to ensure low-cost production is often far too large for such an economy to support.

THE CHANGING TECHNOLOGY OF IRON AND STEEL

Despite detailed improvements, particularly in materials handling, methods of making iron and steel remained essentially unchanged

Table 14-2

Production of Iron Ore, 1963 (Million metric tons)

	ORE PRODUCTION	AVERAGE METAL CONTENT
United States	73.4	54
Canada	27.6	55
West Germany	8.6	30
France	57.6	35
Luxembourg	7.0	30
Italy	1.0	50
Britain	15.6	30
Sweden	23.2	60
Spain	5.3	50
Austria	3.6	30
Mexico	1.9	60
Venezuela	11.6	62
Brazil	10.8	70
Chile	8.4	60
Peru	4.8	60
India	14.8	61
Japan	2.4	55
Malaysia	7.2	60
Philippines	1.2	55
Sierra Leone	1.9	60
Algeria	1.9	55
Morocco	1.2	55
Tunis	0.8	55
U.S.S.R.	135.8	60
Mainland China*	45.0	50–60
Australia	5.7	60
South Africa	4.4	60–65
WORLD TOTAL†	455.0	

* Estimated 1961 figure.
† Excluding mainland China.
SOURCE: United Nations, *Statistical Yearbook*, 1962; *Monthly Bulletin of Statistics*, May, 1964.

for well over half a century before 1939. Since the beginning of World War II, however, very considerable advances have been made, in which certain European producers such as Sweden, Austria, and Belgium have been prominent, and there has been a marked interest on the part of the great chemical companies in new methods of steelmaking. These new technologies, as with the great innovations of the past, must eventually lead to considerable changes in the location pattern of the industry. Indeed, the desirability of effecting such changes has been a major incentive promoting research into iron- and steelmaking; existing technologies not only result in considerable rigidity in the location of the industry in highly developed economies but also operate strongly against the establishment of the industry in countries at lower levels of economic development.

Iron and steel are both alloys of iron and other substances,[2] but the critical difference lies in the proportion of carbon present. In ordinary steels the proportion of carbon varies between 0.1 and 1.4 per cent; the higher the carbon content, the harder the steel, but above 1.4 per cent the metal becomes brittle. Cast iron has a carbon content of about 3 to 4 per cent, and where toughness and durability are required, it finds a wide application. The most valuable property of steel is its high tensile strength, and since cheap steel first became available about a century ago, it has been the principal structural material wherever high tensile strength is necessary. In many employments, however, steel faces powerful competition from a number of newer materials, such as aluminium, plastics, and fiber glass; even for structural purposes aluminum is increasingly preferred wherever lightness is an important consideration. In the early stages of the Industrial Revolution in Europe and in North America the present role of steel was filled by wrought iron, which has a very low carbon content; though relatively unimportant at the present, wrought iron has long been preferred for some uses in which high resistance to corrosion is as important as tensile strength, as in the manufacture of anchors and anchor chains. Specialty steels contain small proportions of other metals, which impart a wide variety of characteristics such as extreme toughness, springiness, ductility, and improved electric properties. Combined with iron in the form of ferroalloys which are added to molten steel, many of these minor metals are virtually the monopoly of one or two restricted areas and hence are of considerable strategic significance. Manganese, however, the most commonly used, is produced in a considerable number of countries.

There are three main operations in the production of finished steel; these are still well defined at present, but it appears highly likely that new processes now under development may telescope them into a single operation. The stages are (*a*) the reduction of metallic iron from its ores, which is effected in the blast furnace, (*b*) the conversion of iron into steel in the steelworks, for which a number of processes may be employed, either singly or in combination, and (*c*) further processing of raw steel in a wide variety of rolling and finishing mills. These three major operations may be carried on in close proximity with each other in integrated plants, or they may be geographically separated. Integrated plants offer the maximum opportunities for economies of scale and usually have coke ovens and ore-treatment units. Such a concentration of activities in one spot enables the fullest use of waste gases and permits the greatest conservation of heat.

[2] Absolute purity of a metal—or of any other substance—is impossible of attainment; the greater the degree of purity required, the higher the cost. For some purposes it is necessary to refine metals so that impurities amount to less than one part in ten thousand.

The Blast Furnace

The blast furnace, with associated stoves for preheating the air blast that gives the furnace its name, is the most fundamental and conspicuous piece of equipment of an integrated iron- and steelworks (Fig. 14-2). The blast furnace has several shortcomings; it is very expensive, requiring with its ancillary equipment an investment of up to $10 million; it needs coking coals, which are often in short supply, and it does not remove all the impurities in the ore, a fact of considerable significance for steelmaking. Its great advantage, however, is that it permits a *continuously* high rate of production; once a furnace is lit, it remains in operation until its refractory brick lining requires attention, a matter of some years. Modern blast furnaces may have a hearth diameter exceeding 30 feet and an internal height of 120 feet or more; such a furnace can produce upwards of 600,000 tons of pig iron per year, and there are some monsters that can produce more than 2,000 tons per day. Charging and tapping are highly mechanized and often automatically controlled, the gaseous products of combustion being used for heating the blast and for generating electricity.[3]

Since the end of World War II the productivity of blast furnaces has been greatly raised through the following techniques:

1. *Beneficiation and sintering.* These processes remove earthy and clayey material, increase the iron content by magnetic separation, convert the ore

[3] Though large producers of electricity, iron and steel plants can seldom meet more than about half their requirements, the balance being purchased from the local supply enterprise.

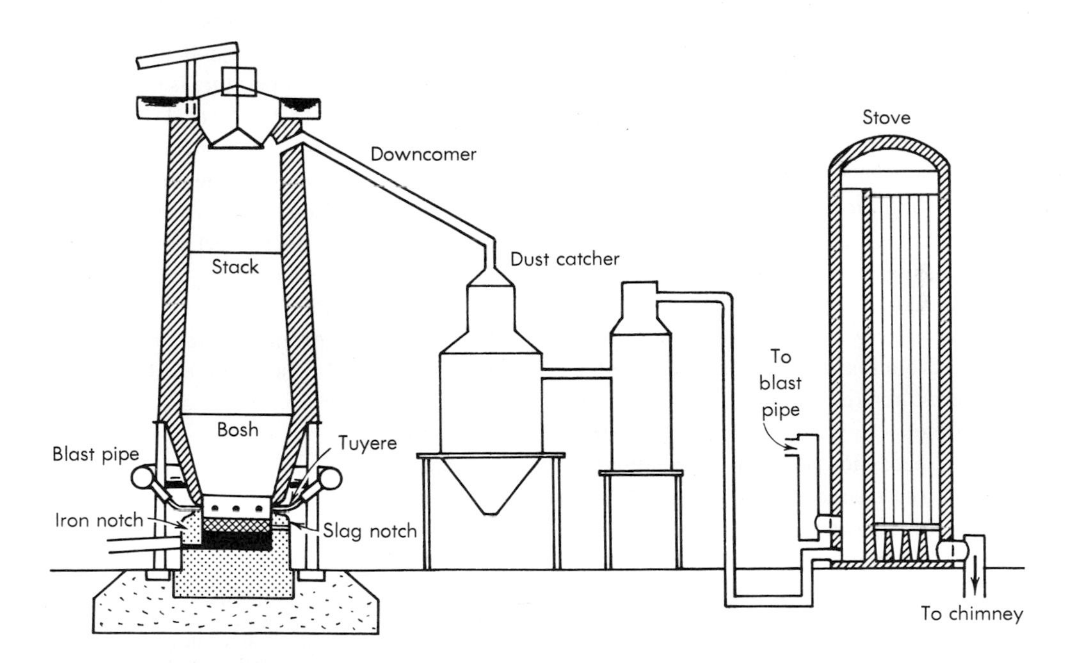

Fig. 14-2 The blast furnace.
Three stoves are usually "on gas" (heating up) while one heats the air blast.

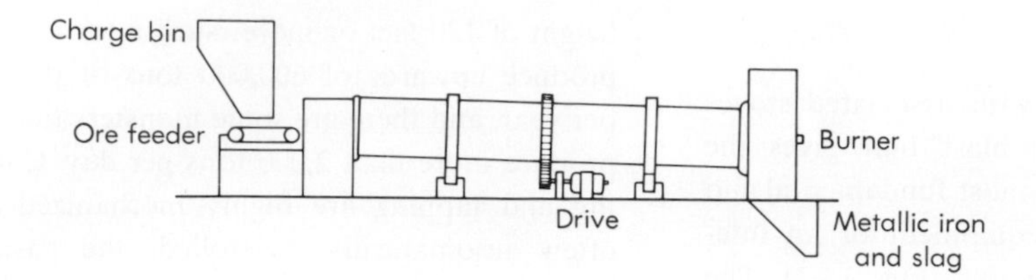

Fig. 14-3 The Krupp-Renn furnace can use many types of fuel.

into pieces of uniform size and quality, and add fluxing material. As coke is used to roast the ore in the sintering process, this takes place at the site of the blast furnace itself; preliminary beneficiation, however, is increasingly common for ore that has to be moved large distances, and is carried out at or near the mine, or at loading points on tidewater.

2. *High top pressure.* This technique, developed by the Republic Steel Corporation, restricts the escape of gases from the furnace top so that fewer iron particles are blown out. Although the field of application is still not clearly defined, all new blast furnaces have provision for pressurized tops, and where they can be employed substantial reductions in fuel consumption are possible.

3. *The oxygen blast.* The use of oxygen is revolutionizing steelmaking, and it seems assured of an increasingly important role in the blast furnace. Oxygen speeds the reaction, shortening the time the charge spends in the furnace.

4. *The injection of a spray of fuel oil into the blast pipe.* Through this technique the consumption of coke per ton of pig produced has been considerably reduced since 1940, and may be less than three-fifths of a ton under favorable conditions.

Nevertheless, the blast furnace remains essentially unchanged despite these detailed improvements, and while it will continue to produce the greater part of the world's output of new pig iron for some time to come, other methods of iron smelting are certain to become of increasing importance. The *low-shaft* blast furnace avoids the great crushing effect of the heavy charge of the normal blast furnace, thus making possible the use of soft cokes or even brown-coal coke. In various types of rotary furnaces, such as those employed in the R.N. process of Republic Steel and in the Krupp-Renn process, the temperature is not enough to melt the iron (Fig. 14-3). The coal or coke in the charge acts merely as a reducing agent, heat being supplied from an external source; the resulting sponge iron is separated magnetically from the gangue. Other direct reduction methods employ gaseous reducing agents, such as hydrogen and carbon monoxide, which are easily produced from natural gas or coal, magnetic methods also being used to separate the sponge iron.[4]

Essentially, most of these new processes represent a return to the "batch" method of production employed by the charcoal furnaces of the pre-Industrial Revolution era; the con-

[4] **Almost every major steel company in the free world has research and development units engaged in new methods of iron smelting, of which there are now a considerable number, for example, the H-iron process of Bethlehem Steel, the Swedish Wiberg-Soderfors process, the Mexican Hojalata-y-Lamina process, and the Esso-Little process of Jersey Standard.**

tinuity of output of the conventional blast furnace is sacrificed. They need very high-grade ores with few impurities, and can only be employed in small units. Nevertheless, several underdeveloped economies possess large quantities of such ores, lack hard coking coals, and find the necessity to restrict production to units of small size no disadvantage at all. In the United States particularly, such new processes offer to steel producers the possibility of exploiting new markets in the areas of expanding population in the West and Southwest, which, though deficient in coking coal, possess several other hydrocarbon fuels.

The Steelworks

Some pig iron may be used for castings, usually after being reheated in a cupola furnace, and a little may be made into wrought iron, but in most countries the greater part of the output of the blast furnace is steel pig destined for further processing in steelworks. Prior to the middle of the nineteenth century steel was almost a luxury product; the old "cementation" process in which bars of pure iron were heated up in contact with charcoal was improved by Huntsman's crucible process of 1740, but steel manufacture remained a slow and expensive business. Then followed the discoveries that made cheap steel possible, and that still form the basis of modern steelmaking. These were:

The *Bessemer process,* introduced in 1856; though usually attributed to the Englishman Henry Bessemer, it was discovered independently by ironmasters in both Western Europe and the United States. In this method of steelmaking a charge of molten pig is placed in a large pear-shaped vessel, or converter, which is then swung into a near-vertical position; a blast of air is then passed through the contents from a pipe in the base. The carbon is rapidly burned out in a violent reaction, the desired proportion being added later in the form of spiegeleisen.[5] The Bessemer process has many advantages; capital costs are modest, it has a high rate of output, and as it needs no extra fuel, its operating costs are low.

The *open-hearth process,* which dates from 1865, developed by Siemens and Martin. This process uses a regenerative furnace; the charge is placed in a large open bath, and the carbon is slowly burned out by passing a blast of hot air and gas over the surface of the charge. The heat of the waste gases is conserved or regenerated by being made to heat a firebrick "checkers," which in turn heats the blast of fresh incoming air. The capital cost of the open-hearth process is high and the rate of output low, although progressive increases in the size of hearths have partially offset this shortcoming; some furnaces have a capacity exceeding 300 tons. The process also needs extra fuel, formerly in the form of coal gas or producer gas; natural gas or fuel oil is usually employed at present. The long duration of the process allows fine control over the reaction, so that it has generally been preferred for high-quality steels. Another substantial advantage is that up to one-half of the charge can consist of scrap, so that the possibility of steelmaking is open to countries that possess little coking coal or ore; the disparity between pig-iron and crude-steel production shown in Table 14-1 is very largely a reflection of the importance of scrap in various producing countries.

The *electric furnace,* of which there are several types. Use of the electric furnace, introduced around the beginning of the present century, was once closely restricted by the limited availability of hydroelectricity, but it has become steadily more important as the

[5] **This substance also contains the simpler ferroalloys ferromanganese and ferrosilicon.**

output of electricity has expanded. The absence of combustion permits steels of very high quality to be produced, and the furnace is also employed for the manufacture of the more complex ferroalloys.[6] Such furnaces are increasingly used in combination with other processes.

While the blast furnace eliminates many impurities, there are some that remain unaffected, the most important of which is phosphorus. As originally developed, neither the Bessemer nor the open-hearth process could remove this substance, the presence of which renders steel brittle. Ores containing more than a trace of phosphorus were thus unsuitable for steelmaking. This shortcoming was remedied by the development of the *Gilchrist-Thomas,* or *basic, process,* in which the acid silica-firebrick lining of the converter or open-hearth furnace is replaced by one of dolomite, or magnesian limestone. This combines with any phosphorus present, and when saturated can be ground up to form a valuable fertilizer, Thomas meal. The basic process took long to become established, but now accounts for the greater part of the world's steel output.

Each process is best suited to ores of particular phosphorus content. The acid processes[7] are employed for ores with a phosphorus content of less than 0.2 per cent; within the range 0.2 to 1.5 per cent the basic open-hearth process is employed, and where the phosphorus content exceeds this figure, the basic Bessemer process is without a rival.[8] The basic Bessemer process is most important in Continental Western Europe—particularly Luxembourg, Belgium, and France, whose iron and steel industries depend largely on limonitic ores of high phosphoric content. In the United States, in Britain, in much of the U.S.S.R., in Japan, and in most other minor producers the basic open-hearth process is dominant. West Germany is unique in placing almost equal emphasis on the basic Bessemer and the basic open-hearth processes. Although everywhere of increasing importance, electric furnaces only account for a major share of total steel output in Sweden, which in consequence has a vital place in the world industry despite its modest total output.

The relative advantages and disadvantages of these various types of steelmaking have been greatly modified since World War II, however, as a result of extended use of oxygen, the greatest technical innovation since the introduction of the Gilchrist-Thomas process. As a result of the development of "tonnage" oxygen plants, oxygen has become available in large quantities and at low cost for the first time; as they produce oxygen in gaseous form, tonnage plants have to be erected on the site where the gas is to be employed. The use of an oxygen blast in a Bessemer-like process eliminates one of the major defects of Bessemer steel, that is, nitrogen absorption, and for most purposes renders it the equal of open-hearth steel. With the highly phosphoric ores of Western Europe the bottom-blown oxygen-Bessemer process is used, but ores of lower phosphoric content can also be oxygen-treated in essentially Bessemer-like processes. Moreover, the extra heat generated by the use of oxygen raises the proportion of the charge that can consist of scrap from less than 5 per cent in the standard Bessemer process to almost 30 per cent under certain conditions.

The most important of these new oxygen processes, the LD (Linz-Donawitz) process, is named after the two Austrian steelmaking

[6] Simpler ferroalloys such as ferromanganese and ferrosilicon may, however, be produced in blast furnaces.

[7] The reader will avoid confusion by recalling that the terms "acid" and "basic" refer to the nature of the furnace lining employed and also to steels produced from furnaces with acid or basic linings.

[8] A phosphorus content of more than 1.2 per cent is necessary in this process, as the process depends upon the heat of combustion to keep the reaction going.

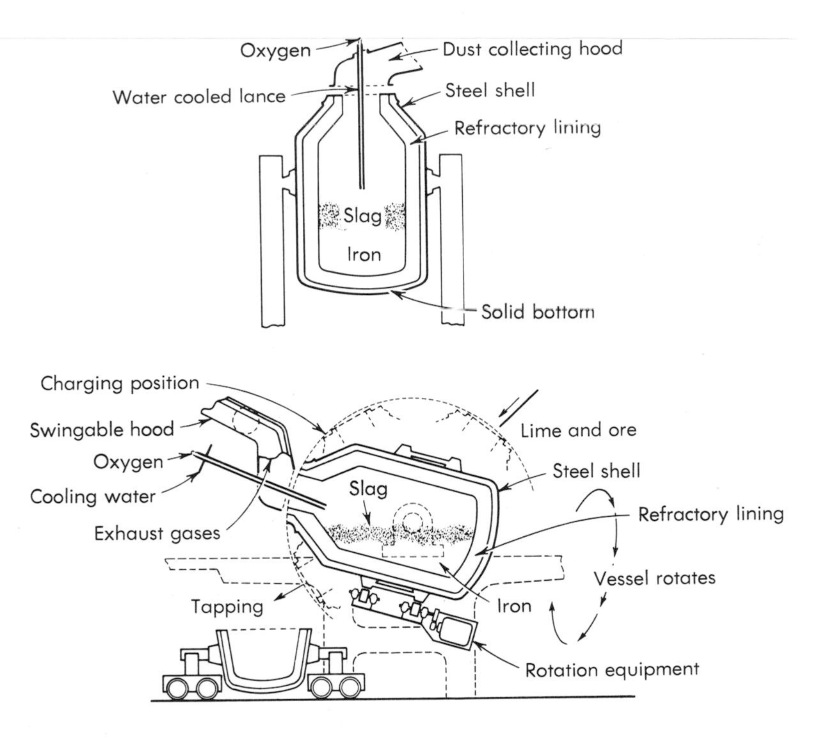

Fig. 14-4 The LD and Kaldo processes.
In the LD process a supersonic blast of oxygen is directed on the charge, up to 30 per cent of which may consist of scrap. The LD-AC process, developed for ores of higher phosphoric content, is essentially similar but uses a blast of oxygen and powdered lime, with a second blow after the primary slag is tipped. The rapidly rotating Kaldo furnace may also be employed either with single or two-stage blowing and permits the production of a wider range of steels than the LD processes; as much as 50 per cent of the charge may consist of scrap. (British Iron and Steel Federation.)

centers where it originated during World War II. The LD process uses a top-blown converter in which a jet of oxygen and powdered lime is directed at the surface of the charge. The original LD process, which employed a single blow and slag-tipping process could only be used with ores in which the phosphoric content did not exceed 0.4 per cent. Development of two-stage blow and slag-tipping operations in the LD-AC process (Fig. 14-4), however, has permitted the use of ores of substantially higher phosphoric content, and this modification of the original LD process is fast becoming one of major world importance (Fig. 14-5). Another oxygen process likely to be of increasing significance is the Swedish Kaldo process, which uses a rotary converter. The oxygen "lance" has also been used in the basic open-hearth process, where it has greatly raised productivity, but the balance of advantage appears to have swung towards the cheap and rapid Bessemer-like processes. During the early Sixties steelmakers in many countries began to convert open-hearth plants into LD, or LD-AC, plants.

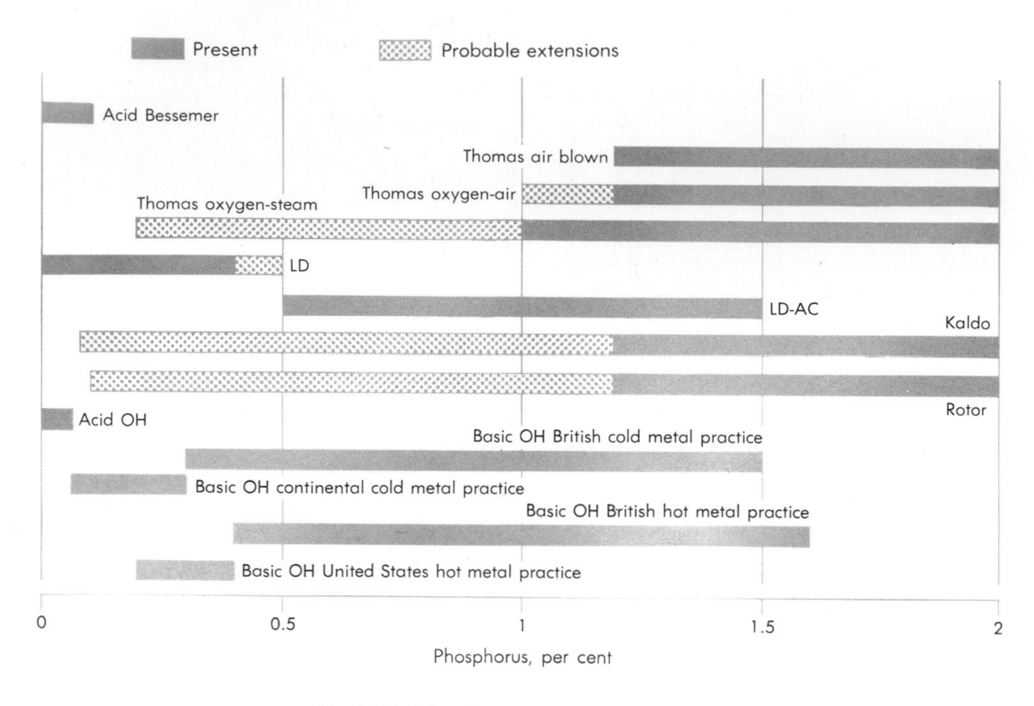

Fig. 14-5 Phosphorus and steelmaking. (British Iron and Steel Federation.)

Present evidence thus appears to suggest that in place of the few processes of the past steelmaking is likely to be carried out in a multiplicity of processes, each specifically suited to the ores and fuels available in each producing area. The desire of all iron and steel companies, however, is a single continuous process that will enable iron ore to be converted into finished steel products; this is still some way off, but there are already a number of projected pilot plants for the production of certain types of steel products using such continuous processes.

Final Processing

From the steelworks ingots are moved to the rolling and finishing mills, which in an integrated works may account for a very large part of total site area. No section of the industry has experienced such rapid technological progress over the past half-century. Most outstanding, perhaps, has been the development of continuous production methods. Continuous strip mills and electrolytic-tinning plants have steadily replaced older discontinuous methods; the continuous sheet mill has also appeared since World War II, and for certain purposes casting may also be carried out continuously. The employment of natural gas and fuel oil in steelworks has steadily expanded; such fuels fire the "soaking pits" in which ingots are kept at the correct temperature for rolling, and have made possible the establishment of rolling mills in areas of petroleum refining, strengthening the desire for at least this final portion of the industry in underdeveloped economies that are substantial petroleum producers.

THE IRON AND STEEL INDUSTRY OF THE UNITED STATES

Both by volume of employment and value of output, the iron and steel industry ranks among the premier industries of the United States. For almost half a century from 1905 onwards the United States accounted for about one-half of the total world output of steel, and shortly after World War I its share almost reached two-thirds. Since 1955, however, its share of world steel output has fallen to about one-third, and the laws of mathematics make it inevitable that this proportion will fall still further in the future. Between the end of World War II and 1960 some 50 million tons of new capacity was added to the steel industry of the United States, about equivalent to twice the total capacity of Britain in the latter year; the industry was then capable of producing some 140 million tons[9] of crude steel, more than twice the annual output of the U.S.S.R. and its satellites. Nevertheless, over this period much capacity remained underemployed; since 1958 crude-steel output in the U.S.S.R. has not been greatly inferior to that of the United States, where steel has encountered acute competition from substitutes in many traditional uses. After 1960, however, American steelmakers belatedly began converting plants to the new LD processes, and it is likely that by 1965, capacity may approach a level of almost 200 million tons.

Historical Development

The rudimentary iron and steel industry of the colonial period was based on scattered small pockets of iron ore occurring along the middle Atlantic coast and charcoal from the eastern hardwood forests. With the westward advance of population and the discovery that anthracite could be used in the blast furnace, the early nineteenth century witnessed the establishment of the industry on the anthracite fields of eastern Pennsylvania. By mid-century the excellent coking properties of the Pittsburgh seam had become known; coke from the Connellsville area, in conjunction with small deposits of local iron ore, laid the foundations for the dominance of the Pittsburgh area that was to last for more than half a century from the end of the Civil War. From this stimulus Pittsburgh never looked back; improvements in navigation and transport facilities on the Great Lakes assisted the development of the high-grade hematite ores of the Lake Superior area, whose existence was in fact known even before the Civil War; the important Mesabi Range, however, whose Hull-Mahoning mine near Hibbing, Minnesota, is still the largest iron mine in the world, did not come into production until after 1890. The high iron content of the Superior ores and their low proportion of phosphorus greatly facilitated the changeover from iron to steel, but by 1905 the basic open-hearth process, particularly suitable for Mesabi ore which possesses a higher phosphoric content than that from other Superior iron ranges, had become dominant in steelmaking.

After 1910 new influences operated to produce several changes in the location of the industry, although Pittsburgh still enjoyed a substantial advantage until 1924 through the pricing policy of the largest producer. Foremost among these was the development of the Midwest as the largest steel market in the country; much of this growth resulted from the demand of new industries, above all the automobile industry. Scrap iron became of increasing importance in steelmaking. The output of crude steel first exceeded that of pig iron in 1914 and

[9] **To facilitate international comparison, metric tons have been used throughout this chapter. One United States, or short, ton is equivalent to nine-tenths of a metric ton.**

thereafter drew steadily ahead; by this date also the industry had become extinct in the anthracite area. Meanwhile, the progressive deterioration in the quality of Lake Superior ores as a result of the removal of the best and most accessible deposits rendered preliminary processing increasingly desirable and led to a search for alternative sources of supply in the form of high-grade foreign ore.

As a result of these influences, the Chicago area, which received its first large integrated works in 1911, and the Erie lakeshore expanded production so rapidly that by 1960 they both possessed an ingot capacity exceeding that of the Pittsburgh district. During the interwar period the middle Atlantic seaboard became once again an attractive area for steelmaking. World War II made so great a demand on the Superior ores that their position in the industry appeared uncertain. Although the development of techniques for mining and processing the exceedingly tough and intractable taconite ores that occur in large quantities in the Superior area has done much to maintain the special position of Superior ores in the industry, it is clear that they will never have the importance in the future that they have enjoyed in the past. Over 25 per cent of the iron ore consumed in the United States in 1960 was imported, and by 1975 this figure is expected to reach 40 per cent. Of more than 25 million tons of foreign ore consumed in 1961, Canada and South America (principally Venezuela) supplied almost equal quantities, but West Africa was also a supplier of some significance.

World War II also resulted in a considerable extension of steelmaking capacity in the West, which has since been augmented as a result of heavy postwar immigration. The West stands to gain more than any other area from the commercial application of direct reduction smelting methods, but so long as the blast furnace remains the only practicable way of smelting iron in large quantities, the Appalachian coalfield will continue to be a dominant influence in the industry. On the other hand, the principal ore-producing district has attracted little development to it; deprived of any large local market, the Duluth steel industry, established largely in response to local pressure for a greater share in the utilization of a major Minnesota resource, has failed to participate in the general expansion of the United States steel industry.

Structure of the Industry

The capital-intensive nature of the industry compels its organization in large integrated units; the giant corporations that dominate the industry in the United States own their own coal and ore mines, operate mining concessions overseas, and possess their own shipping fleets for the transport of raw materials. For some time, however, there has been a tendency for each major producer to confine its activities to the area in which it originated and within which it possesses a substantial degree of natural protection. While the "gentlemen's agreements" on which such self-limitation is based are no longer quite so respected or so respectable, competition between steel manufacturers is minimal, despite the fact that they frequently extol its virtues for others.[10] The tendency for the smaller producers to specialize has also helped to reduce the field for competition. Although entry into the industry is extremely difficult, it is not impossible; Kaiser Steel came into existence at the end of World War II,[11] and small producers can show very high growth rates, as the records of Kaiser and

[10] Steel is an "administered price" industry, and occupies a key position among the inflationary forces in the economy. See J. K. Galbraith, *The Affluent Society,* Houghton Mifflin Company, Boston, 1958, pp. 88, 167–171.

[11] The capital cost of the original Kaiser plant, however, was met by government.

of National Steel, an amalgamation effected in 1929, testify. Further concentration in the industry may prove difficult; a proposed merger between Bethlehem Steel and Youngstown Sheet and Tube was rejected in 1958 as contrary to antitrust legislation.

Outstanding in the industry is "Big Steel," the United States Steel Corporation; formed from the complex of Carnegie interests in the Pittsburgh and Chicago areas, the corporation's activities now extend into virtually every steelmaking district. Undisputed leader of "Little Steel," the name by which the six next largest companies are collectively known,[12] is the Bethlehem Steel Corporation, whose main interests have always been on the eastern seaboard; it was the first to establish an integrated works directly on the coast to use imported ore, and this plant, at Sparrows Point, Maryland, is now the largest in the country. Bethlehem's stake in the Midwest, however, is small in relation to its standing in the industry, and the company has long sought additional capacity to supplement its plants in Buffalo and in Johnstown; hence its interest in the Youngstown corporation.

Most of the other companies of Little Steel have strong regional affiliations. Republic Steel, the third-largest producer, operates on the Erie lakeshore and in the Mahoning Valleys region between the latter and Pittsburgh, an area that is also a major interest of Youngstown Sheet & Tube. Jones & Laughlin Steel is the only Little Steel member with substantial interests in Pittsburgh, but it also operates on the Erie lakeshore. National Steel is particularly associated with Detroit, and Inland Steel, a single-plant company, with Chicago, where it is the second-largest producer, after United States Steel; Youngstown and Republic, however, also have plants in the Chicago area. Armco Steel has widespread geographic interests, but its main plant is in the Cincinnati area where the company originated. Kaiser Steel, pacemaker for the industry with the highest rate of growth, is confined to the west coast, where it operates the only integrated plant, and regards itself as quite distinct from the Little Steel group.[13]

12 The members of "Little Steel" are small only in relation to "Big Steel"; collectively their capacity exceeds that of the United States Steel Corporation. They are also giants in relation to units of the industry in the rest of the Free World; only Japan's Yawata Steel can be regarded as being in the same class.

13 During the strike of 1959, the worst in the postwar history of the industry, Kaiser Steel continued in production, much to the annoyance of the eastern steelmakers.

Steelmaking Districts of the United States

The fortunes of each steelmaking district are closely linked with those of the dominant company in that area and with particular market that is the main preoccupation of that area; Chicago and the Erie lakeshore are thus more sensitive to changes in the level of activity in the automobile industry than is Pittsburgh, while the Atlantic seaboard is particularly affected by the volume of large-building construction in New York and in other large east coast cities (Fig. 14-6).

Pittsburgh has been synonymous with iron and steel for almost a century. Once it was without a rival, but its relative importance has been declining for some time as the expansion of its steel capacity has failed to keep pace with that of the industry as a whole. With the inclusion of the Youngstown district and the upper Ohio valley, however, with which the Pittsburgh area forms one closely knit industrial district, the region's share of national steel capacity is raised to about one-third. Pittsburgh's greatest assets have always been the excellence of its coking coals, the ease with which they can be mined, and low-cost transportation on the Ohio headstreams; but im-

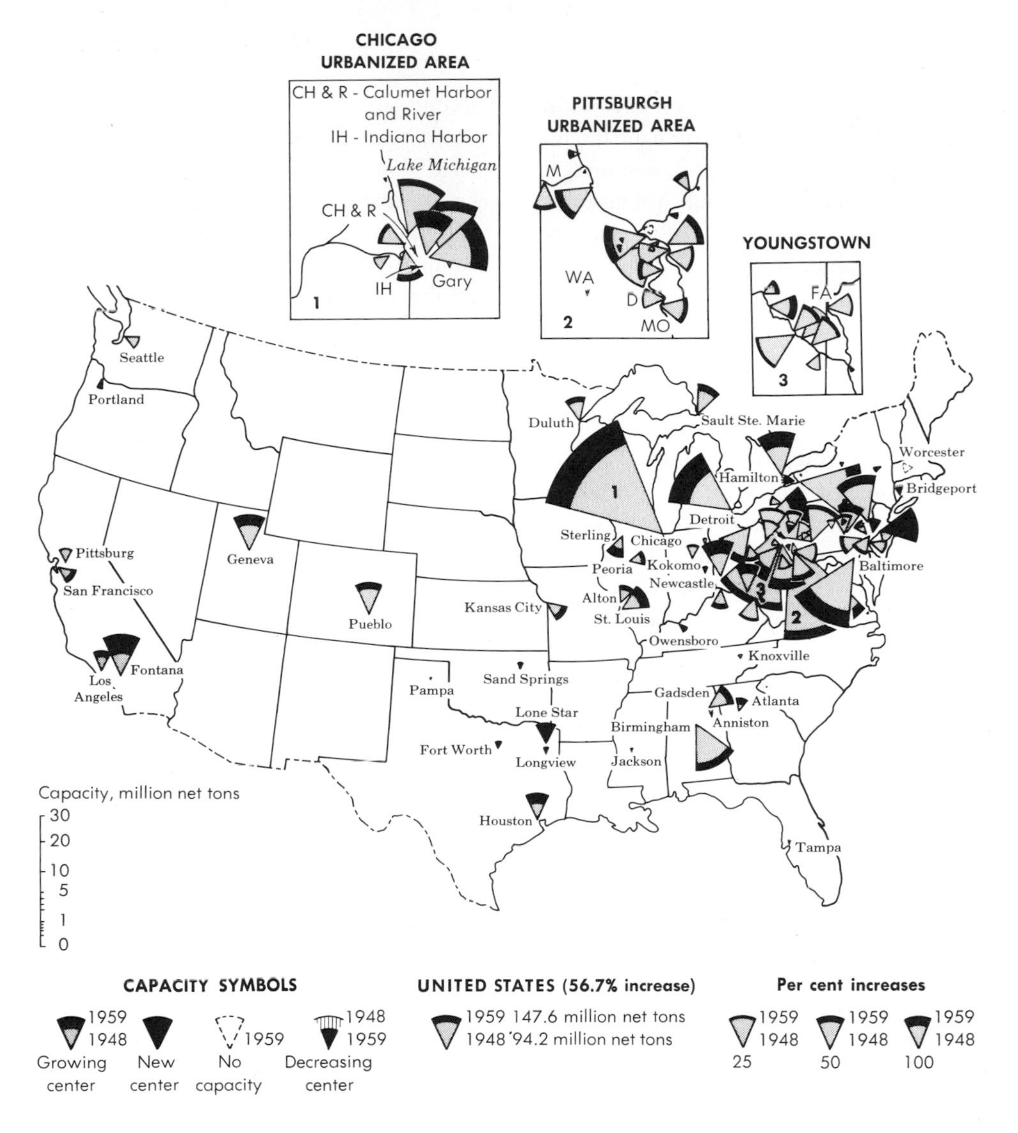

Fig. 14-6 Steel capacity in the United States, 1948–1959.
(By permission of Gunnar Alexandersson and the Editor, *Economic Geography*.)

provements in fuel technology have made these assets now much less significant than in the past, and the narrow, cramped, and congested valleys have tended to repel the establishment of modern plants, whose finishing mills need a very large floor space.

The "Pittsburgh plus" system adopted in 1903 by the United States Steel Corporation was a basing-point method of pricing in which steel prices quoted by all of the company's plants irrespective of location were kept equal to the Pittsburgh price plus the cost of transportation from Pittsburgh to the consumer. As the other steel companies followed the lead of

United States Steel, the effect of the system was to deny any local protection to plants outside the Pittsburgh area, and it probably operated to retard the growth of the industry in areas better placed to take advantage of technological and economic change. Nevertheless, two world wars, with their urgent necessity for immediate expansion of steel output regardless of cost, were perhaps equally important in enabling Pittsburgh to remain the most important producing area for longer than might otherwise have been the case. Since the end of World War II the steel-ingot capacities of both the Chicago area and the Erie lakeshore have overtaken that of the four counties that constitute the Pittsburgh area proper, and it appears likely that the capacity of the Atlantic seaboard area will also do so in the near future.

The *Chicago* area is the giant of the industry, with a steel-ingot capacity of some 25 million tons in 1960, about equivalent to that of Britain; although the number of plants is substantially smaller than in the Pittsburgh area, the average size is very much larger, the plants at South Chicago, Indiana Harbor, and Gary being three of the five plants in the country with an annual ingot capacity exceeding 5 million tons. In marked contrast to the situation in Pittsburgh and the Valleys, plant expansion is easily accomplished through dumping slag into Lake Michigan. The handicap of a long rail haul from east Kentucky or from West Virginia, which supply all but a small proportion of the Michigan lakeside's requirements of coking coal, has been partly offset by improvements in fuel economy; future ore supplies have been safeguarded by the development of Minnesota taconite and by the opening of the St. Lawrence Seaway, which has facilitated the import of Canadian ore from the Burnt Creek area of the Labrador-Quebec boundary. The area is extremely well placed to supply the automobile industry and the midwestern construction industry, the nation's largest consumers of finished steel. During the early Sixties, all the Chicago-area steel companies were making considerable extensions to capacity and changing over from the basic open-hearth to the LD steel-making process. By 1975, it is possible that the area will have an ingot capacity of around 50 million tons.

The *Erie lakeshore* region is an older iron and steel producer than is Chicago, the Lackawanna plant, the largest in the region, having commenced operations shortly after the turn of the century. The region, however, may be taken to include not only the Buffalo, Cleveland, and Toledo districts, in which the industry is old established, but also the Detroit district, in which it is a comparative newcomer. The late and slow development of Detroit as a steel producer appears anomalous in the light of the tremendous growth of the automobile industry; even in 1961 the three integrated plants of the Detroit area supplied only a small proportion of the automobile region's steel requirements. The whole Erie area, however, is heavily specialized in products required by the volatile automobile industry and other consumer-durable industries such as domestic appliances, and therefore experiences considerable changes of fortune.

The *Atlantic seaboard* is both the oldest and one of the newest iron- and steelmaking districts. Since the middle of the nineteenth century the area has suffered from the necessity of having to rail coking coal from the Appalachian field, and has come to rely upon the East Coast market in which it has been protected through progressive increases in transport costs on steel products from Pittsburgh. In the present century, however, the great expansion of the construction industry in New York and, to a lesser extent, the growth of the shipbuilding industry laid the basis for a large increase in capacity, which became increasingly attractive as high-grade imported ore became competitive with that from Mesabi. In 1914 the Bethlehem Steel Corporation began production at its Sparrows Point plant near Baltimore, the largest in the country in 1960 with an annual ingot capacity of almost 7.5 million tons; ore for the Bethlehem plants has been obtained from Cuba, northern Chile, and, in the postwar period, from Venezuela. Since 1951 the monopoly position of the Bethlehem company has been challenged by the development of the United States Steel Corporation's Fairless plant on the Delaware River opposite Trenton, which also uses Venezuelan ore. As foreign ore becomes still more important to the industry, it is highly likely that the share of the middle Atlantic seaboard in total steel production will grow; several other producers are showing a marked interest in the area.

The crude and widely scattered iron industry of the *South* did not survive the Civil War, and not until the last two decades of the nineteenth century did the industry again firmly establish itself. The Birmingham area is unique in possessing all the raw materials for the iron and steel industry in close proximity, but in a region of markedly below-average per capita income and little industrial development, this advantage has carried little weight. The ores of the Birmingham district, moreover, are expensive to extract and contain much silica; silica, while discouraging steelmaking, gives molten iron great mobility, so that the district has specialized in iron pipes and other castings. For these reasons, the charge that the expansion of steel production in the area has been hindered by the largest producer, the United States Steel Corporation, out of deference to its major interests elsewhere is not easy to substantiate; in addition, when demand did quicken during World War II, capacity was greatly expanded. The increase in electricity generation through TVA has produced a minor revolution in steelmaking in the South, and several steelworks now use the electric furnace exclusively.

The *West* had likewise to wait for World War II for a larger share of national steel capacity. Previously this region was limited to one integrated works at Pueblo, Colorado, and to a few small steel-fabricating and -processing plants dependent upon eastern pig iron or scrap; the Pacific war necessitated the construction of new capacity that would have been out of the question under normal economic conditions. On the west coast a great new shipbuilding industry sprang up, gas, oil, and chemical production expanded greatly, and defense establishments of all kinds proliferated. To support these activities three new integrated plants were established by the government, two of which, at Geneva, Utah, and at Fontana in the Los Angeles area, were intended to produce plate for the shipbuilding industry. At the end of the war these plants passed into the possession of the steel companies, and their future appeared uncertain; that at Geneva possessed both local coal and iron ore but had a minuscule market, while that at Fontana had the burden of long and expensive rail hauls from the Utah coalfields. Nevertheless both have survived, and with the postwar influx of new industry and population into southern California, the Fontana plant, acquired by Kaiser, has become the largest steel producer in the West, marketing almost two-thirds of its products, chiefly in the form of sheet, pipe, and tinplate, within the Los Angeles area.

The third wartime plant, at Houston, Texas, also survived; now operated by Armco Steel, it has benefited from the great development of the Gulf Coast in hydrocarbon fuels and raw materials for the chemical industry. Further expansion in this area appears certain in view of the close connection now existing between steel producers and the great chemical companies in the development of "direct reduction" processes. Dangerfield, where a wartime blast furnace was constructed to utilize the iron ores of east Texas, has also been expanded into an integrated plant, and a similar development is possible for the present cold-metal steelworks of the United States Steel Corporation at Pittsburg, California, on the Carquinez Strait. A high rate of growth of steel production in the West and the South seems assured, although no real challenge to the supremacy of the present major producing centers yet appears.

THE BRITISH INDUSTRY

With a crude-steel capacity of about 25 million tons, Britain ranked fourth among world steel producers in 1962. Though Britain was the birthplace of the modern industry, substitution of steel for iron in the latter half of the nineteenth century presented many difficulties for the British industry, which were not entirely overcome even by World War I. During the interwar period, however, considerable reorganization took place, and the industry was able to face World War II in a much more efficient state. Since 1945 Britain has shared in the high rate of growth of steel output common to all Western European producers.

In its multiplicity of producing regions and in the many changes in its location pattern over time, the British industry closely resembles those of the two largest producers, the United States and the U.S.S.R., and contrasts with those of its European rivals and of new producers such as Japan and China. This situation reflects the large number of productive coalfields in Britain and the long history of technical innovation.

Historical Development

As in other parts of Western Europe, the pre-eighteenth-century industry was located in those areas where iron ores occurred in conjunction with copious supplies of timber. The supremacy of coke over charcoal as a fuel was first demonstrated by the Darby family, who, at Coalbrookdale in the small Shropshire coalfield, initiated the new location pattern of the industry. In several of Britain's coalfields, particularly the Staffordshire, South Wales, and Lanarkshire fields, bands of ironstones were interbedded in the coal seams. The Coal Measures ironstones remained the main source of ore until well into the latter half of the nineteenth century, when they began to be displaced by the bedded ores of the scarp lands that extend across England in a belt between the Severn and the Tees and by imported ores.

First extensively worked in the Cleveland Hills of Yorkshire, the ores of the scarp lands are plentiful and can often be extracted in open quarries or strip mines. Their iron content, however, is low, and because of their relatively high phosphoric content they proved unsuitable for the original Bessemer and S steelmaking processes. The only British ores suitable for acid steel are the hematites of north Lancashire and of Cumberland. Their supply, however, is limited, and with the progressive working out of the most accessible ironstones by 1870, a new steelmaking pattern with coastal integrated works based on high-grade nonphosphoric imported ores appeared. South Wales, Scotland, and the northeast were all affected by this development, the old inland centers being compelled to specialize or cease operations. Nor did the basic process, although a British invention, speedily bring about a greater utilization of the scarp-land ores for steelmaking. In part this was a consequence of locational changes that had already occurred and of the continuously high demand for iron plates from the shipbuilders of Clydeside and the northeast coast; in contrast to the situation in the United States, the greatest period of railroad construction in

Britain took place during the "wrought iron age," and until replacement of equipment became necessary, railways did not constitute a large market for steel products. Such explanations, however, appear inadequate; the basic process was merely one of a series of major technical innovations pioneered in Britain but developed overseas, largely through the failure of British industry to replace its empirical outlook with a scientific one. Not until World War I did the basic process really come into its own in Britain, and from then on the scarp-land ores became of increasing importance; mined mainly in Northamptonshire, Lincolnshire, and in Oxfordshire, they now account for all but a very small proportion of the approximately 20 million tons of ore produced in Britain, the balance largely consisting of hematites.

Domestic ores account for about 60 per cent by weight of all ore consumed by the British industry, but as their iron content averages only half that of imported ores, the respective contributions to pig-iron production are almost reversed. Spain, Sweden, and North Africa have long supplied ore for the British furnaces, but since the end of World War II Venezuela and Canada have become the largest suppliers. While foreign ores serve the coastal producing districts, domestic ores are mainly consumed in the east Midlands and in Lincolnshire. As in the United States, the basic open-hearth process dominates steelmaking. Nevertheless, yet another major technical change is now taking place; Britain has taken up the LD and LD-AC processes much more quickly than has the United States, and these appear certain to become of major significance in the near future. As in all other major producers, electric furnaces have accounted for a progressively larger share of total steel output since the end of World War II. Imports of iron ore are handled by a central organization serving all steel companies.

Structure and Locations of the Industry

There are over three-hundred firms engaged in the iron and steel industry in Britain, but as in the United States, a few large organizations account for the greater part of the output; twenty-five enterprises produce about 95 per cent of all crude steel. The immediate postwar attempt to nationalize the industry proved abortive, but one of the largest organizations, Richard Thomas and Baldwins, remains under public ownership, and through the operations of the Iron and Steel Board the government exercises a considerable degree of control over the industry. Since the Great Depression the siting of new plants has been a particular concern of government; several large plants have been located in conformity with social policy aimed at increasing employment in depressed areas. Since World War II public funds have been provided for the modernization and extension of plants in areas of high unemployment. As in the United States, each major steel-producing area tends to be the preserve of a particular company, although some, such as United Steel, Guest, Keen and Nettlefolds, and Richard Thomas and Baldwins, are represented in several producing districts. There is a remarkable geographic diversity; some areas are mainly producers of finished steel in integrated plants, some produce pig for conversion to steel elsewhere, one large steelmaking district produces virtually no pig, and areas which were formerly important steelmaking centers now possess little but rerolling plants. Nevertheless, there appear to be too many producers and too many plants for Britain's scale of steel output; the average plant size is too low to realize all the economies of scale. In what is by far the most significant development in the world industry, the *really* large integrated plant (that is, with an ingot capacity exceeding 5 million tons) located on tidewater, Britain also appears to be lagging behind its European rivals and Japan.

South Wales is Britain's principal steel producer, accounting for about a quarter of total output, a proportion that is likely to enlarge. The industry grew up in the valleys of the northeastern portion of the coalfield, but with the working out of the "clayband" ironstones and the coming of cheap steel processes the main center of activity shifted to the coast. At present it is the section from Port Talbot to Llanelly that is of greatest importance; here, at Margam near Port Talbot, the Steel Company of Wales[14] operates what has been claimed to be Europe's largest integrated plant. South Wales has two of the four continuous strip mills in the country, one at Margam and the other at Ebbw Vale in the northeast; the latter location was selected shortly before World War II as a result of government pressure to alleviate chronic unemployment in what had become one of the most depressed areas in Britain. There is also a large integrated plant at Cardiff, and the Spencer works of Richard Thomas and Baldwins near Newport, which uses the LD process of steelmaking exclusively, is claimed to be the first completely automated integrated plant in the world. The Spencer works was completed in 1962, but despite the fact that it uses imported ore exclusively, it is not located on tidewater. A specialty of south Wales has long been tinplate, but since 1945 the industry has been revolutionized by the introduction of continuous electrolytic plants, and many small plants in the Swansea-Llanelly area have been closed down.

The *northeast,* or *Teeside, area,* is the second steelmaking district of Britain, where the industry grew rapidly in the third quarter of the nineteenth century on the basis of Durham coking coal and ore from the nearby Cleveland hills. Cleveland ore has long been inadequate, however, and as with south Wales, the area now largely depends on imported ore. Plates and structural steel are the main products of the northeast region, which is closely identified with the Dorman Long company. The isolated plant of Consett in Durham is an example of an old manufacturing center that has successfully adapted to changed technological and economic conditions.

In the *East Midlands* the industry is carried on in a number of centers scattered over five counties; here iron and steel production is largely a twentieth-century industry, and the region is unique in Britain in being entirely independent of foreign ore. The Scunthorpe-Frodingham district of north Lincolnshire resembles Teeside in being mainly a producer of plate and heavy structural products; the Appleby-Frodingham plant of United Steel operates the largest blast furnaces in Britain, working 100 per cent sintered ore. At Corby, Northamptonshire, Stewarts & Lloyd operates a large integrated works, originally designed to produce steel pipe and tubes; because of the particular suitability of the local ore and the nature of the product, the basic Bessemer process was adopted, but the greatly enlarged plant now also possesses open-hearth and electric furnaces. The other centers of the east Midlands are mainly producers of foundry pig for conversion or for further fabrication elsewhere.

Scotland was once the foremost pig-iron district of Britain, and even as late as 1920 still produced almost a quarter of the national steel output. But decline was rapid as Scotland's heavy industries languished under acute depression, and by 1960 Scotland's share of steel output had fallen below 10 per cent. The original basis of the Lanarkshire industry was

[14] **This company is largely owned by other major steelmaking companies.**

"blackband" ironstone and "splint" coal, but with the working out of the former, ores were imported from Spain. Scotland never developed a pattern of large integrated works sited on the coast as in south Wales or in the northeast; right up to World War II the Scottish industry consisted of a collection of small independent plants specializing in heavy products, with little development of the highly mechanized finishing mills, whose main markets are the "growth" industries, above all, the automobile industry. This handicap has at last been overcome with the aid of very considerable state financial assistance. Additional ingot capacity at the Ravenscraig (Motherwell) plant of Colville & Co., the largest Scottish producer, serves a new continuous strip mill that with associated finishing mills and an alloy-steel plant is designed to supply the new automobile plants that Scotland has also received through state intervention.[15]

Sheffield is Britain's principal producer of electrical and alloy steel; it makes little pig but uses large quantities from the east Midlands, as well as importing high-grade bar iron (wrought iron) from Sweden. Though Sheffield is famous for its cutlery, heavy products, which include forgings of the most massive kind, are of considerably greater importance.

The now minor *northwest region* is of considerable historical significance. At Brymbo in the North Wales coalfield, "iron-mad Wilkinson" made the cylinders for Watt's first steam engines, and the first basic open-hearth furnace in Britain was put into operation. The region includes the Cumberland-Furness district, which originally used local hematites but now depends largely on foreign ore and is anomalous in producing acid Bessemer steel. At Shotton, on Deeside, the continuous wide-strip mill of John Summers, erected shortly before World War II, has been "integrated backwards" into a major plant.

The *West Midlands,* where the Industrial Revolution may perhaps be said to have begun, is now mainly engaged in producing steel from scrap; in the old Black Country of south Staffordshire iron smelting has virtually ceased. With the exhaustion of its ores and the depletion of its fuel supplies, the continuance of steelmaking in this area reflects the accumulation of labor skills and the large diversified industrial market, which also generates much scrap.

IRON AND STEEL IN WESTERN EUROPE

The EEC, or Common Market, is the world's second-largest producer of steel, and in few parts of the globe has the postwar increase in steel production proceeded faster (Fig. 14-7). It was in the ECSC (European Coal and Steel Community) that the six countries that formed the EEC began their experiment in economic cooperation that led in 1958 to the establishment of the broader organization.

There is a tradition of international cooperation in the European steel industry, which in large measure is rendered inevitable by the distribution of ore and fuel; several great organizations have long conducted operations across international frontiers, and in 1926 most Western European countries were signatories of the International Steel Cartel. This agreement was essentially restrictive, however, whereas the objective of the ECSC is the unification of the six national economies through the establishment of a common heavy-industrial base. To achieve this end the Community aims at the eventual removal of all internal obstacles to the free flow both of raw materials for the steel industry and of finished

[15] See p. 463.

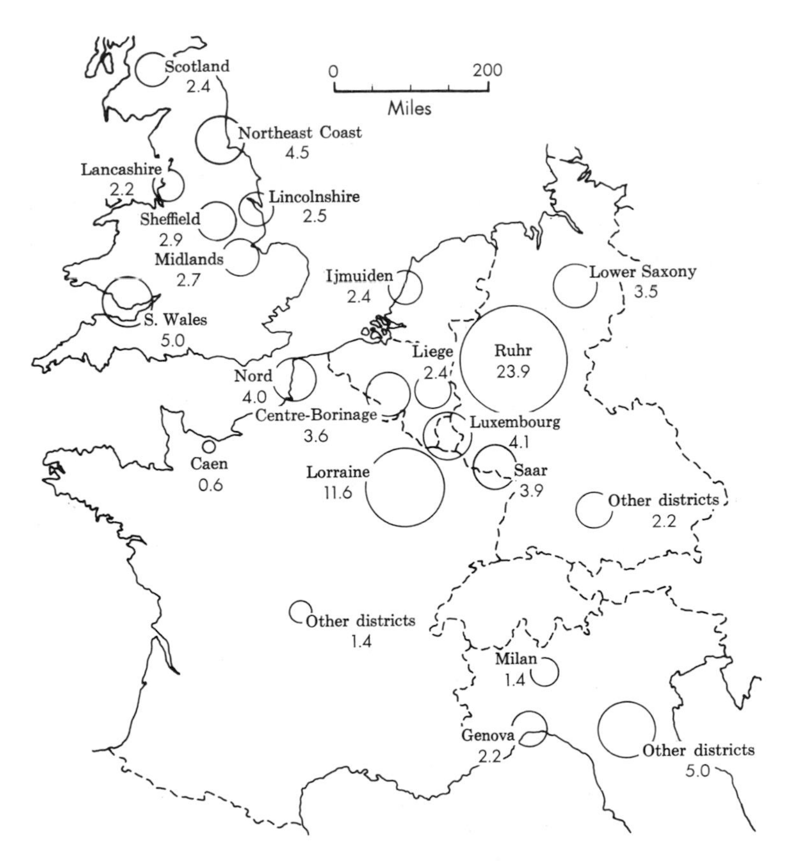

Fig. 14-7 Crude steel production in Western Europe, 1961.
Figures are in millions of metric tons. (EEC.)

iron and steel products; quotas, embargoes, tariffs, export taxes, subsidies, and discriminatory pricing and freight rates are all to be abolished. The various sections of the coal and steel industries would thus gravitate to the most efficient locations, and high-cost producers and districts would lose their present protection; maximum economies of scale would be realized, and the establishment of a large common market would give a great impetus to European economic development.

Since 1953, when the Community first began to function, there has been a substantial increase both in steel production and in trade in raw materials and finished products. In Western Europe's booming economy, however, the general increase in production and in all trade between members has been proportionately greater; moreover, a common pricing system for steel products has yet to appear in the face of the determination of some governments to retain pricing systems based on national economic interests. Yet, whatever its economic success, the Community has greatly assisted the promotion of its real objective. The Community's governing body, the High

Authority, has dealt successfully with both national governments and the great cartels; it has established a common contingency fund for coal and steel and a common organization for the collection of scrap and for the import of foreign ore. This experience of international cooperation undoubtedly assisted the crystallization of public feeling for a higher degree of political unity and paved the way for the EEC itself, in which the whole of the national economies of the six countries are to be merged.[16]

Despite the existence of the Community, however, the organization of the European iron and steel industry continues on essentially national lines; no member exports as much as one-fifth of its output, for the existence of the iron and steel industry tends to encourage the growth of steel-consuming industries in its vicinity.

West Germany

Of the total EEC output of more than 54 million tons of pig iron and more than 73 million tons of steel in 1961, West Germany produced almost half. Germany surpassed Britain's steel output about the turn of the century, and until the rise of the U.S.S.R. in the period between the two world wars it remained the world's second-largest producer. All but a very small portion of Germany's steelmaking capacity before 1939 was located in what is now West Germany. The West German industry made a very rapid recovery from the destruction of World War II following the removal in 1948 of Allied restrictions on steel output; by 1955 West German steel production had once again surpassed that of Britain, and has since gone further ahead. Its new equipment, financed in part by the Allies, makes the West German industry an extremely efficient one, but rapid regeneration was undoubtedly assisted by the great geographic and structural concentration of the industry. In contrast to the British industry, more than 80 per cent of the Federal Republic's steel is produced in the 50- by 25-mile belt that constitutes the North Rhine–Westphalia industrial area. In some other respects, however, there is a considerable degree of similarity; both industries use about the same proportion of domestic ore, both are largely self-supporting in their coke requirements, and their respective patterns of steel utilization closely coincide.

The first coke-fired blast furnace in Continental Europe was erected in Silesia in 1796, but the introduction of the new British techniques of smelting and puddling made little headway in the Ruhr until the middle of the nineteenth century, a somewhat surprising development in view of the fact that the Rhine highlands with their numerous ore deposits and copious supplies of timber had constituted one of the foremost ironworking regions of medieval Europe. This relatively late development was not without advantage, however, for Germany was virtually able to step straight into the steel age; despite its "blackband" ironstone ores the Ruhr thus never developed as a large producer of pig and wrought iron, as did South Wales, but based its steelmaking on ores of low phosphoric content from the Siegerland. These were later supplemented by similar ores imported from Sweden, Spain, and North Africa. Less than a decade after German unification the Thomas process made available for steelmaking the immense ore deposits of the north German plain and Lorraine.

The low iron content of these domestic ores necessitated their smelting on the ore fields

[16] **Britain refused an invitation to become a foundation member of the ECSC, thus forfeiting the opportunity of entering the Common Market *ab initio*. The belief that such Pan-European institutions could not be made to work was to cost Britain dearly.**

themselves; nevertheless, the Ruhr remained the dominant center for steelmaking (Fig. 14-8). The abundance and excellence of its coking coal, the steady improvements in water transport which facilitated ore imports, the growth of coal- and steel-consuming industries in the Ruhr which provided both markets and scrap, and the superiority of open-hearth over Bessemer steel all contributed to ensuring its supremacy. The Ruhr has continued to depend mainly on high-grade foreign ores; since 1918 Lorraine ores have never been of any real significance in the German industry except briefly during World War II.

Great concentrations of iron smelting and steelmaking occur both in the Duisburg, Rheinhausen, Oberhausen, and Muelheim area at the western extremity of the Ruhr industrial district and at Dortmund and Hoerde at the eastern. Though the former has the larger output, the largest plant is that of the Dortmund-Hoerde Huettenunion organization, which in the late Fifties closely vied with the plant of Margam, south Wales, for the title of Europe's largest integrated works. Steelmaking is also carried on at Bochum, but generally the central Ruhr area is a district of steel-consuming and -fabricating industries; Essen, most famous of all German steel towns, ceased to be a steel producer with the dismantling of the great Krupp plant at the end of World War II.

Outside the Ruhr there are only two large integrated plants. One is the nationalized Salzgitter integrated plant, formerly the Hermann Goering works; this uses local low-grade iron ore, produced by underground mining, and has a large market in the nearby Volkswagen plant at Wolfsburg. The other plant is that of the Kloeckner group, situated at Bremen; intended ultimately to have an ingot

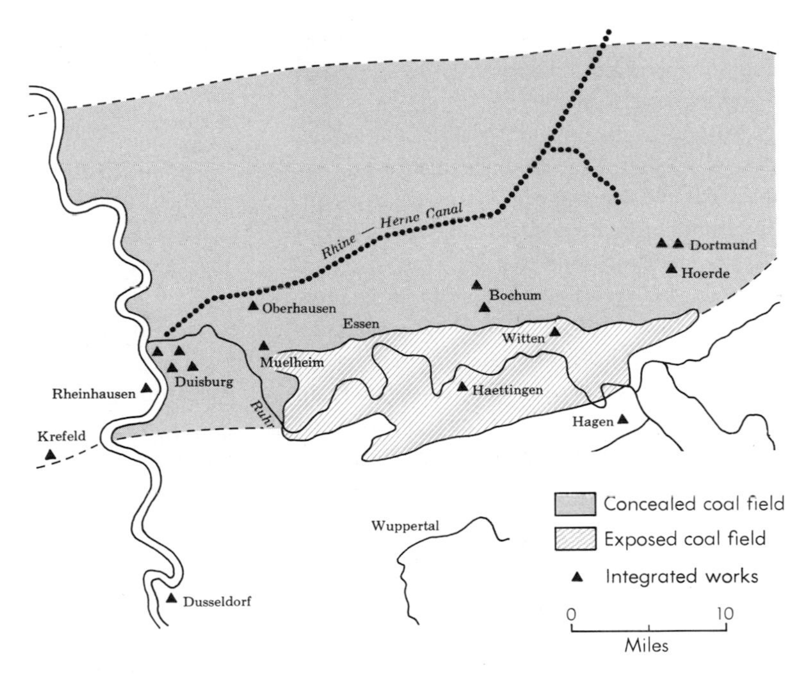

Fig. 14-8 The Ruhr.
The Ruhr is by far the most important steelmaking region in Western Europe.

capacity of about 4 million tons per year, this works is ideally placed for the import of foreign ore and American coal, and may well inspire the construction of similar plants along the North Sea coast.

The remaining steelmakers, which are of minor significance, include the Ilsede Peine works near Hannover, where steel production based on local ores began towards the end of the last century, a number of small establishments in the Siegerland, and an integrated works at Salzbach near Nürnberg. These outlying plants have largely survived through preferential freight rates on Ruhr coal, but if these are eliminated by the Community, the minor producing areas may not survive.

The Saar produces a little more than 3 million tons of crude steel annually; however, its limited dependence on Ruhr coal, the use of the low-shaft blast furnace and Lorraine ore, and the close connections with the adjacent French industry sharply distinguish the Saar iron and steel industry from that of the rest of the Federal Republic.

Although the greater part of Germany's steel is produced by the basic-hearth process, the basic Bessemer process is much more important than in Britain, accounting for about 40 per cent of total output; the share of Bessemer-like processes is certain to enlarge, however, as the LD and LD-AC processes displace the open-hearth furnace.

The extreme concentration of the German iron and steel industry is one of its most striking features and is all the more remarkable in that ownership is not widely disseminated between a multiplicity of shareholders but is solidly in the hands of a few families. Some ten concerns produce more than three-quarters of the total steel output, and the proposed reunion of the Thyssen and the Phoenix-Rheinrohr interests, separated by the Allies after World War II, would create the largest group in the European industry. The domination of the industry by the steel princes has some sinister associations for some of them were accused of aiding both Imperial and Nazi Germany to wage aggressive war; the breakup of the holdings of the great families, and especially of the most famous dynasty of all, the house of Krupp, was a declared Allied war aim.[17]

West Germany's great competitivc strength was expected to result in a considerable increase in exports of iron and steel products to other members of the ECSC. This in fact occurred, but has been offset by considerable purchases of iron and steel from other members, particularly France; in some years West Germany has even been a net importer of steel. All the evidence points to a further substantial increase in West German steel production in the future; an output of about 40 million tons of crude steel forecast for 1975 may well be exceeded.[18]

France

France is the second-largest steel producer in the ECSC, and its iron-ore output is exceeded only by that of the United States and the U.S.S.R. The extensive and easily worked ores of Lorraine, however, were long regarded as of little value and between 1870 and 1914 were largely lost to Germany. In relation to the numerous and large ore deposits, supplies of

[17] Alfred Krupp von Bohlen, head of the family, was indeed jailed and stripped of his possessions, but on his release all his property was returned to him. The Krupp organization still produces steel at its great Rheinhausen plant, but its main interests now lie in heavy engineering and in other steel-consuming industries. The great integrated plant at Essen was in fact dismantled by Krupp subsidiaries, and it is unlikely that the concern was in any way weakened by Allied policy. For similar action in respect of IG Farben, Germany's giant chemical organization, see p. 521.

[18] United Nations Economic Commission for Europe, *Long Term Trends and Prospects in the European Steel Industry,* **Geneva, 1959.**

coking coal are meager, a shortcoming that has been made good by imports. These come chiefly from the Ruhr, but the thesis that the maldistribution of coking coal and iron ore between France and Germany has been a major cause of conflict cannot stand critical analysis.

France experienced the impact of the Industrial Revolution earlier than did Germany, and as in Britain the iron and steel industry was established in a number of centers whose physical resources subsequently proved slender. With the exhaustion of the numerous local ore and coal deposits and the coming of cheap steel, the French industry faced difficult problems of adjustment; right up to 1939 the industry consisted of an assemblage of small independent units, often poorly located and with much obsolete equipment. From this stagnation the industry was rescued, as in Britain, by a massive investment and modernization program, and since 1945 steel output has expanded greatly.

The small coal basins of the Massif Central, particularly those of Le Creusot and St. Étienne, were the earliest centers of the industry, and by the early nineteenth century the northern coalfield had become an important producer of wrought iron. Few of France's numerous ore deposits were suitable for making acid steel, and the development of the Lorraine ore fields had to await the Thomas process. Lorraine "minette" is low-grade ore and has to be extracted by underground mining; nevertheless, it occurs in large deposits, the coincidence of siliceous and calcareous ore in it simplifies blast-furnace charging, and its high phosphorus content makes it eminently suitable for the basic Bessemer process. The nearest source of fuel is the Saar coalfield and its Lorraine extension, but this field produces poor metallurgical coke, and some recourse has always been necessary to Ruhr coal. By judiciously blending Ruhr and Saar-Lorraine coals, and more recently, by utilizing new methods of coal carbonization, the proportion of Ruhr coke consumed in Lorraine furnaces has been reduced to only one-third of the total; there has, however, been little diminution in total coal and coke imports from the Ruhr. These will be greatly facilitated by the Moselle canalization project, completed in 1964.

Most of the new integrated works of postwar development schemes lie at the foot of the Moselle scarp in the Longwy and Thionville districts. Lorraine produces about two-thirds of the steel of France and about 80 per cent of its pig iron; the other major producing area is the northern coalfield, which accounts for a little over a fifth of total steel output; here the basic open-hearth process is used to consume Bessemer scrap from Lorraine and local scrap originating from the area's many heavy industries. The balance of the French steel output is derived from a number of small units in the Massif Central and the Alpine region and from a few coastal plants. The old basis of the industry in the Massif Central has largely disappeared, for all the steel of the Centre-Midi (that is, the combined Massif-Central and Alpine areas) now consists of quality alloy steel, produced in the electric furnace. The expansion of hydroelectricity generation and the postwar concentration of specialty steel in one large combination has revitalized this old area, and its steel output is now greater than in the past. The coastal plants are small, but with the construction of a large integrated plant at Dunkerque to use imported ore, France is at last following the example of all the other major producers of the noncommunist world.

Although it avoided nationalization, the French industry is subject to a very high degree of regulation and control; it has received low-interest state loans for modernization and for new equipment, and has been given a high degree of priority in raising funds in the capital market. Concentration of the industry has been encouraged; four great postwar groupings together with the old established de Wendel organization now account for about two-thirds of total steel output; the largest of these is Usinor, which controls production in the northern coalfield region. Heavy investment in coal carbonization, in ore mining, and in new blast furnaces and steelworks has substantially raised the competitive efficiency of the French industry and has even enabled its products to penetrate into the south German market; it can, indeed, meet the Community's removal of protective barriers and restrictive practices with composure.

Other Countries

The remaining countries of the EEC are only minor producers. As in France, Belgium experienced the Industrial Revolution earlier than Germany, for the English ironmaster Cockerill established blast furnaces at Liége early in the nineteenth century. Originally based on local raw materials, the Belgian industry has had to supplement high-cost domestic coal and ore by imports; nevertheless, the main centers of the industry remain the Liége-Seraing and Charleroi areas, where the industry first became established. Luxembourg also mines minette ores but imports additional supplies from across the French frontier; it is entirely dependent on its neighbors for fuel. Lacking heavy steel-consuming industries, Luxembourg is mainly a producer of pig iron and semifinished steel, which are exported for further fabrication. Both Belgium and Luxembourg make extensive use of the Thomas, or basic, Bessemer process. The Netherlands possesses a large integrated plant at IJmuiden, using imported ore and American and Ruhr coal, and a large new steelworks in the Rotterdam district also appears probable with the development of the Europort project, Rotterdam's bid for a larger share of the expanding trade of the EEC.

Long mismanaged and heavily protected, Italy's steel production has increased greatly since the end of World War II, and is expected to double again before 1975. The great disparity between the country's pig-iron and steel production clearly reveals the dependence on scrap, large quantities of which are imported from the United States. Italy has five large coastal integrated plants, situated at Genoa, Piombino (Tuscany), Naples, Trieste, and Taranto, and one inland at Aosta. The Taranto plant, begun in 1959, was part of the Cassa per il Mezzogiorno's plan for revitalizing the backward south. Numerous small steelworks are scattered throughout northern Italy, and these make use of local scrap, which is charged into electric furnaces or natural-gas-fired open-hearths. Industrial concentration and the increased employment by hydroelectricity and natural gas have greatly raised competitive efficiency and have offset a heavy reliance on imported raw materials. In relation to its total steel output Italy's output of quality steel is higher than that of any other EEC member. The greater part of the Italian industry is under public ownership.

Outside the EEC the only steel producers of note are Spain, Austria, and Sweden. Spain's heavily protected industry, confined to the Asturian coast, shows no sign of the postwar virility of its Italian counterpart. The Erzberg mines of Austria have produced ore since the Middle Ages, but the lack of nearby coking coal is a major handicap. Austria's great contribution to the industry is the LD process.

Sweden's small steel industry has an importance out of all proportion to its size. Swedish ores are of fundamental importance to Britain, West Germany, and other Western

European steel producers, but the great mining centers of Kiruna and Gallivare that produced them have no significance for the domestic industry, which is based on ores of the *Bergslagen* districts of central Sweden. The low-phosphoric ores of Dannemora and of Grangesburg and unlimited charcoal were the basis of the famous bar-iron (wrought-iron) industry that provided Sweden's principal export right up to the nineteenth century. These ores are still of great significance to the domestic industry; ores of higher phosphoric content, which also occur extensively in the Grangesberg district, were little worked until the Thomas process rendered them suitable for steelmaking, and are largely exported. Sweden's specialty is high-quality steel, for which its very pure ores, hydroelectric power, and long tradition of iron and steel production give it special advantages; it is the only noncommunist country that makes substantial quantities of charcoal iron, still necessary for the manufacture of certain kinds of steel, and almost half its steel output is produced in electric furnaces. Until World War II Sweden had a virtual monopoly of certain types of quality steel such as razor-blade steel, and its high-speed steel is widely exported. For its ordinary steels, however, the country is largely dependent on imports, although a new plant at Oxelosund using the Kaldo process is now producing tonnage steels at fully competitive prices.

THE RUSSIAN INDUSTRY

With an estimated crude-steel output of about 80 million tons in 1963, the Soviet Union is the world's second-largest steel producer, and both in the interwar period and after World War II the rapid growth of the Russian steel industry represented a prodigious achievement. Nevertheless, Russian capacity is still substantially below that of the United States, and since 1945 a number of countries have equaled or exceeded the rate of increase of Soviet steel production.

Development of the Modern Industry

The foundations of the modern Russian industry were laid by Peter the Great, who established the first state furnaces and forges in the Urals at the end of the seventeenth century. During the eighteenth century state and private plants based on numerous small but high-grade ore deposits, local charcoal, and serf labor proliferated in the central and northern Urals, and a large export trade in bar iron was built up; by the end of the century Russia vied with Britain for the position of world's leading iron producer. Late in the nineteenth century, technical change and emancipation of the serfs strongly worked against the old Ural area. Coke-fired blast furnaces did not become common in Russia until the last quarter of the nineteenth century, but their appearance then led inevitably to a movement of the industry to the Ukraine, where the coking coal of the Donbas and the hematite ores of Krivoy Rog offered the industry an assured basis for expansion; as in the Urals, state participation in the new area was very substantial.[19] After 1890 growth was very rapid; by 1913 steel output has reached almost 5 million tons, a level not regained until 1929.

The First Five Year Plan (1928 to 1932) exploited the large deposit of magnetite ore of the southern Urals and the coal of the Kuzbas through the famous Ural-Kuznetsk *kombinat*. Iron and coal had been worked at opposite ends of its 1,500-mile axis since the eighteenth cen-

[19] The very large share of the Russian economy that was controlled by the state even before the revolution is perhaps insufficiently appreciated.

tury, and in view of the unsuitability of Ural coal for metallurgical coke, a linkup had long been suggested. Transport appeared an insoluble problem, however, and the development of the *kombinat* was only possible through a substantial subsidy borne by the railroads. Increasing congestion made some relief for the overloaded rail network essential; the Second Five Year Plan (1933–1937) greatly enlarged the output of Karaganda coal (which nevertheless makes poor coke) for the Magnitogorsk furnaces in the Urals, and greater utilization of local ore was made in the blast furnaces at Novokuznetsk in the Kuzbas. By 1947 over 70 per cent of the ore consumed in Kuzbas plants was locally produced.[20]

As a result of the First and Second Five Year Plans the U.S.S.R. claimed that a substantial share of the iron and steel industry had been moved to the eastern regions, that is, the Urals and Soviet Asia. Nevertheless, substantial investment was also made in the Ukraine and in the central industrial area, and in the three years before World War II the share of the eastern regions in Russian steel production actually declined; the eastward migration of the industry only became a reality with the German occupation of the Ukraine. Postwar reconstruction in the Ukraine, however, was rapid; and with the exhaustion of their best and most easily won ores and coking coals, less has been heard of the further expansion of capacity in the eastern regions since the termination of the Fourth Five Year Plan (1946 to 1950). Even with the completion of the Seven Year Plan of 1959 to 1965, the proportion of the national steel output derived from the eastern regions will be less than that of 1950, despite the proposed creation of a "third metallurgical base" linking Kemerovo (Kuzbas) coal with ore from the middle Angara basin.[21]

[20] M. Gardner Clark, *The Economics of Soviet Steel,* Harvard University Press, Cambridge, Mass., 1956, p. 220.

Locations, Organizations, and Prospects

Three major iron- and steel-producing regions are recognized in most Soviet publications (Fig. 14-9). The greatest concentration is still found in the *southern,* or *Ukraine, region,* which produces about half the national output of pig iron and some 40 per cent of Russia's crude steel. Integrated plants are located at Krivoy Rog, on the Dnieper River between Dneprodzerzhinsk and Zaporozh'ye, and in the Donbas itself between Donetsk (formerly Stalino) and Voroshilovsk. With increasing use of sintered Krivoy Rog ores productivity of furnaces in the Ukraine has been raised greatly, and it is likely that real costs are no greater than those of any newer area; however, Zhdanov (formerly Mariupol) has an integrated plant using the very poor ores of the Kerch' peninsula, and must incur a heavy cost penalty. The second producing area is the *central region,* that is, the Moscow-Tula-Lipetsk area, which is mainly a producer of steel rather than of pig iron. The third, and most important steel producer is the *eastern regions,* the enormous area that includes the Urals and all Soviet Asia, collectively accounting for about half of the country's crude-steel output. Magnitogorsk, the largest single center of the industry in the U.S.S.R., is now compelled to mine poorer ores and to use poorer cokes than in the past, but the large integrated plants of Chelyabinsk, Sverdlovsk, and Nizhni Tagil still mainly depend on good Kuzbas coke. During World War II the need for production at any cost and the heavy burden on the transport system led to a resuscitation of charcoal-iron production, and a number of new furnaces were constructed. Despite the high cost, for which a low sulfur and phosphorus content do not entirely compensate, charcoal

[21] United Nations Economic Commission for Europe, *Economic Survey of Europe in 1959,* Geneva, 1960, pp. 20–21.

Fig. 14-9 Iron and steel centers of the U.S.S.R. (British Iron and Steel Federation.)

iron has continued to be produced on a substantial scale in the postwar period, a further indication of the heavy pressure on Kuzbas coking coals. Though backward in this respect, the Ural area, however, is the principal producer of specialty steels.

East of the Urals the only large integrated plant is at Novokuznetsk (formerly Stalinsk); its output of steel is exceeded only by that of Magnitogorsk. Much publicity has been given to the construction of new plants in Soviet Asia and in the Far East, but work on these projects has proceeded very slowly. Temir-tau in Kazakhstan now has blast furnaces in addition to the steelworks established during the war and uses Karaganda coal and local ore; in the whole of eastern Siberia and the Far East, however, the industry in 1960 was represented only by two small plants, at Petrovsk and Komsomol'sk-na-Amure. There is also a small integrated plant at Rustavi, near Tiblisi, which makes use of local deposits of ore and coal, and a considerably larger plant at Cherepovets, equidistant from Leningrad and Moscow in the so-called "northwest region," which uses ore from Karelia and coal from the Pechora Basin.

In an industry which inevitably demands large units for efficient operation, the Russian iron and steel plants are outstanding; and they are particularly noted for the extremely high productivity of blast furnaces, open-hearths, and other items of capital equipment. The productivity of labor is low, but to stress capital equipment makes good sense for a country which is essentially at a semideveloped stage of economic development. In the past the location of new large plants has been little geared to considerations of transport costs, and the movement of raw materials and of finished products has involved heavy burdens on other sectors of the economy. For the largest units, however, the market has been compelled to move to the source of supply; thus great complexes of steel-consuming industries have been located in the Urals and in the Kuzbas.

The future location pattern of the industry does present many problems. The U.S.S.R. possesses numerous deposits of both iron and coal scattered widely through the country, but they are poorly located in relation to each other and in relation to the existing distribution of population. Even in the largest coalfields, coking coals do not constitute more than a very small proportion of total reserves and are markedly inferior in quality to the coking coals of the major producers of the noncommunist world. Ores all too often contain harmful and injurious impurities, and although new deposits are continually being discovered, the best have long been known and worked. It would appear, therefore, that future expansion will demand a proportionately larger investment both in beneficiation of coal and ores and in transport improvements than has been the case in the past. Also, since the tenor of Soviet economic development has been continually to seek ways of improving the efficiency of capital, the most promising line of expansion would seem to be through additions to existing plants rather than through the construction of very capital-consuming new plant complexes.

The location pattern of the Russian industry may thus not differ very greatly in the future from that of the other major producers; the dominance of the present major centers is likely to be confirmed, although the rate of growth of steel output may be much faster in newer areas. However, any attempt by Moscow to implement its promises of more consumer goods or to follow the growing world trend of importing ore would probably operate further to enlarge the importance of the major producing area, the Ukraine. Expansion, at least, is assured; by the conclusion of the Seven Year Plan in 1965 steel output should reach about 90 million tons, while a level of 117 million tons is possible a decade later.[22]

The Soviet Satellites The satellite countries of Eastern Europe are also poorly supplied with raw materials for the iron and steel industry; coking coal is almost everywhere in short supply, ore resources are little better, and imports from the U.S.S.R. have been necessary. Poland and Czechoslovakia each accounted for about a third of the 21 million tons of crude steel produced by the six satellite countries in 1961. The two countries share the Upper Silesian coalfield, which, despite its poor coking coal, has long been the chief focus of the industry in Eastern Europe; Poland's largest postwar plant, however, is located east of Kraków at the new town of Nova Huta. Czechoslovakian steel production is shared by northern Moravia and the coal basins of Bohemia. Despite difficulties over raw materials, both Poland and Czechoslovakia have planned to raise steel output to about 10 million tons by 1965.

OTHER PRODUCING COUNTRIES

Several smaller producers of iron and steel are of particular interest. India, with excellent supplies of ore, will almost certainly become a producer of greater significance than at present; after a considerable period of stagnation the British, West German, and Russian projects at Durgapur, Rourkela and Bhilai, respectively, and the expansion of the Jamshedpur plant will give the country four modern integrated works in the area between the Chota Nagpur plateau ore fields and the Damodar valley coalfields. Brazil, with equally good resources of ore and almost equally in need of a

[22] *Ibid.* By this date the United States is expected to produce almost 150 million tons.

higher level of economic development, has not so far attracted a similar international rivalry to aid its struggling domestic industry. The Union of South Africa has a small but flourishing producer in its nationalized steel industry, and production in Australia is in the hands of a single company (the Broken Hill Proprietary Company, or BHP) which has long claimed to be the cheapest producer of steel in the world. Only Japan and China, however, already have well-developed iron and steel industries which can scarcely fail to become of even greater importance.

Japan

In 1960 Japan's crude-steel output exceeded 20 million tons for the first time, and in the following year the country displaced Britain as the world's fourth-largest producer, an incredible performance for a country in which large-scale, capital-intensive iron and steel production dates only from the establishment of the Yawata ironworks in 1896, and which, even at its peak war effort in 1943 and with all the material resources of mainland East Asia at its disposal, could produce only a little over 7.5 million tons of crude steel. It is true that without enormous American assistance this rapid postwar growth would have been impossible; since the end of the Korean conflict, however, the main impetus for expansion has come from Japan's own booming economy. This achievement is all the more remarkable in view of the very slender resource base for the industry in the Japanese islands; it is striking testimony to the already noted limited influence of domestic raw-material resources in economic development.

A heavy dependence on imported raw materials is a major characteristic of the Japanese iron and steel industry, as indeed it is of many Japanese industries. Neither of the country's two major coalfields, which lie towards the opposite extremities of the Japanese islands, produces good metallurgical coke, and domestic resources of iron ore are meager and are of such low grade that beneficiation is mandatory. Japan has thus concentrated largely on steelmaking in view of the growing demand for steel products and the need to conserve shipping space and to reduce transport costs.

Before World War II Japan made heavy imports of scrap, principally from the United States, and imported pig iron from Manchuria and Korea. Iron smelting became increasingly important with the establishment of a war economy, but even in 1939 imports of scrap and pig still substantially exceeded domestic pig-iron production. Since World War II, however, the industry has undergone a fundamental change as scrap has become progressively more expensive. Now based on imported coking coal and ore, pig-iron production has grown rapidly; the present ratio of steel production to pig-iron production does not differ greatly from that of the United States or West Germany.

Before 1941 coking coals from north China and Manchuria were imported for blending in coke ovens with domestic coals, but the main source of supply at present is the United States; balance-of-payments problems, however, compel the largest possible utilization of relatively high-cost domestic coals. Ore is imported from Malaya and the Philippines as before World War II, but India, including Goa, is now an important supplier, and Japan will have to look further afield as its steel output rises; both Africa and Latin America are possible new sources.

The nature of the industry in the past led to a preponderance of small steelworks and rolling mills, but since 1945, the integrated plant has become the dominant type of unit. The extensive use of imported raw materials has made it possible to locate the industry in proximity to the main markets of the great port cities, and Japan is unique among major producers in that all its large integrated plants are located on tidewater. The Hanshin area (Osaka-Kobe) has the greatest concentration of plants, but it still possesses many small steel mills as well as large integrated plants (Fig. 14-10). The Keihin (Tokyo-Yokohama) area is the second most important area, and has made somewhat greater progress in modernizing smaller nonintegrated works and in eliminating smaller marginal units. Northern Kyushu, the

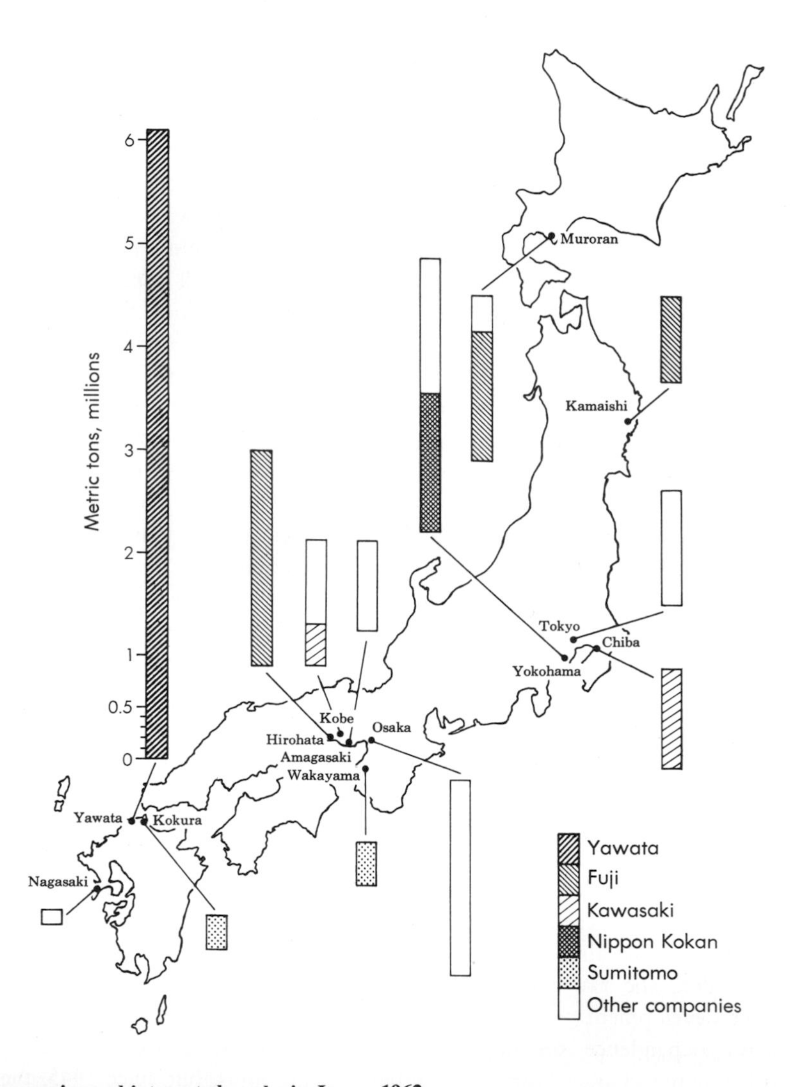

Fig. 14-10 Steel companies and integrated works in Japan, 1962.
Japan is unique among major producers in that all its integrated works are coastal. Some two-thirds of its crude steel production in 1961 was produced in the integrated plants shown here. (British Iron and Steel Federation.)

birthplace of the modern industry, owes its origin to the Chikuho coalfield and remains the preserve of the large integrated plant; its Yawata plant is the largest in the free world outside the United States. Nagoya, the third great metropolitan focus of Japan, also possesses a small integrated plant and steelworks, and further expansion here is likely in view of Nagoya's role in the rapidly expanding Japanese automobile industry. There are also works at Kaimaishi on the ore fields of northern Honshu and at Muroran (Fuji steel) in Hokkaido.

As in Russia, the development of the industry owed much to the imperial government, which established the Yawata works largely for military reasons, and the pattern of steel utilization has long been governed by military considerations. Right up to World War II pig-iron production was entirely controlled by the state, and although steel production was shared with the great *Zaibatsu,* government exercised a firm control. Military and naval requirements no longer dominate the industry, but plate and structural steel are still of greater significance than in Western producers. The growth of Japanese automobile production and other consumer-durable industries, however, suggests that in the near future sheet and strip will become of increasing importance.

Its dependence on imported raw materials with heavy transport charges (which virtually double their cost), means that Japan is a high-cost steel producer. Nevertheless, it has developed a considerable export trade in certain finished products, and the great steel companies Yawata, Sumitomo, and Fuji are becoming widely known. It is probable that Japanese steel production, having already exceeded that of Britain, will come to equal that of West Germany soon after 1965; per capita consumption, however, would still be very much lower than in either of the two leading Western European producers.

China

Since 1950 China has set about the task of making itself a major iron and steel producer with an awe-inspiring intensity; by 1975 China will probably be producing more than 50 million tons of steel, an output that took the U.S.S.R. more than forty years to achieve. The country certainly possesses the physical resources to achieve an output of this level, and as its first goal set itself to surpass the steel output of Britain.[23]

Coal and iron of some sort occur in every province of China, but while three-quarters of the coal reserves lie in Shensi and Shansi, about 50 per cent of the estimated ore reserves occur in south Manchuria, now part of the northeast region. As in the U.S.S.R., only a small proportion of the coal deposits produces metallurgical coke, and ore bodies are generally of low quality and small size. In view of the paucity of communications, mining of coal and iron deposits has been largely governed by proximity to major centers of population, and more distant deposits, even when of higher quality, have in the past been largely unworked. Under such conditions, therefore, it is scarcely surprising that attempts to create giant capital-intensive complexes on the model of those of the U.S.S.R. has produced severe problems in the development of resource-oriented iron and steel complexes in China's pioneer regions, and China's railroads are probably under even greater pressure than those of the U.S.S.R.

Though the industry began in the Yangtze valley towards the end of the nineteenth century, south Manchuria is by far the most important producing area, probably accounting for almost two-thirds of China's pig-iron production. The Manchurian industry, located

[23] To achieve a comparable per capita steel consumption, and in the absence of further population increase, China would have to produce more than 360 million tons per annum, an obvious impossibility in the foreseeable future.

over 400 miles distant from the Peking-Tientsin area, the main urban and industrial focus of north China, was begun by the Japanese during their temporary occupation in World War I. The Japanese initially regarded Manchuria as a source of pig iron for Japanese steelworks; that Peking eventually acquired in Manchuria a self-contained industrial area with steelworks, finishing mills, and associated steel-consuming heavy industries was largely a consequence of the colonizing activities of the Japanese Kwantung Army, which in the decade before World War II virtually treated Manchuria as its own private possession.[24]

[24]The Russians removed much of the equipment from the former Japanese plants in 1945 but with the change of regime in China later found themselves obliged to replace what they had taken.

These small-capacity blast furnaces were under construction at a coastal site in Chekiang during China's "great leap forward."

China's attempt to expand iron and steel production through the use of primitive furnaces such as these of a north China commune (at left) ultimately proved abortive.

The basis of the Manchurian industry is the iron ore of the Anshan-Kung-ch'ang-ling district and coal from Fu-shun and Pen-ch'i; when mixed, these coals produce acceptable coke. Coking coal and iron ore also occur further east along the Yalu valley, where Japanese attempts to establish the industry in the Tung-pien-tao area were arrested by World War II; Peking, however, appears to have neglected this development and has concentrated its efforts on expanding the Anshan-Pen-ch'i-Fu-shun complex of plants.

A second complex is growing out of a number of former small plants in Hopeh and in Shantung. This includes plants at Shih-ching-shan west of Peking, at Tientsin, and at T'ang-shan and a new steelworks at Peking itself. None of these are large integrated plants, but such a plant was provided for in the First Five Year Plan, to be situated at Pao-t'ou, in Inner Mongolia, and now part of the north China region. Construction of the Pao-t'ou plant was long delayed, however, and its situation is not clear. There is also small integrated works at T'ai-yüan in Shansi, and a number of new steelworks are planned or are under construction in Shensi.

The Yangtze valley is the third of China's iron and steel producing areas. Some of the plants here date from the nineteenth century, but others came into existence after the outbreak of the Japanese war in 1937. This area possesses numerous ore deposits, of which that at Ta-yeh in Hupeh is the most important, and it enjoys the best transportation facilities in China. Small integrated plants exist as Shanghai in Anhwei and at Ta-yeh and Han-k'ou in the Wu-han three-city area, often identified as the logical capital of China. This has been selected for the development of a giant complex of works that will eventually rival Anshan; its new blast furnaces, designed and erected by the Russians, are said to be among the very largest in the world. Finally, the plant at Chungking, one of the main arsenals in the long struggle against Japan, has been re-equipped and modernized and now produces heavy rails and sections.

Though a number of small plants were constructed in the south and southwest China during the Japanese war, the industry here is very poorly developed. The First Five Year Plan, however, envisaged the construction of a number of new plants in Kweichow, which were presumably to be linked with the railroad extensions planned for this part of the country.

China is anomalous in producing more pig iron than steel; the low level of economic development and the shortage of scrap make it very difficult to economize in capital investment in blast-furnace construction, although the Japanese built a number of small Krupp-Renn plants before World War II. It was partly this consideration that prompted the great proliferation of peasant and backyard furnaces and converters in 1958, and in a country with very poor communications, copious labor, and small but widely scattered deposits of raw materials, the maximum utilization of local resources had much to commend it. Iron was smelted in furnaces with a life of only three days, and numerous small side-blown converters produced a steel-like substance. Many Western observers, however, declared this product quite unsuitable for modern industrial uses, and these observations in fact proved to be correct; moreover, it appeared that the intense drive for scrap had to some extent deprived the modern capital-intensive industry of much-needed raw materials. It was therefore announced that from 1959 onwards indigenous-style production would not be included in national planning, though some of the better-located small-scale indigenous establishments are likely to be retained as training centers, and may eventually be upgraded as modern plants through further capital investment.

Thus China's experience has shown that

there is no shortcut to the creation of a large ferrous-metal industry. Also, even more important than capital in modern industrialized society is skilled labor, and though Peking could effect some economies in the former, it could not overcome the handicap of an almost complete absence of the latter.

SELECTED REFERENCES

Alderfer, E. B., and H. E. Michl: *Economics of American Industry,* McGraw-Hill Book Company, New York, 1957, pp. 25–86.

Alexandersson, Gunnar: "Changes in the Locational Pattern of the Anglo-American Steel Industry, 1948–1959," *Economic Geography,* vol. 37, pp. 95–114, 1961.

Allen, G. C.: *British Industries and Their Organization,* Longmans, Green & Co., Ltd., London, 1959, pp. 110–126.

American Iron and Steel Institute: *Steel in the Soviet Union,* New York, 1958.

Anglo-American Council on Productivity: *Iron and Steel,* London, 1952.

Brandt, D. J. O.: *The Manufacture of Iron and Steel,* English Universities Press, London, 1960.

British Iron and Steel Federation: "Cartels and Concentration in the ECSC," *The Steel Review,* no. 22, pp. 24–29, 1961.

———: "China and Her Race for Steel Production," *The Steel Review,* no. 15, pp. 8–19, 1959.

———: "Cooperative Arrangements in the ECSC," *The Steel Review,* no. 29, pp. 42–48, 1963.

———: "France: Her Steel Industry," *The Steel Review,* no. 17, pp. 28–33, 1960.

———: "New Processes in Steel," *The Steel Review,* no. 12, pp. 25–34, 1958.

———: "The Russian Steel Industry," *The Steel Review,* no. 6, pp. 24–48, 1957.

———: "Steel in the German Economy," *The Steel Review,* no. 14, pp. 10–25, 1959.

———: "Structural Change in World Ore," *The Steel Review,* no. 30, pp. 18–30, 1963.

Burn, Duncan: *The Economic History of Steel Making,* Cambridge University Press, Cambridge, 1961.

———: *The Steel Industry: A Study in Competition and Planning,* Cambridge University Press, Cambridge, 1961.

Clark, M. Gardner: *The Economics of Soviet Steel,* Harvard University Press, Cambridge, Mass., 1956.

Commonwealth Economic Committee: *Iron and Steel and Alloying Metals,* H. M. Stationery Office, London, 1962.

Erselcuk, Muzaffer: "The Iron and Steel Industry of China," *Economic Geography,* vol. 32, pp. 347–371, 1956.

Martin, J. E.: "Recent Trends in the Lorraine Iron and Steel Industry," *Geography,* vol. 43, pp. 191–199, 1958.

Organisation for Economic Cooperation and Development: *The Iron and Steel Industry,* Paris, 1961.

Pounds, N. J. G.: *The Geography of Iron and Steel,* Hutchinson & Co. (Publishers), Ltd., London, 1959.

———: *The Ruhr,* Indiana University Press, Bloomington, Ind., and Faber & Faber, Ltd., London, 1952.

——— and W. N. Parker: *Coal and Steel in Western Europe,* Indiana University Press, Bloomington, Ind., and Faber & Faber, Ltd., London, 1957.

Rodgers, Allan: "Industrial Inertia: A Major Factor in the Location of the Iron and Steel Industry of the United States," *Geographical Review,* vol. 42, pp. 56–66, 1962.

———: "The Iron and Steel Industry of the Mahoning and Shenango Valleys," *Economic Geography,* vol. 28, pp. 331–342, 1952.

United Nations: *Survey of World Iron Ore Resources,* New York, 1955.

United Nations Economic Commission for Europe: *Comparison of Steel Making Processes,* Geneva, 1962.

———: *Long Term Trends and Prospects in the European Steel Industry,* Geneva, 1959.

White, Langdon, and George Primmer: "The Iron and Steel Industry of Duluth: A Study in Locational Maladjustment," *Geographical Review,* vol. 27, pp. 82–91, 1937.

Woytinsky, W. S., and E. S. Woytinsky: *World Population and Production,* The Twentieth Century Fund, New York, 1953, pp. 1099–1143.

Yamamoto, T.: "The Steel Industry in Japan," *Oriental Economist,* vol. 26, pp. 539–542, 1958.

Chapter 15

NONFERROUS-METAL INDUSTRIES

To the layman the nonferrous-metal industries include the production and fabrication of all metals other than iron and steel, but to the mineralogist and to the metal industries themselves the term "nonferrous metals" has a more restricted meaning. Usage is far from uniform, however, and for convenience the following groups of metals may be recognized:

The *noble,* or *precious,* metals, which include gold, silver, and platinum.

The *base* metals, originally all nonnoble metals but now usually regarded as comprising copper, lead, zinc, and tin (and occasionally nickel and aluminum).

The *light* metals, aluminum, titanium, and magnesium.

Ferroalloying metals, such as chromium, cobalt, manganese, molybdenum, nickel, tungsten, and vanadium.

Metals of particular significance to the electronics industry, such as cadmium and mercury.

Metals associated with the production of atomic energy and other new metals of significance to missile industries, whose properties are still imperfectly understood. This group includes the heaviest metals, such as uranium and thorium, and the lightest, such as lithium and beryllium.

Most of these have much in common from the economic standpoint, but the precious metals have quite different economic characteristics from the rest.

To stress the importance of the nonferrous-metal industries in economies at a high level of development is but to labor the obvious. The production and transmission of electric energy, the electronics industry, and the manufacture of aircraft, motor vehicles, and missiles are all particularly dependent on the nonferrous-metal industries; it would not, however, be too much to claim that there is almost no manufacturing industry in which they do not find some application.

Moreover, their importance is certain to augment in the future. The United States, which already accounts for about one-half of the total world consumption of many metals and for a very much higher proportion of some, will need increasingly large quantities of all in the near future. In 1952, the President's Materials Policy Commission estimated that by 1975 the United States would consume some 20 per cent more tin, 40 per cent more copper and zinc, 50 per cent more lead, 80 per cent more antimony, 100 per cent more nickel and chromium, 300 per cent more bauxite and titanium, and almost 2,000 per cent more magnesium than it did in 1950. The rate of increase in nonferrous-metal consumption of other countries at a high level of economic development is likely to be even more rapid, and the demands of the present underdeveloped economies will be raised considerably by their national development plans. Thus there has been some anxiety over the future availability of certain metals, and the fact that the West is becoming increasingly dependent on the underdeveloped economies for its supplies of these metals gives rise to considerable political and strategic problems. Nevertheless, it is necessary not to overstate the case; the value of the total world output of all nonferrous metals is considerably less than that of the output of iron and steel products in the United States alone; moreover, despite long-term concern there is a chronic tendency for most nonferrous metals to be in oversupply, and their price fluctuations contrast markedly with the strong price stability of iron and steel products. In many employments nonferrous metals face growing competition from metal substitutes.

GENERAL CHARACTERISTICS OF THE INDUSTRIES

Production of nonferrous metals is carried out in two stages. The first involves extracting the ore, and converting it into a concentrate, and in some instances, the preliminary reduction of the metal. The second stage consists of further refining and fabrication. These two stages may be carried on at the same location, or they may be widely separated geographically. With the exception of aluminum, there is generally little further fabrication by metal producers themselves; that is, there is little "forward integration."

Modern mining of nonferrous metal ores depends on the economies of large-scale operations; for the great increase in world demand could never have been met from the limited deposits of high-grade ore. Mechanization of mining and improved techniques of smelting and refining have made possible the profitable working of ores of very low grade—provided that the ore body is large enough to amortize the heavy initial capital investment in mine and smelter equipment. The metallic content of most nonferrous metal ores now being worked is thus much lower than is the case with iron ore; for the world as a whole copper ores average about 3 per cent, lead ores some 7 per cent, and zinc ores about 15 per cent metallic content. Malayan alluvial deposits have an average tinstone content of about 0.3 pound per cubic yard, and in lode deposits throughout the world the metallic content seldom exceeds 5 per cent. Bauxite, the principal ore of aluminum, is anomalous, however; profitable working requires an ore with a metal equivalent of not less than 45 per cent. As a result there is a considerable world trade in bauxite, but long-distance transport of other nonferrous-metal ores is clearly out of the question. The preparation of concentrates, or preliminary reduction of the metal, has to take place in close proximity to the mine; further refining to produce the high-quality metals demanded by modern industry can then take place in the vicinity of the market.

The development of modern techniques of large-scale mining, ore treatment, and refining has meant in practice that the production of one metal often involves the production of others; that is, metals tend to be joint products. Several ores contain minerals from which a number of metals can be extracted; galena, the principal lead ore, is almost invariably argentiferous and often occurs in association with sphalerite, or zinc blende, the main ore of zinc. In the past the recovery of such subsidiary metals was impossible, and much potentially valuable material was dumped as waste. The treatment of complex ores has been greatly facilitated by the technique of selective flotation, a process which uses the affinity of very small particles of concentrated ore for certain oils. In this process, the finely crushed ore is mixed with water, chemicals, and oils and is agitated in a tank, or cell; particles of the desired mineral attach themselves to the oil-coated bubbles that are formed, and rise to the surface of the cell, where the froth is removed. By varying the chemicals used, the successive extraction of a number of metallic minerals is possible, and although the producer cannot alter the proportions of the minerals present in his ore, he can modify the extraction rate to obtain a high-grade concentrate of one metalliferous mineral and a lower-grade concentrate of another.

Thus the profitability of a mine can well turn upon what are essentially by-products, and the output of one metal can depend on the level of output of another. The development of new technologies and new demand patterns is continually converting former wastes into valuable resources, as has been the case with the mine dumps of the Witwatersrand, or simply Rand, goldfields of South Africa, which are being reworked for their uranium content. Many of the newer metals used in the production of missiles are derived from what were formerly waste products from base-metal refining.

Another important characteristic of the nonferrous metals is that they generally do not undergo any fundamental and irreversible change of form in their usual employment, which is in the production of durable goods. When these have reached the end of their economic life the metals in them can often be recovered and used again. In some employments, of course, metals may undergo chemical changes which render this impossible, but newer techniques of metal recovery have progressively raised the share of recovered metal in total metal production. Thus new-metal producers compete not only with each other but also with the producers of recovered, or secondary, metal—for in the absence of much forward integration, all have an identical product to sell.

Price and Price Instability

A characteristic of the nonferrous-metal industries that gives rise to the most intractable economic and political problems is their chronic price instability. In this respect the nonferrous metals stand with agricultural products and differ sharply from manufactures, whose prices on the whole are remarkably stable.

In general, the higher the average price of the metal, the greater the price fluctuations. The aristocrat of the nonferrous metals is tin, the price of which exceeded $1.90 per pound (£1,520 per long ton)[1] at one time during the Korean conflict; less than two years later tin

[1] While £1 = U.S. $2.8 (approx.), U.S. cents per pound × 8 = £ Sterling per long ton.

was priced for a time at below 80 cents per pound, but in the fall of 1964 it soared to a record $2.00 per pound. The temperature of the cold war is thus clearly a factor of considerable importance. Nickel ranks below tin in the price scale, but its average price level is substantially above that of all other base metals. Copper is usually about a third to a quarter the price of tin, and aluminum is cheaper still. Lead and zinc stand together at the bottom of the price scale with a price level about a third that of copper.

Each metal has uses for which it is particularly suitable, but there are others for which substitutes will serve almost as well; in fact, none of the nonferrous metals can be regarded as indispensable, although it is extremely inconvenient to have to do without a particular one, even for a limited period. Thus when a metal appreciates considerably in price, it is possible to transfer part of its field of employment to a metal of lower price rank; new techniques also help to economize in the use of the more expensive metals such as tin and nickel.

Given the nature of modern mining, short-term inflexibility of supply is inevitable. An increase in the price of a metal will certainly encourage larger supplies of recovered metal, but to increase the output of new metal is not something that can be accomplished overnight. As the price increases, recently closed marginal mines reopen, and if the higher price is expected to endure, investment in new capacity will eventually be made; at least two to three years, however, must elapse before a large new mine can come into operation. On the other hand, reductions in price cannot speedily cause a decline in mine output, for in order to cover its high overhead costs, a large mine must operate close to capacity; these costs remain high whatever the level of production.

The greatest hardships and dislocations resulting from unstable prices are largely borne by countries at a low level of economic development, for these are fast becoming the most important producers of new metal. Production of lower-cost recovered metal, of course, is highest in countries that are large consumers, namely, those at a high level of economic development; recovered-metal producers in economically advanced countries immediately benefit when prices rise and cut output quickly when they fall.

All mining tends to involve increasing costs as the richer ores and veins are worked out, but the substantial differences in costs of production between the various producers further aggravate the effects of price instability. Such cost differences reflect not only the richness of ores and the geologic conditions in which they occur but also differing national price and income structures. In times of high or rising prices, low-cost producers make windfall profits; when prices fall, high-cost producers suffer first, but low-cost producers are also affected, for insofar as their low costs come from operation at or near capacity, their opportunities for reduction of output are limited.

The production of most metals is in the hands of a small number of large organizations, often with strong international connections. The great metal-producing companies have interests in areas with varying cost levels and claim that the profits on their low-cost operations are used to assist production in areas of high cost, thus extending the life of the world's mineral reserves. Whether there is any substance in this argument or not, the fact remains that in several countries at a low level of development, exports of metal account for a very large share of foreign earnings; a fall in the price of metal on the world market can thus be offset by devaluating the local currency, so that even severe price declines may have little or no effect in discouraging output in high-cost producers. But producers are opposed by the "countervailing power"[2] of a few large buyers, mainly producers of electric equipment, iron and steel, chemicals, etc., for whom the costs of nonferrous metals are only a small part of total costs; these users promptly adjust their purchases to changes in business activity. Producing states, therefore, have endeavored to strengthen their economic position by formal international agreements or by so-called "study groups," which have attempted, with singularly limited success, to allocate markets or quotas and to maintain floor and ceiling prices through the operation of buffer stocks.

For reasons of national security the United States government also holds substantial metal stocks. Before World War II the United States was not only the largest producer but also the largest exporter of many nonferrous metals. Its situation has since changed dramatically; domestic production is now incapable of meeting demand, and the country has become the world's largest importer of almost all nonferrous metals. The greater portion of these metal imports is derived from foreign operations of American mining companies or from foreign companies (mainly British) in which American capital has a substantial interest. Nevertheless, the growing dependence of foreign sources of supply has obvious dangers; nationalism in several underdeveloped countries is proving heady stuff.

The problems faced by the United States are particularly acute in face of a mounting demand and a growing disparity between domestic and foreign costs of metal production. Mining interests in the country assert that the maintenance of a high level of national security necessitates high protective duties to keep the capital and labor at present engaged in nonferrous-metal production from moving into other employments. Others take the view that the maintenance of high-cost domestic mining through government support assists a more rapid depletion of limited national resources and weakens the country's defenses.[3] National security in this context is usually equated with sectional self-interest; domestic producers with foreign interests speak in a different tone from those without such connections. The external problems are just as acute, for underdeveloped economies regard the downswings of metal prices as another example of perpetual exploitation by the industrialized countries, pointing out as evidence the relative decline in the prices of primary products compared with those of manufactures since the end of World War II.

COPPER AND ALUMINUM

Copper heads the nonferrous metals in value of output. Since 1954 the output of primary copper has been exceeded by that of aluminum, but the output of recovered copper is larger than that of aluminum, and in 1961 copper still occupied the premier position in terms of total output. Nevertheless, aluminum's present rate of increase in output suggests that by 1970 the light metal will be the leader both by value and quantity.

The Metals Compared

Copper was probably the first metal to be worked by man; aluminum is a product of the past century. Copper is easily extracted from its ores, but the reduction of aluminum is a complex operation that at present requires the consumption of enormous quantities of electric energy; its lower price is an eloquent testimony

[2] See **J. K. Galbraith,** *American Capitalism: The Concept of Countervailing Power,* **Houghton Mifflin Company, Boston, rev. ed. 1956, chap. 9.**

[3] **Percy W. Bidwell,** *Raw Materials: A Study of American Policy,* **Harper & Row, Publishers, Incorporated, New York, 1958, p. 129.**

to the economies that follow from large-scale operations.

A comparison of the properties of the two metals reveals many opportunities for substitution. Both metals are attractive in appearance and resist corrosion; aluminum in particular can be given a wide variety of attractive finishes. Both metals are extremely ductile, being easily worked by drawing and extrusion, and are excellent conductors of heat and electricity. Aluminum's conductivity is only two-thirds that of copper, and both are inferior to silver, but the high price of silver limits its employment to specialized uses in which the maximum of conductivity is essential. Copper, however, is a heavy metal, having a specific gravity greater than that of iron, and it is also relatively weak. The addition of almost any metal hardens copper, but as this results in a substantial increase in resistance, the metal is used unalloyed in many applications.[4] As aluminum has a specific gravity less than one-third that of copper, an aluminum line is a better conductor than a copper one of equal length and weight. For this reason and also because of its price advantage, the steel-cored aluminum cable has largely replaced copper as a medium for high-voltage transmission. Aluminum has also displaced copper in other electrical uses in which its higher resistance incurs no real penalty, for instance, in fractional-horsepower motors, but for numerous employments in electricity generation and distribution copper admits of no real substitute. The ease with which it can be soldered is another substantial advantage of copper over aluminum and, in conjunction with its excellent heat-conducting properties, has so far caused it to be preferred for use in automobile radiators; but the lighter metal may well be increasingly used for this purpose in the future. Copper can be alloyed with zinc to produce brass and with tin to produce bronze. Many varieties of these alloys are produced and the range of other copper alloys is very wide indeed.

Aluminum's greatest asset is its lightness. Its low specific gravity, in fact, largely compensates for the high consumption of energy involved in producing it, for the energy required to produce a cubic foot of aluminum is only 2.8 times that of producing a cubic foot of iron. Moreover, alloyed with small quantities of copper, magnesium, nickel, and other metals, aluminum can be given the tensile strength of mild steel. Automobiles, buses, trucks, railroad rolling stock, and especially aircraft (of which over a third of the total weight may consist of aluminum alloys) are familiar fields of application, but shipbuilding is also likely to provide an increasing demand for this versatile metal. The rest of the world has lagged considerably behind the United States in the use of aluminum in building and construction, and a substantial increase in the use of the metal in this industry appears certain in other highly developed economies. The world's first aluminum bascule bridge at Sunderland, England, foreshadows a large increase in the consumption of aluminum in civil engineering. Aluminum is thus a steel substitute as well as a copper substitute. There are many ways in which the aluminum industry more closely resembles that of iron and steel than the other nonferrous-metal industries. Its high-grade ores which can withstand the cost of transportation over considerable distances, its heavy power requirements and complex technology which have largely confined its production to countries at a high level of development, its considerable degree of forward integration and its administered price—all these strongly recall the iron and steel industry.

In consequence of the structure of the aluminum industry the greater price stability of aluminum than copper is a further factor

[4] **Where high conductivity and considerable strength are necessary, as in telegraph lines, an alloy containing about 3 per cent of cadmium provides the best compromise.**

making for substitution. It is already evident that a world per capita copper consumption equivalent to that of the United States at present is beyond the capacity of the world's known copper resources, and in the long run the two metals are more likely to be complementary than competitive. Aluminum will probably take over more and more of copper's traditional employments, thus freeing the scarcer metal for those uses in which it has the greatest comparative advantage; aluminum will, in effect, ensure that the world's limited resources of copper are stretched very much further.

Copper

Copper produces more minerals than any other metal; it can even occur as native, or pure, copper, although such deposits are now of negligible commercial importance. The history of copper mining has shown a progressive shift from the working of native copper to vein-type oxide ores deposited by hot ascending solutions and, in turn, to the so-called "porphyry" coppers—low-grade sulfide ores widely disseminated through immense quantities of rock. Vein deposits are worked by underground mining, but the porphyry coppers are mainly worked in great open-pits or strip mines. Germany, Sweden, and Spain were the principal sources of copper in the Middle Ages, but in the first half of the nineteenth century the principal producer of copper, as indeed of almost all metals, was Britain. After 1850 Chile assumed the premier position, and in 1883 the United States became the leading producer, a position which it has held ever since. Until almost the turn of the century the United States produced from a half to two-thirds of the world's copper; in the present century, however, its share of mine production has progressively fallen with increased production from Chile, Canada, and, after 1930, the Belgian Congo and Northern Rhodesia. Formerly a substantial net exporter, the United States has become the world's largest importer since World War II.

Major Producers of the World Until about 1880 the principal copper-producing district in the United States was the Keweenaw range of Michigan, famous for its native copper; this district still contains immense copper deposits, but much must be regarded as uneconomic at the present. The period from 1880 to 1910 was associated with the growth of vein oxide-ore mining and particularly with the development of the Butte district of Montana, "the richest hill on earth," which gave to the Anaconda Corporation a position of almost complete dominance in the industry. After 1910, however, its supposed monopoly was broken by the development of the porphyry coppers of Utah and Arizona and the growth of the two other giants of the copper industry, the Kennecott and Phelps Dodge corporations. On a state basis Arizona is the largest copper producer, but its total output of not far short of half the national total is made up from a number of mining districts in the southern portion of the state—Morenci, Miami, Ray, Ajo, Bisbee, and others. Utah produces about a quarter of the national output of mine copper, but this is derived from virtually one enormous mine, the great open-pit at Bingham operated by Kennecott. This company also controls production in New Mexico and in Nevada, the other important producing states, but Arizona remains largely the stronghold of Phelps Dodge.

As the average copper content of ores worked in the United States is no more than 1 per cent, the country is a comparatively high-cost producer. Higher-grade foreign ores have thus exerted considerable attraction for the large copper companies; more than two-thirds of the total output controlled by Anaconda comes from abroad. Phelps Dodge, however, has remained largely a domestic producer.

Higher-grade ore bodies of enormous size and lower labor costs go far to explain the competitive position of Chile, second-largest producer of the free world; these advantages offset heavy export taxes and the costs inseparable from production in a desert environment. In contrast to that of the United States, which has more than thirty large mines, Chile's output largely comes from but four large mines; the dozen or so medium mines and the numerous small mines produce less than 5 per cent of total output. Three large mines operated by subsidiaries of Anaconda—Chuquicamata, Potrerillos, and El Salvador—lie in the virtually rainless desert of northern Chile. Chuquicamata, which lies inland from Antofagasta, is the world's largest copper mine and apparently contains the largest reserves; Potrerillos and El Salvador are situated to the south, inland of Chañaral; El Salvador is a post-1956 development, but production at the other large Chilean mines began before 1920. At Sewell, southeast of Santiago, is situated the large El Teniente mine of Braden, a Kennecott subsidiary.

Physical difficulties, such as the problem of water supply and a progressive diminution of the metallic content of ore from the 1.6 per cent or more of the past, are now of less significance than those arising from the political environment; in Chile as in other countries at a low level of economic development, the large foreign-owned corporation has become a favorite target of nationalism. The investment plans of the American companies in 1961 envisaged an eventual increase of 100,000 tons in the country's copper output, but despite this the Chilean government in the same year proposed to force foreign companies to increase output by 15 per cent every three years, to refine all mines output in the country, and to export more copper in fabricated form. These extreme demands may perhaps be modified, for in the long run the interests of the copper companies and the state closely coincide; nevertheless, foreign mining companies may have to face more formidable difficulties than any they have encountered in the past. Some two-thirds of Anaconda's copper production was refined in the country in 1960, but such considerations cannot be expected to carry much weight in view of the considerable irrational content of much nationalist opinion and the demands of extremists for nationalization.[5] Yet Chile's political problems appear mild in comparison with those of what is, in effect, the world's largest copper-producing region, the copper belt of Katanga and Northern Rhodesia.

This central African region has the lowest costs of production in the world, a result of the relatively high metal content of its sulfide ores, which can amount to 6 per cent or more. Moreover, the ores occur in bedded deposits continuous over considerable horizontal distances, and, though the ores are extracted by underground mining instead of by open-pits as in the United States and Chile, low-cost African labor goes far to offset this disadvantage.[6]

Physical isolation long retarded the development of the African copper belt, but the restrictive policy of the American-controlled copper cartels of the Twenties accelerated British investment in the industry, and the completion of the Benguela railway in 1931 went far to solve the area's transport problems. The pace of expansion of copper output, how-

[5] See p. 86 for a comment on nationalist attitudes to foreign estate companies; it applies equally to mining companies.

[6] Africans, however, are denied all opportunity to learn skilled trades by the white unions, and during 1963, prolonged strikes by white workers to enforce job segregation disrupted production in many mines. With the transformation in 1964 of Northern Rhodesia into the independent state of Zambia, a showdown on this issue appears unavoidable. The new African government, aware of its formidable economic and social problems, may well adopt a tolerant attitude to the operations of the British copper companies, but adamantly refuses to pay royalties to the British South Africa Company.

ever, has been such that power supplies, labor, transport, and other facilities have long been fully extended.

Copper mining began in the early years of the century in the Elisabethville district of Katanga, but in the interwar period production in the Northern Rhodesia section of the copper belt drew ahead and has since increased its lead, and further expansion is planned, contingent upon the completion of the Kariba gorge hydroelectricity project on the Zambezi River (Fig. 15-1). The copper industry of south central Africa was initially financed by British, Belgian, and other Western European capital, but there is now a very substantial American interest in it, although the area's main market, in contrast to that of Chile, is Western Europe. In the former Belgian Congo production is entirely controlled by the Union Minière du Haut Katanga, itself part of a larger enterprise, the Société Générale, with considerable interests in estates, in manufacturing industries, and in commerce and transport. In Northern Rhodesia production is limited to a few large mines situated between Ndola and Chingola, closely interlocked in two large holding companies[7] which also have connections with the Union Minière.

[7] **Rhodesian Anglo-American Ltd. and Rhodesian Selection Trust Ltd. Despite its name, there is little American interest in the former group, which is closely linked with South African gold mining.**

Fig. 15-1 The copper belt of Katanga and Northern Rhodesia. Underground mining is being supplemented by open-pit working using bucket-wheel excavators, as at N'Changa.

Although Katanga copper production was hardly affected by the turmoil that accompanied the birth of the Congo Republic (Léopoldville) in 1960, the future of the central African copper belt is obscure, to say the least. Much depends on the relationships of the mining companies with the new governments of the Congo (Léopoldville) and Northern Rhodesia (Zambia); in every direction, however, the outlets from the copper belt pass through areas in which African nationalism is becoming more militant. Not only are the copper producers of Katanga and Northern Rhodesia closely interlocked; they also have considerable connections with the mining industries of South Africa, and these links are likely to come under heavy fire from African nationalism. It is just possible that Northern and Southern Rhodesia—the latter's Wankie coalfield is indispensable to the copper belt—may avoid the head-on interracial clash that appears increasingly probable in South Africa. The cardinal rule for the conduct of a large foreign enterprise in a country at a low level of economic development is to remain aloof from politics, however great the temptation, and this has in general been the policy of the copper companies. Nevertheless, the fact that their related companies in South Africa have to practice rigid discrimination makes operations in the copper belt the hostage of political fortune, and it will need the greatest fortitude on the part of the rulers of Zambia to restrain the more extreme demands of their people.

Other Producers The only other really large producers of copper are the U.S.S.R. and Canada (Table 15-1). The U.S.S.R. has reported large deposits of copper ores, principally in the Urals and in Kazakhstan, and the country's output appears to be about equivalent to that of Northern Rhodesia. Nevertheless, output does not meet domestic requirements, and the U.S.S.R. regularly imports substantial quantities. It would appear, therefore, that the metal is not one with which the country is well endowed.

Canada is unique in that its large copper output is derived either as a by-product of the mining of more valuable metals, such as gold and nickel, or from mines whose main interest is in lead and zinc. Rouyn and Noranda in Quebec (gold), Sudbury in Ontario (nickel), Flin Flon, Manitoba, and Kimberley, British Columbia (lead and zinc) are responsible for the bulk of Canada's copper output. Only about one-third of Canada's copper, however, finds its way to the United States.

Apart from the large producers there are numerous medium-sized producers which collectively appear to be of increasing importance; they include Australia, Mexico, Japan, Yugoslavia, South Africa, and Peru. Japan has been a substantial producer for a long period of time, and the metal is the only one with which the country could be said to be well provided, although its production is carried on at high cost. Australia's growing output now comes largely from the Mount Isa district of Queensland, where the ore body averages more than 3 per cent metal content, a high figure by world standards. Since World War II, control of this increasingly important area has passed to American companies, and there are substantial American interests in copper production in Canada, Mexico, Peru, and the Philippines.

Production Processes It is clear that with ores of such low grade, a considerable mine treatment is necessary. Copper smelting is broadly similar to that of iron; ore is first roasted to remove sulfur and is then transferred to a reverbatory furnace not unlike an open-hearth furnace. Considerable quantities of fuel are required for these processes, and though coal is extensively used in many places, fuel

Table 15-1

Copper Production, 1963 (Thousand metric tons)

	SMELTER*	REFINED†
United States	1,176	1,728
Canada	338	343
Mexico	52	
Peru	156	37
Chile	537	259
West Germany	68	302
Britain		214
Belgium		271
Sweden	19	46
Yugoslavia	51	48
Japan	280	295
Northern Rhodesia	576	439
Congo (Léopoldville)	270	135
Australia	78	92
South Africa	54	15
Poland	24	30
Bulgaria	20	18
U.S.S.R.‡	470	
Mainland China‡	60	
WORLD TOTAL§	3,910	4,600

* Virgin copper recovered from domestic and imported ores and concentrates.
† Including recovered copper.
‡ Estimated 1960 figures.
§ Excluding U.S.S.R. and mainland China.
SOURCE: United Nations, *Monthly Bulletin of Statistics*, May, 1964; Overseas Geological Surveys, *Statistical Summary of the Mineral Industry*, 1963.

oil or natural gas is more usually employed. The black, or matte, copper is further refined in a converter broadly similar to the Bessemer converter and is transformed into blister copper 99 per cent pure. Copper of low electric resistance is produced by further electrolytic refining, and this is always done where minute quantities of precious metals are present.

Alternatively, copper ores can be subjected to chemical leaching and the metal directly recovered by electrolysis. Electrolytic refining may be carried out either in areas where low-cost electric energy is available or in close proximity to the main copper-fabricating and -using industries. In the United States more than half of the electrolytic refineries are situated on the middle Atlantic seaboard, the balance being located in the West, usually at the nearest site to the mine where generation of low-cost electricity is possible; the Anaconda refinery at Great Falls, Montana, and the Phelps Dodge refinery at El Paso, Texas, are examples of this type of location.

In underdeveloped economies, particularly where the scale of production is large, it is often advantageous to smelt or even to refine the metal at, or in close proximity to, the mine itself; moreover, as in Chile, further pressure to expand the production of refined metal can be expected from host governments. Conventional smelters and electrolytic refineries have to be of large size for low-cost operation, and the capital cost of such equipment may be beyond the reach of the smaller producers; new chemical methods of refining, however, offer to such producers the possibility of low-cost refining and fabrication. The Sherritt Gordon process, which employs ammonia leaching, gaseous reduction, and new methods of rolling, is claimed to possess a substantial cost advantage over conventional smelters and refineries, both in operating and in capital costs, and appears very suitable for employment in medium-sized units; the process also produces ammonium sulfate as a by-product, a valuable fertilizer for underdeveloped economies which lack heavy-chemical industries. The first such plant is scheduled to come into operation in Mindanao in the Philippines in 1964, and should make the country self-supporting in many of its fabricated-copper requirements.

Finally, some countries which were formerly important producers of copper also possess large refining industries, Britain and West Germany being the outstanding examples.

Aluminum

The rapid growth of the aluminum industry has few parallels in the world economy. After its beginnings about 1880 production increased slowly and was still less than 100,000 tons in 1914; but the great advantages of the metal slowly became realized, and by 1929 world output had attained some 300,000 tons. Despite the Great Depression, the growth of output continued, and was, of course, greatly assisted by the rearmament programs of the Great Powers and by the recognition of the fundamental importance of air power, particularly by Germany. As the Luftwaffe expanded, so German aluminum production grew; by 1939 Germany had displaced the United States as the world's leading producer and had also become the only substantial producer of magnesium, an even lighter metal than aluminum.[8] But aluminum's growth had only just begun; during World War II world production increased almost fivefold, and although the end of the war brought some retrenchment, output had surpassed the wartime peak by 1954 and has since gone steadily upwards. Expansion schemes already decided on and in course of implementation should raise world output of aluminum to over 8 million tons by 1970. Aluminum has thus joined the select group of industries whose output doubles approximately every decade.

Production Patterns and Methods Several similarities between the aluminum and steel industries have already been indicated, and there are also others that suggest themselves. As with steel, the production of ingot aluminum is a two-stage operation, the first stage involving the preparation of pure aluminum oxide (alumina) and the second the reduction of the metal. Moreover, again as with steel, which is experiencing a technological revolution after a long period of relative stagnation,

[8] Magnesium requires even more energy to produce than aluminum, and despite its lightness and improved methods of production, the metal has failed to live up to its expectations. Its largest single commercial user in the noncommunist world is the Volkswagen automobile plant.

new methods of producing aluminum are being actively pursued; it is highly likely that in the near future the virtual monopoly of bauxite will be broken and that other aluminum-bearing minerals will become of importance, as they already are in the U.S.S.R., which works extensive deposits of nepheline.

Bauxite ores were first worked in temperate countries—in France (whose district of Les Baux has given its name to the ore), in Hungary, and in the United States. The main centers of production, however, have now moved to the humid tropics, where the mineral appears to be produced by the chemical weathering of clayey limestones; its occurrence in areas of higher latitudes is evidence of the existence of such climates in past geologic time. After 1939 bauxite production in Surinam and British Guiana increased very rapidly, but both of these have been eclipsed by Jamaica, which has become the largest producer since the end of World War II (Table 15-2). Over 90 per cent of the bauxite deposits of the United States lie in Arkansas. The best of these were heavily depleted by the demands of World War II and there appeared little future for the remaining leaner ones. New technical advances have made possible the economic working of lower-grade ores and have enabled the country to remain a major producer, but some three-quarters of the bauxite consumed in the country in 1961 was imported.

The Western Hemisphere could well lose its supremacy in bauxite production in the near future in view of the plans that have been made to develop the great deposits discovered in both Africa and Australia. The Weipa district of the Cape York Peninsula of Queensland is claimed to have the most extensive deposits in the world, but it is probable that other large bauxite deposits are still awaiting discovery. Also, while the technology of aluminum production is so complex and its energy requirements so enormous that metal production has so far been largely a monopoly of economies at a high level of economic development, there is plenty of evidence that this situation is about to change.

Bauxite is first crushed and dried, an operation which involves a weight loss of about 15 to 20 per cent, and is then shipped to plants producing pure oxide, or alumina. This stage, which involves a weight loss of 50 per cent or more, is effected through the Bayer process, which makes use of the fact that aluminum oxide dissolves in heated caustic soda but impurities do not; the high silica content of some ores, particularly the poorer ores of Arkansas, created some difficulties, but these have been overcome by a refinement of the Bayer process in which the silica is simultaneously removed. Substantial quantities of fuel are required, both to generate steam for dissolving the oxide and to drive off the water from the hydrated alumina.

The availability of fuel supplies, soda ash and lime, and easy means of importing foreign bauxites have been the major factors influencing the location of alumina plants, which in the United States have tended to be geographically separated from reduction plants. For a long time the only alumina plant in the country was at East St. Louis, but the use of lower-grade Arkansas ores and the increasing importance of bauxite from South America and the Caribbean have led to the construction of new plants on bauxite fields and along the Gulf Coast, most of which make use of natural gas. In Canada, however, and in many other countries integrated plants in which alumina production is located alongside reduction plants are the rule, and this pattern will probably be maintained in some projects for the expansion of aluminum production in African territories. Jamaica has already become a substantial producer of alumina, and an increasing proportion of world alumina output may be expected to take place at or near the site of bauxite mining in the future.

The only commercially practicable way of

Table 15-2

Production of Bauxite and Aluminum (Thousand metric tons)

	BAUXITE 1961	ALUMINUM 1963	
		PRIMARY	RECOVERED
United States	1,503	2,100	456
Canada		626	
Jamaica	6,615		
Surinam	3,405		
British Guiana	2,412		
France	2,190	300	50
West Germany		209	156
Britain		31	147
Norway		220	
Italy	322	91	
Switzerland		60	
Austria		76	
Greece	1,300		
Yugoslavia	1,232	36	
India	476	49	
Japan		203	89
Indonesia	420		
Malaysia	416		
Cameroun		48	
Guinea	1,767		
Hungary	1,357	56	
U.S.S.R.*	4,000	700	
Mainland China*	400		
WORLD TOTAL†	25,090	4,350	

* Estimated, 1961.
† Excluding U.S.S.R. and mainland China.
SOURCE: United Nations, *Statistical Yearbook*, 1962; United Nations, *Monthly Bulletin of Statistics*, May, 1964; Overseas Geological Surveys, *Statistical Summary of the Mineral Industry*, 1963.

producing aluminum metal from the oxide is by electrolysis, in the so-called "Hall-Hérault" process. The oxide will not melt so that electrolysis can take place until a temperature of 2000°F is reached, but its melting point can be reduced by the addition of cryolite and other fluorides; cryolite was formerly a monopoly of the Ivigtut mine in Greenland, but it is now also produced synthetically. The metal is produced in small pots of steelplate with a thick carbon lining which constitutes the cathode; the anode consists of carbon rods of pitch and

Coils of rolled aluminum await treatment in the annealing furnace before passing on to the finishing stands.

petroleum coke which are gradually consumed as reduction proceeds. The manufacture of a ton of metal involves the consumption of more than half a ton of carbon anodes, so that their cost is substantial. Reduction is accomplished by passing through each cell a very large direct current at low voltage arranged by wiring long lines of pots, or cells, in series.

Production in North America and Western Europe As 20,000 kilowatt-hours of electric energy are needed to produce 1 short ton of metal, aluminum reduction plants must be located where electricity is obtainable at very low rates. The search for cheap power is clearly visible in the growth of the industry in the United States, although it must be emphasized that power is only one item in total costs. From its establishment in Pittsburgh, reduction moved first to New Kensington a few miles to the north, where natural gas was available, and then to Niagara Falls, the first major hydroelectricity development. When power supplies there were outgrown, a further move was made to Massena, New York, where power from the Canadian Cedar Rapids development was used. New reduction plants at Badin, North Carolina, took advantage of the electric power from the Yadkin River, while that of Alcoa, Tennessee, used power from TVA. All of these plants were operated by the Aluminum Corporation of America, which until World War II had a complete monopoly of aluminum production in the United States.

The tremendous increase in demand for aluminum resulting from World War II led to heavy government investment in the industry, five large plants being established in the Pacific Northwest where cheap power was available from installations on the Columbia River; a considerable number of other plants were constructed in parts of the country where power costs were appreciably higher, but these did not survive the wartime emergency. In accordance with government policy of encouraging competition in the industry, the economic plants were disposed of to two new producers, Reynolds, originally an aluminum fabricator, and Kaiser.

Further government encouragement to expanded production came as a result of the Korean conflict, in the form of tax concessions to permit rapid amortization and guarantees of loans and markets. As a result the capacity of existing producers was raised, and another newcomer, Anaconda, made plans to commence production. Anaconda's Columbia Falls plant in Montana produced its first metal in 1955, and the number of producers was later expanded by two additional entrants, Harvey and Ormet, the latter a joint interest of Revere Copper and Brass and Olin, a large chemical corporation.

Although plants located in the Pacific Northwest continue to enjoy the lowest-cost power, since World War II other areas have shown some advantages for aluminum reduction. Natural-gas-powered dc generators are used in plants in Arkansas and Texas, and the latter state is also finding a use for its long neglected lignite; in these states higher-cost power is offset by reduced transport and labor costs. The technical changes in conventional thermal coal-fired plants described in Chapter 13, together with proximity to fabricators and markets, have greatly enhanced the attractiveness of the Ohio valley, and it is quite possible that the establishment of the Kaiser plant at Ravenswood, West Virginia, and that of Ormet at Hannibal, Ohio, will attract other producers to this area (Fig. 15-2).

In structure and in location, therefore, the aluminum industry of the United States is

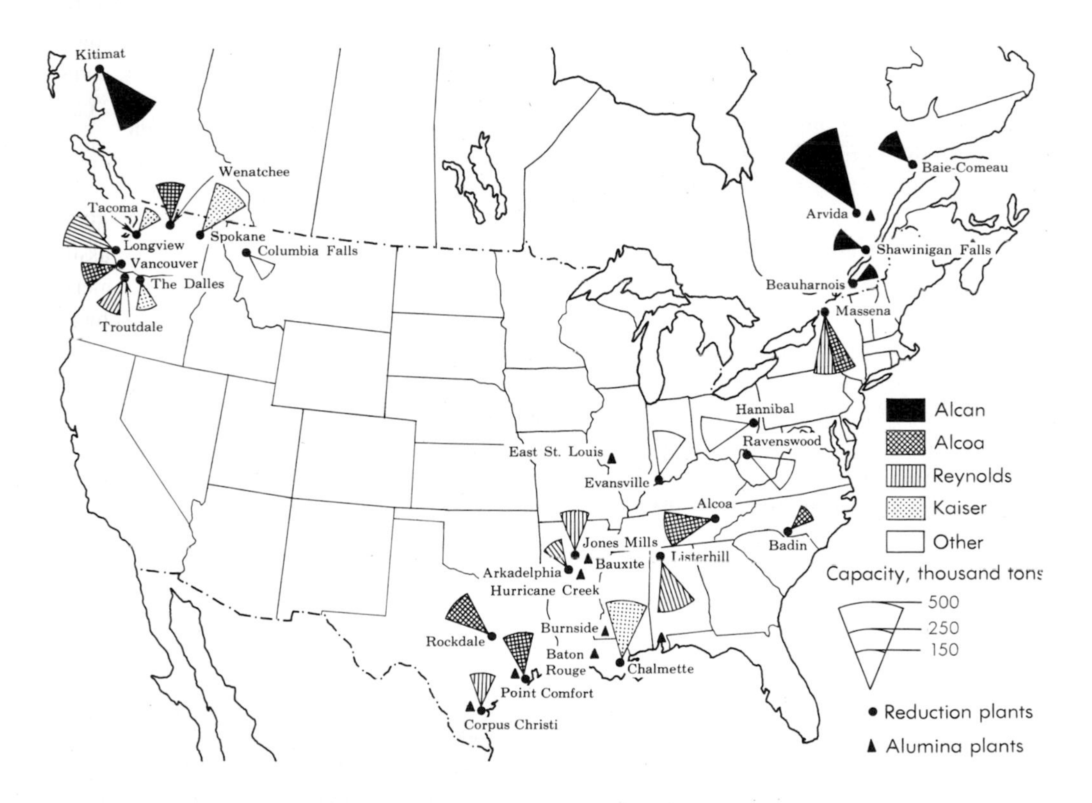

Fig. 15-2 Alumina and aluminum reduction plants in North America.

quite different from that of 1939. The capital costs of integrated operations, however, are so enormous that they must act as a major deterrent to prospective new entrants, particularly as there may also be very heavy capital costs for power. Nevertheless, several companies with interests in other nonferrous metals are interested in entering aluminum production. Moreover, the competition between the American producers has now become a vigorous worldwide activity, providing a desirable degree of competition in several countries where formerly the industry was under monopolistic control.

Despite its greatly expanded production, the United States makes substantial imports of metal from Canada, the world's second-largest producer, which achieved a sixfold increase in output during World War II. Canada's industry is highly localized, and produces metal largely for export; hence cheap power has been a consideration of overriding importance. Canada's industry is entirely controlled by the Aluminum Corporation of Canada (Alcan) in which the Aluminum Corporation of America (Alcoa) has a substantial interest, and is carried on in giant plants which have the lowest costs of production in the world, despite the fact that all bauxite is imported, principally from Jamaica and from British Guiana. The Arvida plant of Alcan on the Saguenay is the world's largest integrated plant, and at Baie-Comeau on the lower St. Lawrence a new plant has been constructed especially to serve the expanding European market. At Kitimat, British Columbia, Alcan is developing what will become the world's largest reduction plant, designed for an ultimate output of 550,000 tons of metal per year from Jamaican alumina. The Kitimat plant, which lies 400 miles north of Vancouver, uses power transmitted via a 50-mile line from the Kemano power station, which will have an ultimate capacity of 1,700 megawatts. The plant produces ingot for export, and is well placed to supply not only the Pacific Coast but also the growing markets of the Far East.

In other European countries cheap power has also been a factor of the greatest importance in the location of the aluminum industry. Since World War II France has regained its position of the early Twenties, when it was Europe's largest producer; in view of its large bauxite deposits, its ample facilities for the generation of hydroelectricity, and its early start in the industry, it is difficult to see why France later lagged behind Germany and Scandinavia in development. Until World War II France was the world's largest producer of bauxite and supplied not only the domestic aluminum industry but also that of Germany, Switzerland, and other producers. In the Alps, the Massif Central, and the Pyrenees, France has numerous sites for hydroelectricity generation, which have been supplemented since World War II by the large schemes in the Rhône valley such as the Donzère-Montdragon Dam. A significant new development is the construction by the Péchiney and Ugine companies, which share French production, of two reduction plants in the Lannemezan plateau of the Pyrenean foothills which operate on power produced from natural gas; similarly based developments in northern Italy may well follow.

Since 1959 Germany has had a close rival for the position of Europe's second-largest producer in Norway; production in Norway has grown remarkably, a fact which is largely responsible for the high national plant-utilization factor in electricity generation. Hydroelectricity is also the basis of the industry in Sweden, Austria, Switzerland, and Italy; Germany is unique in being the only large producer that has long derived much of its production from electricity generated by thermal plants fired by brown coal. Before World War II Germany imported its bauxite from Hungary, then the world's second-largest producer, but this supply has now been cut off. Britain has a substantial output of recovered metal, but its primary production is small; this is in part a consequence of the lack of low-cost electricity from hydro plants, but more importantly it reflects the substantial British interest in low-cost aluminum production in other countries, especially in Canada and Norway. But domestic production may rise as a result of the acute competition among the American producers for a larger share of the anticipated growth of the European market.

The Growth of Other Producers The greatest new developments in aluminum production, however, may take place outside the traditional areas of North America and Western Europe. Africa has proved to have enormous bauxite deposits, and the continent has an enormous hydroelectricity potential. Vast capital investment will be needed to harness these resources, but the desirability of assisting African economic development and the anticipated growth in free world consumption make it fairly certain that some of the proposed schemes for the production of alumina and ingot in African territories will come to fruition. With guarantees of financial support from the World Bank and the American and British governments, the long delayed Volta River scheme of Ghana finally began to appear possible late in 1961. First discussed as long ago as 1924, the production of hydroelectricity from the Volta River for the reduction of metal from the bauxite deposits of the Yenahin area west of Kumasi appeared a practical possibility with the conclusion of an agreement between the British and Gold Coast governments and private capital in 1953 for the construction of a dam some 50 miles from the mouth of the Volta and a smelter to produce 210,000 long tons of metal per annum. Financial and political difficulties hindered the implementation of this agreement, but the Volta project looked commercially attractive to American producers, and under the leadership of the Kaiser company the Volta Aluminum Corporation (Valco) was established, in which Reynolds, Alcoa, Olin, and Alcan also participate. Valco plans a 178,000 tons per year alumina plant.

Nevertheless, the Volta development still depends on the ability and willingness of the Ghana government to finance its share of the power agreement, and the scheme has now to be seen in the light of subsequent plans for the exploitation of the resources of other parts of West Africa. Extensive bauxite deposits have been located in Sierra Leone, Guinea, the Ivory Coast, the Cameroun, and the two Congo republics. Any large investment in Ghana could well lead to a demand from these other African states for similar assistance in developing their respective bauxite deposits.

Another development of possible major significance is the association of certain Australian lead- and zinc-producing companies with American aluminum producers; one consortium intends to produce alumina on the Weipa bauxite field of Cape York Peninsula and to establish a reduction plant, possibly in New Zealand, using power from Lake Manapouri, while another is to develop the bauxite deposits of the Darling Range of western Australia. These new discoveries of bauxite would support an industry much larger than that required to satisfy the domestic market, and it would appear that the companies concerned are looking to the expanding markets of Japan and of other countries of East and Southeast Asia as a major outlet for ingot.

The anticipated expansion of aluminum production in the free world will thus largely arise from the wider foreign operations of leading American producers, acting in conjunction with other nonferrous-metal and chemical companies. It would not be surprising if the leaders of the iron and steel industry decided to enter the aluminum industry, following the example of the Kaiser group.

The U.S.S.R. has been comparatively slow in developing its aluminum industry, for although it possesses ample resources of power, the demands made on them are extremely heavy, and the lack of high-grade bauxite deposits has compelled the use of alunite and nepheline, which involve higher costs. In 1950 Soviet aluminum production was only some 100,000 tons, but in the succeeding decade this output increased sevenfold. Russia's principal deposits of bauxite and substitute ores lie mainly in the northwestern region and in the northern Urals, but the greatest resources for the low-cost generation of electric power lie in the south and in the east. Four new large reduction plants, situated at Volgograd, Pavlodar, Krasnoyarsk, and Irkutsk, using power derived from existent or projected large new hydroelectric installations on the Volga, Irtysh, Yenisey, and Angara Rivers, respectively, will help to raise output still further; by 1970 Soviet production should reach 1.75 million tons.

LEAD AND ZINC

Lead and zinc possess fewer common physical and chemical properties than copper and aluminum, so that opportunities for substitution are relatively fewer. Ores of lead and zinc, moreover, usually occur in association, and the fact that the two metals are produced in almost equal quantities results in a low price difference which further reduces substitution. Lead ores can, however, occur in isolation, as in southeast Missouri, and the Franklin Furnace district of New Jersey is an important producer of zinc without lead. The world appears better endowed with zinc than with lead; in most lead and zinc ore associations the zinc content usually substantially exceeds that of lead, often by a margin of two to one. Long-term prospects for lead supplies are not reassuring, and it is probable that the price difference between the two metals will grow with the passage of time; zinc compounds have already replaced those of lead in the manufacture of certain paints and pigments, and further substitution of zinc for lead is possible. Zinc, however, is largely expended in use and its recovery rate is low, while lead is mainly employed in uses which permit a high rate of recovery; over one-third of United States lead consumption is normally accounted for by storage batteries, which having a relatively short life enable much lead to be recovered within two years.

World demand for lead and for zinc has grown more slowly than that for either copper or aluminum, for the two cheap base metals still find their main employment in traditional uses and have had limited success in invading the "growth" industries. Zinc has had the better fortune, however, for zinc-alloy die castings have become widely used in the motor-vehicle industry; the average American automobile contains about 60 pounds of such castings, and zinc in this form accounts for about one-third of United States consumption. The largest new use for lead is probably in the manufacture of tetraethyl lead, a gasoline additive; this employment amounts to about 15 per cent of United States annual lead consumption, but as there is no possibility of recovery, this proportion might well have to be reduced in the future. Lead is also used to screen atomic reactors and other radioactive operations.

The principal attractions of both metals are their resistance to corrosion and the ease with which they can be cast and worked. The largest use for zinc is in the production of galvanized sheeting, and being easily alloyed and cast, zinc has been able to participate in the expansion of the electrical industries through its contribution to brass. Lead forms the most suitable covering for cables in exposed positions, but its softness and low tensile strength are major disadvantages; it can be hardened by the addition of antimony, and such alloys, with the addition of a little tin, are used for the production of type metal. Lead is very easily extracted from its ore; zinc presents greater difficulty because it vaporizes in the smelting process and must be kept from contact with air. The greater portion of the world's zinc output is now produced by electrolysis, but there is considerable scope for improvement on the largely traditional techniques of smelting and refining both metals. A recent development of some importance is a process for continuous electrolytic plating of zinc from concentrates, thus avoiding the normal smelting process.

Producing Areas There are many lead producers, and world trade in the metal is smaller than that in zinc; the latter, however, is the only nonferrous metal of which Europe is still a large producer (Table 15-3). The United States supplanted Spain as the world's principal producer of lead about 1880 but did not achieve the premier position in zinc until about the turn of the century; it is still the world's leading zinc producer, but since 1957 it has had to

Table 15-3

Production of Lead and Zinc, 1961 (Thousand metric tons)

	LEAD		ZINC	
	MINE	PRIMARY	MINE	PRIMARY
United States	238	431	421	768
Canada	209	156	377	243
Mexico	181	176	269	52
Peru	137	77	174	32
West Germany	50	141	87	186
Sweden	64	39	78	
Spain	83	66	89	42
Belgium		99		245
Yugoslavia	97	90	60	37
Italy	48	45	129	78
Australia	274	214	293	141
Japan	46	76	168	207
Poland	38	40	140	182
Bulgaria	91	41	74	22
U.S.S.R.*		370		400
Mainland China*		70		90
WORLD TOTAL†	2,030	1,930	2,810	2,690

* Estimated, 1961.
† Excluding U.S.S.R. and mainland China.
SOURCE: United Nations, *Statistical Yearbook*, 1962; Overseas Geological Surveys, *Statistical Summary of the Mineral Industry*, 1963.

yield first place in mine lead production (that is, new lead resulting from domestic mining production) to Australia. However, the latter's production of recovered lead is small, while in the United States such secondary production normally exceeds mine output by a substantial margin. United States lead and zinc output reached a maximum in the Twenties; by 1960 primary lead output (that is, domestic mine production plus new lead from imported concentrates) had fallen to about one-half that of the peak output. Output of zinc rose during World War II, to approach the high level of the Twenties, but it has since fallen considerably.

As a result of a long period of intensive exploitation, costs of lead and zinc production in the United States are appreciably above the level of those of the other major world producers; this situation has given rise to demands for a high level of protection for domestic producers. Diminishing output and increasing consumption have led to a great increase in imports, which now substantially exceed the level of domestic primary production.

The principal lead-producing district of the United States has long been the Bonne Terre area of southeast Missouri, followed by the Coeur d'Alene district of Idaho. Utah is also an important lead producer, but the output of Bingham, Park City, and Tintic is dwarfed by the state's production of copper. In zinc production the tri-state area of Missouri, Kansas, and Oklahoma long was first, but output from this district has now very greatly declined, and those western states in which lead and zinc production closely coincide are now of major significance. New Jersey, New York, Tennessee, and Virginia also make a considerable contribution to the national zinc output. In southeast Missouri and in the tri-state area the metallic content of ores is low in comparison with that of other districts; nevertheless, costs of production also are comparatively low, in general, as the ore bodies are larger than those of western states and physical conditions permit a high degree of mechanization.[9] The total number of lead and zinc producers is very large, but some ten companies produce some 65 per cent of primary lead output, and a similar number of companies account for about 60 per cent of that of zinc; seven companies are common to both branches of production. However, even the largest producers have neither the resources nor the status of the leaders of the copper and the aluminum industries.

Australia's lead and zinc production has expanded considerably since the end of World War II. The principal producing area is Broken Hill in far west New South Wales, followed by the Mount Isa district of Queensland. In contrast to the United States, Australia produces no refined lead; Broken Hill ores are smelted at Port Pirie in south Australia, the bullion being exported for further treatment abroad by the English parent company. Canada's large lead and zinc production is largely derived from the great Sullivan mine at Kimberley, British Columbia, the largest lead and zinc mine on the continent. Ores from this mine are smelted at Trail.

Other large producers of both metals are Mexico and Peru, the latter country being another producer whose output has grown considerably since World War II. One large prewar producer, on the other hand, has virtually disappeared; this is Burma, whose great Bawdwin mine in the Shan plateau worked the richest lead-zinc-silver ores in the world; its demise is largely the result of unsettled political conditions. Other lead producers include South Africa and Yugoslavia, and Poland, Italy, and Germany are considerable producers of zinc. Britain and Belgium,

[9] **Percy W. Bidwell,** *Raw Materials: A Study of American Policy,* **Harper & Row, Publishers, Incorporated, New York, 1958, p. 67.**

though now negligible producers of mine lead and zinc, have large refining industries. In no country of the free world, however, is lead and zinc production really important in the national economy, nor do these metals ever, as is sometimes the case with copper, form a major item in the export trade.

In the U.S.S.R. production of both metals began comparatively late; zinc was not produced at all until 1932. As in the rest of the world zinc supplies are more plentiful than those of lead, but output of both has been raised very greatly, and the country is now the third-largest producer in the world of both lead and zinc. The principal source of supply of both metals is the Mednogorsk area of Kazakhstan, but production is also carried on in the central Urals and in the Far Eastern maritime region. The Soviet bloc also possesses the long worked lead and zinc deposits of Upper Silesia, now in Poland.

Prolonged depression in the lead and zinc industries has proved difficult to combat; the multiplicity of producers with varying cost levels hampers international agreement, and several European producers continue to subsidize high-cost domestic lead and zinc production. Whether a formal international agreement would prove more effective than the postwar informal study groups in matching production to consumption is very uncertain.

TIN AND NICKEL

Tin and nickel, the former worked in prehistoric times, the latter little more than a curiosity before the second half of the nineteenth century, are extensively employed in alloys with other nonferrous metals, but are more important as complements to the iron and steel industry. Tin is used in bronzes, type metal, and solders, but by far its largest single use is in tinplate, consumed in tremendous quantities by the food-canning industries. Nickel is a very versatile metal; it is used in electroplating and as a catalyst both in the hydrogenation of fats and in petroleum refining. But it is principally used in alloys, either with other nonferrous metals or with iron and steel; many nickel alloys possess toughness, resistance to corrosion and heat, and remarkable electric and magnetic properties. Nickel forms a wide range of alloys with copper, and special heat-treated alloys of nickel and chromium are of fundamental importance in many branches of engineering. The great toughness of nickel steels first found wide application in warship armor plating, but they are now also used wherever great stress or high temperatures are encountered, as in steam-turbine blades and in the crankshafts, gears, and transmissions of motor vehicles and locomotives. Stainless steel, which contains about 18 per cent of chromium and about 8 per cent of nickel, is widely used in food industries, pharmaceutical industries, and many branches of transportation, and is the fastest-growing commercial use for nickel. Nevertheless, it is still broadly true that nickel is a metal for which military uses are paramount.

Both metals are expensive. The high price of nickel arises not so much from absolute scarcity, for it is relatively much more abundant than copper, lead, or zinc, as from the dearth of high-grade deposits and the difficulties of separating nickel from the ore complexes in which it occurs; techniques of nickel smelting and refining first developed by the German chemist Mond were for long closely guarded trade secrets. Some Bolivian low-grade tin ores are also particularly difficult to smelt, but other contributory factors to the high price of tin are a shortage of high-grade deposits and the labor-intensive nature of much tin mining.

In contrast to the situation with other metals, tin production and nickel production have failed to grow rapidly since the end of

World War II. Increases in nickel output are brought about by a rise in defense requirements, and when such emergencies have passed, the nickel industry faces the problem of considerable surplus capacity; the increase in United States defense spending from the middle Fifties onwards, however, did lead to a search for new deposits.[10] On the other hand, tin production in 1961 remained substantially below the maximum production of nearly 250,000 tons in 1941, despite the fact that world consumption has gone steadily upwards. This paradoxical situation has arisen through new techniques of metal recovery and the more economic uses of the metal developed during World War II, when the Japanese, by overrunning the whole of Southeast Asia, obtained control of some 70 per cent of the world's tin supply. The United States now meets about a third of its requirements from recovered tin, while newly developed thin tinplates contain less than 0.1 pound of tin in a 45-pound pack. Tinplate, moreover, has encountered acute competition from other packaging materials, particularly aluminum and plastics, since 1950.

Production and Trade Patterns The geography of nickel production is simple. There are only two substantial producers, Canada, which is by far the larger, and the U.S.S.R.; the balance of world output is largely provided by the French island of New Caledonia and South Africa. The United States, which consumes about one-half of the free world's supply, itself produces only minimal amounts of primary metal. Virtually all of Canada's nickel output, some 60 per cent of the world total, is derived from the Sudbury area of Ontario, and this geographic concentration of production is matched by an equally remarkable economic concentration; the International Nickel Corporation (Inco), an amalgamation of several former producers, accounts for almost 80 per cent of the Canadian output. Smelting is carried out at nearby Copper Cliff, but Inco has refining and fabricating interests in Britain and in the United States that are substantially older than its refinery at Port Colborne, Ontario, established during World War I.

Since 1939 the dominant position of Inco has been somewhat reduced through the United States government policy of broadening the field of competition when underwriting expansion of metal production for defense purposes. As a result, the small Falconbridge Company, which also operates in the Sudbury area, has slightly enlarged its share of the market, and the expanded demand for nickel after 1952 arising from increasing defense expenditure led to the discovery of a number of new deposits in Canada. Substantial investment has been made in developing the northern Manitoba discoveries in the Lynn Lake district, both by Inco and by a new producer, Sherritt Gordon. The growing shortage of nickel also led the United States government to reactivate the World War II plant at Nicaro in eastern Cuba, where large nickel deposits had long been known to exist. Shut down after World War II as uneconomic in the face of lower-cost Canadian production, Cuba's renewed production proved to be short-lived, for the enterprise was taken over by the Castro regime in 1960. The only other producer of note in the noncommunist world, New Caledonia, was long the world's principal nickel producer before the discovery of the Sudbury. Distance from markets, shortage of fuel supplies, and, above all, labor problems have hampered the development of the New Caledonian industry. The substantial Russian output is derived from the southern Urals, the Kola Peninsula, and the former Finnish area of Pechenga.

[10] In 1948 only 3.6 per cent of the United States nickel supply was consumed by defense departments, but by 1956 this proportion had risen to 42.8 per cent. Bidwell, *Raw Materials: A Study of American Policy,* p. 136.

The production of tin is geographically more widespread than that of nickel, but there are only three important producing areas (Table 15-4). The world's greatest stanniferous zone extends southwards from the Yünnan plateau of China through western Thailand into the Malay Peninsula and into the Indonesian islands off the east coast of Sumatra. Malaya and the Netherlands Indies normally occupied the first and second positions among tin producers, and have the lowest costs of production, and their ores and concentrates are easily smelted. Since achieving independence, however, Indonesian tin production has fallen off. The second major tin-producing region is the high plateau of Bolivia; the third is intertropical Africa, where tin production is carried on in the Jos area of Nigeria and in Rwanda-Burundi. Until the end of World War II the U.S.S.R. was a substantial importer of tin, but since that time domestic production, mainly from the Khapcheranga district of eastern Siberia, has expanded greatly, and in the late Fifties a new phenomenon in the world tin market was the dumping of Russian tin. In contrast, there is not one tin mine in the

Table 15-4

Tin Production, 1963 (Thousand metric tons)

	CONCENTRATES	REFINED METAL
United States		3.1
Bolivia	22.8	
Britain	1.2	18.0
Netherlands		5.1
Belgium		7.2
Malaysia	61.2	85.2
Thailand	15.6	
Indonesia	13.2	
Burma	1.1	
Congo (Léopoldville)	7.2	1.2
Rwanda	1.2	
Nigeria	8.9	9.2
South Africa	1.6	1.0
Australia	3.1	0.3
Mainland China*	24.4	
WORLD TOTAL†		146.0

* Estimate, 1961.

† Excluding U.S.S.R.

SOURCE: United Nations, *Monthly Bulletin of Statistics*, May, 1964; Overseas Geological Surveys, *Statistical Summary of the Mineral Industry*, 1963.

United States, nor is there a large supply in adjacent territories as is the case with other base metals.

Malaya's low costs of production result from the nature of its ores, which have been deposited as stanniferous gravels along the junction of its granitic ranges and the plains. Tin is mined in several states, but the main centers are the Kinta valley of Perak and the Kuala Lumpur district of Selangor (Fig. 15-3). The alluvial tinstone is most cheaply won by the large European-owned dredges, which produce about two-thirds of Malaya's output and can operate profitably on deposits containing only 0.2 pound of tinstone per cubic yard; the balance is mainly derived from Chinese-owned gravel-pump mines. The gravel-pump mine needs much less capital investment, and its equipment is more easily moved to new mining sites; it needs considerably richer *karang* (ore-bearing ground), however, and as costs of production are higher than for dredges, gravel-pump mines are usually the first to reduce output when the price of tin declines. New technical innovations in Malayan tin mining include the bucket-wheel excavator, a machine developed in German brown-coal mining, and the hydrocyclonic jig, a method of tinstone separation that permits a much higher recovery rate than in the past; these introductions may well offset the necessity of having to mine lower-grade deposits in the future.

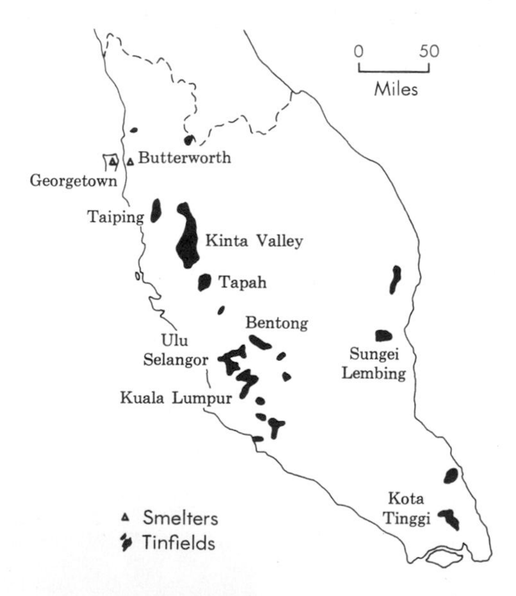

Fig. 15-3 Tin fields of Malaya.
Most of the unnamed fields are of historical importance only.

Little is known about the structure of Chinese mining in Malaya. On the other hand, European companies, though superficially numerous, are closely linked through managing agencies and holding companies; three London holding companies largely control European tin mining in Malaya. These companies are also closely linked with producing interests in Thailand, Nigeria, and the Congo, and before the nationalization of 1957 were closely linked with those of Bolivia. The world tin industry is thus considerably cartelized.

In Indonesia, where the physical conditions governing tin mining are identical with those of Malaya, the industry is entirely in the hands of the state, and is operated with Chinese labor; output, however, declined substantially in the late Fifties. Bangka, Belitung, and Singkep, the tin-producing islands, contain a number of mines that have not been reactivated since the Japanese occupation. Production in peninsular Thailand is virtually an extension of that of Malaya, but unsettled political conditions have impeded the restoration of the industry in the adjacent portion of Burma.

Bolivia's large output—the country has been second to Malaya since 1959—is derived from the ranges to the east of the Altiplano, from lode-type ores that have to be followed deep underground. Mining at elevations of over 12,000 feet involves a heavy cost penalty; moreover, the barilla ores, particularly of the lower grades, are difficult to smelt. Production in Bolivia began only in the present century and

Indian women move a car of tin ore at a Bolivian mine 15,000 feet above sea level.

By means of a bucket ladder, this large electric tin dredge, near Kuala Lumpur, Malaya, can excavate tin gravels more than 120 feet below water level.

was long under the control of a few powerful families. A long period of labor disputes and political instability culminated in the nationalization of the industry in 1957, but expropriation of the Patino and Hochschild interests, the largest producers, did little to solve the long-term problems of the industry.

Bolivia's very high costs of production are of fundamental significance in the world tin situation. It is true that tin in Malaya represents the second-largest source of export income, but its contribution to the national total does not normally exceed about 15 to 20 per cent. In Bolivia, on the other hand, tin provides almost two-thirds of total export income; even with substantial falls in price Bolivian output often drops little, the country meeting such eventualities by devaluating its currency. Bolivian production, moreover, is of special significance to the United States, for it represents the nearest large source of supply.

The low-cost producers of Southeast Asia have always been the leading advocates of international control, and international cooperation in tin marketing dates back to the agreement between the Malayan and Netherlands Indies governments of 1922. Not until after World War II, however, did consumers gain any representation on international regulation bodies. The International Tin Council established after World War II now includes almost all producers and consumers (except the United States) in the noncommunist world, and has attempted to fix ceiling and floor prices and to operate a buffer stock. Its success has been meager; apart from Russian incursions into the market, an important factor making for price instability is the size of the United States government's strategic stocks, which in 1961 amounted to the equivalent of two years' free world production of new metal.

Tin smelting, which shows a marked divorce from tin mining, is very largely in British hands. Malaya possesses two smelters, at Butterworth and Penang, which also handle ores from Burma and Thailand. Concentrates from Southeast Asia and from Africa move to smelters in Belgium, the Netherlands, and Britain. Before World War II Bolivian ores were also shipped to Britain; during the war, however, a smelter to handle low-grade Bolivian ores was established at Texas City. It seems highly unlikely that smelting could ever be carried out economically in Bolivia itself, despite a Russian offer to provide the country with the equipment.

THE PRECIOUS METALS

By convention the precious metals include gold, silver, and platinum; traditionally they are set apart from the base metals by their high price, but the price differentials between the precious metals themselves are far greater than those separating them from base metals. Despite the fact that its price has been some fifteen to twenty times that of tin in much of the postwar period, silver is not really precious at all in the sense that it is a very expensive metal. Silver shares with gold a long history of use for monetary purposes, and though this is now of declining importance, dealings in silver are still closely regulated, and this constitutes a major obstacle to a greater use of the metal for industrial purposes. Nevertheless, industrial uses are growing substantially, and in the near future silver may be regarded as just another nonferrous metal. Gold is some thirty-five times the price of silver, but it is still far from being the most expensive metal; platinum is three times as expensive again, and some rare metals of potential significance in missile technology are virtually priceless. Platinum is largely used for jewelry and for industrial purposes, and has never been of any real monetary importance.

Gold

Gold is unique in almost every way; being extremely malleable and ductile and having a bright untarnishable surface, it is the ideal metal for ornamental purposes and for jewelry. But all the industrial uses for gold only account for about one-quarter of the total free world output—the balance is consigned to the vaults of treasuries and central banks, or finds its way by various channels into the hands of hoarders and smugglers. Throughout history gold has been the standard by which the soundness of a currency has been judged, and its influence still appears as strong as ever. Some view the continuing importance of the yellow metal for this purpose as an intolerable legacy of man's superstitious past, and since 1950 a number of schemes have been suggested for limiting the role of gold as an arbiter of international financial relations; though these have failed to gain any wide measure of support, the central banks of the free world have shown an increasing willingness to cooperate in order to make gold do their bidding, and thus to ease the pressure on the dollar and sterling, the two great currencies of international trade.

Whether used for industrial or monetary purposes, little gold is ever completely consumed; as a result, annual gold production is only a small proportion of the total world stock—perhaps about 2 per cent. The large holders of gold, and particularly the United States, which in the immediate postwar period may have held as much as half the stock of the noncommunist world, can thus considerably influence the price of the metal; though there are minor fluctuations, in practice the price of gold in legal markets is determined by what the United States Treasury will pay for it, which since 1934 has been $35 per ounce. This stability of gold contrasts markedly with the price oscillations of the base metals; activity in gold mining thus is greatest during depressions when the general level of prices is low and falls off during booms as rising cost levels eat away profit margins. The more or less continual postwar inflation has made gold mining relatively unprofitable in many parts of the world, and in some areas such as western Australia gold production only continues because of a considerable subsidy. An increase in the price of gold would greatly stimulate gold mining throughout the world, but this would involve a devaluation of the dollar; this the United States government appears determined to resist. Whether the price of gold should be raised substantially, as the gold mining industry and many financial experts urge, cannot be debated here; on the face of it, digging up gold from enormous holes in the ground in one part of the earth and burying it in other holes elsewhere does not appear a very rational activity whatever the price level.[11] Much depends on the success or otherwise of governments in controlling inflation; it is likely that given a stable general price level, central bank cooperation will enable the present gold price to be maintained.

South Africa and Other Producers Gold production is one of the most widely distributed mining industries, there being very many producers; but only five—South Africa, the U.S.S.R., Canada, the United States, and Australia—produce more than a million fine ounces annually. Free world gold production in 1961 amounted to about 35 million fine ounces, or rather less than 1,100 metric tons. Though this amount is minute in comparison with the scale of output of the nonferrous metals, gold is won by processing enormous quantities of rock; the average tenor of ores in

[11] One reason for the shortage of gold is that so much of new output is acquired by hoarders and smugglers, who frequently absorb more than the world's central banks. The world's largest market for smuggled gold is India. See Paul Ferris, *The City,* Victor Gollancz, Ltd., London, 1961, p. 166.

the Rand goldfield of South Africa is now less than 0.2 fine ounces per ton, and almost 100 million tons of Rand ore are treated annually, a figure that can stand comparison with that of any iron- or nonferrous-mining area.

Gold is extremely stable, and nearly all the world's output consists of "native" gold; alluvial deposits, or "placers," were of considerable importance in the past, but are now of declining significance. Since the turn of the century gold mining has been dominated by South Africa, which now produces two-thirds of the total free world output. The steady expansion of world production since the end of World War II has been almost entirely accounted for by South Africa, which virtually doubled its output during the Fifties.

South Africa possesses the deepest mines in the world—mining now takes place below 11,000 feet on the central Rand—and some of the most profitable. Its low costs of production largely arise from the remarkable bedded deposits of very finely divided gold in reefs, or "bankets," which are continuous over considerable areas; low-cost African labor and the availability of low-cost coal at close hand are, however, also factors of the utmost importance. Since its discovery in 1884 the Rand field, extending roughly east to west through Johannesburg for a distance of more than 50 miles, has been the most important goldfield in the world.

From the central Rand in the vicinity of Johannesburg, production has spread eastwards and westwards since 1920, eclipsing that of the older central portion of the field. Since 1945 development has been particularly active in the so-called "Far West Rand," where a handful of large mines produce over a quarter of the total Rand output; the West Driefontein mine, working some of the richest ores in the Rand, is claimed to be the first mine in the world to produce a profit of more than 2.8 million dollars (1 million pounds sterling) in its first year of operation, and when in full production will produce gold at a value rate of almost $50 per minute. The postwar period has also witnessed a considerable expansion of output in the long known but formerly little-worked Klerksdorp field and in the Orange Free State field near Odendaalsrus, discovered shortly before World War II.

The gold-mining industry of South Africa was largely created by British capital, but there is now a substantial American interest. Within thirty years many of the mines in the older portions of the Rand will be exhausted, but the new mines now in production or planned will have a life expectation of some sixty years, and output could grow for some considerable time to come. But over the country hangs the challenge of African nationalism; it can only be a question of time before the Republic has an independent African state as a neighbor, a development which would have enormous repercussions. As a largely British creation, the mining industry since its earliest days has been opposed to Afrikaner racialist and nationalist policies; its impotence to arrest the course of events since the Nationalist Party came to power in 1948 is a striking illustration of the inadequacy of the Marxist conception of history. The loss of overseas confidence following the Sharpville massacre of 1960 suggested that the industry will have to rely on its own resources for further finance,[12] which in view of its high degree of concentration and extreme profitability is certainly within its capacity. Despite South Africa's large African population, the mining industry is chronically short of labor; the recruiting of additional labor outside the Republic, at present essential to the industry, is

[12] **After 1961 there was a considerable increase in overseas confidence, and gold shares appreciated considerably. Another major incident, however, could occur at any time, and this would profoundly affect foreign investment in South Africa, a major contribution to the country's considerable post-1961 prosperity.**

likely to become progressively more difficult, although this might be offset by further mechanization.[13] But so long as the South African government remains wedded to policies which in the opinion of the entire civilized world deny to the African basic human rights, it is impossible not to have the greatest misgivings over the long-term future of the industry.

The world's second-largest producer of gold is believed to be the U.S.S.R., but no figures have been published since the Thirties and the present level of output is one of Moscow's most closely guarded secrets.[14] Gold, curiously enough, is given a position of considerable importance in Marxist-Leninist economic theory, and although Russian costs of production are undoubtedly very high by world standards, mining has long been facilitated by the use of forced labor. Some gold is produced in the Urals, but the main centers lie in Transbaikalia and in the Lena and Kolyma valleys. From time to time considerable quantities of Russian gold are sold in Western markets, usually to finance an expanded volume of imports. The large Russian exports of gold that reached London in 1964 to pay for Russia's enormous wheat imports, added considerably to international liquidity.

Canada and the United States occupy the third and fourth positions among world producers. Canada's output is won by deep underground mining of lode deposits in a number of centers in Ontario—Porcupine, Kirkland Lake, Rouyn, and Noranda. The United States is virtually alone among the larger producers in deriving about a quarter of its output from dredging alluvial deposits, as in California and in Alaska; by far the largest producer, however, is the Homestake mine of the Black Hills of South Dakota. Australia's substantial level of production is only maintained by a considerable subsidy; the greater part of its output comes from the Kalgoorlie area of western Australia, the balance being accounted for by a number of scattered centers situated mainly in Queensland. Producers of lesser importance include Ghana, Southern Rhodesia, the Philippines, and Colombia.

Silver

World production of silver is about six times that of gold, but its value is only one-sixth as large. The New World has dominated silver production since the seventeenth century, and at present accounts for about 70 per cent of free world output. Unlike that of gold, silver production has failed to expand in recent years, and the level of output in 1960 was still below that of the immediate prewar period; this is largely because silver production is closely associated with that of lead and zinc, metals which have experienced only modest fortunes since World War II.

Silver is still extensively used for monetary purposes, particularly in the United States, where the political strength of the western silver-producing states has long maintained legislation to support the price of the metal. In 1961, when industrial demands were at a very high level, the President recommended that the silver-purchase legislation should be repealed and that the country should move towards the demonetization of silver. Not surprisingly, no action was taken by Congress to implement such a policy. Silver's close relationship with

[13] South Africa's mining industries use labor drawn from almost all of Africa south of the Sahara, but principally from ex-British and the present Portuguese territories. Even Ghana, leader of the anti-South Africa movement among new African nations, supplies workers who are drawn to Johannesburg by the relatively high wages offered by the gold mining industry. It is only a question of time before African governments impose restrictions on the free emigration of labor to South Africa.

[14] Some London bullion dealers believe that Russia's gold output may be as large as that of South Africa. See Ferris, *The City*, p. 162. In 1964, London's largest bullion dealer estimated that the Central Intelligence Agency's figure of Russian gold production was about one-third of the actual Soviet output.

the base metals makes it very unsuitable as a monetary standard, a fact which has largely been responsible for the failure of bimetallic monetary systems.

Silver has remarkable chemical and physical properties, which are making it extremely attractive to some of the most rapidly expanding industries; it is the best conductor of heat and electricity and also the most reflective of all metals, and the sensitivity of silver halides to light is the basis of photography. The rapidly expanding postwar demand for the metal from the chemical, photographic, and electronics industries has, in fact, arrested the long process of silver depreciation in relation to gold; since 1940 the price of silver has been raised from about one-hundredth of that of gold to about one-thirtieth, the ratio existing around the turn of the century. In 1961 the United States Treasury was obliged to suspend sales of silver to domestic industry, and in 1964 speculators were exchanging notes for silver dollars up to the maximum permitted—what they could carry away unaided from the Treasury. Only the misfortunes of China, which have caused it to make large offerings from its silver hoard, have enabled world industrial demands to be met.

The world's largest silver producer has long been Mexico, which is unique in producing substantial quantities of straight silver, unassociated with lead and zinc production. Most of the mines lie in Sonora and Chihuahua, but there are some important centers further south, such as Fresnillo and San Luis Potosí. Much American capital is involved in Mexican silver production. The desire to maintain good relations with a neighboring state and to assist the economic development of Latin America has also been a factor in United States silver-purchase legislation, for this acts also as a subsidy to foreign producers as well as to domestic ones. As the Western Hemisphere produces more than 70 per cent of the world's supply of new silver, a number of countries other than Mexico have benefited from this policy, particularly Canada, whose Sullivan mine is the largest producer of silver in the British Commonwealth, and Peru. In both countries silver production is a by-product of other mining industries and has considerably expanded since 1950; in the latter it has been mainly associated with the increased copper production of Cerro de Pasco. Outside the New World the only large silver producer is Australia; in contrast to its position as a large gold producer, the U.S.S.R. is believed to be only a very minor silver producer.

Platinum

Platinum is another metal for which industrial uses have expanded very rapidly since the end of World War II, for it has many applications in the chemical and electronics industries. The largest producer has long been Canada, where the metal is a by-product of nickel production, but since 1953 the Rustenburg area of South Africa has assumed the premier position.

SELECTED REFERENCES

Alderfer, E. B., and H. E. Michl: *Economics of American Industry,* McGraw-Hill Book Company, New York, 1957, pp. 87–116.

Alexander, W., and A. Street: *Metals in the Service of Man,* 4th ed., Penguin Books, London, 1962.

Bidwell, Percy: *Raw Materials: A Study of American Policy,* Harper & Row, Publishers, Incorporated, New York, 1958, pp. 64–172.

Collier, J. E.: "The Aluminum Industry of Europe," *Economic Geography,* vol. 20, pp. 75–108, 1946.

Courtenay, P. P.: "International Tin Restriction and Its Effects on the Malayan Tin Mining Industry," *Geography,* vol. 46, pp. 223–231, 1961.

Duncan, Craig: "The Aluminum Industry in

Australia," *Geographical Review,* vol. 51, pp. 21–46, 1961.
Ferris, Paul: *The City,* Victor Gollancz, Ltd., London, 1961, pp. 158–168.
Jones, W. R.: *Minerals in Industry,* Penguin Books, Harmondsworth, 1955.
Mouzon, Olin T.: *International Resources and National Policy,* Harper & Row, Publishers, Incorporated, New York, 1958, pp. 471–515.
Ooi Jin Bee: "Mining Landscapes of Kinta," *The Malayan Journal of Tropical Geography,* vol. 4, pp. 1–55, 1955.
Organisation for European Economic Co-operation: *The Non-ferrous Metal Industry in Europe,* Paris, 1956.
Overseas Geological Surveys: *Statistical Summary of the Mineral Industry, 1956–61,* H. M. Stationery Office, London, 1963.
Powelson, John P.: *Latin America: Today's Economic and Social Revolution,* McGraw-Hill Book Company, New York, 1964, pp. 127–138.
President's Materials Policy Commission: *Resources for Freedom,* vol. 2, *The Outlook for Key Commodities,* Government Printing Office, Washington, 1952.
Robertson, W.: "The Tin Experiment in Commodity Market Stabilization," *Oxford Economic Papers,* vol. 12, pp. 310–333, 1960.
Scott, Peter: "The Witwatersrand Gold Field," *Geographical Review,* vol. 41, pp. 561–589, 1951.
Shimkin, Demitri B.: *Minerals: A Key to Soviet Power,* Harvard University Press, Cambridge, Mass., 1953.
Steel, R. W.: "The Copper Belt of Northern Rhodesia," *Geography,* vol. 42, pp. 83–92, 1957.
The Mining Journal Annual Review, London, annually.
The Mining Yearbook, W. E. Skinner and the Financial Times Ltd., London, annually.
Union Minière du Haut Katanga: *Union Minière du Haut Katanga 1906–1956,* 2d ed., Cuypers, Brussels, 1956.
U.S. Department of the Interior, Bureau of Mines: *Mineral Facts and Problems,* 1960.
———: The Minerals Yearbook, annually.
Zimmermann, Erich W.: *World Resources and Industries,* rev. ed., Harper & Row, Publishers, Incorporated, New York, 1951, pp. 691–754.

Chapter 16

ENGINEERING INDUSTRIES

The engineering industries comprise a large, heterogeneous, yet at the same time closely interconnected group of industries that in all highly developed economies account for a large proportion of the labor force in manufacturing industries. Although other materials such as plastics, nylon, and rubber are also used, engineering industries are primarily metal-using industries, taking the end products of the iron and steel and nonferrous-metal industries and subjecting them to further processing. The processed parts are then assembled into final products, either capital goods or consumer durables, which for the most part consist of engines and machines or vehicles driven by engines.[1]

Processing and assembly may be carried on as integrated operations in one establishment, or they may be geographically separated. Heavy engineering[2] requires such a large capital investment that it is usually confined to a small number of large enterprises. In other branches of engineering a multiplicity of producers is found, and in yet others, giant corporations exist in symbiosis with numerous small producers. The latter situation is found in industries that involve the assembly of a large number of parts or subassemblies; through the practice of subcontracting, the specialist firm can concentrate on the production of a particular component for supply to the assembler. There is, nevertheless, a marked tendency for large organizations to interest themselves in many lines of production; the General Electric and English Electric corporations, in addition to a wide range of electric equipment, produce aircraft, jet engines, locomotives, missiles, and components for atomic reactors. Examples of similar horizontal integration occur in every country of Western Europe and in Japan, and in the U.S.S.R. the *kombinat* occupies a position essentially

[1] **Wilfred Smith,** *An Economic Geography of Great Britain,* **2d ed., Methuen & Co., Ltd., London, 1953, p. 372.**
[2] **See p. 266 for a definition of heavy industry.**

similar to that of the great engineering corporations of the West.

The structural diversity encountered in the engineering industries is paralleled by a considerable locational diversity. In highly developed economies there is a close correlation between the distribution of engineering industries and the general distribution of population. Some industries are fixed, or "rooted," in their locations by virtue of exacting physical requirements, as is the case with shipbuilding, or because they are heavy consumers of fuel, as is the case with locomotives, heavy castings and forgings, and some branches of marine engineering. Other engineering industries are fixed because of the specialized and localized markets they serve, as is the case with textile and mining machinery. Several, on the other hand, demonstrate a high degree of indeterminacy in their location pattern, a situation that obtains in the motor-vehicle industry and in the manufacture of electric appliances. But the overall distribution pattern is continually changing, and it is doubtful if any other branch of manufacturing shows greater mobility; the continuing attraction of the great metropolitan areas and capital cities for new engineering industries is very evident. Many branches of engineering have shown a remarkable capacity for growth; the average size of engineering establishments, to judge by numbers of persons employed, is substantially greater than the average for all manufacturing industries,[3] and although it is not possible to prove the point, a similar relationship probably holds in respect of floor space.

Any brief treatment of engineering industries must necessarily be selective; the motor-vehicle and aircraft industries, however, because of their importance in the economies of most Western countries and their many special problems, are given separate treatment in the next chapter.

[3] Smith, *op. cit.*, p. 378.

AGRICULTURAL MACHINERY

The production of agricultural machinery is widely dispersed for obvious reasons. The inventors of most farm machines were practical farmers, and proximity to farms for the testing of equipment is essential. The range of agricultural machinery is very wide, and no single manufacturer makes all types of machine. Machinery for crop cultivation tends to be manufactured by large organizations, but there is still scope for the specialist producer, especially in dairy engineering. The mechanization of agriculture in highly developed countries has led the producers of tractors—and the tractor is by far the most important farm machine—to take up the production of large agricultural implements; conversely, large-implement producers have found themselves obliged to enter tractor production, as the trend of development has been to integrate equipment and tractor in one machine. The close connection of this branch of agricultural engineering with the motor-vehicle industry has resulted in its concentration in the hands of a few large firms which have interests that are worldwide.

Although the earliest machines of the agricultural revolution, such as the seed drill, originated in Britain, the agricultural-equipment industry at present is dominated by the large American producers and their foreign subsidiaries. The shortage of labor and the desire of immigrants to acquire their own land, the physical suitability of great areas of the interior lowlands and the Great Plains for mechanized agriculture, and the opportunity of reaching new markets through the extension of the railroad network all help to explain the higher growth rate of the agricultural-equipment industry in America than in its country of origin in the latter half of the nineteenth century. The early centers of the agricultural-equipment industry lay in New England and on the Atlantic seaboard, areas that possessed a wide variety of hardwoods suitable for the fabrication of largely wooden implements. Inevitably, however, the industry followed the advancing frontier of settlement, establishing itself in almost all fitting-out centers for settlers moving west. McCormick's reaper was manufactured in Cincinnati in 1847, but with continued westward expansion of agriculture, production was later moved to Chicago; from such beginnings developed the giant International Harvester Corporation with subsidiaries in many foreign countries. The growth of the iron and steel industry west of the Appalachians and the gradual adoption of steel as the main constructional material confirmed the advantages of the new centers of the industry.

The great agricultural heartland of the United States is now the world's leading producer of agricultural equipment; from Ohio westwards to Minnesota most large cities and many smaller ones have a share in the industry, although California is also an important producer of certain kinds of equipment. The capacity of the industry is larger than the domestic market can support, and there is a substantial export trade, much of it directed to Europe; Europe is itself a large producer of agricultural equipment, but the small size of the local market in many European countries prohibits the manufacture of certain large and complex machines, such as the combine harvester.

Britain is the second-largest producer of agricultural equipment in the free world, and here the industry is largely concentrated in the towns of East Anglia, Lincolnshire, and eastern Yorkshire, the part of Britain in which plow agriculture has always been most important; this area lies in close proximity to the iron and steel industry of the east Midlands and to Britain's major coalfield. The long decline in the area under crops in Britain, however, has presented considerable problems for the industry and has led to several manufacturers taking up additional lines of production, such as mobile cranes, industrial trucks, earth-moving machinery, and bearings. Not unexpectedly, the production of dairying equipment is largely carried on in the more westerly portions of the country, where grassland farming predominates; a similar situation is found in the United States, in which Wisconsin, Minnesota, and New York are the main producers of equipment for the dairying industry. In dairying, however, the distinction between agricultural machinery and food-processing machinery is rather tenuous.

The British agricultural-machinery industry has long largely depended on export markets, particularly the countries within the British Commonwealth; but in most countries of Western Europe the industry relies on the home market. As the level of farm mechanization is lower than that of Britain, the Continental industry has been confined to a collection of small national units. Denmark, Switzerland, the Netherlands, and Sweden, however, have all made considerable contributions to dairy technology. Outside Europe the only other large producers of agricultural machinery are Canada, Australia, and the U.S.S.R. Although the agricultural-machinery industry of the two Dominions now has close American connections, much of it represents indigenous growth; Australia's "stump jump" plow and "stripper" harvester materially assisted the spread of commercial grain farming in the continent.

The large-scale production of agricultural machinery in the U.S.S.R. dates from the First Five Year Plan; the industry has been greatly favored by Soviet economic planners because it has made possible the release of large numbers of rural workers for other employment. The main centers of production lie in the central industrial region at Tula and Lipetsk and in the Ukraine at Kiev, Kharkov, Rostov, and

Volgograd. Russian farm equipment, however, is often of low efficiency and underpowered; this is particularly true of tractors. The U.S.S.R. is the only country to have made extensive use of electrically powered machines.

The production of food-processing machinery is sometimes combined with that of agricultural machinery, but for the most part is structurally a separate industry. The production of crushing and grinding equipment for cereals, oilseeds, beverages, sugar, and other tropical produce is definitely a heavy industry, and is largely carried on at great port cities situated within easy reach of centers of the iron and steel and related heavy engineering industries. In the United States food-processing machinery is produced on the middle Atlantic seaboard, but most of the larger cities of the Middle West take part in the industry. In Europe the concentration of production in a few great ports—Liverpool, Glasgow, Belfast, Antwerp, Amsterdam, and Hamburg—is striking.

MACHINE TOOLS

Though not a large branch of engineering by any criterion, the machine-tool industry is an extremely important one; machine tools are essential for the manufacture of all other machines, and a nation's ability to provide itself with the greater part of its machine-tool requirements is indicative of an advanced level of industrialization. The products of the industry are very varied, ranging from light drills and lathes to enormous presses and planing machines and giant multipurpose "transfer machines" used in the automobile industry. No one manufacturer is engaged in all types of production, and the numerous small firms both in the United States and in Europe indicate the numerous opportunities open to the specialist producer. The industry still uses a large proportion of highly skilled labor, despite the tendency for semiskilled and unskilled workers to increase their share of employment in almost every type of manufacturing as operations become steadily more mechanized and automatically controlled. The greater importance of skill as compared with cost of raw materials goes far to explain the development of the industry in Switzerland, whose machine tools have acquired a high reputation. The industry is also characterized by great fluctuations in output; this situation is common to most branches of capital-goods production, but manufacture of machine tools is especially hard to combine with other activities, so that skilled labor is relatively difficult to regain if discharged during slack periods.

The machine-tool industry is as old as the Industrial Revolution, and without the work of such pioneers as Maudslay, Whitworth, Bramah, and Nasmyth, industrialization could not have progressed far. The machine-tool industry began in Britain, where it grew out of the textile-machinery industry; the two great textile-producing areas of Britain, south Lancashire and the West Riding of Yorkshire, still constitute two of the three main machine-tool-producing areas in the country. But as in many other lines of industrial activity, Britain fell behind the United States and Germany towards the end of the nineteenth century; in many British factories American machine tools now outnumber domestically produced machine tools. For the relative decline of the British industry the substantial number of small firms, many privately owned, may in part be responsible; certainly the limited financial resources of even the largest firms in the industry have been an obstacle to research.[4]

[4] In 1961 the Department of Scientific and Industrial Research produced a report on the British machine-tool industry which at the time of writing remains unpublished. It is known, however, to be highly critical of certain aspects of the industry, particularly the failure to engage in research.

This defect is now in part being overcome by the establishment of a central research organization to serve the whole of the industry.

Since the end of World War II the rapid growth of the British motor-vehicle industry has greatly enlarged the demand for machine tools and has materially assisted the attainment of a higher level of efficiency in the industry. As a result the west Midlands, which contains a large share of the British motor-vehicle industry, has become the most important area in the country for the production of machine tools, although the larger and heavier types of machine are still the prerogative of the more northerly areas. The Greater London area has also obtained a larger share of production, particularly of the smaller types of power tools.

The American machine-tool industry does not have, perhaps, the world importance of the American agricultural-machinery industry, but American machine tools can be found in every large industrial establishment in the world. The original home of the industry was southern New England, where, as in old England, the connection with textile-machinery production was very marked. New England still remains an important producer, but machine-tool manufacture was also compelled to follow the westward movement of iron and steel production and other metal-using industries. On a state basis Ohio accounts for the largest share of national machine-tool production and contains two of the largest firms in the industry, the Cincinnati Milling Machine Company and Warner Swasey at Cleveland; Michigan and Illinois contend for second position.

The rapid expansion of American industrial production in the present century—above all, the enormous growth of the motor-vehicle industry, which constitutes by far the largest market for machine tools—has compelled the adoption of mass methods of machine-tool production, while in the smaller domestic markets of most European producers "batch" methods of production are more commonly employed. In this system a manufacturer organizes production in a series of discontinuous runs or batches; after the appropriate number of units has been produced, production of the line ceases and the plant is reorganized to produce another line of output. In this way a small manufacturer can produce a number of products, but of course, he can never realize the economies that come from large-scale output with runs in mass or flow production. It is doubtful that the American machine-tool industry could ever adopt the oligopolistic structure of many leading American industries, but the existence of a number of small firms has not been incompatible with research.[5] Machine tools become steadily more specialized; general-purpose machine tools such as the lathe and the drill tend to be replaced by a special machine designed for a particular task, capable of carrying out the multiplicity of operations formerly undertaken by separate machines. The apogee of special-purpose machines is the "transfer machine," used in all large automobile-engine plants for machining cylinder blocks; once fed into the machine, blocks move forward automatically to the next station as each operation is completed, the whole machine constituting a miniature production line.

Other important producers of machine tools include West Germany, now the leading producer in Western Europe, France, Belgium, Switzerland, Sweden, and Italy. The connection between machine-tool production and textile engineering is again visible in West

[5] "Small" has to be understood in an American context; many such firms would be regarded as large in most European countries; it is only in the petroleum industry and in chemicals that foreign firms can match the size of the largest American corporations. It is not true, however, that only large organizations with substantial research budgets can achieve major technological invention. See J. Jewkes et al., *Sources of Invention,* Macmillan & Co., Ltd., London, 1958.

Germany, for the Ruhr industrial area is not a particularly important producer. The main centers of the industry are the Krefeld–München Gladbach–Aachen area, an old textile district, the Rhine-Main region, one of the major centers of the German automobile industry, and Stuttgart.

The U.S.S.R. has paid particular attention to the development of a machine-tool industry, but it is only since World War II that the country has become a major producer. In the late Fifties considerable quantities of Russian lathes and other general-purpose machine tools were offered on the world market for the first time and proved to be soundly constructed and very competitively priced. Russian machine tools are manufactured in modern, highly mechanized factories, principally in the Leningrad and central industrial regions, although some machine-tool production occurs in all the major centers of metal making.

TEXTILE AND MINING MACHINERY

The production of textile and mining machinery is closely tied to the specialized markets that these industries serve. The weight of raw materials in textile machinery is not very substantial, and their cost is only a small proportion of total production costs. The textile-machinery industry would thus inevitably tend to be market-oriented, but also, close working contact between machinery manufacturers and mills is essential. This contact, however, appears to have resulted in a preoccupation with immediate problems, for over the past half century there has been comparatively little technical innovation. The long life of textile machinery has helped to confirm the textile industry's adherence to established methods. Modern machines, however, greatly speed up the traditional methods of textile production, but it is perhaps significant that many recent technical innovations have come from relatively new producers of textile machinery such as Japan and Switzerland.

The close relationship between the production of textile machinery and textile manufacture is most marked in Britain; the manufacture of cotton-textile machinery is located in south Lancashire and in the adjacent portion of Cheshire; woolen and worsted machinery is restricted to the West Riding, and the production of knitting frames and lace-making machinery takes place in Leicestershire and Nottinghamshire. In Lancashire, moreover, although there is a more or less even dispersal of textile-machinery production over the whole textile area, spinning machinery is chiefly made in districts specializing in cotton spinning, and weaving machinery is produced in weaving districts.[6]

As the world's largest textile producer, the United States has a substantial textile-machinery industry. The manufacture of such machinery has not so far followed the migration of the textile industries themselves, and is still largely confined to southern New England; however, some shift in location might be expected in the future. Since the end of World War II new textile machinery has shown considerable technical advance as textile manufacturers, faced with increasing low-cost foreign competition in what is essentially a technologically simple industry, have clamored for machines of higher productivity. Domestically produced cotton machinery, however, finds competition from Japanese machinery particularly acute; Japan, in fact, must now be regarded as the world's leader in cotton-textile machinery.

Textile machinery has a comparatively long life, so that its replacement can be deferred, and

[6] Smith, *op. cit.*, p. 386.

is inexpensive in comparison with most other types of industrial machinery. Also, the growth rate of many textile industries is slow. It is therefore not surprising that the textile-machinery industry is far from flourishing and that there is considerable overcapacity. Exports of machinery have long been necessary in some areas such as Lancashire to sustain the volume of output; in a sense, Lancashire helped to kill Lancashire through providing the equipment that enabled many countries that were once large importers of Lancashire cotton to establish their own domestic textile industries. There are now comparatively few countries that do not possess a cotton-textile industry, and the scope for an increase in world exports of textile machinery does not appear large.

The manufacture of mining machinery is another market-oriented industry, but in addition raw materials are relatively costly, their bulk is substantial, and fuel costs tend to be considerable. Every consideration, therefore, compels the production of mining equipment on, or in close proximity to, coalfields. In contrast to the situation in the textile-machinery industry with its slow rate of growth, output of mining equipment trends steadily upwards in response to the world's insatiable demands for more fuel and metalliferous minerals; moreover, mining machinery tends to become of progressively greater size and complexity. In part this change reflects the necessity for offsetting the heavy loss of labor in mining, a loss which, though particularly severe in the case of coal mining, is also marked in many areas of metalliferous mining; isolated and often elevated environments offer a life which is increasingly unattractive in highly developed economies. The trend towards open-pit working, particularly in coal mining, has provided a large market for the earthmoving- and excavating-equipment industry; the world's largest shovels and draglines are now employed in the mining of coal and iron ore. Manufacturers of such equipment serve a much wider market than that provided by the mining industry, however, and therefore have a wider choice of location; one successful small American producer is located at Salt Lake City, and many firms originally concerned with agricultural engineering in eastern England now find the manufacture of excavating machinery a more remunerative activity.

Pennsylvania, Ohio, and Illinois produce the greater part of the output not only of specialized mining machinery in the United States but also of general excavating and earthmoving equipment. In Britain, south Lancashire, west and south Yorkshire, and Lanarkshire are the major producing regions; for some reason the production of mining machinery has never been important in South Wales, despite the fact that it has long been a major coal-mining area. The Franco-Belgian field and the Ruhr are also important producers of mining machinery. Poland and Czechoslovakia, the largest coal producers of Eastern Europe, have considerable mining-machinery industries, but under Comecon agreements each Eastern European satellite is to specialize in a particular line of machinery in order to avoid wasteful duplication of productive facilities. Sweden is particularly important for the production of certain types of mining equipment, especially for rock drilling. The production of drilling and other specialized equipment for the petroleum industry, however, is virtually a monopoly of the United States, and is heavily concentrated in the most important oil-producing states, that is, Texas, Oklahoma, California, and Louisiana. The only other mining-machinery producer of consequence is the U.S.S.R., whose equipment is of a high standard; however, it is unlikely to be employed outside the Soviet bloc, except in conjunction with Russian economic aid.

LOCOMOTIVES

The manufacture of railroad and industrial locomotives is definitely a heavy industry and so tends to be carried on in areas of coal or iron and steel production and associated heavy industries. Locomotives are mobile, however, and as all areas of heavy industry are well supplied with rail facilities, it is also possible to produce such equipment at some distance from areas of heavy industry. The location of the industry therefore largely turns on whether railroad systems produce their own locomotives, as was the case with the major British roads, or prefer to purchase locomotives from specialist producers. The latter policy has been followed by most United States railroad companies, but British Dominions have tended to follow the example of Britain in their largely state-owned systems. On the European Continent, where railroads are also largely state-owned, both policies have been followed. Where locomotives have been built by operating companies for their own use, their production has tended to take place at convenient points on the respective systems, and there has thus been a certain degree of indeterminacy in location; private specialist builders, on the other hand, are always located in areas of heavy industry or at major nodal points in close proximity to such centers.

Locomotives are capital goods with a long expectation of life; a steam locomotive will last for thirty-five years or more. Their replacement can therefore be deferred, and the industry shows marked oscillations in output, varying with the general level of business activity. Maintenance, however, cannot be postponed, and in the case of steam locomotives this has always been considerable; thus all railroads have been obliged to establish maintenance and minor-repair shops at strategic points throughout the system. Steam locomotives were largely custom-built (and indeed still are); although some manufacturers relied on subcontractors for boilers and other parts, the larger manufacturers produced frames and all major components.

The post-World War II revolution in rail transport brought about by adoption of the diesel locomotive has considerably changed this industrial pattern. Locomotives are now largely standardized, and their considerably greater complexity has resulted in a manufacturing process that is largely an assembly of components produced by specialists. The use of diesel engines has encouraged the entry of the large motor-vehicle corporations into the industry, and the use of electric transmissions (and often also the acquisition of firms producing large diesel engines) has stimulated producers of heavy electric equipment to undertake locomotive production; as a result, famous names dating back to the earliest days of railroading have been eclipsed by such newcomers as General Motors, General Electric, and English Electric. Moreover, the high service availability of the diesel locomotive has meant that the necessity for dispersed maintenance plants has disappeared. Even before World War II, however, the progressive contraction of the railroad mileage in all highly developed economies and the declining share of total freight traffic handled by railroads had resulted in considerable surplus capacity in steam-locomotive manufacture. Where railroad systems still construct their own locomotives, private production has been concentrated in the largest and most efficient plants. Some specialist builders have been obliged to find alternative employment for their plant, but most have successfully adapted themselves to the greatest technical change in railroad history since George Stephenson firmly established the steam locomotive as the principal source of railroad motive power.

Until World War II Britain was both the world's largest producer and the world's largest exporter of locomotives on a numerical basis,[7] production being shared between the railroads and private companies. The major roads had always supplied their own requirements, and their works were established at points on their respective systems whose selection is now difficult to explain; Derby, Doncaster, Eastleigh, Brighton, Darlington, Swindon, and Crewe thus became major centers of the British locomotive-building industry. Minor roads were supplied by specialist builders, but with the gradual absorption of the smaller systems by the large networks, specialist builders came increasingly to rely on export markets, which were in large part created by the expansion of the overseas empire and by heavy British investment in foreign railroad construction. The private builders of steam locomotives are all situated in close proximity to coal- and steel-producing areas; the major centers are Glasgow, Manchester, Leeds, and Newcastle. Following the marked decline in foreign orders consequent on the Great Depression, private builders took increasingly to the building of small diesel locomotives for industrial and switching purposes, even supplying the major roads with their requirements of new yard switchers; it is not surprising, therefore, that in the postwar period their share of total output has increased and that most main-line diesel locomotives for the nationalized railway system have been supplied by them.[8]

As a result of technical change new producers have entered the industry since World War II, notably English Electric, a company which produces both large diesel engines and electric transmissions and from whose Manchester plant have originated the largest and most powerful locomotives ever used on British railroads, and Brush of Loughborough, another major producer of electric equipment. British locomotive exports are still considerable, although United States manufacturers have been keen competitors in the postwar period.

Broadly similar locational factors have operated in several European countries (Fig. 16-1). In France, Le Creusot and Lille, both centers of heavy industry and iron and steel, and Paris are the main locomotive-building centers, and in Germany, the third-largest producer before World War II, locomotive manufacture is carried on at Essen, Kassel, and Berlin. German builders have pioneered with the large diesel-hydraulic locomotive, which gives a very favorable power-weight ratio, but have also undertaken the building of American-designed locomotives under license.

In the United States the construction of locomotives has always been left to the specialist producers, some of which, like their British counterparts, originated in the earliest days of railroading. Nodality has been a factor of importance in the location of the industry, and one of the earliest centers of locomotive construction was Philadelphia, where the Baldwin Company eventually grew to become the largest unit in the industry. Other major centers of the industry are Schenectady, where the American Locomotive Company is located, Pittsburg, Lima, Erie, and Chicago. Leadership of the industry, however, now resides with

[7] **The average weight of a main-line locomotive in Britain in 1935 was only 83 tons, however, compared with an average of more than twice this weight for American locomotives. Smith, *op. cit.*, p. 383.**

[8] **The changeover to diesel haulage in Britain's railroads was greatly retarded through preoccupation with the problems of the coal industry. All four main rail systems were large coal producers, and both the railroads and the coal industry passed into the hands of the state following World War II. Partly to assist the coal industry and partly to conserve foreign exchange, the decision was taken in 1945 to reequip Britain's roads with new steam locomotives. This policy retarded the attainment of a higher level of competitive efficiency by the railroad system, and its deficit grew. The introduction of diesel haulage means that many comparatively new steam locomotives have had their expectation of life greatly reduced, and will not yield an adequate return on the capital invested in them.**

Fig. 16-1 Locomotive works in Western Europe.

corporations whose principal interests are in the automotive and electrical fields,[9] and several of the older producers have been forced to take up additional lines of production. The reequipment of the American railroads with diesel locomotives produced boom conditions in the industry, but since the changeover, completed about 1952, the industry has actively sought markets abroad, and exports have become relatively much more important than in the past.

[9] **General Motors has been charged with using its large railroad-freight business as a lever to persuade railroads to purchase its locomotives.**

SHIPBUILDING

Shipbuilding is a branch of heavy engineering whose location is rigorously determined both physically and economically. It requires deep navigable water either on the coast itself or on a river or inlet; just as essentially, it requires a large area of level land close by on which components and subassemblies can be erected. Ships are almost always custom-built. Considerable standardization of vessels was achieved in both world wars, but in normal times such vessels are uneconomic, as the enormous tonnage of laid-up liberty ships

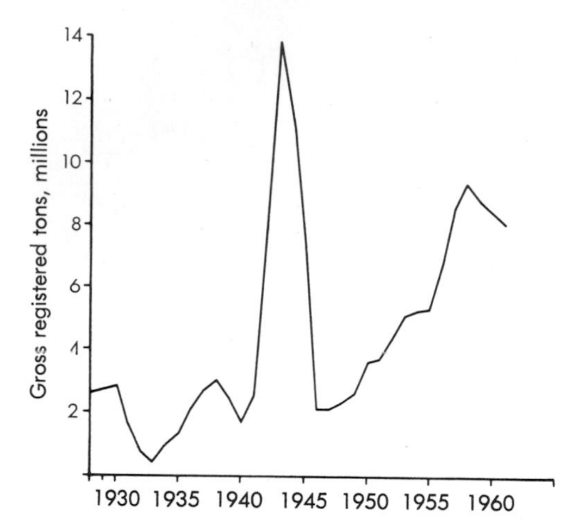

Fig. 16-2 Merchant vessel launchings, 1928–1961. The Great Depression, World War II, and the postwar boom are all reflected in this graph of world merchant vessel launchings.

testifies; the variety of cargoes, the diversity of shipping routes, and the great differences in the equipment and facilities of ports of call necessitate that the purchaser has a vessel designed for his particular purpose.[10] (Fig. 16-2). For bulk cargoes such as petroleum and iron ore some degree of standardization is perhaps possible, however, and it is precisely in such carriers that shipowners have been exploiting the economies of operation that ensue from the use of vessels of large size.

The shipbuilder must have good access to an iron- and steel-producing center, for the transport costs on plates, angles, and heavy sections are high. Many large shipbuilding companies also own plants producing propulsion machinery, boilers, and other equipment, but others purchase such items from specialist producers. These tend to be located in close proximity to areas of shipbuilding, but this is not always the case, for some suppliers may serve many areas.[11]

Few other types of heavy engineering can show technical advances over the past two decades as shipbuilding. There has been a marked tendency for the number of components supplied by specialists to increase as vessels grow increasingly more complex. Loading and discharging equipment has been greatly improved to speed up turnaround at ports; electrically operated hatch covers, improved ship's gear and heavy-lift booms, side hatches, and internal conveyors all help to reduce the time a ship lies idle in port. Other major innovations are the extended use of aluminum superstructures, which permit extra decks and thus greater earning capacity, and the rapid increase in power output of diesel engines, which are now manufactured in sizes large enough for supertankers. The use of more efficient engines permits not only a reduction in machinery space, thus increasing carrying capacity, but also higher speed, which further augments earning capacity. The fully automated ship in which all operations are controlled from the bridge is still some way off, but considerable progress has been made in this direction, particularly in Japan, and progressive reductions in the size of crews can be anticipated.

These technical advances and the increasing size of many classes of vessel are leading to a concentration of shipbuilding in those areas possessing the best physical conditions for the adoption of modern building techniques. The extended use of welding, the prefabrication of large sections, and the employment of very large cranes to lift completed assemblies into position all require large areas of space, and these are often out of the question in old industrial areas, where shipyards are hemmed in by docks, warehouses, and other industrial

[10] **A leading British shipbuilder, however, now offers standardized ships at a substantial discount.**

[11] **Dudley in the west Midlands is Britain's major center for the production of anchors and chains and is as far from the sea as is possible in Britain. See P. Sargant Florence,** *Logic of British and American Industry,* **Routledge & Kegan Paul, Ltd., London, 1953, p. 87.**

buildings. Among major shipbuilding nations these changes have operated strongly to the disadvantage of Britain, which possesses many yards with limited opportunities of acquiring the land required for the adoption of these techniques.

Great Britain, the World Leader

Since wooden ships were supplanted by those made of iron and steel Britain has been the leading shipbuilding nation in the world (Table 16-1). It is true that in the late Fifties both West Germany and Japan in some years launched a greater tonnage, but a larger proportion of British building consisted of passenger vessels and other specialized vessels of higher value than those of Germany and Japan, both of which built a larger tanker tonnage; in value of output, therefore, Britain still easily outpaces its rivals.

The traditional centers of shipbuilding in Britain were on Thameside and on the south coast adjacent to supplies of timber. But with the adoption of iron and steel as the principal structural materials, in the second half of the nineteenth century the focus of the industry shifted to Scotland and the north, where coal and iron production abutted on the coast.[12] Before World War I the northeast coast, with shipyards along the Tyne, the Wear, and the Tees, was the principal shipbuilding area, but Clydeside is now dominant. The reasons for this change are not entirely clear. Though the increasing size of ships has undoubtedly been

[12] The considerable tidal range of the Bristol Channel seems inadequate to explain the failure of the industry to establish itself in South Wales, and this is clearly related to the absence of other branches of heavy engineering. The lack of interest in the manufacture of heavy machine tools, locomotives, mining machinery, heavy electric equipment, as well as shipbuilding, is remarkable in an area that has long been the principal steel producer in the country and an important area for the smelting of nonferrous metals.

Table 16-1

Merchant Vessels Launched and Under Construction, 1963 (Thousand gross registered tons)

	LAUNCHED	UNDER CONSTRUCTION
United States	296	335
West Germany	980	686
France	445	518
Italy	516	686
Netherlands	376	269
Belgium	98	107
Britain	936	1,421
Sweden	868	757
Norway	336	365
Denmark	296	297
Japan	2,375	1,570
WORLD TOTAL*	8,550	8,400

* Excluding U.S.S.R. and mainland China.
SOURCE: United Nations, *Monthly Bulletin of Statistics*, March, 1964.

a factor, the northeast coast has built some large vessels of all types, including modern tankers; tanker construction, in fact, has been a specialty of the area since the early Twenties.

Clydeside, in addition to constituting the principal shipbuilding area of Britain, possesses the largest concentration of marine-engineering establishments. Noted chiefly for its large transatlantic liners from the John Brown & Co. yard at Clydebank, Clydeside produces vessels of all types. The largest class of building has become of minor importance since the end of the war, and it is indeed doubtful if vessels comparable with the *Queens* will ever be produced again, for neither their construction nor their operation can now be regarded as economic.

The Belfast shipyards are anomalous in that Northern Ireland possesses no local steel or other heavy industry and raw materials are imported, principally from Clydeside and from west Cumberland. The Belfast yards of Harland & Woolf, the largest company in the area, are capable of building vessels of the very largest size,[13] and have been responsible for a long series of large passenger liners in the postwar period, including the *Canberra,* the largest liner to be built in Britain since the war.[14] Other areas capable of constructing large vessels are Barrow in Furness, Lancashire, where Vickers Ltd. has built many large postwar liners including the *Oriana,* and Birkenhead on Merseyside. Both of these northwestern areas are also noted for their naval construction, especially submarines.

While no British shipping line operates its own shipyards, there has been a strong tendency for the major lines to give their orders to firms that have served them in the past; thus Cunard has been associated with John Brown, Union Castle with Harland & Woolf, and the Orient Line with Vickers; the P & O Company, however, the world's largest shipping organization, has shared its orders among a number of builders. Shipbuilding is notoriously susceptible to cyclical fluctuations of activity, and the prolonged interwar depression in Britain resulted in heavy unemployment and considerable social distress in all major shipbuilding areas. Since the end of the war, however, shipyards have on the whole been very active, and Britain's difficulties have come more from uncertain delivery dates than from an absolute shortage of orders. Perhaps the greatest obstacles to the attainment of a higher level of efficiency in the British industry are strongly entrenched union privileges and rigorous division of work, which prevent the optimum deployment of labor. Although the pioneer of steam propulsion, Britain has lagged behind Scandinavia in the use of the large marine diesel engine[15] and the bulk carrier; some responsibility for this technical shortcoming, however, must also be borne by the British shipping lines.

Japan

The most remarkable development in the world shipbuilding industry in the present century has undoubtedly been the growth of Japan

[13] **Every major shipbuilding area in the United Kingdom tendered for the construction of the first replacement for the *Queens*, for which government had guaranteed a large subsidy, and for a nuclear-powered vessel to be built for the British government. Neither project is to be proceeded with.**

[14] **Among many innovations on the *Canberra* are an aluminum superstructure, side hatches and transverse conveyors for rapid loading and unloading, a transverse propeller permitting lateral movement, turboelectric propulsion, and all machinery aft, which with the absence of top hatches and derricks gives an uninterrupted deck space. With a speed comparable to that of the largest transatlantic liners, the *Canberra* brings Fremantle, western Australia, within twenty-one days of Southampton.**

[15] **Britain's lack of interest in the compression-ignition engine—now universally known by the name of its pioneer, Dr. Rudolf Diesel—is all the more difficult to understand in that Stewart-Ackroyd, a British engineer, has a claim to prior discovery. The reason probably lies in the enormous importance of coal in the British economy before 1914.**

as a major producer. In 1913 Japan accounted for only some 2 per cent of the total world tonnage launched, and even by 1950 the country accounted for no more than 10 per cent, compared with 38 per cent for Britain. Thereafter growth was extremely rapid; in 1956 Japan surpassed Britain in tonnage launched and has maintained its lead ever since. Following the Suez crisis of 1956 Japan became particularly important as a builder of supertankers, in which the country has no rival either for speed or cheapness of construction. Japan's heavy dependence on tanker construction, however, presents considerable dangers in view of the mounting world oil surplus and the growing difficulty experienced even by modern tankers in obtaining employment.

This development has been all the more remarkable in that Japan is a relatively high-cost producer of steel; its low shipbuilding costs arise primarily from heavy investment in providing shipyards with the most modern techniques. Much of this development has been financed from abroad, in particular from the United States, and was made possible through the immense physical destruction of World War II. Japan, it must be emphasized, is not now a particularly low-labor-cost area, but the absence of irritating and expensive restrictions on the deployment of labor has been a factor of great importance. The costs of producing large tankers have been estimated at about 10 per cent lower than for European yards and as almost half those of American yards.[16] Japan has also taken up the manufacture of European-designed diesel engines under license, and its reputation for speedy and low-cost work has ensured that its ship-repairing facilities have been heavily patronized.

The best-known Japanese shipbuilding center is probably the former Kure Navy Yard, acquired and completely reequipped after the war by an American concern, National Bulk Carriers Inc. The Kure yard has turned out a succession of increasingly large tankers culminating in the *Universe Daphne* of 110,000 deadweight tons.[17] Other major centers of shipbuilding are Nagasaki and Sasebo on Kyushu, Shimonoseki, Hiroshima and the Hanshin area (Osaka-Kobe), all on the Inland Sea, Nagoya, and the Keihin area (Tokyo-Yokohama). In 1962 the Sasebo yard completed the world's largest commercial vessel, the *Nissho Maru* of 132,000 deadweight tons, for a Japanese oil company; this yard has declared its ability to build bulk carriers of up to 150,000 deadweight tons.

Other European Nations

Britain's traditional rival in shipbuilding has long been Germany, and the postwar resurrection of the West German shipbuilding industry has been remarkable. As in Japan, the destruction of the old shipyards, together with substantial foreign aid, has enabled the industry to make use of the most modern equipment. Not unexpectedly, the German shipbuilding industry shows greater concentration, both structurally and geographically, than its British counterpart. The principal center of both shipbuilding and marine engineering is Hamburg, where Bloehm and Voss, the most famous German shipbuilding concern, is located. Hamburg is also the site of the Schlieker company yards; this fast-growing postwar newcomer to the industry built some very large tankers before its quite unexpected failure in 1962. This shock, together with growing labor unrest, suggested to many that the postwar Ger-

[16] *Petroleum Press Service,* vol. 27, p. 11, London, 1960.

[17] Tankers are usually measured in deadweight tons, that is, cargo capacity. The tonnage measurements for most vessels are capacity measurements. By legal definition, 100 cubic feet is equivalent to 1 ton, so that gross tonnage is the internal volume of the ship (less certain exempted spaces) in cubic feet divided by 100. Net tonnage represents the earning space after the deduction of propulsion machinery, crew's quarters, etc.

The turbine rotor being machined in a Leningrad plant illustrates the heavy division of electrical engineering; the manufacture of domestic electricity meters, as in this plant in Taipei, is clearly a light industry.

man "economic miracle" was coming to an end. The observation was premature, but even up to 1964, no use had been found for the Schlieker yards. Bremen and Kiel also have extensive shipyards. Though not part of the German industry, the important shipbuilding and marine-engineering industries of Rotterdam share the same material base as West Germany.

Scandinavia's importance as a major shipbuilding area is insufficiently appreciated. The annual tonnage launched by Sweden, Norway, and Denmark combined is little inferior to that of West Germany, and no other shipbuilding area has made a greater contribution to technological progress; Sweden, which has experienced a very rapid increase in tonnage launched since 1945, pioneered with all-welded-construction techniques and has been largely responsible for the development of the giant marine diesel engine of more than 20,000 horsepower. Göteborg is the main center of the Swedish shipbuilding and marine-engineering industry and is likely to be the first European center capable of producing supertankers of upwards of 100,000 deadweight tons. Other Scandinavian yards are located at Malmö in Sweden, in the Oslo district of Norway, and at Copenhagen and Odense in Denmark. Despite an apparently unfavorable geographic position in relation to supplies of iron and steel—Sweden, as pointed out earlier, is largely dependent on imports for its tonnage steels—the Scandinavian builders are all comparatively low-cost producers. Sweden's highly automated yards—

New techniques of shipbuilding, involving prefabrication and the use of dry docks in place of launching slips, are illustrated by this Sasebo yard, in Japan. The vessel under construction is the *Nissho Maru* of 132,000 tons dw, the world's largest bulk carrier; the completed vessel is seen after being towed out of the flooded dry dock.

where a new process has been developed for building ships stern first, completely under cover, so that no loss of time is incurred through inclement weather—justify emphatic rejection of the argument that high-labor-cost areas cannot be competitive in the shipbuilding industry; also, the long established Swedish principle of one labor union per industry has meant a complete absence of restrictions on the deployment of labor and freedom from the endless demarcation disputes that plague the British industry.

Of the remaining European shipbuilders, both France and Italy are capable of producing all types of vessels including large, fast, and handsome passenger liners; but both are high-cost producers, and their industries have long depended on heavy subsidies. France has shipyards at Dunkerque, but the main shipbuilding area is on the west coast, far removed from supplies of finished iron and steel products. From St. Nazaire, however, some magnificent vessels have appeared; the *France,* which will almost certainly be the last giant transatlantic liner, is the longest ship ever built. Other west coast shipbuilding centers are Brest (a naval dockyard) and La Pallice. Italy's industry is mainly located at Genoa, site of the country's largest integrated iron and steel works, and at Trieste and Naples.

The United States

The United States is normally of small importance as a shipbuilder and is also a very high-cost producer, for both shipbuilding and marine engineering are largely custom operations demanding a very high labor input. Before the Civil War the United States was the foremost shipbuilding nation of the world; the industry was heavily concentrated on the New England coast, which possessed raw materials in abundance and a long tradition of shipbuilding and seafaring. After the war the changing technology of shipbuilding and the decline of the wooden sailing ship operated strongly against the New England industry, which lacked access to coal and iron; moreover, opportunities for more profitable investment in railroads and in internal economic development attracted capital away from shipping and shipbuilding alike. Nevertheless, government has always considered it necessary to maintain the industry in being for reasons of national security.

Large vessels are now built in the United States only for the Navy or when special considerations such as the award of a large subsidy are involved.[18] Nevertheless, when cost is of secondary consideration, as in a war emergency, the United States has shown itself capable of the most stupendous feats of construction. More than 2,000 ships were built during World War I by the Emergency Fleet Corporation, and in the peak year of 1943 during World War II some 12.5 million tons of shipping were produced, about half as much again as total world launchings in 1961. This prodigious output was achieved by the adoption of simplified and standardized designs and by the maximum of prefabrication; as a result, the construction time for a vessel of 8,000 gross tons was finally reduced to less than three days. This tremendous wartime tonnage inevitably acted as a severe postwar depressant on the industry, and by 1955 American launchings had declined to less than 20,000 gross tons; shipyards either closed down or found alternative employment. Between 1958 and 1962, however, launchings averaged about 120,000 tons annually, about 5 per cent of total world launchings.

Despite its small overall size, the United

[18] Some very large tankers have been built by the Bethlehem Steel Corporation's shipbuilding subsidiary for the Niarchos group, as part of an agreement permitting Niarchos to transfer surplus American vessels to foreign registration. Bethlehem Steel's own large ore carriers, however, are Japanese-built.

States shipbuilding industry possesses some of the world's largest yards. Shipyards are situated on all three coasts and on the Great Lakes, and many smaller World War II craft began their existence on the Ohio, the Tennessee, and other rivers. The most important shipbuilding area is the middle Atlantic coast. This portion of the country contains many major ports, but its intense urbanization and industrialization heighten the difficulties of retaining skilled labor in a very volatile industry; the steady expansion of the iron and steel industry in the area, however, is likely to be of considerable assistance to the industry in reducing costs. At Sparrows Point the Bethlehem Shipbuilding Company possesses yards capable of building tankers of over 100,000 deadweight tons. The same company possesses yards at Quincy, Massachusetts, that have also turned out some very large vessels; this is now the only important commercial shipbuilding center in New England, but the region has a large defense establishment in the Navy's Groton yards, which have long specialized in submarines. The United States Steel Corporation, in contrast, has displayed only a limited interest in shipbuilding, although it does possess a subsidiary company in the industry. Other major shipbuilding concerns are located at Newport News, where the *United States,* present holder of the Blue Riband of the North Atlantic, and such giant carriers as the *Forrestal* and the *Constitution* were built, and Camden, New Jersey, where the world's first atomic-powered freighter, the *Savannah,* was constructed. Brooklyn's navy yard is almost as well known as its bridge and enjoys the distinction of having built the world's largest vessel, the aircraft carrier *Constellation.*

The Erie lakeshore and southern Wisconsin also enjoy the advantage of local iron and steel industries and build vessels of large size; before World War II it was often claimed that the average size of ships operating on the Great Lakes exceeded that of vessels operating on the world's oceans, but with the great proliferation of large tankers since 1945 this claim can no longer be sustained. Since the opening of the St. Lawrence Seaway this interior shipbuilding region has lost its natural protection, although Great Lakes vessels can be built with less longitudinal strength than those intended for oceanic service, and are therefore somewhat cheaper to construct.

The other shipbuilding districts all suffer from the disadvantage of having only minor iron and steel industries in their immediate vicinity to support them. The Gulf Coast can draw upon the Alabama section of the iron and steel industry for some raw materials, and at Pascagoula, Mississippi, the Ingalls Company, drawing on the same source, has built some large passenger liners, a surprising postwar development. The connection of the western iron and steel industry with the wartime shipbuilding industry of the Pacific Coast has already received some attention.

The high cost of shipbuilding in the United States raises difficult problems, as a nucleus of skilled labor must be preserved in the industry in the national interest. Both the construction and the operation of ships are heavily subsidized, and large vessels for commercial purposes usually incorporate features desirable from the standpoint of the defense departments. But broadly similar considerations apply in the case of many other shipbuilding nations; most transatlantic liners now in service were built with the aid of a subsidy of some kind.

THE ELECTRICAL INDUSTRIES

Electrical engineering is in some ways the epitome of the engineering industries. Some of the electrical industries are among the heaviest of all industries and have rigidly determined locations; others are essentially light industries whose location is largely indeterminate. Some branches of production are dominated by a handful of giant enterprises, while others are shared between a multiplicity of producers in a fiercely competitive market. There is a measure of overall unity, however, arising from the interest of the largest organizations in virtually all branches of production, and the expenditure on research is very high. Very broadly the electrical industries fall into three divisions: (*a*) equipment for the generation, transmission, and distribution of electric energy; (*b*) equipment and appliances for converting electric energy into heat, light, and mechanical energy; and (*c*) electronic equipment.

In electrical engineering the employment ratio of ferrous to nonferrous raw materials is lower than in any other engineering industry, with the possible exception of aircraft production; indeed, nonmetals are also of considerable importance, particularly in the electronics division. The production of turboalternators, large motors, switchgear, and transformers requires massive castings or forgings, special alloy steels, and large quantities of copper, so that proximity to centers of metal making and heavy industry is essential. For the manufacture of the heaviest cables and particularly submarine cables, a waterside location is very desirable. Close liaison with manufacturers of boilers, water turbines, and diesel engines is also necessary. The growing importance of the diesel engine for small power stations and the development of a wide range of "packaged" power plants have resulted in many combinations between engine producers and manufacturers of generating equipment; integrated operations of this kind are very attractive to organizations with large financial resources. The heavier sections of electrical engineering are thus characterized by an oligopolistic structure in which a few large producers share the market—General Electric, Westinghouse, Lincoln, and Allis-Chalmers in the United States, English Electric and the Associated Electrical Industries (AEI) group in Britain, Siemens and Allgemeine Electricität Gesellschaft (AEG) in Germany, Toshiba and Hitachi in Japan.

Manufacture of heavy electric equipment is largely a custom operation, so that in this branch the United States enjoys no special advantage; indeed, foreign firms have consistently bid lower than domestic firms for the supply of equipment for large United States government projects. The manufacture of smaller motors and appliances, however, readily lends itself to flow production, so that in this section of the industry the United States has no rival. There is also room for smaller firms, some of which may be little more than assemblers. As raw materials are of limited bulk and the value added in manufacture is high, a wide choice of locations is possible; large metropolitan centers, however, constitute a major attraction.

The electronics branch of electrical engineering is perhaps the most remarkable of all; it is essentially a *communications* industry, concerned with the recording, transmission, and processing of intelligence in a variety of forms. In contrast to other branches of electrical engineering, it makes use of currents at high frequencies and depends heavily on tubes, transistors, and other semiconductors. Its raw materials are most diverse and generally of small value in relation to the value of the finished products; it also needs few of the machine tools employed in the production of generating equipment and appliances. Though a very young industry with an astronomical growth rate, it is an outgrowth of the older branches of electrical engineering, so that all of the large firms in the industry have a share in it; these, however, are challenged by a number of specialist firms, some of which, such as RCA, Sylvania, and Raytheon, are also of large size. In addition, since the most fundamental requirement for entry is scientific knowledge and the ability to sustain research, many other large organizations such as International Business Machines (IBM), Burroughs, and Sperry Rand, whose main interests were originally in other fields, have also entered the electronics industry. Nor is this all, for the basic items of equipment in the industry are few and are relatively cheap,[19] so that the assembler with limited capital but with the appropriate scientific knowledge can also enter the industry with fair hopes of success; some of the most rapidly growing concerns in the industry are those orginally formed by breakaway groups of scientists from the large enterprises. An industry which brings together the giants of heavy electrical engineering, motor vehicles, aircraft, business machines, its own autochthonous large enterprises, and small independents must be regarded as unique.

The Leading World Producers

Though many nations have contributed to the development of electricity generation, transmission, and utilization, until 1914 leadership of the electrical industries rested with Germany. The country enjoyed no special geographic advantages to help account for this fact, and an explanation has mainly to be sought in the social and institutional environment of Imperial Germany, which was also mainly responsible for its strong grip on the chemical industries.[20] After World War I the United States assumed the premier position, but the field is now far too wide for any one nation to achieve clear technical or economic superiority in every branch of production; much electronic engineering, moreover, now consists of defense production, for which many governments, directly and indirectly, provide large research funds. In types of production in which flow methods with relatively low labor input are possible, above all in the appliance section, the United States is preeminent; it also has a commanding position in the manufacture of the largest types of computers. Nevertheless, it is clear that in some lines of production other countries have strong competitive positions. Japanese electronic equipment is of a very high technical standard and is relatively inexpensive, and the country has also some cost advantages in the production of heavy generating equipment; France excels in the production of high-voltage switchgear, while Britain has played a major part in the development of the very large turboalternator. Several countries at a high level of development, in fact, can point to some branch in which they enjoy either a technical or an economic advantage.

The electrical industries of the United States are very widely distributed, and decentralization has been a marked feature of the policy of the large electrical corporations. The General Electric Corporation has more than 130 plants scattered through nearly thirty states;[21] the greatest concentration of plants, however, is in the heavily populated northeast portion of the country extending between southern New England and the Mississippi and lying mainly north of the Ohio, an area that also contains most of the plants of the Westinghouse Corporation, which number about a hundred. Production of the largest and heaviest items of equipment is of necessity located either at, or in close proximity to, centers of the iron and steel industry and related heavy industry, for example, at Pittsburgh, Buffalo, Cleveland, Sharon, and Chicago. Cities on

[19] Essentially, the resistor, capacitor, inductor, and semiconductors such as the tube, transistor, or some similar device; such products account for about one-third of the value of total output of the electronics industry of the United States.

[20] See pp. 501–503.

[21] Not all of these, of course, are engaged in the electrical industries.

major lines of communication, such as Schenectady, long synonymous with General Electric, and several in the Ohio valley and on the middle Atlantic seaboard, also participate in the heavier branches.

While some of the large specialized electronic-equipment producers such as Sylvania have also pursued a policy of decentralization, this devision of the electrical industries is on the whole becoming more highly localized. As markets are more important than raw materials and scientific knowledge more important than either, this industry is definitely attracted to the largest metropolitan centers, which are important markets and also have by far the greatest number of institutions from which scientifically trained personnel can be recruited. The share of electronic production accounted for by consumer goods tends progressively to decline; by 1960 it was scarcely a fifth of the total value of output, and had experienced relatively little growth in the preceding decade.[22] The largest market for electronic equipment now lies in guidance and control systems for missiles and rockets and in other military uses; the prospect of a continued high level of defense spending makes it certain that the growth rate of the electronics industry will remain high.

The largest center of electronics production is now southern California, the state as a whole accounting for about a fifth of national production by value. The electronics industries of the Los Angeles area have in part arisen from the increasing demands of its local aircraft industry, but many have also developed in response to the amenities that have long constituted one of the principal inducements to industrialization in the area; these climatic, academic, and recreational advantages are heavily stressed by local companies as inducements to scientists to join their staffs. This heavy concentration of production has obvious military dangers, and rival lobbies agitate for and against a wider allocation of defense spending.

Both in their structure and location pattern the electrical industries of Britain resemble those of the United States. The heaviest branches are largely shared between two large organizations, English Electric and AEI; both groups are involved in the production of diesel engines and locomotives. The two principal areas for heavy electrical engineering are south Lancashire and the West Riding, in both of which these two groups possess plants; the industry is also important, however, in certain Midland cities such as Stafford, Rugby, and Loughborough, which, though not themselves centers of heavy industry, lie on the main lines of communication between such centers and the metropolis. Greater London's interest in heavy electrical engineering is largely confined to heavy cables, a type of production which is shared between Thameside and Merseyside (Liverpool). The capital, however, is extremely important for the production of appliances and electronic equipment, activities which are very well represented among the great concentrations of industry to be found in the northern and northwestern outskirts.

In the six countries of the EEC electrical industries are also located either in the metropolitan centers or in areas of heavy industry. In Germany, however, the Ruhr was closely challenged even in 1939 in the production of the heaviest types of equipment by Berlin; electrical industries were the largest industrial employers in the former German capital, where the plants of Siemens and AEG were among the largest of their kind in Europe. The division of Germany has reduced the importance of the former capital in electrical engineering, although the enormous Siemens plant at Siemenstadt (Spandau) in West Berlin has been rebuilt and extended. Both Siemens and AEG possess several plants in other parts

[22] *The Economist,* **vol. 201, p. 137, London, 1961.**

of the country; the Rhine-Main region, Nürnberg, Stuttgart, and Munich have all shared in the expansion of the electrical industries. The Netherlands, while lacking a heavy electrical industry, possesses one of the largest and most famous producers of electric appliances and electronic equipment, Philips, whose headquarters and largest plant are situated at Eindhoven. Both Philips and Siemens have numerous foreign subsidiaries.

Outside Europe and North America only two producers of electric equipment are of major significance, the U.S.S.R. and Japan. Leningrad was long the principal center of electrical engineering, but the industry is now widely distributed. Japan's booming electrical industries have made a major contribution to the country's phenomenal postwar economic growth; they are heavily concentrated in the three great industrial nodes of the Keihin and Hanshin cities and Nagoya.

SELECTED REFERENCES

Alderfer, E. B., and H. E. Michl: *Economics of American Industry,* McGraw-Hill Book Company, New York, 1957, pp. 117–148.

Allen, G. C.: *British Industries and their Organization,* Longmans, Green & Co., Ltd., London, 1959, pp. 133–172.

———: *Japan's Economic Recovery,* Oxford University Press, Oxford, 1960, pp. 93–99.

Azami, E.: "Changing Japan: The Shipbuilding Industry Past and Present," *Japan Quarterly,* vol. 5, pp. 370–380, 1958.

Gibbs-Smith, A. J.: "World Machine Tool Analysis," *The Times (London) Review of Industry,* vol. 16 (new series), no. 189, p. 57, October, 1962.

Jones, Leslie: *Shipbuilding in Britain,* University of Wales Press, Cardiff, 1957.

Malik, Rex: "Electrical Engineering in Europe," *The Times (London) Review of Industry,* vol. 16 (new series), nos. 187–190, August-November, 1962.

———: "The Siemens Empire," *The Times (London) Review of Industry,* vol. 17 (new series), no. 192, January, 1963.

Minin, P. I.: *Development of Agricultural Machine Building in the U.S.S.R.,* United States Joint Publications Research Service, New York, 1958.

Organisation for European Economic Cooperation: *The Engineering Industries in Europe,* Paris, 1960.

Parkinson, J. R.: *Economics of Shipbuilding in the United Kingdom,* Cambridge University Press, Cambridge, 1960.

Smith, Wilfred: *An Economic Geography of Great Britain,* 2d ed., pp. 372–414, Methuen & Co., Ltd., London, 1953.

U.S. Department of Agriculture: "The Development of the Tractor," Yearbook of Agriculture, 1960.

Woytinsky, W. S., and E. S. Woytinsky: *World Population and Production,* The Twentieth Century Fund, New York, 1953, pp. 1144–1163.

Chapter 17

MOTOR-VEHICLE AND AIRCRAFT INDUSTRIES

The motor-vehicle industry is perhaps the most remarkable "growth" industry of the twentieth century, and has come to occupy a key position in the economies of several countries at a high level of development. Until World War II the United States completely dominated both the production and the use of motor vehicles; but since 1945 Western Europe has become of increasing importance, and rapid expansion of vehicle production has been a major factor in the maintenance of a high level of economic growth. Outside North America and the European Continent motor-vehicle production, as opposed to assembly of motor vehicles from imported parts, is only well established in Australia and Japan, where postwar expansion has also been rapid, but the foundations for the industry have been laid in a number of countries in Asia, Latin America, and Africa. In Eastern bloc countries generally the industry is still of limited significance, a result of investment policies which channel resources into expanding heavy industries and which enforce maximum utilization of the railroad system.

The aircraft industry has also demonstrated remarkable capacity for growth, but except for relatively brief periods its commercial markets have always been secondary to military ones; it has therefore received greater emphasis in Eastern bloc countries than has the motor-vehicle industry. Until the end of World War II the two industries were very closely connected, for many motor-vehicle manufacturers were also involved in the production of aircraft or aircraft engines. Since then, however, the pace of technological change in the aircraft industry has been so rapid that many of these former links have been broken, to be replaced by new bonds with the burgeoning electronics industry.

The products of the motor-vehicle industry include motorcycles, automobiles, buses, trucks, and tractors; some manufacturers also produce industrial trucks, stationary engines, and marine engines. Outside the Eastern bloc and Japan, the production of automobiles is by far the most important section of the industry, but in Western Europe generally, commercial-vehicle production is relatively more important than is the case in the United States. Japan and Italy, with their lower level of per capita incomes, are very large producers of motorcycles.

The production of motor vehicles involves the assembly of a large number of individual parts; their number and variety, in fact, is so great that it is virtually impossible for even the largest manufacturers to make them all. In the United States there has been a strong tendency for the large automobile manufacturers to absorb component-making firms, but subcontracting for the supply of parts from independent producers is still widely practiced, and a delicate balance between internal production and "buying out" has long been regarded as an essential for success. Manufacturers generally undertake the production of the most complex and expensive components such as motors, chassis, and transmissions themselves and buy out other parts. Even when components are produced by subsidiaries, some buying out is still practiced, for this enables manufacturers to keep their own component plants operating near capacity during periods of depression and also reduces the possibility of a production delay through labor disputes when times are good. Specialist component manufacturers can also enjoy the advantages of lower unit costs through longer production runs.[1]

The substantial economies achieved through large-scale operations have been a powerful incentive towards concentration of production in the hands of a few large producers, particularly in the automobile industry. Long runs not only permit lower costs but also make possible rapid amortization of expensive capital equipment, a necessity in the United States where the automobile industry has adopted a policy of annual model changes. Large-scale operations are also necessary in the automobile industry because of its notorious susceptibility to cyclical fluctuations; large financial resources are necessary to withstand heavy losses during poor years and to ensure that capacity exists to take advantage of any upturn in the market. The production of commercial vehicles, however, still leaves considerable room for the small specialist producer, although in all producing countries the greater part of the output of commercial vehicles is derived from the automobile manufacturers.

THE MOTOR-VEHICLE INDUSTRY OF THE UNITED STATES

The United States produced some 55 per cent of the world output of automobiles and 30 per cent of that of commercial vehicles in 1962 (Table 17-1); this is a substantial share, but in 1929 the respective proportions were 85 per cent and 70 per cent. The growth rate of the United States industry has thus been lower than that of the world as a whole, but this fact has to be considered in the light of the very large and increasing interest of American manufacturers in foreign production.

Historical Development and Present Situation in the World

One of the most remarkable facts about the American motor-vehicle industry is the rapidity with which it attained maturity. By 1905, a date which marks the end of the period of basic experiment with the form and structure of the automobile, the United States had wrested the leadership of the automobile industry from its original home, Europe, and by 1912 American production attained an output of half a million

[1] **Subsidiaries of General Motors produce almost every kind of component and supply rival manufacturers as well as the parent organization. The corporation has stated on occasions, however, that any division can purchase a part from outside the organization if it can obtain a lower price.**

Table 17-1

Production of Motor Vehicles, 1963 (Thousands)

	AUTOMOBILES	COMMERCIAL VEHICLES
United States	7,632	1,464
Canada	520	99
Argentina	96	36
Brazil	97	84
EEC	3,992	536
West Germany	2,412	252
France	1,452	254
Italy	1,104	75
Netherlands	24	5
Britain	1,608	408
Japan	408	979
India	22	28
Australia	216	36
East Germany	72	8
Czechoslovakia	56	43
Poland	18	20
U.S.S.R.	168	564
WORLD TOTAL*	16,150	4,380

* Excluding mainland China.
SOURCE: United Nations, *Monthly Bulletin of Statistics*, May, 1964.

vehicles. Production had then already become concentrated in the hands of a few large enterprises, some seven firms accounting for about one-half of the automobile production. Rigorous standardization of parts, a concentration on relatively low-priced vehicles, the production of a limited number of models, and the adoption of flow methods of assembly sharply differentiated the United States industry from that of Europe, which remained devoted to the production of expensive vehicles with a limited market, produced by methods of assembly that involved a high labor input. The mass-production techniques employed so successfully by the American automobile industry were already in use in other industries, but in Ford's Highland Park plant of 1914, the first to use a moving assembly line, they were carried to their logical conclusion. By concentrating on the production of but one model, the famous model T, and by successive reductions in price made possible through economies of scale, Ford achieved an industrial leadership that lasted until the technical shortcomings of his vehicle were so obvious that they could no longer be offset by a low price.[2]

[2] The assembly line has a long history, and considerably predates the automobile industry and the Highland

The greatest period of growth was the decade following World War I, which witnessed a trebling in the number of automobiles registered, the passing of the leadership of the industry to General Motors, and the rise of the Chrysler company. By 1929 the present structure of the industry was virtually established; in that year the motor-vehicle industry, which produced over 4.5 million automobiles and 750,000 commercial vehicles, stood at its high-water mark in the American economy. It did not again achieve such a level of production for another two decades.[3] The automobile industry is still the principal consumer of steel, rubber, plate glass, and several nonferrous metals, but its overall importance in the economy is now much less; in 1960 automobile workers accounted for only some 2 per cent of the total labor force.

The maturity of the automobile industry of the United States has resulted in its market being mainly a replacement market, although since World War II considerable success has been achieved in persuading Americans to become two-car families.[4] The purchase of a new car can thus be deferred, and there has been a general tendency for the expectation of life of the average automobile to increase. Since the pent-up World War II demand was satisfied, automobile production has fluctuated between a high of almost 8 million cars in 1955 and a low of a little more than 4 million in the recession year of 1958. The succeeding years epitomize the kaleidoscopic fortunes of the automobile industry; from 1958 to 1960, the industry operated at little more than 60 per cent of capacity, but then followed three years of extraordinary prosperity, and in 1964, it seemed that the industry would at long last attain its goal of 8 million cars in a year. Three giant corporations, General Motors, Ford, and Chrysler, the "Big Three," dominate the industry and account for some 95 per cent of the automobile market. General Motors alone, the world's largest industrial enterprise,[5] accounts for about 50 per cent, Ford and Chrysler in most years sharing an almost equivalent proportion between them. This relationship fluctuates little; the smaller corporations have appeared largely incapable of taking a significant volume of sales from General Motors. The balance of the automobile market is shared by two independents, American Motors and Studebaker-Packard; there has been no successful new entrant into the industry since 1929, although Kaiser came within an ace of success in the late Forties.[6]

The reasons for this extreme concentration may be summed up in the oft-noted fact that success breeds success. The industry has always held that a "complete line," that is, models for every gradation of the market, has been indispensable for success. The Big Three have long offered such a complete range, and possess a volume of production that permits substantial economies of scale. Nevertheless, this observation may no longer be so valid as in the past, for it has been conclusively shown that a single successful model can not only save a firm from extinction, as the Rambler did for

Park plant. It was first used in the manufacture of railroad box cars in the Eighties of the last century, the assembly line originally consisting of a length of railroad track along which the cars were drawn as each operation was completed. The real credit for the success of the Ford company appears to have been largely due to James Couzens, Ford's partner. See J. K. Galbraith, *The Liberal Hour,* Houghton Mifflin Company, Boston, 1960, pp. 141–163.

[3] Automobiles, of course, became steadily more complex and powerful, so that numerical comparison of output levels over time is somewhat misleading.

[4] Some 18 per cent of car-owning families are said to possess two cars. *Time,* July 28, 1961, p. 61.

[5] This is certainly true by most criteria by which a commercial enterprise can be judged. The United States Atomic Energy Commission, however, might also be justifiably awarded this distinction.

[6] In 1964, the Studebaker Corporation ceased assembly at its South Bend, Indiana, plant, although automobile production is to continue at its Hamilton, Ontario, establishment. The number of independents remains unchanged as the Checker Company of Kalamazoo, Michigan, a specialist producer of taxicabs, has commenced marketing of private automobiles.

American Motors, but can even carry its manufacturer to the very forefront of the industry, as has been the case with Volkswagen. Perhaps the factor that has most strongly operated against the independents in the postwar period has been the low trade-in value of their products, which has reflected, very largely, public concern about the future continuity of production. That the American public was not entirely satisfied with the products of the domestic industry is suggested by the great success of European imports; their sales, though virtually negligible in 1950, had by 1959 come to account for about 8 per cent of total sales. Together with the smaller car of American Motors, these imports were responsible for forcing the production of more economical "compact" cars on the Big Three.[7] Since 1960, however, the attraction of the small foreign car has declined, and manufacturers have again emphasized greater size, power, and comfort in American automobiles. The belief at the turn of the decade that the American public was evincing a more mature outlook, with a greater appreciation of sound and sensible engineering, may thus have been premature; fashion seems as important a factor in the automobile industry as in any other consumer-goods industry.[8]

Not all the many independents squeezed out of automobile production since the Great Depression by the relentless pressure of the three giants have been lost to the motor-vehicle industry; some, such as Willys, have found refuge in the production of commercial vehicles, which also supports several major component producers formerly engaged in the automobile industry.

Despite its oligopolistic structure the automobile industry is fiercely competitive, but as with all industries with a similar structure, price competition is largely avoided. Competition mainly takes the form of attempts to maximize consumer appeal through distinctive styling, gadgets, special equipment, and other features; engineering excellence per se is generally conceded to have relatively little to do with success, as is evidenced by the oscillations in the fortunes of Chrysler, whose products have always been noted for their quality engineering; Chrysler's customary prewar 20 per cent share of the market has been cut to less than half this figure in some years. The Big Three are well placed to take advantage of changes in the public taste for automobiles; however, the survival of the independents now looks more likely than it did in the middle Fifties, and even if they should pass from the scene, their demise would considerably strengthen the demand for a compulsory separation of some of the interests of General Motors, a proposed policy that attracted considerable political support after the successful revolt of dealers following the 1958 depression against having automobiles forced on them by manufacturers. There is also reason for believing that, notwithstanding the development of progressively more powerful engines and of automatic transmissions, concentration has impeded basic research; Detroit never questioned its traditional conception of the automobile until the European imports forced it to do so.[9]

Partly through the greater cost of the elaborate, overpowered American automobile and partly through the general postwar dollars shortage, the United States automobile indus-

[7] Kaiser's failure in the early Fifties at popularizing the smaller car may have misled the larger manufacturers. It may well have been that until the memory of wartime shortage and austerity had receded, such cars could not have appealed to the American public.

[8] Partly to counteract a general world impression that American automobiles are overostentatious, and partly for the convenience it offers, the severe and functional Checker has been adopted by several United States' overseas legations for personal transportation.

[9] General Motors' Charles Wilson may be somewhat maligned by the attribution to him of the dictum, "What's good for General Motors is good for the United States"; nevertheless, his opposition to basic research was notorious.

try has lost the large export market it enjoyed before World War II. In 1937 almost 400,000 cars were exported, but in 1960 only 177,000; throughout the world the role of the tough prewar American car with its high ground clearance and ability to go almost anywhere has been largely usurped by the Volkswagen. It is unlikely, moreover, that large foreign sales will be regained. The export market, admittedly, has always been of minor significance in comparison with the domestic one, but its loss may well have operated very strongly against the independents.

The desire to participate nonetheless in fast-growing overseas markets has been a major reason for the heavy investment of American automobile manufacturers in foreign production. The increase in demand for new cars in the United States is not expected to be much above that of the projected growth rate of population, that is, about 2 per cent per annum; the demand of Western Europe, on the other hand, is growing very rapidly, and by 1970 annual sales may be not greatly inferior to those in the United States itself. Substantial shares of the automobile industries of Western Europe and of Australia are already in the hands of the Big Three, as is the whole of the Canadian industry; foreign profits are estimated to account for some 17 per cent of the total earnings of Ford and 14 per cent of those of General Motors.[10] The Chrysler company has been slower to realize the potentialities of foreign-based production. However, it remedied this deficiency in 1962 by acquiring a controlling interest in the French Simca concern, and for some time previously had endeavored, as had the independents, to broaden the field of its foreign operations through licensing agreements to local manufacturers and assemblers; in 1964 it obtained a substantial interest in the British Rootes organization. Thus, although the direct share of the United States in automobile production has diminished, its degree of control over the world industry has not and indeed, it may well increase in the future.

[10] *Time*, **July 26, 1961, p. 61.**

Locations

The United States motor-vehicle industry is at once geographically concentrated and widespread. It is widespread in that the production of components, accessories, and equipment embraces virtually every state; on the other hand, the manufacture of the largest subassemblies and components such as motors, transmissions, wheels, and bodies is concentrated in western New York and in the lower Lake states, and the final assembly of motor vehicles is still more highly localized, the two major centers being southern Michigan and southern California. Detroit is the undisputed center of the world automobile industry.

The motor-vehicle industry as a whole provides numerous examples of plants whose location appears largely fortuitous, and it is not easy to provide a convincing explanation for the dominance of the southern Michigan area in the United States automobile industry. It is true that many of the pioneers of the industry resided in Michigan and that some were involved in the manufacture of carriages, from which early autos differed very little save in their possession of a primitive gasoline motor. There was also a considerable supply of capital accumulated through the Michigan lumbering industry: capital which, with the logging out of the state, was looking for profitable, even speculative investment. While the initial establishment of the industry in southern Michigan is, therefore, understandable, it is not clear how it came to outpace the numerous other centers; in 1921 Chicago, Cleveland, Indianapolis, St. Louis, and New York were still important centers of automobile assembly, as they had

Fig. 17-1 Automobile assembly plants in the United States. (After Boas.)

been from the earliest days of the industry.[11] Detroit was then the headquarters of the two largest producers, General Motors and Ford, as it was soon to become of Chrysler. As the founder of the Chrysler concern was a former General Motors executive, Chrysler's establishment in Detroit is scarcely surprising or indicative of the inherent superiority of the Detroit area. Moreover, there is little reason for believing that had either or both of the industry's two leaders been located elsewhere in the lower lakes region, they would not have prospered. The most probable explanation for the dominance of southern Michigan is that its units attained a size that gave them substantial economies in production earlier than the units of other centers and that this advantage became greater with the passage of time. Also, the automobile industry has largely created its own labor force, for, contrary to general reputation, it does not require highly skilled labor; in southern Michigan is enjoyed little competition from other industries, while this was certainly not the case in the Chicago, Indianapolis, or Erie lakeshore area. It may well have been that in the rapidly expanding post-1918 economy the automobile industry needed an absence of local competition for labor.

[11] **Charles W. Boas, "Locational Patterns of American Automobile Assembly Plants,"** *Economic Geography,* **vol. 37, no. 3, pp. 225–226, July, 1961.**

Although Detroit is the headquarters of the Big Three, only Chrysler has its main productive facilities in the city (Fig. 17-1). Ford's huge integrated plant is located at Dearborn some ten miles from the city center, and General Motors assembly operations in Detroit are confined to the Cadillac plant. General Motors activities are considerably decentralized, Buick and Chevrolet vehicles being produced at Flint, the Oldsmobile at Lansing, and the Pontiac at its namesake city; the great World War II Willow Run plant at Ypsilanti which turned out countless Liberator bombers now produces GM automatic transmissions. The two independents are located outside Michigan; Studebaker-Packard is at South Bend, Indiana, and American Motors has its final assembly plant at Kenosha and its body plant at Milwaukee. Most of the older centers of automobile production still retain a considerable stake in the motor-vehicle industry as producers either of components or of commercial vehicles; Ford engines are produced at Cleveland, the Chevrolet motor plant is at Buffalo, Willys vehicles are manufactured at Toledo, and specialist producers of heavy commercial vehicles are mainly located in the Cleveland and Chicago areas.

Detroit and southern Michigan now assemble only about a third of the total output of automobiles; since the transport of finished vehicles involves much expensive air space, manufacturers have established regional assembly plants. These materially lower costs, for the transport of parts from the parent factory is very much less expensive than that of assembled vehicles. The greatest concentration of final-assembly plants outside southern Michigan is found in California, the state with the highest ratio of vehicles to population; no less than eight such plants are located in the Los Angeles area, and there are two in the San Francisco Bay area. These large urban agglomerations some 2,000 miles distant from the southern Michigan area are obvious locations for regional assembly; similar plants are situated at major regional centers serving large populations, such as Chicago, Kansas City, St. Louis, Dallas, Atlanta, Jersey City, and Boston.

THE MOTOR-VEHICLE INDUSTRY IN WESTERN EUROPE

The motor-vehicle industry began in Western Europe, and until 1905 the combined production of France, Britain, and Germany was equivalent to that of the United States. After that date, however, the disparity in production mounted rapidly as the American industry adopted the techniques of mass production; not until after World War I were such methods widely practiced in the European industry. Behind substantial tariff barriers the respective national industries then grew rapidly, particularly in Britain, where a horsepower tax, which tended to favor the small car, provided further protection.[12] As a result European vehicle production continued to rise throughout the Great Depression, output in Britain reaching a level of almost 400,000 automobiles and 120,000 commercial vehicles shortly before World War II.

This expansion of European vehicle production was virtually confined to Britain, Germany, France, and Italy, for only these countries possessed a broad base of engineering industries capable of producing the many components required (Fig. 17-2). It was also accompanied by a marked concentration of production as flow methods of assembly became more widespread, but this was much more pronounced in the three main producers of Continental Europe than in Britain. Before World War II entry into the British industry was relatively easy, and even at the present it is far from impossible. In France, on the other hand, almost 70 per cent of vehicle output was in the hands of three firms by 1928, and a similar situation was attained in Germany in the following decade.[13] Shortly before World War II the six leading British producers had come to control about 90 per cent of the output of automobiles, but they produced many more models than their large Continental European counterparts and, in fact, continued to do so long after the war. In 1956 about 60 per cent of West Germany's automobile production was accounted

[12] This tax, which led to the development of small, long-stroke engines, is now generally conceded to have been a disservice to the British industry. It not only promoted the fragmentation of the domestic market and the production of a multiplicity of models but also hindered the development of an export trade. See G. C. Allen, *British Industries and Their Organization,* Longmans, Green & Co., Ltd., London, 1959, pp. 182, 197–198.

[13] Ingvar Svennilson, *Growth and Stagnation in the European Economy,* United Nations Economic Commission for Europe, Geneva, 1954, p. 151.

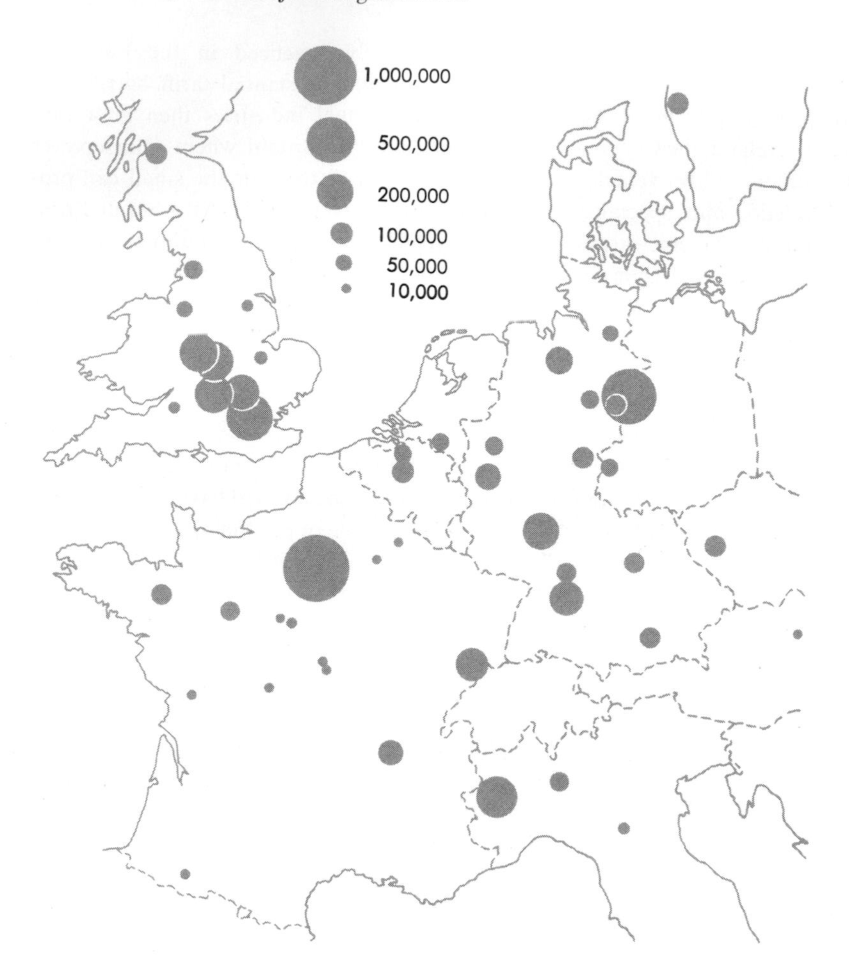

Fig. 17-2 Automobile and commercial vehicle production in Western Europe, 1961.
Although Europe's largest vehicle plant is at Wolfsburg, Paris is the foremost center of the European vehicle industry. (EEC.)

for by three models, about 75 per cent of French production by four basic models, and nearly 65 per cent of the Italian output by only two models; the 90 per cent of the output controlled by the now five leading British producers, however, was shared between nine models.[14] This dissemination of effort has long been held to be a major shortcoming of the British industry. In the past, in fact, British automobiles, except for sports cars, have found considerable difficulty in competing in markets in which they receive no preferential treatment; with a large number of models, production runs were seldom large enough to realize the full economies of scale.

The interwar expansion of the European

[14] "Competition in the Car Market," *The Economist*, vol. 193, p. 10, London, 1957.

motor-vehicle industry was further accelerated by the establishment of subsidiaries of both Ford and General Motors behind the British and German tariff barriers. Ford also began production in France, but the more highly concentrated French industry proved a less congenial environment; after World War II Ford's interests were sold to a domestic producer, Simca, in which Chrysler now has a 65 per cent share.[15] The British and German subsidiaries, which are now entirely owned by their respective parent organizations, have, however, become major producers; General Motors' success in Germany has been relatively greater than in England, but Ford's experience has been the reverse.

The destruction of much of the Continental European industry during World War II and the inability of the United States quickly to satisfy the pent-up domestic demand for automobiles left Britain with a clear field in export markets after 1945. Through rigorous restriction of home demand exports grew rapidly, British vehicles penetrating into markets, such as the United States, which before World War II had been virtually closed to them. Until 1956 Britain was the world's largest exporter of motor vehicles, as well as the second-largest producer; with the rehabilitation of the Continental European industry, however, its share of the export trade was bound to decline, although the spectacular success of Volkswagen, whose rapid growth carried German automobile production above that of Britain after 1956, was largely unforeseen. Further expansion of the British automobile industry was hindered not only by the policy of producing a large number of models but also by the British government's repeated imposition of anti-inflationary measures which bore down very heavily on the automobile industry.

In the mid-Fifties a pattern of production involving national specialization was beginning to emerge in Western Europe. Britain's strength lay in sports cars, for the production of which it had long held a competitive advantage, and in medium-sized automobiles whose production had been encouraged by the abandonment of the old horsepower tax; France and Italy had a clear advantage in small economy cars, while Germany produced vehicles of intermediate size. This pattern did not long endure, however; both Germany and France became increasingly successful in medium-sized cars, while Britain itself began to produce small economy vehicles. All the major automobile makers took steps to strengthen their competitive position as internal tariffs within the Common Market were reduced, and by 1961, as Britain's entry began to look probable, the situation had become extremely fluid. Numerous interlicensing schemes foreshadowed further concentration in the industry; Fiat planned to assemble in Germany and, through Simca, in France, but could expect competition in the home market from Renaults assembled by Alfa Romeo and from British Motor Corporation (BMC) products assembled by Innocenti, one of Italy's largest manufacturers of machine tools and motor scooters. In the expectation of enlarging their share of the European market, American-owned subsidiaries have made further heavy investment in capacity, but so, indeed, have domestic producers. In 1961 it was forecast that by 1965 Western Europe could attain a capacity of 9 million cars and 1.5 million commercial vehicles, and that automobile sales might amount to as much as 6 million.[16] The growth of output, in fact, proved faster than expected, and in 1964 it appeared that the European automobile industry would produce

[15] The French government viewed with concern this acquisition of a controlling interest in a major French producer by one of the American Big Three; legislation was threatened to prevent further major French industries from passing into American control.

[16] *The Economist*, vol. 201, p. 246, London, 1961.

about 8 million cars, a level of output approximately equal to that of the United States. With a scale of output at the American level, it seemed likely that the European industry would be forced to adopt the American policy of a diversified range and frequent model changes; manufacturers were finding that newer models were accounting for much of their increase in sales.

Development of the British Industry

The British motor-vehicle industry grew out of the cycle industry, which in the last two decades of the nineteenth century had established itself in the Birmingham-Coventry area. The Birmingham district had become the principal center of the gun-making, lock and chain, and nonferrous-metal trades, and many firms took up the manufacture of components for the new cycle and motor-vehicle industries; until the Great Depression some were engaged in the simultaneous production of cycles, motorcycles, and automobiles, occasionally within the same plant. Birmingham and Coventry still dominate the British industry; of the "Big Five" producers (the reduction of one from the prewar "Big Six" resulted from the merger of the Austin and Morris concerns in 1952 to form BMC, the largest unit in the industry) only Ford and Vauxhall (General Motors) are located elsewhere. BMC's Longbridge (Birmingham) plant is claimed to be the largest automobile plant in Britain, and the company has other factories in the Birmingham area producing engines and commercial vehicles. In addition to its large share of final assembly the Birmingham area is the principal producer of components and subassemblies, many of which are common to all makes. British-made components are already used to some extent by Continental manufacturers and may well be more extensively employed in the near future; in brakes and steering gears, particularly, Britain appears to have a considerable technological advantage. Coventry contains the plants of the two smallest members of the Big Five (Rootes and Standard-Triumph) as well as those of specialist manufacturers such as Jaguar and Daimler; its total vehicle output is less than that of Birmingham, but a higher proportion of its labor force is engaged in the motor-vehicle industry, and it might, therefore, be regarded as the Flint of Britain.

The location of the other major plants of the British automobile industry is less easily explained. The former Morris plant at Oxford, now part of the BMC organization, arose in the hometown of the founder of the Morris company, and its location appears largely fortuitous. It could draw on no fund of local skilled labor (though, as already pointed out, this is not essential for the industry) and from the beginning depended on immigrant labor. For the supply of components, however, Oxford is very conveniently situated in relation to Birmingham, where, indeed, the Morris company produced its commercial vehicles. A somewhat similar situation holds in relation to the Vauxhall plant at Luton, Bedfordshire. The Vauxhall company was originally based in London and was acquired by General Motors following its move to Luton after World War I. Luton lies on a main line of communication between the metropolis and the Midlands; it lies outside the higher London wage area[17] but is close enough to the capital to enjoy all the advantages of a metropolitan location.

London, the most important center of carriage making, early became one of the leading areas for the new automobile industry, and its western and northwestern suburbs still

[17] Several assembly plants of American and Continental producers were located in the Greater London area in the interwar period; these nearly always selected sites just outside the area within which employers were compelled to pay the higher London wage rate.

contain many specialist builders of bodies for both automobiles and commercial vehicles. Also it is a major producer of components, has a substantial share of the production of the heaviest type of commercial vehicles, and contains the plants of a number of formerly very famous names in the automobile industry whose interests now lie largely in aircraft. The capital also possesses the second-largest producer in the British industry, Ford, whose main plant is located at Dagenham in east London. This works possesses the only blast furnace in southern England and, with its neighboring plants for the production of bodies and wheel and brake assemblies, exemplifies Ford's integrated method of vehicle production. Though obligated since 1945 to establish new plants elsewhere as a result of official limits on the employment permissible at Dagenham, the company contrasts markedly with the decentralized BMC, which much more closely resembles General Motors in its general location pattern. Ford moved to Dagenham from Manchester in 1930, a migration which appears to owe much to the attraction of the large metropolitan market; the plant possesses excellent waterside facilities of which fullest use is made, both for the import of ore and for the export of finished vehicles. Oddly enough, the company's new plant at Liverpool is not far removed from its original location.

The rapid expansion of the British motor-vehicle industry in both the interwar and post-war periods has been productive of so many pressing social problems that under the Distribution of Industry Act the government has prevented further expansion on existing sites and has directed investment in new capacity to the development areas of south Wales, Lancashire, and Scotland.[18] Of the locations offered Merseyside (Liverpool) has proved the most attractive, where Ford, Vauxhall, and Standard-Triumph have new plants; BMC tractors and commercial vehicles are produced at Bathgate (Edinburgh), Rootes has selected a site near Glasgow,[19] and Rover is to assemble in south Wales. All manufacturers are adamant that the refusal of government to allow them to expand in their present locations will result in higher costs, but it is the tendency for the two largest organizations, BMC and Ford, to enlarge their share of the domestic market that actually may spell difficulties for the expansion plans of the smaller producers.

The West German Industry

West Germany is the largest motor-vehicle producer in Western Europe, but the structure of the industry is not very different from that of Britain. Four large organizations—Volkswagen, Opel, Daimler-Benz, and Ford—account for about 85 per cent of total output, but there still are numerous small firms, including that rarity, the privately owned concern; in 1961 there were eight automobile producers with an annual output of less than 50,000 cars.[20] Over half the total output, however, originated from one producer, Volkswagen; neither in the British nor in the United States industry is there any equivalent of this manufacturer or, indeed, of Daimler-Benz, a highly competitive producer of heavy trucks, commercial vehicles, and industrial and marine engines as well as of quality automobiles. The share of the American-controlled organizations in total output is lower than the share they possess in Britain (some 30 per cent as opposed to 40 per cent),

[18] Mergers offer a way of defeating the act, however; Jaguar has acquired considerable new capacity in Coventry through the acquisition of Daimler.

[19] Scotland was an important center of automobile production in the early days of the industry, but its distance from the main component-producing area, the west Midlands, eventually told against it; some 80 per cent of the components used in the new Rootes Linwood, plant, west of Glasgow, come from suppliers more than 300 miles away. Scotland has remained, however, a minor center of commercial-vehicle production.

[20] *The Economist,* vol. 201, p. 246.

This sign at the NSU plant in south Germany illustrates West Germany's debt to foreign workers in achieving its "economic miracle."

Cars travel along final assembly lines of the Volkswagen plant at Wolfsburg, the world's largest automobile plant outside the United States.

but this may increase in the future as the investment plans of Ford (Taunus) and General Motors (Opel) come to maturity.

As in other major producers, the location of the West German industry shows little close relationship with that of the iron and steel industry. The earliest centers of the industry lay mainly in south Germany, but of the "Big Four" only Daimler-Benz with its main plant at Stuttgart is now located in this region, although there are numerous small producers of specialty vehicles located in Munich, Nürnberg, and Stuttgart. The main centers of the vehicle industry now lie in the north German plain and in the Rhine valley. Germany's largest industrial establishment of any kind is the giant Volkswagen plant at Wolfsburg near Braunschweig, only a few miles from the border with East Germany.

Wolfsburg is a new town which owes its existence entirely to the Volkswagen plant; there appears to be no particular reason for its location except its position almost equidistant from Berlin, the Ruhr, and Hamburg, the three greatest urban concentrations of Germany, although it lies close to the great Salzgitter steel plant. The Volkswagen plant was established as a national enterprise by the Third Reich and was to produce a revolutionary "people's car" (Volkswagen translated); contributions were invited in advance from prospective customers to help finance construction of the plant, but no private deliveries were ever made, and the Volkswagen became the workhorse of the Wehrmacht. The plant was a battered wreck when occupied at the end of World War II by the British Army, which then offered the car to every major British manufacturer; none could see any future for it—perhaps the supreme example of the inability of the leaders of the industry to foresee changes in public taste. In default of finding a manufacturer, the British Army entrusted the plant to an ex-Opel executive to manage, and success was rapid. The tough, go-anywhere Volkswagen proved equally as suitable for the primitive roads of Africa, Asia, and Australia as for the highways of Europe; moreover, it proved highly acceptable to many Americans desiring a change from the products of Detroit. By concentrating on the production of one model, Volkswagen successfully reaffirmed the model T formula for success; extended several times, the plant, with its daily output of almost 4,000 vehicles, is the world's largest automobile works outside the United States. As European automobile production grew rapidly in the Sixties, however, the one-model policy was clearly losing sales to the company, and the Volkswagen share of the West German market dropped considerably in the face of competition from the new models of Opel and Taunus. An additional model was added to the range and further diversification seems possible in the future.

It appears odd that such a plant could for so long have no legal owner, but in 1961 the legal difficulty was resolved by the West German government in an unparalleled capital operation. Some 60 per cent of the capital of the fourth-largest automobile enterprise in the world was sold to over 1.5 million buyers, few of whom had ever held any kind of stock before. Purchase of shares was limited in the first instance to low-income groups and to workers in the Volkswagen plant, most of whom bought their shares at substantial "social discounts"; elaborate precautions effectively prevented speculation and the exercise of any kind of control over management by shareholders. This unusual and complex operation was, of course, the result of a long conflict of political interests between management and labor, and between the Federal and Lower Saxony governments, which together hold 40 per cent of the shares.[21]

[21] So long as the organization possessed no legal owner, it was impossible for disgruntled prewar subscribers to bring suit against it. It was therefore in the interests of both management and the Federal government to maintain the *status quo* for as long as possible.

Opel, Germany's second-largest producer, has its main plant at Rüsselheim in the Rhine-Main region and has new capacity at Bochum in the Ruhr; the Ford plant is located at Cologne. The post-1960 expansion plans of both General Motors and Ford were mainly directed at the production of small cars to compete with Volkswagen, a policy in which the two companies have achieved considerable success. The Borgward concern of Bremen, which enjoyed considerable success in the middle Fifties, appeared to be the exception to the rule that the privately owned company no longer has a place in the industry; however, the company later ran into financial difficulties and has been purchased by a Mexican syndicate. One potential weakness of the German industry appears to be its excessive dependence on export markets; these absorb between 40 and 50 per cent of automobile output. Nevertheless, the German industry enjoys little protection and is strongly competitive; with a greater degree of economic unity in Europe it should maintain its present advantages.

The Industries of France and Italy

For a time, at least, a greater degree of economic unity could react unfavorably on the French and Italian industries, which, despite their enormous postwar growth, appear to be high-cost producers. France first produced more than 1 million vehicles in 1960, and its level of output has since been virtually equal to that of Britain. As already remarked, the industry is highly concentrated, automobile production being almost entirely in the hands of four producers—Renault (a state-owned enterprise which behaves exactly like any corporation and which is by far the largest producer), Citroën (which is largely owned by the Michelin Tire Company), Simca, and Peugeot. The geographic concentration of the industry is also very marked; three of these four automobile manufacturers are located in the Paris region, which has been an important center of the industry since the early experimental period, and the capital is also by far the most important producer of components. The smallest of the four, Peugeot, is located at Sochaux, near Belfort, in eastern France. As in Britain, the state has endeavored to prevent new capacity being created in the metropolis; Renault's expansion is located at Le Mans, that of Citroën at Rennes. Lyon is the main center for the production of heavy commercial vehicles.

The Italian industry is perhaps the closest approach to a monopoly encountered in any major producer; Fiat, one of Europe's largest industrial empires, accounts for 85 per cent of automobile production and almost 70 per cent of that of commercial vehicles. This situation is largely the result of the extreme protection given to the industry by the Mussolini regime. The limited size of the Italian market allowed only one manufacturer production runs long enough to achieve substantial economies of scale; once Fiat had attained such a position, it became impossible for any other to duplicate its success. Prohibitive tariffs and import quotas made foreign competition exceedingly difficult, so that unless he was fortunate enough to be able to afford a high-priced custom-built car, the Italian buyer had to have a Fiat or nothing. Fiat's grip on the industry is strengthened by its control of the production of almost every kind of component, but the company also engages in the production of numerous articles which have nothing to do with the vehicle or aircraft industries.[22] Many of the raw materials for the Italian industry have to be imported, but Fiat is an exceedingly efficient producer, and its two large plants at Turin produce every kind of motor vehicle; it strongly

[22] See p. 268.

pressed for Italy's entry into the Common Market, in marked contrast to the protectionist attitude of most Italian manufacturers.

Italy's famous specialty automobile producers are all located in the north Italian plain; the Lancia company also has its main plant in Turin, but the small state-owned Alfa Romeo concern is located at Milan; through license arrangements to produce Renault and BMC products, Milan, Italy's foremost industrial city, could also become a major center of automobile manufacture. Even the briefest reference to the Italian motor-vehicle industry must include mention of the motor scooter, one of Italy's pleasantest contributions to the postwar world; from the plants of Innocenti and Piaggio, of Milan and Genoa, respectively, more than half a million motor scooters issue each year, a large proportion of which are exported.

THE AIRCRAFT INDUSTRY YESTERDAY AND TODAY

Before World War II the aircraft industry could be divided into three sections—the production of engines, of propellers, and of aircraft frames, or airframes. A few European producers undertook the manufacture of all three, while some firms produced both aircraft frames and engines. More commonly, however, the aircraft manufacturer relied on specialist firms for engines and propellers. Many of the firms in the industry had entered it from the motor-vehicle industry and continued to engage in both types of production, as certain European concerns still do; Ford invested heavily in the industry in the interwar period but later withdrew, and General Motors is still a producer of aircraft engines. The interconnection between the two industries became most marked during World War II, for it was mainly to the motor-vehicle industry that the British and American governments initially turned when the war began for an immediate expansion of aircraft production and for the operation of much hastily constructed new capacity. During the peak year of the United States war effort some 96,000 planes were produced, a feat that might be considered the apogee of mass-production techniques applied to precision engineering. After a postwar cutback the aircraft industry received a temporary stimulus from the Korean conflict, but not until the later Fifties, when the immense progress made by the U.S.S.R. in nuclear devices and in rocket and missile technology became obvious, did the industry receive sufficient new investment to restore it to a very high level of activity.

In the meantime the organization of the industry had changed markedly as a result of a fantastic rate of technological change. Production of supersonic aircraft and guided missiles required techniques very different from those involved in the production of the bombers and fighters of World War II; in the field of commercial aircraft the size and cost of the new jet airliners gave rise to problems for both producers and commercial airlines that may not be entirely resolved before the supersonic airliner makes its appearance. It is scarcely surprising that some producers have found these changes too much for them and have moved into other lines of production. More importantly, these changes have opened the way for a great penetration of the industry by electronics and electrical companies; in addition, although famous names such as Lockheed and Northrop still produce conventional aircraft, they also produce a variety of components for missiles and space research equipment, as well as undertaking their final assembly. Thus, it is no longer correct to speak of the aircraft industry without realizing that it is now essentially absorbed in a larger and vastly more complex "aerospace industry."

The greater part of the cost of a missile is incurred in its instrumentation and in its electronic guidance and control systems; as it may contain upwards of a million parts, the number of component suppliers is very large, so that the boundaries of the aerospace industry are exceedingly difficult to determine. In the United States it embraces not only aircraft producers proper but also the giants of the electronics and electrical industries and of the motor-vehicle industry and a very large number of small specialist firms, many of which have grown enormously as a result of a government contract.

Firms engaged in the aircraft and aerospace industry spend a higher proportion of their revenue in research than any other industry; even so, the bulk of research expenditure is borne by government. The industry is highly speculative, for costs can seldom be accurately forecast. Except for the smallest types of civilian plane, aircraft development costs are often enormous, and these are often further inflated by changes in specification and performance demanded by defense departments even when the aircraft has finally reached the production stage. Production costs are also prodigious. In contrast to the motor-vehicle industry with its need for comparatively little highly skilled labor, a considerable proportion of the employment in the aircraft industry consists of qualified technicians and other skilled workers, and missile production additionally involves large numbers of highly trained scientists, enough of whom can seldom be recruited. The materials used are also expensive; steel is of small significance to the aerospace industry, which depends heavily on expensive alloys of nonferrous metals, alloys which have become progressively more complex and thus more expensive with the development of jet engines and rocket motors. Moreover, aircraft and missiles cannot be produced with the tolerances acceptable in vehicle production; every part has to be manufactured and assembled with the greatest accuracy possible and is meticulously inspected.

The stretching machines, extrusion presses, and other specialized equipment used in airframe manufacture not only are extremely costly but can seldom be amortized over long production runs because of the continuous introduction of new models to meet demands for improved performance. The aircraft industry therefore tries to reduce costs by broadening the field of employment for existing craft in production, usually by modifying military aircraft for commercial use. Many large jet airliners in service at present are modified military types, a fact that goes far to explain why they have not always been entirely satisfactory. At the same time, a few jet liners can perform the work of a much larger piston-engined fleet, so that the number of new craft required as replacements and to cater for traffic growth is much less than in the past; the industry has thus found itself producing a small number of very expensive machines.[23] The enormous financial resources required for the development of these new large aircraft have placed great strains on aircraft manufacturers and may well lead to further concentration. Even in the United States where concentration in the aircraft industry is already well advanced, there are grounds for believing that the number of airframe manufacturers is too large for the commercial market.[24] The American aircraft industry has thus tended to become a relatively unprofitable part of the much larger aerospace industry, which since 1955 has displaced the

[23] **The lower operating costs of jet airliners should have permitted lowering of fares, thus stimulating traffic and leading eventually to an increased demand for aircraft. In practice, however, the expected lowering of fares did not materialize.** **See p. 570.**

[24] *Time,* **Aug. 18, 1961, p. 55. In 1961 the General Dynamics Corporation recorded the largest loss ever experienced by an American company; this arose largely from the company's attempts to break into jet airliner manufacture in competition with Boeing and Douglas.**

This model of a projected Boeing supersonic airliner is designed to fly at 1,800 miles per hour. Wings are shown in the landing position and folded back for flight. The formidable engineering problems presented by such aircraft demand special research equipment, such as the wind tunnel at Farnborough, England, shown here, constructed for the development of the Anglo-French Concorde airliner, which will have a cruising speed of 1,500 miles per hour.

automobile industry from its long-held position as the premier industry of the United States by value of output.

Free World Locations and Structure

In contrast to the American motor-vehicle industry, which has tended to be highly localized, American aircraft production has shown considerable fluidity in its location pattern, and the aerospace industry as a whole is dispersed throughout the length and breadth of the country (Fig. 17-3). Before World War II airframe production in the United States was divided between eastern manufacturers which had grown out of pioneer firms established in the early years of the century and manufacturers on the Pacific Coast. Among the more important centers of the eastern industry were Dayton, the oldest established center of the industry, Buffalo, Detroit, and New Jersey. These locations all lie within the heavily industrialized northeast portion of the country, and it seems probable that given suitable sites (an airframe plant not only requires a large floor space for final assembly but also needs to be located alongside a flying field), a location anywhere within this region would have succeeded. The eastern area is still the principal producer of engines and propellers, the main centers being Detroit, Paterson, Indianapolis, and Hartford.

The interwar period witnessed a considerable growth of airframe production on the Pacific Coast; so rapid was the growth of the industry in southern California in the years preceding World War II that this area came to account for about half of the total weight of airframe production. With the plants of Douglas, Lockheed, North American, and Northrop, Los Angeles became the major focus of the industry, but San Diego (Convair) and Seattle (Boeing) also shared in this western expansion. It is not easy to provide a convincing explanation for this western growth, and it has been frequently remarked that from the strategic standpoint, a more unsatisfactory location for

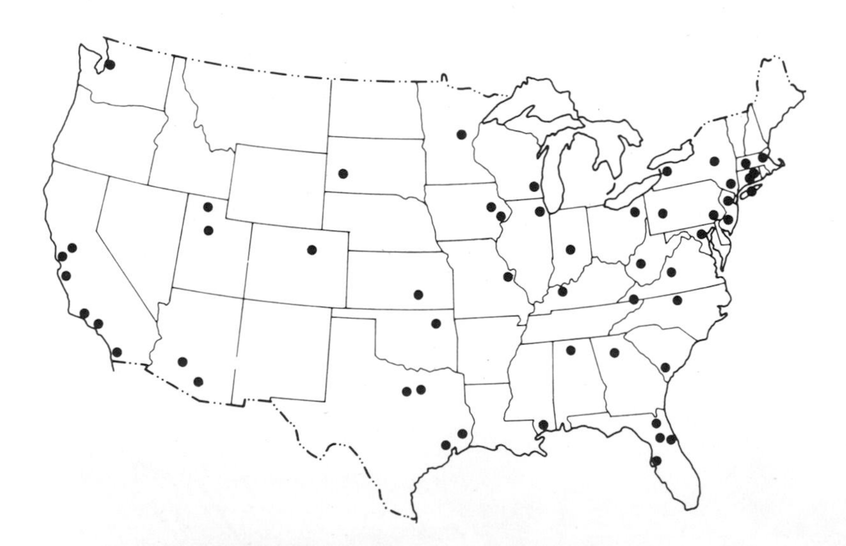

Fig. 17-3 Aircraft and aerospace contractors.
This map of major aircraft and aerospace contractors suggests that the aerospace industry has penetrated into almost all parts of the country.

the industry could scarcely have been chosen. It may have been that the mild climate and generally good flying conditions enjoyed by southern California were of some assistance to the industry, but this influence must have been marginal, for airframe production also prospered in areas with very different climate conditions. It is likely that a more important factor was the strong attraction of the highly speculative aircraft industry for a region that had become accustomed to the equally speculative motion-picture industry and was on the lookout for further quick gains; moreover, aircraft possessed some of the glamor associated with the motion-picture industry.

Yet even in southern California the aircraft industry was not of major significance in 1939; it was World War II that converted the industry into a giant. The west coast fully shared in the general expansion of the industry as the danger of Japanese attack receded, but new plants were also erected in parts of the country considered less strategically vulnerable, particularly in the Midwest and in the south central states; St. Louis, Wichita, Fort Worth, and Dallas also emerged as important centers. Southern California still remains the leading center of airframe production, and the three producers of large commercial aircraft are all located on the west coast. A second area of airframe production lies on the opposite coast in Long Island and in Connecticut, where the Grumman, Republic, United Aircraft, and Sikorsky companies are located. In both foci, the production of manned aircraft has become a minor activity for all major airframe makers.

The U.S.S.R. is the world's second-largest aircraft producer, but the only other country of major significance in the free world is Britain. Though considerably smaller than its American counterpart, the British industry contains almost as many airframe producers, many of which also produce engines. This situation has created many difficulties in the greatly changed conditions of the postwar period, and it is highly likely that a more concentrated industry would have been able to capitalize on Britain's early and commanding lead in the production of jet engines and of turbojet and pure-jet commercial aircraft. The industry, however, slowly appears to be passing into the control of two combinations—the Hawker group, which includes De Havilland, Blackburn, and Avro, with plants in Greater London, the Midlands, Manchester, and east Yorkshire, and the British Aircraft Corporation, a grouping of Bristol, English Electric, and Vickers. Britain's aircraft manufacturers have been denied a major part in missile production through the decision to rely on United States weapons, a policy that, though a blow to national pride, makes good economic and political sense, incidentally. With the declining demand for manned aircraft the airframe manufacturers have therefore sought diversification in the fields of electric and atomic energy, in "ground effect" craft, and in other employments for the diesel engines and gas turbines that many of them also manufacture.

There is a broad coincidence between the location patterns of the vehicle and aircraft industries in Britain, but Greater London, with a number of plants of both major aircraft groups, is the undisputed focus of the industry. Southern England, however, possesses a major nonmetropolitan producer in the Bristol Company, which is also a leading manufacturer of gas turbines. The leadership of southern and southeastern England in this new industry is scarcely surprising, for favorable physical conditions add to the strong economic forces that have attracted most new industries to the capital. London shares with the west Midlands the production of engines, an activity which before World War II was closely connected with automobile production and which is still not entirely divorced from it. Perhaps the most respected firm in the British industry, and certainly one of the most successful, is the Rolls Royce Company of Derby and Crewe, whose engines, made under license in a number of foreign countries, have found extensive employment in American and in other European aircraft as well as in aircraft produced by domestic manufacturers. The company still produces an automobile that is often regarded as the epitome of quality. Another old automobile producer with a similar history is the west London firm of Napier, whose late-World War II products represented, perhaps, the apogee of the piston engine. Both of these manufacturers have found additional interests in the production of diesel engines for vehicles and for general industrial purposes.

Most other countries of the North Atlantic Treaty Organization (NATO) have small and heavily subsidized aircraft industries. Canada produced some successful commercial aircraft in the immediate postwar years, but the growing complexity and increasing cost of the jet airliner and the supersonic fighter presented the small industry with problems that it found difficult to resolve. British manufacturers possessed a considerable stake in the Canadian industry, which is mainly located in Ontario and the St. Lawrence lowlands, but when the Canadian government abandoned its plans for domestic production of a supersonic fighter, the British-owned companies withdrew much of their interest in Canadian production. France's largely state-owned industry has achieved considerable success in the production of both supersonic fighters and medium-sized commercial jet airliners; Paris and Toulouse are the two main centers. Since 1945 the production of all but light aircraft has been forbidden in both Germany and Japan, but a revival of the manufacture of other types seems virtually certain in the near future.

SELECTED REFERENCES

Aerospace Yearbook, 1960, American Aviation Publications, Washington, 1960.

Alderfer, E. B., and H. E. Michl: *Economics of American Industry,* McGraw-Hill Book Company, New York, 1957, pp. 149–180.

Allen, G. C.: *British Industries and Their Organization,* Longmans, Green & Co., Ltd., London, 1959, pp. 172–206.

"Automobiles," *Oriental Economist,* vol. 26, pp. 417–426, 1958.

Boas, Charles W.: "Locational Patterns of American Automobile Assembly Plants," *Economic Geography,* vol. 37, No. 3, pp. 218–230, July, 1961.

"British Motors in the European Lead," *The Economist,* vol. 211, pp. 611–612, London, 1964.

Cunningham, W. G.: *The Aircraft Industry: A Study in Industrial Location,* L. L. Morrison, Los Angeles, 1951.

Fryer, D. W.: "The British Vehicle and Aircraft Industry," *Geography,* vol. 33, pp. 136–149, 1948.

Hurley, Neil P.: "The Automotive Industry: A Study in Industrial Location," *Land Economics,* vol. 35, pp. 1–14, 1959.

Maxcy, George, and Aubrey Silberston: *The Motor Industry,* George Allen & Unwin, Ltd., London, 1959.

"Motors 1961," *The Economist,* vol. 201, pp. 243–258, London, 1961.

Organisation for European Economic Cooperation: *Some Aspects of the Motor Vehicle Industry in the U.S.A.,* Paris, 1953.

"The Aerospace Industry," *Time,* Oct. 27, 1961.

"The Nation and Its Industry in Space," *Fortune,* June, 1962.

Chapter 18

TEXTILE INDUSTRIES

Textile industries differ considerably from the capital-intensive "growth" industries already examined; in the highly developed economies the role of textile industries is a relatively small one, and in most such economies the problem of surplus capacity is often acute. Clothing, however, is a basic and universal need of mankind, and the textile industries are perhaps the most widespread of manufacturing industries. Their role as agents of economic development, moreover, merits some attention; in the present highly developed economies the textile-machinery, machine-tool, and heavy-chemicals industries all grew rapidly with expanding textile production. Finally, although handicraft production may still satisfy a substantial proportion of local cloth requirements in some countries, the present century has witnessed an extension of factory-based production using power-driven machinery to many countries at low levels of economic development; several nations of Asia and Latin America already possess sizable textile industries, and the development of such industries in the emergent nations of Africa can confidently be predicted. From a world standpoint, therefore, the importance of textile industries is very considerable.

The textile industries produce yarn and cloth for apparel, industrial, and household purposes from both natural and man-made fibers. Apparel is by far the most important use in the world as a whole, but in highly developed economies, industrial and household demands can account for a substantial proportion of total textile consumption; in the United States apparel accounts for about 55 per cent of total textile-fiber consumption and industrial and household purposes account for some 25 per cent and 20 per cent, respectively. The products of the industry are thus largely consumer nondurables needing periodic replacement, and there is a close relationship between the general level of economic development and per capita consumption of textile fibers (Table 18-1). This correlation is not greatly affected by climatic influences; Malaya has a higher per capita consumption

Table 18-1

Per Capita Fiber Consumption (Kilograms)

	COTTON		WOOL		RAYON AND ACETATE		SYNTHETICS	TOTAL	
	1949	1959	1949	1959	1949	1959	1959	1949	1959
U.S.A.	12.0	10.2	1.8	1.1	3.2	2.8	1.38	16.9	15.5
Canada	8.6	6.3	2.4	1.4	2.2	2.5	0.91	13.3	11.1
Britain	6.8	5.7	2.7	2.5	2.0	2.9	0.84	11.6	11.9
Australia	5.6	5.9	3.6	2.4	1.9	1.8	0.52	11.1	10.6
New Zealand	4.9	5.0	4.7	3.2	1.6	1.9	0.30	11.2	10.4
W. Germany	3.1	5.7	1.0	2.1	2.8	3.3	0.55	6.9	11.7
Japan	1.2	4.4	0.1	0.9	0.6	2.2	0.8	1.9	8.3
Italy	3.0	3.4	1.2	0.9	0.8	1.8	0.39	5.0	6.5
Argentina	5.9	5.4	1.9	1.0	0.6	0.8	0.1	8.4	7.3
Venezuela	2.3	2.7	0.2	0.3	1.1	1.1	0.2	3.6	4.3
Malaya and Singapore	3.1	2.3			0.6	1.3	0.03	3.8	3.7
India	1.9	2.0				0.1		1.9	2.1
Philippines	1.4	1.6			0.9	0.3	0.03	2.3	1.9
U.S.S.R.	3.7	6.2	0.5	1.0	0.2	1.2	0.07	4.4	8.5
China	1.3	2.5		0.1				1.1	2.6
E. Germany	1.3	6.1	0.1	0.3	3.4	7.2	0.42	4.8	14.0

SOURCE: FAO, *World Per Caput Fiber Consumption Levels,* Rome, 1960. FAO, *Monthly Bulletin of Statistics,* January, 1962.

of textile fibers than South Korea, which experiences quite severe winters and a very much higher per capita consumption then Indonesia, which has a climate that closely resembles Malaya's. Per capita fiber consumption in the world as a whole increases only very slowly, and in the decade following 1950 there was even a tendency for such consumption to decline in economies at a high level of economic development.

The textile industries are broadly divisible into two major groups. The *old,* or *traditional,* textile industries use raw materials which consist of vegetable or animal fibers. These are technologically simple industries requiring a relatively modest capital investment, and as the economies of large-scale operations are not very marked, they are generally organized into units of small size. Their structure is mainly competitive, and, as is usual with industries possessing a competitive structure, research expenditure is relatively small. The traditional industries still account for the larger share of world textile-fiber consumption, but their share is a slowly declining one.

The *modern,* or *rational,* textile industries, on the other hand, use man-made fibers, and their technology is essentially scientific. The technology of the old textile industries was developed long before the chemical and physical properties of their raw materials were clearly understood; in modern textile industries these properties have been manipulated to impart to the finished cloth highly desirable qualities, absent in the products of the traditional industries. In modern textile industries the economies of scale are considerable, so that large units are essential. Modern textile industries thus possess an oligopolistic structure, in some countries a monopolistic structure; they possess many close connections with the chemical industries, out of which they have largely grown, and spend large sums on research. Numerous international licensing and marketing agreements further emphasize the contrast with the cutthroat competition common in the traditional textile industries.

Nevertheless, the various branches of the modern textile industries compete vigorously with each other as well as with the older traditional industries; the expansion of rayon, which earlier in the present century made great inroads into markets formerly held by silk, cotton, and wool, has been checked by the competition of nylon and of other noncellulose synthetic fibers. Moreover, the distinction between the two divisions is slowly becoming blurred through the increasing importance of blended fabrics employing mixtures of traditional and modern fibers.

The manufacture of textiles involves the production of yarn and its subsequent conver-

Hand operations are still of considerable significance in Japan's silk industry.

sion into cloth; the manufacture of garments from finished cloth is the concern of the structurally separate clothing industries, although the boundary between textile and clothing industries is not a sharp one. In most traditional textile industries—cotton, wool, linen, and silk—the methods of manufacture are essentially similar. Yarn is produced by spinning, a process in which a twist is imparted to the fibers. This, however, is the culmination of a lengthy series of operations in which the fibers are cleaned and then carded or combed, and the resulting ropes, or "slivers," of clean fiber are gradually drawn out to fit them for the spinning frames; "doubling," i.e., the twisting together of spun yarns to make a stronger thread, is carried out in the case of warp yarns and hosiery yarns. Silk, however, does not require spinning; the long filament from the silkworm cocoon is merely "reeled," and the reeled silk is subjected to a doubling, or "throwing," operation. The finished yarn is then woven into cloth on some kind of loom, and the fabric is subjected to a series of finishing operations.

The mechanization of textile production, which began in eighteenth-century Britain, was an important part of the Industrial Revolution; the new techniques first established themselves in the British cotton industry, a somewhat surprising development in the light of the great historical importance of the woolen industry in Britain, and their adoption in other traditional textile industries came considerably later. Hargreaves's spinning jenny (1765), originally a hand-operated machine, helped to overcome the deficiency of yarn that had become acute with the adoption of the flying shuttle, invented by Kay about 1733, which had greatly increased the productivity of the handloom weaver. With Arkwright's water frame (1767) and carding machine (1775) the foundations of modern spinning technology were laid. Arkwright's machines used several features of the jenny and of an earlier invention by Lewis Paul, and were soon superseded by Crompton's mule (1779) and the ring spindle frame (1830). Arkwright, nevertheless, was a pioneer of major status; he can be regarded as the real founder of the modern factory system of mechanized production.[1]

The mechanization of weaving, the principal method of making cloth from yarn, came considerably later; Cartwright's loom of 1787 was not a commercial success, and not until about 1840 did the power loom begin to assume its modern form. The Jacquard loom of 1801, which weaves complicated patterns and designs by following the hole patterns of a chain of punched cards inserted in the loom, can perhaps be considered one of the earliest examples of automation. The greatest advance, however, came with the introduction of the Northrup battery loom of 1895, which ejected the empty shuttle from the loom and automatically replaced it with a full one. The Northrup loom was later equipped with an automatic "stop motion" which operated whenever a breakage of the weft occurred; a weaver could thus supervise many more automatic than ordinary looms.

An important alternative method of making a fabric is knitting, the principle of which is looping a continuous thread. In contrast to the loom, which is of great antiquity, the knitting (or stocking) frame dates only from the late sixteenth century. Modern knitting machines produce either flat or circular fabrics and make possible the production of garments in one operation. The knitwear and hosiery industries have taken full advantage of the properties of the man-made fibers, and in highly developed economies their general prosperity is often in marked contrast to the parlous situation of traditional textile industries; their

[1] **Paul Mantoux,** *The Industrial Revolution of the Eighteenth Century,* **Jonathan Cape, Ltd., London, 1961, p. 234.**

location pattern, moreover, is usually very different from that of other textile production.

Another method of making a fabric is by twisting threads around each other, thus producing lace. The Levers lace-making machine dates from the early nineteenth century, and until World War I the lace industry enjoyed considerable prosperity; lace, however, has long ceased to be fashionable for household purposes, and, once a principal field of employment, and the industry has greatly declined. But all textile industries are vulnerable to changes of fashion; this is, indeed, a major factor making for instability.

COTTON

Cotton is by far the most important and widespread of all textile industries and accounts for nearly 70 per cent of total textile consumption (Table 18-2). It was the first industry to pass into the factory system, and in many countries its establishment has constituted the first step towards industrialization.[2]

Three main periods of development can be recognized. Prior to the beginning of the eighteenth century, cotton was a handicraft industry confined to raw-cotton-producing countries. India was then a major producer, and through the activities of the British East India Company a large and valuable export trade in finished yarns and cloths was built up. In Europe, however, cotton was a high-priced and relatively unimportant fabric. Following the removal of legal sanctions against cotton manufacture in the first half of the eighteenth century, the manufacture of cotton cloths, or cotton-wool mixtures (fustians), slowly began to grow in Britain as the advantages of the fabric became more widely recognized.

During the Industrial Revolution (1750 to 1850), however, cotton supplanted wool as the premier textile in Western Europe. The use of steam-driven machinery in cotton mills spread from Britain to Belgium, France, the United States, and Germany. There was a remarkable international specialization during this period, raw-cotton producers exporting their raw material to industrializing countries and receiving finished cotton cloth in exchange.

The third period commenced about 1850. Further dispersal of the cotton industry gathered momentum and in the twentieth century was carried to almost every part of the world. Mechanized production spread first to southern and eastern Europe, then to India, Japan, China, Brazil, Argentina, and other Latin

[2] **Australia, New Zealand, and the Scandinavian countries, however, have all achieved a high level of industrialization without developing a cotton-textile industry of any significance.**

Table 18-2

Percentage Consumption of Apparel Fibers by Types

	1938	1959	1961
Cotton	77	69	67
Wool	12	10	9
Rayon and Acetate	11	18	18
True Synthetics		3	6
	100	100	100

SOURCE: FAO, *World Per Caput Fiber Consumption Levels,* Rome, 1960. FAO, *Monthly Bulletin of Agricultural Economics and Statistics,* January, 1962.

American and Asian countries. In older producers the cotton industry continued to grow until World War I, though in most it experienced a marked change of fortune after 1920. The period from 1850 to the present also witnessed the apogee and decline of the international trade in cotton textiles. In the Eighties of the last century only half the output of cotton cloth was consumed in countries in which it was manufactured; by 1955 this proportion had risen to almost 90 per cent, by which time total world output had increased 3½ times.[3]

The reasons for the progressively wider distribution of the cotton industry are fairly clear (Fig. 18-1). Its techniques are well known; modern machinery is relatively inexpensive and is capable of being used by a largely unskilled labor force; the use of ring-frame spinning and the automatic loom, moreover, permits a high output per worker. The industry is relatively labor-intensive and provides a large number of employment opportunities which can be further stretched by rotating work; a high labor turnover is a distinctive feature of the cotton industry in several countries. It also provides a market for locally produced raw materials, and its products are assured of a considerable local demand, for over much of the intertropical world, cotton is not only a very suitable crop for peasant cultivation but also by far the most suitable apparel fiber.

[3] **International Federation of Cotton and Allied Textile Industries,** *The Cotton Industry in a World Economy,* **Manchester, 1958, p. 20.**

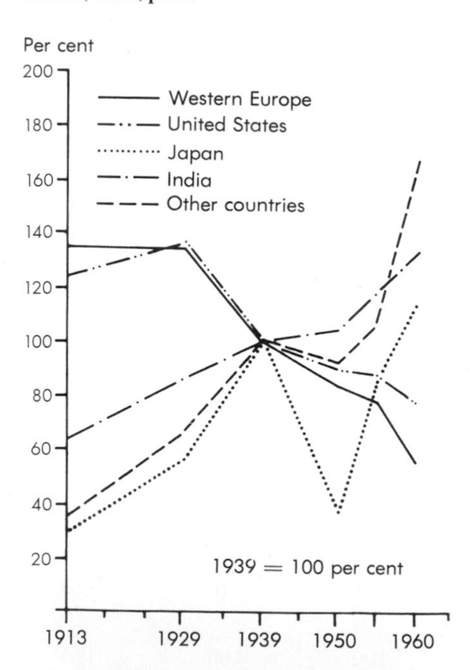

Fig. 18-1 Percentage increase in cotton-spinning capacity.
International Federation of Cotton and Allied Textile Industries.

In the past imports of cotton cloths have constituted a large item in the import trade of many countries at low levels of development, necessitating substantial allocations of scarce foreign exchange. Many such countries have not only developed a domestic industry capable of satisfying their own requirements but have themselves entered the export trade, greatly to the discomfort of the older producers. The irritation of cotton manufacturers in older producing countries with imports from low-labor-cost areas is understandable, and the United States and the EEC have taken action to protect their industries from such competition. Yet it should be borne in mind that although the wages of the Japanese, Indian, or Hong Kong worker are low in relation to those of his or her American counterpart (for much of the labor force in the industry consists of female workers), they are not low in relation to the general wage level in these countries. It is a waste for the highly developed economies to maintain a large capital investment or labor force in what is still, essentially, a technologically simple industry; the acceptance by such economies of an appreciable level of manufactured imports with a high labor content would be, in fact, an excellent way of assisting the underdeveloped economies in escaping from their present dependence on the highly volatile earnings of primary products. The difficulties of the older producers in part arise from their own shortcomings as well as from foreign competition; there is a long history of resistance to technical innovation, as a result of which much old and obsolescent equipment has been maintained in existence, and the ease with which output can be increased by multiple-shift working has also discouraged investment in new plant.

There are five major producers of cotton textiles in the free world—the United States, India, Japan, the EEC, and Britain (Table 18-3). The U.S.S.R. and China are also very large producers, but in these countries the problems of the industry are entirely different from those of the rest of the world. Neither plays any part in world trade in cotton textiles, or even allocates sufficient resources to the industry to satisfy the domestic demand for cotton textiles, and their participation in that of raw cotton is largely a matter of political convenience.

The United States

In raw-cotton consumption, production of finished cotton, and productivity per worker,

Table 18-3

Capacity and Production of the Cotton-textile Industry, 1961

	RING SPINDLES (MILLIONS)	POWER LOOMS (THOUSANDS)		YARN OUTPUT (THOUSAND METRIC TONS)
		ORDINARY	AUTOMATIC	
United States	19.6		315	1,646*
Argentina	1.1	5	15	88
Brazil	3.9	76	27	65
EEC	18.2	132	228	1,102
West Germany	5.8	39	69	403
France	5.4	44	62	314
Italy	4.5	17	77	206
Netherlands	1.0	15	18	76
Belgium	1.5	17	12	103
Britain	6.7	117	47	266
India	13.9	189	18	862
Japan	13.3	331	55	545
Hong Kong	0.6	5	15	97
Eastern Europe†	6.5	113	41	517
U.S.S.R.	10.8	125	98	1,165
Mainland China	9.6	115	40	1,632
WORLD TOTAL	123.2	1,420	1,120	

* 1958.

† Bulgaria, Czechoslovakia, East Germany, Hungary, and Romania, 1960.

SOURCE: United Nations, *Statistical Yearbook*, 1962.

the United States cotton-textile industry is easily the world leader.

As in many other countries, the cotton industry grew up in areas associated with the much older woolen industry, which had established itself in New England and on the middle Atlantic seaboard. The presence of copious soft water, numerous sites for waterpower, and a humid climate which assisted spinning were substantial physical advantages.[4] Profits of the trading and whaling industries seeking speculative outlets found the new industry attractive, and with the imposition of protective tariffs against British competition after the War of 1812, cotton-textile production increased rapidly. Not until the eve of the Civil War, however, did British imports cease to be of significance and the domestic industry become capable of supplying the greater part of the national demand. The introduction of the steam engine led to a concentration of manufacture at ports and estuaries where coal imports were possible, replacing the dispersed location pattern of the earlier waterpower era. New Bedford and Fall River thus became the centers of major significance.

A far more important territorial change occurred after 1880 with the establishment of a cotton-textile industry in the Piedmont area of the South; after somewhat slow beginnings, the southern industry grew very rapidly in the years between 1910 and the Great Depression, and in the latter part of this period a definite physical migration of industry took place, several northern mills transferring their operations to southern locations. The reasons for this shift have been much discussed, but the move is analogous to the general world trend of the industry to gravitate towards lower-labor-cost areas. The particular factors that operated most strongly in the expansion of the industry in the South appear to have been limited unionization, lower resistance to the introduction of such laborsaving techniques as high-draft spinning, the automatic loom, and multiple-shift working (which became standard practice in the South after World War I), and concessions from public authorities in the form of cheap land and lower taxes. Augmented by the expansion of hydroelectricity generation in the Piedmont all these factors favored the construction of large single-story plants with individual motors on each machine, a practice conferring maximum flexibility of operation, in contrast to the rigidity inevitable with multiple-story layout of the old New England mills, built when machinery had to be driven by lines of shafting. In any case, the cramped and congested condition of most New England textile centers with their high land values hindered the construction of modern mills. Shortly before the Great Depression the number of operating spindles in the South surpassed that of New England; moreover, the southern spindles were much more productive. The problem of redundant capacity was thus largely confined to the old northern section of the industry.

The American cotton-textile industry has a typically competitive industrial structure, with numerous small firms, none of which is able to produce the whole range of products turned out by the industry but each of which nonetheless retains a considerable capacity for switching from one line to another with changes in market conditions. No one manufacturer has more than 5 per cent of the industry's total capacity, but some units such as the Burlington and Stevens corporations are enormous by

[4] **The importance of this climatic factor in the localization of the industry both in North America and in Europe nonetheless appears to have been overstressed. In the early days the tendency of warp threads to break was a difficulty which was reduced by spinning in damp atmosphere. A major contribution to the solution of this problem was made by Radcliffe in 1804, through the introduction of the "slashing" process, that is, steeping the warp yarns in boiling starch.**

European standards and rank among the largest American companies.[5] Although there are many independent specialist concerns, there is a considerable degree of integration, spinning, weaving, and finishing being frequently undertaken in the same plant. The American industry is much more highly capitalized than its European counterpart, and productivity of both labor and capital is very much higher. The United States produces very much more cloth than the EEC countries and Britain combined, although it has less than one-half as many spindles and only a little more than one-third as many looms; the industry's labor force, moreover, is less than half that of the European industry.

Nevertheless, the American industry has shared the generally depressed fortunes of cotton textiles in other highly developed economies, and there is a tendency for the large units to spread into other branches of textile production and into chemicals and plastics. One of the industry's major difficulties arises from the United States government's price-support policy for raw cotton; the effect of this is to make the cost of raw material to the domestic manufacturer considerably higher than to the foreign buyer who benefits from the subsidy on raw cotton exports. Since raw materials account for about 50 to 60 per cent of the total cost of production, this disadvantage is a considerable handicap; as manufacturers have pointed out, the taxpayer is subsidizing their foreign competitors. As a result, a supplementary duty to offset the effects of the subsidized export of raw cotton has been imposed on imports; official pressure has also been brought to bear to persuade Japanese and Hong Kong manufacturers to place physical quotas on their exports. On balance, however, the United States is a substantial exporter of cotton textiles, and foreign competition is not a factor in many lines; imports amount to less than 5 per cent of domestic production, as against one-third to one-half in the case of Britain.[6] Far more serious is the loss of markets to man-made fibers, in both apparel and industrial applications, as a result of the cotton support policy. But despite apparently unpropitious conditions, American cotton-textile manufacturers have invested considerable sums in modernization, and when supported by scientific research, cotton has shown that it can be an effective competitor to the newer textile fibers.[7]

Western Europe

Western Europe, which for convenience may be taken as the six countries of the EEC and Britain, is the world's second-largest producer of cotton textiles (Fig. 18-2); its capacity, however, is greater than that of the United States, and the problem of redundant spindles and looms is considerably more acute (Table 18-4). Nowhere is this more pressing than in Britain, which in 1913 possessed about 40 per cent of the world's total spinning capacity and about 30 per cent of all power looms. In 1956 Britain still had about half of all spindles and about two-thirds of all looms in place in Western Europe, but the annual hours of operation of active spindles and looms were among the lowest of any producing country. The proportions of spindles and looms in place, however, fell dramatically after 1959 with the implemen-

[5] In 1963 these two concerns occupied the forty-eighth and ninetieth positions, respectively, in *Fortune*'s list of the 500 largest United States industrial corporations. See *Fortune*, July, 1964.

[6] If all textiles are considered, however, the United States has been a net importer since 1956.

[7] Although the cotton-textile industry's annual investment between 1947 and 1957 averaged some 450 million dollars, expenditure on research was, nevertheless, inadequate. See International Federation of Cotton and Allied Textile Industries, *op. cit.*, pp. 54, 130.

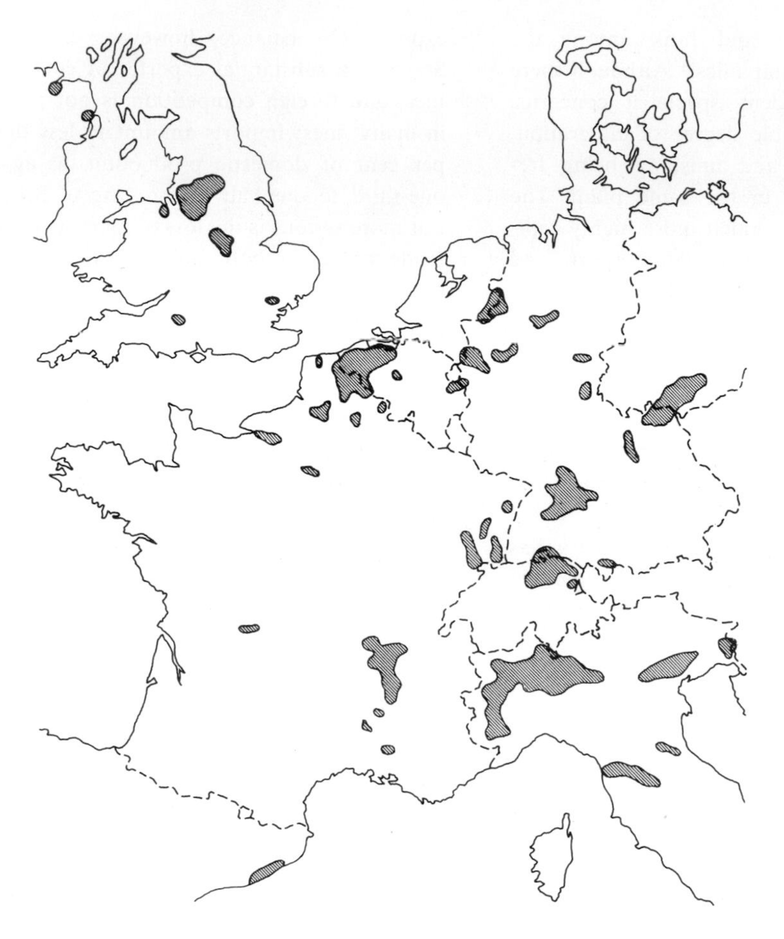

Fig. 18-2 Textile areas of Western Europe. Numerous minor centers have been omitted.

tation of a state scheme for scrapping redundant and obsolescent machinery.

Britain is, in fact, only a minor producer of cotton textiles at present, but the cotton industry has such particular associations with Lancashire and the influence of cotton manufacturers was for so long a time of major importance in British economic policy that the industry merits more than a passing reference; moreover, the location of the cotton industry in Britain appears highly anomalous in comparison with that of Continental Europe. Its geographic concentration is extreme, for it is virtually restricted to eastern and southeastern Lancashire and the adjacent portions of Cheshire and Derbyshire; every other major producer, on the other hand, possesses a number of distinct cotton-manufacturing regions.

The traditional home of the textile industries in Europe was the flanks of the Hercynian uplands—the Vosges, the Rhine plateau, the Bohemian massif and others—and certain other areas such as the plain of Flanders and northern Italy. These originally possessed local wool or flax (though several districts came to be dependent on imported supplies with the passage of time), soft water, and waterpower, as well as a population willing to supplement the farm income by working under the domestic system of industry, and the cotton industry grew up in these old textile areas. In Britain this did not happen, largely because of the political strength of the highly influential wool manufacturers, who were long able to maintain irksome restrictions on the new industry; there were few parts of the country which satisfied the physical requirements of the cotton industry and were free of restrictions. Of the three districts in which it succeeded in establishing itself, Derbyshire, east Lancashire, and the Glasgow area, east Lancashire proved to possess the best endowment for growth; it was able to take advantage of technological change, and the "external economies" that result from a concentration of production soon made the appearance of any other producing regions impossible. Glasgow, which could have been a competitor, found its iron and steel, shipbuilding, and other heavy industries more profitable.

Lancashire's 150 years of uninterrupted expansion of cotton-textile production were firmly based on the export trade, and in the nineteenth century Lancashire was extraordinarily successful in adapting itself to the changing pattern of world demand; exports were first directed mainly to Europe and North America, later shifted to Central and South America, and around the turn of the century moved mainly to Asia and Africa. In 1913 the output of cotton cloth reached 8 billion yards (six times that of 1960); of this total some four-fifths was exported, a proportion that remained unequaled until 1950 when Hong Kong began to export a similar proportion of its output. The home market is now of overwhelming importance, as with all Western producers, and the country has become a major importer. The decline of the Lancashire cotton industry did not result from foreign competition in its export markets, but was largely a consequence of the establishment of a domestic mill industry in those markets themselves, above all in India, which in 1913 took nearly half of Lancashire's cotton exports.

Lancashire was also anomalous in its long adherence to mule spinning, which even before

Table 18-4

Hours of Operation of Active Looms and Spindles in the Cotton Textile Industry of Western Europe, 1956

	SPINDLE HOURS OF ACTIVE SPINDLES*	LOOM HOURS OF ACTIVE LOOMS*
Belgium	4,280	
France	3,416	3,172
West Germany	3,845	3,534
Italy	3,604	2,962
Netherlands	4,072	3,040
Britain	2,007	2,248

* The hours of operation of active looms and spindles reflect the varying importance of multiple-shift working; it was little used in Britain, where there was considerable overcapacity.

SOURCE: International Federation of Cotton and Allied Textile Industries, *The Cotton Industry in a World Economy*, Manchester, 1958.

the Great Depression had ceased to be of any real significance anywhere else in the world. Mule spinning is very suitable for spinning the finer yarns, or higher counts,[8] but its productivity is low as a result of an intermittent action, and it requires a male labor force; its retention partly reflects the gradual preoccupation with finer-quality yarns as Lancashire's competitive margin in the coarser yarns was reduced. Resistance to the use of the automatic loom and to multiple-shift working was so great that in 1960 only about one-third of the looms in operation were automatic and only a third of those worked under a system of three shifts per day. Moreover, the old horizontal form of industrial structure that grew up after 1840 in response to the growth of the export trade remains essentially unchanged. Spinning, weaving, finishing, and marketing are largely performed by specialists, and each operation is geographically restricted. Spinning and doubling are largely the prerogative of southeast Lancashire, Oldham spinning the lower counts and Bolton the higher; weaving, though spread throughout the cotton area, is a particular specialty of the towns north of the Rossendale upland; and finishing is carried on in the Manchester-Oldham area. This fragmentation has assisted the entry of imported cotton products into the British market, for each specialist is interested in getting his raw material from the cheapest source, whether internal or external.

The prolonged contraction of the British cotton-textile industry prompted the government during the Great Depression to provide financial assistance to bring about a greater measure of rationalization and to scrap redundant machinery; on the whole, however, these operations were of limited success. In 1959 a new scheme, described at the time as "the cotton industry's last chance of modernization," was introduced; this provided compensation for scrapped machinery, and as a result, over 7 million mules and nearly 3.5 million ring spindles, together with over 100,000 looms, were scrapped. With the progressive expansion of double-shift working, an innovation in Lancashire, Britain's reduced equipment has since worked at a much higher proportion of capacity. Imports of cotton goods from Commonwealth countries (in practice from India, Pakistan, and Hong Kong) entered the country duty-free until 1959, and the success of the redundancy scheme was held by British manufacturers to be conditional on some limitation of these imports. Since that date, Commonwealth suppliers have since been obliged to impose "voluntary restrictions" on their exports, but the whole question of the importation of cotton textiles from low labor-cost producers into the highly developed economies is one that gives rise to considerable controversy in Britain, particularly as countries of the EEC have taken strong action to exclude imports of cotton textiles from low-labor-cost areas.

The largest producer of cotton textiles in Western Europe is West Germany, but France is only little inferior. Germany's textile industries are widely scattered, a result of late political unification, but with the division of Germany after World War II the Federal Republic retained the greater part of the cotton industry; the larger part of the woolen industry passed to East Germany. Saxony was the foremost textile area of both Imperial and interwar Germany, but another area of considerable significance was the lower Rhineland, where textile production had long been established in the Aachen–Düren–München Gladbach area and in Wuppertal; expansion of cotton and woolen industries in this region has compensated for the loss of the production of

[8] **Cotton, wool, and linen use the count system for grading yarns, that is, the number of hank lengths that weigh 1 pound; these lengths are 840 yards, 560 yards, and 300 yards, respectively. The productivity of the ring spindle is half as much again as that of the mule spindle.**

Leipzig, Chemnitz, and Plauen, and some of the textile centers of south Germany have also revived. West Germany's cotton exports are only a very small fraction of total output, and the needs of the buoyant home market have necessitated substantial investment in new plant; the annual hours of operation of active spindles and looms are very high by European standards (Table 18-4). The French cotton industry began in Alsace, where the industry appeared in the late eighteenth century, but Rouen and the northeast industrial area (Lille–Roubaix–Tourcoing) later drew ahead. Both in France and West Germany integrated operations are the rule.

While not themselves centers of textile production, the three great cotton ports of Western Europe—Liverpool, Le Havre, and Bremen—play a vital part in the industry.

Asia

In the present century the production of cotton textiles in Asia has increased enormously, and Asian countries now dominate world trade. China, India, and Japan are all producers of the first rank, and since 1945 the industry has grown rapidly in Pakistan and in Hong Kong. The very limited development of the cotton industry in Indonesia, a large textile consumer, is thus highly anomalous and reflects the ineptitude of the Indonesian government.

India, now the second-largest individual producer of the free world, has always been an important one. The first power-using mill was established as long ago as 1854, but the development of the mill industry was very slow in the face of Lancashire competition; its real chance did not come until World War I, when British exports were cut off and large Allied armies in the Middle East had to be supplied from Indian bases. In the interwar period India's greater fiscal autonomy enabled the industry to receive a measure of protection, but Japanese competition became increasingly severe. World War II provided a further fillip to growth, and since Indian independence in 1947 the industry has grown rapidly, comfortably attaining the targets set in the First and Second Five Year Plans; its growth, in fact, has had to be limited by government action in the interests of the old handicraft industry, which, never entirely destroyed by foreign competition and supporting perhaps as many as 10 million people, has considerable political strength. Thus the production of certain types of cloth is reserved to the handloom section, an excise duty is levied on all mill production, and penal duties are imposed on output in excess of production quotas. Nevertheless, the mill section accounts for about three-quarters of India's total production of cotton cloth, and it is doubtful if the handicraft industry could survive without its considerable protection. The restrictions imposed on the mill section of the industry in its home market and the growth of a cotton industry in Pakistan have been important factors in encouraging interest in export markets outside the subcontinent. Bombay and Ahmadābād are the principal centers of the Indian industry, but inland cities such as Sholāpur, Nagpur, and Coimbatore have shown faster rates of growth in production in recent years; the migration of the industry to centers within the Indian cotton belt suggests a parallel to that of the industry in the United States.

Japan's cotton-textile industry began later than that of India, but its growth was much more rapid; as in India it was World War I that provided the first major incentive to growth, but in the case of Japan, this even provided an opportunity for invading Lancashire's markets. With its low-cost labor, modern machinery, multiple-shift working, and the depreciated yen, the Japanese industry had a substantial cost advantage. Indeed, it was largely unaffected by the Great Depression; in 1933 Japan became for the first time the world's largest exporter of cotton cloth and though eclipsed during World War II, it regained the position of leading exporter in 1954. The level of exports, however, is much below that of the late Thirties, and the direction of cotton-exports has largely shifted from East, Southeast, and South Asia to the Americas and Africa.

Japan's approaching industrial maturity is indicated by the steady decline in the proportion of the total industrial labor force engaged in the textile industries; also, the share of raw cotton in the import trade and that of cotton textiles among exports have fallen substantially since the end of World War II. Labor is now strongly unionized, and the system adopted by Japanese factories in 1959 of operating 15.5 hours per day, divided between two shifts, certainly cannot be regarded as "sweated labor." Moreover, the beginnings of overcapacity can be detected; since 1956 the government has had the power to instruct manufacturers to dispose of equipment deemed redundant, and all spinning and weaving equipment has to be registered. As in the older producers, the cotton industry in Japan does not possess the oligopolistic structure typical of iron and steel, electric machinery, and other metal-making and -fabricating industries. Spinning is largely in the hands of the so-called "Big Ten" integrated concerns, but there are still numerous small spinning establishments, and only about one-sixth of all registered looms are owned by integrated concerns. The latter are also engaged in other branches of textile production, and to prevent diversion of looms from one type to another, equipment has to be specifically registered for either cotton or rayon.

The location of the Japanese cotton industry is broadly coincidental with that of manufacturing industry as a whole, but the Hanshin area (Osaka-Kobe) is by far the most important, followed by the Keihin (Tokyo-Yokohama) and Nagoya areas. Weaving is more widely distributed; though most important in the three great industrial foci it is also carried on in many cities along the Inland Sea and on the Japan Sea, as well as in those of the basins of central northern Honshu.

The Eastern Bloc

The U.S.S.R. and China rank among the world's largest producers of cotton textiles; their per capita consumption, however, is low. The Russian cotton industry grew up in what were the Polish portions of Imperial Russia, and its capital and labor force were largely non-Russian. Later the industry was established in the central industrial area, and with the loss of the western territories the Moscow-Ivanovo district became, and has since remained, the main center of the industry. While there has been some attempt to introduce a mill industry into the cotton-producing areas of Soviet Asia, this does little more than meet local demand. Broad economic considerations —and the congested conditions of Russia's railways—would suggest that a major relocation of the industry is highly desirable, but the consumer status of the industry gives it a low priority in the allocation of resources. The 1959–1965 Seven Year Plan envisaged an increase of cotton-cloth production from 5.8 billion to nearly 8 billion meters;[9] this target, however, is below the 1958 production level of Western Europe.

China's mill industry dates from the end of the Sino-Japanese War in 1895, which almost involved a share-out of China among the Great Powers. The industry was established in a number of centers within the various spheres of influence to the powers—in south Manchuria, Tientsin and Tsingtao, and Shanghai and Canton—but though foreign capital from a number of sources participated in the indus-

[9] United Nations Economic Commission for Europe, *Economic Survey of Europe 1959,* Geneva, 1960, p. A. 13.

try, Japanese interests soon predominated. The period from 1914 to 1920 was one of exceptionally rapid growth; during this period much of the industry passed into Japanese hands, and Shanghai was confirmed as the major center of the industry. The Japanese attempt to reduce China to economic vassalage and World War II and its aftermath were great setbacks to the industry; after 1949 much capital and physical equipment was moved to Hong Kong, where production, largely for export markets, has grown tremendously since 1950. In the late Fifties the Chinese cotton industry again grew extremely rapidly; by 1960 it had probably overtaken that of the U.S.S.R. both in the number of installed spindles and in the number of looms, and Shanghai had become one of the leading cotton-textile centers of the world. For a brief period in the middle Fifties it appeared that China planned to become a major exporter, but the flood of Chinese cotton goods into Asian and African markets that began at that time was not maintained; with the growing shortage of cotton consequent on the failure of the agricultural program and increasing industrial dislocation, the threat passed. By 1962 China's cotton industry may well have been the largest in the world; yet it was able to provide the Chinese people with only a few yards of cloth per head annually, and consumption has been severely rationed.

WOOL

The woolen industry plays a much smaller part in the world economy than the cotton industry, and is still largely confined to countries at a high level of development situated in the temperate latitudes. Since the end of World War II, however, Japan has become a major producer, and it is possible that China may also do so in the future.

Many factors operate to check a wider dispersal of woolen-textile production. Wool is a high-cost and specialized fiber without the numerous applications of cotton, and is mainly employed for apparel purposes in countries with distinct winters. The woolen industry is more complex than that of cotton; it is not one industry but two, for the woolen-cloth and worsted divisions use different raw materials, have different organizations, and serve different markets. Although wool technology does not differ very greatly from that of cotton, the fiber is more difficult to handle and requires a high degree of skill on the part of operative. The manufacture of woolens and worsteds requires a higher proportion of male labor than the cotton industry requires and also is more time-consuming, making physical output per worker lower; more than 90 per cent of cotton cloth is woven as "gray" cloth, but worsteds are patterned on the loom, as are tweeds in the woolen section. Because both woolen industries produce largely for domestic consumption and because international trade in wool textiles does not involve countries with wide labor-cost differentials, the woolen industry has generally experienced rather better fortunes than has the cotton industry; the United States, however, appears to be an exception.

Woolen cloths are made from short fibers, or "noils," which are separated in the combing process from the longer "tops" destined for the worsted section. Woolens, however, also use considerable quantities of old and reconstituted wool, known as "shoddy" and "mungo." Mule spinning is still of considerable importance, particularly in Europe, where it is the dominant process in the woolen section. Woolen cloths are usually dyed in the piece and are often heavily fulled, so that the weave is inconspicuous or invisible. Worsted yarns are almost entirely made from new wool and are spun on ring frames or, as in Britain, on broadly similar cap and fly frames; hard and highly twisted, worsted yarns are woven into conspicuous patterns.

There is a tendency in most countries for worsted to become of greater importance than woolens, but both have experienced considerable competition from textiles manufactured from man-made fibers. Wool's share of total textile-fiber consumption has thus been falling for some time, and the process appears likely to continue (Table 18-2); total production of woolen textiles of all kinds, however, should increase with the achievement of higher living standards in those parts of the temperate climatic zone still at low levels of development. But much more intensive research will be necessary to withstand competition from man-made fibers; wool can be made shrink-proof, can be given permanent pleats, and can be woven into ultralightweight cloths, but these improvements should have been introduced before they became selling points for synthetics.[10]

The Major Producers

There are only four large producers of woolen textiles—Western Europe, the United States, the U.S.S.R., and Japan (Table 18-5). Through most of the period between the world wars the output of woolen textiles in the United States was the largest in the world, although Britain possessed a greater capacity. Nevertheless, apart from the temporary stimuli of World War II and the Korean crisis, the American woolen industry has fared poorly since the early Twenties. In part this has been the result of changed ways of living, which have reduced the necessity for warm clothing, and of competition from man-made fibers; for its failure to adapt to changes of fashion, however, the industry has only itself to blame.

Production of woolen fabrics was widespread in the colonial period, but with the advent of power-driven machinery, factory production established itself in southern New England and on the middle Atlantic seaboard. Substantial tariff protection was necessary to enable the industry to meet British competition, and not until after the Civil War did the worsted section of the industry become really important.

Since 1945 the flight of the cotton industry to the South has been followed by a similar movement of both sections of the woolen industry, and for essentially similar reasons; the greater part of the industry's capacity, however, is still located in northerly areas. The South has been relatively more attractive to the worsted section than the woolen. This may have arisen from the greater conservatism of the woolen section, which has found it hard to break away from its traditional dependence on long runs of staple product such as serges and uniform cloths, but the proximity of the main centers of rayon and other man-made fibers production to southern mills enhances the opportunities of the worsted section for producing the lightweight blends that are increasingly in demand. The strong competitive position of the South is indicated by its acquisition of a larger share of capacity while the woolen industry was experiencing an overall decline.

As in the cotton industry, government policy in relation to domestic raw-material production has enhanced the industry's difficulties. Wool output in the United States has long been declining, and the attempts to increase the proportion of home-produced wool in the industry's total consumption has had the effect of pushing up prices until wool has almost become a luxury fabric. As a result, synthetic substitutes are considerably cheaper, and United States consumption of wool per head has dropped substantially; in 1960 it was less than half that of most countries of Western Europe.

[10] The basic scientific discovery for putting permanent pleats in woolens and worsteds was made as far back as 1930.

Table 18-5

Capacity and Production of the Woolen Industries, 1961

	SPINDLES (THOUSANDS)	LOOMS		WOOLEN YARNS (THOUSAND METRIC TONS)
		AUTOMATIC	TOTAL	
United States	1,347	11,700	12,900	303
EEC	4,760	10,840	66,520	533
West Germany	1,190	2,660	15,940	114
France	1,280	4,950	16,070	147
Italy	1,560	1,790	24,040	194
Britain	2,590	11,700	43,900	240
Japan	1,800		34,150	144
U.S.S.R.				232

SOURCE: United Nations, *Statistical Yearbook*, 1962.

The woolen industry was long Britain's most important manufacturing industry, and though eclipsed by the rise of Lancashire cotton in the nineteenth century, it has regained its position as Britain's leading textile industry since 1945. Although it is not so highly localized as the cotton industry, its geographic concentration is striking enough, about three-quarters of all employment in the industry being located in the West Riding of Yorkshire. Before the late eighteenth century the West Riding was but one of a number of woolen-producing areas, and it could not match the quality of either the Cotswolds woolens or the worsted of East Anglia. It was, however, well placed to adopt the technological innovations that had been developed across the Pennines in Lancashire and was situated in the northwestern portion of what was to become Britain's major coalfield. By about 1830 the worsted section had passed into a factory system, and the two branches of the woolen industry had already outgrown the supply of British wool; the woolen section, however, retained features of the old domestic system until late in the century.

The West Riding woolen industry has differed importantly from the Lancashire cotton industry in several ways. The West Riding never developed the extreme concentration on export production that was so marked in Lancashire; only about 40 per cent of the total production of woolens and worsteds was exported in 1913, and the trade had long been declining with the growth of woolen industries in the United States and in Continental Europe. The industry even then possessed a much more integrated structure than the Lancashire cotton industry, although in the worsted section a tendency towards a more horizontal form of organization slowly became apparent in the period between the wars. The geographic specialization of Lancashire has been largely absent; in the nineteenth century woolens were relatively more important in the south and southeast of the great West Riding conurbation and worsteds in the north and northwest, but this pattern has virtually disappeared as both sections of the industry have spread through the whole of the area. Largely because of these structural differences the West Riding lacks a metropolitan center of the status of Manchester which provided the numerous specialist services and acted as intermediary for the atomized cotton industry. Bradford is the major center of production but shares metropolitan functions with nearby Leeds, whose manufacturing industries mainly involve engineering and ready-made clothing.

While woolen exports have continued to decline and in 1960 represented only about 20 per cent of total production, the British woolen industries have nevertheless fared very much better than the cotton industry; though much machinery is elderly, productivity per worker is not markedly lower than elsewhere.

The close geographic coincidence of cotton and woolen industries in Continental Europe has already been emphasized; the most important woolen-textile area is that shared by France and Belgium, that is, the Lille-Roubaix-Tournai district. French woolen output has been virtually unchanged since the period between the two world wars, but that of West Germany, as in cotton, is substantially above the level for the Third Reich. Most remarkable, however, is the postwar growth of the woolen industries in Italy, output in 1960 being more than twice that of pre-World War II years. Italy is a very old producer of woolens, for the industry was the basis of the prosperity of a number of medieval Italian city-states, particularly Florence. Eclipsed during the Industrial Revolution, the industry revived about the end of the nineteenth century when the development of hydroelectricity began to lay the foundations of the present Italian industrial economy, but the emphasis was then on the coarsest and cheapest cloths. Italy now produces the finest worsteds and woolens, and Italian designs, as in many other industrial arts, are standards for the world to follow.

This development in Italy is largely the result of a very high postwar rate of economic growth and consequent higher living standards which have created a preference for more expensive fibers. Precisely similar trends are observable in Japan and in the U.S.S.R. Since 1958 Japan has become Australia's best customer for raw wool, and by 1960 output of woolen textiles was almost four times the prewar level. Japanese woolen production is almost entirely destined for the home market, and the relatively low per capita consumption and continuing ebullience of the Japanese economy suggest considerable capacity for further growth. The Japanese woolen industry is organized in large integrated units, but its geographic distribution largely coincides with the major centers of the cotton industry.

The post-World War II expansion of the Russian woolen industry has made the U.S.S.R. probably the world's largest producer on a national basis, but present per capita consumption of wool is no higher than in Japan. Russian woolens are of poor quality, being largely produced from domestic wools. By far the most important focus of the industry is the Moscow-Ivanovo region in the central industrial area.

MAN-MADE FIBERS

Man-made fibers were first produced commercially shortly before the end of the last century and have since had a meteoric rise to a position of substantial importance in the world economy. By 1914 world output has attained a level of about 25 million pounds; the industry was then firmly established in most countries of Western Europe, where the initial research and development was carried out, and in the United States. Production in Japan began during World War I. After 1920 world output and the number of producers grew extremely rapidly; in the following decade total output increased more than fourteen times, and a very high growth rate was maintained right through the Great Depression up to the outbreak of World War II, by which time the man-made-fiber industry had displaced wool from its position as the world's second most important apparel fiber.

After 1945 the industry was established in yet more countries, and by the mid-Fifties the level of output was almost twice that of 1939; thereafter, however, the rate of growth slowed very considerably, and production of some types of fiber actually declined. Whether the man-made fibers can improve on the 22 per cent share of free world apparel-fiber consumption that they held in 1960 is conjectural, but it would appear that the future rate of growth of the industry is likely to be only modest in comparison with past performance. The reasons for the abrupt change that has already occurred is the stationary or declining per capita fiber consumption in many countries at high levels of economic development; consumers in such countries appear to want to spend more of their enhanced incomes on other goods than textiles.

There are many man-made fibers, but they can be grouped into four main classes (Table 18-6):

1. The cellulose fibers rayon and acetate,[11] which together account for about 75 per cent of total man-made-fiber production. Cellulose is a complex organic substance present in all plants, but the main raw materials used are spruce wood pulp and cotton linters, the burr adhering to the cottonseed after ginning.
2. The protein fibers, which are produced from organic substances, such as milk protein, or from proteins derived from corn, groundnuts, or other vegetable matter. First commercially produced in the period between the two world wars, the protein fibers have proved unprofitable, and are of small and diminishing importance.
3. The true, or noncellulose, synthetic fibers, whose development has largely taken place since World War II. The true synthetics are produced from a few basic organic raw materials, such as bituminous or brown coal, petroleum, or natural gas, by the creation of complex long-chain molecules in a process known as polymerization. The most important is the polyamide fiber nylon, but there are very many true synthetics, some of which possess a variety of names according to the country of manufacture. Some true synthetic fibers have failed to find employment as apparel fibers but are well established in household and industrial uses.
4. The inorganic fibers such as those produced from glass or asbestos, whose application is entirely outside the apparel field.

[11] **Before 1951 the term "rayon" was used in the United States to denote all types of cellulose fibers; this is still the practice in Britain, although there is an increasing tendency to follow current American usage, which is to restrict the term "rayon" to fibers made by the viscose process, and to use the term "acetate" for those made by the rival acetate process.**

Rayon and Acetate

All but about 10 per cent of total world production of cellulose fibers consists of *viscose* rayon or, simply, rayon. The viscose process was developed in Britain at the end of the nineteenth century, and uses as its raw material sheets of almost pure cellulose derived from spruce pulp. These are treated with caustic soda and carbon bisulfide, and the resulting viscose solution is forced through the orifices of a thimble-shaped "spinneret" into a coagulating bath; spinning is performed by collecting and twisting the coagulated filaments in a rapidly revolving "box." The rival acetate process, developed almost simultaneously, was not used to any appreciable extent until after World War I. In this process cotton linters and wood

Table 18-6

Man-made Fibers

- Cellulose
  - Rayon
  - Acetate
- Protein
  - Lanital
  - Merinova
  - Vicara
- True Synthetics
  - Polyamides
    - Nylon
    - Perlon
    - Amilan
    - Rilsan
  - Polyesters
    - Terylene
    - Dacron
    - Tetoron
  - Polyacrylics
    - Orlon
    - Acrilan
    - Creslan
    - Zefran
    - Dynel
    - Courtelle
  - Polyvinyls
    - Avisco
    - Mewlon
    - Vinylon
  - Polyvinylidene
    - Saran
    - Velon
  - Polyethylene
    - Reevon
    - Wynene
    - Velon
    - Courlene
  - Polypropylene
    - Meraklon
    - Moplen
  - Polystyrene
    - Shalon
- Inorganic
  - Glass
  - Asbestos

Table 18-7

Percentage Capacity of Cellulose Fibers by Type

	CONTINUOUS FILAMENT			STAPLE FIBER	
	HIGH-TENACITY RAYON	REGULAR RAYON	ACETATE	RAYON	ACETATE
United States	43	22	35	84	15
Britain	42	34	24	94	6
Italy	19	68	13	100	
West Germany	40	54	6	97	3
Japan	19	72	9	99	1
France	36	51	13	96	4
WORLD TOTAL	30	53	17	96	4

SOURCE: CEC, *Industrial Fibres*, 1962.

pulp are treated with acetic acid and acetic anhydride, and the resulting cellulose acetate is dissolved in acetone; filaments are extruded in a current of warm air. A third process, the cuprammonium process, now accounts for less than 1 per cent of total cellulose-fiber production, having lost much of its former market in the hosiery industry, its principal former employment, to nylon. Acetate and cuprammonium are usually marketed under their respective trade names, Celanese and Bemberg.

Because of its superior dyeing properties, acetate became of increasing importance as an apparel fiber from about 1930 onwards, but outside the United States and Britain it has never been of any appreciable significance; in the former it accounts for about one-third and in the latter for about one-quarter of the output of continuous filament. Apart from a slightly lower cost, rayon has two advantages over acetate—it is better suited for the production of staple fiber and for high-tenacity tire cord (Table 18-7).

Though rayon was first marketed as "artificial silk," it was found that by cutting filaments of appropriate thickness and length into staple fiber and spinning on cotton, woolen, or linen spindles, it was possible to give rayon the appearance and some of the properties of the traditional textiles; staple fiber, or staple, as it is often called, can also be used in mixtures with natural fibers. Production of staple began in the blockaded central European powers during World War I in substitution for natural fibers, but its production did not grow rapidly until the onset of the Great Depression. By the outbreak of World War II, however, output had almost overtaken that of filament; rayon staple was produced on a very large scale by the Axis Powers, Germany, Italy, and Japan, which lacked control over supplies of raw cotton and wool; by 1939 these three countries accounted for about 90 per cent of world staple-fiber output. In the United States and in Britain, where supplies of traditional fibers were assured, staple-fiber production was slow to develop, but in both countries output grew very rapidly after World War II. The United States, however, is now anomalous among major rayon producers in having a larger output of continuous filament than of staple fiber, an indication of the abundant availability of almost all types of fiber in the country (Table 18-8).

Costs of raw materials in all man-made

Table 18-8

Production of Rayon and Acetate (Thousand metric tons)

	1948		1963	
	FILAMENT	STAPLE	FILAMENT	STAPLE
United States	388	122	322	290
Brazil	12	1	31*	10*
EEC	148	109	274	421
West Germany	30	40	79	187
France	44	30	59	84
Italy	48	18	89	112
Netherlands	16	10	34	17
Belgium	10	11	13	21
Britain	66	39	150	176
Spain	7	9	19	41
Japan	16	16	133	329
East Germany	6	39	26	114
U.S.S.R.	6	5	132*	98*
WORLD TOTAL†	708	445	1,220	1,833

* 1961.
† Excluding mainland China.
SOURCE: United Nations, *Statistical Yearbook*, 1962; *Monthly Bulletin of Statistics*, May, 1964.

fiber industries are proportionately very much less than in the older textile industries, but as the economies of scale are very substantial, large production units are mandatory (Fig. 18-3). Moreover, the price stability possessed by man-made fibers in consequence of the organization in a few giant units is a powerful factor in their competitive struggle with natural fibers. The heavy capital costs and the patent rights associated with rayon production encouraged international cooperation and marketing agreements almost from the beginning; the old British silk firm of Courtaulds, which acquired the patent for the viscose process, had interests in the Italian Snia Viscosa and Dutch Enka concerns; all were parties, in concert with other producers, to agreements restricting competition. Such international agreements have long obtained in the chemical industries, of which the man-made-fiber industry is really an outgrowth. Several of the largest chemical corporations are now themselves producers of rayon and acetate, and firms whose activities were restricted to the cellulose fibers have entered the field of the true synthetics since World War II; ties with the chemical industries have thus tended to become still closer.

In its preponderantly male labor force the man-made-fiber industry contrasts sharply with the traditional textiles; in large part this is a consequence of the limited interest of fiber producers in further processing, for which large-scale operations confer no particular advantage. Spinning of staple fiber, weaving, and knitting are largely performed by independent firms on cotton machinery, which, as already noted, can be interchanged between cotton and rayon. European fiber manufacturers generally show a higher degree of forward integration than their American counterparts; the British Celanese Company, now merged with Courtaulds, not only produced finished fabrics but undertook all stages of manufacture, including that of certain chemical raw materials, in one enormous integrated plant. The Celanese Corporation of America, however, also has considerable interests in weaving and knitting.

The production of cellulose fibers (and, a fortiori, that of true synthetics) is confined to countries able to support a substantial heavy-chemicals industry, and within such countries,

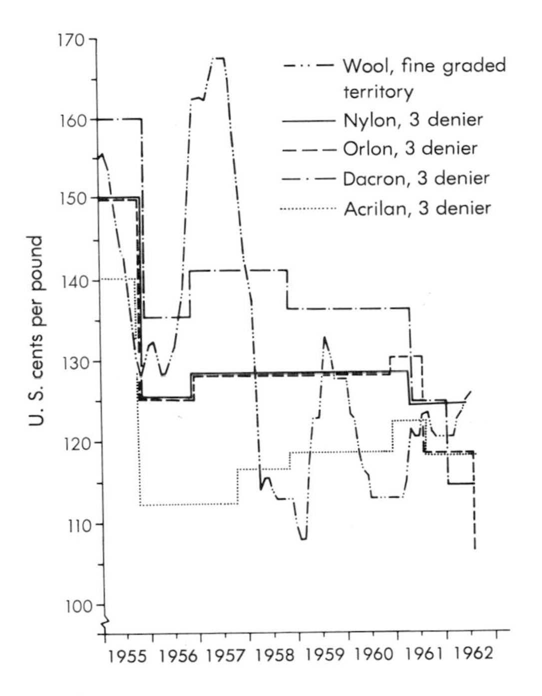

Fig. 18-3 Wool and synthetic prices.
Price stability and lower prices with increasing output are the main advantages of the true synthetic fibers. Denier is the weight in grams of a 9,000-meter length of yarn. (Textile Organon.)

siting factors are often more important than locational factors. The man-made-fiber industries require enormous quantities of water and a means of disposing of very large amounts of waste products; with progressively severer penalties for river pollution and stricter control over effluent disposal, the location of man-made-fiber plants frequently gives rise to considerable problems in highly industrialized and densely populated areas, where demands on water supplies are often rising at a rate to cause considerable concern. There is thus a tendency to locate new plants on coastal sites or well removed from competing claimants on water.

The United States is the largest producer of both cellulose and true synthetic fibers; in the former, however, its margin over Japan, the second-largest producer of both types, is slender. The American rayon industry was virtually monopolized by foreign capital for a very long period; even as late as 1929 three foreign-owned corporations controlled about three-quarters of total output. The largest of these was the American Viscose Corporation, a subsidiary of the British firm of Courtaulds; when sold at the nadir of Britain's fortunes during World War II, it was the largest British investment in the country. Experience and control of patents gave Europeans a firm grip on the newly introduced rayon industry, and the duty on imported rayon encouraged them to set up plants behind the American tariff barrier. American Viscose is still the largest producer, but second is the giant chemical organization, Du Pont; Courtaulds recommenced production in the United States in 1953. The Celanese Corporation of America is the leading producer of acetate.

The earliest location of the rayon industry was in eastern Pennsylvania and on the middle Atlantic seaboard; the industry, however, has tended to move westwards and southwards, and the greatest concentration of plants is now in Virginia and Tennessee. The factors that

Rayon cord is produced at a Krasnoyarsk mill in the U.S.S.R.

have attracted the cotton industry to the South have also operated in the case of rayon and acetate production; however, there is no close coincidence with cotton-textile production, and rayon plants are more widely dispersed.

In Japan also the rayon industry began in affiliation with European companies. During the interwar period production increased at a prodigious rate, and although international trade in rayon has never been proportionately as large as that in cotton textiles, Japan acquired a firm grip on the world's export trade during the early Thirties and, apart from World War II, has held it ever since. Rayon production was of necessity organized in large units from the beginning, but the weaving of rayon fabrics is carried on by a multiplicity of firms, most of which began in silk weaving. Before World War II Japan used substantial quantities of low-grade domestic and Manchurian pulp for the cheaper rayons; production of better fabrics has always largely depended on imported North American pulp. Japan is especially notable for its enormous production of rayon staple fiber, which was extensively used as a wool substitute; with increasing prosperity and growth of the woolen industry, staple-fiber production has been virtually stationary since the middle Fifties.

Apart from its temporary eclipse by the United States in the years immediately following World War II, Western Europe has always been the leading rayon-producing area. The industry first developed rapidly in Britain, which until 1913 was the world's leading producer. After 1920, despite considerable absolute growth, Britain's rayon production was exceeded in turn by that of the United States, Italy, Germany, and Japan. Britain's relative position among major producers improved considerably after 1945, however, as a result of a great expansion in the output of staple fiber; as in the United States, the greater part of the expansion of low-tenacity filament has consisted of acetate.

The British industry was long dominated

by two giant producers, Courtaulds, the old established Essex silk-weaving firm that pioneered the viscose process, and British Celanese, leaders of the acetate section. Courtaulds plants are located in most of the major traditional-textile areas, but some are situated in parts of the country where textiles have never been of significance; British Celanese, on the other hand, had all its facilities in one integrated plant near Derby.[12] Since 1957, when the two companies merged, production of cellulose fibers in Britain has been in the hands of a virtual monopoly.

Noncellulose or True Synthetic Fibers

The production of the true synthetic fibers is a part of the chemical industries; their development in the United States and the commanding position that the country holds in total world production—it accounted for about half the world output of over 1 billion pounds in 1960—indicate the enormous stature of the American chemical industries. In 1963 world production of true synthetic fibers approached that of rayon in the years before World War II (Table 18-9); it is, however, unlikely that the subsequent expansion of rayon output can be matched, in view of the slow growth of world textile consumption. In the late Fifties there was, in fact, considerable evidence of overcapacity; yet many countries were making substantial investment in additional true-synthetic-fiber plants. The best prospects for rapid growth of the true synthetics may well lie in greatly extended industrial applications, where many have indeed already made considerable penetration. Their most profitable employment at present, however, is as apparel fibers.

The true synthetics have many valuable properties; most resist abrasion, creasing, and shrinking and possess high tenacity and elasticity. On the other hand, while each is well fitted for a particular purpose, all have some disadvantages, and their high price in any case

[12] The location of this plant on the Derwent River would not have been possible if the present regulations concerning effluent disposal had been in force at the time of its establishment.

Table 18-9

Production of Noncellulose Synthetic Fibers, 1963 (Thousand metric tons)

	FILAMENT	STAPLE
United States	320	200
West Germany	58	50
France	38	28
Italy	49	29
Britain	52	31
Japan	109	131
U.S.S.R.*	11	18
Poland	48	56
WORLD TOTAL†	1,297	

* 1961.

† Excluding mainland China.

SOURCE: United Nations, *Monthly Bulletin of Statistics*, May, 1964.

prevents them from acting as general-purpose fibers. Increasing scale of operations, however, has already produced remarkable reductions in price.

About half the present output of true synthetics consists of polyamide-type fibers (nylon, Perlon); these are largely used unmixed, so that they are mainly produced as continuous filament, as is also the case with the polyacrylic fibers, the second most important group. The increasingly important polyester fibers (Terylene, Dacron) are mainly used in blends, however, so that production of polyester staple exceeds that of filament. The blending of true synthetics with natural fibers or with other synthetic fibers is becoming increasingly common, for in this way it is often possible to combine the desirable features of two fibers in one fabric. The polyacrylic fibers (Orlon, Acrilan, Courtelle), however, were largely developed as wool substitutes, and for certain purposes, such as women's knitwear, have proved superior to wool in some ways. While no synthetic fiber is likely to possess all the properties of wool, every one of wool's uses can expect to meet increasing competition from a particular synthetic fiber; the claim that "there is no substitute for wool," as the world's wool-growing and -marketing organizations constantly reiterate, is unlikely to be effective when it is abundantly clear to every housewife that there are many such substitutes.

It would seem that there are already too many true synthetic fibers; certainly there are many whose best fields of employment are still not entirely clear. This multiplicity of fibers arises from the number of competing chemical corporations, each with its own fiber or group of fibers, seeking a share of the market. Nevertheless, licensing agreements have permitted the production of the more important by companies other than the originators; Du Pont, discoverers of nylon, now produces only a small proportion of the nation's nylon output; Terylene, first developed in Britain, is produced by licensees in many other countries. While nylon-type fibers everywhere predominate, the availability or otherwise of local raw materials and the particular interests of the chemical companies concerned have produced certain national specialties; the United States, where wool is a high-cost fiber, is notable for its relatively large production of polyacrylic fibers; Japan is the world's largest producer of polyvinyl fibers; and Italy is acknowledged leader in polypropylene fibers.

The capital costs of a true-synthetic-fiber plant are huge, being some three times those of a rayon plant of equivalent output; for the production of polyester fibers a minimum plant capacity of 11 million pounds per year is necessary for economic operation.[13]

The location of the true-synthetic-fiber industry in the United States broadly corresponds with that of rayon and acetate; Virginia, Maryland, Pennsylvania, and Ohio have the largest number of plants, but manufacture is very dispersed, extending into southern New England, the Deep South, the Erie Lakeshore, the Ohio valley, and even into southern California. All of these are important centers of chemical production; the pull of the chemical industries thus appears greater than that of the textile areas; this observation also holds for Europe, where most plants are located in close proximity to major chemical-producing centers.

SELECTED REFERENCES

Airov, Joseph: *Location of the Synthetic Fiber Industry,* The Technology Press of the Massachusetts Institute of Technology, Cambridge, Mass., and John Wiley & Sons, Inc., New York, 1959.

Alderfer, E. B., and H. E. Michl: *Economics of American Industry,* McGraw-Hill Book Company, New York, 1957, pp. 323–432.

[13] Commonwealth Economic Committee, *Industrial Fibres,* H. M. Stationery Office, London, 1960, p. 105.

Allen, G. C.: *British Industries and Their Organization,* Longmans, Green & Co., Ltd., London, 1959, pp. 211–294.

———: *Japan's Economic Recovery,* Cambridge University Press, London, 1960, pp. 80–92.

Asian Textile Annual: Far Eastern Economic Review, Hong Kong, annually.

Board of Trade: *Working Party Reports,* H. M. Stationery Office, London, *Cotton,* 1946, *Hosiery,* 1946, *Lace,* 1947, *Wool,* 1947.

Commonwealth Economic Committee: *Industrial Fibres,* H. M. Stationery Office, London, annually.

Hague, D. C.: *The Economics of Man-made Fibres,* Gerald Duckworth & Co., Ltd., London, 1957.

International Federation of Cotton and Allied Textile Industries: *International Review,* Manchester, 1959, 1960, 1961, 1962.

———: *The Cotton Industry in a World Economy,* Manchester, 1958.

Keizo Seki: *The Cotton Industry of Japan,* Tokyo, 1956.

Nihon Boseki Kyokai: *The Story of the Japanese Cotton Textile Industry,* Osaka, 1957.

Ohara, S.: "From Cotton to Vinylon: A Short History of the Textile Industry," *Japan Quarterly,* vol. 4, pp. 510–518, 1957.

Organisation for Economic Cooperation and Development: *The Textile Industry in Europe 1960–61,* Paris, 1962.

Organisation for European Economic Cooperation: *The Future of the European Cotton Industry,* Paris, 1957.

Robson, R.: *The Cotton Industry in Britain,* Macmillan & Co., Ltd., London, 1957.

———: *The Man-made Fibres Industry,* Macmillan & Co., Ltd., London, 1958.

Rodgers, T. B.: "The Changing Geography of the Lancashire Cotton Industry," *Economic Geography,* vol. 38, pp. 299–314, 1962.

Smith, D. M.: "The Cotton Industry of the East Midlands," *Geography,* vol. 47, pp. 256–269, 1962.

Smith, Wilfred: *An Economic Geography of Great Britain,* Methuen & Co., Ltd., London, 1959, pp. 415–499.

Wallwork, K. L.: "The Cotton Industry in North West England," *Geography,* vol. 47, pp. 241–255, 1962.

Wool Trade Directory of the World, Thomas Skinner & Co. (Publishers), London, annually.

Chapter 19

CHEMICAL INDUSTRIES

Chemical industries rank with the fuel and power and metal industries as one of the main foundations of modern industrialized societies; hence, the encouragement of various kinds of chemical production receives considerable emphasis in the national development plans of many underdeveloped countries. In the more highly developed economies several branches of chemical production possess growth rates that are among the highest of any manufacturing activity.

So vast is the scope of the modern chemical industries that any definition of their content is largely arbitrary. In the United States it has been customary to distinguish between chemical-*manufacturing* industries directly engaged in the production of inorganic or organic chemicals and chemical-*processing* industries, such as the manufacture of soap, which use chemicals and other raw materials. This division, however, is extremely tenuous; almost all large producers of chemicals find themselves involved in processing in order to achieve economies of scale and to find markets for by-products, while large firms engaged in chemical-processing industries find themselves drawn into chemical manufacturing for similar reasons. The United States Census of Manufactures has an elaborate classification of "chemicals and allied products" which distinguishes the following major divisions, each of which is further subdivided: industrial inorganic chemicals; industrial organic chemicals; soap, detergents, and related products; drugs and medicines; paints, varnishes, and allied products; gum and wood chemicals; vegetable and animal oils; fertilizers; and miscellaneous chemical products. An even broader but very practical grouping is that used by Britain's Ministry of Labour, which in addition to the above activities includes coke ovens and gas manufacture and petroleum refining and related activities such as petrochemicals production within its "chemical and allied trades."

Any brief treatment of such a vast assemblage of activities must be highly selective, and in this chapter attention will be focused on the heavy-chemical industries (acids, alkalis, and certain organic chemicals), drugs and fine chemicals, plastics, and petrochemicals, the newest and one of the fastest-growing members of the diverse family of chemical industries.

HISTORICAL DEVELOPMENT AND WORLD ORGANIZATION

Chemical industries may be said to have commenced with the discovery of the art of smelting metals, and some knowledge of chemical processing must have been accumulated even in prehistoric times. The use of alum for tanning leather and for dyeing cloth was known to the Egyptians. The foundations of chemistry, however, were laid by the Arab alchemists who, in pursuing that chimera the transmutation of metals, acquired a considerable store of empirical knowledge and were the first to identify and use the important mineral acids. The Arabs were in all probability the first to use mineral substances in the treatment of disease, thus initiating the long and close connection of the chemical industries with medicine, a union that produced its first important fruit in the sixteenth century through the work of Paracelsus.

The growth of scientific inquiry from the seventeenth century onwards greatly expanded chemical knowledge; the work of Boyle, Lavoisier, and Dalton not only provided a rational explanation for much accumulated chemical knowledge but also made possible the enormous expansion of chemistry and its industrial applications during the nineteenth century. Not until the Industrial Revolution was well under way, however, did the full benefits of scientific reasoning become apparent; until 1845 the only formal training in chemistry available in Britain was that given in medical schools, and the first professor of the Royal College of Chemistry established in that year was a German.[1] The rapidly expanding British textile and metal industries involved an enormous increase in the production of acids, soda ash, and other chemicals, and from 1750 to about 1870 Britain maintained a supremacy in chemical production that matched its lead in the mechanical arts. But the founders of the British chemical industry, like their counterparts in textile and metal production, were largely practical men; until 1870 chemical industries remained largely extractive in character, being heavily dependent on the mining of bulky raw materials of relatively low value such as limestone, salt, pyrites, and coal, and chemical production itself remained largely empirical.

After 1870 the general chemical industries experienced a profound change; organic-chemicals and processing industries became of increasing importance, and natural products were supplemented, and in some cases supplanted, by chemically synthesized ones. England remained the largest producer of most acids and alkalis until the end of the century, but leadership of the chemical industries as a whole, and particularly of the organic section, passed to Germany, and shortly after the turn of the century both the United States and Germany surpassed Britain's production of heavy inorganic chemicals. Britain and the United States both depended heavily on Germany for their supplies of dyestuffs and other organic chemicals until World War I, when necessity forced a great development of organic-chemical industries in both countries.

The supremacy of Imperial Germany in the

[1] **T. K. Derry and T. I. Williams,** *A Short History of Technology,* **Oxford University Press, London, 1960, p. 271. The Royal College itself was largely established through the interest of Prince Albert, the German consort of Queen Victoria.**

chemical industries did not result from a superior endowment of physical resources. The country possessed valuable deposits of potash in Saxony and in Alsace, abundant lignite and bituminous coal, and an excellent system of water communications ideally suited for the carriage of bulky raw materials, but these advantages scarcely appear greater than those of England, where, in Lancashire and Cheshire and on the northeast coast, coal, limestone, and salt deposits occurred in close proximity. Moreover, Britain should have been the first to develop a large organic-chemicals industry, for Perkin, a young student of the new Royal College of Chemistry, discovered the first aniline dye in 1856 and was the first to begin production of this valuable range of coal-tar dyes. Thirteen years later Perkin was unfortunate in that his discovery of a method of synthesizing alizarin, the dye of the madder plant, had been independently discovered by Caro, a German chemist who had also worked in England and who had filed his patent a day earlier.

By 1870, however, the initiative had already been lost;[2] the old British empirical outlook contrasted strongly with the scientific tradition of the German universities and technical schools, and the close connections that were maintained between German universities and industry enabled new discoveries to be quickly exploited. The considerable encouragement to scientific investigation given by the German state strongly contrasted with the indifferent attitude of British officialdom, and with the passage of time this encouragement became powerfully reinforced by Germany's political ambitions; the country's dependence on imported industrial raw materials, which could always be cut off by British naval strength, could be reduced by the development of synthetic substitutes produced at home. In some cases these ersatz materials proved superior to the natural product and cheaper to produce; many German techniques eventually came to be widely copied, as was the case with the Haber-Bosch process for the fixation of atmospheric nitrogen. World War I, however, provided the stimulus to the British chemical industry that had so long been lacking, and shortly afterwards a fusion of the four leading chemical companies produced the giant Imperial Chemical Industries (ICI) organization, at present the largest chemical enterprise in Western Europe.

The chemical industries of the United States were slow to develop, although the largest chemical manufacturer, Du Pont, traces its origin to a black-powder mill erected in 1802. Heavy-chemical production only really commenced on a large scale after the Civil War; by the turn of the century, however, the United States had achieved the premier position in the production of sulfuric acid. This late start was in some ways advantageous; the United States never had a Leblanc soda plant and was able to use the experience of Europe in adopting the most efficient production techniques. In organic chemicals, the United States was scarcely less dependent than Britain on imports from Germany before World War I. The large orders placed by Britain and France with American manufacturers had already greatly stimulated the production of organic chemicals before the country entered World War I, however, and as German patents became available to American manufacturers, output rose rapidly. By 1920 the United States possessed the world's largest chemical industry.

After World War I the German chemical industry showed remarkable powers of recovery, and through the work of the I.G. Farben company the Germany of the Thirties became the world's largest producer of synthetic rubber, synthetic petroleum, synthetic nitrates, rayon staple fiber, aluminum, and

[2] The first research laboratory established by a British chemical company did not appear until 1891.

magnesium; as a result, Hitler's Germany was an even more formidable adversary than that of Wilhelm II. These powers of recovery were again strikingly demonstrated after World War II.

Russia and Japan both began their chemical industries much later than the other major producers, and in both the state took an active part in development. Until World War I Japanese chemical production was very small—the country produced less than 100,000 tons of sulfuric acid in 1914—but with the cutting off of imports Japanese chemical production rapidly expanded, and it maintained a very high growth rate throughout the interwar period; by the outbreak of World War II Japanese production of sulfuric acid exceeded that of every other producer except the United States. Russian chemical production was only slightly larger than that of Japan before World War I, and the appearance of the country as a major producer of heavy chemicals came only with the First and Second Five Year Plans. The U.S.S.R. is now the world's second-largest producer of most acids and alkalis, but output is still only about half that of the United States.

Structure and Characteristics of the Industries

The chemical industries produce an enormous variety of substances, whose range continually increases. Output of many of these newer products has shown an especially high growth rate in the United States; some 40 per cent of the gross sales of American chemical companies is made up of products unknown some two decades ago.

There are more than 3,000 chemical firms operating in the United States, but many of these are blenders or processors of chemicals produced by others; the output of key inorganic and organic chemicals is everywhere in the hands of a few giant corporations, and the structure of the chemical industries is mainly one of monopolistic competition or oligopoly; in several countries, indeed, the production of these key chemicals is monopolized by one organization. It is only in chemicals and petroleum production that the size of units in other major producers matches the giant enterprises of the United States, and the national economies of most European countries can only support one such organization—ICI in Britain, Rhône-Poulenc in France, Union Chimique in Belgium, Montecatini in Italy, and I.G. Farben in interwar Germany. The economy of the United States, however, supports about a dozen really large units of which three—Du Pont (which slightly outranks ICI for the position of the world's largest chemical organization), Union Carbide, and Montsanto are of outstandingly large size.

In many branches of chemical production, and particularly in heavy chemicals, which make use of raw materials of considerable bulk and low value, large units are mandatory as the economies of scale are very great. Also, many chemical reactions yield by-products, and manufacturers are often drawn into other lines of production in order to provide a market for them. The fact that the industry is its own best customer, recycling many products into other branches of production, also encourages the development of great integrated organizations (Fig. 19-1); by reaching backwards to the control of the raw materials, such as salt, pyrites, anhydrite, limestone, and even coal, and forwards into the production of dyes, textiles, paints, fertilizers, and pharmaceuticals, the great chemical companies are able to secure the maximum number of openings for both main and subsidiary products. The corrosive nature of many chemical processes and the rapidity with which plant and processes become obsolete necessitate access to vast financial re-

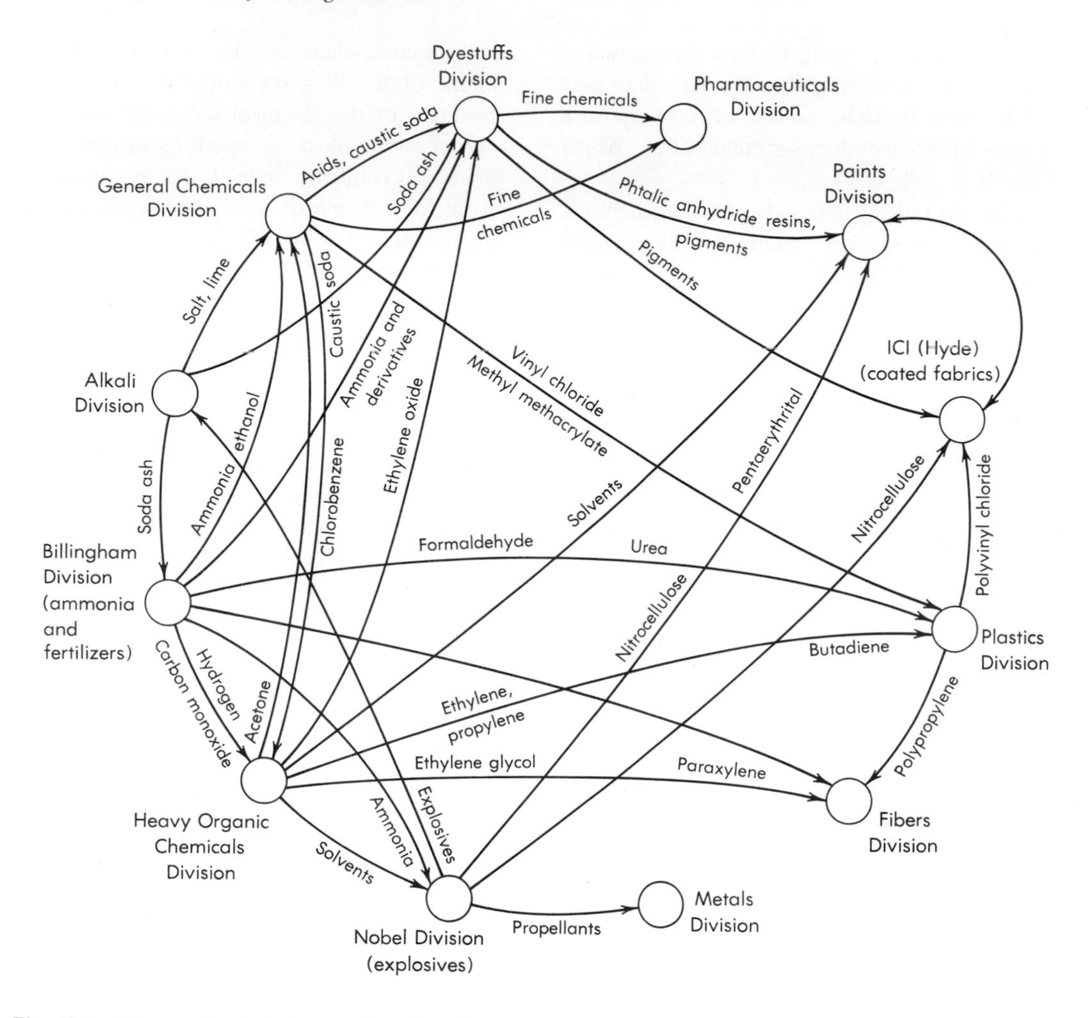

Fig. 19-1 The complex interchange of products between divisions.
The Imperial Chemical Industries is Europe's largest chemical corporation. (ICI.)

sources and so also make for concentration. Built-in obsolescence may perhaps be said to originate in the chemical industries; few other industries regularly spend such a high proportion of gross receipts on research, and many old established chemical industries have been wrecked by the introduction of lower-cost processes. Concentration avoids such problems, and ensures that the very large research budget pays handsome dividends; to produce nylon involved the Du Pont Company in an expenditure of some 45 million dollars.[3]

As in the automobile and steel industries, price competition between the major chemical producers is virtually absent; each respects the others' price structure, and there are "gentle-

[3] **Terylene was discovered by the British Calico Research organization with only a very modest expenditure; but British Calico Research was unable to use the discovery, and to bring Terylene into commercial production involved ICI in an expenditure of some 30 million dollars.**

men's agreements" over division of territories. Until 1952, when they were terminated by Federal injunction, Du Pont had numerous connections with ICI; and the two companies operated joint-owned subsidiaries in a number of countries. Before World War II, I.G. Farben also had a number of agreements with American chemical companies, as a result of which some of the most famous American firms in chemicals were convicted of having conspired to withhold certain essential chemicals from the Allies. It is rare that one or another of the great American companies is not facing an antitrust suit, a situation that has encouraged the practice of licensing patents to other producers.

From time to time the development of new products has resulted in outbreaks of price competition through dumping, as producers endeavor to keep plants operating at capacity by exporting marginal output at very low prices; protected by an extremely high tariff wall, American producers have occasionally found this solution to the problem of temporary overcapacity irresistible, much to the irritation of smaller European chemical producers. But on the whole, the rate of growth of the chemical industries leaves scope for almost every producer, and in the United States some of the smaller companies have had extremely high growth rates in comparison with the leading companies. Moreover, increase in scientific knowledge is so rapid that it cannot be monopolized even by the largest producers; the way is thus still open for new entrants, and newcomers continue to achieve considerable success, in the pharmaceuticals and fine-chemicals sections particularly.

Chemical plants tend to employ little labor in relation to the large floor space they occupy; because most operations are automatically controlled, a small highly trained technical staff can operate a large plant with only a small unskilled labor force.

HEAVY CHEMICALS

The heavy-chemicals division of the chemical industries usually includes the production of certain key chemicals such as mineral acids, alkalis, soda ash, and, among organic chemicals, alcohols and their derivatives; it can also include the gasification and hydrogenation of coal or lignite, the manufacture of fertilizers and explosives, electrochemicals, and a considerable portion of the petrochemicals industry. All these activities constitute heavy industries as defined in Chapter 11, and so will be dealt with in this section, with one exception: for convenience, and in view of its close connection with petroleum refining, the petrochemicals industry will be considered separately.

The heavy chemicals are produced in very large quantities—world output of sulfuric acid in 1960 was about 60 million tons—from bulky and inexpensive raw materials (Table 19-1). Although much electric energy is used in the production of certain alkalis and fertilizers, the heavy-chemicals division uses considerable quantities of fuel, especially coal, which is frequently an important raw material as well as a source of heat. The manufacture of heavy chemicals also requires copious quantities of water and generates considerable quantities of effluent and waste products. The British Alkali Act of 1863, designed to restrain soda manufacturers using the old Leblanc process from liberating toxic hydrochloric acid gas into the atmosphere, was the first of many regulations aimed at preventing stream and air pollution. Economic efficiency reinforces such legal sanctions by compelling manufacturers to find uses for all by-products wherever possible, but the necessity for effluent disposal is still an important factor in the siting of heavy-chemical plants. Certain types of production, in which workers come in contact with poisonous or injurious substances or in which toxic sub-

Table 19-1

Production of Sulfuric Acid, 1963 (Thousand metric tons)

United States	18,610
Canada*	1,760
West Germany	8,640
France	2,150
Italy	2,510
Belgium*	1,580
Britain	2,930
Spain	1,440
India	520
Japan	4,990
Australia	1,270
U.S.S.R.	6,900
East Germany	860
Poland	880
Czechoslovakia	720
Mainland China†	1,100
TOTAL	56,860

* 1961.
† 1959.
SOURCE: United Nations, *Statistical Yearbook*, 1962; *Monthly Bulletin of Statistics*, May, 1964.

stances are emitted into the air or into rivers, are legally designated "noxious industries"; for such production the siting of plants and their effluent disposal are rigorously controlled.

Sulfuric Acid Sulfuric acid is probably the most important product of the heavy-chemicals division in that it is essential for the preparation of most other acids and alkalis and of an enormous range of organic chemicals. It is used in the manufacture of fertilizers, particularly superphosphates; fertilizer production accounts for about one-quarter of total consumption in the United States and Britain. It is also used in the manufacture of rayon and paper, in petroleum refining, and in glassmaking. Like many chemicals, sulfuric acid is not, of course, a homogeneous product; for many industries a cheap, relatively weak, and impure acid is perfectly satisfactory, but for the manufacture of coal-tar dyestuffs, explosives, and other organic chemicals, a pure and highly concentrated acid (commercially known as oleum) is necessary.

Sulfuric acid is produced by burning sulfur or pyrites; in Britain, Japan, and the United States elemental sulfur is mainly used, but in Continental Europe pyrites is the main raw material. Britain imports considerable quantities of sulfur from the United States, where it occurs in association with the salt domes of the Gulf Coast of Texas and Louisiana; the Frasch process introduced in 1898 enabled sulfur to be raised very cheaply and greatly stimulated sulfuric acid production. American sulfur reserves, however, gave rise to some concern, and in the Fifties the long worked deposits of Sicily began to receive new attention. Sulfur deposits occur in many volcanic areas, but isolation and costs of extraction limit production except where large markets exist close at hand, as in Italy and Japan.

Sulfuric acid was first made in industrial quantities in the eighteenth century; in 1746 Roebuck introduced the "lead chamber" process, which, with modifications, was of major importance in Britain until World War I. Though satisfactory for many purposes, chamber acid was unsuitable for the rapidly expanding organic-chemicals industry; but suitable concentration acid could be cheaply produced by the "contact" process, in which sulfur dioxide is made to combine with oxygen by passing the gases over finely divided platinum, which acts as a catalyst. Discovered in 1831 by Phillips, a Bristol vinegar manufacturer, the new process, like the later discoveries of Perkin and of Gilchrist and Thomas, did not establish itself in the land of its origin; in Continental Europe, however, and particularly in Germany, the contact process made great strides, particularly after 1870. German chemists discovered how to substitute cheaper catalysts for expensive platinum; in the United States, where the process spread rapidly after 1890, vanadium was also employed. Small-scale production of oleum by the contact process began in Britain in the last quarter of the nineteenth century, but it was not until World War I, when new plants had to be hastily constructed, that the process began to achieve the significance that it had acquired elsewhere. Some sulfuric acid is also produced as a by-product of coal gasification and petroleum refining, and some from lead and zinc smelters.

Alkalis Although sulfuric acid has wide industrial applications, usually about 40 per cent of the output is consumed where produced, mainly in the manufacture of other acids, alkalis, fertilizers, and organic chemicals. Alkalis are extensively used in the manufacture of glass, textiles, and soap, and their production has been the subject of fierce and prolonged competition between rival processes.

The beginnings of the modern alkali industries date from the discovery by the French chemist Leblanc of a method of making soda ash in commercial quantities from common salt by treating the salt with sulfuric acid and heating the product with limestone and coal. The Leblanc process was developed in France at the end of the eighteenth century in order to offset that country's inability to import natron in the face of British sea power, but it was Britain that prospered most from the new process. Having a very favorable juxtaposition of the required raw materials, Britain was scarcely challenged in soda production until the appearance of the Solvay, or ammonia soda, process, first used in Belgium in 1863. The Solvay process produced purer soda, and at lower cost, than that made by the old Leblanc process, which for every ton of soda ash produced two tons of foul-smelling alkali waste. The competition of ammonia soda led to combination among the Leblanc producers and to attempts to recover salable products from the waste materials; as a result the old process continued in operation for a further half-century, but it is now entirely defunct.

Both the Leblanc and Solvay processes yield caustic soda as a by-product, but in the last quarter of the nineteenth century a number of methods were introduced for producing caustic soda by electrolysis of brine. This also liberates chlorine, which is much used in the preparation of bleaching powder for the textile and paper industries, and is also essential in intermediate stages of synthetic-dye manufacture.

Caustic soda is an important raw material

of the soap and glass industries, but as other raw materials are of greater significance to these industries, the major chemical companies do not themselves engage in soap or glass manufacture. Soap is prepared by boiling fats with caustic soda, and preoccupation with vegetable and animal fats and oils can lead to the development of great vertically integrated enterprises. The world's largest producer of soap, margarine, and hydrogenated fats is the British-Dutch Unilever combine, one of the world's largest enterprises, with plantations in Africa, Southeast Asia, and the Pacific islands and with large interests in trading and in the food industries. The manufacture of improved and special-purpose soaps, however, brings the soap manufacturers squarely into the compass of the chemical industries, for by the addition of active oxygen in the form of persulfates, percarbonates, and perborates, soap can be given valuable bleaching and disinfecting properties. Over the last decade soap has received considerable competition from the soapless detergents made by sulfonating fatty acids, a development which, as already noted, has greatly affected the market for vegetable oils.[4] Unilever's principal competitor is the American Procter & Gamble organization of Cincinnati, which also has many foreign subsidiaries; but the variety of soaps and toilet preparations is so wide that many manufacturers still survive despite the extravagant advertising budgets of the giant international corporations.

Fertilizers Closely associated with the manufacture of acids is the production of artificial fertilizers. Ammonium sulfate, a nitrogenous fertilizer, is produced as a by-product of coal gasification and coke ovens, but towards the end of the nineteenth century attention was turned towards supplementing the world's deposits of natural nitrates by artificial fertilizers produced by the fixation of atmospheric nitrogen. Some of the earlier methods such as the arc and cyanamide processes used considerable quantities of electric energy and so were restricted to areas of cheap hydroelectric power; they were rendered obsolete, however, by the Haber-Bosch process, perfected in 1913, in which hydrogen and nitrogen under pressure are made to combine to form ammonia. The Haber-Bosch process is one of the greatest of the many German contributions to the chemical industries, and although it considerably increased Imperial Germany's military strength, its positive benefits have been profound. Synthetic fertilizers produced by this process now account for more than two-thirds of world nitrogenous-fertilizer production; the first British plant came into operation in 1925 and the first American plant in 1927. The erection of Haber-Bosch plants occupies a prominent place in the development plans of many underdeveloped countries.

Phosphatic fertilizers are produced by treating natural phosphates with sulfuric acid, thus producing superphosphate; phosphate rock deposits occur in Florida, in North Africa, and in the Pacific on Nauru, Ocean, and Christmas Islands.

Explosives The manufacture of synthetic dyestuffs and explosives requires fuming sulfuric acid (oleum), but strictly speaking, both are branches of the organic-chemical industries. Nitrocellulose, the first major advance on gunpowder, which had remained virtually unchanged since the thirteenth century, was first manufactured commercially in the middle nineteenth century by treating cotton with nitric and sulfuric acid, and another powerful explosive, nitroglycerin, produced by nitrating glycerin (a by-product of the soap and fats industry), was discovered almost contemporaneously. The manufacture of both explosives was attended with great hazard, however. The foundations of the modern explosives industry were laid by the Swedish chemist Nobel, who

[4] See p. 141.

As fertilizer pours from an overhead conveyor in this Japanese chemical plant, it is bagged and loaded by hand. The use of capital-intensive and labor-intensive methods within the same plant is common in several Japanese industries, and reflects the old feudal obligations of the employer towards his workers.

rendered nitroglycerin "safe" by absorbing it in a diatomaceous clay known as kieselguhr, to produce dynamite; gelignite, or blasting gelatin, was first produced commercially by Nobel in the Eighties. Nobel's work, however, also included the development of detonators, without which these "safe" explosives could not be fired. Nobel was granted patents for production in both Britain and in the United States; in the former he came into prolonged legal conflict with the British government, which had developed the highly explosive lyddite (picric acid) by nitrating phenol, a product of the coal-tar industry. Coal tar also yields toluene, by nitrating which the very powerful explosive TNT is produced; toluene, however, can be produced less expensively by petroleum refineries.

The first factories for the production of nitroglycerin were situated on hillsides, and movement of liquids was effected by gravity so that no explosive material could remain in the pumping equipment;[5] and over the years there has been considerable safety-increasing improvement in manufacturing processes. The manufacture of explosives will always retain a certain degree of hazard, however, and works are therefore situated well away from habitation, usually on alluvial marshland.

Alcohol and Fuel-chemical Industries Other important branches of the heavy-chemical industries are the industrial alcohols and the fuel-chemicals industries. Alcohols are widely used for many industrial purposes and are most cheaply produced from grains or from other vegetable material; shortly after World War I, however, I.G. Farben began to manufacture methyl alcohol, formerly derived from wood distillation, by the direct combination of hydrogen and carbon monoxide at high temperature and pressure.

Hydrogen and carbon monoxide are constituents of water gas, which is produced by passing steam over red-hot coke, a process known since the mid-nineteenth century. This process is discontinuous, for in the passage of steam the temperature of the coke is greatly lowered. A number of improvements have been made in this long familiar technique, of which one of the most successful is the Fischer-Tropsch process in which the reaction is rendered continuous, and the resulting gases are combined in the presence of a catalyst into liquid hydrocarbons.

The Fischer-Tropsch process was greatly improved during World War II, when it considerably supplemented Germany's production of synthetic fuels; this had originated before World War I when Bergius succeeded in hydrogenating powdered coal by a blast of hydrogen at high temperature and pressure. The hydrogenation of coal is not normally economic in the face of competition from petroleum, but it was undertaken in interwar Europe to cope with unemployment in the coal industry, and from the strategic viewpoint, it has many attractions for countries rich in coal but lacking petroleum fields. Perhaps the most remarkable example of the application of the Fischer-Tropsch process is to be found in South Africa, where SASOL, a state-owned corporation, is engaged in developing a giant plant at Vereeniging that will make the country independent of oil imports in an emergency. Because of cheap African labor the costs of coal production in South Africa are the lowest in the world, but the project appears largely inspired by political motives.

Shortly before World War II Germany made yet another remarkable contribution to the fuel industries, the Lurgi process, in which brown coal is hydrogenated to produce methane, the main constituent of natural gas. Lurgi plants have been erected to produce methane as a feedstock for the production of organic chemicals in the lignite fields of Texas and

[5] Derry and Williams, *op. cit.*, p. 548.

for the production of gas and synthetic fuels from the brown-coal deposits of eastern Victoria in Australia.

Two further branches of the heavy-chemical industries may be noted—the liquefaction of air to produce industrial gases, and electrochemicals, to which some reference has already been made. Electrochemicals are of particular interest in relation to industrial location, because certain chemical activities can only be carried on where cheap electric energy is available, and in the past this requirement has largely restricted them to areas possessing hydroelectric plants; such activities include the manufacture of calcium carbide and cyanamide, the reduction of aluminum, magnesium, and other metals, and the production of heavy water and other operations of significance in the preparation of fissionable material.

In conclusion, one other locational factor may be mentioned. The close interconnection of certain chemicals, such as sulfuric acid and coal-tar derivatives, which have repeatedly been mentioned above, is a powerful factor making for the appearance of giant agglomerations of heavy-chemical industries in plants that may extend continuously for 2 miles or more. Such concentrations are found on the Gulf Coast and on the mid-Atlantic seaboard of the United States, in the Teeside district of Britain, and in the lower Rhineland of West Germany. The rapid development of the petrochemicals industry is accelerating this trend towards the development of giant complexes of interconnected plants.

FINE CHEMICALS AND PHARMACEUTICALS

In contrast to the heavy chemicals, whose annual production, usually in continuous processes, runs into hundreds of millions of tons, fine chemicals and pharmaceuticals are produced in small amounts, usually by "batch" production methods. Drugs and medicines have to be produced to critical specifications, so that the most rigorous control of ingredients is necessary, and value of output is very high; although drugs and medicines account for only about 0.5 per cent of the weight of synthetic organic chemicals produced in the United States, they make up one-third of the value added in manufacture of organic chemicals. Fine chemicals industries include disinfectants and antiseptics, flavors and essences, veterinary products, rubber chemicals, plastics, and resins; some of these are produced with as meticulous a care as for the production of drugs, but others such as synthetic rubber and plastics, however, are now produced on so large a scale that they merit separate consideration.

The pharmaceuticals industry works so closely with medicine and the medical sciences that although several of the great chemical companies have important pharmaceuticals divisions, that of Bayer being particularly famous, much of the industry is in the hands of specialists. Certain common drugs and medicines are also produced in large quantities by manufacturers with other interests such as soap and toilet preparations, and numerous small enterprises produce proprietary medicines, generally of minimal therapeutic value, from ingredients produced by others. Several countries at a high level of economic development without well-established heavy-chemical industries have developed their own pharmaceutical industries, as the most important requisite for industry is not local physical resources or great accumulations of capital, as in most of the heavy-chemicals industries, but scientific manpower; raw materials are small in bulk and may be easily imported, and small-scale batch methods of production are often mandatory to ensure complete control of quality. The pharmaceuticals industry, however, is expanding even more rapidly than chemical industries as a whole, and for the development of new lines, considerable financial resources are necessary in order to maintain a large research budget. Quantity production of a new drug may also demand considerable feats of pharmaceutical engineering; penicillin was developed in Britain during World War II, but at that time the physical resources for its manufacture could not be made available there, and these had to be sought in the United States.

Even as late as the outbreak of World War II Germany, with its well-organized organic-chemicals industry, occupied a commanding position in pharmaceuticals, but as in organic chemicals the United States is now dominant. Switzerland also occupies a position of considerable significance as a drug producer; American and Swiss firms together control about two-thirds of the drug production of Britain. The foreign manufacturing subsidiaries that have been established by several of the great American drug houses, such as Parke Davis, Pfizer, and Merck, have often done considerably better financially than local companies.[6] This has caused some irritation, but American drug companies insist that as their subsidiaries enjoy the fruits of their parents' research, part of the research cost must be debited to subsidiaries, which must therefore earn a high rate of profit. However, some countries, such as Italy, which have been slow to recognize foreign patents on pharmaceutical products, have been able to undercut the patentee's price, and to build up a considerable export trade in some lines. The most rapidly growing pharmaceutical industry, however, is probably that of Japan, and the widespread incursion of Japanese drugs into world markets can confidently be expected in the near future.

Geographically, the pharmaceuticals industry is a footloose one; raw materials exercise little influence in location, and great metropolitan centers which are the main markets and sources of scientific manpower are a considerable attraction. There are several examples of indeterminacy in the industry's location pattern; one of Britain's largest manufacturers is located at Nottingham, the home of the founder of the company. The desirability of clean air free from contamination has also exerted some influence, so that small country towns have occasionally been selected as sites for the industry.

The very high returns that can be earned in the pharmaceuticals industry are a strong encouragement to new entrants, especially as there is scope for the smaller firm. The industry is increasingly attractive to food manufacturers, particularly those specializing in the production of infant and invalid foods; in Europe these industries also tend to be located in smaller country towns.

In contrast to the heavy-chemicals industries, which employ mainly male labor, pharmaceuticals tends largely to be an industry in which female labor predominates.

PLASTICS

Few branches of manufacturing industry have grown as fast and as late as the plastics; although certain cellulose plastics have been known for over a century, the great expansion of plastics production has come only since 1920. Plastics can be substitutes for metals, glass, wood, or natural fibers, but many have special properties of their own. Some are very

[6] A British investigation of 1961 showed that even allowing to subsidiaries of American drug companies a share of the research costs of their parents, the rate of profit averaged 35 per cent, compared with 20 per cent for British firms and 13 per cent for Swiss firms. (*The Economist,* p. 66, vol. 201, 1961). The popularity of American drugs in Britain is in part based on convenience, for they are marketed under registered names; British manufactured drugs are largely marketed under the chemical name, which can be of considerable length.

cheap and others are very expensive, but an increasing scale of output can be expected to lower the prices of the dearer kinds, and even the fact that some plastics are now highly priced does not mean that articles made from them must also be expensive; the low specific gravity of plastic articles means that a little can go a long way.

The production of plastics underwent a rapid and enforced expansion during World War II, when the substitution possibilities of these versatile materials received maximum emphasis. As a result plastics were sometimes employed in uses for which they were not well suited; since the war, however, there has been a tendency to concentrate more on those uses in which the special properties of plastics can be employed to best advantage. Free world output of plastics appears to have been around 300,000 tons in 1939 and 500,000 tons in 1949, but it was about 8.5 million tons in 1963 (Table 19-2). Such a high growth rate, of course, cannot be sustained indefinitely, and there is a considerable problem of overcapacity in several lines of production.

Plastics are substances that at some stage can be made to flow without losing cohesion; they can be molded into a required shape and made to retain it. The ease with which they can be molded in quantity, the fact that many can be given attractive colors and varying degrees of opacity, and their strength, lightness, and resistance to most chemicals are the main reasons for their widespread use. Plastics consist of long-chain carbon-containing molecules known as polymers; such structures occur naturally in rubber, cellulose, and shellac, but most modern plastics are synthesized from organic raw materials such as coal tar and petroleum products. The silicon atom somewhat resembles that of carbon in its ability to form molecules capable of being polymerized, and there is a range of silicon, or inorganic, plastics; most, however, are too expensive to find wide employment.

Plastics are usually grouped into two classes, the thermosoftening and the thermohardening. The *thermosoftening (thermoplastic) plastics* soften on heating and subsequently harden. Among the more important thermosoftening plastics are the cellulose derivatives; polyethylene, used in the manufacture of

Table 19-2

Production of Industrial Plastics and Resins, 1963 (Thousand metric tons)

United States	3,780
West Germany	1,428
France	322
Britain	796
Japan	1,404
Australia	84
East Germany	96
Poland	92
WORLD TOTAL*	8,300

* Excluding U.S.S.R. and mainland China.

SOURCE: United Nations, *Monthly Bulletin of Statistics*, May, 1964.

squeeze bottles and possessing remarkable electric properties; polystyrene, a cheap plastic easily molded into shapes of great complexity; polyvinyls, of which there is a considerable number and which are capable of forming either soft or hard substances; polyamides, such as nylon; polyacrylics, one of the most important of which is Perspex, much used in the aircraft industry and in dentistry; and polyesters, which in some ways can be regarded as an intermediate group. Many of these thermoplastics can be used to produce fibers, and this was often their first commercial application.

The *thermohardening (thermosetting) plastics,* which harden on heating, are produced in greater quantities and are the older group. They include the dark phenol plastics, much used in electrical appliance moldings, and the similar amino plastics, which can be produced in bright colors. The thermosetting plastics are also employed in the manufacture of laminated materials, adhesives, and protective coatings. The use of polyester and epoxy resins in conjunction with fiber glass produces a material as strong as steel and resistant to corrosion; moreover, since no pressure is needed, the most complex shapes can be cheaply produced.

Industrial plastics are produced as resins, powders, or pellets and in rods, tubes, or sheets for further processing by manufacturers of plastic articles. Thermoset-plastic articles are produced by compression molding, in which the plastic powder is heated and compressed in the mold itself. Injection molding, in which the plastic material is heated externally and is then gradually forced into the mold, is employed for the production of articles from thermoplastics. A somewhat similar technique is extrusion, in which the heated plastic is forced through a die or orifice. The production of industrial plastics takes place in large plants, often themselves part of a larger plant complex. In contrast to industrial plastics production, molding is still a relatively simple industry in which there is a great deal of cutthroat competition.

The United States accounts for about half the free world output of plastics, the next-largest producers being West Germany and Britain; per capita consumption in the two largest European producers, however, is less than half that of the United States.

Synthetic Rubber

Synthetic rubber can be regarded as a special kind of plastic, but the scale of operations and the conjunction of the industrial giants of the petroleum, chemical, and rubber industries set it apart from other branches of plastic production. Synthetic rubber was first developed by Germany and was employed by that country on a small scale in World War I, but acceptable substitutes for natural rubber in most fields of employment did not eventuate until the Thirties; at that time, under its policy of achieving maximum national self-sufficiency, Germany developed the "Buna" rubbers, derived from butadiene, a product of petroleum refining. In 1936 Germany first produced the general-purpose rubber Buna S, a copolymer of butadiene and styrene, which was followed by the special-purpose Buna N, a copolymer of butadiene and acrylonitrile. The U.S.S.R. also took steps in the Thirties to increase its self-sufficiency in rubber, both through the manufacture of synthetic rubbers and through the cultivation of other rubber-bearing plants; at the outbreak of World War II, Germany and the U.S.S.R. were the only synthetic-rubber producers of major significance.

The interest of the United States in synthetic rubber dates from the early Twenties and was sharpened by the Stevenson restriction scheme in British-controlled natural-rubber-producing territories, which forced up the price of natural rubber. Thiokol, a material which possesses some of the properties of natural rubber and which has found new employment as a rocket fuel, was commercially produced in 1931 and was closely followed by Du Pont's acetylene- and chlorine-derived material later named neoprene; butyl, a copolymer of butylene and butadiene, was developed by Jersey Standard shortly before World War II. All of these rubbers, however, were special-purpose rubbers resistant to oils and solvents. The United States, with access to the natural rubber of Southeast Asia, where costs of production were only about a third of those of synthetic general-purpose rubbers, lacked the incentive to develop a large synthetic industry until World War II, when the Japanese occupation of Southeast Asia deprived the Allies of all but a very small proportion of the world's natural-rubber supply.

Under the stimulus of the war emergency a massive synthetic-rubber industry was rapidly created, and at the end of the war the United States emerged as the world's largest rubber producer, a position it has held ever since (Table 19-3). Peak wartime output was nearly 835,000 tons, of which GR-S (government rubber, styrene type), the American designation for Buna S, accounted for some 85 per cent. Some twenty-seven plants were erected, about half of which were located in east Texas and Louisiana and half in the Northeast; one was sited in the Los Angeles area and one in Canada (Sarnia). During the

Table 19-3

Production of Synthetic Rubber, 1963 (Thousand metric tons)

United States	1,633
S-type	1,178
Neoprene	131
Butyl	109
N-type	48
Stereoregular	142
Canada	182
West Germany	108
France	98
Italy	95
Netherlands	86
Britain	129
Japan	87
Poland	36
East Germany	89
TOTAL	2,543

SOURCE: International Rubber Study Group, *Statistical Bulletin*, May, 1964; United Nations, *Monthly Bulletin of Statistics*, May, 1964.

war it was necessary to resort to grain-produced alcohol for part of the butadiene and to coal tar for part of the styrene requirements of the copolymer plants; at present both of these materials are derived from the petrochemicals industry.

In 1955 the United States government sold its plants to private enterprises owned jointly by the "Big Four" American rubber companies and by leading oil companies. In order to safeguard its investment, the United States government compelled rubber manufacturers to use not less than 40 per cent of synthetic rubber in total consumption, but as natural rubber had commanded a premium until 1963 most manufacturers have used a considerably higher percentage than this. The stability of synthetic-rubber prices has also encouraged the use of synthetic rubbers. In 1960 the so-called "stereoregular" rubbers (polybutadienes and polyisoprenes), chemically identical with natural rubber, were introduced, and by 1965 it is possible that rubbers of this type will account for about a fifth of the synthetic-rubber production of the United States.

Natural rubber, however, can be produced at a price no synthetic can match as a result of the development of high-yielding clones yielding up to 3,000 pounds per acre, and it seems probable than the new synthetics will continue to be used in conjunction with natural rubber. It is clear, however, that a steadily larger share of world rubber consumption will be met by synthetic rubber, as the opportunities for the rapid expansion of natural-rubber production are limited, and total consumption is likely to increase steadily as the output of motor vehicles augments and as new uses are discovered for rubber; by 1975 it could reach a level of 7 million tons. The United States output of synthetic rubber is now well above the World War II peak, and several new plants have been built, while the number of synthetic-rubber producers in the world continues to grow. Britain, which has substantial interests in natural-rubber production and whose Colonial Office long opposed the establishment of a synthetic industry, became the third-largest producer of the free world in 1961, and the industry is well established in France, Italy, West Germany, and Japan; the Eastern bloc countries are also endeavoring substantially to raise their production of synthetic rubber. This great expansion of synthetic-rubber production has been closely connected with the growth of the petrochemicals industry.

PETROCHEMICALS

The rapidly increasing importance of the petrochemicals industry has already become apparent; its growth represents, perhaps, the most important development in chemical industries in the present century. The use of petroleum products as a source of chemical raw materials dates from 1922 and originated in connection with early attempts in the United States to produce a synthetic rubber. The period of really rapid expansion, however, did not come until after World War II, and arose from the technological improvements in refining which made a market-oriented refining industry possible. From the Gulf Coast of the United States the petrochemicals industry has spread to all countries that are large consumers of petroleum products and that have therefore acquired large refining industries in the postwar period. It is possible that in the not distant future the petrochemicals industry will also establish itself in the Middle East and in the Caribbean.

The petrochemicals industry is essentially part of the organic-chemicals industries, whose main raw materials have traditionally been coal tar and other products of coal distillation and alcohol derived from grain or molasses. The petrochemicals industry provides hydro-

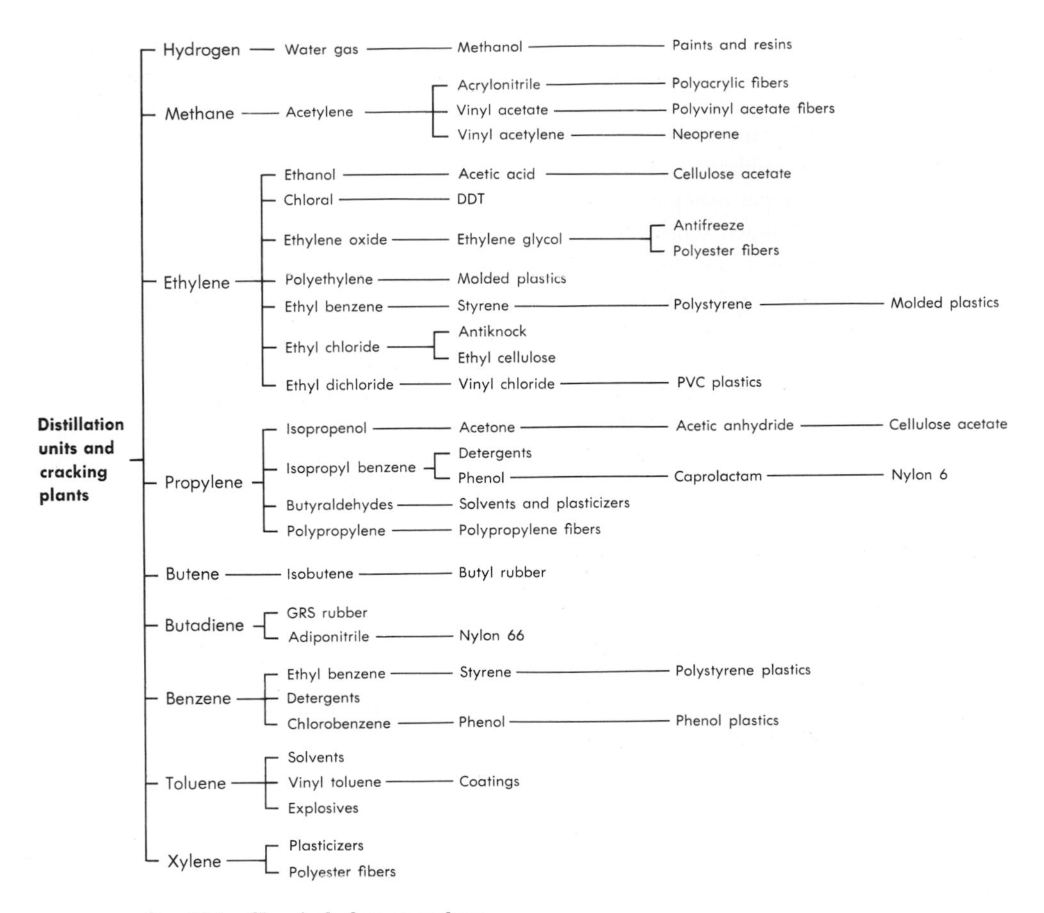

Fig. 19-2 Chemicals from petroleum.

carbons for the synthesis of other organic chemicals very much more cheaply than any other source, and particularly the unsaturated hydrocarbons, which have a remarkable capacity for chemical reaction. Acetylene, ethylene, and propylene are three of the most useful chemical "building blocks" produced by the petrochemicals industry; the first, which is extremely reactive, has traditionally been produced from calcium carbide, the manufacture of which involves the use of considerable quantities of electric energy. From these simple substances a remarkable range of products has been developed, including some which are identical with and compete with coal-tar derivatives but also others which are completely new and have fields of employment that are far from clearly defined. Petrochemical producers, in fact, have been obliged to spend considerable sums in finding uses for the new substances they have produced, for many of these have never before been available in quantity and at prices sufficiently attractive for commercial exploitation (Fig. 19-2). Among the more important products of the petrochemicals industry are raw materials for the plastics and synthetic-rubber industries, pharmaceuticals, insecticides, fungicides, and weed killers; one weed killer, known as 2-4-D, is also finding a use as a yield stimulus in the natural-rubber industry, some slight compensation perhaps for the contribution of petrochemicals to the production of synthetic rubber.[7]

The development of petrochemicals, with which could also be included those chemical industries based on natural gas, not only has made possible the development of large organic-chemical industries in countries such as Italy which were formerly handicapped by lack of raw materials but also has greatly assisted old producers such as Britain which had failed to keep abreast of technology in organic-chemical industries based on other fuels. It has also brought the great chemical and petroleum companies into competition—but on balance there is more collusion than collision. Existing agglomerations of chemical plants have found it highly desirable to add petrochemical plants, while large refineries have found the addition of chemical units equally advantageous. The petrochemicals industry has thus acted as a powerful stimulus to the growth of the giant complexes of chemical plants already noted.

THE UNITED STATES AND OTHER MAJOR CHEMICAL PRODUCERS

The United States possesses the world's largest complex of chemical industries, with a total value of output exceeding that of the EEC and Britain combined; the value of output per worker is more than three times the average for Western Europe, a result of rapid expansion in the most capital-intensive lines of production. What is surprising, in view of the great wealth of the country in raw materials and its high level of economic development, is the comparatively recent date at which this supremacy was achieved; this growth, moreover, took place behind a tariff barrier of enormous proportions considering the country's extraordinarily favorable physical resource basis, and the chemicals industries are still among the most heavily protected industries in the country. American companies, however, through their foreign subsidiaries, have also participated in the rapid growth of chemical industries in the rest of the world; in the establishment of foreign operations many of the smaller companies have been more active than the giants.

The location pattern of the American chemical industries is markedly decentralized; transport costs on heavy chemicals are substantial, and on the whole, markets are of greater significance than proximity of raw materials. Certain areas, however, either because of a wealth of raw materials or because of technological change, have attracted a substantial share of new investment in chemical industries (Fig. 19-3); foremost among these are the Gulf Coast of Texas and Louisiana and the Ohio valley. As in other major industries they tend towards territorial division of company activities; the two leaders, Du Pont and Union Carbide, and Allied Chemical have their plants mainly in the East, but such fast-growing rivals as Dow and Monsanto have their main strength in the Midwest and Southwest.

The oldest area and still one of the leading areas, particularly for heavy inorganic chemicals, is the mid-Atlantic seaboard, home of E. I. du Pont de Nemours & Co., the world's largest chemical organization and the nation's largest producer of synthetic fibers, paints and finishes, synthetic organic dyes, and other organic chemicals. Du Pont's headquarters are in Delaware, where three of the company's plants are located, but it operates nearly ninety plants scattered through twenty-five states; the largest is at Deepwater, New Jersey, built originally for synthetic-dye production. Apart

[7] **The yield stimulus is applied by painting the bark beneath the tapping cut.**

Fig. 19-3 Major centers of chemical production in the United States.

from some synthetic-ammonia production Du Pont has little interest in acids and alkalis, and part of its former explosives interests have been separated to form Hercules Powder. Although it operates the largest nylon plant in the country in the Kanawha valley of West Virginia, it has licensed many other producers, and, unusually for a chemical company, it also has substantial interests in rayon. The company is also anomalous in its retention of a family-dominated organization, although this is common enough in German industry.

The names of Union Carbide and American Cyanamid reveal their origin in the electrochemicals industry, for these substances are produced in arc furnaces; both companies are now heavily engaged in plastics. Allied Chemical and Dye is more specialized in heavy inorganic chemicals than the other large organizations and is the largest producer of synthetic ammonia and fertilizers; its preoccupation with the older products of the chemicals industries is said to have been responsible for a growth rate that has been below that of the chemicals industries as a whole.

Of the midwestern companies Dow was originally based on the brine deposits of Midland, Michigan, but the company has supplemented its large production of inorganic chemicals with plastics and pharmaceuticals, and it is more heavily engaged in petrochemicals than any of the major companies; it is the only American producer of magnesium, which it extracts from seawater at a plant at Freeport, Texas. Monsanto, on the other hand, has followed a reverse policy, moving into heavy inorganic chemicals from the production of organic chemicals derived from coal tar.

World War II saw a great proliferation of new plants based on the remarkable association of raw materials present in the Southwest, and as already mentioned, the Gulf Coast, where salt, sulfur, petroleum, natural gas, and lignite occur in close proximity, is the preferred area for new investment. Many plants began life through government investment, but after the war these were mainly sold to smaller independent companies in order to broaden the field of competition. The development of new chemical industries in the Ohio valley is closely associated with the low-cost production of thermoelectricity and very highly mechanized coal production.

Western Europe

The combined chemical output of Britain and the EEC was somewhat inferior to that of the United States in 1960, but the more rapid growth of chemical production in Europe suggested a real possibility that the United States could be overtaken in the not distant future.

While West Germany is the largest producer, Britain possesses the largest European chemical firm in Imperial Chemical Industries (ICI) (Fig. 19-4). This is by far the largest public company operating mainly in Britain and possesses more than one-hundred plants scattered throughout all of Britain's major industrial regions. More than forty works are situated in Lancashire, Cheshire, and northwest Derbyshire, the original home of the British alkali industry, in all of which areas the chemical industries are largely raw-materials oriented. ICI's largest complex of plants, however, is on Teeside, where the production of synthetic ammonia, coal hydrogenation, heavy organic chemicals, and petrochemicals and synthetic-fiber production are combined to produce one of the most remarkable plant concentrations in Britain. ICI could be likened to a British equivalent of Du Pont and Allied Chemical combined, but the company is progressively shifting its major interest towards the more complex and capital-intensive (and more profitable) branches of chemical production; it has a half interest in British Nylon Spinners, Britain's only producer of nylon, and in 1962 very nearly swallowed its partner in this venture, Courtaulds. In pharmaceuticals, however, ICI's position is challenged by a number of largely foreign-owned specialists, and the major center of production is the Greater London area.

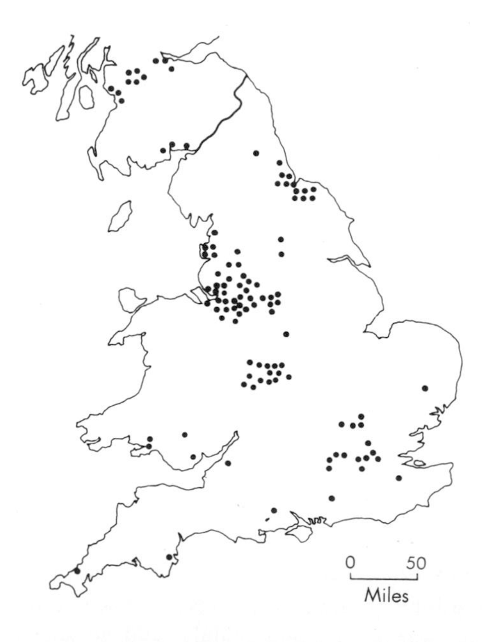

Fig. 19-4 Plants of ICI, Great Britain.
The plants of ICI epitomize the distribution of Britain's chemical industries. (ICI.)

As already noted, West Germany's chemical industries showed a remarkable capacity for regeneration after World War II. Even by 1950 prewar production levels of many heavy chemicals had been regained; both the development of Perlon (nylon 6) despite the Du Pont patents and the recovery of Germany's traditional position as the world's foremost exporter of synthetic organic dyes showed that the German chemical industries had lost little of their creative ability.

Interwar Germany's I.G. Farbenindustrie (Dyestuffs Trust), created in 1925 from a union of a number of large companies which were themselves the product of pre-1914 amalgamations, is probably the most famous—or infamous—of all chemical companies. With the growth of National Socialism, I.G. Farben's ramifications spread wider and wider through the German economy, reaching backwards to the control of basic raw materials and forwards into the fabrication of articles from its chemical products. Hitler's armies marched across Europe on boots made from its synthetic leather and clad in uniforms made from its synthetic fibers; countless millions of Europe's Jews were executed in death chambers with its poisonous gasses; the Wehrmacht's trucks and tanks rolled on its synthetic rubber powered by its synthetic gasoline, while the Luftwaffe absorbed vast quantities of its aluminum and magnesium, of which metals Germany had become the world's largest producer.

The Allies' resolution to dismantle this industrial colossus is hardly surprising, but as with the Krupp organization, it proved impossible to effect in practice. I.G. Farben certainly enlarged the capacity of Nazi Germany to wage aggressive war, but the wider responsibility of the company to the world at large is a question with a large political content.[8] I.G. Farben's dissolution was opposed by Du Pont and Dow, which had prewar agreements with the German company, and all that was done was to divide the company into its three main pre-1925 components—Farbenfabrik Bayer of Leverkusen and Wuppertal, Farbwerke Hoechst of the Rhine-Main region, and Badische Anilin und Soda Fabrik (BASF) of Ludwigshafen. Some of the company's property, however, passed into the hands of the West German government. The many I.G. Farben directors and managers who received prison sentences for "war crimes" in the immediate postwar years were soon released, even those with proved Nazi loyalties; their speedy reinstatement, often in their old jobs, has proved a considerable political embarrassment to the West German government. The three successors to I.G. Farben closely cooperate, and their eventual reunion is by no means unlikely, particularly if, as is expected, Britain is ultimately admitted to the EEC; the creation of ICI in 1926 was very largely the reaction of the four largest British chemical companies at the time (Nobel Industries Ltd., British Dyestuffs Ltd., Brunner, Mond & Co., and United Alkali Co.) to the creation of the German giant. By most tests, at present, ICI is almost twice as large as Bayer, the biggest chemical company in the Federal Republic.

While the Rhine and Ruhr are the leading areas of chemical production in West Germany, control of the second great complex of chemical industries of Germany passed to East Germany after World War II. This is the Bitterfeld-Wittenburg-Leuna area, whose raw-material base consists of the lignite of the middle Elbe basin and the potash deposits of the Stassfurt and Mansfeld districts of Saxony. The Middle Elbe region produces heavy inorganic chemicals, synthetic fibers, and a wide range of organic products synthesized from brown coal; during World War II Leuna possessed Germany's largest nitrogen-fixation plant and a great Lurgi plant for the synthesis of gasoline.

One of Europe's largest chemical complexes is to be erected by Shell and ICI on the Maas river, where Shell already operates Europe's largest oil refinery. Other major centers of Europe's chemical industries are Lyon, home of the largest French producer Rhône-Poulenc, Porto Marghera (Venice), and Fawley (Southampton), where Jersey Standard operates Europe's second-largest refinery.

Under the aegis of the Cassa per il Mezzogiorno, Montecatini (noted for its polypropylene fiber Moplen) has erected a large petrochemicals plant at Brindisi. The company overextended its capital resources, however, and received massive assistance from Shell, which thus acquired a large share of the equity.

[8] For a crushing indictment of the directors of I.G. Farben, see J. E. du Bois and E. Johnson, ***Generals in Grey Suits,*** **John Lane, The Bodley Head, Ltd., London, 1953.**

SELECTED REFERENCES

Alderfer, E. B., and H. E. Michl: *Economics of American Industry,* McGraw-Hill Book Company, New York, 1957, pp. 239–258.

Corbett, W. G.: *The Economic Development of Detergents,* Gerald Duckworth & Co., Ltd., London, 1958.

Haber, L. F.: *The Chemical Industry in the Nineteenth Century: A Study of the Economic Aspect of Applied Chemistry,* Clarendon Press, Oxford, 1958.

Happel, J.: *Chemical Process Economics,* John Wiley & Sons, Inc., New York, 1958.

Manufacturing Chemists' Association: *Chemical Statistics Handbook,* Washington, 1960.

———: *The Chemical Industry Facts Books, 1960–61,* Washington, 1959.

Organisation for Economic Cooperation and Development: *The Chemical Industry 1961–62,* Paris, 1962.

Royal Commission on Canada's Economic Prospects: *The Canadian Chemical Industries,* Ottawa, 1957.

Sheehan, Robert: "Turnaround Year for Montsanto," *Fortune,* vol. 70, no. 3, September, 1964.

Taylor, F. Sherwood: *A History of Industrial Chemistry,* William Heinemann, Ltd., London, 1957.

Theiler, Carl R.: *Men and Molecules,* George G. Harrap & Co., Ltd., London, 1960.

Wilson, Charles: *The History of Unilever,* Cassell & Co., Ltd., London, 1954.

Woytinsky, W. S., and E. S. Woytinsky: *World Population and Production,* The Twentieth Century Fund, New York, 1953, pp. 1176–1209.

Yarsley, V. E., and E. G. Cousins: *Plastics in the Service of Man,* Penguin Books, London, 1956.

PART IV

Service industries

Chapter 20

BUILDING, COMMERCIAL SERVICES, AND GOVERNMENT

Except in the centrally planned economies, employment in service (tertiary) industries substantially exceeds that in mining, manufacturing, and construction (secondary) industries.[1] This is, of course, inevitable; service industries not only include personal and professional services of all kinds, the administrative machinery, and transport and communications, but in the noncommunist world they also involve the ultimate stages of almost every kind of productive activity. In the highly developed economies, in particular, it is difficult to overstate the importance of service industries in bringing producers and consumers into conjunction. Advertising has been described as "the most obtrusive of all economic phenomena"; in the United States expenditure on advertising services was increasing at a rate of more than a billion dollars per year at the end of the Fifties, a sum sufficient to provide every underdeveloped country of Asia or of Latin America with a new steelworks.

The great diversity of the service industries and their concentration in urban agglomerations make geographic analysis particularly difficult. Some service industries, such as laundries, do possess plants which often show clearly defined location patterns, and as in manufacturing industries, there may be a tendency for the larger units to grow in importance as economies of scale become more pronounced. On the whole, however, services tend to congregate, and are consumed where they are produced; except in a few special instances, some industries enjoy a high degree of local and national protection. These special cases, however, may be of extreme importance; among them could be included such giant enterprises as the motion-picture industry, the foremost American industry by value of output

[1] In this chapter, the term "industry" is used in its literal sense, and not restricted to manufacturing industry. Strictly speaking, an industry is the activity of the *employer;* occupation is the activity of the *employee.* It is thus perfectly legitimate to speak of the "wheat industry" or the "building industry." The use of the term "industry" to denote manufacturing is merely a popular convention.

during much of the period between the two world wars, and one of the country's principal sources of foreign exchange before grossly inflated costs and uninspired productions allowed Europe to regain after 1945 the leadership of the industry that it had lost to Hollywood in the first decade of the century. Banking and insurance are also organized in worldwide enterprises; for many years the "invisible exports" represented by the provision of such services to foreigners have enabled Britain to run a large balance-of-payments deficit.

BUILDING AND CONSTRUCTION

The term "building" is generally reserved to the production of houses, dwellings, and industrial and commercial buildings. "Construction," on the other hand, is the term used for the erection of large dams, bridges, harbors, and power stations. There is no significant economic difference between the production of houses and that of automobiles save that the former are fixed and have a long life expectancy. For this reason, building and construction are customarily grouped with manufacturing industries in national income analysis. Nevertheless, in many ways the building industry much more closely resembles service industries in general than it resembles the great majority of manufacturing industries; a very substantial proportion of the industry in all economies is, in fact, concerned with the repair and renovation of existing structures, and the distribution of the building industry, in common with that of most service industries, is closely related to the general distribution of population.

The building industry occupies a key position in economies at all levels of development. It uses a large and diverse range of raw materials and employs a large labor force. In most highly developed economies the proportion of the nonagricultural labor force engaged in building and construction is usually between 5 and 8 per cent, a substantially higher proportion than that in many important manufacturing industries; its share of the male labor force is considerably higher, being about 14 per cent in Britain in 1960. The building industry uses male labor almost exclusively, and wage payments account for a substantial portion of its total payments. Changes in the level of activity are thus speedily communicated throughout the whole economy, and building is often used as a barometer of general business activity. It is, moreover, profoundly affected by the rate of interest, which in turn is largely determined by that important intangible, "business confidence"; buildings are expensive structures and are usually constructed, as well as purchased, with borrowed money. A reduction in the rate of interest markedly lowers costs and permits substantial reductions in rents.

In the highly developed economies the greater part of new housing construction is in one way or another controlled by the state. Even in the richest countries, far too large a proportion of the population is inadequately housed; it is by no means uncommon for families to possess an automobile or a television set but to lack a bathroom and interior toilet. In part this is a consequence of rent-control legislation, which has made the renovation of dwellings financially unattractive and has discouraged the building of new houses for rental. But it also reflects the loss of output through two world wars and social changes which have increased the demand for housing beyond the available supply; in all highly developed economies the average age at which marriages are contracted has declined considerably, and young people who formerly would have lived with their parents for a longer period now desire to set up households of their own. In some highly developed countries, particularly in Australia, a high rate of immigration has also increased the pressure on housing. As it has become accepted that rents should not constitute an unduly high proportion of family expenses, the subsidization of lower-income groups through public housing has expanded considerably in the present century, and housing policy has become a major political issue. As the building industry has such a central place in the economy, moreover, the very large public stake in the industry means that through its housing policy the state has a potent instrument for influencing the general level of business activity.

Much of the capital investment necessary to modernize the underdeveloped economies, moreover, will have to consist of buildings. As the building and construction industries are large consumers of bulky raw materials which cannot be transported far and must therefore mainly be produced locally, and are also large employers of labor, the expansion of building and construction is an obvious line of policy in economic development. Building-material industries are among the first to expand as national development plans are implemented, and the construction of roads, dams, irrigational canals, and other public works by unemployed and underemployed labor has been frequently advanced in "up by the bootstraps" policies for economic development.

The building industry has sometimes been described as the only large and important industry to be unaffected by the Industrial Revolution. The observation is of questionable validity and is in any case totally inapplicable to the construction industry, at least in highly developed economies. Nevertheless, it must be conceded that until comparatively recently a substantial sector of the building industry was little affected by the use of power-driven mechanical equipment; in Europe spoil from building excavations was handloaded and hauled away by horse and cart until well into the Twenties. Over the past three decades, however, a revolution has occurred in both building materials and building techniques. Site preparation and excavation are now highly mechanized, welding has replaced riveting in steel-frame buildings, the use of prestressed concrete has enabled architects to design structures of great strength and beauty, and the vertical transport of materials has been greatly accelerated through the use of tower cranes and elevators. Whole floors of multistory buildings can now be cast in one piece on top of each other, each floor being subsequently raised into its appropriate position. Yet even in large structures the use of traditional materials and hand methods is still abundantly obvious in many countries, and in house building labor-intensive methods are still predominant almost everywhere. Timber and other materials are still cut and prepared on site, and walls and partitions are often laboriously built up brick by brick. The introduction of more efficient methods of building has frequently been resisted, and for the most part successfully, by organized labor, though innovations which have reduced much of the more arduous labor have for the most part been accepted.

The fact that buildings are usually custom-built reduces the opportunities for mechanization and for the employment of standardized techniques; moreover, people on the whole seem less willing to accept a standard house than a standard automobile. Techniques of mass production and prefabrication have thus made little impact on house building so far, although there has been some progress in this direction since the end of World War II. As a substantial part of the cost of housing is incurred in the site and its preparation, prefabrication and standardization do not confer any outstanding advantages.

The limited opportunities for large-scale

The world's largest housing shortages occur in the underdeveloped countries. This simple machine makes bricks of adobe. Below, prefabricated apartment buildings are erected at Krasnodar in the U.S.S.R.

The tower crane, a postwar development pioneered by Sweden and West Germany, has considerably reduced the costs of large building construction.

operations are largely responsible for the competitive structure of the building industry, with its multiplicity of small firms; much business is still performed by skilled workers working on their own account, a state of affairs that is confirmed by the widespread practice of subcontracting particular tasks to specialists. Thus in all highly developed economies the vast majority of firms in the building industry are of very small size; in the Fifties more than three-quarters of all building firms in most countries of Western Europe employed less than ten workers.[2] At the same time, the greater part of the output of new buildings in Western Europe was accounted for by a few large firms (that is, those employing more than fifty workers), and these possessed a very large share of the total labor force in the industry; but firms employing more than one thousand workers are few in number in all highly developed economies, and must be judged of very large size by the general standards of the building industry. The large units almost always have interests that extend beyond construction into some branches of engineering, and in the case of very large units, such as Kaiser or Krupp, even into the iron and steel industry. The large units are capable of constructing a dam, harbor, or, with their associates, a large atomic energy station anywhere in the world, and international competition in this class of work is very keen.

[2] **J. Frederic Dewhurst, et al.,** *Europe's Needs and Resources,* **The Twentieth Century Fund, New York, 1961, p. 223.**

Leading Building Industries of the World It is probable that the U.S.S.R. possesses the world's largest building and construction industry, although comparisons with that of the United States or that of Western Europe are difficult. The U.S.S.R. has a tremendous backlog of housing as a result of its extreme backwardness before the revolution, the destruction during World War II, and the rapid expansion of its urban population. The Russian building industry has been credited with producing 3 million dwellings annually through much of the Fifties, but this figure has to be considered in the light of the rigid rationing of living space and the low investment in each dwelling unit. The cramped and congested conditions of most Russian dwellings, even in new housing blocks, have received frequent comment by Western observers; even in the largest cities, substantial areas of old wooden housing, virtually unchanged since before the revolution, are to be seen; modern housing consists for the most part of large apartment buildings, often of extreme architectural banality. The Russian building industry is organized in large units and is highly mechanized, and in marked distinction to that of the free world, it employs a considerable quantity of female labor. The absence of the small units so numerous elsewhere, capable of effecting the repairs inevitable from time in time in a climate of extreme severity, is one of the principal reasons for the delapidated appearance of much Russian housing; it has been frequently remarked that even newly completed buildings look in poor condition.

The output of the building industry of the United States appears to be approximately equal to that of the EEC and Britain combined; in the peak year of 1959 both the European and American industries produced rather more than 1.5 million housing units. Moreover, investment per dwelling in the United States tends to be much larger than is the case in most countries of Western Europe. The application of mechanization has been pushed much further, and large units are of relatively greater importance, than in the European industry. As a whole, the building industry deserves the epithet of "a shambling giant." Few large industries make such little expenditure on research, although the building industry does receive substantial benefits from that undertaken by the building-materials industries. Both on social and economic grounds, an improvement in the efficiency of the building industry is highly desirable.

LARGE-SCALE COMMERCE AND FINANCE

The scope of commerce is not easy to define, and it is often difficult to measure the employment it provides. Some economists now hold that the share of commerce in total employment can be at any level regardless of the stage of economic development; it is certainly true that in West Africa, for example, commerce in the broad sense occupies a great many people, and collectively they must account for a considerable proportion of the work force. Few of these people, however, are specialists; they are essentially part-time operatives, and their capital is minimal. In countries at a high level of development, on the other hand, commercial and financial activities are highly capitalized and are very often organized in large units; their work force, moreover, consists of full-time specialists working with considerable mechanical and electric equipment. It is, of course, possible that mechanization will ultimately make it possible to dispense with a large labor force in commercial activities, as has already occurred in manufacturing industry; the sheer volume of business now undertaken by banks and insurance companies has led to the introduction of highly mechanized methods of accounting, closed-circuit television, new methods of reproducing and storing documents, and the use of computers, and many of these techniques have also been adopted in government.

Commerce in the broadest sense includes all those activities that bring together producers and consumers, but its range is very great. At the lowest level is retail trading, which with wholesaling may be said to constitute the distributive trades; in economies at a high level of development, these are among the very largest employers of labor. At successively higher levels are all those service institutions engaged in financing and facilitating consumption, distribution, and production, both nationally and internationally. Some of these, such as banking and insurance, are generally very widely available, but the greatest proliferation is inevitably found in great metropolitan centers; the large manufacturing establishment usually deals with its bank's head office rather than with the local branch.

In general, the larger the urban center, the greater the range of commercial and financial services available. Nevertheless, Los Angeles and Chicago, though more populous and with a much higher volume of industrial activity than either Zürich or Amsterdam, count for very much less in the world of international finance, for an agglomeration of functions at this level appears to be closely connected with a large volume of foreign trade. Outstanding, of course, are the two great financial and commercial centers of New York and London, although there is an important distinction to be made between them: though its connections are worldwide, New York is primarily engaged in ministering to a domestic economy which generates over half of total world product; London, on the other hand, is primarily devoted to serving the world economy as a whole, and in this sense is unique. This observation would have been even more true of the period before World War I, when the "bill on London" was the principal means of conducting international trade and the London money market was the main source of funds for development projects all over the world. But London's financial institutions still retain considerable virility, and through its adhesion to the sterling area, much of the world still retains a considerable economic cohesion and looks to London for guidance in financial matters. For London is still, as it has long been, the principal market for most agricultural products entering world trade, even if it no longer exercises a similar function in respect of metals, as it did before World War II. Also, London is almost certainly the world's largest insurance center, and in marine insurance it has no rival.

The City of London Though much modified by the remarkable expansion of the world economy in the nineteenth century which they did so much to facilitate, London's financial and commercial institutions trace their origins to the very beginnings of banking, insurance, and joint stock enterprise; the sense of history and tradition, discernible even to a casual visitor, sharply distinguishes the hub of these institutions, the City of London, from Wall Street, its "upstart rival" across the Atlantic. Since the Great Depression the New York financial markets have been subjected to the fierce light of publicity and to a considerable degree of government surveillance. The City, however, has no equivalent of the Securities Exchange Commission to watch over it, and difficult though it is to believe in view of all that generations of professional economists, financial experts, and journalists have written, many of the operations of the London money market are still shrouded in such a mysterious semireligious mumbo jumbo that they are imperfectly understood even by the market itself; the reticence of the City's most sacred institution, the Bank of England, to explain its operations received some tart comment in an important postwar inquiry into the workings of the London money market.[3]

Unlike the New York financial district, the City of London, or City, as it is invariably called, is a unit of local government, with unique powers possessed by no other authority in Britain. The City has an area of only a little over 1 square mile, and its resident population is only about 5,000; during working days, however, this is swollen to over 500,000. Few of the head offices of the great British mining and manufacturing corporations are found within its boundaries, although Unilever is an important exception; most of these, together with the entertainment and advertising industries, the central administration, and the great retail stores, are to be found in the West End, within the City (Borough) of Westminster.

The core of the city is a circle of a quarter-mile radius centered on the Bank (of England). Within this limited area are located the head offices of the British clearing banks, many British-owned banks operating both within the Commonwealth and in foreign countries, and offices of every foreign bank of any significance, even including the Moscow Narodny Bank, which plays a vital part in Soviet trade with the West. The core also includes the discount houses, once largely concerned with financing international trade through bills of exchange but now earning a profitable livelihood as providers of short-term funds for the British Treasury; the great merchant (investment) banks such as Hambros, Baring, and Rothschild; the London Stock Exchange; and famous commodity exchanges such as the Metal Exchange, the Tea Exchange (which deals in a variety of tropical products), and the Baltic (which deals in grain, timber, and other products formerly imported from the Baltic area). Also included in this limited area are the world's most important gold market, Lloyd's (the world's best-known insurance institution), the head offices of most of the leading plantation companies, those of many of the major shipping companies (some of which, however, are located at Liverpool), and the world's largest tanker-charter market. Serving the main business of the City are a multiplicity of accountancy and law firms and a great deal of printing and publishing; the City's Fleet Street is the home of the newspaper industry, two of the great national dailies having daily circulations exceeding 4 million, an astronomical figure by the standards of most American newspapers. These commercial and financial activities are often closely interwoven by a complicated network of interlocking directorships; personal contact still counts for much in the City, and despite Britain's progression towards a welfare state, a select number of families still control much of the City's business.

[3] *Report of the Committee on the Working of the Monetary System (Radcliffe Report),* **Cmd. 827, H. M. Stationery Office, London, 1959, p. 300.**

Wall Street The New York financial district, the half square mile bisected by Wall Street, has much in common with the City despite a totally different appearance and tradition; stockbrokers advertise openly, a practice that is forbidden in Britain, but the sanctity of the verbal contract, the touchstone of the broking business, is equally revered. Banking, investment banking (underwriting), investment trusts, commodity trading, and their indispensable auxiliaries, law, accounting, and printing, are the main occupations of the financial district, and employ, with supporting services, perhaps more than 100,000 workers.

The necessity for close personal contacts has often been held as the main reason for the extreme concentration of financial services in geographically very restricted areas within the world's great metropolitan centers, but the multiplicity of electronic devices linking banks, brokers, traders, and their clients deprives this argument of much of its validity. The principal reason for concentration is almost certainly tradition, well exemplified in the top-hatted bill brokers of the City, who still make their daily calls on the banks of London. Though the New York financial district has few such customs of the past, personal contact still counts for a very great deal there. Nevertheless, limitations on branch banking in force in most states and the creation of the Federal Reserve districts have prevented New York from acquiring a hold over American banking comparable to that of the City of London in Britain; several important insurance companies, moreover, have their head offices elsewhere, notably in Hartford, Connecticut, which has sometimes claimed the title of "the nation's insurance capital."

While it does not appear likely to affect the standing of their financial districts, the rapid growth of alternative sources of credit in all the highly developed economics has set the traditional suppliers a problem for which they have not yet found a satisfactory answer; prominent among these other sources of credit are hire-purchase, or credit-sale, organizations and building societies. Though the gross volume of such credit is not really large in relation to the total credit outstanding, credit sale has almost become the rule in the purchase of consumer durables, particularly motor vehicles, and has attracted the manufacturers themselves; through its acceptance division, General Motors, the world's largest manufacturer, also has a not inconsiderable stake in the credit business. The Ford Motor Company of Britain in 1963 decided to establish an acceptance company to finance the purchase of its vehicles, an example that may well be followed by other British motor vehicle manufacturers.

Other Financial Capitals Of the other great centers of international finance, only Amsterdam shares with London a tradition of overseas commercial enterprise reaching far back into the Middle Ages; the others, such as Paris and interwar Berlin, have largely been products of nineteenth-century imperial growth. The money markets of Zürich and Geneva are an even more recent phenomenon, owing much to Swiss neutrality in a polarized world and to the renowned discretion of Swiss bankers, which is more to the liking of foreigners than pleasing to the Swiss government; an account number in a Swiss bank may belong to an oil-enriched sheik, a movie queen, an ex-dictator, or even a commissar. The remarkable strength of the Swiss franc in the postwar world has also greatly stimulated the expansion of the Swiss capital market.

A few other centers of financial importance owe their position to the dexterity of their citizens in making and exploiting profitable loopholes in the many regulations governing dealings in gold and foreign exchange in most countries of the world. Beirut in Lebanon is a major Middle East center of banking, and was heavily involved in the so-called "Kuwait gap," by which British holders of sterling were able to purchase dollar securities and other hard currencies; the British government did its best to plug the gap in 1957, but some leakage of sterling undoubtedly continued. It is also the principal center of operations for the smuggling of gold into India and other Asian countries. Hong Kong also operates a profitable free market in foreign currencies, and nearby Macau has a remarkable free market in gold, which is one of the mainstays of its economy. These activities grade insensibly into the provision of services for the smuggling trade, particularly in gold; the insatiable demand for the services of the gold smuggler, particularly in India, makes complete control of such "banking" impossible. In the immediate postwar period Tangier also became a not inconsiderable center of "banking," largely because of the opportunities open for the profitable smuggling of consumer goods into a war-impoverished Europe. With the winding up in 1956 of the international commission that had controlled Tangier since 1923, the city's career as a "banking" center received a sharp check.

DISTRIBUTION: THE MARKETING REVOLUTION

The distributive trades include wholesale and retail selling, and in most cities that do not have large manufacturing plants, they are almost always the largest employers of labor. Many of those engaged in retailing, however, are self-employed, and the means of an independent livelihood through the possession of a small store has long been attractive to a substantial section of the wage-earning class. It is partly this fact that accounts for the very large number of small stores, even in highly developed economies; despite the heavy mortality among such businesses, their numbers are maintained at a high level by a succession of new entrants.

Nevertheless, in the highly developed economies marketing has experienced a technical revolution over the past three-quarters of a century, which may still have some way to run. Although small stores still account for the majority of firms in retailing, their share of total turnover is very much smaller in proportion. In Britain in 1950 single-store units, most of which were small, were estimated to account for about 70 per cent of total retail establishments but handled only 45 per cent of sales;[4] this figure may understate the importance of the small trader, but in 1961 all small independent establishments accounted for less than half the total retail turnover.[5] The situation in the United States is even more striking; in 1954, for example, 30 per cent of all stores had annual sales of less than $20,000, but these stores handled only 3 per cent of all retail sales; all unincorporated stores, which appear to have accounted for about 80 per cent of all retail establishments, performed about half of all retail transactions.

The multiplicity of small stores arises from many causes. The most important is probably convenience; customers like to have a store near at hand for emergency purchases and to avoid the loss of time and expense of traveling. The willingness of small tradesmen to give credit to their regular customers is also an important factor, and a small store can be combined with the exercise of a particular skill. In those advanced economies in which the automobile has not yet come to dominate everyday life, the movement to the suburbs has also helped to enlarge the number of retail outlets. In the United States, on the other hand, the suburban exodus has produced a very different pattern of trading; instead of doing the daily shopping common in Europe, the American housewife makes her purchases once or twice a week from a supermarket or regional shopping center provided with good parking facilities.

The marketing revolution inevitably had to await the development of the mass production of standardized branded articles, the establishment of an efficient transport network, modern techniques of mass advertising, and, most important of all, the rise of a mass market of considerable purchasing power; hence it is not surprising that it did not begin to appear until at least a century after the Industrial Revolution was launched. While the Industrial Revolution came first to Britain, the marketing

[4] James B. Jefferys, *Retail Trading in Britain,* Cambridge University Press, Cambridge, 1954, p. 470.

[5] Census of Distribution, 1961, quoted in *The Economist,* vol. 206, p. 718, 1963.

revolution originated in the United States, which has maintained a commanding lead in the development and application of new techniques of marketing down to the present. There is little doubt, however, that as the use of the automobile expands in Europe, the supermarket and shopping plaza will become as common there as they have become in the United States.

The marketing revolution essentially involved exploitation of the economies of scale and the opportunities this presented for specialization. In the early nineteenth century the retailer often had to exercise considerable skill, and apprenticeship in the trade was common practice; grocers had to blend tea and roast coffee, cure and cut bacon, ham, and other meats, and weigh out and package a multiplicity of commodities. The storekeeper, moreover, had also to be manager, accountant, and often janitor. The rapid growth of the United States economy after the Civil War, however, created conditions under which large-scale retailing could flourish; in the last quarter of the nineteenth century the department store, the chain (multiple) store, and the mail-order house all made their appearance and grew rapidly. Some of the great American chains, especially the F. W. Woolworth Company, whose first store dates from 1879, developed very widespread foreign operations.

The bulk purchases of the large organizations have enabled them to offer substantially lower prices in many lines than those charged by small traders and have also enormously enlarged the range of goods offered for sale. In addition, the large units have been able to exercise considerable countervailing power against manufacturers in the interests of their customers; by threatening to undertake production themselves, the great chains have forced producers to lower prices. Large organizations are usually able to achieve substantial economies in advertising, transport, and warehousing costs and are more able than small organizations to engage in research into new methods of marketing. They can also acquire the best sites for their stores; since the end of World War II the chain stores of Britain and the United States have mainly enlarged their share of total retail turnover by expanding operations in the better-sited stores and have closed down many where trade showed little capacity for growth.

Department Stores, Chains, and Cooperatives Increasing urbanization and the development of efficient city and interurban transport systems initially favored the growth of the department stores, which were almost invariably located in the city center. The department store originated in Chicago, and is particularly associated with the name of Marshall Field, who in 1879 opened the first "modern" department store. The large department store is still a characteristic feature of the downtown area of all large modern cities and even exists in the centrally planned economies; few visitors to Moscow fail to visit Goum, its celebrated department store. Some stores have achieved great size and affluence, with annual sales exceeding 100 million dollars and a work force that may reach or even exceed 5,000 employees. Among the largest of such stores are the R. H. Macy store in New York and that of the J. L. Hudson company in Detroit, but there are several others almost as large, both in the United States and in other countries; among these is the Myer company store of Melbourne, which its proprietors claim is the largest department store in the British Commonwealth.

Generally speaking, department stores have enlarged their share of total retail trade through the greater part of the century; in Britain their share of trade rose from about 1.5 per cent at the beginning of the century to about 6 per cent in 1950, and in that year the share of department stores in total retail turnover in the United States was about 8 per cent; in Continental Western Europe, in contrast, the success of the department stores has not been marked, and their share of retail turnover was still less than 4 per cent even in 1960. Nevertheless, it is fairly clear that the heyday of the department store has passed, for although such stores have continued to raise their share of retail trade, it was in the decade before World War I when their great rivals, the chain stores, were poorly developed, that department stores reached their most commanding position in large-scale retailing.

During the pre-World War I decade, the large department store took on its present characteristics, and its former policy, which was to offer standard lines at lower prices than small traders, perceptibly changed. With increasing size and affluence the department stores catered increasingly to a middle-class market, emphasizing quality and variety in merchandise and progressively extending the range of amenities and free services offered to customers. Stores became more sumptuous and often more ornate, as can be seen by comparing the Macy store of 1902 with the London store that the American Selfridge erected in 1909. The proliferation of department stores changed the character and appearance of city centers; stores were frequently massed side by side, making some streets synonymous with lavish spending.

In the interwar period, however, the department store came under increasingly heavy competition from the chains, or multiples, which have so far been by far the most successful form of large-scale retailing. Prominent among the factors responsible for the growth of the chains were the progressive drift of population to the suburbs and the extended use of the automobile. Also, the chains were much more successful than department stores in tapping the new mass markets that were developing with increasing incomes and in catering to many classes of consumers; department stores have always appealed mainly to women customers and have long depended on clothing and drapery for the greater portion of their sales. Groceries and meat proved particularly suitable for handling by the chains, and several developed a vertical as well as a horizontal organization; some of the British grocery chains acquired control of tea plantations in Ceylon, *estancias* in Argentina, and wheat farms in Canada.

Sharing in this expansion of chain-store retailing in Britain were the cooperative societies, descended from the "Rochdale pioneers" of 1844, who established the first successful consumers' cooperative. The individual societies were served by so-called "wholesale societies," which became among the largest manufacturers of food products in the country. Britain's cooperatives have been linked throughout their history with the socialist movement, and since 1945 an adherence to doctrinaire socialist trading attitudes has been responsible for some decline in their fortunes. Nevertheless, in 1960 they still accounted for about 11 per cent of all retail business in Britain, and there was some evidence of a growing willingness to adopt the methods of the more successful chains. In the United States, however, cooperation has never made much headway in retailing, and cooperatives still account for less than 1 per cent of sales; they have, however, been moderately successful in handling agricultural supplies. Almost certainly, it was the extremely rapid growth of the American economy that militated against the cooperatives. The apogee of consumer cooperation is to be found in Northern Europe; in Finland and in Iceland nearly a third of all retail trading is in the hands of cooperatives.

In the decade after World War I the growth of chain-store trading in the United States was almost explosive; during this period chains enlarged their share of total turnover from less than 5 per cent to more than 20 per cent and moved from groceries into furniture, motor-vehicle supplies, variety goods, optical goods, drugs, beauty parlors, and many other lines of business.

Legal Developments The rapid expansion of the chains in the United States caused consternation among the politically powerful small traders, and as a result, several states passed tax laws aimed at hampering the expansion of chains. Small traders have also been among the most vociferous advocates of so-called "fair trade" laws; these prevent price cutting by allowing manufacturers of branded products to fix the prices at which their goods are offered to the public and, in effect, endeavor to prevent large units from realizing the full economies of scale. On the whole, these measures have achieved little success, partly because of the traditional American hostility toward "restraint of trade," and partly because rigorous enforcement of such laws merely results in a loss of trade to neighboring states without such legislation. In Britain, Australia, and most other countries of the British Commonwealth, resale price maintenance has been rigorously enforced, not by legislation, but by the concerted action of manufacturers wishing to isolate themselves from competition. Manufacturers refused to supply traders selling below stipulated prices; the development of cut-price stores in Commonwealth countries was thus greatly hindered, although in some lines, such as chocolates and confectionery, price-cutters were often very successful. There were, however, few legal forms of discrimination against the chains, and in 1960 a Restrictive Practices Court was established in Britain to review manufacturer's agreements. Where these can be shown to be in the national interest, such practices receive, in effect, official approval, but a number of agreements have been struck down by the Court so that the way is being opened for the operations of price cutters.

In most countries of Western Europe, the interwar period produced very considerable antichain legislation in favor of the small shopkeeper. As a result the concentration of distribution in large units has proceeded very much more slowly than in the United States or in the British Commonwealth; in 1960 multiples handled less than 10 per cent of the retail trade of West Germany, compared with some 30 per cent in the case of Britain. These restrictions, of course, also retarded the establishment of American chains, which had achieved considerable success in British territories, and their appearance in West Germany is largely a postwar development, but in France, where small shopkeepers are perhaps more powerful than elsewhere on the Continent, the door has remained closed to the foreign-owned chains.

The Newer Forms of Retailing The success of the chains inevitably stimulated other forms of large-scale trading to improve their competitive position. In the United States between the wars, department stores began to set up branches in the suburbs, a development that was pioneered by the two great mail-order houses, Sears, Roebuck and Montgomery Ward. Mail-order retailing is an activity that has achieved little success outside the United States, and even within the United States its share of total retailing is very small; for some considerable time the mail-order houses have derived the greater part of their income from their stores. Large downtown stores have set up suburban branches or have merged themselves into "department-store chains"; even so, few such combinations can hope to achieve bulk purchases as large as those of the chains, and the department stores' future position is questionable. In Britain the postwar period has witnessed a considerable concentration among department stores, the great majority of which by 1963 were controlled by a handful of large organizations which covered the whole country. Nevertheless, even this has not prevented some decline since 1950 in the share of department stores in retail turnover.

The most striking development in retailing in the postwar period has undoubtedly been the rapid growth of the supermarkets. These are typically self-service grocery stores, and the term has generally been reserved to those with annual sales exceeding $100,000; very many, however, have a turnover of more than ten times this figure. Supermarkets originated in the Depression and were pioneered by independent operators; their success has encouraged the chains to enter the self-service business themselves. Nevertheless, independent operators (that is, with up to ten stores) have held their own, and by combining in "voluntary chains," even individual stores have been able to realize some of the economies of large-scale operations. The very success of the supermarkets has, in some parts of the United States, almost defeated itself; so many stores have been constructed that the "catchment area" of many has been reduced below the economic level for profitable operation. Supermarkets have reacted to this situation by broadening the range of goods handled, and many have become miniature department stores. The one-stop-shopping appeal of such supermarkets, supported by heavy advertising and good parking facilities, is often very effective, but there is clearly a limit to the number of such units that a community can support.

Another important postwar retail development, still largely confined to the United States, is the growth of discount-house trading. The rise of the discounter reflects the dissatisfaction of the more enterprising traders with retail-price maintenance; in many lines it has proved possible to reduce margins and yet raise profits, by encouraging a larger turnover. The discounter offers no services and subjugates every consideration to that of the lowest possible price; discount stores have been particularly active in handling electric and household appliances.

But the postwar trends in retail trading in the United States are best exemplified in the shopping plazas, or regional shopping centers, which in the later Fifties were developing around the margins of many cities. Around a large parking area, vital for their very existence, the plazas usually contain a large branch store, perhaps of a department store in the local metropolitan center but more probably of one of the two great mail-order houses; representative stores of the principal chains, some of which might also reach the proportions of minor department stores; and invariably one or more large supermarkets.

The United States and Europe Today It is not easy for the average American, for whom familiarity breeds its inevitable accompanying degree of contempt, to appreciate how little the rest of the world has been affected by the marketing revolution; even in Western Europe many of the postwar American innovations have still to make their mark. In Britain, which after Anglo-America has experienced the greatest impact of the changes in distributive techniques, supermarkets were becoming extremely common in the later Fifties, but they were largely located in existing shopping areas, usually lacked any parking facilities, and were generally little more than small self-service grocery stores. Rapid expansion of supermarket chains in Britain speedily exhausted the small supply of managerial talent experienced in such operations, and several chains ran into difficulties. In 1960 there was no equivalent of the large American shopping plaza anywhere in the country, although the first such development in Australia commenced operations in 1960 in a Melbourne suburb through the initiative of the city's largest department store.[6]

Britain shares with the United States a pattern of retailing in which by far the greater part of the work force consists of employees, more than half of whom are female. In Continental Western Europe, working proprietors account for a much larger share of the retail labor force, and the proportion of female workers is significantly lower. These facts, of course, reflect the limited development of large-scale retailing on the European Continent. It is difficult to see how this situation can fail to change with the progressive realization of the complete Common Market.

GOVERNMENT SERVICES

One of the largest and most rapidly growing service industries is government. In economies at all levels of development the state is usually by far the largest employer, and in underdeveloped countries that have recently received political independence, the rate of increase in official employment has often been staggering; by 1960 Indonesia possessed more than three times as many public employees as the Netherlands Indies of 1939, although the general level of economic activity was considerably lower. The relatively enormous bureaucracy of the underdeveloped countries is, in fact, a form of welfare service for the politically important literate section of the community; having played an important part in the national revolution, this section has had to be rewarded, although there is often little for the new bureaucrats to do.

In Britain, Australia, and the Scandinavian countries—generally considered welfare states—government service accounts for about 25 per cent of all civilian employees. In New Zealand, where large corporations, the principal private employers in most highly developed economies, are notably absent and an unusually large proportion of the total work force is self-employed, the state employs nearly 30 per cent of all wage and salary earners (Table 20-1).

However, only a small proportion of total government employment in these countries and in Western Europe is directly engaged in

[6] **It could be argued, of course, that the shopping centers of Britain's New Towns, eight of which are located in the Greater London area, are shopping plazas, for they possess all the essentials; they are, perhaps, the first shopping areas in Britain to recognize the existence of the automobile. Nevertheless, they were not privately financed, and the first such regional shopping center, located near Nottingham, began operations in 1964.**

Table 20-1

Government Employment in Selected Countries

	PERCENTAGE OF TOTAL WORK FORCE	PERCENTAGE OF TOTAL SALARY AND WAGE EARNERS
United States	11.2	13.5
New Zealand	20.4	29.1
Australia	21.6	26.0
Britain	22.3	24.4

SOURCE: Various official publications. The figures relate to the situation in the middle Fifties.

administration; by far the largest share is absorbed in postal services, telecommunications, transport, power supplies, health and sanitation, and education services. In the United States, where many services that in Western Europe and in the British Dominions are the concern of the state fall within the private sector, the share of government in total employment is considerably lower. Western Europe's appreciably higher rate of economic growth than that of the United States in the decade starting in 1950 thus suggests that the progressive expansion of the Washington payroll may not be the unmitigated tragedy it is sometimes claimed to be.

The apparently inexorable tendency of the state to enlarge the number and variety of its activities is the subject of the well-known law of the German economist Wagner, who as long ago as 1876 held that the encroachments of the state would progressively reduce the field of private economic activity. It is possible to argue that nineteenth-century *laissez faire* was merely an interlude and that a high degree of state control over the national economy is more normal. It is doubtful, however, that the enlargement of the field of state interest has materially reduced the scope for the exercise of private enterprise, at least in advanced economies. For the most part the new services provided have consisted of those for which the expectation of return on capital is too low to be attractive to private enterprise; nobody can seriously argue that the Germans suffer from a lack of openings for entrepreneurial ability, despite the fact that they have been longest exposed to the operations of the welfare state.

In underdeveloped economies, on the other hand, shortage of capital and managerial ability makes it inevitable that the state must supply much of these itself in the implementation of its national development plans. Many countries, moreover, have adopted political systems that discourage capitalism in theory and occasionally in practice, as in India, Indonesia, and Egypt, in all of which a form of state socialism has been made the national goal. Under such considerations the creation of an inflated bureaucracy is unavoidable.

The Location of Government While the distribution of most service industries reflects the general distribution of population, government is concentrated in relatively few centers. Administration has always been a powerful factor in city development. The preindustrial city of Europe was almost invariably an administrative center of importance, and even towns of religious significance usually exercised important administrative functions. The indigenous cities of Asia were major administrative or religious centers. Several great cities founded in more modern times—Berlin, Madrid, St. Petersburg (Leningrad), Bangkok, Washington, and in the present century Canberra, New Delhi, and Brasília—owe their existence to their selection as administrative centers. Many of these possessed no advantage save political expediency, being originally located in unattractive or even repellent environments. Canberra and Washington, moreover, have largely failed to attract either commerce or manufacturing, and remain devoted to the business of government. It is highly likely that Brasília will follow a similar course of development, if, indeed, this city can ever survive at all, for it is clear that Brazilian politicians have so far been quite unwilling to accept it as a permanent home for the administration.

In most European countries the national capital not only contains the central administration but also is the principal financial, commercial and industrial center. As attempts at controlling the expansion of commercial and industrial activities in national capitals have usually proved abortive—and there are strong economic reasons, in many cases, for allowing them further growth—the question arises of the possibility of decentralizing the administration itself in order to reduce the imbalance in employment opportunities and living standards between the metropolis and the provinces. The governments of highly developed economies, however, while usually extolling the virtues of decentralization for others, appear singularly reluctant to adopt such a policy themselves. With modern methods of communication, arguments for a heavily centralized government machine have little validity; moreover, in all highly developed economies it is common knowledge that arrangements for decentralizing government in the event of a nuclear attack are far advanced. If such a development is possible in an emergency, it is certainly possible under normal conditions, and in several European countries an attractive case can be made out for such a decentralization policy. The expansion of office building continues to be a major factor in the increasing congestion of many great metropolitan areas, and in many instances governments are the principal offenders; though committed in theory to limiting the growth of office employment in the London area, the British government has itself erected enormous blocks in the heart of London and has rented much additional space from private developers. Excessive centralization of government in France has long been a principal cause of conflict between Paris and the rest of the country; a decentralized French administration, however, appears as unlikely as a decentralized Russian one. Evidence of the depressing and disturbing effects on the Russian economy produced by the highly centralized planning mechanism is now abundantly obvious, even to the Russians themselves, but fear of the wider repercussions on society of any decentralized decision making prevents the government from making any substantial changes in its present highly centralized system, with its plethora of central coordinating organizations.

SELECTED REFERENCES

Allen, G. C.: *British Industries and Their Organization,* Longmans, Green & Co., Ltd., London, 1959, pp. 295–315.

Cohen, Saul B.: "Locational Research Programming for Voluntary Food Chains," *Economic Geography,* vol. 37, pp. 1–11, 1961.

Dewhurst, J. Frederic, et al.: *Europe's Needs and Resources,* The Twentieth Century Fund, New York, 1961, pp. 213–245.

Epstein, Bart J.: "Evaluation of an Established Planned Shopping Center," *Economic Geography,* vol. 37, pp. 12–21, 1961.

Ferris, Paul: *The City,* Victor Gollancz, Ltd., London, 1960.

Green, H. L.: "Planning a National Retail Growth Program," *Economic Geography,* vol. 37, pp. 22–32, 1961.

Hall, Margaret: *Distributive Trading,* Hutchinson & Co. (Publishers), Ltd., London, 1949.

Jefferys, James B.: *Retail Trading in Britain,* Cambridge University Press, Cambridge, 1954.

———and Derek Knee: *Retailing in Europe: Present Structure and Future Trends,* Macmillan & Co., Ltd., London, 1963.

Mayer, Martin: *Madison Avenue, U.S.A.,* Harper & Row, Publishers, Incorporated, New York, and John Lane, The Bodley Head, Ltd., London, 1958.

———: *Wall Street: Men and Money,* rev. ed., Harper & Row, Publishers, Incorporated, New York, 1959.

Phillips, Charles, and Delbert Duncan: *Marketing: Principles and Methods,* 3d ed., Richard D. Irwin, Inc., Homewood, Ill., 1956.

Robbins, S. M., et al.: *Money Metropolis: A Location Study of Financial Activities in the New York Region,* Harvard University Press, Cambridge, Mass., 1960.

"The Distribution Upheaval," *Fortune,* April, May, and July, 1962.

Westing, J. H.: *Readings in Marketing,* Prentice-Hall, Inc., Englewood Cliffs, N.J., 1957.

Chapter 21

TRANSPORTATION INDUSTRIES

Transport and communications constitute a major division of the service industries; possibly as many as 25 million people are employed in these activities throughout the world.[1] Although they never account for a substantial proportion of the national work force, transport and communications in general possess a share of total national employment broadly commensurate with the level of economic development. In highly developed economies this proportion appears to be between 7 and 10 per cent; in semideveloped economies the range is between 3 and 5 per cent; in underdeveloped economies the share of transport and communications in total employment is usually below 2 per cent. Countries with an unusually large per capita foreign trade not unexpectedly possess an unusually large proportionate employment in transport as is evidenced by New Zealand and Malaya. Norway, with one of the world's largest merchant marines, has some 14 per cent of its total population engaged in transport and communications, a very high figure indeed. These figures, however, understate the importance of transport as an employer of labor, for a considerable share of road transport is undertaken by nonspecialists—farmers, merchants, and manufacturers who have often found it more convenient to move their produce or merchandise in their own vehicles.

It is significant that specialist transport workers are among the most highly organized in the national labor force irrespective of the level of economic development, and almost everywhere have taken a leading part in the growth of the labor movement.

[1] **W. S. Woytinsky and E. S. Woytinsky,** *World Commerce and Governments,* **The Twentieth Century Fund, New York, 1955, p. 319.**

TRANSPORT IN THE WORLD ECONOMY

Transport is so intimately connected with both production and trade that it is often very difficult to separate the three activities; in the modern world economy each involves the other two, and the development of transport facilities capable of overcoming distance at relatively low cost was an essential prerequisite for the development of large-scale production and regional specialization; without such a simultaneous "expansion of the market," the Industrial Revolution would have been impossible. The construction and operation of transport systems, moreover, provided valuable technical and managerial training in the rationale of large-scale enterprise in general; the large organization with enormous physical capital, with a board of directors exclusively concerned with major issues of policy, and with large and specialized technical, commercial, and operational staffs scarcely existed before the coming of the railway. The new techniques of business organization developed by railroad and steamship companies were widely adopted in manufacturing and in commercial enterprises, and though transport industries may have lagged in the use of new business techniques over the past 25 years, it is well to remember that the modern corporation is largely their creation.

Improved transport made possible accelerated urbanization and industrialization and was a powerful factor in the development of national states and colonial empires. The social and political repercussions of transportation were also profound, and in practice cannot be separated from economic considerations. Transport is a subject of acute political controversy in countries at all levels of economic development, and as the state is often a participant in transport industries, its own economic interests are often directly involved. In the last analysis all solutions to transportation problems have to be politically acceptable.

It is difficult to estimate the relative importance of the various types of transportation facilities in the world as a whole; even for individual countries the statistical picture is far from complete, as much road transport goes unrecorded. Excluding intracity transport, which is performed through the road system, railways appear the most important freight carriers, handling perhaps two-thirds of the world's total freight tonnage: however, as the average journey of oceangoing vessels is considerably greater than that of railway trains, oceanic shipping is responsible for a greater ton-mileage. Air transport is relatively insignificant for freight purposes; in 1961 freight ton-miles moved by civil airlines amounted to less than one-thousandth of those moved by railways. In passenger traffic, however, the disparity, though still considerable, was very much less in that year, railways accounting for ten times as many passenger miles as airlines. In all economies at an advanced level of development road transport accounts for the greatest number of passenger-miles and an increasing share of intercity freight.

Transport media may be complementary or competitive or both. Oceanic shipping experiences little competition in freight traffic, but in passenger traffic competition from airlines is acute. On the other hand, oceanic and inland navigation, railways, and airlines all rely in part on road transport for the carriage of goods and passengers to and from their terminals, as few customers possess their own docks or sidings. Technical change continually modifies the scope of competition and cooperation. While the railway led to a decline in intercity stagecoaches and wagon services, it greatly stimulated other kinds of road transport serving points on the rail system. In turn the motor vehicle won back for the roads a substantial share of intercity freight, but the introduction of "piggyback" services may again swing the balance of advantage in favor of the railways.

It is unrealistic to divorce the main transport media from those ancillary facilities that make them effective. Shipping lines do not provide the docks and harbors used by their vessels, nor do airlines supply their own landing fields and ground navigational aids; trucking and bus companies are not responsible for the provision or maintenance of the road system used by their vehicles. Most of these ancillary facilities are provided at public expense and represent inherited social capital; as a result, it is often a matter of considerable difficulty to determine the true economic costs of many types of transport. Such "subsidized competition" has long been decried by the railways, which claim, with some justification, that they alone have to meet their full costs including the maintenance of roadbed and terminal facilities. In point of fact, however, much railway construction was also subsidized in one way or other.

It is also extremely difficult to assess the real return on investment in transport, for although the direct return may be small in comparison with that offered in other lines of investment, indirect returns, such as the stimulation of other economic activities, may be very substantial. Transport is the only industry which affects all other economic activities; indeed, it touches the life of the citizen at almost every point. Transportation economics is thus a formidable and complex subject, and the realization of the ideal of the economist—that the production of every good or service should cover its full economic cost—is virtually impossible. How does one apportion the costs of thousands of road casualties or the pollution of the atmosphere resulting from innumerable automobiles? How does one view the miserable return of a commuter railway whose low fares have stimulated the development of a distant suburb and its profitable distributive industries? These are questions that can only be resolved in the political arena.

By its very nature, therefore, transport becomes a highly regulated industry; with the exception of agriculture, which in all highly developed economies is elaborately protected from the free play of market forces, it is doubtful that any other activity is the subject of so much state control. Some types of transport have to be operated as monopolies if they are to run at all; early attempts to treat railways as if they were akin to roads, on which all could ply vehicles subject to the payment of a toll, speedily collapsed. But uncontrolled monopoly is socially and politically undesirable; the railroads' gross exploitation of monopoly position and the adoption, in the words of one of the most celebrated railroad barons, of a "public be damned" attitude inevitably led to the imposition of controls in the broad public interest.

Nowadays, entry into most kinds of transport is rigorously controlled by the state, usually on grounds of maintaining a high standard of safety and quality of service but in practice because of the political expediency of maintaining the level of incomes of those already participating. A New York taxi fit only for the scrap heap can still command a high price if it possesses a valid license plate capable of being transferred to another vehicle. Nevertheless, a substantial share of road transport is subject to no regulation in most economies at advanced levels of development, including goods carried by private traders or manufacturers in their own vehicles and within certain territorial limits and personal transport of many kinds. It is doubtful, moreover, that much of this is susceptible to regulation, unless the solution of the centrally planned economies is envisaged, in which for all but the privileged

Few more effective stimuli to economic development exist in the underdeveloped world than the construction of good all-weather roads. Below, a new railroad, financed by the World Bank, under construction in the Gabon, will facilitate the shipment of iron ore. New railroad construction in highly developed countries is now rare.

elite personal transport is virtually confined to what can be provided by a very inferior pair of shoes.

An efficient and coordinated transport system in which all wasteful duplication is avoided and every system covers its full costs is an unattainable ideal; those who cry that all that needs to be done to set the transport industries aright is for government to get out of the business completely exhibit a gross naïveté.

RAILWAYS

Panegyrics on railways are seldom heard at present, but in the past they were common enough; and as their composers correctly foresaw, few inventions have so changed the face of the earth and the lives of its peoples. Apart from their immense stimulus to production and to the mobility of labor, the railways in a sense created their own capital equipment through their association with the coal and iron industries in a self-sustaining "virtuous circle" of rapid economic growth. In this dynamic process, by which a largely traditional economic society was transformed into a modern, rational, and capital-intensive one with a high built-in rate of economic growth, the railway system grew extremely rapidly. In Britain the fastest growth was experienced during the "railway mania" of the 1840s; in Continental Western Europe the greatest spurt in construction occurred between 1860 and 1870, in the United States and Canada between 1880 and 1890, and in Japan, Argentina, and Australia during the decade after 1900. The railway could not always trigger a takeoff, however; in many dependent territories such as India, the Netherlands Indies, and the African colonial possessions, even a heavy investment in railways failed to produce such a beneficial effect, partly because all the equipment was provided from outside and was not an autochthonous economic creation and partly because political and military considerations usually outweighed economic ones in the alignment and development of the railway system.

The period of rapid growth was succeeded in most countries by a slow but steady expansion of the route mileage until about 1930, when the world possessed a total of some 768,000 miles of line.[2] Since then, there has been a slight contraction as many branch lines in the highly developed economies have been abandoned, but to some extent this has been offset by continued construction in the Eastern bloc, both the U.S.S.R. and China having increased their mileage very substantially; indeed, China's most rapid period of growth may well appear to have commenced in 1950. The total passenger and freight traffic carried by the world's railways has continued to augment, but in most countries at an advanced level of economic development railways have accounted for a declining share of the total traffic carried by all forms of transportation over the past three decades.

The Railway and Other Forms of Transport The greatest advantage of the railway is its ability to move a very large load at high speed with only a modest expenditure of energy, and for the overland conveyance of bulk cargoes—wheat, coarse grains, coal, or iron ore—the railway is usually essential. It is also unrivaled as a means of moving very large numbers of people quickly, as the experience of two world wars eloquently testifies. In cities with underground railway (subway) systems, these account for an increasing share of commuter traffic as congestion on the roads steadily increases; after several decades of allowing public transport to decay, several major North American metropolitan areas are about to construct new subway systems. The disad-

[2] **Woytinsky and Woytinsky,** *World Commerce and Governments,* **p. 341.**

vantage of the railway is its inflexibility; it is poorly equipped to assemble small lots of miscellaneous freight into trainloads and to distribute these lots over a wide area. Nevertheless, through the introduction of new technical equipment, the railway is now showing itself capable of competing strongly with trucking even in traffic of this kind.

The railway has also proved extremely vulnerable to competition in intercity passenger traffic, the branch of transportation in which it made its first great impact. Over short distances it has encountered strong competition from the automobile and bus and over longer distances from the airplane. It is possible, however, that some of these losses may be won back for distances of up to 300 miles. Traveling time between airports and city centers offsets the gain made during flight by aircraft, and frequent high-speed electrified services of the type operating between Tokyo and Osaka averaging well over 100 miles per hour cannot be matched by bus lines or automobiles even on superhighways. But while the town or regional planner looks with increasing favor on the railway as a means of reducing road congestion in urban areas and the consequent strangling of the city center, it remains true that for the world as a whole rail passenger traffic is of declining significance. In most highly developed economies passenger traffic accounts for less than one-third of railway revenue, and in the United States for less than 10 per cent.

Condition of the Railways of the Western World Railways share with coal mining the distinction of being the sickest industries in Western countries. United States railways earned less than 2 per cent on their invested capital in 1961, and many systems had heavy losses; the railways of Britain, Continental Western Europe, and Canada, as well as Australia, were in equally poor financial condition. In large part this depression is a legacy of the past. As a result of Federal or state subsidies, several railways in the United States were built primarily for the profits of construction, and never possessed any possibility of profitable operation. Many parts of Britain possess far more lines than were ever warranted by the expectation of traffic, and were built because capital sought speculative employment (indeed, at the time, there were only limited opportunities for investment open to the general public). In the wheat belts of Australia, the Prairie Provinces of Canada, and the wheat regions of the United States the belief that wheat could never be grown economically more than 30 miles—less than an hour's trucking time—from a railway led to many more lines being laid than are now necessary. In many of the western United States lines were built not with any strong expectation of financial return but to promote settlement and to open up the country. In some countries military considerations frequently conflicted with economic ones and strongly influenced the alignment of routes; the peculiar Russian gauge of 5 feet was intended to impede invasion by neighboring powers that had adopted the English, or standard, gauge, and in the German Empire no track could be laid or moved without the consent of the General Staff.

Even where railways were privately owned and operated, a high degree of regulation was imposed, and this has since been maintained even though the former power and influence of the railways has largely vanished. Thus railways have been forced to become common carriers, obliged to accept all traffic offered even though its carriage may involve a loss; rates have been fixed, and discrimination between users has been forbidden; the closure of unprofitable branches has been made an operation of the greatest difficulty, and mergers of competing systems have been discouraged. Nevertheless, while the removal of these disabilities would strengthen the competitive position of railways, in research expenditure and in the application of rigorous costing procedures railways have long lagged behind the standards of manufacturing industry.

World Utilization of Railways The density of the rail network varies very widely throughout the world, and in the past the route mileage in relation to the total national area has often been regarded as an indicator of economic progress; maps of the rail network of Eastern Europe show a remarkable difference along the 1914 boundaries of the German and Russian empires. But the degree to which the rail system is utilized also varies very considerably, and examination of the ton-miles and passenger-miles in respect of each mile of line is even more instructive (Table 21-1). By these criteria the railways of the U.S.S.R. and Japan are unique; the world's densest networks, those of Western Europe and of eastern North America, do not appear to be worked anything like as hard. The intensity of freight traffic over the whole system is more than five times as great in the U.S.S.R. as in the United States, and it is also considerably higher in the Eastern European satellites and somewhat higher in Japan than in the United States. The discrepancy between the United States and Russia in part arises from the fact that the freight traffic of the United States—and indeed, of that of most highly developed economies—is heavily concentrated on a few routes constituting a small proportion of the total rail mileage, whereas large parts of the U.S.S.R. have been provided

Table 21-1 *Railway Mileage and Utilization, 1961*

	MILES OF LINE (THOUSANDS)*	PASSENGER-MILES PER MILE OF LINE (THOUSANDS)	TON-MILES PER MILE OF LINE (THOUSANDS)
United States	217.5	92	2,340
Canada	44.2	45	1,420
Britain	18.5	1,160	980
West Germany	22.6	1,250	1,600
France	24.3	990	1,510
Netherlands	1.9	2,530	1,060
Belgium	2.9	2,120	1,560
Switzerland	3.2	1,460	850
Italy	13.2	1,320	860
India	34.9	1,430	1,420
Indonesia	4.1	1,350	180
Japan	17.2	4,690	2,390
Australia	26.3		360
New Zealand	3.3		370
U.S.S.R.	78.0	1,280	11,800
Czechoslovakia	8.1	1,600	3,960
Poland	14.5	1,350	3,210

* 1952 figures.

SOURCE: The Statesman's Yearbook, 1961. United Nations, *Monthly Statistical Bulletin*, April, 1963.

with no alternative transport facilities as a matter of policy, so that the overall freight load is inevitably high. But the discrepancy also reflects the considerably longer hauls in the U.S.S.R.; rail hauls of coal, iron ore, timber, grain, and ferrous metals all average around 600 miles.[3] The high figure of ton-miles per mile of line in Japan also reflects the general absence of an all-weather road network.

In the intensity of passenger traffic over the rail system the United States and Canada occupy a very striking position; no underdeveloped economies record anything like such a low utilization; indeed, in several underdeveloped economies the number of passenger-miles per mile of line is exceedingly high by comparison. In both countries of Anglo-America the number of passenger-miles has fallen by more than half since 1945 and is still declining; this trend, of course, has been largely accounted for by the fall in intercity travel, for most commuter lines continue to find their services subject to increasing pressure. As it is impossible to provide employment during off-peak periods for the equipment that is necessary to handle peak loads, overheads on commuter lines the world over are extremely high, and attempts to improve the often very unsatisfactory peak services only increase the railways' financial difficulties.

Japan has by far the highest passenger traffic per mile of line in the world; it is also one of the very few countries in which revenue from passenger traffic exceeds that earned by freight. This heavy traffic includes not only a large volume of commuter traffic but also an increasing volume of intercity travel; despite the fact that in the decade after 1950 the number of registered motor vehicles in Japan quadrupled, passenger rail traffic during this period more than doubled. In contrast to the high utilization of railways for freight purposes in the Eastern bloc, passenger rail utilization is little greater than in most highly developed economies of Europe; travel for other than official purposes is heavily discouraged, and for many years the U.S.S.R. maintained an internal pass system to control the movement of population, as China indeed still does. Western Europe contrasts strongly with the United States in its high passenger rail utilization; in Switzerland and the Netherlands passenger rail utilization is unusually high, a fact that largely explains why these two countries' state-owned rail systems make a profit on their operations.

[3] **Woytinsky and Woytinsky,** *World Commerce and Governments,* **p. 369.**

The Railways of the United States

With about 30 per cent of the world's total railway mileage, the United States has the largest route mileage of any country in the world and still has more than twice that of the U.S.S.R. By 1850 the country had come to possess almost as great a mileage as the rest of the world, and half a century later it still possessed about 40 per cent of the world total. Railways in the United States have always been privately owned and operated except for a brief period during World War I, but in practice they have long been regarded as a public institution, and still are—the public knows that commuter trains will continue to run however much their operating companies may be driven into the red.

The 231,000 miles of line existing in 1960, almost 7.5 miles for every 100 square miles of territory, are very unevenly distributed, the network of lines being greatest on the middle Atlantic coast and in the lower Lake states and least in the arid Southwest (Fig. 21-1).

One of the most remarkable features of the railway system, especially to a European, is the multiplicity of operating companies and the absence of a transcontinental system such as exists in Canada, where there are, indeed,

Fig. 21-1 Railroads of the United States.

two such systems, both of which also own and operate railways in the United States. In part this is a reflection of the traditional resistance to the formation of monopolies, though since 1920 there has been serious official study of consolidation, and in the Twenties and again in the Fifties, certain financial groups endeavored to consolidate several of the major roads. In practice, however, about a dozen large units control most of the nation's 110 Class I systems; three, the Santa Fe, Milwaukee, and New York Central, possess more than 10,000 miles of line each, and the Union Pacific and the Pennsylvania systems also closely approach this figure. A considerable degree of greater consolidation now appears inevitable, and several proposed mergers are being discussed at the time of writing; much debate concerns the respective merits of "parallel" mergers, such as that proposed between the New York Central and Pennsylvania systems, and "end on" mergers, such as would be created by an amalgamation of the Southern Pacific and Union Pacific systems.

Until the Great Depression the railroads remained on the whole prosperous; but when the Depression hit, they began to decline. In the Twenties about 70 per cent of all intercity freight was moved by railways, but by the Fifties this share had shrunk to only a little over 40 per cent. Over the same period the automobile, bus, and airplane heavily eroded the railways' passenger traffic. The incidence of this competition in both freight and passenger traffic, however, fell unequally over the whole railway system, and the fact that the different operating companies enjoy such varying fortunes has hampered the industry both in dealing with government and in meeting competition from other forms of transport.

The most prosperous systems are the western roads, the so-called "transcontinentals," particularly those serving California. These enjoy long hauls, for the most part of valuable and perishable freight, and operate in a part of the country where alternative forms of transport are relatively limited. They have virtually no commuter traffic, and passenger services largely consist of fully booked long-distance trains for riding on which a premium fare can be asked as they provide an opportunity for seeing in comfort some of the nation's most spectacular scenery. Some lines were also perspicacious enough to enter trucking and pipeline operation when entry was easier than at present, and several obtain a substantial income from the production of petroleum and natural gas on property derived from land grants. The western railroads, moreover, continue to benefit from the rapid expansion of population and new industrial development in the West and Southwest.

Another group of prosperous railroads consists of the coal-originating systems of the Pocahontas Region (West Virginia and Virginia) of the Interstate Commerce Commission. These lines carry very little passenger traffic and derive most of their income from the transport of coal, westwards to the Erie lakeshore and eastwards to the Hampton Roads; as coal exports have attained a high level since 1950, the latter movement has been of considerable significance.

The most depressed railroads are those serving the populous Northeast, where two of the largest and most important roads in terms of total revenue—the Pennsylvania and New York Central—are located. This area has suffered most severely from the competition of trucking; also, the bus, plane, and particularly the automobile have greatly eroded intercity passenger traffic, while the flight to the suburbs has aggravated the commuter burden.

In contrast to the situation in Western Europe, where almost all lines are double-tracked, only a very small proportion of the American roads are of this type; capacity of lines, however, has been greatly enlarged through improved signaling and the adoption of central traffic control (CTC), in which the movement of all trains on a section is controlled from one point. Multiple tracking is largely confined to the northeast, and between Albany and Cleveland on the New York Central and New York and Pittsburgh on the Pennsylvania Railroad are the longest stretches of quadruple track in the world. The latter section carries the heaviest freight traffic in the country. As this suggests, about 10 per cent of the total route mileage, situated in the Northeast, carries about half the ton-miles moved by the nation's railways.[4] Less than 2 per cent of the railway mileage in the United States is electrified, the lowest proportion recorded in any advanced economy, but American roads were the first completely to abandon the steam locomotive and to substitute diesel haulage, a development which was largely completed in the five years after 1948. Diesel locomotives achieve very high utilization factors and are extremely reliable, but their costs are high—more than three times those of steam locomotives of equivalent power—and it is not clear that their greater work availability entirely compensates for higher interest and amortization charges.

Several remedies have been proposed for the ills of the American railroads—tax relief, closure of branch lines, mergers, a reduction of labor "featherbedding," greater freedom from regulation, and a reduction of "concealed sub-

[4] **Edward L. Ullman, "The Railroad Pattern of the United States,"** *Geographical Review,* **vol. 39, no. 2, p. 242, April, 1949.**

sidies" to roads, airlines, and inland water transportation.[5] Greater competitive efficiency may be achieved through the extended application of "piggybacking," in which trailers are loaded on flatcars for long-distance haulage, being conveyed by road from the terminal to their final destination. This simple and by no means new technique is working a revolution in freight rates, for it has enabled railroads to quote rates for moving a "cube" of space, avoiding the multiplicity of rates in force in the past. In this development, freight forwarders, specialists who make up such lots for shipment, may have an increasingly important part to play.[6] Although subsidies are regarded with horror by many Americans despite the fact that agriculture and the largest and most rapidly growing industry, defense production, are heavily subsidized, some subsidization of commuter services may well be inevitable. New York's antiquated subway system is kept in operation through large disbursements from public funds, and the State of Massachusetts has subsidized commuter lines threatened with closure by the operating company.

The Railways of the U.S.S.R.

While the railways of Western Europe, apart from their shorter average hauls, closely resemble those of the United States in their operations and general problems, the railway system of the U.S.S.R., the second-largest national network in the world and the largest under one ownership, offers many points of contrast. During the decade following 1950 freight ton-mileage on the Russian system moved far ahead of that conveyed over American railroads. The railways move about nine-tenths of the total freight ton-mileage in Russia, the balance consisting largely of traffic on inland waterways, which are frozen over for the greater part of the year. This heavy load on the railway system has been confirmed in successive development plans.

From the beginning Russian railway construction was strongly influenced by strategic considerations, and although economic factors have been of increasing importance, those of strategy have never been overlooked. Over the wide plains of Russia the physical environment favors railways more than other forms of transportation; road metal is in short supply both in the glaciated expanses of the north and in the loessial steppes of the south, and railways can operate in all weathers. Grades are extremely modest, and lines can often take a straight course, as is well shown by the alignment of the Moscow-Leningrad route. Conditions are severer, however, in the more mountainous western Siberia and in central Asia, in both of which areas extreme cold and aridity have necessitated the equipping of steam locomotives with condensing tenders.

Long hauls have always been a feature of the Russian railways, for the concept of regional specialization did not begin with the revolution; moreover, hauls have gradually lengthened despite all the efforts of Soviet planners. Particularly heavy traffic is carried over the three truck lines linking Moscow and the Donets and on the western section of the Trans-Siberian railway; other "transcontinentals" carrying a heavy traffic are the Kazakhs-

[5] The adoption of the diesel locomotive, which unlike its steam predecessor requires no fireman, was mainly instrumental in bringing railroad management and labor into head-on collision. The railroad unions have steadfastly resisted any attempt by management to reduce labor costs by discharging redundant workers, while management has insisted that only in this way can railroads be made fully competitive. For many years, the nation has lived with the threat of a major national strike, and on a number of occasions, an uneasy truce has been established through government intervention. The issue is still far from resolved, but in 1964, President Johnson persuaded the unions to accept the principle that redundant labor must be eliminated (although in practice no discharge of labor from the railroads will take place). In return for granting higher pay and fringe benefits to workers, the railroads received substantial tax concessions.

[6] See "Freight Goes Forward with Forgash," *Fortune*, July, 1962.

tan lines serving the Karaganda coalfield and the TurkSib railway. The Trans-Siberian line completed in 1904 was built to serve mainly military interests, but its role changed considerably with the development of heavy industry in the so-called "eastern regions" under the First Five Year Plan. Since the end of World War II the Trans-Siberian line has been double-tracked, and the section between the Kuznetsk Basin and Chelyabinsk in the Urals was converted to electric traction in 1953. Further relief to the hard-pressed line resulted from the completion of the South Siberian railway, providing direct connection between Magnitogorsk and the Kuznetsk Basin via Akmolinsk and Barnaul (Fig. 21-2). However, the proposed Baikal-Amur railway connecting Bratsk on the Angara River with Sovetskaya Gavan' on the Pacific coast and passing north of Lake Baykal appears to have been dropped.

Despite their heavy traffic the equipment of Russian railways is inferior to that of railways of Western Europe and of North America. Several trunk lines are doubled-tracked, and a considerably higher proportion of the system is electrified than in the United States. Rails are generally lighter in weight, however, so that trains are much lighter than in the United States; in 1955 some 40 per cent of Russia's main lines were equipped with rails weighing more than 88 pounds per yard and only 18 per cent with rails weighing more than 101 pounds per yard; the corresponding figures for the United States were 75 per cent and 60 per cent,

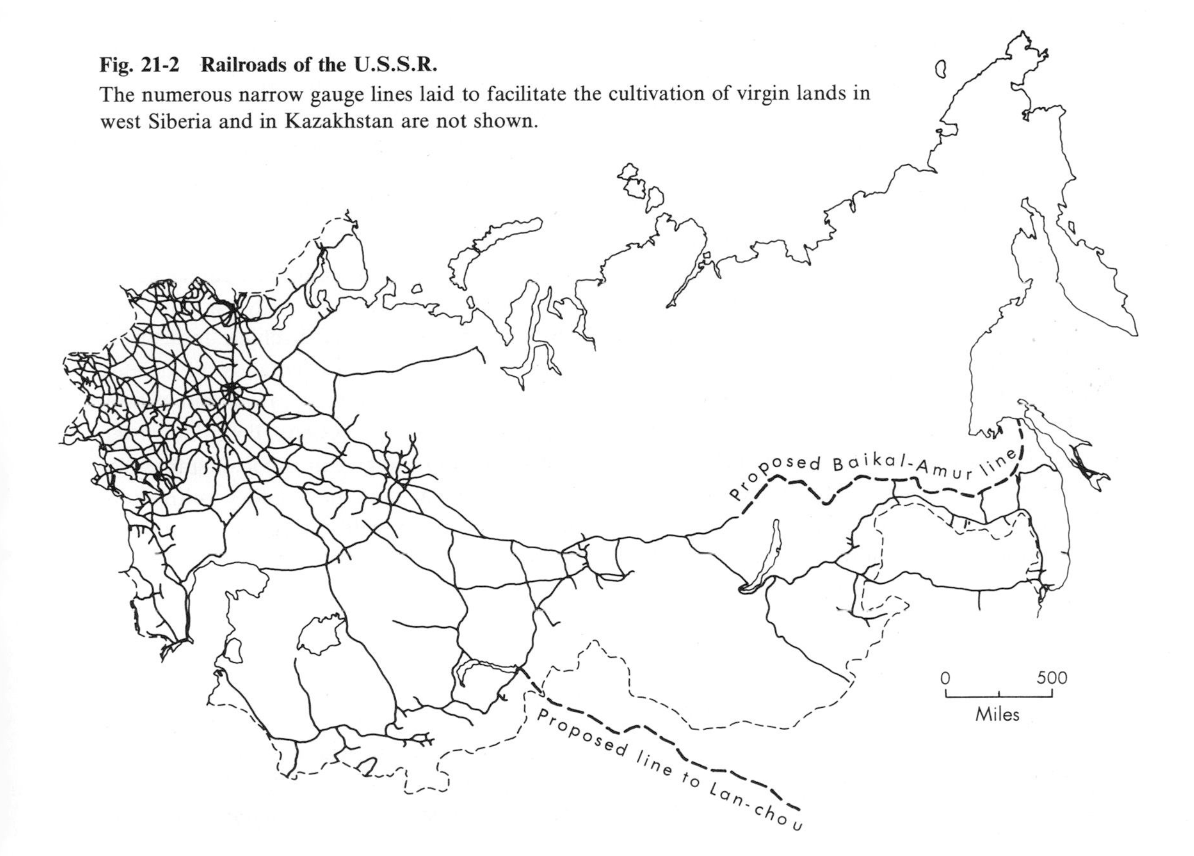

Fig. 21-2 Railroads of the U.S.S.R.
The numerous narrow gauge lines laid to facilitate the cultivation of virgin lands in west Siberia and in Kazakhstan are not shown.

while 20 per cent of the United States had rails weighing more than 130 pounds per yard.[7] Signaling systems have lagged behind modern practice, and very limited employment is made of CTC, which is not particularly effective in increasing capacity under Russian conditions in view of the limited number of passing loops provided on single-track routes. The application of diesel haulage has been long delayed, and is still far from completed, and the relatively light rails have prevented maximum employment of the largest types of locomotives. Steam locomotives are still extensively used, including many acquired from the United States during World War II, and are much used in classification (marshaling) yards, a further source of delay.[8] Such glaring deficiencies suggest that the railway system of the country requires the investment of considerably more resources than has been accorded it in the past; even with the enforcement of a Draconian labor discipline the railways of the U.S.S.R. require the deployment of a labor force estimated at more than three times that of railways of the United States.

It is highly likely that all the shortcomings of the Russian railroads are present in even more acute form in the railways of China. China is supplementing the Chinese Eastern Railway, its old connection with the U.S.S.R., with two new links, one between Ulan Bator and Ulan Ude and another from Lan-chou through Ti-hua to connect with the Turksib at Aktogai near Alma-Ata. The withdrawal of much of Russian technical and economic assistance from China following the post-1959 estrangement between the two countries may sharply reduce the expectation of traffic over these lines.

[7] **Interstate Commerce Commission,** *Sixty-eighth Annual Report on Transport Statistics in the United States,* **p. 9.**

[8] **Robert N. Taafe,** *Rail Transportation and the Economic Development of Soviet Central Asia,* **University of Chicago, Department of Geography Research Paper No. 64, Chicago 1960, p. 97.**

The Railways of Japan

Japan possesses what are certainly the best narrow-gauge railroads and possibly the best railroads of any type in the world, and the general prosperity of both national and private systems is in such contrast to the general world railway situation that some explanation appears desirable. As in so many other branches of the Japanese economy, the state provided the main impetus to railway construction; the first railway in Japan, a line connecting Tokyo and Yokohama, was opened in 1872, and the state has since retained ownership of all main trunk lines, though branch lines are in private hands. Strategic considerations were very strong in the alignment of the railway network; although the population of the main island is markedly coastal, lines were often set back out of range of hostile warships, and the numerous tunnels piercing the hill masses that lie between Japan's many small coastal plains were considered a positive advantage.

The terrain, the absence of good all-weather roads, and the unwillingness to sacrifice cultivable land for road construction in view of the past need for maximum self-sufficiency in food greatly benefited the railways; the slow development of the motor-vehicle industry in view of the overriding demands of defense production also encouraged a maximum utilization of the railway system. Japan, however, could well afford to give up a considerable area of the marginal land now under cultivation; the motor-vehicle industry is flourishing, and the beginnings of a good road system are now in evidence. The railway system, nevertheless, has maintained its competitive efficiency; extensive use of electric traction has enabled it to retain its grip on intercity passenger traffic, and the new standard-gauge Tokaido line between Tokyo and Osaka, providing an hourly service at an average speed of more than 100 miles per hour, sets a standard in intercity passenger services unmatched anywhere in the world. It is inevitable that the Japanese railways will lose some business to road transport, but the concentration of Japanese industrial activity in a few major nodes will continue to operate to the advantage of railways.

ROADS

If railways still constitute the backbone of the transportation system in most advanced economies, the road system is the flesh and blood.

The first roads were constructed to serve the military and administrative needs of the state, which alone could command the resources necessary for their construction, and numerous military roads have been constructed in more modern times, such as those built in the Scottish Highlands after the Forty-five rebellion and the famous Burma and India roads of World War II. The outstanding road builders of the past were the Romans, whose durable constructions constituted the main road system of Western Europe for the best part of two millenia. Until quite modern times —and even today in the U.S.S.R. and in other Eastern bloc countries—the traditional method of road construction and maintenance in most countries was the *corvée,* or compulsory labor service, which was organized by the local authority. Constructed and "maintained" by a recalcitrant and largely unpaid labor force, using whatever local materials were immediately at hand, it is scarcely surprising that the roads of pre-eighteenth-century Europe left much to be desired.

The Roman art of building good all-weather roads was revived in the eighteenth century with the work of Telford, McAdam, and Metcalfe, whose methods were adopted by the "turnpike trusts." These joint stock companies charged a toll for the use of their property and flourished in the latter half of the eighteenth century in both Britain and the United States, but were eclipsed by the coming of the railway. The greatest impetus to road improvements and new road construction came with the development of the motor vehicle at the end of the nineteenth century. Just as the railroad had done before it, the automobile triggered a remarkable quickening in the pace of economic development in many countries; it changed the whole pattern of life and consumption, promoted an economic maturity with emphasis on the production of consumer durables, and ushered in an era termed by one economic historian the era of "high mass consumption."[9]

Roads vary so widely in quality and in carrying capacity that figures of road mileage often convey little meaning; even in advanced economies a considerable part of the road system is primarily for access to dwellings and carries little traffic. The total world road mileage is more than ten times that of railways, but only one-third is hard-surfaced and less than one-fifth has improved drainage and is properly graded.[10] On a per capita basis the highest road mileages are found in recently settled but still sparsely populated countries with advanced economies, such as Australia, which has by far the highest figure in the world, Canada, and New Zealand. The very high road mileage in relation to the population of these countries imposes a very substantial financial burden in road maintenance, and it is impossible to keep more than a small proportion in good condition. The United States has a very large sparsely populated area and a considerable mileage of dirt roads, although it also possesses a hard-surfaced road network unequalled elsewhere in the world which mainly serves the densely populated eastern portion of the country. Its per capita road mileage occupies

[9] W. W. Rostow, *The Stages of Economic Growth,* Cambridge University Press, Cambridge, 1961, p. 10.

[10] Woytinsky and Woytinsky, *op. cit.*, p. 401.

a median position between that of the British Dominions and densely populated Western Europe, where nearly all highways are hard-surfaced.

Throughout the world, road mileage is still expanding very rapidly, even in several underdeveloped economies, where road construction has often been advocated as a means of employing underutilized labor in "up by the bootstraps" policies. The centrally planned Eastern bloc countries are anomalous, however, for they have little wish to promote a greater mobility of labor or to invest substantially in a motor-vehicle industry. For roads and the motor vehicle form an indissoluble union (a considerable objection to "up by the bootstraps" construction, which is to little purpose unless the capital equipment can be provided to make use of it), and as one of the prime initiators of the era of high mass consumption, the automobile constitutes a serious threat to the ruling communist elite.[11] Hence there is a preoccupation with tractors and commercial vehicles (which, however, do not appear to have received sufficient investment for the maintenance of high agricultural productivity) and a policy of minimum road construction and improvement. This deliberate flouting of what is without question one of the most important social and economic changes of modern times may yet cost the U.S.S.R. dearly.

Over the world's highways move something like 100 million automobiles and about 25 million trucks and commercial vehicles, but their distribution is very uneven; about two-thirds of the former and half of the latter are located in the United States, although these shares must progressively decline with the expansion of the motor-vehicle industry in other parts of the world. It is doubtful which has had the greater social impact—the increased personal mobility resulting from the use of the bus and automobile or the carriage of goods by commercial vehicles.

The great advantage of road transport of goods is its flexibility and its avoidance of break of transit; it serves almost every house, and door-to-door delivery is a convenience that is often worth the payment of a substantial premium. Also, the capital investment required for entry is relatively little, for much is provided from inherited social capital, and the degree of skill required to drive a motor vehicle is very modest and can be readily acquired even by peoples of low literacy and little formal education; thus road transport sharply contrasts with railways, which usually necessitate heavy capital investment and require a high degree of skill from most operatives.

All these advantages make road transport ideally suited for the carriage of perishables and finished manufactures of high value and relatively small bulk, that is, traffic capable of paying the highest rates. It cannot handle the bulk movement of primary products and minerals, which it leaves to other forms of transport. Through skimming off what was the cream of the railways' freight traffic and concentrating on the most frequented and therefore the most profitable routes, road transport has done the railways of the world much damage. The fact that much road transport has always been unregulated undoubtedly helped to promote its expansion, but that its use represented a considerable convenience to many users is perfectly clear. In the United States the share of road transport out of a steadily augmenting volume of intercity freight has progressively enlarged; from less than 5 per cent in 1929 the share of road transport had risen to nearly 10 per cent in 1949 and to over 20 per cent in 1960.

Road-rail competition is universal in the free world, and in many countries has been heightened by the construction of new roads parallel to existing railways. However, some

[11] Rostow, *op. cit.*, p. 133.

Table 21-2

Motor Vehicles in Use, 1961 (Thousands)

	AUTOMOBILES	COMMERCIAL VEHICLES	MOTOR VEHICLES PER THOUSAND OF POPULATION
United States	63,274	10,572	415
Canada	4,326	1,157	300
Mexico	549	352	25
Argentina	473	396	41
Brazil*	570	367	13
West Germany	5,167	783	110
France	6,158	1,723	170
Italy	2,443	477	59
Netherlands	620	185	73
Belgium	837	181	110
Britain	5,993	1,531	144
Sweden	1,304	118	190
Switzerland	579	65	116
Japan	569	1,552†	21
India	312	263	1
Malaysia	191	53	24
Australia	2,064	843	277
New Zealand	541	132	280
South Africa*	895	227	85
Poland	135	132	9
Yugoslavia	78	42	6
WORLD TOTAL‡	102,900	25,910	

* 1960.
† Including three-wheeled vehicles.
‡ Excluding U.S.S.R., Bulgaria, Czechoslovakia, East Germany, Hungary, Romania, and mainland China.
SOURCE: United Nations, *Statistical Yearbook*, 1962.

countries with state-owned rail systems have taken strong action to limit such competition, partly to safeguard railway revenues and partly to prevent damage to poor road surfaces by an unrestricted volume of heavy truck traffic. In South Africa long-distance trucking is virtually forbidden, and it is rigorously controlled in New Zealand. In Australia the freedom of interstate commerce is guaranteed by the constitution, and effective control has proved difficult; intrastate traffic by roads, however, is effectively regulated by the states. Most European countries impose regulations on road transport, particularly in long-distance trucking; the most extreme case is perhaps that of Britain, which has a Transport Commission charged with responsibility for operating all forms of transport within the country.[12]

Since the Thirties there has been a considerable increase in the mileage of limited-access multilane highways, in which sharp curves and steep grades are avoided and the traffic streams are physically separated. The first such roads were the *autostrade* of Italy and the *autobahnen* of Germany, constructed in the Thirties to serve military ends; the construction of such superhighways for commercial purposes soon spread to the United States, which now accounts for a very large share of their total extent. The new limited access roads, of which the Pennsylvania Turnpike was the first, were financed by local bond issues, and the costs of construction were recovered by the imposition of a toll. This twentieth century turnpike era came to an end with the decision of the Federal government to construct a network of superhighways spanning the entire country, incorporating part of the existing turnpike network. The benefits of this new system of roads are difficult to assess; there was certainly strong political pressure for their construction, generated by the manufacturers of motor vehicles and earthmoving and construction machinery and by the oil companies. Where such road building was intended to relieve congestion in urbanized areas, it has been entirely abortive; each new highway has become saturated within a short period of its opening.

The costs of road construction have been considerably reduced by the remarkable machines that have been developed in the United States for road building, which offer the possibility of constructing intercontinental highways even in the difficult physical conditions of the intertropical world. Considerable progress has been made with the construction of the Pan-American highway linking most of the Latin American capitals with the United States, and proposals for a Trans-African and a Trans-Asian highway have been made. A long awaited Trans-Canada highway was completed in 1962.

INLAND WATERWAYS

It is sometimes difficult to appreciate the supreme importance of rivers, lakes, and coastal waters as a means of transportation in earlier times, so completely have these media been eclipsed by overland transportation in most advanced economies. The principal advantage of inland waterways is that they are largely provided by nature and the capital equipment required to make use of them is small; water transport, moreover, makes possible the movement of very heavy loads with the minimum application of energy, and transport costs are therefore very low. The shortcomings of natural waterways, however, are very considerable; rivers frequently flow in directions which discourage their use as arteries of commerce, and their sinuous courses and the fact

[12] The carriage of a manufacturer's goods in his own vehicles is, however, largely free, and there has been considerable denationalization of road transport since 1951.

that traffic is usually compelled to travel at low speeds mean that such transportation can only be used where time is not a pressing factor. Natural waterways may also be closed for a considerable portion of the year, either because of the lack of water during dry seasons or, at high latitudes, through freezing.

The utility of natural waterways can often be greatly enhanced through dredging, the construction of locks and other regulation works, and canalization; there are, in fact, relatively few important inland waterways that have not required some improvement of this kind. In the late eighteenth and early nineteenth centuries the construction of artificial waterways, or canals, became joint stock enterprises of major importance in Western Europe and in North America; with the coming of the railways, however, many canals fell into disuse. Inland navigation at present is very largely a state responsibility, and new canal construction or river improvement is often part of multipurpose schemes for utilizing water resources. In effect, water transport is often as heavily subsidized as road transport.

The Great Lakes and Other Waterway Systems

Although inland waterways may be of considerable local or regional importance, there is only one system (excluding the Suez and Panama canals, which are primarily used by oceangoing vessels engaged in international trade) that can be regarded as of major significance in the world economy as a whole—the Great Lakes of North America. Before World War II the average size of cargo vessels operating on the Great Lakes was larger than that of those on the open oceans, and the annual tonnage of shipping passing through the Sault Ste. Marie (Soo) Canals connecting Superior and Huron frequently exceeded that of the Suez and Panama canals combined. The growth of the world's tanker fleet and the tremendous increase in oil exports from the Middle East have invalidated both these statements, but traffic on the lakes is impressive enough; the total freight tonnage moved by "lakers" is about one-tenth of that carried by all international seaborne shipping, though on a value basis, of course, their share of freight is very much less. The greater part of this tremendous freight tonnage consists of eastbound iron ore, limestone, and wheat; coal is the principal westbound cargo.

An extraordinarily favorable combination of geographic circumstances is largely responsible for the tremendous importance of the Great Lakes in the economy of North America; they span the considerable distance that separates the most important sources of iron ore from those of metallurgical coking coal, and they bring the spring-wheat region within easy access of the populous northeastern markets and the great ports of the Atlantic coast. Apart from the Soo Canals and the Welland Canal, which overcomes the obstacle formed by the Niagara escarpment between Erie and Ontario, few major improvements have been necessary. Many lakeside ports, moreover, have overcome a problem that continues to bedevil many of the world's greatest ports—how to achieve rapid turnaround of vessels. Elaborate equipment for rapid loading and discharging is installed at all important lake ports, for with a closed season of four months' duration rapid turnaround of vessels is essential.

Long accessible to specially constructed ocean vessels capable of negotiating the old shallow-draft canals around the rapids of the St. Lawrence River, the Great Lakes could also be entered by more than three-quarters of the world's total shipping tonnage after the St. Lawrence Seaway was completed in 1959. Though bitterly opposed by the railways and by the Atlantic ports, the much-discussed seaway project finally became a reality as a result of the determination of the Canadian government to construct it unaided if necessary. Its first two navigational seasons did not come up to the expectations of its supporters or of those lakeside cities that had invested heavily in port improvements in the hope of attracting a share of the nation's overseas trade. Nevertheless, there is a good reason for believing that the long-term effects of the seaway will be profound.

The glaciated plain of northern Europe also possesses an important system of waterways, formed by generally south-to-north rivers linked by east-west canals. The main focus of the system is the lower Rhine and Maas, where two great ports, Antwerp and Rotterdam, compete for the trade of the Rhine valley. The political division of Germany, however, has reduced the usefulness of the formerly important Mittelland Canal, which connects the three principal rivers of north Germany. As on the Great Lakes, raw materials for the iron and steel industry form the most important traffic on the waterways of northwest Europe. Considerable sums are being invested by the EEC countries in waterway improvements in connection with development plans for the iron and steel industry and the Europort project; of particular importance is the Moselle Canal.[13] This long-discussed scheme was finally brought to fruition in 1964, making the Lorraine iron and steel area accessible by the largest Rhine barges. The EEC has now decided to construct a Rhône-Rhine canal and to make other navigational improvements that would permit large barges to operate between Rotterdam and Marseille.

The U.S.S.R. also possesses what appears from the map to be a first-class system of inland waterways, and by means of canal interconnections it is now possible to transport goods between all the marginal seas of European Russia. The usefulness of the Russian waterways, however, is greatly reduced by the fact that navigation is only possible for eight months of the year in the southern portion of the country and for a considerably shorter period in the north. Much improvement of waterways originated in vast multipurpose and capital-intensive schemes of the late Stalin era, schemes which are difficult to justify on economic grounds. Only a small proportion of Russia's total inland freight traffic passes over its waterways, and of this it is estimated that the Volga alone accounts for about half. Timber, coal, petroleum, grain, and cotton are the principal freights, and the use of the waterway system is encouraged by rates considerably lower than those levied by the railways. However, there appears to be a strong preference for the railways in order to avoid delays and damage in transit, and attempts to encourage the use of the Caspian-Volga route for the transport of cotton from Soviet central Asia have not been successful. Petroleum shipments, moreover, will decline considerably with the extension of the pipeline network.

OCEAN TRANSPORT

Ocean transport outranks all others on a ton-mile basis and is the medium most closely associated with international trade. A certain amount of domestic trade is also carried on by seagoing coasting vessels, but in most countries this trade is steadily declining. The coasting trade is usually reserved to ships of the country concerned (cabotage), and such is the case in the United States, which is a high-cost shipping operator. But congestion and delays in turnaround in port often offset the low costs that coastal shipping can offer for bulk cargoes; in Europe the declining importance of coal as a source of energy has also led to a reduction in the coastal trade.

[13] See p. 385.

The size of the world's merchant marine has grown *pari passu* with the increasing volume of international trade and in 1961 stood at 40 million gross registered tons.[14] It is customary to divide shipping services by distinguishing between liners, operating on fixed routes and schedules, and tramps, which are nonscheduled and seek cargoes wherever available, though the distinction is not a hard-and-fast one in practice. There is a general tendency for liners to enlarge their share of world trade. In part this is a reflection of technological progress; vessels tend to become more specialized and to operate at higher speed, but tramps must be unspecialized and to maintain a cost advantage operate at modest speed. Even before World War II many new freighters had speeds of 16 knots, but by 1960 19 to 20 knots was increasingly common; to a ship operating on Australia-to-Europe or transpacific runs, such an increase in speed makes possible an extra round trip in the year. The reduction in coasting trade has also affected tramp shipping, but probably the most important factor in its relative decline has been the subsidization of national shipping fleets by the autarchic policies of many governments.

The most important development in the composition of the world's shipping fleet in recent years has been the rapid growth of tanker fleets, which in 1962 accounted for nearly one-third of the total registered tonnage. Scarcely less remarkable, however, has been the increasing size of tankers themselves; in the early Fifties vessels of 30,000 deadweight tons were considered very large, but by the middle Fifties 60,000 deadweight tons was by no means uncommon for new tanker construction, and at the end of the decade 100,000 deadweight tons had been exceeded in a number of vessels. The oil industry is the only industrial enterprise that is heavily in the shipping business;[15] about one-third of the total tanker tonnage is owned and operated by oil companies themselves and is kept fully employed, the balance consisting of vessels that are owned either by specialists such as the well-known groups of Niarchos and Onassis or by regular shipping lines and that operate under charter.

Shipping Nations of the World

With its far-flung colonial empire, its great and still expanding foreign trade, and the commanding lead it had enjoyed in the construction and operation of the steam-powered ship, Britain in 1914 dominated the world shipping scene, possessing about half the total tonnage. By 1962 Britain's merchant marine was but little larger than on the eve of World War I, and its share of the total world tonnage had fallen to but 16 per cent. Britain, moreover, no longer possessed the world's largest merchant fleet, that distinction having been assumed by the United States as a result of its tremendous World War II construction. However, a very large part of the United States merchant fleet is inactive and consists of general-purpose carriers designed for rapid construction; though uneconomic to operate under present conditions, a large fleet is preserved for use in an emergency, and a large part is used for the storage of surplus agricultural commodities. Britain thus retains the world's largest active merchant marine (Table 21-3).

Britain's progressively declining share of world shipping reflects its diminishing share of world trade. However, an increasing proportion of Britain's own trade has been carried on by foreign vessels, a fact which suggests some shortcomings on the part of Britain's ships and

[14] As noted on p. 443, the gross tonnage of a ship measures the volumetric content of the ship in units of 100 cubic feet, less certain deductions.

[15] The iron and steel industry also has a considerable interest in shipping, but its scale of operations is very much smaller.

Table 21-3

Merchant Shipping Fleets, 1962 (Millions of gross registered tons)

	TANKERS	TOTAL
United States	4.7	23.3
Panama	2.2	3.8
Liberia	6.7	10.6
Britain	7.5	21.7
Norway	6.7	12.5
Sweden	1.4	4.2
Denmark*		2.4
West Germany*		4.9
France	2.2	5.2
Italy	1.9	5.4
Netherlands	1.5	5.2
Greece*		6.5
Japan	2.3	8.9
India*		1.0
Poland*		0.9
U.S.S.R.*		4.7
WORLD TOTAL	45.3	140.0
Steamships		73.7
Motorships		66.3

* Division unobtainable.
SOURCE: United Nations, *Statistical Yearbook*, 1962.

ports; Britain was comparatively slow to adopt the motor ship, which has been such an important factor in the growth of the Scandinavian merchant fleet, and was even slower to build and operate the profitable large bulk-carriers turned out by Japanese and Scandinavian yards. Another reason for the relative decline of British shipping has been the autarchic policies followed by many nations in subsidizing their respective national fleets; France, Germany, Italy, and the United States have done their best to reserve their overseas trade to vessels flying the national flag, and the United States requires that at least 50 per cent of the shipment of goods provided under foreign aid schemes and of surplus agricultural commodities shall be made in American vessels. The logical consequences of such policies, as is pointed out by British shipowners, who have never been subsidized to any degree by their government, is that a substantial part of the cargo fleet of the world will be compelled to travel one way in ballast. Britain's shipping interests are still worldwide, however, and its P & O (Peninsular and Oriental) group is the world's largest shipping organization.

Greece, the Netherlands, and Norway resemble Britain in their strong maritime traditions, and all have large merchant fleets in relation to their populations. The Norwegian economy is particularly outstanding for the large contribution the national income receives from shipping services, and the country, in contrast to Britain, has enlarged its share of the world's merchant marine; in 1962 its merchant fleet was considerably more than twice as large as it was in 1939. As Denmark and Sweden have also considerably expanded their tonnage, the three Scandinavian countries collectively occupy an important position in the world shipping industry, and their combined fleets are little inferior in magnitude to that of Britain.

The large merchant fleets of Germany, Italy, and Japan in 1934 were almost entirely destroyed during World War II; since 1945, however, their recovery has been rapid, and another development of considerable importance has been the growth of registrations under the "flags of convenience," particularly those of Panama and Liberia. Panamanian registration was used by owners of tankers and of general-cargo vessels even before World War II; but Liberian registration has been closely connected with the growth of the oil export trade of the Middle East, and the greater part consists of American- and Greek-owned tanker tonnage. The principal reason for the use of such flags is to avoid taxation and to escape from regulation, particularly in respect of wages. The payment of registration fees to governments has traditionally been made in return for services rendered by governments to companies registering ships at their ports, but the governments of the flags of convenience scarcely provide any such services, and the use of such registrations has been vigorously opposed by the seamen's unions of every important shipping country. It is notable that British shipping and oil companies have made relatively little use of such registrations, largely for patriotic reasons.

Newly independent countries have also shown considerable interest in the development of national fleets in order to improve their balance-of-payments positions; India's merchant fleet slightly exceeded 1 million tons in 1962. The U.S.S.R., on the other hand, is an unimportant shipping nation, a fact that reflects its small share of world trade and its limited extent of ice-free coast; it is, however, acquiring a large mainly foreign-built tanker fleet. Russia's sudden and unpredictable ventures into foreign trade are usually handled by chartering; it has made much use of chartered vessels to fulfill its new commitments to Cuba.

Shipping Routes

Shipping moves across the oceans of the world in certain well-defined lanes a score or more miles in width, usually following great circles but deviating to avoid natural obstacles and occasionally shifting with the passage of the seasons, moving polewards in summer and equatorwards in winter for better weather. Sometimes the two causes of deviation are combined. This is the situation with the world's most important route, that across the North Atlantic, where the danger from icebergs, which enter the ocean in large numbers with the coming of spring, has been effectively held in check since the *Titanic* disaster of 1912 by the operations of the International Ice Patrol.

Despite numerous predictions during the century that its role would be usurped by the Pacific, the North Atlantic still remains by far the most important artery of international commerce and is crossed by several routes, of which the most important is the northerly one between Western Europe and eastern North America. A second route diverges southwards to the Caribbean and the Panama Canal and is used by lines connecting Europe with the west coast of North and South America, the Pacific islands, and New Zealand and by cer-

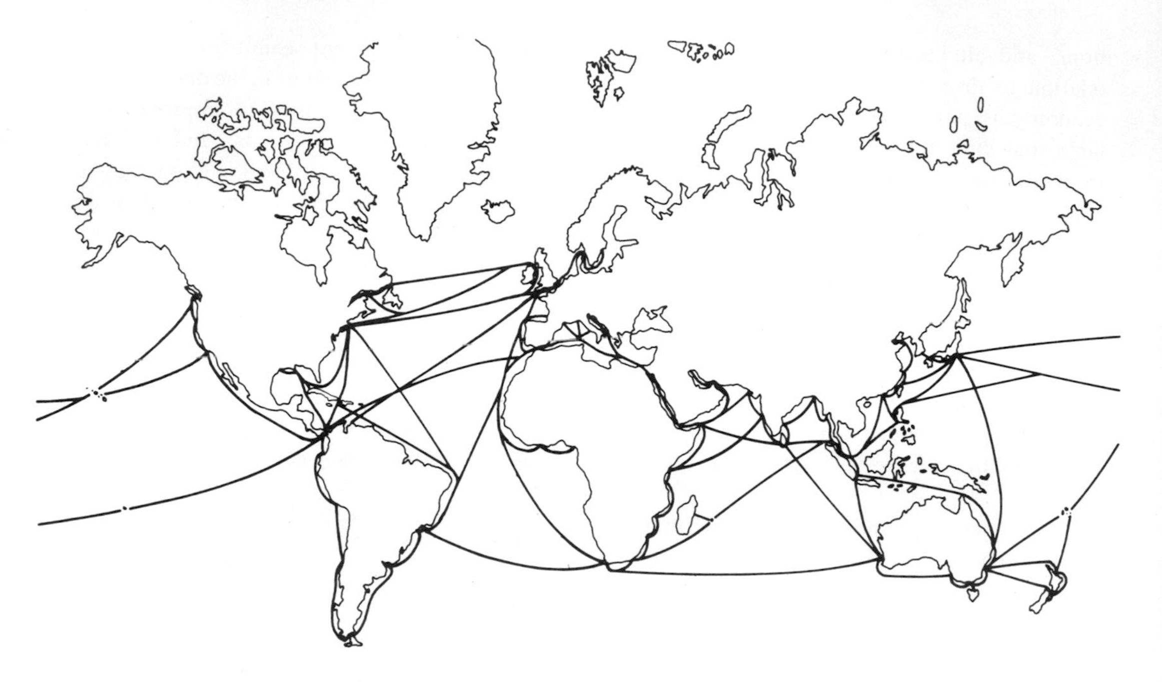

Fig. 21-3 World shipping routes.

tain round-the-world routes; the southernmost route makes for the ports of southeast Brazil and the La Plata estuary. These three routes coalesce to the southwest of the English Channel with those from the Cape and the Mediterranean in the "Western Approaches" of the British Admiralty, scene of one of the key battles of World War II, where is normally to be found the greatest concentration of shipping at sea in the world (Fig. 21-3).

The second major shipping route is of considerable antiquity and connects Western Europe (and increasingly, eastern North America) via the Mediterranean and the Suez Canal with the Persian Gulf, India, Southeast Asia, the Far East, and Australia. This route has sometimes been called the lifeline of the British Empire, so essential was it to the preservation of the imperial territories; commercially, however, it has never been as important to Britain as the northernmost route across the North Atlantic. This Eastern route was also of considerable significance to France and the Netherlands, both of which had colonial possessions in Southeast Asia. The opening of the Suez Canal in 1869 was mainly responsible for the rise of this Eastern route to a position of major importance in the world economy, but the rapid development of the oil industry of the Middle East after 1930 has been of scarcely less significance. Since 1939 traffic on the Suez Canal, both in terms of the tonnage of vessels making transits and in terms of cargoes, has more than quadrupled; so important had the canal become to Europe's energy supplies that its closing in 1956 precipitated a major fuel crisis. This great pressure on the canal has necessitated the adoption of the convoy system, the use of passing sections in the Bitter Lakes and in a special cut, and repeated dredging to accomodate the increasing size of tankers; in all probability the duplication of the existing canal will also have to be undertaken. Despite prophecies in 1956 of dire disaster the nationalized canal administration has proved equal to every demand made upon it.

All other ocean shipping routes are of minor importance in comparison; these include the route from Europe to the Indian Ocean via the Cape, which becomes of major significance only in emergencies, as during World War II and in 1956; the route from eastern North America via Panama to the west coast; and the routes across the North and South Pacific. Japan's increasing trade with North America has resulted in some slight increase in the importance of the North Pacific route, but for Japan itself the route southwards to Southeast Asia and the Indian Ocean is of greater significance. Though traffic through the Panama Canal since 1945 has not increased at anything like the rate of that passing through the Suez, the growth in the number of vessels making transits has produced considerable congestion, particularly through the locks (from which Suez is free); a number of preliminary investigations for an additional canal across the isthmus of Central America have been made, but it seems likely that, if undertaken, a second route through the territory of the Panama Republic will be selected. The political problems are formidable, for rising Latin American nationalism has confronted the United States with a situation not unlike that faced by Britain and France in Egypt before the Suez crisis of 1956. The Panama Canal forms part of the main route from New Zealand to Britain and is used by a number of interesting round-the-world routes. These were pioneered by Dutch and Japanese shipping interests before World War II and have since been successfully revived; certain British companies serving South Africa, Australia, and New Zealand have also shown increasing interest in such services.

While the route between Europe and the United States has long been the most profitable in passenger traffic, with increasing competition from the air this is rapidly ceasing to be the case, and the prospects for transatlantic passenger services look far from promising. On the other hand, the Suez route to Australia has become steadily more important and has shown itself less vulnerable to air competition; the latest vessels placed in service are quite the rivals of most Atlantic liners in size, speed, and opulence, as well as a good deal more profitable. In part this prosperity is a result of a heavily subsidized immigration policy—more than 1 million immigrants entered Australia in the decade after 1948—but the prospect of varied ports of call, the certainty that the greater part of the journey will be performed under ideal weather conditions at almost any time of year, the strong ties between Australia and Britain, the very high Australian per capita income, and a remarkably strong valuation placed by Australians upon leisure all assist in ensuring a high level of bookings in the return direction. In contrast, traffic on the North Atlantic shows a heavy bias in one direction at certain times of year, towards Europe in the spring and summer, and towards North America in the fall.

Structure of the Shipping Industry Shipping is by its very nature an activity open to every nation with access to the sea, and international competition is fierce. But many countries that are high-cost operators possess large merchant fleets, as for one reason or another many governments subsidize their national shipping fleets. American shipping lines depend heavily on subsidies to remain in operation, and France has also long been noted for the substantial assistance given by the state both to shipbuilding and to ship operation. Even with the payment of considerable subsidies, United States shipping is not competitive; the main reason for this, so owners assert, is that they are forced to pay wages far above those paid by competitors. Wages are not, however, the only item in costs even if they are an important one; the United States has been even slower than Britain to exploit the economic motor ship.

Wherever competition is fierce, attempts are made to mitigate its severity, and the shipping industry is no exception, particularly as vessels are becoming steadily more costly to construct and to operate. Amalgamation offers the possibility of a more economic deployment of capacity, and some very large combinations, such as Britain's P & O and Ellerman groups, are virtually worldwide in their operations. The state may have a partial or sole interest in certain shipping lines; the Italia-Lloyd Triestino group is owned by the Italian government, and before World War II the Japanese government also had a very large interest in overseas shipping. Several newly independent nations—Israel, Ghana, India, and Indonesia—possess national shipping lines. But despite the tendency towards larger groupings, many small enterprises continue in existence, particularly in tramp shipping.

Another method frequently adopted to reduce competition has been the conclusion of formal or "gentlemen's" agreements to maintain freight rates at a given level; all main routes at one time or another have been the subject of such "conferences," as they are called in shipping circles, but their preservation is a matter of some difficulty—there is always a strong temptation for some operators to remain outside and to profit by the price umbrella of the participants.

The Ports of the World

Though not part of the shipping industry, ports render services which are essential to oceanic transportation.

The ports of the world total many thousands, but the number of those of major significance to the world economy is very small. Only about 160 have shipping arrivals exceeding 2 million net tons per annum, and less than 30 of these have arrivals exceeding 10 million tons; 4 ports—New York, Antwerp, London, and Rotterdam—have entries exceeding 20 million net tons per annum.[16]

Perhaps a more satisfactory index of the importance of a port, however, is the tonnage of goods loaded and unloaded; on such a basis Aden, one of the world's greatest ports from the standpoint of tonnage entering, dwindles to minimal significance. In 1960 there were 28 ocean ports of the world handling mainly general cargoes with a combined freight tonnage exceeding 10 million tons; 9 of these were located in the United States, 8 in the EEC countries, 4 in Japan, 3 in Britain, and 2 in Canada. A further 19 ocean ports handling mainly petroleum also exceeded this figure, as did 2 ports mainly handling coal and 8 United States Great Lakes ports (Table 21-4).

It is a striking fact that the great ports of the world almost always record a considerably larger tonnage of goods unloaded than goods loaded, that is, that on a tonnage basis, imports tend to exceed exports. For some of the very largest ports—New York, London, Rotterdam, Philadelphia, Hamburg, and Yokohama—the disparity is particularly heavy. Two factors account for this: great ports are almost always of major importance as industrial and distributive centers and thus attract a very large share of the import trade, whereas exports, particularly those of a bulk nature, are often shipped through minor ports close to the point of origin. Ports with a substantial export surplus on a tonnage basis are usually heavily specialized; they include, above all, those handling petroleum (Mena al Ahmadi, Kuwait, handles by far the largest export tonnage of any port in the world), coal, iron ore, and mineral

[16] **F. W. Morgan,** *Ports and Harbours,* **rev. ed., Hutchinson & Co. (Publishers), Ltd., London, 1958, pp. 18–20.**

Table 21-4

Seaborne Freight Traffic at World Ports, 1960 (Tons of cargo loaded and unloaded)

OVER 50 MILLION	30–50 MILLION	15–30 MILLION	10–15 MILLION	7–10 MILLION
New York	Maracaibo, Venezuela*	Hamburg	Singapore	Tampa
Rotterdam	Aruba, N.W.I.*	Bandar Mashur, Iran*	Bremen	New Castle, Pa.
Mena al Ahmadi, Kuwait*	Curaçao, N.W.I.*	Baltimore	Puerto Ordaz, Venezuela*	Narvik, Norway†
London	Houston*	San Francisco	Le Havre	Naples
	Antwerp	Ra's Tannūrah, Saudi Arabia*	Baton Rouge, La.	Sydney
	Puerto La Cruz, Venezuela*	Southampton	Sept-Iles, Canada†	Casablanca
	Philadelphia	Norfolk, Va.	Abādān, Iran*	Santos, Brazil
		Los Angeles	Fao, Iraq*	Melbourne
		Marseille	Newport News, Va.	Hull
		New Orleans	Vancouver, B.C.	Copenhagen
		Amuay Bay, Venezuela*	Mobile, Ala.	Portland, Ore.
		Banias, Syria*	Paulsboro, N.J.*	Swansea
		Punta Cardon, Venezuela*	Tokyo	Durban
		Beaumont, Tex.*	Osaka	Bristol
		Boston	Kobe	Hong Kong
		Yokohama	Buenos Aires	Szezecin, Poland
		Port Arthur, Tex.*	Amsterdam	
		Sidon, Lebanon		
		Montreal		
		Liverpool		
		Genoa		
		Portland, Me.*		

* Petroleum ports.
† Iron-ore ports.
Note: Since 1962, Rotterdam has been the world's largest port.
SOURCE: United Nations, *Monthly Bulletin of Statistics*, January, 1961.

fertilizers. In the United States, ports with a surplus of tonnage loaded over tonnage unloaded include New Orleans, Houston, Galveston, a number of minor Gulf petroleum ports, and the coal ports Newport News and Norfolk; in Canada, Vancouver, Halifax, and the iron-ore port of Sept-Iles occupy a similar position. Rangoon and Bangkok, the two principal rice-exporting ports of the world, are anomalous in that although they are the principal ports of their respective countries, export tonnage exceeds import tonnage.

Ports vary tremendously in their equipment, according to the physical setting of the port itself, on the one hand, and according to the nature of the traffic handled and the market or hinterland served, on the other. Of these two sets of factors the second is by far the more important, and numerous examples can be quoted of artificial harbors that have been created in response to the demands of a growing volume of traffic. Ports, in fact, grow steadily more artificial as the size of vessels increases; the total number capable of handling supertankers of 100,000 deadweight tons and upwards is less than a dozen, and virtually none of these is natural. It scarcely need be said that specialized ports and terminals have elaborate facilities for the rapid loading and discharging of their respective cargoes, so that the turnaround of tankers and ore carriers is extraordinarily rapid. General-cargo ports in the highly developed economies have a multiplicity of devices for rapid discharging of cargoes—cranes, grabs, elevators, belt and chain conveyors and transporters—and the degree of mechanization is being steadily enlarged. In contrast to the multiplicity of dockside cranes in most major European ports, ports in the United States generally rely on ships' gear for the discharging of general cargoes. The situation in ports of countries at lower levels of development is similar to that of the United States; though it ranks among the first twenty ports of the world by any criterion, Singapore has few dockside cranes, and all general cargo is handled by ships' gear.

Ports compete vigorously among themselves; only specialized ports can possess a geographically distinct hinterland, and the vast majority compete on varying terms with near or distant neighbors for traffic in every item of freight. Improved handling and storage facilities or better transport to and from the port may succeed in attracting a larger share of traffic in a particular commodity. One of the principal factors in port competition at the present, however, is the question of labor relations. Port employment resembles coal mining in possessing an exceedingly bitter history of labor relations; the work is heavy, dirty, and not infrequently dangerous; above all, however, it has been casual, resulting in highly erratic earnings and considerable periods of unemployment, and in the past port workers have often been grievously exploited. The complete elimination of casual labor in ports is impossible, although in many countries much has been done to mitigate its consequences through unemployment and guaranteed wage schemes. Nevertheless, much of the traditional hostility between employers and labor remains, and the introduction of more mechanized methods of moving cargo has been fiercely resisted by organized labor, even though this has removed much of the hard work previously inseparable from port employment. In some areas mechanization has only been introduced after prolonged struggles and on terms under which the greatest benefits have accrued to labor.

Increased mechanization and rapid turnaround of vessels are essential if owners are to profit from the higher operating speeds of modern freighters. In many countries turnaround is very protracted, even where considerable mechanical equipment is installed; nowhere is the situation worse than in Australia and New Zealand. Extreme militancy of labor in a port is often accompanied by a high incidence of damage and pilfering, and ports where such conditions are much in evidence are tending to lose ground to others that can compensate for less favorable locations or facilities by better labor relations. New York has been losing trade to Philadelphia and New Orleans, and London to Continental ports precisely for these reasons. Trade once transferred from one port to another cannot easily be attracted back.

AIR TRANSPORT

Regular commercial air services date only from the end of World War I, but by the end of the interwar period a considerable network of routes had been created and only the North Atlantic remained to be spanned. Since 1945 air travel has grown enormously; between 1948 and 1960 the number of passenger-miles flown increased more than fivefold and in the latter year totaled about 70 billion; about two-thirds of this was accounted for by services provided within the United States and by flights to and from the country. Freight traffic has shown a similar rate of growth, but nonetheless still accounts for an insignificant fraction of total freight traffic.

As air transportation involves a very heavy expenditure of energy, it is prohibitively expensive for most types of freight and can only be employed in the case of goods of small bulk and high value or of extremely perishable nature. Mail services formed the sole support of many early airlines, and mail is still the most important freight item; orchids and other exotic flowers and fruits and radioactive isotopes for medical or for scientific purposes are now extensively transported by air. However, spare parts for machines or even complete machines are now airlifted if the high cost of doing so is less than that resulting from loss of production entailed by the employment of alternative methods of transport.

For passenger traffic, on the other hand, the cost of air travel is little if at all greater than that of travel by sea, and in most cases the convenience and speed of the modern airliner is often worth the payment of a premium; since 1960 the number of passengers traveling by air across the North Atlantic has exceeded that traveling by sea.

Aircraft operate in a continuous medium and can therefore fly in great circles between their starting point and destination. In practice air routes avoid major physical obstacles such as high mountains wherever possible, and they have to select alignments that offer the maximum possibility of traffic. In every country landing rights and permission to pick up and to set down passengers are strictly controlled, but there are usually granted to foreign airlines on a *quid pro quo* basis; the right to pick up and set down passengers within the same country is nevertheless regarded as a form of cabotage and is generally reserved to airlines of the country concerned. Every phase of the air-transport industry is strictly regulated by national or international authority, in part in the interest of safety and in part in the interest of economic efficiency.

Air transport is more heavily subsidized than any other kind of transport, either through mail subsidies and the provision of landing fields, terminals, and navigational aids or through operational subsidies. In many countries airlines are opened by state agencies; the United States is unique in the free world in the retention of a largely private-enterprise air-transportation industry. Considerations of national prestige are primarily responsible for this world situation, for the expectation of a profitable return on investment is so slender and the capital requirements of a modern airline are so large that few private entrepreneurs would be willing to engage in such an activity. The possession of a national airline is frequently regarded as essential by many underdeveloped countries just to show that they are truly independent; that they are thus committed to a heavy outlay of scarce foreign exchange, are compelled to employ a considerable highly paid foreign labor force, and can expect a minimal return counts for little where national pride is involved.

Despite the heavy subsidies paid by governments, the return on invested capital in air transportation in the early Sixties was equivalent to that in railways and coal mining; it cannot compare with that of the "growth" industries. The main reason for this situation is that the industry has grown too rapidly, that capacity has outstripped demand. The use of aircraft of progressively larger size has resulted in considerable economies of scale, but the introduction of jet aircraft not only very greatly enlarged carrying capacity but also threatened to terminate the still useful lives of the last generation of piston-engined craft. The high cost of jet-engined airliners (about 8 million dollars) necessitates their maximum employment; this, however, has been hampered by the higher fares that operators of older aircraft have forced upon jet operators for equivalent services and by the fact that very many airlines are too small to justify the employment of jet aircraft. Nevertheless, most of the world's national airlines and all of the large American companies have reequipped with jet airliners since 1959, with the result that for several years planes have operated far below the load factor necessary for profitable operation. It would seem that further combination is necessary in the air-transportation industry before the world's airlines are called upon to invest in the still larger and more expensive supersonic craft on the drawing boards.

SELECTED REFERENCES

Alexandersson, Gunnar, and Göran Norström: *World Shipping,* Almquist & Wicksell, Stockholm, and John Wiley & Sons, Inc., New York, 1963.

Ballert, Albert G.: "The Great Lakes Coal Trade: Present and Future," *Economic Geography,* vol. 29, pp. 48–58, 1953.

Bigham, Truman C., and Merrill J. Roberts: *Transportation: Principles and Problems,* McGraw-Hill Book Company, New York, 1952.

Buchanan, C. D.: *Mixed Blessing,* Leonard Hill, London, 1958.

———: *Traffic in Towns,* H. M. Stationery Office, London, 1963.

Chang, Kuei-sheng: "The Changing Railroad Pattern in Mainland China," *Geographical Review,* vol. 51, pp. 534–548, 1961.

Fair, Marvin L., and Ernest W. Williams: *Economics of Transportation,* rev. ed., Harper & Row, Publishers, Incorporated, New York, 1959.

Gorter, W.: *United States Shipping Policy,* Harper & Row, Publishers, Incorporated, New York, 1956.

Harper, D. V.: *Economic Regulation of the Motor Trucking Industry by the States,* The University of Illinois Press, Urbana, Ill., 1959.

Hunter, H.: *Soviet Transportation Policy,* Harvard University Press, Cambridge, Mass., and Oxford University Press, London, 1958.

International Labour Organisation, Inland Transport Committee, 7th Session: *Social Consequences of Changing Methods and Techniques in Railways and Road Transport,* Geneva, 1961.

Marx, D., Jr.: *International Shipping Cartels,* Princeton University Press, Princeton, N.J., and Oxford University Press, London, 1953.

Morgan, F. W.: *Ports and Harbours,* rev. ed., Hutchinson & Co. (Publishers), Ltd., London, 1958.

Neft, David: "Some Aspects of Rail Commuting: New York, London and Paris," *Geographical Review,* vol. 49, pp. 151–163, 1959.

O'Dell, Andrew: *Railways and Geography,* Hutchinson & Co. (Publishers), Ltd., London, 1956.

Organisation for European Economic Cooperation: *Federal Regulation of Transport in the U.S.A.,* Paris, 1953.

———: *Maritime Transport,* Paris, 1957.

———: *Railroads in the U.S.A.,* Paris, 1952.

Rees, Henry: *British Ports and Shipping,* George G. Harrap & Co., Ltd., London, 1958.

Sealey, Kenneth R.: *Geography of Air Transport,* Hutchinson & Co. (Publishers), Ltd., London, 1957.

Sturmey, S. R.: *British Shipping and World Competition,* Athlone Press, London, 1963.

Taafe, Edward J.: "*Air Passenger Hinterland of Chicago,* University of Chicago, Department of Geography Research Paper No. 24, 1952.

———: "Air Transportation and United States Urban Distribution," *Geographical Review,* vol. 46, pp. 219–238, 1961.

Taafe, Robert N.: *Rail Transportation and the Economic Development of Soviet Central Asia,* University of Chicago, Department of Geography Research Paper No. 64, Chicago, 1960.

Ullman, Edward L.: *American Commodity Flow,* University of Washington Press, Seattle, 1958.

———: "The Railroad Pattern of the United States," *Geographical Review,* vol. 39, No. 2, pp. 242–356, April, 1949.

Wallace, W. H.: "Railroad Traffic Densities and Patterns," *Annals of the Association of American Geographers,* vol. 48, pp. 352–374, 1958.

Wheatcroft, Steven: *Economics of European Air Transportation,* Harvard University Press, Cambridge, Mass., and Manchester University Press, Manchester, 1956.

Woytinsky, W. S., and E. S. Woytinsky: *World Commerce and Governments,* The Twentieth Century Fund, New York, 1955, pp. 305–559.

Chapter 22

INTERNATIONAL TRADE

International trade is but a part of trade in general, and it does not differ essentially from any other kind of trade save that many more restrictions are often placed in its way; but as it takes place across national frontiers, it is often spoken of as if it involved transactions between countries. The right of governments to regulate foreign trade has never seriously been questioned, but except in the centrally planned economies and occasionally in countries with chronic balance-of-payments difficulties, government-to-government trading is comparatively rare. In the free world the great majority of transactions in international trade are concluded between individuals, or more usually between corporations, that may also carry on a large domestic trade. Some countries at a high level of development, however, have state marketing agencies for certain of their primary products and these agencies either trade on their own account or allocate consumption between home and foreign use; also, international agreements have been concluded to regulate foreign trade in wheat, sugar, coffee, and tin, and several more such agreements appear probable in the future. It is thus convenient to speak of international trade between countries, but in considering its many problems it is often better to regard it as involving transactions between *producers* and *consumers*. These, of course, do not deal with each other directly but through intermediate merchants, precisely as in domestic trade.

THE BASES AND TRADITIONS OF WORLD TRADE

Nations engage in trade for many reasons. An obvious one is that they wish to acquire commodities that for physical reasons they are unable to produce themselves; countries in temperate latitudes thus import many foodstuffs and agricultural raw materials from tropical lands. Nations also import ores, metals, or supplies of fuel from countries where these commodities are in plentiful supply, in order to make good any domestic deficiency. In practice all nations have to engage in trade of this kind; none is large enough or sufficiently well endowed with physical resources to be independent of the rest of the world except for short periods or emergencies, and then only at considerable cost and inconvenience. But important though this trade is, it accounts for a minor proportion of world trade as a whole, for nations import many goods that could be produced at home; economies at an advanced level of development both import and export automobiles, machinery, electric apparatus, chemicals, and textiles, and the list could be extended almost indefinitely.

That nations trade in this manner follows from the advantages of international specialization and the application of the principle of *comparative costs.* First stated by the economist Ricardo over a century ago, the principle argues that nations are better off if they specialize in the production of goods in which they hold the greatest comparative advantages and leave the production of those in which they are at a comparative disadvantage to others; it is thus the *differential ratios* between the costs of producing different goods in various countries, rather than the absolute difference in international cost levels in the production of particular commodities, that motivate trade. A country may acquire a comparative advantage in a line of production in a number of ways; it may arise from the greater bounty of nature, the skill acquired through long tradition, or the intensity of capitalization; not infrequently all these factors reinforce each other.

International trade is reciprocal; a country can only import so long as it can acquire the foreign exchange with which to pay its suppliers either from the earnings of its exports or through the receipt of loans or capital donations. Equally, a country cannot continue to export without being prepared to absorb imports unless it or some other country is prepared to finance the purchase of such exports. In practice, therefore, exports pay for imports. It is not necessary or even desirable that a country should achieve an exact balance with every trading partner. In the long run, however, there exists a broad correspondence in value between a country's imports and its exports; if at any time there is surplus of exports over imports, the balance of trade is said to be favorable, while an excess of imports signifies an unfavorable balance of trade.

These terms are relics of the mercantilist policies pursued by all nations in the sixteenth and seventeenth centuries; an export surplus was considered desirable because it encouraged an inflow of gold and bullion in payment, while a surplus of imports, so it was agreed, tended to deplete a country's stock of gold and reduced national strength. These arguments were demolished in Adam Smith's famous *Wealth of Nations* almost two centuries ago, but many politicians and businessmen still regard a surplus of exports as being in some way beneficial and a surplus of imports as highly detrimental. Actually, large export surpluses are usually characteristic of underdeveloped economies, which have to achieve them in order to meet interest charges on foreign loans and dividends on foreign investment, as well as to pay for current imports. Some such countries it is true, such as India and China, do possess large unfavorable trade balances, but large import surpluses may nevertheless be accompanied by a very rapid growth of national production, as is exemplified by colonial North America and by modern Japan. For a country at a high level of development to have a very large export surplus, as was the case with the United States during the period between the world wars and the early post-World War II period, is a questionable luxury; in the United States this was largely financed by private and government loans and by the import of gold.

Trade is only one item of the financial transactions between countries that make up the balance of payments; import surpluses may be offset by "invisible exports," such as shipping, insurance, and other services provided for foreigners, or by the remission of interest and dividends on overseas loans and investment, transactions which largely made good the situation of Britain's import surplus in the interwar period. The remissions of emigrants have long been of major significance to Italy, Greece, India, and China; tourism, which has long been an important source of foreign earnings to the first two countries, is of increasing general significance.

Protection and Free Trade

Mercantilism involved a massive state interference and regulation of the national economy, but towards the end of the eighteenth century a new economic philosophy based on the writings of Adam Smith and the French physiocrats appeared, and in the nineteenth century it achieved a wide measure of acceptance. This was the doctrine of *laissez faire*—that government should refrain from interfering in economic life and that international trade should be free of restriction. For almost a century the principle of free trade was the economic lodestone of Britain, and the example of Britain was widely copied. And the growth of international trade in the nineteenth century was undoubtedly impressive; allowing for changes in prices, the volume of world imports and exports appears to have expanded about fifty times between 1820 and 1913.[1]

For Britain with its early industrialization, free trade was undoubtedly the correct policy; what was not so clear was whether it served equally well for countries whose industrialization came later and which were therefore faced with strong British competition. In the United States Alexander Hamilton and in Germany Friedrich List argued for the imposition of tariffs in order to protect "infant industries," and their arguments have been reiterated with various refinements down to the present. The debate is still unresolved, although the great majority of economists strongly support free trade, at least for countries at a high level of economic development. The case of underdeveloped economies, which have to modernize their economies under conditions far less favorable than those formerly enjoyed by the present advanced economies, is another matter; but even the most massive protection is unlikely to be sufficient to create a self-sustaining industrialization, and additional assistance apart from protection is generally required.

This is not to say, of course, that there may not be good cause for the imposition of tariffs in certain circumstances, particularly where they may make possible economies of scale, but in general, tariffs favor one section of the community—the protected producers, their suppliers, and their workers—at the expense of the whole; the high level of protection in the United States and in many European countries reflects the opportunities presented by their respective political systems for the exercise of pressure on behalf of sectional or regional interests.

Tariffs are sometimes classified as either protective or revenue-raising, but the distinction has little practical validity. There are a number of other methods of granting protection such as import quotas or exchange control, devices frequently adopted even by highly developed economies when they have temporarily severe balance-of-payments problems. Also, duties may be placed on exports, and

[1] **W. S. Woytinsky and E. S. Woytinsky,** *World Commerce and Governments,* **The Twentieth Century Fund, New York, 1955, p. 39.**

several underdeveloped economies have long derived the greater part of their revenues from such taxes. A greater problem to international trade, however, is posed by the subsidization of exports, usually of primary products, by the state, a common practice in many economies at a high level of development, and by dumping, that is, selling abroad by manufacturers below the price at home or even below cost of production. Most nations have antidumping legislation, but dumping is not easy to prove. In its dealings with other governments, each country tends to adopt a holier-than-thou attitude; Australia, for example, complains of the heavily subsidized exports of United States wheat but itself subsidizes the export of butter and sugar.

In 1914 there was a worldwide international economy with remarkably few restrictions on trade or on the mobility of factors of production. In the aftermath of World War I Russia made itself a self-contained economic unit, and barriers were placed on the flow of world trade which became progressively higher with the deepening of the Great Depression. The United States, traditionally a high-tariff country, in the Hawley-Smoot Tariff of 1930 imposed the highest duties in its history, and as each nation in turn raised duties and followed deflationary "beggar my neighbor" policies, the volume of world trade declined precipitately.

Recovery was to some extent assisted by attempts to expand trade through reciprocal agreements, and at the end of World War II the President of the United States was given further powers to negotiate tariff concessions. The world economy was reduced by the loss of further territory to the Soviet bloc, however, and with the rapid resuscitation of Europe's manufacturing industries reaction set in and the "escape clause" was often invoked to protect American industries. Nevertheless, the world appears to be moving towards a greater degree of trade freedom. The success of the EEC produced a long queue of applicants for either full or associate membership, and the Trade Expansion Act of 1962 places the President of the United States in a better position to negotiate reciprocal concessions with this important new economic unit and with other foreign countries.

THE COMPOSITION OF WORLD TRADE

The magnitude of world trade is eloquent testimony of its benefits; in 1960 the combined value of world imports and exports exceeded 260 billion dollars, a figure that was more than five times that for 1938.[2] Such a comparison ignores the problem of changing price levels, but even on a volume, or quantum, basis, world imports and exports over this period appear to have doubled. Great structural changes have accompanied this substantial increase in world trade, and although much depends on the method of classification of products adopted, the overall trend is clear.

Manufactures One of the most significant changes in the composition of world trade has been the steadily increasing importance of manufactures; its corollary is that the share of highly industrialized nations in world trade has also considerably enlarged (Table 22-1). In 1913 manufactures and machinery accounted for about one-third of the total value of world exports; by 1929 this share had risen to about 40 per cent, and in 1960 it was almost one-half.

This expansion may appear somewhat surprising in view of the ever wider dissemination of industrial activity about the world, and in

[2] The value of imports exceeds that of exports because it includes the cost of the imports themselves, insurance, and freight charges (c.i.f.); exports are valued on board (f.o.b.).

Table 22-1

Percentage Share of World Trade Turnover, 1960	
United States	13.3
Canada	4.3
EEC	22.6
West Germany	8.2
Belgium-Luxembourg	3.0
Netherlands	3.2
France	5.0
Italy	3.2
EFTA	15.6
Britain	8.5
Sweden	2.1
Switzerland	1.6
Denmark	1.2
Japan	3.3
Australia	1.7
Venezuela	1.3
South Africa	1.1
Middle East	3.6
Eastern bloc	11.8
U.S.S.R.	4.3
East Germany	1.5

SOURCE: Calculated from United Nations, *Yearbook of International Trade Statistics, 1960,* New York, 1962.

part it reflects changes in the "terms of trade"; the prices of agricultural products have declined relatively to prices of manufactures, largely because the world is maintaining far too many farmers of low productivity.[3] But the expansion also mirrors an important change in the composition of manufactures entering world trade. On the eve of the Great Depression (and a fortiori in 1914), exports of manufactures possessed a high content of consumer nondurables, particularly cotton textiles; such products, however, are among the first to be manufactured in newly industrializing countries, and it is scarcely surprising that their proportionate share in world exports has progressively declined. But as the industrial structures of the highly developed economies have progressively shifted towards a greater emphasis on metal-making, metal-consuming, and other capital-intensive industries, so too have their exports; consumer nondurables have tended to be replaced by capital goods, chemicals, and consumer durables, particularly motor vehicles. Such exports usually account

[3] While this statement in general is true, the reader is warned against drawing too much from it. Prices go up as well as down, and when primary producers talk about a fall in prices, they mean, in fact, a decline from the *previous peak.* It was inevitable that agricultural prices should fall after the scarcity of the immediate postwar years was overcome. Over the past half century, primary producers have done better than producers of manufactured products, if times of high prices are considered as well as periods of low prices. Moreover, primary products have remained largely unchanged by time; a modern motor vehicle is a considerable improvement over its prewar counterpart, and its "real" price is higher.

for one-half to two-thirds or more of the total value of exports of the highly developed economies,[4] and it is significant that the same structural changes are clearly visible in the recent history of Japan's export trade.

Moreover, although the highly developed economies compete to supply capital equipment to industrializing countries, they show an increasing disposition to trade with each other. This paradox was noted even before World War I, when Germany and Britain, although competing fiercely in world markets, nevertheless became increasingly important customers of each other. Since 1945 the economic resurgence of Europe has been accompanied by a remarkable increase in trade between the member countries of the EEC and between Western Europe and Anglo-America. Ultimately this situation arises from expectations of a continued high rate of economic growth, which translates a high rate of technical progress into heavy investment in capital-good industries. It seems reasonable to assume that as industrialization proceeds around the world the share of machinery and other "higher" manufactures in world trade will steadily enlarge.

Fuels, Ores, and Nonferrous Metals It is only to be expected that fuels, ores, and nonferrous metals, constituting as they do the underpinnings of the capital-intensive industries of the highly developed economies, should have increased very substantially in importance in world trade since 1939. Outstanding, of course, is the case of petroleum. Shortly before World War II petroleum products (crude and refined) displaced cotton as the leading commodity in world trade, and they have since far outranked all others; between 1937 and 1960 the share of petroleum products in the total value of world exports virtually doubled (Table 22-2), and the day may not be far distant when petroleum products account for 10 per cent of the value of all exports. The reasons for the tremendous expansion of the petroleum trade were made clear in Chapter 11. The tremendous growth of market-oriented refinery industries has inevitably affected the pattern of trade in petroleum products; in contrast with the prewar situation, crude oil is proportionately very much more important than refined products. The direction of trade in petroleum has also greatly changed with the rise of the Middle East as the major exporting region and the shift of the United States from the position of world's largest petroleum exporter to that of the world's largest importer.

The growth of the petroleum trade has more than compensated in the fuels commodity group for the decline in exports of the older mineral fuel, coal. The world coal trade reached its maximum level in 1913, when coal exports outranked in value those of any other commodity save cotton, but since then there has been an almost continual decline not only in the relative importance of coal in world trade but also in the gross volume of exports. Nevertheless, this has also been accompanied by dramatic changes in the direction of trade in coal, and the future of the coal trade is by no means bleak. The great European producers that dominated the pre-1914 and the interwar export trade have become importers, and the United States, once a minor exporter, now occupies the key position. European importers, particularly the iron and steel companies, would take substantially larger quantities of low-cost American coal if their governments would allow them to do so; the government of the United States may be expected to press for a reduction in discrimination against American coal.

On a volume basis, exports of almost all metals and metalliferous ores have increased

[4] **The most striking exceptions are Australia and New Zealand, which in 1960 recorded proportions of approximately 13 per cent and 5 per cent, respectively.**

Table 22-2

Percentage share of Foodstuffs and Raw Materials in World Exports

	1937	1960
Petroleum	3.47	6.07
Pulp & Paper	1.84	2.06
Coffee	1.21	1.61
Cotton	3.16	1.91
Wheat	2.20	1.64
Timber & Lumber	1.29	1.66
Wool	1.84	1.26
Natural Rubber	1.84	1.39
Copper	1.24	1.21
Sugar	1.35	1.11
Coal	1.99	0.77
Tobacco	1.09	0.65
Rice	1.01	0.48
Tea	0.78	0.48
Cocoa	0.41	0.44
Jute	0.70	0.44
Butter	0.91	0.33
Fish	0.43	0.65
Tin	0.74	0.27
Iron Ore	0.38	0.87

SOURCE: *International Financial Statistics*, 1961.

substantially since before World War II (Table 22-3). The only important exception has been that of tin; in 1960 world exports of tin were still well below those of 1939, largely as a result of the great technical progress made in the recovery of secondary tin and in more economic use of tin metal.[5] It may be noted, however, that only iron ore and the aluminum group (bauxite, alumina, and aluminum metal) have enlarged their share of total world trade; in general the nonferrous metals have slightly declined in relative importance.

As in the case of fuels, recent changes in the direction of world trade in metals and ores have been very striking. The United States has become the leading importer of iron ore, as it is also of copper, lead, and zinc, despite the fact that it was a major exporter of base metals through much of the interwar period.[6] Latin America and Africa have become increasingly important as suppliers of ores and metals, and the significance of the latter appears certain to augment in the near future.

Foodstuffs and Agricultural Raw Materials Foodstuffs and agricultural raw materials collectively account for about one-third of the total value of world exports and this group

[5] See p. 420.

[6] Although the United States was the world's largest copper exporter right up to the outbreak of World War II, large-scale exports of lead and zinc ceased in the early Twenties.

Table 22-3

*Indices of Volume of World Exports, 1958**

Food, vegetable oils, and tobacco	107
Beverage crops	138
Agricultural raw materials	105
Ores and nonferrous metals	179
Petroleum	779
Manufactures	203

* 1928 = 100.
SOURCE: United Nations, *World Economic Survey, 1958,* New York, 1959.

includes the "big six" commodities—cotton, wheat, wool, coffee, sugar, and rubber—that for decades have dominated world commodity markets. While exports of almost all items in this group have increased in value above the prewar level, the expansion has been very modest in relation to the growth of world trade as a whole, and the group's share of total world exports is steadily declining. This development is of particular consequence for many underdeveloped economies, several of which are heavily dependent on the export earnings of but one commodity and lack alternative foreign exchange earning capacity. The great beverages of international commerce—coffee, tea, and cocoa—might be excepted from this generalization, although the fortunes of coffee and tea producers, at least, do not appear to have been appreciably better than those of producers of other agricultural commodities. Largely in consequence of an appreciable increase in the level of prices and a considerably enlarged output, coffee since the end of World War II has become the foremost agricultural product by value of exports; in most prewar years it was generally the least important of the "big six."

The reasons for the declining share of foods and agricultural raw materials in world trade have already been analyzed. The demand for foodstuffs is relatively inelastic; rising real incomes produce an increased demand for food, but the increase is usually less than the rise in incomes, and at very high levels of income consumption per capita of some staples of diet may actually decline. Many countries, particularly in Western Europe, have followed agricultural policies that have resulted, admittedly at very high cost, in a very large volume of domestic food production. As Western Europe is collectively by far the most important market for almost all kinds of foodstuffs, these policies have reduced the opportunities open to underdeveloped economies to obtain a small share of the postwar European prosperity; a larger proportion of Europe's available supplies of wheat, coarse grains, sugar, meat, and oils and fats is now met from domestic sources than was the case before World War II (Table 22-4). Additionally, some formerly important exporters of certain commodities now no longer have so much to offer for sale abroad as a result of a higher level of domestic consumption, a situation that has largely arisen from a rate of population growth in excess of the rate of increase in output. India, formerly a substantial exporter of wheat and cotton, now imports large quantities of both commodities, and the volume of rice exports from mainland Southeast Asia is markedly lower than in the interwar period.

The share of agricultural products in world trade would probably have fallen still more had it not been for the fact that these changes have been partially offset by a great increase in

Table 22-4

Domestic Food Production as Percentage of Total Food Supplies in Europe*

	PREWAR AVERAGE	1956–1960
Bread grains	74	85
Coarse grains	73	78
Sugar	54	69
Meat	88	93
Oils and fats	52	55

* OEEC countries.

SOURCE: United Nations, *World Economic Survey, 1958,* New York, 1959. OEEC, *Twelfth Annual Economic Review,* September, 1961.

heavily subsidized agricultural exports from the United States. As a result of such subsidization, the United States now possesses a larger share of world exports of wheat, corn, barley, oats, and soybeans than it did before World War II; as already noted, a heavily subsidized cotton export program was instituted in the Fifties to retain for the country its "fair historic share" of world raw-cotton exports.

Other Primary Products The fortune of international trade in the products of other primary industries has been somewhat different; demand for timber and timber products is usually enhanced by an increase in real incomes, and for the reasons advanced in Chapter 8, world demand for forestry products seems certain to expand very rapidly.[7] The value of exports of timber, lumber, and wood pulp already exceeds the value of exports of any agricultural commodity. The extraction of timber, however, is frequently integrated with the production of pulp, paper, and cellulose, so that the great expansion in the value of exports of forest products in part reflects the increasing importance of manufactures in world trade; the manufacture of pulp and paper, to stress a point already made, is an extremely capital-intensive industry. Fish and fish products, largely as a result of a considerable increase in exports of fish oils, fish meals, and quick-frozen fillets and fish sticks, have also enlarged their share of world trade.

[7] See p. 218.

THE NETWORK OF INTERNATIONAL TRADE

While it is abundantly clear that a handful of countries dominate the world trade picture, the relative importance of international trade to the national economy varies so greatly from country to country that it is difficult to make generalizations of broad validity. Per capita foreign trade does not appear to bear a close relationship with the level of economic development. Very populous countries at a low level of development such as India and China certainly possess a very low per capita foreign trade, but the low rank of the U.S.S.R. arises not so much from a low level of development as from a deliberate policy of national self-sufficiency. At the other end of the scale of riches, United States per capita foreign trade is exceeded by that of several countries at all levels of economic development. For many years before 1959 the highest figures were those recorded by New Zealand and Iceland, but since World War II the oil sheikdoms of Kuwait, Qatar, and Bahrain have moved far into the lead.

A considerable number of countries at relatively low levels of economic development record surprisingly high figures of per capita foreign trade; in general, these possess small populations whose economic interests are divided between subsistence agriculture and the production of foodstuffs and raw materials for export. Perhaps the most striking example is Malaya, which in some years before the Great Depression occupied the second-highest position through its exports of rubber and tin. Other countries in Asia in a broadly similar position include Sarawak and North Borneo (Sabah), now incorporated with Malaya in the Federation of Malaysia, Brunei, Ceylon, and Hong Kong, which holds its high position by virtue of its entrepôt trade and exports of cheap manufactures based on imported raw materials. A number of countries around the Caribbean—Cuba, the former British West Indies, Venezuela, and the Guiana territories—are similarly situated; in Africa, Ghana and the North African territories could also be assigned to this so-called "poor trading" group.

Many countries at high levels of development, however, do possess a very large per capita foreign trade, such as Belgium, Switzerland, the Netherlands, Denmark, and Britain, all countries of small size. Small countries, of course, can only attain a high level of development through a very large volume of foreign trade; they cannot indulge in the variety of regional specializations possible in countries of continental dimensions and must concentrate on a few lines of production. But large countries at high levels of development can also have a very large per capita foreign trade, as is the case with Canada and Australia. Per capita foreign trade is not, therefore, a satisfactory index of the level of economic development, but it does assist in identifying unusual cases or classes of countries (Fig. 22-1).[8]

The Flow of World Trade

The flow of world trade is extremely intricate, as it involves a large number of countries each engaged in a multiplicity of commercial relations with the rest of the world. This multilateral pattern is largely a heritage of the remarkable economic expansion of the nineteenth century and the creation of a world economy which reached its widest geographic extent on the eve of World War I. Not only was there then a minimum of restriction on the flow of international trade, but most currencies were freely convertible in terms of each other and into gold. In this situation a country's trading deficit in respect of country A or B could be offset by a positive balance with D, E, or F; at its apogee the whole system was retained in overall balance by the outflow of capital from Europe, particularly from Britain, and by that country's willingness to accept an import surplus.

World War I and the Great Depression considerably damaged this intricate multilateral pattern; the imposition of exchange control and import quotas by many countries led to the growth of bilateral trade agreements, sometimes involving barter. By such means Nazi Germany reduced much of southeast Europe to economic and political vassalage, and since 1945 the U.S.S.R. has endeavored to follow a similar policy with certain neutral underdeveloped economies, whose chronic balance-of-payments difficulties and dissatisfaction with the prices earned by their primary products have rendered them susceptible to Soviet blandishments.

At the end of World War II much of

[8] **Norton Ginsberg,** *Atlas of Economic Development,* **The University of Chicago Press, Chicago, 1961, p. 104.**

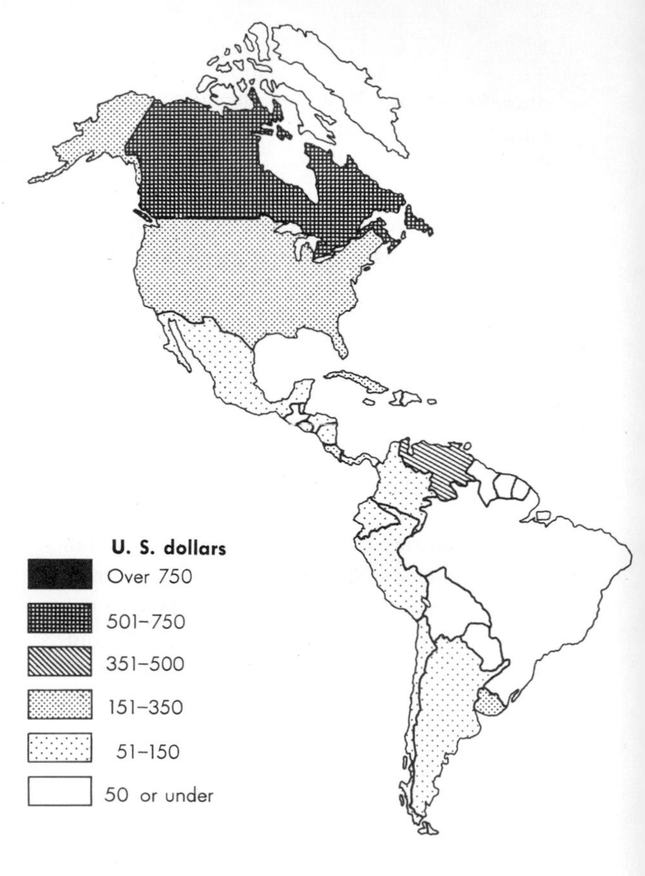

Fig. 22-1 Per capita foreign trade turnover, 1960. (After Ginsberg.)

Europe's industrial and agricultural capacity was destroyed, and the early postwar years witnessed an immense outpouring of United States foodstuffs, raw materials, and manufactures to devastated parts of the world. The limited foreign exchange earning capacity of Europe produced a "dollar problem" of considerable severity, particularly for Britain, which had been compelled to liquidate many of its foreign assets in order to prosecute its war effort, and the enormous United States export surplus was largely financed by loans and aid schemes. Europe's resuscitation was rapid, however, and the dollar shortage disappeared by the end of the Fifties. With greater convertibility of currencies, multilateral trade was again firmly established, but many countries of Asia and Latin America continued to experience balance-of-payments difficulties, often because of "forced draft" industrialization programs. Egypt, Burma, Ceylon, Indonesia, Brazil, Argentina, and the Eastern bloc continue from time to time to engage in government-to-government bilateral trading.

A greatly simplified diagram of the flow of world trade appears in Fig. 22-2; the overwhelming importance of trade across the North Atlantic is clearly visible, a situation that is also strikingly illustrated in Table 22-1. Western Europe (that is, noncommunist Europe) and the United States and Canada together account for some 55 per cent of world trade turnover;[9] the two largest trading nations, the United States and Britain, alone account for some 22 per cent.

Western Europe's 40 per cent share of world

[9] That is, imports plus exports.

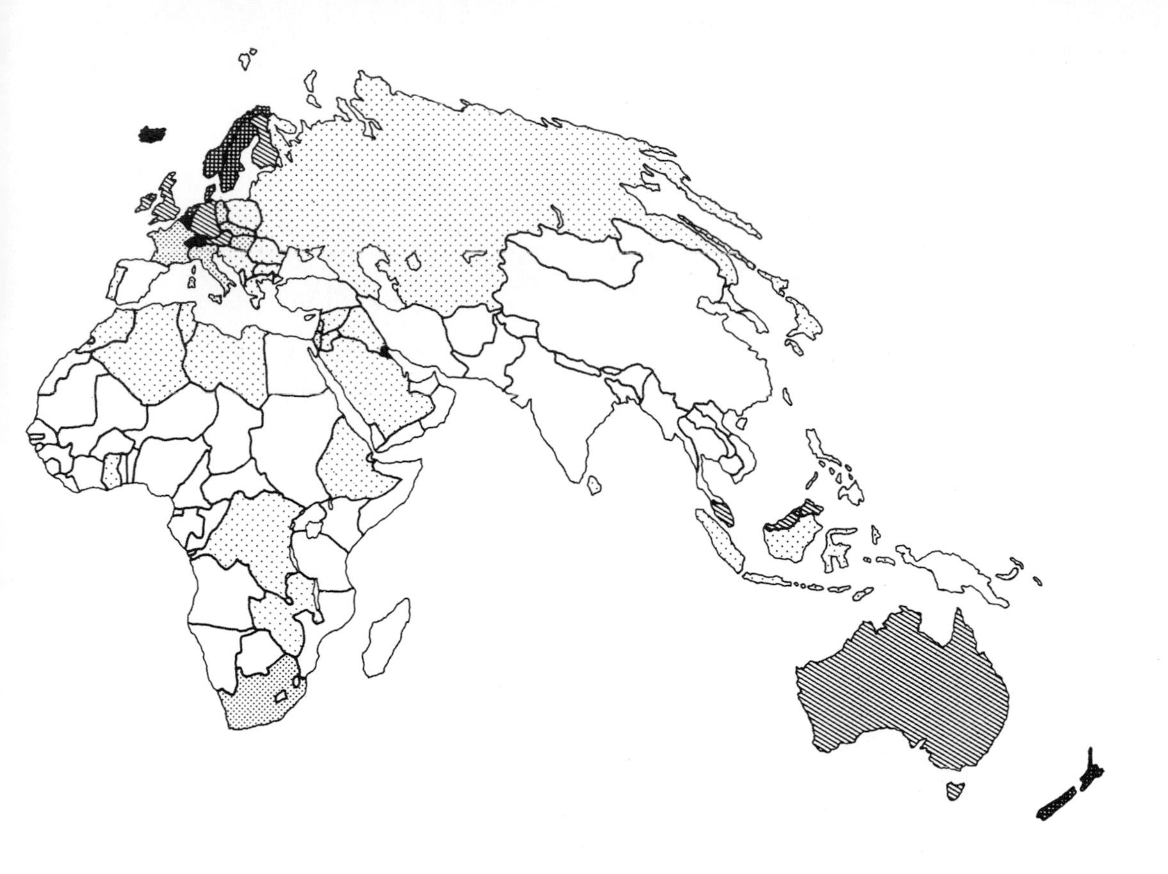

trade turnover in 1960 is certainly an impressive proportion, but in large measure it is a consequence of political fragmentation—more than 55 per cent of its foreign trade is carried on between constituent territories, and this proportion is certain to increase in the future. The achievement of political unity in Western Europe would therefore lower substantially its share of world trade; the continent would then be in a position similar to that of the United States, whose great foreign trade is dwarfed by the volume of domestic transactions. Nevertheless, Western Europe's trade with the rest of the world is still greater than the total foreign trade of the United States, a situation that is largely accounted for by the fact that as the world's largest market for most foodstuffs, Europe's import bill is considerably the larger.

There is a considerable difference between the trade patterns of the EEC and the EFTA; extra-European trade is relatively much more important to the latter group, but the difference largely arises from Britain's trade connections with British Commonwealth countries. The EEC and EFTA are, respectively, each other's best customer and chief supplier; in each also the United States is the second-largest supplier of imports, but as an export market the United States is less important to the EEC than Africa, and is outranked by the British "white Dominions"[10] in the case of the

[10] The pre-1939 Dominions, Canada, Australia, New Zealand, and South Africa. The last is no longer a member of the Commonwealth, and its population is largely non-white, but as its trade pattern closely resembles that of the other Dominions, the convention is retained. The term "Dominion" before 1939 indicated a self-governing territory of the British Empire, acknowledging allegiance to the Crown. In the postwar Commonwealth, the term has disappeared.

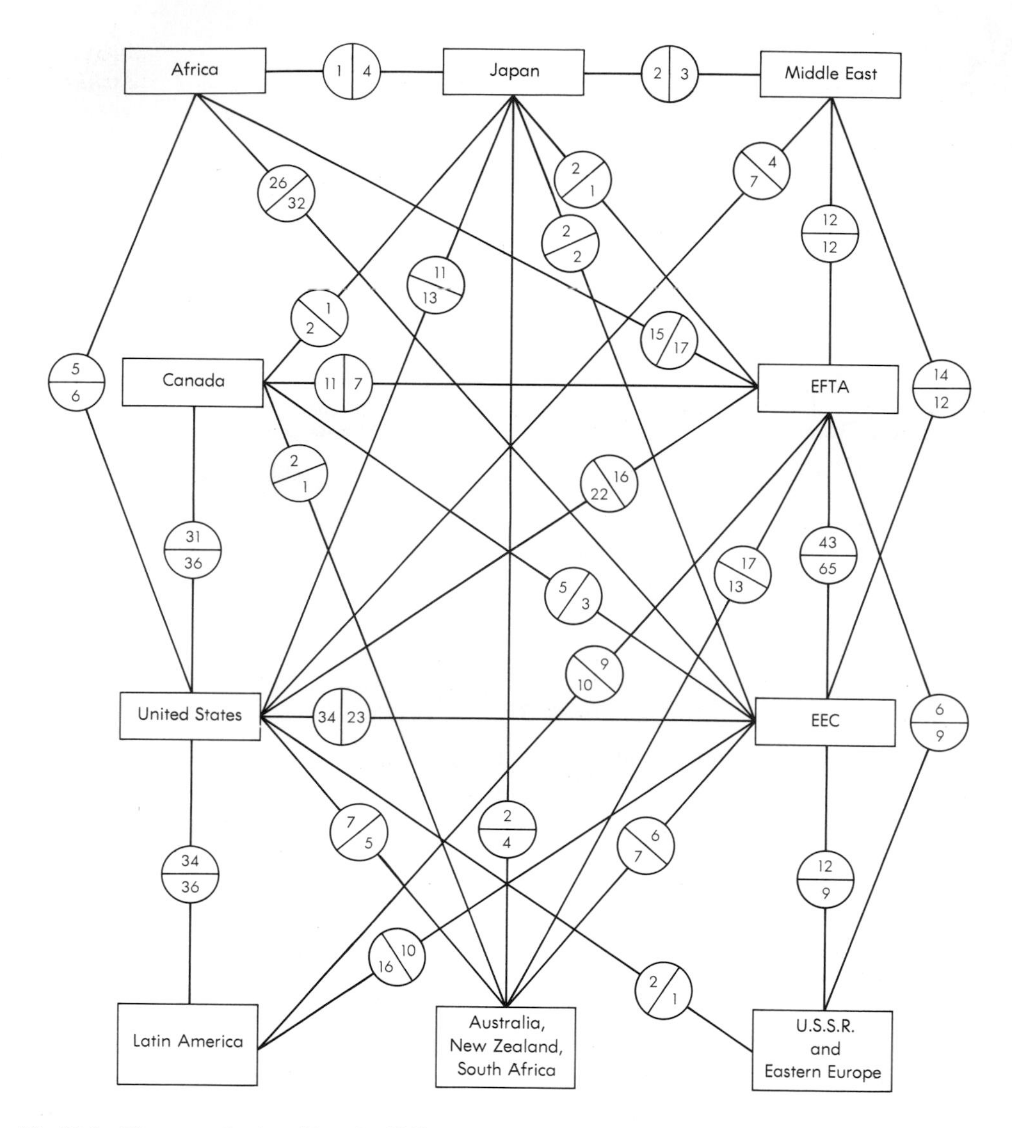

Fig. 22-2 The network of world trade, 1960.
Figures in the semicircles represent the value (in $100 millions) of exports from originating countries; exports worth less than $100 millions have been excluded. (United Nations, *Yearbook of International Trade Statistics,* 1960.)

EFTA. Latin America is an important source of Europe's imports and outranks Asia, but it is of considerably less importance to Europe as an export market.

The United States shares with Europe a worldwide trade pattern, and not unexpectedly, the American continent accounts for a large proportion of United States trade; Canada and Latin America are virtually equal to each other both as suppliers of imports and as markets for exports, and together these areas account for some 40 per cent of total United States trade turnover. Europe, however, outranks either area as a trading partner in American import and export trade, and its contribution to the United States trade turnover is increasing (Fig. 22-3).

Africa and Asia in large measure still maintain the trade patterns that were instituted when the greater part of these continents consisted of dependent territories. Former British African territories continue to trade mainly with Britain and view its proposed entry into the EEC with considerable alarm, while former French territories trade mainly with France and have the status of "associated states" with the EEC. Among former British colonial possessions, Malaysia is exceptional in that its main export markets have always been the United States and Continental Europe. Some former colonial possessions such as Indonesia and India have achieved a much wider geographic dispersal of their foreign trade since gaining independence, but others, among which the Philippine Republic is outstanding, have made little progress in this direction, even though in this case dispersal seems essential for long-term economic development.

The most significant changes in Asia's trade pattern since World War II have occurred in the Far East and in the Middle East. China has withdrawn into the largely self-contained Eastern bloc, but Japan's economic breakthrough to the threshold of becoming a highly developed economy has been accompanied by far-reaching changes in the direction and composition of its foreign trade. Before World War II Japan's principal trade connections were mainly with its imperial possessions, China, and South and Southeast Asia; its main trading partner in a greatly expanded volume of postwar trade has been the United States, and the North American continent is virtually as significant an export market as Asia. Japan has also succeeded in establishing new trade links with Africa and Latin America, but perhaps a

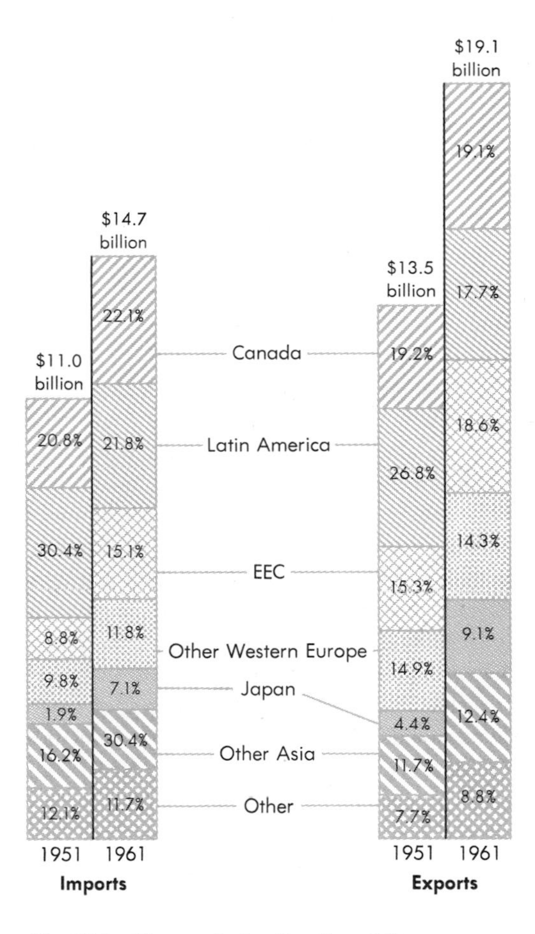

Fig. 22-3 Changes in the direction of the foreign trade of the United States, 1951 and 1961.

more important development is the rapidly expanding two-way trade between Japan and Australia and New Zealand. Japan has been the principal buyer of Australian wool since 1958, and its heavy adverse trading balance with Australia has provided the leverage to enable it to persuade Australia to allow a greater freedom of entry to Japanese manufactures. Japan is also an increasingly important customer for Australian sugar and coarse grains and for New Zealand's dairy products; both Australia and New Zealand, moreover, look mainly to an expansion of trade with Asia to compensate them for any losses which might result from Britain's entry into the EEC. In the period of June, 1963, to June, 1964, Japan for the first time supplanted Britain as the leading buyer of Australian products.

TRADE BLOCS AND TRADE AGREEMENTS

Since the end of World War II a number of organizations for the expansion of trade have been established, some of almost worldwide application and others of more specifically regional significance. In part this development was the result of an almost universal desire to restore the world economy to health after the ravages of war, but it also reflected the growing awareness in several countries of the necessity for a higher degree of specialization than was possible under the existing pattern of trade relations, much of which was a legacy of the Great Depression. In Europe particularly, the growing menace of the Soviet Union has also been a powerful factor in the promotion of a sense of community that has transcended older national rivalries and that has made possible, among other things, a great increase in intra-European trade.

The General Agreement on Tariffs and Trade

The General Agreement on Tariffs and Trade (GATT) came into existence as a result of the Geneva Conference of 1947 and is the survivor of an abortive attempt by the United States to sponsor an international trade organization as a special agency of the United Nations. In 1960 GATT contained some thirty-five members which together accounted for more than three-quarters of world trade turnover, but several other states were indirectly associated through agreements made with GATT members. GATT's permanent organization is an extremely small body, and the agreement largely operates through its periodic conferences, five of which were held between 1947 and 1962. GATT might be described as a market and clearinghouse for trade concessions; nations select items on which they are prepared to make tariff concessions in return for appropriate counterconcessions in the form of tariff reductions and increasingly, although strictly this is a breach of one of the principles of the agreement, in the form of amelioration of quantitative restrictions on imports. Once negotiated, these concessions have to be extended by contracting parties to all third parties with whom they possess most-favored-nation agreements; such agreements, which are a feature of most trade treaties, grant to the goods of a country with which agreement is reached treatment no less favorable than that accorded to the goods of any other country. By bringing together a multiplicity of trading parties, GATT conferences greatly speed up negotiating procedure; in March, 1962, for example, the United States and the EEC, the United States and Britain, and the EEC and Britain concluded a three-way 20 per cent reduction in certain tariffs (the "Dillon round").

GATT also requires members to refrain

from granting any new trade preferences, requires them not to practice dumping or subsidization of exports (although subsidies on exports of primary products are not expressly forbidden), and strongly discourages the imposition of quantitative restrictions on trade. Such restrictions are permitted, however, in the case of countries in acute balance-of-payments difficulties, but as a temporary measure only, and may be imposed in order to protect essential industries in newly industrializing countries; in certain circumstances and with prior notice, they may also be imposed to protect newly established industries in countries at advanced levels of economic development.

It must be admitted that the policies followed by many GATT signatories run counter to the letter and the spirit of the agreement, which has never been popular with the Congress of the United States. Britain has continued to grant preferences to Commonwealth countries, and quantitative restrictions on imports of agricultural produce into the United States in combination with its large volume of subsidized agricultural exports have considerably irritated many foreign countries, particularly Canada. The rise of Japan as a major trading nation has also produced many problems. Japan was admitted to GATT in 1956, but many members, fearing the competition of its cheap exports, continued to impose strict quotas on Japanese products; Britain and the EEC discriminate very heavily against Japan under an article which permits established members to withhold the granting of most-favored-nation concessions to new signatories. GATT has nevertheless undoubtedly helped to free many channels of world trade, particularly between the economically advanced nations, which have most to gain from the greater specialization that becomes possible through lower tariffs; but the fate of the 1964 "Kennedy round" hinges on agricultural problems.

The European Economic Community

The European Economic Community (EEC), or Common Market, is important not so much for what it is as for what it may well become—a political unit with a population and productive capacity greater than that of either the United States or the U.S.S.R. At the time of its formation through the Treaty of Rome in 1957 the Community consisted of a union of six members of the Organisation for European Economic Cooperation (OEEC)—France, the German Federal Republic, Italy, the Netherlands, and the Belgium-Luxembourg economic union. The OEEC was originally established in 1948 to assist in the distribution of American aid to Europe under the European Recovery Program (Marshall Plan); it survived the termination of American aid in 1951 and remained an important research and advisory body for its eighteen European members. It concerned itself with the coordination of general economic and financial policies, energy requirements, productivity, technical and scientific training, the development of nuclear energy, the allocation of raw materials in such emergencies as the Korean conflict, and the provision of special assistance to less advanced areas within the Organisation, which lie mainly in the Mediterranean. The OEEC was an extremely successful body—so much so that the Inner Six that were planning their own closer economic union were determined that its influence should be contained; largely through their pressures the OEEC was reconstituted in 1960 as the Organisation for Economic Cooperation and Development (OECD), including the United States and Canada as full members instead of associated members as previously.

While the OEEC had long been concerned with the possibility of establishing a European free trade area, the six members of the Euro-

Up to 1,750 Volkswagen cars can be conveyed on each trip by this converted vessel operating between Hamburg and the United States. On its return voyage, the vessel carries bulk cargoes.

pean Coal and Steel Community (ECSC), which were also linked after 1956 in the European Atomic Energy Community (Euratom), proceeded to create a much closer economic and trade union in the EEC. The preamble to the Treaty of Rome states that member states will create a common market and a common external tariff, with common policies for agriculture, transport, labor, and other sectors of the economy, and Article 1 adds that the aims of the Community are "the achievement of a harmonious development of the economy within the whole Community, a continuous and balanced economic expansion, increased economic stability, a more rapid improvement in living standards and closer relations between member-countries." Such an objective goes far beyond that of a trade treaty and clearly implies a supranational political unit to which all members would eventually have to surrender sovereignty.

The removal of customs duties and quantitative restrictions on trade between members was to take place in stages; a twelve- to fifteen-year transitional period was originally provided for the establishment of the full Common Market. But the rate at which successive reductions of tariffs were to take place has been speeded up, and at the beginning of 1962 it was decided that the Common Market in industrial products was to be achieved by 1967 and the full Common Market by 1970. Agreement on the creation of the Common Market for agricultural products has caused special difficulty in view of the high degree of protection afforded to farmers by most members and the dependence of the French and West German governments in particular on the rural vote. It is apparent that for products of temperate agriculture the EEC will possess an internal price level above that of the outside world, but by how high a margin is not yet clear.

As a major trading group the EEC more closely resembles the United States than Britain, in that it is not normally a large importer of foodstuffs, and has been on occasions a considerable exporter; only in the case of fats and oils is the Community substantially in deficit. Its exports, however, closely resemble those of Britain in consisting largely of manufactures. About one-third of the trade turnover of the EEC consists of transactions between member states, but there are considerable differences in their directions of trade patterns. West Germany, which accounts for about one-third of the total trade turnover of the EEC, conducts about one-half of its total trade in Europe, but the balance is widely distributed. The performance of Germany in world export markets has been perhaps the most impressive part of the German "economic miracle." Germany displaced Britain as the world's second-largest exporter of manufactures in 1958 and has closely challenged the United States for the premier position since 1963. Germany has gained a larger share of the import markets of every major trading group, but its gains have been greatest in the United States and in the part of the sterling area outside Europe; not surprisingly, the products that have spearheaded Germany's export success are organic chemicals, machinery, and motor vehicles.

As already suggested, Europe counts for less in the trade pattern of France than it does for the other members of the EEC, largely because of French connections with former African colonial possessions in the Union Française; these provide about one-quarter of its imports and take about one-third of its exports. French exports find a wide geographic distribution outside Europe and Africa, but this "rest of the world" market is of much less significance than in the case of Germany. Belgium and the Netherlands, on the other hand, conduct about two-thirds of their trade with other European countries, but the Netherlands is anomalous in the EEC for conducting a higher than average proportion of its trade with Britain. Not much more than 1 per cent of the imports of the Netherlands now originate from Indonesia, the former Netherlands East Indies.

The success of the EEC has been very great. Between 1958 and 1961 the value of trade between member states increased by more than 50 per cent; trade with the rest of the OEEC area and the remainder of the world also increased substantially, but less rapidly. By 1962, a considerable number of other European countries had applied for full or associate membership, and it seemed that by 1964, the EEC would embrace all of Western Europe. This was not to be; Greece did become an associate member in 1963, but early in that year the EEC received a major setback through the French rejection, against the declared wishes of the remaining five members of the Community, of Britain's long debated application for membership. It remains to be seen how serious the damage to the concept of European political and economic unity will prove. France's action was largely politically inspired, and in view of the close identity of British and American views on the position of Europe in the postwar world, it was a direct rebuff to the United States.

Britain and the Commonwealth

From the early eighteenth century to the outbreak of World War I, Britain was the leading trading nation in the world; it regained this position in the Thirties after temporarily losing it to the United States, but following World War II Britain was again reduced to second position in total trade turnover by the

United States, and since 1959 it has been supplanted as the world's second-largest exporter by West Germany. While it is certain that Britain will never regain the dominant position in world trade that it occupied in the nineteenth century, Britain nevertheless is of crucial importance. It is unique in being the only really large trading nation that is regularly a very large importer of foodstuffs as well as of raw materials and manufactures, although it is possible that in the not distant future Japan will occupy a similar position; thus about one-third of Britain's imports are made up of foodstuffs as compared with about one-fifth in the case of the United States, one-sixth in that of the EEC, and about one-eighth in that of Japan.

This large food component gives to Britain's trade a constancy that is in marked contrast to the trade fluctuations of other nations, which closely follow swings of the business cycle. Britain is the chief market for exports of cereals, meat, dairy products, tea, fruit, and vegetables, and is exceeded only by the United States as a market for sugar; for some food products, such as butter, Britain is the *only* market open to exporters. Britain is also a very important market for exports of raw materials such as tobacco, rubber, textile fibers, vegetable oils, ores, metals, and fuels, although its imports of most of these products are exceeded by those of the EEC and the United States. Britain is, however, by far the largest importer of timber and wood pulp.

Britain's exports have long consisted largely of manufactures, but before World War I coal and cotton textiles were of particular importance. The decline of the British coal and cotton export trade during the interwar period has already received comment; at the present these former mainstays of the British economy provide less than 2 per cent of Britain's export earnings. Motor vehicles and machinery dominate Britain's exports, together accounting for about 40 per cent of the total value in most postwar years; the balance is largely contributed by chemicals, iron and steel, base metals, and woolens and worsteds.

While the United States is by far the most important single trading partner of Britain, over 40 per cent of Britain's trade is conducted with the Commonwealth. The Commonwealth, however, is far more important to Britain as an export market than as a source of imports, for there are several commodities in which the Commonwealth is a deficit area—cotton, coffee, tobacco, and, above all, petroleum. Almost 20 per cent of Britain's trade is conducted with Canada, Australia, New Zealand, and South Africa.[11] The preferences granted to the senior Dominions by the Ottawa agreement of 1932 have dwindled in significance with the passage of time, however, and the determination of many Commonwealth countries vigorously to prosecute their industrialization programs makes them as adamantly opposed to "empire free trade" as they were in the days of the Great Depression. The continually declining proportion of its trade that is conducted with the Commonwealth and the increasing, even if smaller, proportion of trade with the EEC have been powerful factors motivating Britain's attempt to seek entry into the Community; between 1956 and 1961 the share of the EEC in Britain's foreign trade rose from about 13 per cent of total value to nearly 20 per cent.

Moreover, the former senior Dominions are themselves showing a more widely dispersed direction of trade; between 1956 and 1962 Britain's share of the total trade of Australia and New Zealand fell heavily, although Britain still remained, of course, their chief trading partner. New Zealand, which sends more than 60 per cent of its exports to Britain, would be severely hit by the imposition of

[11] **South Africa ceased to be a member of the Commonwealth in 1960 but continues, nevertheless, to enjoy its former preferences in the British market.**

tariffs arising from Britain's entry into the EEC, and its special position received sympathetic consideration in the negotiations over Britain's entry. Australia, on the other hand, has achieved considerable success both in diversifying its export structure and in finding new markets, and can face the prospect of Britain's entry with some confidence. Broadly similar considerations apply in the case of Canada; although the British market has been of generally increasing importance to Canada, in the Fifties Britain still took only some 14 per cent of Canada's total exports, at a time when Canada's exports were achieving some success in penetrating into the EEC.

The European Free Trade Association

The European Free Trade Association (EFTA), in which Britain is associated with Portugal, Austria, Switzerland, Denmark, Norway, and Sweden, came into being in 1960 as a result of the Convention of Stockholm in the previous year; it arose from the failure of the attempt to establish free trade within the whole of the OEEC area. The Stockholm signatories proposed to establish within their territories a free trade in industrial products to be achieved, in stages, by 1970. EFTA lacks the political motivation of the EEC and contains no provisions for broader social and economic integration; it does not possess the basic economic cohesion of the EEC, with which, indeed, several EFTA members conduct the greater part of their trade. Britain has had a trade treaty with Portugal since the fourteenth century and with Sweden since the early seventeenth century; in 1961 the EFTA nevertheless accounted for only about 13 per cent of Britain's total trade by value, although this proportion is steadily rising.

Following Britain's application in 1961 to be admitted to the EEC, EFTA lost much of its vigor, and all other members hastened to make similar applications. With the summary rejection of Britain's application in 1963, however, the EFTA received a new lease on life, and its progressive tariff-reduction plan has been pushed ahead. Fantastic though it may have appeared in 1962, the EFTA may well achieve a common market *pari passu* with the EEC, unless its other five members can persuade France to have second thoughts on Britain's entry. Since 1963, France has indicated that it is prepared to accept certain EFTA members within the EEC (but not Britain); these, however, have remained loyal to EFTA.

The Foreign Trade of the United States

Following World War II the United States regained the premier position among the world's trading nations which it had lost to Britain as a result of the Great Depression, and its total trade turnover has since grown steadily. In 1960 the total dollar value of the foreign trade of the United States was some five times that of 1930; by volume, imports were 2½ times and exports 3 times as great as on the eve of the Depression. This greatly expanded trade reflects not only considerable changes within the American economy itself but also the greatly altered position of the United States in the world as a whole.

In most years of the nineteenth century the United States had a favorable balance of trade but overall remained in deficit. From 1900 onwards, however, really large export surpluses were recorded, and after World War I the United States displaced Britain as the world's chief creditor nation. World War I also made the country the largest exporter in the world, a role which was never subsequently relinquished. World War II and its aftermath saw United States exports again enormously enlarged; in 1960 they still amounted to more than two-thirds those of the EEC, despite the high growth rate of the Western European economy, and were greater than those of the EFTA. The growth of the import trade has been slower, and not until the middle Fifties did the United States attain the premier position.

The tremendous size of the American export surplus and its inexorable tendency to rise is one of the most striking features of international trade. This largely arises from the fact that the United States is a major exporter of every class of commodity—foodstuffs, agricultural and mineral raw materials, manufactures, and machinery. Canada's export trade is broadly similar, although in value it is only about one-quarter that of the United States, and in many postwar years Canada has had a slight trading deficit.

This many-sided character of the United States export trade is a comparatively recent development; the same, indeed, is also true of Canada. At the turn of the century, crude and processed foodstuffs and raw materials of all kinds accounted for about two-thirds of the total value of exports; among individual items cotton was easily the most important and continued to be so almost to the outbreak of World War II. After the turn of the century, exports of American wheat, meat, and other animal products declined in significance, and the role of world's largest food exporter was gradually assumed by Canada. The great growth of exports of manufactures dates from about 1910; from then on the relative contribution of this item in total exports progressively enlarged, attaining a level of about 50 per cent in 1930 and about 65 per cent in 1960.

The United States again became a large food exporter after World War I, but the stimulus was temporary. World War II, however, saw a great increase in agricultural output that was later sustained; reverting to a position it had occupied half a century earlier, the United States again became the world's largest exporter of food as well as of agricultural raw materials. A major difference from the earlier period, however, was that these exports were heavily subsidized; in addition, considerable quantities were given away for relief aid or for economic development in backward areas.

Great changes have also occurred in the pattern of trade in raw materials. Before World War II the United States was the world's largest exporter of petroleum, a commodity that ranked second to cotton in export items, and was the leading exporter of most base metals. At present the United States is the world's largest importer of petroleum, iron ore, and base metals, and imports of most kinds of raw materials appear certain to increase.

The pattern of industrial exports has also experienced considerable changes. Never an important exporter of textiles, the United States built up its exports of manufactures on the small machines and gadgets for which the country has become famous—hand tools, sewing machines, typewriters, business equipment, electric and telephonic apparatus, and automobiles. In many of these lines the United States no longer enjoys a very appreciable technical or economic advantage, however, and the emphasis in manufactured exports has progressively shifted towards more complex and capital-intensive types of machinery and apparatus, such as machine tools, mining and excavating machinery, materials-handling equipment, computers, aircraft, and pharmaceuticals.

The growth of the United States economy and its expanding demand for raw materials of many kinds have made it easier for the producers of such products to find a market in the United States; many such materials come from former colonial possessions of European powers, and frequently their expanded output is the result of American investment. Petroleum products, ores, and metals together make up about one-quarter of the total value of American imports. Foodstuffs, on the other hand, have never been important items of imports save for certain tropical products; more than half the total value of imports of foodstuffs is accounted for by coffee and cane sugar. Though it has been generally hostile to international commodity agreements, the United States has nonetheless agreed to underwrite the level of export earnings of Latin American producers by participating in the International Coffee Agreement, and the value of coffee imports appears likely to remain at a high level. Among agricultural raw materials wool and natural rubber are of major significance, although neither accounts for more than about 2 per cent of the total value of imports.

Although the United States is the world's largest exporter of manufactures, it is also the largest importer after the EEC. The value of manufactured imports has doubled in the decade from 1950, and in 1960 accounted for about 40 per cent of the total value of imports. In part this increase reflects the extreme competitiveness of the products of other industrialized countries as a result of considerable investment in new capital equipment since the end of World War II, but the increase in imports is also indicative of a growing awareness of the folly of enabling European and Japanese industry to enlarge their respective productive capacities while at the same time refusing entry to their products. In sum, the changing pattern of trade of the United States epitomizes the changing composition of world trade as a whole.

These changes in composition have inevitably been accompanied by changes in the direction of United States trade. At the turn of the century Europe was the chief market for American exports and the major source of its imports, but this pattern was considerably altered by World War I, when Canada and Latin America became America's main trading partners. Canada is still by far the largest export market and the main source of imports on a national basis; it is particularly significant to the United States as a source of raw materials, especially metals, natural gas, and forest products. Canada could also become a large supplier of petroleum, and hopes to convert some of its exports of raw materials and semimanufactures into fully manufactured products; its large trading deficit with the United States could well be used as a lever to this end. Latin America is the main source of tropical products, except natural rubber; of the Latin American states Venezuela is the chief source of imports, but Mexico is the leading export market. Latin America is normally the only region of the world with which the United States regularly has a trading deficit.

Since World War II, however, Europe has substantially enlarged its share of American trade; the EEC and the EFTA have combined to restore Western Europe to its traditional place as the main source of American imports, and as an export market Western Europe is now almost as important to the United States as is the rest of the Western Hemisphere. But perhaps more remarkable has been the growing importance of Japan as a trading partner; on a national basis Japan was the second-largest source of imports into the United States in 1961, and as an export market it was only slightly outranked by Britain for the second position.

Political as well as economic considerations make it virtually certain that the foreign trade of the United States will continue to grow in the future. The United States is the keystone of the defense system of the noncommunist world and also bears a substantial degree of responsibility for its economic well-being. Large though its visible balance of trade is, overseas defense expenditure and foreign aid of various kinds have recently placed the

United States in a balance-of-payments deficit, and to check the outflow of gold further exports are being officially encouraged. The Trade Expansion Act of 1962, widely greeted as the most far-reaching document in the history of United States commercial relations, is a commendable attempt to come to terms with the realities of the world economy and to abandon the protectionist outlook of the past, which was perhaps less justifiable for the United States than for any other nation, though in fact, the booming Common Market and the economic offensive of the U.S.S.R. left the nation little choice. Under the terms of the act the President is empowered to reduce all tariffs by up to 50 per cent and to abolish them completely in the case of certain items; these consist mainly of industrial products, in which the United States and the countries of Western Europe are responsible for more than 80 per cent of world output.

The administration has been greatly strengthened by the Trade Expansion Act in negotiations with the Common Market; by offering European producers a chance of competing with domestic producers in the American market, the United States should succeed in obtaining a reduction in tariffs for items in which it has a considerable comparative advantage. Among the products for which export prospects are brightest as a result of the act are coal, earthmoving and excavating machinery, automobiles and trucks, and computers and data-processing equipment. Reductions in European tariffs would also have the effect of discouraging American manufacturers from investment in new plant abroad, a development that has been of considerable concern to organized labor, which, however, has refused to accept the fact that the "export of jobs" is in large measure a consequence of American protectionist policy. Certain American industries will undoubtedly suffer as a result of the enhanced foreign competition that will follow from the implementation of the Trade Expansion Act. These are likely to be industries that already rely on a heavy degree of protection for survival, such as watchmaking and woolen textiles. The act provides for the retraining and redeployment of displaced workers from such affected industries.

The Latin American Free Trade Association and Other Trade Groups

Regional trade groups are far from new; the Prussian Zollverein (customs union) played an important role in the unification of Germany, and from 1918 Britain operated a customs union and common market between its East African territories of Kenya, Uganda, and Tanganyika which, however, appear unlikely to survive now that all of these territories have become independent; in 1964, Tanganyika declared its intention of imposing duties on imports from Kenya and Uganda. The success of the EEC, however, has greatly stimulated interest in regional common markets, and one organization outside Europe which may eventually prove to have far-reaching consequences has already come into being. This is the Latin American Free Trade Association (LAFTA), which was created as a result of the Montevideo Treaty of 1960.

The initiative for LAFTA came from Brazil, which approached the United States and other Latin American states urging the creation of an economic union along the lines of the EEC. The signatories of the treaty, which included Argentina, Brazil, Chile, Mexico, Peru, Paraguay, and Uruguay, undertook to create a common market within twelve years of the date of effect of the treaty (1962) by the progressive removal of tariffs and quantitative restrictions on imports and agreed to work for convertibility of their currencies. They also agreed to coordinate their agricultural development and industrialization policies and to consider ways of assisting economically less developed member states. Following the signing of the treaty Colombia, Ecuador, and Venezuela indicated their intention of joining, but Bolivia has stated that it will stay outside.

It would be easy to be pessimistic about the future of LAFTA; its members for the most part have competitive economies and conduct relatively little trading with each other; many have chronic balance-of-payments difficulties and, it would not be too much to say, have economies that for years have appeared on the verge of chaos. Political instability and social unrest are a commonplace. Nevertheless, as the experience of the EEC has conclusively shown, it is not so much knowledge of what such an association can accomplish as the observed and observable desire and willingness of members to make international institutions work that is the passport to success. Granted such a desire, LAFTA may yet prove to be the key by which the Latin American states can overcome their pressing economic, social, and political difficulties.

Embryonic similar organizations can be detected in Asia and Africa. The idea of a common market between the members of the Association of Southeast Asian States (ASA), which includes Malaysia, Thailand, and the Philippines, has already been ventilated, and at the Lagos Conference of 1962, twenty-nine members of the Organization of Inter-African and Malagasy States declared their intention of establishing a common organization for economic cooperation and development. The proposed organization would work for the removal of restrictions on trade between member states and for the coordination of their economic development plans.

SELECTED REFERENCES

Aubrey, H. G.: *United States Imports and Foreign Trade,* Oxford University Press, London, 1957.

Barr, Robert J. (ed.): *American Trade with Asia and the Far East,* Marquette University Press, Milwaukee, 1959.

Economist Intelligence Unit: *The Commonwealth and Europe,* London, 1960.

General Agreement on Tariffs and Trade: *Trends in International Trade,* Geneva, 1958.

Grotewald, Andreas, and Lois Grotewald: "Geographical Aspects of International Trade," *Economic Geography,* vol. 33, pp. 257–266, 1957.

Hilgerdt, Folke: *The Network of International Trade,* League of Nations, Geneva, 1942.

Kaufmann, Johan: "Trends in United States Tariff Policies," *Kyklos,* vol. 6, pp. 55–74, 1954.

Kitzinger, U. W.: *The Challenge of the Common Market,* Basil Blackwell & Mott, Ltd., Oxford, 1961.

Maizels, Alfred: *Industrial Growth and World Trade,* Cambridge University Press, Cambridge, 1963.

McDougall, G. D. A.: "Britain's Foreign Trade Problems," *Economic Journal,* vol. 57, pp. 69–113, 1947.

Meyer, F. V.: *The Seven,* Barrie & Rockliff and Pall Mall Press, London, 1960.

Nove, Alec, and Desmond Donnelly: *Trade with Communist Countries,* Hutchinson & Co. (Publishers), Ltd. (for Institute of Economic Affairs), London, 1960.

Scott, N. B.: "Sino-Soviet Trade," *Soviet Studies,* vol. 10, pp. 151–161, 1958.

Tarshis, Lorie: *Introduction to International Trade and Finance,* John Wiley & Sons, Inc., New York, and Chapman & Hall, Ltd., London, 1955.

United Nations, Department of Economic Affairs: *Relative Prices of Exports and Imports of Under-developed Countries,* New York, 1952.

———: *World Economic Survey, 1962, Part I,* New York, 1963.

———: *Yearbook of International Trade Statistics,* New York, annually.

United Nations Economic Commission for Asia and the Far East: "Asia's Trade with Western Europe," *Economic Survey of Asia and the Far East 1962,* pp. 5–134, Bangkok and New York, 1963.

Yates, P. Lamartine: *Forty Years of Foreign Trade,* George Allen & Unwin, Ltd., London, 1959.

PART V *Conclusion*

Chapter 23

TOWARDS FIVE BILLION PEOPLE

"Better fifty years of Europe than a cycle of Cathay," sang a popular nineteenth-century poet, a sentiment that would probably still receive the approbation of the great majority of people in the Western world. Life would be less disturbed were China still the sleeping dragon, a distant land of "lesser breeds without the law" counting for little in the councils of the world. But for good or bad China forcibly protrudes itself; the half-century from 1950 is likely to see changes with that country as profound as those occurring within any period of equivalent length in Western history. Throughout the world, indeed, traditional societies are in the throes of the "revolution of rising expectations" as their peoples seek to achieve the higher living standards that Western contact and influence have demonstrated is possible.

Major world catastrophe such as a thermonuclear war excepted, can such standards be achieved in view of the apparently inexorable tendency in many areas of the world for the rate of population increase to outstrip the rate of increase in production? It is the opinion of the great majority of economists that raising the present low living standards of the vast majority of mankind will constitute by far the most pressing economic problem of the next half-century; beside it, other issues such as the possibility of maintaining full employment without an enormous defense expenditure or the problem of combating inflation dwindle to insignificance.

Varying degrees of optimism are expressed as to the possibilities of a successful outcome. Some believe that the largest and most populous countries such as China, India, Indonesia, and, one might also add, Brazil have already commenced their "developmental" takeoff and that other underdeveloped economies will also do so within the next two decades.[1] Others are not sure; one United Nations study has anticipated that the existing relationships between population and resources in underdeveloped countries would continue to worsen, as they are doing, for some time to come.[2]

In the latter case the "revolution of rising expectations" could be thwarted and diverted into forms fraught with danger for the free world. The failure of national revolutions to meet public aspirations can provide fertile soil for the spread of communism, and it demands no great perspicacity to detect a number of countries in which economic, political, and social confusion in the present pre-takeoff period is so advanced as to constitute precisely the setting that, in Rostow's opinion, makes communist seizure of power possible.[3] Hungry and backward nations cannot wage agressive war, it is true, but they could allow others to use their territory for such ends, as the example of Cuba suggests. They could also deny to the free world access to raw materials and minerals,

[1] W. W. Rostow, *The Stages of Economic Growth,* Cambridge University Press, Cambridge, 1960, p. 126.

[2] United Nations, *Determinants and Consequences of Population Trends,* New York, 1953, p. 162.

[3] Rostow, *op. cit.*, p. 163.

for which sooner or later the Soviet bloc is likely to be a competitor; there must ultimately come a time when high-grade foreign mineral deposits prove more attractive to Soviet planners than inaccessible low-grade domestic ones, particularly as modern weapons have removed much of the strategic value of home production.

The continued adhesion of the great majority of the new nations of Africa and Asia to the free world economy is one of the most striking political phenomena of the postwar period. One or two nations have had mild flirtations with the Eastern bloc, and others may be tempted to behave similarly in the future, but in the main the leaders of newly independent nations have been as eager to impress on Moscow as on Washington that they intend to be masters in their own house. The U.S.S.R. has so far failed to attract any appreciable share of the foreign trade of the underdeveloped world. Its economic aid, both actual and promised, has been but a fraction of that of the highly developed economies. In certain countries such as Indonesia and Egypt, the acceptance of large quantities of Soviet military equipment not only has resulted in a mortgaging of exports for many years to come, but also has saddled the nation with a military budget that absorbs an inordinately large share of the national product. There is little doubt, however, that the existence of enormous inequalities in the living standards of the free world continues to be of considerable political and practical value to the Sino-Soviet bloc, where living standards at best are only modest. Self-interest no less than considerations of humanity, then, urges the Western world to bend every effort to reducing the present disparities.

The magnitude of this problem and the challenge it presents to the economically advanced nations are of astronomical proportions. In 1952 the United Nations *Report on Measures for the Economic Development of Underdeveloped Countries* estimated that it would take an annual capital investment of 20 billion dollars in the underdeveloped world to achieve a satisfactory rate of improvement in the productivity of agriculture and industry; this may be compared with an estimated international aid from all sources of about 2.9 billion dollars in 1960.

What would an annual capital investment of this magnitude—equivalent to the gross national product of Italy, or about 5 per cent of that of the United States—do for living standards? Assuming that the rate of increase in the per capita income of India could thus be raised to about 4 per cent per annum, nearly twice that of most of Western Europe in the late Fifties, it would take nearly half a century for the Indian standard of living to rise from one-tenth to one-fifth of that of Western Europe, while the absolute gap in living standards, assuming unchanged rates of advance in Europe and India, would continue to grow for some considerable time.[4] Even under the most favorable circumstances imaginable, a considerable period must elapse before Indian living standards can show any significant improvement. With a 10 per cent annual increase in per capita income, Indian living standards would be raised to about half those of Western Europe in 1960 in about seventeen years, and even a decade of advance at this rate would achieve a substantial amelioration. No country, however, has ever recorded such a rate of economic advance for as long as ten years. In what may well be the most rapid rate of economic growth so far achieved, Japan in the decade after 1951 expanded its real national product by about 9 per cent per annum while population grew at about 1 per cent per annum. The Japanese "economic miracle" is still imperfectly understood, but it is clear that over

[4] P. M. S. Blackett, Presidential Address to the British Association for the Advancement of Science, 1958.

this period Japan possessed exceptional advantages which India has no hope of achieving. A rate of economic growth of such magnitude in India is so remote a possibility that it can be completely dismissed.

PROBLEMS OF THE RESOURCE BASIS

Has the world, in fact, the physical resources to support a universally high living standard? Or to put the matter in another way, does the present high living standard of a small proportion of the world's population condemn the remainder to perpetual poverty? The United States has a per capita consumption of energy almost two hundred times that of India, and its consumption of minerals is virtually as great. It has been pointed out that a world per capita consumption of energy and metals at the present level of that of the United States would substantially exceed known world reserves; world population, moreover, is augmenting rapidly. With a world population of 7 billion, a figure that is quite likely to be achieved at some time in the next century, the total pig-iron "capital" to support a worldwide industrialization at the present level of that of the United States would amount to about 100 billion tons; the total amount of metallic iron present in the world is only a fraction of this figure.[5]

While it is true that at any point of time the stock of a particular resource is finite, it does not follow that the total of all resources is finite, for resources are man-made. It is likely that long before there begins to be real pressure on the world's iron-ore resources, the tasks for which iron is now required will have largely been taken over by other materials whose supply is not rigorously limited—in all probability by man-made substances synthesized from a few basic materials or waste products. Such transformation will certainly require the use of considerable quantities of energy, but it appears possible that a world population of 7 billion could be supported at an appropriately high energy consumption for a very long period of time, even in the absence of fossil fuels.[6]

While it is fit and proper to consider the long-term future of mankind as one United Nations study has urged,[7] the gloomy prophecies made from time to time of man's future in a finite world rest on demographic assumptions that may well prove unfounded. But in the world of the present, it is an indisputable fact that *economic development in the underdeveloped world is part of the nationalist movement, and its motivation is primarily political,* and the author's opinion is that within the next two decades the underdeveloped economies either will have commenced their takeoff and have entered the first stage of the demographic transition within a framework of a free society or will have been forced along the path of rapid economic development by the authoritarian methods of the communists.

It cannot seriously be contended that the world's resources are inadequate to support the simultaneous takeoff of the present underdeveloped countries, whatever political and economic systems they may adopt. As already indicated, even at a growth rate of about 10 per cent per annum in real product it would take the underdeveloped world a substantial time to approach the present consumption levels of the highly developed economies; a rate of growth of even half this magnitude appears a very ambitious target for many countries. A 5 per cent (or even a 10 per cent) growth rate would in no way jeopardize world

[5] Harrison Brown, *The Challenge of Man's Future,* The Viking Press, Inc., New York, and Martin Secker & Warburg, Ltd., London, 1954, p. 196.

[6] *Ibid.*, p. 186.

[7] See p. 36.

resources; indeed, it would materially assist in taking up the slack in the supply situation of many primary products. More than a decade after the President's Materials Policy Commission in *Resources for Freedom* anticipated a sharp increase in the demand for raw materials and energy supplies, there was no prospect of shortage in any item; many commodities, including petroleum, copper, and uranium—the glamour material of the early postwar period—were in embarrassing oversupply.

National Size and Social Organization

While it can be conceded that there is no overall shortage of physical resources to impair economic development in economically backward areas, it remains true that resources are often unevenly distributed and that some countries appear to have far from a fair share; and the smaller the country, the less likely it is to possess an equitable endowment from nature. A nation may be considered small either on the basis of geographic area or in terms of population, but it is clear that since 1950 a number of small nations, under one definition or the other, have come into existence for which it is difficult to visualize much of an economic future. Unfortunately this situation is worst in precisely that part of the world where living standards are lowest and where the problems of economic development appear most formidable. More than 30 African states acquired independence between 1950 and 1964, and it is likely that there will be more than 50 separate African states before the winds of change have blown themselves out. Of the 33 new states, 7 in 1962 had populations of less than 2 million, and 13 possessed a college-graduate population of less than 100. Many of these new political units are not, it is true, of particularly small geographic size—although 3 possess an area of less than 25,000 square miles—but nearly all contain extensive areas of negligible productivity, which are unlikely to become very much more productive, even given an accelerated rate of technological progress.

The Balkanization of Africa constitutes an immense obstacle to development; old colonial boundaries resulting largely from the fortuitous course of exploration have become ossified, severing peoples of similar racial or linguistic groupings and cutting across drainage basins, by far the most important physical units in a continent with a larger proportion of useless land than any other save Antarctica. Political fragmentation, however, is but a facet of the larger problem of tribalism; the granting of independence has almost everywhere been an occasion for settling old scores, and internecine conflict threatens to tear apart several states and prospective states alike—the Congo (Léopoldville), Cameroun, Tanganyika, Kenya, Rwanda Burundi, Uganda, and even Nigeria, the most populous and perhaps the most sophisticated of all new African states.

It cannot, of course, be argued that small geographic size and its concomittant, a small population, are themselves obstacles to the attainment of a high level of economic development; New Zealand, Switzerland, Belgium, Denmark, and Malaya have all reached a higher level than that of their larger and more populous neighbors. None of these countries possesses a large physical resource base, and for the most part the activities that have bought them their opulence were also open to their neighbors as well. If all nations practiced free trade and there were no obstacles to the mobility of factors of production, the size of a country would probably bear no relation to its level of well-being, as the classical economists believed. In the real world, however, trade is not free and there are numerous obstacles to the mobility of factors of production; the size of nations does therefore affect the issue, although it is difficult to make broad generalizations. Small nations possess few capital-intensive industries, although chemical industries are occasionally well developed. Sweden and Australia both have important and rapidly expanding motor-vehicle industries which involve true manufacturing as opposed to assembly of imported parts, although before World War II many economists would probably have denied that such a feat was possible. South Africa, with a much larger population but of considerably smaller purchasing power, is also endeavoring to create its own domestic industry and will probably succeed. Motor-vehicle production, however, is now a well-understood industry, and with technological progress economies of scale often appear with progressively smaller runs; in other words, the scale of output necessary to make production economically feasible is tending to be reduced. There is reason, therefore, for believing that a country with a population of about 10 million is large enough to support almost any industry, and even one with a much smaller population can hope to acquire some of the newer "growth" industries.

This, however, can be of little comfort in the half-million square miles of desert that constitute the Niger Republic, or in the equally parched half-million that make up the neighboring territory of Chad; the only future for these political units is that of pensioners. Several of the states bordering the Gulf of Guinea, Uganda, and Zambia appear to possess considerable physical and human resources, but some kind of integration with better-endowed neighbors seems desirable in the case of many African states, a fact which is conceded by many African leaders, although the obvious ambitions of many of its leading advocates have caused the unification movement to be viewed with suspicion by most Africans. Two blocs with widely differing views on the form of inter-African cooperation and on African relations with the rest of the world have appeared, the "Casablanca" group led by Ghana and Egypt and the "Monrovia" group consisting mainly of former French possessions and Nigeria; these are contesting for the allegiance of the present uncommitted African nations and for the goodwill of African leaders in parts of eastern and southern Africa that have still to gain independence.

Observations broadly similar to those regarding Africa could also be made concerning the relationship of physical resources to the social organizations that attempt to make use of them in the former British West Indies, going their separate ways after the collapse of plans for federation. Jamaica and Trinidad are probably just large enough to form viable political and economic units, but this will greatly enhance the difficulties of the other islands, particularly in view of the fact that since 1962 emigration to Britain has been controlled; interisland migration has long been rigorously restricted. Depressed and overcrowded Antigua, once a bastion of British naval strength, is an economist's despair; the investment in converting a substantial area into a millionaire's holiday resort, whatever its effect on the local economy, does not appear altogether wise, for several political observers have expressed concern at the possible consequences of displays of lavish living in low-income countries, and such investment cannot in any case much increase the capacity of the economy for growth. Certain parts of the West Indies, such as Trinidad and British Guiana, have bitter racial problems resulting from the importation of Indian agricultural workers, and the granting of independence to the latter territory has been repeatedly delayed through outbreaks of interracial violence. Several variations on this island theme of a narrow resource basis, a rapidly expanding population, and acute communal friction can be identified in other parts of the world—Cyprus, Mauritius, Fiji—and on a somewhat larger scale one might almost add Ceylon. Fiji could, perhaps, be transformed into an "Australian Hawaii," but the prospect appears remote.

Limited physical resources, however, are the primary problem of only a small proportion of the population of the underdeveloped world; China, India, Pakistan, Indonesia, and Brazil together account for about 45 per cent of world population. It is scarcely possible to regard the present economic misery of these countries as the result of the niggardliness of nature, for the smallest has an area of nearly 400,000 square miles, while the two largest, with more than 3 million square miles apiece, are virtually subcontinents. The extensive areas of mountain and desert, it is true, are mainly negative for the present agricultural society, but they may prove far from negative for nonagricultural uses. Easily won sources of energy are scanty, but even this does not apply to Indonesia or to Brazil, both of which have substantial petroleum resources; Indonesia allows enormous quantities of natural gas to go to waste for want of a local market, and few parts of China are far from a coal deposit of some kind. It is impossible to escape the conclusion that the obstacles to a higher level of development in these large political units do not lie in the physical environment but in the social and institutional one.

Capital and Its Users

It is often said that the shortage of capital is a major obstacle to economic development in many countries, but as with all broad generalizations, the statement requires qualification. Every Asian and Latin American country at least possesses a wealthy elite with considerable physical assets; in Asia there are hoards of gold, silver, and jewelry which in some countries may amount to more than a fifth of the national income. Perhaps of even greater significance than the shortage of private investment capital is the unwillingness to invest in enterprises which do not offer much possibility of large speculative gains. Utilities and manufacturing industries do not usually offer more than a modest return with the prospect of a long-term capital gain; in countries where the expectation of life is comparatively low and where capricious capital levies are likely to be imposed, such investment is bound to be unattractive. Concern for the future value of money often reinforces the appeal of gold and silver as outlets for wealth; unlike land or property, these can be secreted from rapacious governments. In many underdeveloped economies much investment in productive enterprise is in the hands of immigrant groups or of small religious sects—the Lebanese in West Africa, the Parsees in India, the Chinese in Southeast Asia, the *santri* Muslims in Indonesia. Religious beliefs or social pressures have encouraged such peoples to practice thrift and to regard hard work and risk bearing as virtues. It might therefore be imagined that such groups would be encouraged by governments to extend their activities, but in practice the reverse is usually the case; in many countries, severe obstacles have been placed in the way of their exercise of their traditional employments. Medieval European monarchs knew better.

Nevertheless, the opportunities for private investment in most underdeveloped economies are bound to be limited for a reason already stated, namely, that the prime motivation for economic development is political. Thus by far the largest share of investment will continue to be undertaken by the state, and political necessity dictates that the largest allocations will be for utilities, irrigation, agricultural credit and marketing, education, and social services. Capital-intensive industry is likely to be reserved to a state monopoly or, where governments are still anxious to attract foreign capital, a state partnership with foreign enterprise.

The various methods by which government can increase the rate of capital accumulation and finance development plans cannot be discussed here, but it is no uncommon experience in underdeveloped economies for government to find that it is unable to make all the investment for which funds have been made available and for investment that is made to yield nothing like the return anticipated. Among the more important reasons for failures of this kind is the shortage of technical and administrative ability, and assistance in overcoming this bottleneck is one of the most effective forms of economic aid. The shortage of technical personnel exists at all levels, but it is most acute in the middle and lower echelons—the supervisors, foremen, straw bosses, and technicians who have to implement, and often to interpret, the decisions of higher management. Without an adequate supply of such people, there is a real danger that investment in producing highly trained graduate and postgraduate engineers and scientists will largely be wasted, for without their supporting workers such highly qualified personnel cannot be employed in the jobs for which they are qualified. As a result of this shortage of ability, new plant seldom operates at planned capacity in underdeveloped economies, and cost levels are often extremely high. Ultimate responsibility for this situation, however, must rest with defective government machinery.

It is only very recently that nations at an advanced level of economic development have learned to create incorruptible and efficient government machinery, and it is scarcely surprising that virtually no underdeveloped economies have yet acquired the trick; indeed, it can be argued that efficient and incorruptible government is a product of a higher level of development, not a precondition. In most underdeveloped economies politicians and civil servants are almost expected to take every opportunity of enriching themselves; indeed, they are considered fools if they do not, and protestations of innocence are unlikely to be widely believed, Corruption need not, moreover, constitute an obstacle to economic development; under certain circumstances it may even encourage it, as several periods of the history of the United States might testify. It is not surprising that the discharge of a greatly expanded government business, including the implementation of a complex development plan by a public service with a large number of relatively young and inexperienced senior officials who have attained high office through rapid, perhaps overrapid, promotion as a result of political change, occasionally results in scandal, bottlenecks, and breakdowns. The advanced economies should adopt a tolerant attitude towards such demonstrations of inefficiency and malpractice; when faced with bringing about changes of equal magnitude in the shortest time, as in the organization of a maximum war effort, all the resources of government and private *expertise* available to a highly developed economy are not proof against the commission of appalling bungles.

The connection between efficient government and a rapid rate of economic growth can clearly be seen in the case of Malaysia, which could well be the next Asian country after Japan to break through to the age of high mass consumption. Malaya is the most development-conscious of all newly independent Asian nations, and has inherited and maintained a public service whose competence and integrity are in marked contrast to the those of most of its neighbors. As a result, its realistic development plan is being rapidly and efficiently prosecuted, and the increase in national product between the achievement of independence in 1957 and 1962 averaged almost 6 per cent per annum in some years; such a rate does not compare very unfavorably even with that of Japan, although with one of the highest rates of population increase in the world, the increase in output per head in Malaya has been modest. In every way, however, the contrast with Ceylon, a country with which Malaya is often compared in respect of its economy and its plural society, is marked; communal conflict and widespread corruption have been largely responsible for Ceylon's failure to enlarge its margin of economic advantage over India and Pakistan.

In short, it seems that in underdeveloped economies, as well as in more advanced ones, economic development more and more depends on the quality rather than on the quantity of the capital equipment in use, and on the skill and intelligence of those who use it.[8]

The Problem of Agriculture

The supreme necessity of raising agricultural productivity in the underdeveloped countries is universally conceded, partly because of rapidly increasing populations and limited possibilities of extending the cultivated area but also because it is clear that any higher rate of capital accumulation will mainly have to originate in the agricultural sector. Technically it should be possible to double agricultural productivity in most underdeveloped countries within a reasonably short period without far-reaching changes in agrarian organization. From a level of productivity in 1880 not greatly different from that of much of East and Southeast Asia at present, Japan took about three decades to perform such a feat with its own unaided resources. This increase in productivity was largely drained off by taxes, and the proceeds were applied by the government to financing the expansion of other sectors of the economy.

It is comparatively easy to impose such a tax when productivity is rising, but outside the largely foreign-owned estate sector, agricultural productivity in most underdeveloped countries is either static or declining. It is possible that in some circumstances the imposition of additional taxes would stimulate greater production, and in some countries, such as Indonesia, it has been claimed that there is considerable scope for such action. But perhaps the first and most obvious step is to eliminate the worst excesses of landlordism and its closely associated problem of rural indebtedness; it has often been remarked that it is folly to expect the peasant to produce two bags of rice where only one could be raised before if both are to go to the landlord. In many countries, the national revolution that brought independence did little or nothing to modify the power of the landlord class. Governments might take over landlord rights, as has occurred in Japan, Mexico, and Egypt, but the state can be more rapacious than even the most grasping landlord. The slogan "the land to the peasants" has been perhaps the most powerful source of support for communism in Asia; the peasants, however, have invariably lost their land with the creation of a communist society. But if the psychological climate for a greater agricultural productivity could be created by offering the peasant better incentives through the elimination of the excesses of landlordism or through the opportunity of acquiring much desired consumer goods, such as bicycles,[9] extended use of fertilizers in conjunction with improved seed of proved high response could produce decisive results, even with the present small fragmented farms, crude implements, and other associated handicaps; all of these difficulties will prove more tractable if productivity can be given an initial upward impetus and it becomes possible for the more efficient farmers to acquire holdings of larger size.

[8] J. K. Galbraith, *The Liberal Hour,* Houghton Mifflin Company, Boston, 1960, pp. 44–45.

[9] The bicycle is a very desirable piece of property in much of the underdeveloped world. It is an almost essential piece of farm equipment in Southeast Asia, and in India and Africa, it is as much coveted as an automobile in wealthier countries.

The problem of raising agricultural productivity is not confined to the underdeveloped economies; it is also acute in the centrally planned economies. In Eastern Europe and in the U.S.S.R. there is, of course, no question of starvation; diet is adequate if dull. But there are persistent shortages in those foods that acquire greater consumer preference with increases in income, particularly meat, milk, butter, dairy products, and fruit. The U.S.S.R. showed some appreciable advance in agricultural output in the early post-Stalin era, although probably not as large as was claimed, and it was proudly announced that Russian per capita consumption of meat and butter would exceed that of the United States in the very near future; since 1958, however, agricultural output has been virtually stationary, and there is apparently no prospect of fulfilling the ambitious targets for 1970.[10] The reasons for this mediocre performance lie in the failure of Russian agriculture to obtain sufficient investment and the continuation of administrative policies which have the effect of minimizing incentives. The necessity of meeting whatever volume of output happens currently to be the subject of a plan leads to the neglect of other lines of production; thus seed grain may be dispatched to meet cereal quotas, and breeding stock may be slaughtered to fulfill target output.

While the economically advanced members of the Eastern bloc have gone on vainly struggling to implement rash promises of higher meat and dairy output, the optimism of the Chinese "great leap forward" of 1958 has been swept away by a torrent of natural and man-made disaster. Drought, floods, and pests took their time-honored toll of China's crops, but worse was the reduction of peasant incentive through the imposition of the "higher cooperative" and the *commune.* With an annual increment in population of more than 15 million, China faces a grim battle for survival; while it has so far managed to fend off starvation, largely through administrative efficiency in managing food stocks and through better transport, undernourished workers cannot create the new industrial society that has been planned. In the early Sixties it appeared far from certain that, shackled by its ideologies and denied Russian economic assistance, China could ultimately escape from a situation of being able to offer its people only the barest minimum of subsistence.

It is clear that whatever the shortcomings of peasant agriculture in the underdeveloped world, collectivization on the traditional communist pattern is no solution at all. Paradoxically, the quickest and simplest way to obtain a higher agricultural output in Russia—and almost certainly in China and Cuba also—would be to enlarge the private sector. Ideologically, of course, this is completely unacceptable; indeed, the Russian rulers would like nothing better than to eliminate completely the private plots of the peasants as Castro has done and as Khrushchev himself once planned to do through his "agrotowns"; the consequences to agricultural output, however, would be so disastrous that they are compelled to stay their hand. It is a striking fact that it is in those countries that have not imposed collectivization or have reversed the collectivization policy, such as Poland, that the agricultural sector has given least trouble to the communist world. China's failure to sustain a higher agricultural output has deeper implications, for China has claimed to be the champion of the new nations of Asia and Africa, and has branded the U.S.S.R. as essentially a European power. If China cannot launch its takeoff through its agricultural revolution, it can hardly be expected that similar methods will succeed elsewhere, a fact that should be of significance to Indonesia, where the world's largest Commu-

[10] **Alec Nove, "Soviet Agriculture Marks Time,"** *Foreign Affairs,* **vol. 40, p. 593, 1962.**

nist party outside the Sino-Soviet bloc itself views the mounting social and economic chaos in that country with considerable satisfaction. The great decline in production that has followed the Cuban revolution is further evidence of the sterility of the communist agricultural program.

It is often forgotten that the Russian Revolution inherited a substantial industrialization, the greater part of which was already in the hands of the state, and an agriculture which, though backward by the standards of Western Europe or North America, was considerably more advanced than that of the present underdeveloped economies. The Non-European world never possessed these advantages, and if they cannot solve their agricultural problems, as it appears they cannot through collectivization, their chances of emulating the spectacular industrial advance of the U.S.S.R. will not be very great.

INTERNATIONAL AID FOR ECONOMIC DEVELOPMENT

Whether the estimate given earlier of the capital to provide an effective stimulus to economic development in the underdeveloped world is an over- or an underassessment is not really important. The sum is undoubtedly a very large one—although in relation to Western defense expenditure it is not really large at all—and it is undeniable that what is forthcoming from both internal and external sources is only a fraction. The desirability of a great increase in external aid to economically backward countries is thus often conceded, but there is no unanimity as to how such aid should be raised among donors or how it should be distributed among recipients. Approximately 90 per cent of all aid to underdeveloped countries since the end of World War II has been bilateral, that is, government-to-government aid, and there is little question that this fact alone has greatly limited its usefulness. Of the total free-world bilateral aid of about 15 billion dollars between 1956 and 1960, about 90 per cent has been provided by the United States, which has also made by far the largest contribution to multilateral aid.

While the desire of the United States to apportion foreign aid to those governments it regards as friendly is perfectly understandable, particularly as the Eastern bloc has endeavored to extract the maximum publicity value from its own very limited foreign aid, underdeveloped countries find the actual and implied conditions attached to such aid extremely distasteful. Moreover, much United States aid has been for military purposes, and general aid has been mainly directed to those countries where military or strategic problems have existed rather than to those countries whose need is the greatest. Thus until about 1958, Indonesia, India, and Pakistan had received little in comparison with Japan, Korea, Taiwan, the Philippines, and Vietnam. American aid to Japan has certainly paid handsomely in terms of economic development, and considerable development has also been recorded in Taiwan despite a vast budget for military expenditure. The economic situation in the Philippines has improved since 1958, but the anticipated effects of American aid were a very long time in coming; Korea, on the other hand, still has little to show so far for the vast sums it has received.

After 1958 India and other previously ignored Asian countries began to acquire very substantial assistance indeed. Unfortunately, however, apparent American preoccupation with the problems of Asia has had repercussions in Latin America, which has felt itself neglected in the matter of aid; even the President's Alliance for Progress scheme was largely seen as a reaction to the challenge of Cuba rather than as a spontaneous attempt to cope

Major construction projects in the underdeveloped world not only produce a direct return but also an important indirect one, as they encourage the acquisition of skills and attitudes of mind previously in short supply.

Above, a class of workers receives instruction on constructional methods during the building of the Kariba dam.

Center, a traveling industrial exhibition from West Germany about to leave on a tour of Africa. In relation to its resources, the Federal Republic's contribution to foreign aid appears distinctly meager.

Below, an Indian Colombo Plan student receives managerial training at a British mine.

with Latin America's pressing economic issues. Moreover, the continuing unwillingness of Congress to provide funds for long-term aid programs has been responsible for the spawning of a multiplicity of agencies administering aid in a multiplicity of forms, a factor which has also tended to reduce the effectiveness of much American aid.

The balance of bilateral aid, apart from that provided by the Eastern bloc, which is estimated at about 4.4 billion dollars between 1955 and 1961, has been provided by France and Britain, mainly to their former colonial territories. The magnitude of French aid which goes far to explain the adhesion of the former French possessions to French institutions, is little appreciated. Even beside the volume of French aid, to say nothing of that provided by the United States, the contributions of Britain appear very small. Nevertheless, the aid provided by Britain, Canada, Australia, and New Zealand in the so-called "Colombo Plan" has been extremely effective. This is not really a plan at all but a collection of *ad hoc* projects involving donations of food, raw materials, or equipment or the provision of technical assistance and training; however, the regular meetings of donors and recipients and the strong sense of local responsibility have been able to create an active public interest which other agencies, both bilateral and multilateral, have been unable to match.

Although the special agencies of the United Nations such as FAO, the World Health Organization (WHO), and UNESCO are indirectly involved in economic aid, this is the

Aid where it is most needed—on the personal level. A Peace Corps agricultural scientist at work in Pakistan.

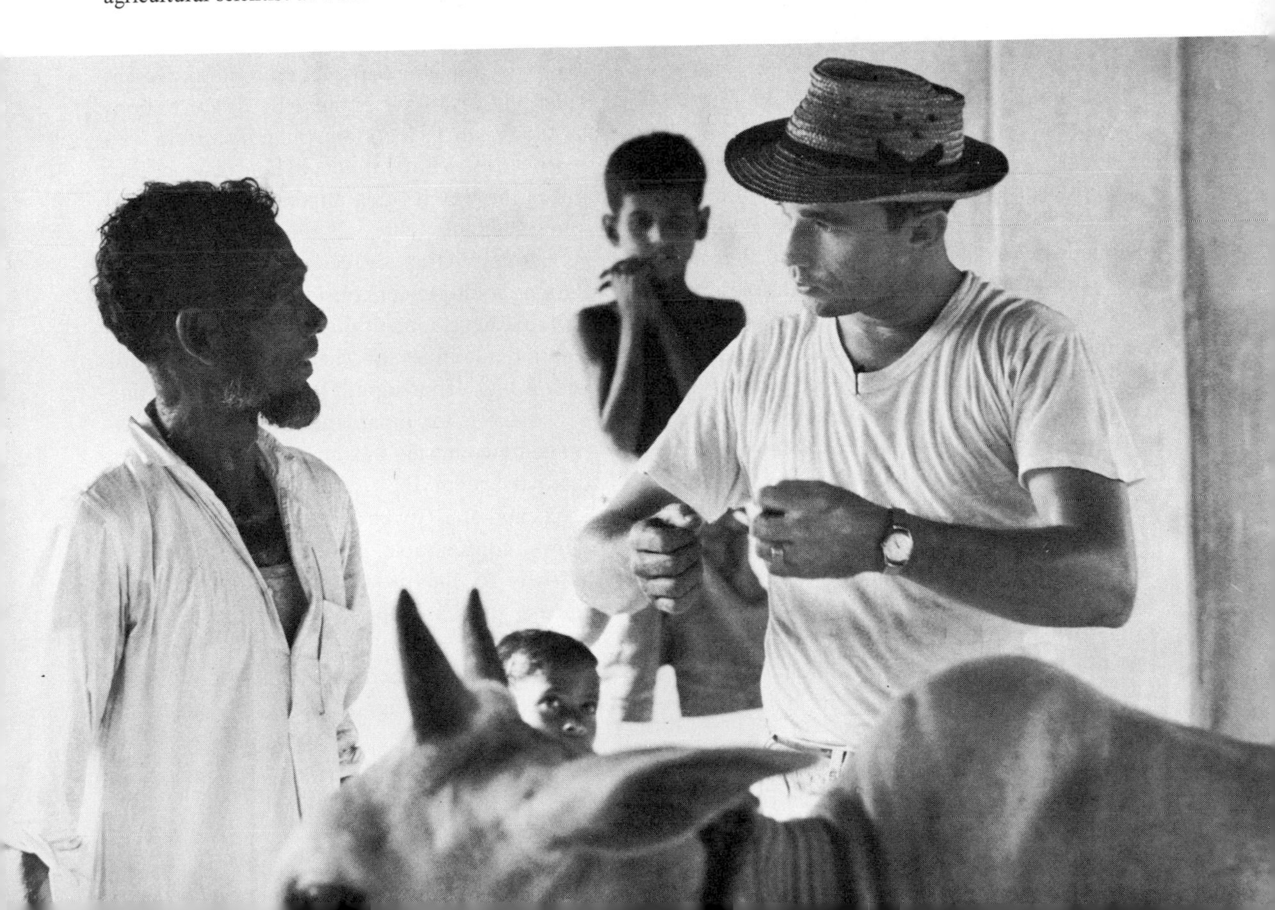

particular concern of the International Bank for Reconstruction and Development (the World Bank) and the Expanded Program for Technical Assistance (EPTA). The World Bank, supported by almost sixty nations but with one-third of its capital subscribed by the United States, lends money to governments for development projects; but again, its aid has largely gone to the most credit-worthy nations rather than those with the greatest need— indeed, the Bank has been inordinately proud of its adherence to established business criteria. India and Japan have both received substantial sums, but so also has Australia, which, despite the fact that it is sometimes called underdeveloped by economists who should know better, has one of the highest per capita incomes in the world. Since 1957 the International Finance Corporation has supplemented the work of the Bank by lending to private business, but the scale of its operations is small. EPTA operates largely through other agencies and has specialized in a worldwide interchange of experts; its valuable work, however, has been gravely handicapped by the smallness of its financial resources.

Despite the small scale of multilateral aid operations, aid of this kind is infinitely preferred by the underdeveloped economies, which would like to see all aid channeled either through the United Nations or through some special body such as the OECD; the latter course would avoid the complications and disagreements which would be certain to arise through having to include the U.S.S.R. as a partner in aid operations. For some years the underdeveloped countries have been pressing for a Special United Nations Fund for Economic Development (SUNFED), to which all members would contribute 1 per cent of their national income. The effect of this would be greatly to increase the present aid expenditure of the United States, which already carries a very large share of the financial burden of the United Nations, and the proposal has therefore been strongly resisted, and not without some justification. Other countries, however, could certainly contribute very much more to aid; this is particularly true of the EEC countries, but Britain, Canada, Australia, New Zealand, and Japan could also contribute much more than they do at present.

The total aid received annually by underdeveloped economies seldom amounts to more than about 10 to 15 per cent of their export income, so that fluctuations in the prices of export commodities may more than wipe out any gains from international aid. Commodity-stabilization schemes have had little success so far, and it is doubtful that these price oscillations can ever be completely ironed out. The highly developed economies all protect their farmers from the consequences of such fluctuations, and it might well be asked why they should not be prepared to extend such assistance to the farmers of the underdeveloped economies. It would certainly be an excess of cynicism to claim that bilateral aid at present is largely a subsidy granted by donor nations to their own farmers and manufacturers who receive orders or contracts in consequence, but this is the way it often appears to the political and economic elite of the underdeveloped economies. Also, the economically advanced nations could render considerable assistance to national development plans by importing substantial quantities of cheap consumer goods with a high labor input. The need for creating new markets for Japan and other newly industrializing countries was an important factor in the passage of the Trade Expansion Act of 1962, and it is to be regretted that the EEC shows considerable reluctance to open its markets to the products of industrial newcomers such as Japan, India, Pakistan, and Hong Kong.

On the whole there can be little doubt that competition in foreign aid is likely to be much more rewarding for the economically advanced nations than accepting the challenge of the U.S.S.R. to a battle in space research or a battle for maximum production.[11] Large and populous countries such as Brazil and Indonesia received very little direct aid from the West until the eleventh hour. The greatest asset of the free world is still its capacity for social and economic change; whether our free society can endure may well depend on how rapidly the economic geography of the world can be transformed.

SELECTED REFERENCES

Belshaw, J. P.: "Social and Economic Revolution for the Development of Backward Countries," *Economic Record,* vol. 32, pp. 319–322, 1956.

Benham, F. C.: *Economic Aid to Under-developed Countries,* Oxford University Press, London, 1961.

Berliner, J. S.: *Soviet Economic Aid,* Frederick A. Praeger, Inc., New York, 1958.

Berrill, Kenneth (ed.): *Economic Development with Special Reference to East Asia,* Macmillan & Co., Ltd. (for International Economic Association), London, 1964.

Brown, William A., and Redvers Opie: *American Foreign Assistance,* The Brookings Institution, Washington, D.C., 1953.

Coale, Ansley J., and Edgar M. Hoover: *Population Growth and Economic Development in Low-income Countries: A Case Study of India,* Princeton University Press, Princeton, N.J., 1958.

Colombo Plan: *Annual Report,* H. M. Stationery Office, London, annually.

Ellis, H. S. (ed.): *Economic Development for Latin America,* Macmillan & Co., Ltd. (for International Economic Association), London, 1961.

Galbraith, J. K.: *Economic Development in Perspective,* Harvard University Press, Cambridge, Mass., 1962.

Lewis, W. Arthur: *The Theory of Economic Growth,* George Allen & Unwin, Ltd., London, 1960.

Robinson, E. A. G. (ed.): *Economic Consequences of the Size of Nations,* Macmillan & Co., Ltd. (for International Economic Association), London, 1960.

Rostow, W. W.: *The Stages of Economic Growth,* Cambridge University Press, Cambridge, 1960.

Shonfield, Andrew: *Attack on World Poverty,* Random House, Inc., New York, and Chatto & Windus, Ltd., London, 1960.

"Technology and Economic Development," *Scientific American,* vol. 209, no. 3, September, 1963.

United Kingdom Parliament: *The Colombo Plan for Co-operative Economic Development in South and South-east Asia,* H. M. Stationery Office, London, 1950.

United Nations, Department of Economic Affairs: *Commodity Trade and Economic Development,* New York, 1953.

———: *International Compensation for Fluctuations in Commodity Trade,* New York, 1961.

———: *World Economic Survey,* New York, annually.

Wharton, C. R.: "The Nature of Technical Assistance for Economic Development," *Economic Development and Cultural Change,* vol. 6, pp. 109–128, 1958.

[11] It is not suggested, of course, that the U.S.S.R. should be allowed to achieve any military advantage through its plans for space exploration. The military value of landing men on the moon or probing Venus has, however, been questioned by many scientists.

PHOTOGRAPHIC CREDITS

Part I World Bank
Part II National Film Board of Canada, Ottawa
Part III Westinghouse photo
Part IV New York Stock Exchange

Page 15, USDA photo *17 above,* Marc Riboud, Magnum *17 below,* Burt Glinn, Magnum *20 above,* United Nations *20 below,* FAO photo by C. Bavagnoli *21,* Werner Bischof, Magnum *22 above and below,* Marc Riboud, Magnum *34 above and below,* Division of Air Pollution, U.S. Public Health Service *35,* Burt Glinn, Magnum *52 above left and right, center,* USDA photos *52 below,* UPI photo *53 above,* Elliott Erwitt, Magnum *53 below,* USDA photo *77 above,* Belgian Government Information Center *77 below,* USAID *101,* FAO photo by A. Defever *108,* FAO photo *109,* Swiss National Tourist Office photo by B. Schocher *135 above,* FAO photo by S. Bunnag *135 below,* USDA photo *181 above,* Werner Bischof, Magnum *181 below,* Natural Rubber Bureau *194 above,* FAO photo by M. Ganzin *194 center,* USDA photo *194 below,* Australian News & Information Bureau photo by W. Brindle *196 above,* Edison Electric Institute *196 below,* USDA photo *226 above,* United States Pulp Producers Association *226 below left,* National Film Board of Canada, Ottawa *226 below right,* USDA photo *241,* Rene Burri, Magnum *246 above,* FAO photo by Alan Glanville *246 below,* U.S. Bureau of Commercial Fisheries *262 above left,* Information Service of India *262 above right,* United Nations *262 below,* Ford Foundation photo by Homer Page *263 above,* Eastfoto *263 below,* Ford Motor Company *284 above,* Standard Oil Company (N.J.) *284 below,* Cities Service Company photo by Clyde Hare *285 above,* Sovfoto *285 below,* Standard Oil Company (N.J.) *328 above and below,* German Information Center *342,* Edison Electric Institute *343 above,* General Electric Company *343 below,* Allis-Chalmers Manufacturing Company *348,* World Bank *394,* Henri Cartier-Bresson, Magnum *395,* Eastfoto *412,* Aluminum Company of America *423 above,* United Nations *423 below,* The Malayan Tin Bureau *444 above,* A. Cheprunov from Novosti Press Agency *444 below,* USAID *445 left and right,* Sasebo Heavy Industries Co., Ltd. *464 above,* German Information Center *464 below,* Volkswagen of America *469 above left and right,* The Boeing Co. *469 below,* Paris Match *475,* Werner Bischof, Magnum *496,* Y. Rumkin from Novosti Press Agency *509,* USAID *528 above,* CARE photo *528 below,* UPI photo *529,* Turner Construction Company *545 above,* World Bank *545 below,* United Nations photo *588,* Volkswagen of America and German Information Center *598,* ILO photo *608 above,* World Bank *608 center,* German Information Center *608 below,* Britain's Information Services *609,* Charles Harbutt, Magnum and the Peace Corps.

INDEX

Aachen, coalfield, 327
  cotton textile industry, 484
Abaca, 176–177
Acetate (*see* Rayon and acetate industry)
Acid steelmaking processes, 368
Acreage controls, 127, 140
Acrilan (*see* Noncellulose synthetic fibers)
Aden, 566
Adit mines, 312
Africa, agriculture, 70, 72, 74, 90–91, 103
  bauxite and aluminum, 415
  coal, 315, 332
  coffee, 88–89, 157–158
  cooperatives, 89
  copper, 405, 407
  corn, 72, 138
  cotton, 74, 82, 167, 172–175
  developmental problems, 601
  fishing, 248
  forests, 219–221
  gold, 425–427
  hydroelectricity, 346, 415
  iron ore, 362, 378
  livestock, 197, 207
  oil palm, 87, 89, 143–144
  petroleum, 300
  population, 29
  regional groupings, 602
  sugar, 152
  tea, 161
  tin, 422–424
  (*See also* specific countries and products)
African States, Organization of, 595
Afrikaners, 103
Agency houses, 86
Agha Jari oil field, 294
Agrarian Law (Netherlands Indies), 179
Agricultural Adjustment Act, 127
Agricultural cooperation, 65
Agricultural credit, 64–65
Agricultural machinery, 431–433
Agricultural productivity, 25–26, 605–607
  (*See also* specific products and countries)
Agricultural products, elasticity of demand for, 48–49, 579
  gross value of, 120
  price support (*see* Price support for agricultural products)
  terms of trade of, 576
Agricultural products (*See also* specific products)
Agricultural revolution, 104, 431
Agricultural structure, 54–66
Agricultural surpluses, 51–54
  (*See also* specific crops)
Agricultural Trade Development and Assistance Act, 127–128, 137, 172
Agriculture, centrally planned economies, 50–51, 606–607
  criteria of classification, 68–69
  electoral representation of, 54
  fixed costs in, 48
  highly developed economies in, 14, 51–54
  labor force in, 10, 14, 16, 19
  level of economic development and types of, 116–117
  livestock, place of, in, 192
  major world types of, 68–69
    commercial crop and livestock farming, 104–107
    commercial grain farming, 94–99
    commercial grazing, 92–94
    crop farming and horticulture with subsidiary livestock, 100–104
    dairying, 107–112
    intensive dry-field, 81–83
    pastoral nomadism, 90–92
    plantation crop, 83–90
    primitive subsistence, 70–75
    sawah, 76–80
    specialized horticulture, 113–116
  semideveloped economies in, 16
  subdivision and fragmentation, 56
  subsistence and commercial, 47–48
  underdeveloped economies in, 19, 605
  (*See also* specific products and countries)
Aid, international, in economic development, 607–611
Air pollution, 269, 319, 505
Air transport, 569–570
Aircraft, and aerospace industry, 467–472
    Canada, 472
    Great Britain, 471–472
    structure and organization, 467–468
    U.S., 468–471
    Western Europe, 472
  pasture improvement with, 212
  rice cultivation with, 137
Alabama, 201, 319, 376
Alaska, 288*n.*
Alberta, 96, 299
Alcoa, Tennessee, 412
Alcohols, 510
Alexandria station, 54
Alfa Romeo S.p.A., 461
Alfalfa, 94, 98
Algeria, agriculture, 100
  petroleum, 300
Alkalis, 507–508
Alkylation, 301
Allgemeine Electricität Gesellschaft, 448
Alliance for Progress, 607
Allied Chemical and Dye Corporation, 519
Allis-Chalmers Corporation, 448
Alps, 344, 347, 414
Alsace, 485
Aluminium Corporation of Canada (Alcan), 414
Aluminum, employment and properties of, 403
  growth of production, 409
  smelting technology, 409–412
Aluminum Corporation of America (Alcoa), 412, 414
Aluminum production, Alpine region, 414
  Australia, 415
  Canada, 414
  France, 414
  Germany, 414
  Ghana, 415
  Great Britain, 415
  Norway, 414
  U.S.S.R., 416
  U.S., 411–414
Alunite, 416
American Cyanamid Corporation, 519
American Independent Oil Co. (Aminoil), 296
American Locomotive Company, 438
American Motors Corporation, 455, 456, 458
American Rolling Mill Corporation (Armco), 373, 376
American Viscose Corporation, 495
Ammonia synthesis, 508
Amsterdam, 433, 533
Amu Dar'ya, 91
Anaconda Corporation, 404, 405, 413
Angara river, 349*n.*, 416
Angola, 158

Anhydrite, 503
Anshan, 333, 396
Antarctica, 250
Anthracite, 311
  in U.S., 317, 319–320
Anticlinal structure, 280
Antigua, 602
Antimony, 417
Appalachia, poverty in, 14*n.*
Appalachian coalfield, 318–319
Appalachian oil fields, 288
Apparel fibers (*see* Textile industries)
Apsheron peninsula, 297
Arabia, 293, 294
Arabian American Oil Company (Aramco), 296
Area Redevelopment Act, 270
Argentina, agricultural work force, 16, 26
  alfalfa, 94, 98
  beef production and exports, 201–203
  cattle distribution, 201
  estancias, 60
  corn production and exports, 139–140
  cotton, 174
  flax, 98
  industrialization, 124
  level of economic development, 16
  livestock ranching, 92–94
  petroleum, 292
  railways, 546
  sheep distribution, 209–210
  trade, 125, 594
  wheat production and exports, 98, 124–125
  wool, 210
Arizona, copper mining, 404
Arkansas, bauxite and aluminum, 410, 413
  rice, 137–138
Arkwright's water frame, 476
Aruba, 290
Arvida, 414
Asia, direction of trade, 585
  population, 29, 36, 42
  (*See also* specific countries)
Asphaltic-base crudes, 279
Assam, tea estates, 159–160
Assembly-line production, 454–455
Associated Electrical Industries Ltd. (AEI), 448, 450
Association of Southeast Asian States (ASA), 595
Aswan Dam, 173, 349*n.*
Atlantic Ocean, fisheries, 240, 242–245
  shipping lanes and routes, 563–564
Atomic energy, 355–358
  Great Britain, 355–356
  power stations, location of, 356–357
  technology, 355
  U.S., 355–356
  Western Europe, 358
Atomic Energy Commission, 350, 356
Australia, agricultural cooperatives, 65
Australia, agricultural machinery, 432
  agricultural marketing, 65
  agricultural work force, 25
  barley, 105
  bauxite and aluminum, 410, 415
  beef production and exports, 201, 202
  butter production and exports, 205–206
  cattle, 92–94, 201
  coal mining, 332
  copper, 407
  cotton textile industry, 261
  crop and livestock farming, 107
  dairy farming, 100, 110
  economic growth, rate of, 14
  gold mining, 427
  government, employment in, 540
  industrialization, 25
  iron and steel industry, 391
  lead and zinc, 418
  motor vehicle industry, 452, 457, 602
  multipurpose water projects, 349–350
  oats, 105
  pasture improvement, 94, 213
  petroleum imports, 300
  ports, 569
  railways, 546, 547
  regional shopping centers, 539
  rice, 134
  roads, 555, 558
  sheep, 92, 93, 210–211
  shipping services, 565
  Snowy Mountains scheme, 349
  sugar, 146, 149, 150
  trade, 577*n.*, 586, 591
  urbanization, 10
  wheat, 98–99, 124–126, 129
  wool, 210–211, 213
Austria, hydroelectricity, 347, 348
  iron and steel industry, 364, 386
Automation, 260, 434, 476, 530–531
Automobile industry (*see* Motor vehicle industry)

Bacon and ham, 110, 215
Badische Anilin und Soda Fabrik Gmbh, 521
Bagasse, 338
Bahrein Islands, 296
Baie-Comeau, 414
Bajrah, 82
Baku, 297
Balance, of payments, 574, 582
    U.S., 593–594
  of trade, 573
    U.S., 592–593
Baleen whales, 250
Bali, 19
Baltic Exchange, 532
Baltimore, 376
Bananas, 86
Bank of England, 532
Banking, 531–534
Barbados, 144
Barents Sea, 243
Barilla ores, 422
Barkly Tableland, 54
Barley, 99, 105, 121
Barter trade, 581, 582
Basic process, 368
Basic slag, 368
Bast fibers, 176
Batch production, 434
Bauxite, 399, 410, 415
Bayer, 511, 521
Bayer process, 410
Baykal-Amur railway, 533
Beef cattle, 83, 195–201
Beef production and trade, 201–203
Beehive coke ovens, 322
Beet sugar (*see* Sugar)
Beirut, 533
Belfast, 433, 442
Belgian Congo (*see* Congo Republic [Léopoldville])
Belgium, canals, 560
  chemical industries, 503
  coal mining, 326–327
  farm size, 55
  greenhouse cultivation, 113
  iron and steel industry, 364, 386
  per capita product, 7
  power stations, location of, 354
  textile industries, 477, 482
  trade, 589
Bemberg, 493
Beneficiation and sintering, 365–366
Benelux union, 587
Bengal, 165
Bergius process, 510
Bergslagen, 387
Bering Sea, 250
Berlin, 33, 267, 450
Beryllium, 398
Bessemer process, 367–368
Bethlehem Steel Corporation, 359, 373, 376
  shipbuilding, 446, 447
Beverages, 153–163
Bicycle industry in Britain, 462
Bicycles in underdeveloped economies, 605
Big Inch pipeline, 290
Bihar iron ore, 332
Bimetallic standard, 427–428
Bingham, Utah, 404
Birmingham, Alabama, 319, 376
Birmingham, England, 267, 268, 462
  (*See also* Black Country)
Birth rates, 37, 39, 42
Bituminous coal, 310–311
  (*See also* Coal)
Black Country, 268, 380
Black Hills, 229, 427
Blast furnace, 365–366
Bochum, 383, 466
Boeing Aircraft Corporation, 470
Boerde lands, 200
Bolivar oil field, 290

Bolivia, tin mining, 422–423
 trade, 595
Boll weevil, 169, 171
Bombay, cotton textile industry, 485
Bonneville Dam, 351
Borgward Gmbh, 466
Bovoids in agriculture, 192
Bowater Co., 231, 232
Boyle, Robert, 501
Braden Copper Co., 405
Bradford, 490
Brahmaputra River (Tsangpo), 346
Brasília, 540
Bratsk power station, 349*n.*
Brazil, agricultural productivity, 148–149
 cattle, 198, 201
 coffee, 154–157
 cotton textile industry, 477
 fazendas, 60, 155
 forests, 221
 iron and steel industry, 390
 livestock ranching, 94
 resources, adequacy of, 603
 sugar, 148–149, 154
 trade, 125, 594
"Brazils," 154
Breeding, animal, 193
Bremen, 383, 445, 466, 485
Bristol Aircraft Co., 471
Bristol and Somerset coalfield, 325
British Aircraft Corporation, 471
British Borneo (*see* Sabah; Sarawak)
British Columbia, aluminum, 414
 forests, 232
 lead and zinc, 418
British Commonwealth (*see* Commonwealth)
British Guiana, 152, 409, 602
British Motor Corporation, 268, 461–463
British Petroleum Co., 282, 286, 293–294, 296
British West Indies, 146, 152, 602
 (*See also* Barbados; Jamaica; Trinidad)
Broadleaf forests (*see* Forests)
Broiler industry, 215
Broken Hill, 418
Broken Hill Proprietary Ltd., 391
Brown coal, 309–310
 (*See also* Coal)
Brussels convention, 152
Buenos Aires, 33, 567
Building and construction industry, 526–530
Buna rubber (*see* Synthetic rubber)
Burgan oil field, 294
Burma, fish consumption, 237
 lead and zinc, 418
 moneylenders, 65
 rice, 76, 134–137
 tin, 422
Burundi, 158
Butadiene, 514–515
Butane, 301
Butte, Montana, 404
Butter consumption, 204
 surpluses and trade, 205–206
 (*See also* Dairy farming)

Cacao cultivation, 86, 161
 (*See also* Cocoa)
Cadmium, 398, 403
Calcium carbonate (*see* Limestone)
Calcutta, 33
California, agriculture, 114–115
 aircraft industry, 470–471
 cotton, 171
 electronics industry, 450
 industrial expansion and population growth, 267–268
 iron and steel industry, 377
 motion picture industry, 471, 525–526
 motor vehicle industry, 459
 natural gas, 305
 petroleum, 288
 railways, 551
 rice, 134, 137–138
 sugar beets, 151
Calorie consumption, 49–50
Caltex Corporation, 286
Cambodia, 19, 134, 136, 182
Cameroun, 87, 601
Camphor, 89
Canada, aircraft industry, 472
 aluminum, 414
 copper, 404, 407
 fisheries, 244–247
 forest industries, 231–232
 gold, 427
 hydroelectricity, 347–349
 inland waterways, 351*n.*, 559–560
 lead and zinc, 418
 livestock ranching, 92
 motor vehicle industry, 457
 natural gas, 305
 nickel, 420
 petroleum, 299
 railways, 549–550
 silver, 428
 trade, 591–593
 wheat, 96, 123, 126–127
 wood pulp and paper, 225, 227
Canals, Western Europe, 329, 560
Canberra, S.S., 442
Canberra, 540
Cane sugar (*see* Sugar)
Canterbury lamb, 212
Canterbury Plains, 107
Capital, economic development in, 603–605
Capital-intensive industries, 260–261
 (*See also* specific industries)
Captive mines, 321
Capture, law of, 288
Carbon black, 261
Carbon in steel, 364
Cardiff, 322, 379
Caro, N., 502
Cartels in nonferrous metals, 401–402
"Casablanca group," 602
Caspian Sea, 560
Cassa per il Mezzogiorno, 270, 521
Cast iron, 364
Castor oil, 141
Catalytic cracking and reforming, 301
Cattle, 83, 195–203
 (*See also* Commercial grazing; Crop and livestock farming; Dairy farming)
Caucasus Mountains, 297
Caustic soda, 507
Celanese, 493
Celanese Corporation of America, 495, 596
Cellulose, 223, 234
Cellulose fibers (*see* Rayon and acetate industry)
Central America, coffee, 157
Centrally planned economies, 19–24
 (*See also* specific countries)
Centrals (sugar mills), 148
Centrifugal sugar, 147
Cereals, 120–140
Ceylon, coffee, 154
 communal friction, 603–604
 death rate, reduction of, 37
 economic development, 605
 estates, 84, 87
 population growth, rate of, 42
 rice, 134
 rubber, 179, 182
 smallholders, 182
 tea, 158–160
Chad Republic, 602
Chadbourne scheme, 153
Chain stores, 536–538
Charcoal iron, 387, 388
Checker Cab Co., 455*n.*, 456*n.*
Chemical industries, 500–522
 acid and alkalis, 505–508
 alcohol and fuel chemicals, 510–511
 explosives, 508–510
 fertilizers, 508
 fine chemicals and pharmaceuticals, 511–512
 heavy chemicals, 505–511
 historical development, 501–503
 petrochemicals, 516–518
 plastics, 512–514
 share of industrial work force, 261
 synthetic rubber, 514–516
 U.S., 502, 506, 511, 512, 516, 518–520
 Western Europe, 520–521
Chemical pulp, 225
Chena, 71
Cherepovets, 389
Chesapeake Bay, 245
Chettyars, 65
Chicago, 33, 372, 375, 535
Chikuho coalfield, 393
Chile, agriculture, 102–103
 copper, 404, 405
 estates, 60

Chile, forests, 221
  iron ore, 362
  trade, 594
China, agriculture, 78–84, 606
  coal mining, 315, 333
  cooperatives and communes, 60
  cotton cultivation, 84, 174
  cotton textiles, 486–487
  credit, 64
  energy, use of, 271
  fertilizers, use of, 80
  First Five Year Plan, 256*n.*
  fisheries, 249
  food shortages in, 50–51
  "great leap forward," 23, 259, 606
  Hwang Ho scheme, 352
  iron and steel industry, 393, 396
  land ownership, 59
  migration to cities, 33
  rice exports, 136
  sericulture, 178
  sheep, 207
  small-scale industries, 259
  soybeans, 142, 143
  tea, 160
  tenancy, 64
  tin, 421
  water buffaloes, 195
  wheat, 122, 126
Chinese estate labor, 179
Chlorine, 507
Christmas Island, 508
Chromium, 419
Chrysler Corporation, 455–457
Chuño, 75
Chuquicamata, 405
Cigarettes, consumption of, 186
  (*See also* Tobacco)
Cinchona, 89
Cincinnati, 373, 434, 508
Citriculture, 102, 116
City of London (*see* London)
Clark, Colin, 14*n.*, 25*n.*
Cleveland, Ohio, 375, 434, 457, 459
Cleveland Hills, 379
Clones, 183
Clovers (*see* Pasture improvement)
Clydeside, 442
  (*See also* Glasgow)
Coal, chemical industries in, 510, 517
  energy supplies in, 274
  hydrogenation, 510
  Industrial Revolution in, 308–309
  iron and steel industry in, 362
  nature and occurrence of, 309
  reserves, 315–317
  trade, 322, 323, 330, 557, 590
  types of, 309–311
  utilization, 321–322
Coal mining, history of, 308–309
  technology, 311–315, 320
Coal mining industry, Australia, 332
  Belgium, 326–327
  China, 333
  Czechoslovakia, 330–331
Coal mining industry, East Germany, 330
  France, 326
  Great Britain, 322–326
  India, 311, 332
  Japan, 332
  Netherlands, 327
  Poland, 330
  South Africa, 315, 332
  Southern Rhodesia, 407
  U.S.S.R., 331–332
  U.S., 317–322
  West Germany, 327–330
Coarse grains, concessional sales, 129
  (*See also* Corn)
Coastal shipping, 560
Cochin China, 179
  (*See also* South Vietnam)
Cockerill, John, 386
Cocoa, 161–163
Coconut oil, 141–142
Cod fisheries, 239, 244
Coeur D'Alene, Idaho, 418
Coffee, cultivation and varieties, 153–154
  per capita consumption, 158
  surpluses, 155–156
  trade, 157
  (*See also* International Coffee Agreement)
Coke, metallurgical, 362
  ovens, 322
Collective farms (*see Kolkhozy*)
Cologne, 466
Colombia, coffee, 156–157
  petroleum, 292
  trade, 595
Colombo Plan, 609
Colonial Sugar Refining Co. Pty. Ltd., 89
Colons, 100
Colorado, iron and steel industry, 376
Columbia River, 351
Colville and Co., 380
Commerce and finance, 530–534
Commercial grain farming, 94–99
Commercial grazing, 92–94
Commodity agreements, 65–66, 402
  (*See also* specific agreements)
Commodity Credit Commission, 127, 172
Commodity stabilization, 66, 610
Common Market (*see* European Economic Community)
Commonwealth (British), trade, 590–591
  (*See also* specific countries)
Commonwealth Sugar Agreement, 152
Communal tenure, 56–60
Communications industry (*see* Electronics industry)
Compagnie Française des Petroles S.A., 283
Comparative costs, principle of, 573
Conacre, 49
Concessional sales, 129, 136, 172
  (*See also* Agricultural Trade Development and Assistance Act)
Congo Republic (Brazzaville), 87
Congo Republic (Léopoldville), copper, 404
  estates, 87
  oil palm, 142–144
  tin, 420, 422
Coniferous forests (*see* Forests)
Connally Act, 289
Connecticut Valley, 186, 188
Connellsville coking coal, 371
Consortium (*see* Iranian Exploration and Development Co.)
Continuous strip mills, 370
Convair Corporation, 470
Cooperatives, 60, 65, 89, 110
  consumer, 536
Copper, ores, 404
  price, 401
  production, 404–407
  properties and uses of, 403
  smelting, 407–409
  substitutes, 403–404
Copper Cliff, 420
Corby, 379
Corn, chemicals, 139
  hybrid, 106, 139
  price, 121
  production, 98, 138–140
  surpluses, 140
  trade, 129, 140
  uses of, 138–139
Corn Belt, 106
Corridor system, 74
Corvee, 555
Costa Rica, 157
Cottage industries, 31, 258, 337
Cotton, 82, 84, 167–173
  per capita consumption, 166, 474
  staple length, 167
  surpluses, 172
Cotton textile industry, Australia and New Zealand, 261
  characteristics of, 478
  China, 486–487
  Great Britain, 481–484
  history of, 477–478
  Hong Kong, 485, 487
  India, 485
  Japan, 485–486
  role in economic development, 261
  technology, 476
  U.S.S.R., 486
  U.S., 479–481
  Western Europe, 481–485
Cottonseed oil, 142
Council for Mutual Economic Aid (COMECON), 298, 330
Count system, 484*n.*
Countervailing power, 401–402, 535
Courtaulds Ltd., 494, 495, 497
Coventry, 462
Cracking, 301

Credit sale, 533
Creole Petroleum Corporation, 290
Crewe, 438, 472
Crompton's mule, 476
Crop farming and horticulture with subsidiary livestock, 100–104
Crop and livestock farming, 104–107
Crops, value of output, 119–120
Crucible process, 367
Crustaceans, 238, 245, 250
Cryolite, 411
Cuba, agricultural productivity, 606, 607
nickel, 420
per capita product, 6
revolution in, 148
sugar, 146–148
tobacco, 186–187
trade, 149
Cuprammonium process, 493
Curaçao, 290
Cyanamide process, 508
Cyprus, 602
Czechoslovakia, coal mining, 330–331
heavy industry, overinvestment in, 24
iron and steel industry, 390

Dacron (*see* Noncellulose synthetic fibers)
Dagenham, 463
Daimler Car Co., 463
Daimler-Benz Gmbh, 463–465
Daingerfield, Texas, 377
Dairy cattle breeds, 203
Dairy farming, 107–112
Dairy products, 203–206
Dalton, John, 501
Damman oilfield, 294
Damodar Valley, 332
Dams, regulatory and storage, 346
Darby, Abraham, 323
D'Arcy, William, 293
Darjeeling, 158
Deciduous forests (*see* Forests)
Decortication, 176
Defoe, Daniel, 37
Delaware, 105, 518
Deli Maatschappij NV, 68
Demersal fisheries, 240
Denier system, 495*n.*
Denmark, bacon and ham, 215
cooperatives, 110
dairy farming, 109–110
manufactures, 16*n.*
per capita product, 7
shipbuilding, 445
trade, 591
Department stores, 535–536
Depletion allowance, 288
Derby, 438, 472
Derbyshire coalfield, 323, 324
Deserts, 29
Detergents, 141, 508
Detroit, Michigan, 457, 458, 470
de Wendel, S. A., 386
Diesel engines, 437, 442
Diet and income, 49
Dillon round, 586
Direct reduction processes, 366–367
Discount houses, 532
Discount stores, 538
Distribution, 534–539
Distribution of Industry Act, 269
Dogger Bank, 243
Dollar, value of, 425
Dolomite, 368
Dominican Republic, 146
Dominions, British, 583*n.*
Donets coalfield, 331
Donetsk (Stalino), 388
Donzère-Montdragon Dam, 414
Dorman Long and Co., 359, 379
Dortmund-Ems Canal, 329
Dortmund-Hoerde Huettenunion Gmbh, 383
Douglas Aircraft Corporation, 470
Douglas fir, 229, 230
Dow Chemical Corporation, 519, 521
Drift mines, 312
Dry farming, 97, 102
Dry rice, 72, 83
Dunkerque, 385
Du Pont de Nemours & Co., E.I., 502, 514, 518, 521
Durham coalfield, 324
Durum wheat, 122
Dutch Guiana, 410

East Germany, chemical industries, 521
coal mining, 330
textile industries, 484–485
East St. Louis, 410
Eastern Interior coalfield, 319
Ebbw Vale, 379
Economic Commission for Asia and the Far East (United Nations), 129, 258
Economic development, and capital, 603–605
criteria of, 4–12
and diet, 49
and industrialization, 260–261
and resources, 600–601
Ecuador, cacao cultivation, 162
fishing, 248
trade, 595
Edible oils, 140–141
(*See also* specific oils)
Edjélé oil field, 300
Egypt, African affairs, in, 602
Aswan Dam, 173, 349
cotton, 172–174
irrigation, 82, 172–173
land reform, 174, 605
petroleum imports, 298
population growth, 38
Suez canal, 295, 564–565
Suez crisis, 274
Egypt, trade, 174, 599
wheat, 83
Ejidos, 59–60
Elbe River, 329, 521
Electric furnace, 367–368
Electric power stations, location of, 342, 343, 346, 353–355
Electrical engineering, 447–451
Electricity, consumption of, 336, 337
high voltage transmission, 341
interconnection, 339–345
international interchange, 344
investment in annually, 336
load factor, 338–339
measurement of, 338
plant utilization factor, 340
production, rate of growth of, 335–337
(*See also* Hydroelectricity; Thermoelectricity)
Electrochemical industries, 266, 337, 508, 510
(*See also* Aluminum)
Electrolysis, 507
Electrolytic tinning, 370
Electronics industry, 448–449
Emba oil field, 298
Enclosure movement, 56, 104
Encomiendas, 61
Energy, primary and secondary, 272
solar, 273
Energy consumption, 270–275
manufacturing industries, 272
U.S., 273–274
Western Europe, 274–275
(*See also* specific sources)
Engel's Law, 49
Engineering industries, 430–451
England (*see* Great Britain)
English Electric Co., 430, 450
Enka NV, 494
Ente Nazionale Idrocarburi (ENI), 286
Espirito Santo, 155
Essen, 383
Estancias, 60, 92
Estates, 60–61, 83–90
(*See also* specific crops)
Europe, cattle, 199–200
Eastern, agricultural productivity, 606
coal mining, 330–331
commercial grazing, 92
iron and steel industry, 390
lead and zinc, 419
mining machinery, 436
petroleum, 299
(*See also* Council for Mutual Economic Aid; specific countries)
energy requirements, 272–274
fisheries, 242–244
forests and forest-products industries, 223, 227, 232–234
population, 29, 36, 42
sheep, 207–209
Western, agricultural cooperatives, 65

Europe, Western, agricultural machinery, 432
agricultural organization, 56, 61–62
aircraft industry, 471–472
aluminum, 414–415
building industry, 529–530
chain stores, 537
chemical industries, 520–521
cotton textile industry, 481–485
crop and livestock farming, 104–106
dairy farming, 107–109
horticulture, 113–114
inland waterways, 560
iron and steel industry, 377–387
lead and zinc, 417
locomotive construction, 438, 439
mining machinery, 436
motor vehicle industry, 459–467
petroleum products, consumption of, 301–302
railways, 546–548
rayon and acetate industry, 946–997
shipbuilding, 443–446
tobacco cultivation, 187
trade, 582, 583
wheat, 105, 122–123
woolen and worsted industries, 489–490
(*See also* specific countries)
European Atomic Energy Community (Euratom), 357, 588
European Coal and Steel Community (ECSC), 326, 380–382
European Economic Community (EEC), 104, 129, 158, 583, 587–589
European Free Trade Area (EFTA), 206, 583–584, 591
European Recovery Program, 587
Europort (Rotterdam), 386, 560
Evian agreement, 100
Expanded Programme for Technical Assistance (EPTA), 610
Expectation of life, 40
Explosives, 508–509
Exports (*see* Trade)

Factory ships, 249, 250
Fair trade laws, 537
Falconbridge Co., 420
Falkland Islands, 250
Farbenfabrik Bayer Gmbh, 511, 521
Farbwerke Hoechst Gmbh, 521
Farm size, 54, 55
Fats (*see* Vegetable oils)
Fault traps, 280
Fazendas, 60, 155
Federal Power Commission, 305
Fenlands, 114
Ferroalloys, 364, 368
Fertilizers, 508
Fiat S.p.A., 268, 461
Fiberboard, 227
Fibers (*see* Noncellulose synthetic fibers; Rayon and acetate; Vegetable fibers)
Fiji Islands, 89, 146, 602
Finishing mills, 370
Finland, consumer cooperatives, 536
forest industries, 233
Fischer-Tropsch process, 510
Fish, per capita consumption, 237
Fish catch, composition of, 236, 239
Fish fillets, frozen, 244, 245
Fisheries, 238–250
Japan and Pacific, 248–250
Northeast Atlantic, 242–244
Northwest Atlantic and North America, 244–248
outlook for, 232
Fishing, employment in, 237
methods, 240
"Flags of convenience," 563
Flax, 98, 176
(*See also* Linseed oil)
Flint, Michigan, 458
Florence, P. Sargant, 264, 266, 268
Florida, 116, 188, 508
Flotation process, 400
Flying doctor service, 92
Fontana, California, 376
Food chains, 240
Food processing machinery, 433
Ford Motor Co. (Britain), 463, 533
Ford Motor Corporation, 454, 455, 458
Ford-werke AG, 463
Foreign aid (*see* International aid for economic development)
Forest of Dean coalfield, 325
Forest-products industries, 222–227
Canada, 231–232
Europe and U.S.S.R., 232–235
United States, 227–231
Forestry, employment in, 217
Forestry Commission (Great Britain), 219
Forests, coniferous, 220–221
conservation in newly independent countries, 73
distribution and productivity, 219–222
hardwood (broadleaf), 221–222
world losses, 117
France, agricultural electoral representation, 54
aircraft industry, 472
aluminum, 414
birth rate, 56
coal mining, 326
cotton textile industry, 485
electric power interconnection, 344
horticulture, 114
iron and steel industry, 384–386
location of new industry, 270
locomotive construction, 438
métayage, 102
motor vehicle industry, 459–460, 466
silk industry, 177
France, sugar beets, 146
sugar imports, 152
trade, 589
vegetable oils, 142
wheat, 123, 126
Frasch process, 506
Free trade, 574–575
Freeholds, 61
Freight rates, 267
Frodingham, 379
Fuel cell, 338
Fuel and power in industrial location, 265–266
Fuel wood, 218
Fuji Steel Co., 393

Gach Saran oil field, 295
Galena, 400
Galvanising, 416, 417
Gallivare, 387
Gasoline, 301, 303
Gauge, railway, 547, 554
General Agreement on Tariffs and Trade (GATT), 586–587
General Dynamics Corporation, 468*n.*, 470
General Electric Corporation, 430, 448, 449
General Motors Corporation, acceptance, 533
automobile components, 453*n.*
foreign production, 457, 462, 463
location of plants, 458
locomotives, 437, 439
separation of interests, 456
share of automobile market, 455
Geneva, Switzerland, 533
Geneva, Utah, 376
Genoa, 467
Geographical discoveries, 83
Germany, Democratic Republic (*see* East Germany)
Germany, Federal Republic (*see* West Germany)
Gezira, 65, 175
Ghana, aluminum, 415
cacao, 161
cooperatives, 65
gold, 427
inter-African cooperation, 602
Volta River scheme, 349
Gilchrist-Thomas process, 368
Gippsland, 210
Gladstone, W.E., 173
Glasgow, 433, 438
(*See also* Clydeside)
Glassmaking, 507
Glenrothes, 326
Glucose, 139
Glycerin, 508
Goats, 92, 101, 193
Goering, Hermann, steelworks, 383
Gold, and balance of trade, 573
price of, 424–425

Gold, production, 425–427
smuggling, 425, 533
standard, 581
Government, role in economic development, 603–605
Government service, 539–541
Gracchi brothers, 100
Grain farming (*see* Commercial grain farming)
Gram (chickpea) 82
Grand Coulee Dam, 351
Grasslands, 90, 92
(*See also* Pasture improvement)
Great Britain, agricultural machinery, 432
agriculture, mechanization of, 105
aircraft industry, 471–472
aluminum, 415
atomic energy, 355–356
banking and finance, 531–532
beef production and imports, 203
butter imports, 205–206
butter and margarine consumption, 206
chain stores, 537
chemical industries, 520
coal mining, 322–326
coal utilization, 321
consumer cooperatives, 536
cotton textile industry, 482–484
crop and livestock farming, 104–105
dairy farming, 111, 204
department stores, 535, 536
electric power interconnection, 344
electric power stations, 353–356
electrical engineering, 450
enclosure movement, 56, 104
European Economic Community, 589
European Free Trade Area, 591
farm size, 55
fisheries, 240, 243–244
forestry, 219, 233
government, employment in, 540–541
iron and steel industry, 377–380
locomotive construction, 438
machine tool industry, 433–434
merchant shipping, 561–562
motor vehicle industry, 459–463
Norfolk rotation, 104
occupational distribution, 25
papermaking, 227
population, 37–38
railways, 546–548
rayon and acetate, 496–497
sheep, 206
shipbuilding, 441–442
sugar imports, 152
tenancy, 64
trade, 589–591
urbanization, 11
vegetable oil imports, 142
whaling, 251
wheat imports, 130
Great Britain, woolen and worsted industries, 489–490
Great Circles, 563, 569
Great Depression, international trade, 575
(*See also* specific commodities)
Great Lakes, 447, 559
Greece, currants, 102
merchant shipping, 562
olives, 103
tobacco, 189
Green tea, 158
Greenhouse cultivation, 113
Grimsby, 243
Groton, 447
Groundnut oil, 141–142
Groundwood pulp, 225
Grozny, 297
Guadalquiver River, 102
Guano, 249
Guatemala, 177
Guest, Keen and Nettlefolds Ltd., 378
Gulf, of Guinea, 84
of Mexico, 288
Gulf Coast oil fields, 288
Gulf Oil Corporation, 283, 291, 296
Gur, 147

Haber-Bosch process, 502, 508
Haddock fisheries, 245
Hall-Hérault process, 411
Hamburg, 433, 443
Hamilton, Alexander, 574
Hampton Roads, 551
Handicrafts (*see* Cottage industries)
Hanshin cities (Osaka, Kobe, Kyoto), 392, 451, 486
Harbors (*see* Ports)
Hard wheat, 122
Hardwoods (*see* Forests)
Harland and Woolf Ltd., 442
Harrisons and Crosfield Ltd., 87
Hartford, Connecticut, 470
Hawaii, 85, 146, 150
Hawley-Smoot tariff, 575
Hay, 107, 111, 200
(*See also* Pasture improvement)
Heavy industries, 266
Hematite, 362
Hemp, 176–177
Henequen, 177
Herring fisheries, 239, 243
Highly developed economies, 13–16
unemployment in, 14, 269–270
Hitachi Co., 448
Hochschild, M., 424
Hoechst, 521
Hogs, 110, 192, 195, 213–215
Holland-Amerika Plantage Maatschappij (HAPM) estate, 54
Homestake mine, 427
Hong Kong, 265, 483, 484, 487, 533, 610
Hoover Dam, 342
Hopeh, 84, 396
Horses, 197
Horticulture, 113–117
Hosiery, 476–477
Housing (*see* Building and construction)
Houston, 376
Hudson, J. L., Co., 535
Hué, 133
Hull, 243
Hull-Mahoning mine, 371
Humboldt Current, 249
Hungary, bauxite, 410, 414–415
commercial grain farming, 95
Huntsman, Benjamin, 367
Hwang Ho, 83, 349
Hybrid corn (*see* Corn, hybrid)
Hydroelectricity, 345–352
advantages and disadvantages, 346–347
distribution of generation, 347–349
multipurpose projects, 349–352
Hydrogen, 508, 510
Hydrogenation, coal, 508, 510
oils and fats, 141, 508

Iceland, cooperatives, 536
fisheries, 243, 244
petroleum imports, 298
Idaho, lead and zinc, 418
Ifugaos, 78
I.G. Farbenindustrie AG, 502, 520–521
Iguassú Falls, 346
IJmuiden, 386
Illinois, 106, 319
Imperial Chemical Industries Ltd., 502, 504, 520, 521
Imports (*see* Trade)
Indentured labor, 85
India, cattle, 83, 198
coal mining, 311, 319, 320, 332
cooperatives, 65
cotton, 82, 174
cotton textile industry, 485
Damodar Valley scheme, 349
farm size, 54
foreign aid, 607
gold smuggling, 425, 533
iron and steel industry, 390
irrigation, 82
jute, 165, 176
labor distribution in manufacturing, 261
merchant shipping, 566
millets, 82
rice, 79, 133, 134
small-scale industries, 258, 259
subdivision, 56
sugar, 147
tea, 158–160
water buffaloes, 195
wheat, 82–83, 123, 129
Indian Ocean, fisheries, 248
shipping routes, 564, 565
Indianapolis, 457, 470

Indigo, 85
Indonesia, Agrarian Law, 179
  Asahan project, 349
  cotton textile industry, 485
  estates, 85-87, 179, 184
  foreign aid, 599, 611
  irrigation, 82
  Land Rents Ordinance, 150
  petroleum, 299-300
  population, 37-38
  resources, adequacy of, 603
  rice, 79, 132-134
    (*See also* sawah agriculture *below*)
  rubber, 183-184
  sawah agriculture, 75-80
  smallholders, 182
  sugar, 81, 149-150
  tea, 158, 160
  tin, 420, 422
  tobacco, 186, 187
  trade, 599
Industrial agglomeration, 268
Industrial fibers, 166, 176
  (*See also* specific fibers)
Industrial location, 261-269
  regulation of, 269-270
Industrial Revolution, 37, 308-309, 476, 501
Industrial work force, 32, 260-261
Industrialization and nationalism, 256, 600, 603
Industry, definition of, 525
Infant mortality rate, 39, 40
Infield and outfield, 104
Ingalls Shipbuilding Co., 447
Inland Steel Corporation, 373
Innocenti S.p.A., 461
Insurance, 531-533
Intensive dry-field agriculture, 81-83
International aid for economic development, 607-611
International Bank for Reconstruction and Development (World Bank), 610
International Coffee Agreement, 158, 593
International Nickel Corporation, 420
International Rubber Agreement, 182
International Steel Cartel, 380
International Sugar Agreement, 152-153
International Tea Agreement, 161
International Tin Agreement, 424
International Whaling Commission, 251-252
International Wheat Agreement, 130
Iowa, 201
Iran, petroleum, 293-294, 297
Iranian Exploration and Development Co., 294
Iraq, petroleum industry, 293-294, 306
Ireland, cattle exports, 200
  conacre, 49
  dairy cooperatives, 65
Iron ore, 360-362
Iron ore, in economic development, 600
  (*See also* Iron and steel industry)
Iron and Steel Board, 378
Iron and steel industry, Australia, 391
  Brazil, 390-391
  China, 393-394
  continental Western Europe, 380-387
  Eastern Europe, 390
  Great Britain, 377-380
  India, 390
  Japan, 391-393
  requirements, 360-362
  South Africa, 391
  technology, 362-370
  U.S.S.R., 387-390
  U.S., 371-377
Irrawaddy Delta, 136
Irrigation, China, 82
  Egypt, 172-173
  India, 56, 82
  Indonesia, 82
  Malaya, 56
  Mediterranean basin, 102
  Sudan, 65, 175
  U.S., 94, 115
  (*See also* Sawah agriculture)
Israel, 58-59, 102, 306
Italy, agriculture, 100-103
  autostrade, 558
  battaglio del grano, 102
  Cassa per il Mezzogiorno, 270, 521
  cattle, 199
  chemical industries, 503, 512, 521
  citriculture, 102
  coffee consumption, 158
  economic growth, 16
  estates, 61
  hydroelectricity, 347
  iron and steel industry, 386
  motor vehicle industry, 466-467
  merchant shipping, 563
  mezzadria, 16, 102
  national product, 599
  natural gas, 304
  olives, 103
  petroleum industry, 286
  pharmaceuticals, 512
  sericulture and silk, 177
  wheat, 102, 126
  woolen and worsted industry, 290
  zinc, 418
Ivigtut, 411
Izmir, 102

Jacquard loom, 476
Jaguar Motor Co., 462
Jamaica, 410, 602
Japan, agricultural work force, 26
  chemical industries, 503, 512
  coal mining, 322
  cotton textile industry, 485-486
  crop and livestock farming, 107
  economic growth, 16, 599
Japan, electrical engineering, 449, 451
  employer's obligations, 18
  fisheries, 248-249
  foreign aid, 607, 610
  forests, 227
  hydroelectricity, 347, 348
  iron and steel industry, 391-393
  labor distribution in manufacturing industries, 261
  man-made fibers, 496, 498
  merchant shipping, 563
  motor vehicle industry, 452
  population growth, 38
  railways, 549, 554-555
  rice, 79, 132, 134
  shipbuilding, 442-443
  silk, 178
  small-scale industries, 31, 259
  sugar imports, 152
  tea, 158
  textile machinery, 435
  trade, 585-586, 593
  whaling, 250
  woolen and worsted industries, 490
  Zaibatsu, 393
Japanese Arabian Oil Co., 286
Java, cinchona, 89
  communal tenure, 58
  culture system, 37
  farm size, 54
  population, 29, 38
  rice, 79, 132
  small-scale industries, 258
  tea, 160
  tobacco, 187
  (*See also* Indonesia)
Jevons, Stanley, 316
Jewelry and silverware, 267
Johannesburg, 426
John Brown & Co., 442
John Summers Ltd., 380
Joint products, 142, 193, 400
Jones & Laughlin Steel Corporation, 373
Joplin, 418
Jowar, 82
Jute, 165, 176

Kaiser Aluminum Corporation, 412
Kaiser Motors, 455, 456, 459
Kaiser Steel Corporation, 372, 373, 376
Kaldo process, 368
Kanawha River, 519
Kansas, 96
Karaganda coalfield, 388
Kariba Dam, 406
Katanga, 405-406
Kay's flying shuttle, 258, 476
Kazakhstan, 61, 97
  (*See also* U.S.S.R.)
Keihin cities (Tokyo, Yokohama), 33, 392, 443, 451, 486
Kenaf, 176
Kennecott Copper Corporation, 404, 405

Kennedy round, 587
Kentucky, 188, 208, 319
Kenya, coffee, 89, 158, 594
  wheat, 122
Kerala, 160
Kerosene, 301, 303
Keweenaw Range, 404
Kharif crops, 82
Khrushchev, Nikita, 131
Kibbutzim, 58–59
Kiel, 445
King ranch, 54
Kinta Valley, 422
Kirkland Lake, 427
Kitimat, 414
Kloeckner-Werke Gmbh, 383
Knitwear and hosiery, 476–477
Kola peninsula, 234
Kolkhozy, 59
Kombinat, 387, 430
Korea, 136
Korean war, 322, 350, 400
Kraft paper, 225, 231
Krivoy Rog, 387
Krupp, Friedrich, Gmbh, 384
Krupp-Renn process, 366
Kuala Lumpur, 422
Kure Navy Yard, 443
Kuroshio, 248
Kuwait, 292, 294
Kuwait-Saudi Neutral Zone, 296
Kuznetsk, coalfield, 331–332
  iron and steel, 389
Kwantung Army, 395
Kwashiorkor, 49
Kyushu, 332, 393, 443

La Plata lowlands, 201
Labor force, in agriculture, 10, 14, 16, 19
  manufacturing industries, 260–261
  (*See also* specific industries)
  motor vehicle industry, 458, 462
  textile industries, 478, 485–487
Labor supply in industrial location, 267
Labrador, iron ore, 362
Lace industry, 477
Ladang, 71, 75
Lake Erie, 375, 447, 559
Lake Maracaibo, 290
Lake Superior, 371, 372, 447, 559
Lamb and mutton, 93, 209, 211–212
Lancashire, chemical industries, 520
  coalfield, 324
  cotton textile industry, 482–484
  machine tools, 434
  motor vehicle industry, 463
  textile machinery, 435, 436
Land reform, 55, 56, 61, 174
Land tenure, 56–64
Lard, 214
Latifundia, 55
Latin America, birth rates, 39
  coffee, 153–158
Latin America, copper, 404, 407
  cotton, 174, 175
  foreign aid, 607–609
  forests, 219–221
  lead and zinc, 418
  per capita product, 6
  petroleum, 290–292
  population, 36
  silver, 427
  tierra templada, 75
  trade, 593
  (*See also* specific countries)
Latin American Free Trade Association (LAFTA), 594–595
Lavoisier, Antoine, 501
Law of capture, 288
Laxton, 104*n.*
LD (Linz-Donawitz) and LD-AC processes, 368–370, 375, 378
Le Creusot, 385
Le Havre, 485
Lea Valley, 113
Lead, ores, 400
  price, 401
  production, 418–419
  properties and uses, 416–417
Leaf fibers, 176
Lebanon, 533, 603
Leblanc process, 502, 507
Leduc oil field, 299
Leeds, 438, 490
Leicestershire, 200
  coalfield, 324
Leningrad, 235, 451, 540
Leuna, 521
Levers machine, 477
Leys, 106, 111
Liberia, 563, 602
Libya, petroleum, 300
Liège, 386
Lignite, 309–310
  (*See also* Coal)
Lille, 485, 490
Lime, 362
Limestone, 369, 501, 503, 507
Limon, 146, 200
Limonite, 362
Lincolnshire, iron and steel, 379
Linseed oil, 141
List, Friedrich, 574
Lithium, 398
Little Inch pipeline, 290
Liverpool, 450, 485
Livestock, cattle, 195–201
  hogs, 213–215
  place of, in agriculture, 192–195
  poultry, 214–216
  sheep, 206–213
  work animals, 195–197
  (*See also* Commercial grazing; Crop farming and horticulture with subsidiary livestock; Crop and livestock farming; Dairy farming; Pastoral nomadism)
Livestock ranching (*see* Commercial grazing)
Llanelly, 379
Load factor, 338–339
Location of industry (*see* Industrial location)
Lockheed Aircraft Corporation, 467
Locomotive construction, 437–439
Loess, in China, 82
  in Europe, 146
London, aircraft industry, 471
  City of, 531–532
  electrical engineering, 450
  government services, 541
  industrial expansion and growth of, 269, 270
  motor vehicle industry, 462–463
  population, 33
  port of, 566, 567
  regional shopping centers, 539*n.*
Longwall coal mining, 313–314
Lorraine, iron ores, 382, 383, 385
Los Angeles, aircraft and aerospace industries, 470–471
  electronics industry, 450
  fishing, 247
  industrial expansion and population growth, 267–268
  iron and steel industry, 376
  motion picture industry, 525–526
  motor vehicle industry, 459
  population, 33
  synthetic rubber, 515
Louisiana, 137, 288, 289
Lung cancer, 190
"Lur" brand, 110
Lurgi process, 310, 510
Luton, 462
Luxembourg, 386, 587
Lynn Lake, 420
Lyon, 177, 466, 521

Macau, 533
Machine tools, 433–435
Mackinder, Sir Halford J., 91
Macy, R. H., & Co., 535
Madras, 133
Maghreb, 100
Magnesium, 398, 409, 519
Magnetite, 362
Magnitogorsk, 388, 389
Mail order stores, 537
Malawi, 161
Malaya (*see* Malaysia, Federation of)
Malaysia, Federation of, economic development, 18, 605
  estates and smallholders, 87, 88
  irrigation, 56
  natural rubber, 87, 88, 183–185, 190
  oil palm, 143
  population growth, rate of, 42
  rice, 55, 134
  subdivision, 56, 88
  tin, 420–422

Malaysia, trade, 581, 585
(*See also* Singapore)
Malnutrition, 39, 50
Man-made fibers, types of, 491–492
(*See also* Noncellulose synthetic fibers; Rayon and acetate)
Manchester, 438, 484, 489–490
Manchuria, iron and steel industry, 395
soybeans, 142
Manganese, 364, 367*n*., 368*n*.
Manila hemp (*see* Abaca)
Manitoba, nickel, 420
wheat, 96
Mansfeld, 521
Margam, 379
Margarine, 142, 204, 206, 508
Market gardening, 113
Markets in industrial location, 267–268
Marshall, Alfred, 3
Marshall Field & Co., 535
Marshall Plan, 587
Massif Central, 385
Mauritius, 146, 602
Maykop, 297
Meat (*see* specific products)
Mediterranean agriculture, 100–104
Megalopolis, 16
Mehemet Ali, 172
Mekong Plain, 19
Melanesia, 72
Menam Plain, 136
Mercantilism, 573, 574
Merino sheep, 206, 210, 211
(*See also* Sheep)
Mesabi Range, 371
Meseta, 206
Métayage, 61
Mexico, cotton, 172
henequen, 177
lead and zinc, 418
motor vehicle industry, 466
petroleum, 292
population growth, 38
silver, 428
"Mexico Club," 157
Mezzadria, 16, 102
Michigan, chemical industries, 521
copper, 404
motor vehicle industry, 457, 458
Mid-continent oil fields, 287–288
Middle East petroleum industry, 292–297
costs of production, 294
nature of oil fields, 293
reserves, 292
structure of, 296
U.S. interests in, 295–296
Midland, Michigan, 519
Milan, 467
Milk (*see* Dairy products)
Millets, 82
"Million cities," 33
Mina-al-Ahmadi, 295, 566
Minnesota, 96, 371
Minette ore, 385
Mining, increasing costs in, 401
nonferrous metal ores, 399
opencast, 320, 323
(*See also* specific minerals)
Mining machinery, 436
Missouri, 319, 418
Missouri Valley Authority, 351–352
Mittelland Canal, 329, 560
Mixed farming (*see* Crop and livestock farming)
Molybdenum, 398
Mond, Ludwig, 419
"Monrovia group," 602
Monsanto Chemical Corporation, 503, 519
Montana, 404, 413
Montecatini S.p.A., 503, 521
Monterey pine, 221
Montgomery Ward Co., 537
Moscow, 33, 386, 388, 490
Moscow Narodny Bank, 532
Moselle River, 329, 385
Motion picture industry, 471, 525–526
Motor vehicle industry, 185, 452–467, 602
characteristics and structure, 453
U.S., 453–459
Western Europe, 459–467
Mountains, population of, 29
Mudie Report, 190
Mulberries, 177
Multiple stores (*see* Chain stores)
Multipurpose water projects, 349–352
Mumford, Lewis, 16
Mutton (*see* Lamb and mutton)
Myer Emporium Pty. Ltd., 535

Nagoya, 393
Naples, 386
Nasser, A., 174
National Coal Board, 316, 323
National product, 5–7
National size and economic development, 601
National Steel Corporation, 373
Natural gas, 274, 304–305, 410, 414
Natural rubber, 178–185
yield stimulants, 578
Nauru, 508
Nepheline, 410, 416
Netherlands, butter exports, 206
coal mining, 327
dairy farming, 111
electronics, 451
greenhouse cultivation, 113
iron and steel industry, 386
merchant shipping, 562–563
natural gas, 304
railways, 549
shipbuilding, 445
trade, 589
Netherlands West Indies, 291
New Caledonia, 420
New England, aircraft and aerospace industry, 471
cotton textile industry, 480
dairy farming, 204
shipbuilding, 446, 447
woolen and worsted industries, 488
New Orleans, 567, 569
New South Wales, 92, 99, 110, 149, 332
New York, 33, 375, 531–533, 566, 567, 569
New Zealand, agricultural cooperatives, 65
agricultural work force, 25
aluminum, 415
cattle, 201
crop and livestock farming, 107
forestry, 221
government, employment in, 540
hydroelectricity, 347
lamb, 212
pasture improvement, 94, 213
ports, 569
roads, 555, 558
sheep, 211–212
trade, 577*n*., 590
urbanization, 10
wool, 212, 213
Newcastle-on-Tyne, 438
Newfoundland, 232, 244, 245
Newport, 379
Newport News, 447
Newsprint, 223, 225, 231, 232
Niagara Falls, 412
Niarchos, S., 446
Nicaro, 420
Nickel, 401, 419–420
Niger Republic, 602
Nigeria, cacao, 161
oil palm, 87, 143
petroleum, 306
tin, 420, 422
vegetable oil exports, 143
Nile River, 172
(*See also* Gezira)
Nisshio Maru, S.S., 443
Nitrates, 508
Nitrocellulose, 508
Nitroglycerin, 509
Nobel, Alfred, 510
Noils, wool, 487
Noncellulose synthetic fibers, 492, 497–498
Nonferrous metals, characteristics of, 399–402
classification of, 398
(*See also* specific metals)
Noranda, Quebec, 427
Norfolk, Virginia, 322
Norfolk rotation, 104
North America, commercial grain farming, 94–97
commercial grazing, 92–94
crop and livestock farming, 105–106

North America, dairy farming, 107, 111
horticulture, 114–115
inland waterways, 351*n.*, 559–560
population, 36
railways, 549–552
(*See also* specific countries)
North Auckland, 110
North Carolina, 188
North Dakota, 96
North Rhine-Westphalia conurbation, 33
(*See also* Ruhr)
North Sea fisheries, 238, 243
Northern Rhodesia (Zambia), 404 407
Northrop Corporation, 467
Northrup battery loom, 476
Northumberland coalfield, 324
Norway, aluminum, 414
fisheries, 244
forest industries, 233
hydroelectricity, 344, 347, 348
merchant shipping, 542, 563
territorial waters, 243
whaling, 250–251
Nottinghamshire coalfield, 323, 324
Novokuznetsk (Stalinsk), 388, 389
Noxious industries, 356, 505
Nutrition, 39, 49, 50
Nylon (*see* Noncellulose synthetic fibers)

Oats, 99, 105, 121
Occupations, 24–26, 525*n.*
Ocean Island, 508
Odendaalsrus, 426
Ohio Valley, 354, 413
Oil, crude (*see* Petroleum)
Oil palm, 87, 142–144
Olives and olive oil, 103, 141
Onassis, A. S., 561
Opel, A., Gmbh, 463
Open-hearth process, 367
Opencast mining (*see* Strip mining)
Oranges, 116
(*See also* Citriculture)
Oregon, 229
Ores (*see* Iron ore; Nonferrous metals)
Organization, for Economic Cooperation and Development (OECD), 272, 587
for European Economic Cooperation (OEEC), 272, 587
of Inter-African and Malagasy States, 595
of Petroleum Exporting Countries (OPEC)
Oriana, S.S., 442
Orlon (*see* Noncellulose synthetic fibers)
Osaka (*see* Hanshin cities)
Ottawa agreements, 590
Ottoman Empire, 292
Öxelosund, 387
Oxen, 195
Oxford, motor vehicle industry, 462
Oxygen, 366, 368
Ozarks, 29

Pacific Ocean, fisheries, 245–250
shipping routes, 565
Pakistan, 82, 174, 175
Palm oil and palm kernel oil, 141–144
Palouse, 95
Panama, shipping registrations, 563
Panama Canal, 565
Panama disease, 86
Papermaking, location of, 227
(*See also* Forest-products industries; Newsprint)
Paraffin-base crudes, 279
Paraguay, 594
Paraná, coffee, 155
Paraná pine, 221
Paris, 33, 270, 466, 472
Parity, 127
Particle board, 227
Passenger miles, types of transport, 543
Pastoral nomadism, 90–91
Pasture improvement, 94, 212, 213
Patagonia, 94
Patino interests, 424
Patras, 102
Payments, balance of (*see* Balance, of payments)
Pechenga (Petsamo), 420
Péchiney, S.A., 414
Peking, 396
Pelagic fisheries, 239–240
Penicillin, 512
Peninsular and Oriental Steam Navigation Co. (P & O), 562, 566
Pennsylvania, 311, 318, 320, 558
Perkin, Sir William H., 502
Persia, 283, 292, 294
Peru, copper, 407
cotton, 167, 172
fisheries, 244, 249–250
lead and zinc, 418
silver, 428
sugar, 150
trade, 594
Perusahaan induk, 259
Peter the Great, 387
Petrochemicals, 516–518
Petroleum, advantages of, 278–279
in energy supplies, 274
growth of output, 277
in industrial location, 31
in international trade, 577
nature and occurrence of, 279–282
reserves and recovery techniques, 281–282
surpluses, 282, 286
traps, 280–281
Petroleum industry, in Africa, 300
in Canada, 299
Petroleum industry, in Caribbean and Latin America, 290–292
in Indonesia, 299–300
in Middle East, 292–297
social and political problems, 305–306
structure and organization of, 282–287
in U.S.S.R. and Eastern Europe, 277, 297–299
in U.S., 287–290
in world economy, 276
Petroleum products, consumption patterns, 301–302
trade, 304, 577
Petroleum refining, 300–301
location of, 302–304
Peugeot S.A., 466
Pharmaceuticals, 511–512
Phelps Dodge Corporation, 404
Philadelphia, 33, 567, 569
Philippines, abaca, 177
copper, 409
estates, 60
fish consumption, 237
foreign aid, 607
gold, 427
rice imports, 134
sugar, 89, 152
swiddens, 72
tenancy, 63, 64, 68
Philips Gloeilampenfabrieken NV, 451
Phoenix-Rheinrohr Gmbh, 384
Phosphates, 508
Pig iron (*see* Blast furnace; Iron and steel industry)
Pipelines, in Canada, 299, 305
coal, 320*n.*
in Middle East, 294–295
in U.S.S.R. and Eastern Europe, 298
in U.S., 290
Pisciculture, 79–80, 237, 249
Pittsburgh, 319, 371–375
Pittsburgh plus pricing system, 374
Plains, population of, 29–30
Plankton, 240
Plant utilization factor, 340
Plantation crop agriculture, 83–90
Plastics, 512–514
Platinum, 424, 428
Ploesti, 299
Plutonium, 355
Pocahontas coal, 319
Pocahontas railroads, 551
Poland, coal mining, 330
collectivization of agriculture, 59, 606
heavy industry, overinvestment in, 24
horses, 197
iron and steel industry, 390
lead and zinc, 419
Population, geographical distribution of, 28–30
growth and structure, 36–39

Population cycle, 39–42
Pork, 49
(*See also* Hogs)
Port Colbourne, 420
Port facilities, 568
Port labor, 568–569
Port Pirie, 418
Ports, tonnage loaded and unloaded, 566–568
Portugal, per capita product, 7
fishing, 243
sugar imports, 7
trade, 591
Potash, 502, 521
Potatoes, 49
Potrerillos, 405
Poultry, 213–216
Pratt seam, 319
Precious metals, 398, 424–428
President's Materials Policy Commission (Paley Reports), 399, 601
Price support for agricultural products, 51–54
corn, 140
cotton, 172
dairy products, 204
rice, 137
sugar, 137
wheat, 105, 127–129
Primeurs, 114
Primitive subsistence agriculture, 70–75
Primogeniture, 56
Printing, 532, 533
Procter & Gamble Co., 508
Prorationing, 288–289
Protection, 574–575
Protein foods, 49
Province Wellesley, 58
Public Law 480 (*see* Agricultural Trade Development and Assistance Act)
Pueblo, 376
Pulp and paper, 225
(*See also* Forest-products industries; Newsprint)
Pumping hydroelectric stations, 346
Punjab, 82

Qatar, 293, 294, 296
Quebec, 232, 414, 427
Queensland, bauxite, 410
commercial grazing, 92, 93
dairy farming, 110
sugar, 146, 149
Quinine, 89
Quinoa, 75

Rabi crops, 82
Radioactive isotopes, 355
Radioactive waste, 356
Ragi, 82
Railways, advantages and disadvantages of, 546, 547
condition of, in West, 547–548
Railways, diesel locomotives, 437, 439
expansion of, and economic development, 546
in Japan, 554–555
revenue of, 549
and road competition, 546, 547
in U.S.S.R., 552–554
in U.S., 549–552
utilization of, 548–549
Rand, gold mining, 400, 425–427
Rapeseed oil, 141
Ras' Tannūrah, 295
Ratooning, 150
Raw materials in industrial location, 265
Rayon and acetate industry, characteristics of, 493–495
growth of, 491–492
in Japan, 496
in U.S., 495–496
in Western Europe, 496–497
Redwoods, 229
Reforestation, 233
Régie Renault, 461
Regional shopping centers, 538, 539
Reid Report, 325
Resale price maintenance, 537
Resources, adequacy of, for economic development, 600–601
and national size, 601–603
Retailing (*see* Distribution)
Reynolds Aluminum Corporation, 412
Rheinhausen, 383, 384
Rhine-Herne Canal, 329
Rhine-Rhône Canal, 560
Rhine River, 329
Rhodesian Anglo-American Ltd., 406*n.*
Rhodesian Selection Trust Ltd., 406*n.*
Ricardo, David, 104, 573
Rice production, 131–134
trade, 136–138
in U.S., 136–138
varieties and yields, 134–136
(*See also* Sawah agriculture)
Richard Thomas & Baldwins Ltd., 378, 379
Ridley, H. N., 179
Ring-spindle frame, 476
Rio Grande do Sul, 201
Roads, 555–558
Rockefeller, John D., 283
Rocky Mountain fields, coal, 318
oil, 295
Rolling mills, 370
Rolls-Royce Ltd., 472
Romania, corn, 98, 139
petroleum, 299
sunflowers, 98
Romney Marsh sheep, 210, 211
Rosario, 98
"Rotolactor," 112
Rotterdam, 303, 386, 445, 560, 567
Rouyn, Quebec, 407, 427
Royal Dutch-Shell group, 282, 289, 291
Rubber (*see* Natural rubber; Synthetic rubber)
Ruhr, coal mining, 327–384
iron and steel industry, 382–384
Rüsselheim, 466
Rwanda, 158
Rye, 121
Ryegrass, 110

Saar, coalfield, 327
iron and steel industry, 384, 385
Sabah (North Borneo), 87, 182, 184
Saguenay River, 414
St. Étienne, 385
St. Lawrence Seaway, 351, 447, 559
Sakhalin, 297
Salinas Valley, 114
Salmon fisheries, 247, 249
Salt, 501, 503
Salt domes, 281
Salzgitter, 383
Samoa, 248
San Diego, 247, 470
San Francisco, 459, 567
São Paulo, 155
Sarawak, 182, 184
Sarnia, 515
Saskatchewan, 126
Saudi Arabia, 293, 294
Sawah agriculture, 75–80
Saxony, 326, 484–485
Scientific instrument industry, 267
Scots pine, 233
Scottish coalfields, 324, 326
Scottish iron and steel industry, 379–380
Sea Island cotton, 167
Sears Roebuck Co., 537
Secondary industries, 24
Secondary metal, 400
Securities Exchange Commission, 531
Seining, 244
Semichemical pulp, 227
Semidevelopment economies, 16–18
Semihard wheat, 124
Sennar Dam, 175
Sericulture, 177–178
Shaft mines, 312
Shanghai, 487
Share cropping, 61, 169
(*See also* Tenancy)
Sheep, 93, 206–213
Sheffield, 380
Sherritt Gordon Co., 420
Sherritt Gordon process, 409
Shifting cultivation, 187
(*See also* Primitive subsistence agriculture)
Shipbuilding, 439–447
Shipping conferences, 566
Shipping fleets, 561–563
Shipping routes, 563–565
Shoddy, 487

Siderite, 360
Siemens group, 450
Siemens-Martin process, 367
Silesian coalfields, 326, 330, 382, 390
Silk, 177–178
Silver, 424, 427–428
Silviculture, 217–218
Simca S.A., 457
Sinclair Oil Corporation, 289
Singapore, 568
Sisal, 85, 176, 177
Skim milk, 215
Slash-mulch swidden agriculture, 74–75
Slashing process, 480*n.*
Slavery, 84, 186
Small-scale industries, 258–259
Small stores, 534
Smallholders, 43, 158, 181–184
Smith, Adam, 573
Smith, Wilfred, 266*n.*, 430*n.*
Snia Viscosa, S.p.A., 494
Snowy Mountains scheme, 349
Soap and detergents, 507–508
Socfin group, 87
Socony-Mobil Corporation, 283, 296
Soda, 507
Soft wheat, 122
  (*See also* Wheat)
Softwoods (*see* Forests, coniferous)
Soil Bank Program, 127
Solar energy, 273
Solvay process, 507
Somali Republic, 92
Sorghums, 96
South Africa, Cape region agriculture, 103
  cattle, 201
  coal hydrogenation, 510
  coal mining, 315, 332
  economic dualism, 18
  goats, 92
  gold, 425–427
  iron and steel industry, 391
  platinum, 428
  road-rail competition, 558
  sheep, 212–213
  sugar, 152
South America (*see* Latin America; specific countries)
South Australia, 99
South Georgia, 250
South Vietnam, 133, 134, 136, 137, 179
South Wales, 311, 324, 374
Southern Rhodesia, 18, 186, 189, 407
Soviet Union (*see* U.S.S.R.)
Sovkhozy, 54, 61
Soybeans, 106, 142, 143
Spain, *huertas,* 102
  iron and steel industry, 386
  land ownership, 102
  lead and zinc, 417
  olives, 102, 103
  per capita product, 7
Spain, rice, 134
  sheep, 206
Sparrows Point, 373
Spear grass, 73
Special United Nations Fund for Economic Development (SUNFED), 610
Sperm whaling, 250
Spiegeleisen, 367
Spinning (*see* Textile industries)
Spring wheat, 122
Stainless steel, 419
Standard (timber), 223
Standard Oil Company, of California, 283, 286, 296
  of Indiana, 289
  of New Jersey, 282, 286, 289, 291, 296
Standard Oil Trust, 283
Standard Vacuum Oil Company, 286
Staple fiber, 493
Steam engine, 265, 308
Steel Company of Wales Ltd., 379
Stevenson restriction scheme, 182
Stewards & Lloyd Ltd., 379
Stockpiles, strategic, 402
Strip mining, 320, 323
Studebaker Corporation, 455*n.*, 458
Styrene, 415–515
Sudan, 65, 175
Sudbury, 420
Suez Canal, 295, 564–565
Suez crisis, 274
Sugar, 144–153
  beet production, 151
  cane and beet, costs of production, 143–145
  cane production, 145–151
  markets, 146, 152–153
Sulfate and sulfite processes, 225
Sulfur, 507
Sulfuric acid, 506–507
Sullivan mine, 418
Sumatra, 160, 179, 186, 187, 299–300
  (*See also* Indonesia)
Sunflowers, 98
Supermarkets, 538
Supertankers, 295, 561
Surinam, 410
Sverdlovsk, 388
Sweden, forest industries, 233
  hydroelectricity, 233, 344
  iron ores, 362
  iron and steel, 386
  mining machinery, 436
  motor vehicle industry, 602
  shipbuilding, 445–446
  trade, 591
  wheat, 123
Swiddens, 71–75
Switzerland, banking, 533
  hydroelectricity, 344, 348
  machine tools, 433
  per capita product, 7
Switzerland, pharmaceuticals, 512
  railway utilization, 549
  textile machinery, 435
  trade, 591
  urbanization, 11
Swollen shoot, 162
Sylvania Corporation, 450
Synthetic fiber (*see* Noncellulose synthetic fibers).
Synthetic rubber, 514–516

Taconite, 372
Taiga, 220
  (*See also* Forests, coniferous)
Taiwan, 136, 146
Tanganyika, 176, 594
Tangier, 534
Tankers, 443, 561
Taranaki, 110
Taranto, 386
Tariffs (*see* Free trade; Protection)
Tasmania, 347
Tea, 158–161
Tegalan, 81
Telford, Thomas, 555
Tenancy, 61–64, 105, 173
Tennessee, 188
Tennessee Valley Authority, 349–350
Territorial seas, 242–243
Texaco Corporation, 283, 296
Texas, aircraft industry, 470–471
  aluminum, 413
  chemical industries, 506
  cotton, 170–171
  goats, 92
  iron and steel industry, 376–377
  lignite, 413
  petroleum, 287–289
  rice, 137
  sheep, 207
Textile fiber consumption, 473–474
Textile industries, characteristics of, 474–475
  in Industrial Revolution, 476
  technology, 475–476
  (*See also* specific industries)
Textile machinery, 435–436
Thailand, cooperatives, 65
  fish consumption, 65
  rice, 65, 134–136
  rubber, 182
  tin, 422
Thames-Waikato plain, 110
Thermoelectricity, 352–354
Thomas meal, 368
Thorium, 255
Thyssen Hütte, A., Gmbh, 384
Tierra templada, 75
Tin, price fluctuations, 400–401
  production, 420–423
  smelting, 424
  uses of, 419
Tire cord, 493
Titanium, 398

Tobacco, 185–190
surpluses and export earnings, 188, 189
types of, 186
Tokyo (*see* Keihin cities)
Tokyo Shibaura Co. (Toshiba), 448
Tolai, 89
Toluene, 510
Ton-miles, types of transport, 543
Tonkin, 29
Tops, wool, 487
Tractors, 95, 105
(*See also* Agricultural machinery)
Trade, balance of, 573
barter, 581, 582
blocs and agreements, 586–595
direction of, 577
(*See also* specific items)
free, and protection, 574–575
international, in agricultural products, 578–580
fuels and minerals, 577–578
history and bases of, 572–575
machinery and manufactures, 575–577
network of, 581–586
per capita, 580–581
terms of, 576
Trade Expansion Act, 575, 594
Trade Unions, 442, 446, 542
Tramp shipping, 561
Trans-Arabian pipeline (Tapline), 295
Transcontinental railways, North America, 549–550
Transfer machines, 434
Transport, in industrial location, 266
in world economy, 543–546
(*See also* specific transport industries)
Trans-Siberian railway, 553
Traps, petroleum, 280–281
Trawling, 243, 245
Trent Valley, 354
Trinidad, 602
Tri-state area (Joplin), 418
Trolley locomotives, 319
Truck farming, 114
Tuna fisheries, 247–249
Tung oil, 141
Turboalternators, 340
Turin, 466
Turkey, raisins, 102
tobacco, 186, 187, 189
Turkmen Canal, 91
Turner Valley oil field, 299
Turnpike trusts, 555

Uganda, 175, 594
Ugine S.A., 414
Ukraine, agriculture, 95, 98
coal mining, 331
iron and steel industry, 387, 388
Underdeveloped economies, 18–19, 26, 39
Underdeveloped economies, foreign aid to, 607–611
manufacturing industries, 258–260
problems of development, 595–605
Underground mining (*see* Coal mining, technology)
Unemployment in highly developed economies, 4, 269–270
Unilever Ltd., 508
Union Carbide Corporation, 503, 519
Union Minière du Haut Katanga, 406
U.S.S.R., agricultural machinery, 432–433
agriculture, condition of, 23, 131, 606
aluminum, 416
building, 529–530
cattle, 198
centrally planned economy of, 19–24
chemical industries, 503
coal mining, 331–332
corn, 98
cotton, 174
cotton textile industry, 486
electric power stations, 344, 345, 354
fertilizer consumption, 131
Five Year Plans, 331, 387–388
foreign aid, 599
forests and forest-products industries, 222, 234–235
gold, 427
horses, 197
hydroelectricity, 346, 416
inland waterways, 560
iron and steel industry, 387–390
lead and zinc, 419
machine tools, 435
migration to cities, 33
natural gas, 304
nickel, 420
per capita product, 6
petroleum industry, 277, 297–299
railways, 388, 486, 552–554
roads, 555
sheep, 207
sugar beets, 144, 147
sunflowers, 98
tea, 161
trade, 123, 130–131, 149, 151, 174, 235, 532, 599
(*See also* Council for Mutual Economic Aid)
whaling, 251–252
wheat, 95, 97–98, 123, 130–131
woolen and worsted industries, 490
United Arab Republic (*see* Egypt)
United Fruit Co., 86*n.*
United Kingdom (*see* Great Britain)
United Nations, Special Fund for Economic Development (SUNFED), 610
(*See also* Economic Commission for Asia and the Far East)
United States, S.S., 447
U.S., agricultural cooperatives, 65
agricultural machinery, 431–432
agricultural work force, 14
aircraft and aerospace industry, 468–471
aluminum, 411–414
atomic energy, 355–356
balance of payments, 594
bauxite, 410
building and construction, 530
cattle, 198, 200–201
chain stores, 536–537
chemical industries, 502, 506, 511, 512, 516, 518–520
coffee consumption, 157, 158
coal mining, 317–322
consumer cooperatives, 536
copper, 404, 408–409
corn, 97, 139–140
cotton, 167–172
cotton textile industry, 479–481
dairying and dairy products, 111–112, 204–205
department stores, 535, 536
electric power interconnection, 342, 345
electrical engineering, 449
energy consumption, 273, 274
farm size, 54, 55
fertilizer consumption, 131
fisheries, 245–246
foreign aid, 607–609
forests and forest-products industries, 225, 229–231
gold, 427
gold reserves, 425
government, employment in, 539–540
hogs, 214–215
horses, 197
hydroelectricity, 347–352
inland waterways, 351*n.*, 559–560
iron and steel industry, 371–377
irrigation, 94, 115
labor distribution in manufacturing industries, 260
lead and zinc, 417–418
locomotive construction, 438–439
machine tools, 434
margarine, 142, 206
merchant shipping, 561
mining machinery, 436
motion picture industry, 471, 525–536
motor vehicle industry, 453–459
multipurpose water projects, 350–351
natural gas, 304, 305
noncellulose synthetic fibers, 498
nonferrous metals, future requirements of, 399
per capita product, 6
petrochemicals, 516
petroleum industry, 277, 282–290

U.S., pharmaceuticals, 512
population growth, 38
ports, 566, 567
poultry, 215–216
poverty, 14
price support and large farms, 51
(*See also* Price support for agricultural products)
railways, 549–552
rayon and acetate, 495–496
rice, 133, 136–138
roads, 555, 557
sheep, 207–209
shipbuilding, 446–447
silver, 427
soybeans, 142, 143
sugar, 146, 147, 150–151
Supreme Court, 54
synthetic rubber, 514–516
textile machinery, 435
tobacco, 187–189
trade, 585, 591–594
(*See also* specific products)
vegetable oils, 141–142
wheat, 96–97, 123, 127–129
wool, 209
woolen and worsted industries, 488
United States Steel Corporation, 373, 376
United Steel Co., 378, 379
Upland cotton, 167
Upland rice (*see* Dry rice)
Upper Silesia coalfield (*see* Silesian coalfields)
Ural-Kuznetsk *kombinat,* 332, 387–388
Ural-Volga oil fields, 297
Uranium, 355, 358, 400
Urbanization, 30–36
Uruguay, 94, 201, 208, 210

Valorization, 156
Van Camp Corporation, 247
Vanadium, 398
Vauxhall Motor Co., 462
Vegetable fibers, 165–178
Vegetable oils, 140–144
Venezuela, per capita product, 7
petroleum industry, 290–292
trade, 291, 595
Vickers Ltd., 442
Victoria, 99, 110
Victoria Falls, 346
Vietnam (*see* South Vietnam)
Village industries (*see* Cottage industries; Small-scale industries)
Virginia, 322
Virginia tobacco, 186, 188
Viscose process, 491
(*See also* Rayon and acetate industry)
Viticulture, 102, 114
Volga River, 560
Volgograd (Stalingrad), 345, 416
Volkswagen, 383, 456, 457, 461, 463, 465
Volta River, 415
Voluntary chains, 538

Wachagga, 88
Wagner's Law, 540
Warwickshire coalfield, 324
Washington, State of, 229
Washington, D.C., 540
Waste paper, 225
Water buffaloes, 195
Water projects (*see* Multipurpose water projects)
Weaving (*see* Texile industries)
Weber, Alfred, 261–262
West Driefontein, 426
West Germany, aluminum, 414
autobahnen, 558
cattle, 200
chemical industries, 501–503, 507, 510, 514, 516, 520–521
coal mining, 310, 326–330
coffee consumption, 158
cotton textile industry, 484
dairying, 204
electrical engineering, 449
inland waterways, 329, 560
iron and steel industry, 382–384
locomotive construction, 438
machine tools, 434–435
merchant shipping, 563
motor vehicle industry, 459, 460, 463–466
particle board, 227
per capita product, 6
railways, 546–548
rayon and acetate, 493
shipbuilding, 441, 443–444
synthetic rubber, 514, 516
tobacco consumption, 187
trade, 589
woolen and worsted industries, 490
West Indies (*see* British West Indies; Cuba; Dominican Republic)
West Riding (*see* Yorkshire)
West Virginia, 318–320
Whale oil, price, 141
Whaling, 250–252
Wheat, in major types of agriculture, 82, 94–107
requirements for, 122
surpluses, 127–128
types of, 122, 124
world trade, 123–131, 579
yields, 122, 124
(*See also* specific countries)
Whitefish, 240, 244
Whittlesey, Derwent, 32–33
Wickham, Henry, 179
Wildcatting, 281
Wilkinson, John, 380
Willys Motor Corporation, 459
Winter wheat, 122
Wisconsin, 204
"Witches broom," 162
Wittfogel, Karl A., 79*n.*
Witwatersrand (*see* Rand)
Wolfsburg, 383, 465
Woodpulp (*see* Forest-products industries)
Wool, 213, 498
(*See also* Sheep)
Woolen and worsted industries, 487–490
Woolworth, F. W., Co., 535
World Bank, 610
Wrought iron, 364
Wuhan cities, 396
Wyoming, 288

Yalu River, 396
Yangtze Valley, 322, 396
Yawata Steel Co., 373, 391, 393
Yokohama (*see* Keihin cities)
Yorkshire, coal mining, 323–324
electrical engineering, 450
machine tools, 434
mining machinery, 436
textile machinery, 435
woolen and worsted industries, 489–490
Youngstown, 373
Youngstown Sheet and Tube Corporation, 373
Yucatan, 177
Yugoslavia, 407, 418
Yünnan, 421

Zaibatsu, 393
Zambia, 405–406
Zinc, ores, 400
price, 401
production, 418–419
uses of, 416–417
Zollverein, 594